SOCIAL PROBLEMS

SIXTH EDITION

SOCIAL PROBLEMS

A Critical Power–Conflict Perspective

Joe R. Feagin

Texas A&M University

Clairece B. Feagin

David V. Baker

Riverside Community College

PEARSON

Prentice
Hall

Upper Saddle River, New Jersey 07458

Library of Congress Cataloging-in-Publication Data

Feagin, Joe R.
  Social problems : a critical power-conflict perspective / Joe R. Feagin, Clairece Booher
Feagin, David V. Baker.— 6th ed.
      p. cm.
  Includes bibliographical references and index.
  ISBN 0-13-099927-X
  1. United States—Social conditions—1980- 2. Social problems—United States. 3. Social
conflict—United States. 4. Power (Social sciences)—United States. I. Feagin, Clairece
Booher. II. Baker, David V. III. Title.
  HN59.2.F4 2006
  306'.0973—dc22   2005016123

Publisher: Nancy Roberts
Editorial Assistant: Lee Peterson
Full Service Production Liaison: Joanne Hakim
Senior Marketing Manager: Marissa Feliberty
Marketing Assistant: Anthony DeCosta
Assistant Manufacturing Manager: Mary Ann Gloriande
Cover Art Director: Jayne Conte
Cover Design: Kiwi Design
Manager, Cover Visual Research & Permissions: Karen Sanatar
Cover Art: Sergio Spada/Stock Illustration Source
Director, Image Resource Center: Melinda Reo
Manager, Rights and Permissions: Zina Arabia
Manager, Visual Research: Beth Brenzel
Photo Researcher: Julie Tesser
Photo Coordinator: Robert Farrell
Composition/Full-Service Project Management: Ann Imhof/Carlisle Communications Ltd.
Printer/Binder: Hamilton Printing Company

Credits and acknowledgments borrowed from other sources and reproduced, with permission,
in this textbook appear on appropriate page within text.

Pearson Education LTD., London
Pearson Education Singapore, Pte. Ltd
Pearson Education, Canada, Ltd
Pearson Education—Japan
Pearson Education Australia PTY, Limited

Pearson Education North Asia Ltd
Pearson Educación de Mexico, S.A. de C.V.
Pearson Education Malaysia, Pte. Ltd
Pearson Education, Upper Saddle River, New Jersey

10 9 8 7 6 5 4 3 2 1
ISBN 0-13-099927-X

Brief Contents

Contents

Chapter 3

POVERTY, UNEMPLOYMENT, AND UNDEREMPLOYMENT   79

Chapter 4

PROBLEMS OF RACISM AND RACIAL INEQUALITY   114

Chapter 5

PROBLEMS OF GENDER ROLES AND SEX DISCRIMINATION   150

Chapter 6

PROBLEMS IN EDUCATION   199

Chapter 10

PROBLEMS OF WORK AND WORKER ALIENATION   369

Chapter 11

ENVIRONMENTAL, ENERGY, AND MILITARY-INDUSTRIAL PROBLEMS   408

Chapter 12

REMEDYING SOCIAL PROBLEMS 458

INDEX 507

Preface

This nation was founded with the following dramatic words written mainly by the young revolutionary Thomas Jefferson:

> We hold these truths to be self-evident, that all men are created equal, that they are endowed by their Creator with certain unalienable Rights, that among these are Life, Liberty, and the pursuit of Happiness. That to secure these rights Governments are instituted among Men, deriving their just powers from the consent of the governed, that whenever any form of Government becomes destructive of these ends, it is the right of the People to alter or to abolish it.

Jefferson eloquently expressed here the desires of second-class citizens for equality, liberty, and social justice. Although Jefferson the slaveholder did not have the propertyless, white women, black Americans, or Native Americans in mind when he penned these lines of the Declaration of Independence in 1776, over the course of more than two centuries his ideas have been dramatically expanded to include the democratic demands of all exploited and oppressed peoples for greater control over their political and economic lives.

Fewer than one hundred years later and in the middle of a bitter civil war, President Abraham Lincoln echoed Jefferson's words in his 1863 Gettysburg Address:

> Fourscore and seven years ago our fathers brought forth on this continent a new nation, conceived in liberty and dedicated to the proposition that all men are created equal . . . that government of the people, by the people, for the people, shall not perish from the earth.

Coming in the same year as his Emancipation Proclamation, which officially freed most enslaved black southerners, Lincoln's words at Gettysburg extended certain ideals of liberty and justice to enslaved black Americans.

(Architect of the Capitol)

The history of the United States is a long series of people's movements seeking expanded democratic control not only over the political system but also over the economic system under which they live—from the early farmers' rebellions, to the protests of abolitionists, to democratic socialist movements, to union movements, to community action groups, to the black civil rights movement, to environmental protection movements, to gay rights' protests. Just 128 years after the signing of the Declaration of Independence, Eugene V. Debs, a union leader and presidential candidate, extended Jefferson's ideas to include the U.S. economic system and all the working people of the U.S., especially the propertyless. In 1904, Debs expressed this new interpretation of liberty and justice in a pamphlet, *Unionism and Socialism:*

> Full opportunity for full-development is the unalienable right of all . . . The earth for all the people! That is the demand. The machinery of production and distribution for all the people! That is the demand. The collective ownership and control of industry and its democratic management in the interest of all the people! That is the demand. The elimination of rent, interest, and profit and the production of wealth to satisfy the wants of all the people! That is the demand. Cooperative industry in which all work together in harmony as the basis of a new social order, a higher civilization, a real republic!

Debs insisted on "full opportunity for full development" being the "unalienable right of all."

Later on, the "Universal Declaration of Human Rights" further expanded Jeffersonian ideals when, with the help of progressive U.S. delegates, the members of the new United Nations unanimously passed it in 1948. Its articles echo and dramatically extend the Jeffersonian tradition:

> Articles 1–3: All human beings are born free and equal in dignity and human rights . . . without distinction of any kind, such as race, colour, sex, language, religion, political or other opinion. . . . Everyone has the right to life, liberty, and security of person.
>
> Article 23: Everyone has the right to work . . . to protection against unemployment.
>
> Article 25: Everyone has the right to an adequate standard of living . . . food, clothing, housing, medical, social services.

These articles affirm the *human rights* of a variety of oppressed groups in all nations—including subordinated racial and ethnic groups, women, and political dissidents—and they add the rights to work and to enjoy a decent standard of living to the list of basic human rights.

During the turbulent 1960s, Dr. Martin Luther King, Jr., spoke vigorously of liberty and justice for black Americans from the steps of the Lincoln Memorial in Washington D.C.:

> I have a dream that one day this nation will rise up and live out the true meaning of its creed: We hold these truths to be self-evident; that all men are created equal. I have a dream that one day on the red hills of Georgia the sons of former slaves and the sons of former slaveowners will be able to sit down together at the table of brotherhood.

Working hard to extend the principles of equality and justice to all Americans, Dr. King was killed five years later as he was trying to help garbage workers fight for better working conditions in Memphis, Tennessee.

Among the deepest human desires are those for full human development, equality, democracy, happiness, and freedom from oppressive political and economic conditions. As we will see in the chapters that follow, many Americans have not yet secured the full range of basic human rights. Today, they continue to face class domination, racial discrimination, and gender discrimination.

Many Americans of all backgrounds, in the past and in the present, have become aware of these roots of societal problems and have adopted a power–conflict perspective in interpreting this troubled society. This social-problems textbook develops a critical power–conflict perspective as a necessary step in making sense of the many serious problems facing U.S. society. We will examine the roots of major societal troubles in the patterns of class, racial, and gender stratification and subordination and will give special attention to the connections among numerous societal problems. Problems that are often discussed in this country as separate are in fact closely interrelated. For example, the drive for ever-renewed profit in capitalistic enterprises—profit whose use and reinvestment are ultimately in the hands of the business elite—links together such apparently diverse problems as employment discrimination, environmental pollution, declining real wages for many U.S. workers, the downsizing of corporations, corporate price fixing, and the manipulation of politicians by corporate lobbyists.

The capitalistic drive for private profit regularly creates unemployment and underemployment for millions of U.S. workers, especially in a globalized capitalistic economy where it is profitable to move manufacturing or other business operations from the United States to other countries, such as Mexico, Sri Lanka, or mainland China. This drive for profit also generates corporate crimes, such as illegal price-fixing and insider trading in corporate stock, and it is a major factor in the creation of environmental pollution and the spread of high-tech weapons across the globe. Close examination reveals the interconnectedness of many apparently isolated social problems because the roots of the problems are to be found in the structure and operation of our advanced capitalistic system. These arguments will be fully developed in the chapters that follow.

A major advantage of a power–conflict perspective, compared with the perspectives found in more conventional social science textbooks, is that it can force us to think critically about the stratified operation and fundamental roots of the U.S. social system. Many of us have been told by our parents and teachers, "Never mind what you think; *we* are trying to teach you what to think." Buckminster Fuller expressed it this way in his book *Critical Path*:

> My mother said it. My school teachers said it. . . . "Thinking" was considered to be a process that is only teachable by the elders of the system. "That is why we have schools, dear." Thinking was considered to be an utterly unreliable process when spontaneously attempted by youth.

The first step toward critical thinking about our society and its future is to look systematically into major U.S. social problems and to examine their roots in the underlying class, racial, and gender stratification systems.

More than two centuries ago Thomas Paine, another U.S. founding patriot, wrote in *Common Sense* that "a long habit of not thinking a thing *wrong* gives it the superficial appearance of being *right*." To understand the many social problems of the United States, we must examine critically all the features of U.S. society that we have long taken for granted. We should be willing to study ideas and data that our "elders" have told us are forbidden or foreign. We should keep an open mind and be willing to consider views that challenge our existing ideas about the social world around us. If we let someone else do most of our thinking for us—whether it be parents, spouses, teachers, employers, or the media—we are not using our human capabilities to the fullest.

Recent decades have brought an endless series of crises—toxic waste, homelessness, discrimination, protests over declining real wages, unemployment, corporate flight, air pollution, wars—to our fragile globe; the next few decades will doubtless bring more crises. If we the people of the United States are to successfully deal with these crises, many more of us will have to think much more deeply about the social and economic roots of problems—and about major new solutions for the present and future.

ACKNOWLEDGMENTS

One of the pleasures of writing a book is the exchange of ideas with one's critics and colleagues. We are grateful to the following people for comments on various drafts of the chapters of this text: Gideon Sjoberg, David Perry, Al Watkins, David Snow, T. R. Young, Graham Kinloch, Randy Hodson, Bob Parker, Rose Brewer, Theresa Sullivan, Susan Marshall, Dorie Williams, Mark Warr, Antonio Ugalde, Dale McLemore, Gil Geis, Diana Kendall, Larry Cohen, Sheldon Ekland-Olson, Carroll Price, Madeleine McCulley, Christine Williams, Janice Perlman, Penny Green, Hernán Vera, Walter Firey, Manuel Castells, Carol Rambo Ronai, Michael Radelet, Chris Chambers, and Tiffany Hogan. We are also indebted to several generations of undergraduate students, graduate students, and teaching assistants for providing commentary as the chapters were developed and used in courses.

We thank the numerous reviewers of various editions of this textbook, L. Kay Gillespie at Weber State University and Martin Sugarman at Oxnard Community College. Nancy Roberts, Bill Webber, and Ed Stanford, editors at Prentice Hall, provided guidance in getting the several editions of this book off the ground. We also thank Robert Parker for preparing study questions at the end of most chapters and for contributions to Chapter 10 in the fourth edition and Lester Kurtz for help in drafting an early version of the war section in Chapter 11. We thank Ben Sargent for his permission to use his excellent editorial cartoons for each edition of this textbook. We also thank Tina Baker for help on the index and instructor's manual

We welcome comments and suggestions from the readers of this book, particularly in regard to changes for future editions.

Joe R. Feagin
Department of Sociology
Texas A&M University
4351 TAMU
College Station, TX 77843–4351

Clairece B. Feagin
c/o Department of Sociology
Texas A&M University
4351 TAMU
College Station, TX 77843–4351

David V. Baker
Behavioral Sciences Department
Riverside Community College
4800 Magnolia Avenue
Riverside, CA 92506-1299

SOCIAL PROBLEMS

(New York Convention and Visitors Bureau)

chapter 1

A Troubled Society

Social schizophrenia is present in this nation. One side is the rosy social self we boast of; the other is the seamy social self we alternately worry about and deny. We portray the self we boast of in terms of progress, prosperity, freedom, free enterprise, equal opportunity, and rags-to-riches mobility. In this vision, we are a people born and living free. We see the major problems of social justice that we face—such as class inequality, racism, and sexism— as either cured or on their way to being cured. We say that we live in a society that is the freest on earth. When pressed to justify this image, we may note that our basic documents speak of the "unalienable rights" of "life, liberty, and the pursuit of happiness" and the desire to "establish justice" and "secure the blessings of liberty." If pressed to defend our society, we may cite the dramatic industrialization of the nineteenth century, the incorporation of millions of European immigrants into the cities, and the prosperity of their descendants. We may go on to argue that the United States is the most democratic and affluent country on the planet, a consumer paradise.

This rosy picture is substantially true for a portion of Americans. It is, however, a portrait that obscures much of the reality of social life in the United States; it is to some extent a cover-up portrait that most of us have learned at home, in school, and from the media. Certainly, much truth can be found in these views of U.S. society, but the history of this society also has a seamy side.

Our past and present are haunted by numerous troubling ghosts: many Native Americans massacred in the European American quest for land; brutally whipped African Americans enslaved in chains; women and children working 12 hours a day in firetrap factories; millions of workers unnecessarily unemployed decade after decade; millions of families suffering below the poverty line; industrial workers with high cancer death rates; millions of victims of racial and gender discrimination; workers exploited by employers paying insufficient wages; aged citizens wasting away in scandal-ridden nursing homes; millions of urbanites with lives cut short by foul water and polluted air; countless homeless people living on the streets; a political system tainted by corruption and crime; and many millions of workers in other countries suffering from near-slave wages because of profit-oriented decisions made by U.S. corporations operating around the world. Past and present, U.S. society burdens the lives of ordinary citizens with multiple troubles, many of them rooted in patterns of racial, gender, and class oppression.

Those committed to the rosy picture of this nation may object to such a listing. They may argue, "We are aware of some societal problems, but we disagree with your emphasis." They may say, "These problems are typically the result of lazy or evil individuals, or of the actions of our distant ancestors, for which we are not to blame." Some may claim, "The problems are being worked on, and in any event each only requires a modest remedy. The larger society is fine." One such traditional interpretation has been called "blaming the victim," as it often sees those who are suffering, such as poor Americans or black Americans, as for the most part the cause of their individual and family problems.[1]

This social problems book takes issue with the individualistic or blaming-the-victim approach. Most victims of exploitation and oppression are *not* the victims of isolated errors. The source of many problems lies in the discrimination, exploitation, and oppression rooted in basic societal arrangements—the social patterns and processes that have framed this society from its beginning. Solutions for current problems, including government programs, are often ineffective because of the character of such fundamental arrangements as racism, sexism, class exploitation, heterosexism, and bureaucratic authoritarianism.

We human beings create structured social arrangements within which we carry out everyday activities. Central to this web of social arrangements are complex sets of norms and roles. *Norms* are rules that define what people should or should not do in their relations with other human beings. For example, many Americans have been taught to believe that a woman's proper place in life is only "in the home" as a wife and mother. Moreover, some white Americans believe that black Americans are racially inferior and should not hold positions of authority over whites. *Roles* refer to social positions to which sets of norms regarding duties and privileges are attached. For example, the socially defined role of mother carries with it the duties of childbearing, child rearing, and child care. Occupational roles, such as Wall Street investor, corporate executive, clerical worker, truck driver, and farm worker, all infer their own expectations, duties, and privileges. Combined in complex and changing ways, norms and roles together make up the larger social, economic, and political institutions of U.S. society.

A key feature of these structured patterns of everyday social life, which we illustrate in later chapters, is *stratification*—the relations of domination and subordination in which powerful people control a disproportionate share of such resources as property and wealth and thus shape the lives of the less powerful. From our society's beginnings, class, racial, and gender stratification have set limits on creativity and self-development. Perhaps the inadequate public discussion of these social arrangements is tied to the discomfort that arises from probing the misconceptions about our social existence. In this book, we provide the reader with a *critical power—conflict perspective* that digs deeply into our basic societal arrangements and helps to make sense of the substantial number of serious social problems in the United States.

The United States is highly stratified by class.

GOALS OF THIS CHAPTER

In this chapter, we look first at a few comments from Americans in all walks of life who are trying to make sense of their lives. After highlighting themes in their comments, we explore different approaches to social problems. It is here that we contrast the traditional perspectives on society and social problems with the critical power–conflict perspective. We conclude the chapter with a set of guiding propositions about U.S. society that draw upon the critical power–conflict perspective.

AMERICANS VIEW THEIR LIVES

More than one-third of the adults in nationwide polls state that their families' financial situations are *worse* today than in the recent past, and only one-fifth feel they are better off. Almost two-thirds state that the financial situation of most U.S. families has declined in recent years, and nearly half feel the next generation will be worse off than people are today.[2]

Only a few social scientists and journalists have given much in-depth attention to the expressed views of ordinary Americans on their lives, needs, and troubles. Caught in the often-frustrating web of everyday existence, we human beings do recognize and try to make sense of the troubles we face. The writers who have recorded the observations of articulate

Miners do some of America's most dangerous work, often at a high personal price in terms of dust-related diseases. (Library of Congress)

Americans have presented suggestive portraits of everyday life. As sociological readers, we can search for common themes in the following comments to find insights into the society in which working people live.

Workaday Troubles

First, we hear from Frank, a stonecutter, who is disabled, unemployed, and homeless:

> I'm a skilled stonemason. . . . I take native stone and cut it and put it together to build houses, chimneys, fireplaces, or art work. . . . But cement contains concentrations of calcium carbonate and lime. Because of constant exposure to it I developed. . . . cement poisoning. . . . My skin breaks open, sometimes clear down to the bone.
>
> I worked as long as I could, but due to the cement poisoning I had to quit. Since then I've done very little but minimum-wage jobs. It's all I can get; being a skilled stonemason doesn't help me when I can't do masonry. And I don't know if you've ever been exposed to 'em or not, but a minimum-wage job is slave labor.
>
> And with the rents and everything, if you have a minimum-wage job you get a choice: you can either get a place to live, and starve, or eat and have no place to live. So society oppresses the poor. In fact, they keep us poor, they perpetuate poverty.
>
> So I don't work day labor any more. I'd rather get out here and scrounge on the street. . . . I couldn't afford rent if I was working anyway, so why should I care? And this way I'm nobody's dog.[3]

Because of unemployment, many Americans have become homeless, but they still seek work. Marilyn, a homeless worker in Austin, Texas, describes the exploitation that low-wage workers often face:

We went and worked on this job a week. The boss said he'd pay us at the end of the week. We were there the day he got $2,500. And he took us to the Tamale House and said he was going to go to the bank and cash the check and come back and pay us, but he never came back and nobody got their money. See, he was a subcontractor and there was four of us working for him. . . . And we got the job done and we were down there waiting for him to come back and pay us.[4]

Jane, the wife of a packinghouse worker, talks about the <u>dehumanizing</u> effects of her husband's workplace, an extremely noisy, dangerous, and hierarchical environment:

[In] the packinghouses is a different world from this world. They are changed people when they go in there. They're aggressive; they're hostile; they look out for Number One. People who are the nicest people in the world outside, when they go in there, they're the most bigoted people you'd ever want to meet. It's the packinghouse and that environment that does that. [My husband] comes home from work, shoo[t] man, he's like a totally different person. He is real hostile. He wants to pick a fight with me. He's got everything figured out and whether I like it or not, you know, he's not willing to discuss it. After a while . . . when he gets out of the mood he gets in, in there, in the packinghouse, then he becomes the man I know and love. But that type of environment—hot, dirty, hazardous—everybody looking out for Number One, because if you help a friend out, it's going to be your job too, you know.[5]

The periodic economic recessions of recent decades have brought unemployment to workers who had not experienced joblessness before. For example, Richard, a 29-year-old schoolteacher who was laid off, had been unemployed for nine months when he made these comments to an interviewer:

It was my first and only job out of college, so this is the first time I've ever really been unemployed. When I first found out that I was going to be laid off I had sort of mixed feelings about it. In the beginning I was happy because I was ready to do something else and it forced me to go find some other field. But I was also very scared because it was a "secure job." . . .

When I started looking I had certain standards set. Of course, now I've lowered them. I've considered driving a cab, because I can drive, so at least it's something people couldn't tell me I don't have the experience for. . . . It has gotten really depressing and lately I just started crying like a baby. . . . I always thought being unemployed was something that happened to someone else, that it was someone else's problem. Now when I hear the term hardcore unemployed, I identify very much.[6]

Members of the rapidly growing contingent workforce—temporary, part-time, and contract workers who have no firm attachment to the companies for which they work—speak of the second-class status in the workplace that their tentative employment gives them. Michael, a 29-year-old electrical engineer, and his wife and young daughter still live with his parents. His $16.50-an-hour job as an independent contractor is scheduled to last only a few more weeks.

Any day they can walk in and say: "We don't need you." And that's how we live. . . . How do you plan a future that way?[7]

For two years after Cheryl and her husband, Terrence, were laid off from their full-time high-tech jobs, they hustled to find temporary and consultant jobs to support their three children. Cheryl is a college graduate and Terrence has a master's degree. A move to another state where the unemployment rate was low brought two more years of temporary and contract work before both found full-time jobs. Yet neither expects these jobs to last long. Cheryl states:

> The promise of permanent work at a company isn't there anymore for most people. Certainly, it was not there for us. . . . We have no faith in the corporate life anymore.[8]

Over a ten-year period Frank, age 53, has been laid off from five full-time jobs, including microwave test group supervisor and senior engineering technician, each paying less than the previous one. Now he earns $5.50 an hour as a part-time employee.

> I come home now, and I just don't know what to say to my wife, or to my daughter. I know it's not anything I did wrong. But you have this overpowering sense, this sick feeling that somehow you let everybody down. You have fear.[9]

Frank's wife, Judith, explains:

> We have no security in our lives anymore. . . . We try to maintain things as normal as possible. But when you're always worrying about the next paycheck, it's hard to be normal.[10]

Safety at work is a troubling issue many workers face on a daily basis. Poultry processing plant workers are among the most vulnerable to workplace hazards. Here, a 30-year-old immigrant poultry worker describes the poor conditions at a plant where employers disregard the well-being of workers:

> If we are not done with the truckful of chickens, we cannot leave work at the end of our shift. We are slaves. . . . You just have to be very fast. You're not always working safely because you have to keep up with the production line. The managers always want more production in less time. . . . You have to be careful with the knives and the machines, because everything is so slippery. A lot of fat falls on the machines and the floor. There's fat everywhere. Everything's greasy. So when there's a disk cutter with a rotating blade, your fingers are in danger. . . . Outside it's hot, but inside the temperature has to be under 50 degrees. We get sick year round even if we dress warm. Ice is always falling from the ceiling on your head. Some of it gets on your feet, into your boots. Your back's always cold, and your feet are always wet.[11]

Latinos and African Americans

Francisco is a disabled assembly-line worker. His job had been operating a machine that used rapid-fire pulses of compressed air to pound golf club shafts onto heads. He now receives workers' compensation.

> I made 2,300 golf clubs a day. I worked there 40 hours a week for 10 years. . . . I told them about the pain. They said, "If you don't work, you'll get fired." My supervisor would shake his finger at me. He would kick me. He would tell me, "I don't like you because you're a Latino.". . . . I worked for two years with the pain [because I needed the $5.50 an hour to support my family].
>
> I went to a doctor who told me that little by little the bone had worn away. He said I have a frozen shoulder.[12]

Diana's story ↓

Black anger over racial subordination surfaces in the comments of Diana, a black woman who has been successful in business in a southwestern city. She speaks about what it is like to be black in America:

> One step from suicide! What I'm saying is, the psychological warfare games we have to play every day just to survive. We have to be one way in our communities and one way in the workplace or in the business sector. We can never be ourselves all around. I think that may be a given for all people, but us particularly. It's really a mental health problem. It's a wonder we haven't all gone out and killed somebody or killed ourselves. . . . They say get an education. Go out and be *a* entrepreneurs. Pull yourself up from your boot straps. What boot straps? Hell, we got to first get the boot in order to have the straps. We try to do all these things. We learn the rules of the games, and by the time we have mastered them enough to really get into the economic mainstream . . . they change the rules of the game. The game becomes something else, because now you have learned how to play it. So it changes constantly, constantly. It always keeps us on edge.[13]

The View from the Home

Millions of women spend most of their time as homemakers and mothers. Therese, a wife in an Illinois suburb, critically reviews her life as follows:

> How would I describe myself? I'll sound terrible—just a housewife. (*Laughs*) It's true. What is a housewife? You don't have any special talents. I don't have any.
>
> Somebody who goes out and works for a living is more important than somebody who doesn't. What they do is very important in the business world. What I do is only important to five people. I don't like putting a housewife down, but everybody has done it for so long. It's sort of the thing to do. Deep down, I feel what I'm doing is important. But you hate to say it, because what are you? Just a housewife? (*Laughs*)[14]

Problems with Gender Discrimination: Women Workers

Karen, a computer science professor, tells of the variable treatment she receives from her male colleagues:

> Of the male faculty, I'm pretty good friends with two of the men. We read each other's work, go out to lunch once in a while, drop by each other's office and call each other almost on a daily basis. But if they're going to lunch with a couple of the other guys and I bump into them, they never ask me to join them. They're cool and businesslike and act as though they barely know me. Even worse, when they're in my office, they criticize sexist remarks that they laughed at during a committee meeting two hours earlier.[15]

In another case, Mary Lou tells of her experiences working for an energy company:

> My supervisor came into my office and showed me pictures of himself with a naked woman—absolute pornography. I threw him out of my office. Then I reported this to Employee Relations. Employee Relations [ER] handled the whole situation as poorly as possible. Although they promised me a day to think over the situation and what action I wanted to take before they confronted my supervisor, they did quite the opposite. When I arrived at work the next morning, ER was already meeting with my supervisor and understood the situation entirely—I encouraged such advances by my supervisor. Needless to say, all the men sympathized with my supervisor. They felt I was obviously in the wrong because I'm young and attractive and in being so I must obviously want a man to make advances towards me. This is sick, sick, sick logic on anyone's part.

Even though other women had told me this supervisor had harassed them also, no one was willing to come forward even when asked, and support me. After seeing how I was treated, I really couldn't blame them. Office gossip flourished. I'm surprised no one wanted to attach a Scarlet Letter to my clothes. My reputation and credibility was totally shot. I had to take a week off without pay because the atmosphere was so stressful nearly every day [that] I broke down and cried.[16]

Family Tragedies

Hy, a retired resident of Miami Beach, tells a story of medical malpractice that has destroyed his wife and his own life:

I always worked—made a dollar. Now I wouldn't say that at my age I wouldn't go to work. If my wife was all right, I'd still go to work because at sixty-nine I'm still a young man. But I feel my wife comes before anything else and that's why I'm here with her in the nursing home.

My wife had a hysterectomy; they gave her too much anesthesia and she had brain damage. That was about eleven years ago. . . . It's five years now that she's in a nursing home and I take care of her every day. I stay here seven days a week from seven in the morning until five-thirty at night. I take her out of bed, wash her and feed her, take her down the street. . . . It's very hard, very hard for me to get around. Unfortunately I spent over $65,000 on my wife, all the money I had. It's not a tragedy, it's just one of those things that happens, but it's very tough for me.[17]

Interpreting Life's Troubles

We can see in these comments that for most people, day in and day out, individual and family life flows on as a series of events. Some comments reflect pleasures; some, boredom; many, serious daily troubles. We glimpse personal hopes and recurring societal problems in the quotations. Broader social, economic, and political contexts are here personalized and "family-ized." All these Americans—young and old, male and female, and from various racial–ethnic groups—are aware that some troubles are part of the daily run of events. Interestingly, since the 1500s the Anglo-Saxon word *trouble* has meant "things or events causing stress," in particular the pains of work and unpleasant relations with higher authorities. Today, as in the past, many Americans still run into difficulties with powerful outside groups or organizational higher-ups and still have to deal with related family crises and troubles.

Recurring themes are evident in these portraits of ordinary Americans. We see some people trying to make sense of the daily realities surrounding them. Most describe dilemmas and problems in their lives at work, at home, and in the larger society. Frank speaks of feeling oppressed by his former job and that he is condemned to dangerous, disabling work. Diana describes the difficulties that African Americans, including those who are successful, face in coping with the discrimination imposed by white Americans. Karen speaks of being slighted by her male colleagues in a computer science department. Mary Lou discusses the dangers in sexual harassment at the workplace.

Thinking analytically about these comments, we begin to ask why. Why do workers feel threatened by or at their workplaces? Why are they alienated from their work? Why do they sometimes see themselves as abused and oppressed? Why are chemicals in the workplace a problem? Why do women workers and workers of color face an added type of oppression in the form of everyday discrimination? Why do some African Americans feel they are "one step from suicide"? Why is there so much unemployment? Why is a "woman's place" so often seen as in the home?

Society is made up of the actions of real human beings; it is not just an abstraction of these actions. We human beings work, eat, love, and raise children as best we can. Because of the time pressures of everyday life—of making a living and living as families—most Americans find it difficult to stand back, examine their society in depth, and probe deeply for the systematic answers to basic questions. Yet most of us know that certain human needs, both our own and those of others, are not being met; we are usually not ignorant of the political–economic context within which we live our lives. A number of the rank-and-file Americans quoted have begun to search for broader answers. Often they see their lives and the difficulties therein tied clearly to the institutional structures of the larger societal context.

Sometimes rank-and-file Americans sound rather radical in their assessments of the personal and societal problems they see. They will be critical of automation causing job losses, of big corporations that pollute rivers, of corrupt politicians tied to big corporations, or of recurring racism they face. At other times, however, even in the same breath, they will sound conservative. They will be critical of poor Americans who need welfare, calling them welfare "queens," or they will express the view that the "free" market and private property are very good features of this society and that capitalists have a right to invest and run businesses as they see fit. While some Americans are consistently conservative on many issues, the majority seem to be more inconsistent, sometimes taking a relatively radical position, sometimes a relatively conservative one. Most Americans have come to accept established views of the social world taught to them at home, at church, in the media, and in school, even while the serious social problems in their own lives, in their workplaces and communities, as well as what they see in the mass media, compel them to question the powerful elites and exploitative forces that surround them.

In the chapters that follow, we will see this inconsistency in a variety of beliefs, such as those about the poor, welfare, crime, markets, business, socialism, and the environment. Eric Hobsbawm describes this inconsistency as "prepolitical thought"—that is, as thinking which has not yet reached the level of full political or class consciousness. In modern America, this commonplace prepolitical thinking does not provide a coherent viewpoint or interpretive framework for understanding the deep relationship between personal and societal problems and the underlying foundations of exploitative class, racial, and gender relations. Many Americans have not yet found a consistent language, an integrated perspective with which to express a deeper understanding of their troubled worlds.[18]

SOCIETAL DECLINE: THE GENUINE PROGRESS INDICATOR

Research done by Redefining Progress, a nonpartisan institute, supports and validates the sense that rank-and-file Americans have of growing social and health problems in this capitalistic society. Concerned about society's future health and well-being, public-spirited researchers at this institute constructed a statistical index that measures the economic well-being of the United States much better than the old measures—called the Gross National Product (GNP) and the Gross Domestic Product (GDP)—which are currently the major statistical indicators used by business and government officials. Redefining Progress researchers have shown that the conventional GDP is a poor measure of the nation's well-being and growth because it includes the costs of crime, divorce, and other aspects indicating the breakdown of U.S. society. Money spent on added policing, home security, divorce lawyers, and cleaning up pollution increases the GDP, but these costs represent a loss of national well-being. Similarly, the sale of wood from harvesting redwood trees in old forests adds to the GDP, but the long-term environmental costs of depletions of the country's natural resources are not subtracted from the GDP. Indeed, in ordinary business accounting similar costs would not be counted as income, as they are in the GDP, but as expenses (or depreciation) deducted from income. The policy researchers note that "much of what economists now consider economic growth, as measured by GDP, is really one of three things: (1) fixing blunders and social decay from the past; (2) borrowing resources from the future; or (3) shifting functions from the community and household realm to that of the monetized economy."[19]

In contrast to the GDP, the statistical index called the Genuine Progress Indicator (GPI) deducts social breakdown expenditures for such things as crime, pollution, and divorce and adds in the value of household work and volunteer work. The result is that while the GDP has risen more or less steadily since 1960, the GPI peaked from the mid-1960s to the early 1970s and then started a steady downhill slide. During the period from 1960 to 1970, for instance, the annual growth rate of GDP per capita was 2.2 percent and the annual growth rate of the GPI was also positive at 1.5 percent. However, between 1970 and 1980 the average annual GDP rate continued to rise, at 1.7 percent per year, while the GPI began to decline, at the annual rate of −1.0 percent. By the 1980–1990 period, the GPI was declining more rapidly, at −1.8 percent annually, while the GDP was increasing at 1.7 percent annually.[20] In 2000, the GPI rose a little, by 1.6 percent, while the GDP increased by 3.9 percent.[21] Even with this increase, the GPI is still about $23,947 per capita *below* the per capita GDP. One recent report on the GPI noted that "GDP has overestimated the health of our economy by $7 trillion. Ironically, one of the key factors contributing to this overcounting is the expenditure that has resulted from the accounting scandals at Enron, WorldCom, Arthur Anderson and others. The wrongdoings at Enron alone will contribute up to $1 billion to the US economy, in the form of legal fees, jail time, media frenzy and associated payouts."[22]

Thus, Redefining Progress researchers conclude that sources of the discontent of the U.S. public over the state of the country are measured much better by the GPI than by the GDP. "Honest national accounting would inject a large dose of accountability to the political process. It would stop politicians and interest groups from hiding the implications of bad policy behind what amounts to a rigged set of books."[23]

PEOPLE WORKING FOR CHANGE: SOME EXAMPLES

Americans in many different communities have organized to improve life conditions in many different areas of their lives. The following are some examples.

The United Farm Workers Union

Over the last several decades, the United Farm Workers (UFW) union has forced growers, often-large agribusiness corporations, to make substantial changes in working conditions for migrant farmworkers. Growers once forced low-paid farm laborers to work from 4:00 A.M. until 8:00 P.M. or later, with some putting in 92 hours each week. Out of fear of being fired, workers could not refuse overtime. They had no health care and no toilets or fresh water during long, hot days in the fields. Pressure from the union brought health plans, reasonable working hours, and more humane working conditions to many workers. However, for farmworkers in some areas of the Southwest, low wages, terrible working conditions, and extreme exploitation are still routine. During recent decades, the UFW has fought against the use of deadly chemical pesticides that cause cancer, other health problems, and premature death in large numbers of farmworkers. Growers have required workers to spray fields without protective clothing or masks. Workers have carried home deadly poisons on clothing. Aerial spraying has put poisons into the air and water supplies in towns where farmworkers live. Children in some towns suffer a much higher than normal cancer rate.[24]

The charismatic leader of the UFW, César Chávez, died in 1993, after two days of testimony in a lawsuit brought by a grower against the union because of its boycotts against the company to improve workers' conditions. Some of the UFW's recent efforts have been in court, in attempts to protect the rights of unions to organize and boycott. Despite lawsuits brought by growers to reduce the effectiveness of the union, the UFW continues organizing to improve working conditions of agricultural workers. Recently, UFW lawyers have joined with other farmworker groups in a lawsuit to enjoin the Environmental Protection Agency's approval of two chemical pesticides used by growers. These dangerous poisons continue to contaminate workers and their families. Exposed farmworker children living within a quarter mile of fields where growers use chemicals have four to five times more of these chemicals in their bodies than do other people tested.[25]

Clerical Workers' Unions

Clerical and technical workers won a major victory in 1988 when Harvard University's administration dropped its opposition to the drive to unionize the mostly female clerical and technical workers. Two of the new union's goals were pay equity and child care. The victory of these workers, which came after months of hard work and unpleasant relations with the administration, provided encouragement for women workers attempting to organize in white-collar workplaces across the United States. As the union sought a second contract four years later, it criticized Harvard for unfair bargaining, contracting out work, safety violations, and unfair labor practices. The union sought a wage increase equal to or near the university's annual increases in revenue, insurance coverage for domestic partners, employment security, and improvements in child care benefits.[26]

In the mid-1990s, Harvard's management and its 3,600 office, library, and laboratory workers agreed upon another 3-year plan that included wage increases of nearly 14 percent over the contract period. The agreement also specified new or expanded work and family benefits such as job sharing, flexible work schedules, and child care.[27]

Over the last several years, clerical workers at campuses of the University of California and the University of Minnesota, as well as other college campuses, have unionized and won major concessions to improve the work lives of clerical workers.

Striking for Better Conditions

Several hundred workers at a Chipman-Union plant in Union Point, Georgia, won a new agreement in the mid-1990s that included a significant increase in wages and benefits. The mostly black female workers had voted to be represented by a union of clothing, textile, and garment workers (called UNITE!). For two years, the workers, speaking of problems of sexual harassment and piece-rate wages at the plant, organized demonstrations to improve working conditions. The government's National Labor Relations Board issued complaints against the firm for bad-faith bargaining and firing union activists. The new agreement provided for improved working conditions and reinstatement of fired workers.[28]

Today, the laundry, garment, and retail workers' union represents 250,000 members in the United States and Canada. Its recent organizing campaigns have been against Life Uniforms and Cintas, the country's largest nurses' uniform retailer and the largest uniform provider, respectively. The union argues that Life Uniforms relies on sweatshop labor to produce such private labels as LifeStyles, Angelica, and Life scrubs. The union also asserts that Cintas discriminates against African American and Latino workers in hiring, pay, and promotions.[29] The struggle for better working conditions for U.S. workers continues, in the North and the South.

Protesting Toxic Pollution

Numerous grassroots organizations monitor, and often protest, the actions of industrial corporations and military bases and weapons plants in order to protect local communities and the environment from hazardous wastes. In the 1990s, a coalition of California citizens' groups waged a successful campaign against the toxin-producing open burning of rocket fuel by United Technologies Corporation. Demonstrations by community residents and union members and passage of a zoning ordinance prevented an Oklahoma cement company from burning hazardous waste and spewing toxins into the air of the local community.[30] Concerned citizens in California's Silicon Valley convinced an IBM plant there to phase out use of ozone-destroying chemicals.[31] Grassroots pressure played a major role in ensuring passage of the Federal Facilities Compliance Act (1992), which provides penalties for violations of solid and hazardous waste laws by military bases and other federal facilities—among the country's worst polluters. Prior to the passage of this law, federal facilities often failed to comply with toxic waste disposal laws, openly disregarding public health issues.[32]

An estimated 60,000 industries dump billions of gallons of wastewater into lakes, streams, and rivers. They dump toxic wastes into landfills. Today, some citizens are taking aggressive action against these industrial polluters. The National Environmental Law Center (NELC) has pressed lawsuits to force companies to stop polluting and to clean up hazardous waste in landfills. Taking such firms as Shell Oil, General Electric, ICI Americas Corporation, and numerous others to court, the NELC has won settlements in most lawsuits filed. Courts have imposed nearly $45 million in fines against companies and forced some of the worst polluters to comply with environmental laws. Local environmental groups and agencies have received the money collected under the settlements to clean up local environments. NELC attorneys also settled a suit against one of the largest chemical companies, Dow Chemical. The NELC attorneys aimed the lawsuit at a Midland, Michigan plant that Dow admitted was dumping into the Tittabawassee River (and thus Saginaw Bay) toxic chemicals that significantly exceeded legal limits allowed by federal permits for the disposal of toxic chemicals. The plant has sometimes dumped 137 pounds of phosphorus per day over its legal limit, creating high phosphorus levels in the bay and excessive algae growth. Two other dangerous chemicals—2,4-D and chlopyrifos—have exceeded legal limits by 16 to 138 percent. Alleging a "clear pattern of violations," the NELC sued on behalf of state and local groups to force Dow to meet its obligations under the Clean Water

Act.[33] Dow Chemical eventually paid $800,000 to fund Saginaw Bay environmental projects and agreed to spend more than $30 million to reduce discharge of chemicals into the Tittabawassee River.[34]

In these cases, we see Americans concerned about societal problems organizing and protesting to make the United States a better place to live. In this book, we will not just examine social problems; we will also look at many examples of citizens working for progressive change.

TRADITIONAL PERSPECTIVES ON SOCIETY AND SOCIAL PROBLEMS

Traditionally, many social scientists have been preoccupied with understanding or defending the established social order. How and why do some societies last for centuries? What holds together the different groups and institutions of a complex society? Is the glue for societies a consensus on widely shared values? Many traditional social scientists and other social commentators have preferred answers emphasizing the harmonious working of established U.S. institutions, and when they consider change, they have preferred slow rates of evolutionary change.

Much U.S. and European social science reflects a commitment to the broad contours of the existing order of that political–economic reality we call *capitalism.* There is not, nor has there ever been, a "value-free" social science. The predominant perspective underlying much U.S. social science has gradually evolved from one of a laissez-faire (hands-off) government approach in the late nineteenth and early twentieth centuries—a *conservative order-market view* generally opposed to government intervention in social and economic life—to a *liberal order-market view* in the last century—a reformist perspective that by the early 1900s, a time of growing labor conflict in the United States, accepted some government intervention as necessary. Often the liberal order-market view approach has taken the form of what is called *corporate liberalism.* Seeing capitalists and corporations as necessary and productive but as requiring some government regulation, corporate liberals have supported regulation of corporations and other businesses, plus significant government aid to support corporations when the market fails and enough government aid to working people to keep them from protesting too much. The social science of the founding "fathers" of U.S. sociology and the great European sociologists has often been rooted in this corporate, reformist liberalism.[35]

The European Background

Émile Durkheim (1858–1917), a French sociologist who greatly influenced the sociology of social problems in the United States, was concerned with what holds societies together. He pointed out problems of social integration that exist in a capitalist society because of an increasing division of labor. As jobs, occupations, and other activities become more specialized in modern urban societies, people become less self-sufficient and more dependent on others than in rural areas. From this viewpoint, to keep a complex society such as the United States from falling apart, it is necessary that all social groups agree on basic values, such as the individualistic "work ethic."[36]

Durkheim emphasized a *social strain* theory of social problems. He discussed the strains in societies that he thought led to problems of crime, suicide, and violence. In this view the breakdown of traditional social organization, such as in the presumed loss of respect for traditional authority as farming people move from rural areas to cities, leads to flux and breakdown in traditional values and often to crime, suicide, and urban violence. Rapid changes such as industrialization and urbanization trigger the destruction of respect for the authority of tradition, church, and state. This lack of structure and discipline must be replaced by more structure and discipline under industrial capitalism if the social equilibrium is to be restored. Durkheim did not seriously analyze the role of racism, sexism, or class conflict in modern societies. He hoped that workers and capitalists could somehow work out conflicts and operate in harmony. He thought that expansion of government, with its regulatory programs, was necessary under modern capitalism, and he hoped that capitalism could be reformed. A corporate liberal, Durkheim was linked to progressive groups pressing for reforms of French capitalism. Since his time, Durkheim's emphasis on strain and disorganizing forces such as urbanization have heavily influenced much social science analysis of social problems.

Corporate Liberalism

By the early 1900s, many U.S. social scientists realized that laissez-faire thinking was inadequate for dealing with the changing U.S. economy, one in which a few large companies were increasingly in control of major sectors of industry, such as the automobile and steel industries. Workers and communities were facing problems as multinational (global) corporations expanded overseas to South America, Asia, and Africa. From the late nineteenth century to World War II, many workers protested poor working conditions and participated in union movements. Liberal order–market view advocates in universities, government, and large corporations became committed to some government intervention to help U.S. corporations make a profit at home and overseas, to social welfare intervention to cool down labor unrest, and to government regulation to reduce consumer protests. The ideology of corporate liberalism became the dominant view in social science in the decades after 1900. Corporate liberals recognized that business, labor, and consumer groups were in conflict and that elite leaders had to do something about the conflict. They argued that government intervention could and should solve this social conflict within the framework of a reformed capitalism.

These social scientists called on government to be a neutral judge of competing interest groups in conflict and, to act in the interest of the whole society. They generally ignored the fact that government under capitalism was, and is, substantially dominated by large corporations and investors whose interests often receive more attention than those of ordinary workers, small-farm operators, or small business owners. Such a government could not be neutral; nor would it provide the type of social support programs demanded by workers and consumers to protect and support their families. Nonetheless, prominent social scientists felt that some government intervention was necessary to stave off economic depression, to help troubled enterprises make a profit, to rein in extreme economic competition, and to meet the protests of workers' groups.[37]

Leading sociologists adopted some variant of this liberal order–market view. Early sociologists such as Lester Ward (1841–1913), Albion Small (1854–1926), and E. A. Ross (1866–1951) analyzed critically the social conflict of their times. Their active decades were filled with labor–capitalist battles, extremes in business competition, unionization drives, the imperialist use of U.S. troops in foreign countries, and large-scale immigration to the

United States of workers from southern and eastern Europe. These sociologists wrote in the period called "early monopoly capitalism," a turbulent time in the United States symbolized by growth of large corporations. During this era, force by the police, state militias, and federal troops was used by corporate officials to put down legitimate worker protests, including union movements, directed at improving workplace conditions. For the most part, these sociologists did not take issue with the use of government force as a tool for expanding the interests of the business entrepreneurs. Nor did these social scientists easily take the perspective of working people, immigrants, people of color, or women. Still, they were critical at times of the greed characteristic of the capitalistic society of their day. Sociologists such as Small and Ross did on occasion go beyond the conventional wisdom of the dominant intellectual and business elites to argue that workers should have greater power. In general, capitalists and workers were seen as competing interest groups whose differences could be reconciled within the framework of capitalism and with the help of a reformist federal government. The concern of these sociologists for order reflected their view of the way in which conflicts should be resolved. Stability required the expansion of government, including aid to business, police control of workers' protests, and some welfare-state reforms.[38]

Social Problems: The Durkheimian Tradition in the United States

The intensive study of social problems by U.S. social scientists dates from the decades between 1910 and 1940, as is signaled by numerous textbooks, from C. A. Ellwood's *The Social Problem: A Constructive Analysis* (1915) to C. M. Rosenquist's *Social Problems* (1940). Early texts presented a diversity of societal problems, such as drug addiction and crime, with a little sociological interpretation; any interpretive framework fit into the tradition of social order and strain reflected in the work of corporate–liberal sociologists such as Durkheim. These texts viewed societal problems in terms of personal, family, and other social disorganization, with an emphasis on individual departures from established norms of society.[39]

For example, according to Stuart A. Queen and Delbert M. Mann's textbook *Social Pathology* (1925), a sociological interpretation of social problems accents "maladjustment," "demoralization," and "disorganization."[40] Discussions of divorce, illegitimacy, and mental illness demonstrated this concern with the failure of individuals to fit in with established norms and roles. Economic problems, such as child labor, are sometimes considered, but the typical approach gives great attention to social statistics and little attention to the roots of economic problems, such as child labor, in an aggressively profit-oriented capitalistic system. Sociologists such as Queen and Mann viewed solutions to social problems primarily in terms of individual adaptation to existing norms, roles, and social conditions and, less often, in terms of limited government intervention in the society, such as modest government health programs.

In his 1940 textbook, Rosenquist viewed the existing system as a given: "Perhaps we may be on solid ground through a recognition of the capitalist system and its accompaniments as normal. We may then deal with its several parts, treating as problems those which do not function smoothly."[41] Here again is a reflection of the Durkheimian functionalist tradition. The existing capitalistic order is considered normal, and areas that do not function smoothly are seen as abnormal and as social problems.

Like later textbooks, these books reveal a strong concern with the functioning of individual Americans and their adjustments to the existing social order. Troubled individuals are often described as "pathological," "disorganized," or "maladjusted." While these texts recognize industrial and urban changes as forcing individuals to adjust to new situations, they give little attention to the problem-generating character of the capitalistic, race-stratified, gender-stratified order of the larger society. They usually reject the laissez-faire view of no government intervention, and they often cast solutions in corporate–liberal terms, with, as one early sociologist said, an eye toward avoiding "revolutions on the one hand, and reactions on the other."[42]

Mainstream Social Science Views of Social Problems

Between the 1930s and the 1970s, theorist and social analyst Talcott Parsons (1902–1979), with his followers, brought to contemporary sociology a continuing concern with social order grounded in an ideology of corporate liberalism. Optimistic about technological and societal change, Parsons rejected critical power–conflict theories that were skeptical about the long-term survival of capitalist societies and that forecast periodic rebellions by oppressed groups. Parsons's underlying values reflected a liberal order–market view commitment to moderate government reform and orderly change. Parsons was optimistic about a growing agreement on values between groups in conflict, such as whites and African Americans in the civil rights movement, and a decline in injustice in capitalistic societies, so much so that he became convinced that sociologists in the next generation would write of slow evolution, not of revolution, in Western societies. Parsons played a major role in emphasizing social consensus, equilibrium, and slow evolutionary change to the point of seriously downgrading theoretical analysis of class, racial, and gender conflict. While Parsons has been heavily criticized, the sociological perspective he reflected is today implicit in, or compatible with, that of many social scientists who analyze social problems.[43]

One influential social-problems textbook in the 1960s and 1970s period was *Contemporary Social Problems* by prominent sociologists Robert K. Merton, a student of Parsons, and Robert M. Nisbet. There, Nisbet defines a social problem as behavior patterns regarded by much of society as "being in violation of one or more generally accepted or approved norms."[44] Nisbet rejects the idea that social problems are so deeply rooted in the framework of society that "a total change of society" is required. Given his acceptance of the existing capitalistic order, Nisbet argues for a value-free, scientific approach to studying problems. If provided scientific knowledge about problems, existing government policymakers can then take the appropriate action. In the concluding chapter, Merton agrees that a social problem "involves a discrepancy, judged unacceptable, between social standards and social actuality."[45] Merton also argues for value-free analysis and objective data collection, so that existing government policymakers can make use of the data collected. In effect, Merton suggests that the existing capitalistic system is healthy and can be reformed with the aid of presumably neutral academic and government experts. Social-problems textbooks and research over the last several decades have in many ways reflected this general approach.

Indeed, since the 1960s federal government attempts to deal with problems of such groups as poor Americans have varied but have regularly been piecemeal measures, such as the poorly funded War on Poverty programs of the 1960s and the underfunded housing programs for poor families developed in more recent decades. When government programs have involved sociologists, those who get the call are usually the social statisticians who make much use of government-generated statistics, too often uncritically, in their analyses. The tendency is to study many problems in terms of (often limited) government statistics. Government data tend to neglect those with the greatest power in society. Basic and revealing data on corporate executives' actions and attitudes or on major real estate firms' discrimination against people of color or women, to take just two examples, have not been systematically gathered by the government analysts or mainstream social scientists. In addition, social problems are often studied in isolation from one another, from their historical context, or from the larger frameworks of class, racial, and gender stratification. While many social scientists are aware of these criticisms of traditional social-problems analysis, their actual research and teaching practices frequently reveal their commitment (or resignation) to an ahistorical and noncontextual approach to social problems. In recent decades, when some government-sponsored approaches did not solve social problems—when problems such as poverty persisted in spite of modest government programs—some prominent social scientists have reacted by rejecting government intervention and have thus forsaken the liberal order–market view perspective for a neoconservative, and renewed laissez-faire, approach.

A CRITICAL POWER–CONFLICT PERSPECTIVE

For decades, the mainstream social science emphasis on order and on competing labor–business groups managed by a neutral government has been challenged by some power–conflict analysts of U.S. society. These social scientists give much greater emphasis than mainstream social scientists—both conservative and liberal order–market view analysts—to the great inequalities of power, wealth, and resources in society, to inequalities along class, racial, and gender lines, and to how these inequalities shape an array of societal problems. They have focused on why and how hierarchies of dominant and subordinate groups are established, maintained, and replaced. Most social scientists in this critical tradition give greater attention than mainstream order–market view analysts and researchers to the regular exploitation of the powerless by the powerful and to ongoing conflicts between powerless and powerful groups. Such an approach, they argue, is the only way to get beneath surface appearances.

Critical power–conflict analysts recognize that orderly normative arrangements exist, but they argue that the existing social structure of capitalism, such as the great wealth of corporate capitalists and the modest conditions of many workers, creates an exploitative and conflict-ridden system. Such troubling arrangements represent a social order that seems stable but harbors seething inequality-spawned conflicts below the surface, conflicts that can break forth in protests, riots, or revolution. A radical (from the Latin *radix,* meaning "root") power–conflict perspective looks critically at often-hidden roots of social problems in exploitative, discriminatory, and alienating social behavior. The roots stressed in this textbook are capitalism, racism, and sexism. Attention is given to the institutionalization and bureaucratization of exploitation and inequality in organizations, communities, corporations, and governments. Many power–conflict sociologists adopt a bottom-up perspective and examine social problems from the viewpoints of oppressed groups.

Today, power–conflict social scientists are a diverse group, including not only a variety of neo-Marxists (who tend to focus on class) but also feminists (who focus on gender exploitation), racial–ethnic analysts (who focus on racial or ethnic exploitation), gay–lesbian researchers (who focus on heterosexism), and critical state analysts (who focus on antidemocratic governments). Important differences exist among these perspectives, but many of them deeply analyze the roots of problems in dominant institutions and develop major critical or radical solutions to social problems. Unlike some conventional perspectives, no unified body of power–conflict theory and analysis exists yet. Many analysts, however, provide thought and analysis that create a foundation for the sustained critical power–conflict perspective on social problems presented in this book.

Background: The Influential Thought of Karl Marx

In recent decades, numerous social scientists and other Americans have become aware of the importance of the Marxist intellectual traditions for building an adequate understanding of U.S. society, including its serious social problems. More so than in most western European countries, in the United States certain Marxist and neo-Marxist ideas, books, organizations, and even college teachers have been repressed since the late 1930s. In the 1940s and 1950s—the era of McCarthyism—thousands of people (such as TV writers and college teachers) were fired from their jobs or prevented from taking jobs was the slightest indication that they held a power–conflict point of view, whether it was feminist, Marxist, or antiracist. Official witch-hunts were conducted for "disloyal" (meaning "critical") Americans in many institutions, including government agencies and universities. This political repression had a chilling effect on the social sciences, so much so that it has only been since the late 1960s that U.S. scholars and researchers have felt they had the *freedom* to discuss and write critically about the ideas and impact of the Marxist and other power–conflict traditions.

Karl Marx (1818–1883) was perhaps the first social science thinker to put power and class conflict issues at the center of his interpretation of the social structure of capitalist societies. These societies, at their most fundamental level, are characterized by ongoing conflict between major social classes, especially the capitalist class (the owners or controllers of the means of production) and the working class (the workers hired by capitalists). Marx recognized other social classes, such as mom-and-pop grocery store owners (the petty bourgeoisie), but he gave emphasis to the fundamental split between the controllers of factories and offices and those who work for them. The capitalistic structure of production and distribution results in direct control over and exploitation of masses of struggling workers by a small group of (often wealthy) capitalist owners. The owners' profits, to a substantial degree, are derived from the work efforts of their workers, who must sell their labor to capitalists so they and their families can survive. For Marxists, this unequal class structure has greatly influenced the development of politics, law, and education in countries such as the United States. In spite of recent assertions by U.S. media pundits that "Marx and Marxism are dead," Marx's ideas and analyses remain highly accurate and very relevant for understanding the problems and developments in advanced capitalistic countries, including the United States.

Marx emphasized that human beings are born into social classes and ideological frameworks not of their own making. Individuals and their need for material goods, as well as their need for self-mastery and creativity, are the core reality, but human beings are hemmed in by the actions of many others. Exploited workers find themselves fighting for their interests, for better wages or working conditions, in an ongoing struggle with capitalists. Workers are alienated from their work and workplaces because they do not control them. Because of its ownership and control over the means of production (such as offices and factories), the capitalist class has *much* greater socioeconomic resources and economic and political power than the working class. The employers' view of the world becomes the ruling ideology in a capitalistic society. This great power imbalance, Marx argued, will periodically generate worker protests, including large-scale movements on the part of the workers conscious of workplace exploitation. Recurring economic and political conflict is fostered by the presence of clear class enemies and of good communication within one's own class, be it capitalists or workers. Neither individual pathologies and maladjustments nor large-scale disasters are necessary for social problems to occur. To understand major problems in societies, Marx argued, look for exploitation between groups, and thus for regular conflicts in basic social interests.[46]

An important feature of Marx's analysis, and of those drawing on his ideas ever since, is the view that government under capitalism is not an independent force separated from the capitalist class. Governments in a capitalist society usually are not neutral. They are dominated by the capitalist class directly, through actual participation, and indirectly, through the requirements of a capitalist economy to which government officials must respond. Unlike most corporate liberals presented previously, those in Marx's tradition see government as very substantially biased by its links to capitalism. Societal problems typically cannot be solved simply by appeals to government for reforms. A bit more government regulation here, a few more social programs there, can make life more bearable for many Americans, but government reforms are always in danger of being rolled back. Capitalistic countries have governments that reflect in their programs struggles between capitalists and ordinary working people, but they nonetheless remain capitalist-dominated governments.

Capitalists use their money in attempts to control state and federal governments.

Contemporary Social Class Perspectives

Many social scientists have grappled with the "ghost of Karl Marx," but in U.S. sociology only a few social science researchers, until relatively recently, have pressed forward in discussing the ideas of Marx in analyzing social problems. One exception was C. Wright Mills (1916–1962), who developed a strong power–conflict perspective that borrowed important ideas from the Marxist tradition but used traditional social science ideas as well. Mills, who called himself a "plain Marxist," viewed a Marxist approach as a lasting contribution to social science. In his view, probing beneath everyday events to major resource and power inequalities shaping them leads to fundamental insights into the importance of economic factors in human history; and social-problems analysis should be grounded in examining age-old conflicts between oppressor and oppressed, between rulers and ruled.

Mills noted new developments in U.S. capitalism. He documented the fact that, within the broad classes of capitalists and workers, new intra-class divisions had arisen. As he saw it, the subgroup of white-collar workers—a group composed of sales clerks, clerical workers, and salaried professionals—has recently come to center stage in modern capitalistic economies. Most of these better-paid workers are relatively propertyless, just as factory workers are. A critical dividing line, Mills argued, is the amount of prestige: "People in white-collar occupations claim higher prestige than wage-workers, and as a general rule, can cash in their claims with wage-workers as well as with the anonymous public." Mills also accented the growth of a managerial group working for the capitalist class. In *The Power Elite* (1959) Mills documented, at the helm of U.S. society, a small tripartite elite—those few people (almost all white men) in big business, big government, and big military institutions who make the society's most important decisions.[47]

Highlighting the interrelationships of the economic, political, and military sectors of U.S. society, Mills saw government as being tied closely to the economy. Government intervention in the form of welfare programs and military programs has actually supported capitalism when it was threatened. Advanced capitalism has so far saved itself from the death Marx predicted by extensive government and military programs. Government contracts and subsidies support the profits of many corporations, especially in agriculture and the military-industrial complex. Government subsidies, loans, and tax credits aid many firms in the private sector, from farmers, to aircraft manufacturers, to oil companies. Government aid to poor and other rank-and-file Americans has periodically expanded (or contracted), in the form of welfare, unemployment benefits, and housing programs. Such social reforms are usually forced by the protests of working-class Americans and workers' organizations. Mills's analysis has more radical implications for the scale of societal change needed in society than do traditional order–market view approaches. Mills made use of Marxist theories, but he was critical of some Marxist ideas. For example, he rejected the idea that the working class is necessarily the most important agent for social change in capitalist societies.[48]

Numerous social scientists working in the Marxist tradition emphasize the problematic character of work, the workplace, and the working class. For example, in *Labor and Monopoly Capital* (1974), Harry Braverman uses much research data to show how the growing group of white-collar workers is for the most part made up of relatively low-wage workers, including a large group of women clerical workers. Their workaday lives are just as hemmed in by bosses, strict supervision, workplace and work alienation, and repetitive job activities as are those of most blue-collar workers. Braverman, himself a veteran of skilled manual work, presents evidence that weekly wages of many groups of clerical workers are lower than those of skilled blue-collar workers. These white-collar workers are thus firmly in the working class.[49]

Braverman emphasizes the *deskilling* of many jobs. Over several decades, mechanization has reduced the skill levels necessary for many jobs, so that many workers are too highly educated for jobs they have or are likely to have for the rest of their lives (a fact well-known to many college graduates). The average blue-collar worker and the average white-collar (clerical or sales) worker today need relatively modest education and training to perform their jobs. In part, this deskilling process reflects a class struggle, since deskilling is the intended result of the management procedures used in corporations and businesses for bringing workers under closer control (see Chapter 10). Today, many categories of workers no longer control as much knowledge as they once did, and this lack of personal knowledge gives capitalist employers and managers more power. This lack of worker control contributes to the persisting problem of worker alienation. Braverman's analysis goes to the roots of problems in the workplace today, including lack of control over work, alienation, low wages, and unemployment. The work of Marxist and neo-Marxist researchers contains many important insights that we can draw on to better understand the social problems of the United States today.

Even some contemporary non-Marxist social scientists have found themselves discussing class contradictions of modern capitalism in quasi-Marxist terms. For example, we note in Chapter 2 that the real (inflation-adjusted) income of average Americans has been declining for decades as U.S. capitalists disinvest in the U.S. economy, export jobs, and seek out low-wage workers and more profitable investments in lower-wage countries around the globe. Marx's analysis of capitalism would incline one to expect this result, with a long-term demise of capitalism being the likely result. However, government intervention in economies such as that of the United States has so far staved off the ultimate economic decline. Today, nonetheless, economic deterioration—such as the loss of good-paying jobs—is proceeding in the United States, as well as in Europe and Japan.

A few mainstream economists are beginning to recognize the significance and meaning that this economic decline has for theories of capitalism. For example, in *The Future of Capitalism,* influential MIT economist Lester Thurow has noted that historically "democratic governments, not the market, built the middle class. . . . Democracy cares about capitalistic economic inequality and is working to reduce it. The combination worked. The potential conflict between capitalistic power and democratic power did not explode."[50] However, the current scene is different from that of previous economic crises, such as those during the Great Depression of the 1930s. Indeed, over the last two decades, we have seen *increasing* income and wealth inequality in the United States but, unlike in previous periods, the majority of business leaders or senior government officials as yet show little interest to do anything significant about these growing economic inequalities. Thurow underscored a basic problem of capitalism, and one foreseen by Marxist analysts: "If an American worker has a falling real standard of living, a government that does nothing about it, and no political parties that even promise to do something about his or her major problem, what then?"[51] The implied answer is economic chaos and social revolution.

Perspectives Emphasizing Gender and Race

In addition to the emphasis on class, one finds an emphasis on racial stratification and gender stratification among many social scientists who adopt a power–conflict point of view.

Orthodox Marxists often explain racial and gender problems in terms of capitalism and class relations; they tend to accent the ways in which the class patterns of capitalist societies have led to subordination of women and people of color. Other social scientists, however, probing deeply the roots of problems in this society, see racial and gender discrimination as substantially independent of, though intertwined with, the social class relations of modern capitalism.[52]

For example, some feminist scholars have noted that certain problems of women cut across class lines—problems such as patriarchal (male-dominated) families, wife beating, rape, access to abortion, and adequate child care—and thus they take issue with too heavy an emphasis on class. These feminist scholars have noted that patriarchal arrangements, with men as a group having great family, economic, and political power over women as a group, existed before capitalism became significant in world history. Many feminist analysts have viewed the U.S. system of male–female power and resource inequality as rooted in women's societally defined reproductive roles and sexuality.[53] In contrast, for many orthodox Marxists the inequality of wives in the home and the family and the "wage slavery" of husbands outside the home are both the result of capitalism. The fact is usually missing in such an analysis that the preexisting patriarchal structures of most precapitalist societies greatly shaped the emerging capitalist system of the fifteenth and sixteenth centuries. Thus, eliminating class exploitation will not necessarily free women from gender subordination inside and outside the home.[54]

A combined and interactive analysis—one accenting the gender stratification and class stratification that women face—has been accepted by many neo-Marxists and other power–conflict analysts as the more fruitful approach to understanding problems of women in contemporary societies. Class oppression imposed by a powerful employer class and patriarchal oppression by men are different, but often related, types of social oppression. The gendered division of labor in the home and in the workplace benefits capitalists as capitalists and men as men. The gendered division of labor can be seen today in families and workplaces, but this division is ancient, and most men in all classes have profited from the subordinate position of women in societies, past and present. Feminist researchers such as Zillah Eisenstein have shown that today the United States is still a patriarchal system in which women must struggle vigorously for maximum liberation, creativity, and a positive sense of self.[55]

Gender stratification is similar in some—although by no means all—respects to racial stratification; both involve inequality defined by birth, not by achievement. In both cases, the relationship is one of dominance (powerful position) and subordination (less powerful position). Gender and racial stratification both have a concrete *material* basis: gender stratification in the division of labor within the family and in the capitalistic economy outside the family, and racial stratification in the division of labor by racial group in the economy.

A number of power–conflict analysts accent the importance of racial domination and exploitation for understanding U.S. society and its problems. Racial domination as we have come to experience it in the Western world has its roots in the expansion of capitalism in the fifteenth through nineteenth centuries. Expansionist in orientation, many European investors, merchants, and slave traders pursued overseas exploitation and colonization from the 1400s to the 1900s. Robert L. Allen notes that wherever Europeans went, the indigenous populations were reorganized into capitalist labor systems, with a local workforce subordinated onto plantations, into mining operations, and into factories controlled by European colonizers. Local, self-sufficient agriculture was transformed into commercial agriculture for

Latina Sexual Slavery in the United States

In April 2000, a young girl named Rosa testified before a U.S. Senate Foreign Relations Committee investigating the trafficking of women and children from foreign countries to the United States. In her testimony, Rosa explained that when she was 14 years old and working cleaning hotel rooms in Veracruz, Mexico, a man came to her parents' house and asked if Rosa would be interested in making more money doing similar work in the United States. The man promised Rosa and her parents that she would be safe and that she would meet other young Mexican girls working in hotels in the United States. Rosa persuaded her parents to let her go, and the man smuggled Rosa into the United States through Texas, and eventually to Orlando, Florida. Once there, the smugglers told Rosa that her job did not involve cleaning hotel rooms but having sex with men for money. Since Rosa had never had sex before, the men initiated her by repeatedly raping Rosa "to teach her how to have sex." Over several months, the smugglers took Rosa to different trailers and forced her to have sex with men throughout most of the day. When Rosa became pregnant, the smugglers forced her to have an abortion. Rosa told the committee that years after her ordeal she still feels disgraced and shamed, and that she is mistrustful of people.

Appearing before the same committee, but in disguise because she feared for her safety and that of her family, Maria told a story similar to Rosa's. Maria explained that she was 18 years old and working as a domestic servant in Veracruz when a friend approached her and told her about jobs in restaurants and bars in the United States where she could make more money. A "coyote" brought Maria to Texas and eventually to a safe house in Florida. Once in Florida, Maria's smugglers told her that she would be working in a brothel as a prostitute and forced her to work 12 hours a day, six days a week, servicing 32 to 35 men a day (far more on the weekends), ostensibly to pay off her smuggling debt. There were four girls to a brothel, and every 15 days their capturers transported them to another trailer in an isolated area of another city. The armed bosses would regularly rape and beat the girls to keep them in control. Maria's ordeal lasted for several months, although the smugglers held other young girls much longer. Maria's sexual enslavement ended when federal law enforcement agents raided the brothel. Federal authorities revictimized Maria when they kept her incarcerated in a detention center for several more months.

Rosa and Maria's stories of forced sexual "slavery" are not unique in the United States—they are just 2 of more than 20,000 young girls smuggled from Mexico and Central American countries every year and forced into the sex slave industry, an industry that is one of the most critical human rights violations confronting the United States today. One state department official estimates that if one considers adult persons trafficked to the United States from other countries, 30,000 to 50,000 sex slaves are in captivity in the United States at any given time. Child-victims of the United States sex trade often end up in the rural outer reaches of large metropolitan regions in Maryland, Virginia, Texas, New York, New Jersey, and California.

One reason why U.S. government officials can only estimate the number of sex slaves in this country is because law enforcement is not looking for them, and in some cases they are actually participating as patrons of the illicit sex enterprises. One of the worst cases of law enforcement's indifference to child sex trafficking in the United States occurred in San Diego County in California—"a paradise for thousands of children who year after year visit SeaWorld and the Wild Animal Park at the San Diego Zoo." Ten years *after* local law enforcement first learned about the local sex slave market, federal agents and county sheriffs finally

continued on next page

raided the camps and discovered smugglers had kidnapped hundreds of young Mexican girls between the ages of 7 and 18 for the rape camps in San Diego County. Adult men raped the young girls every day in homes and brothels in mostly rural, agricultural camps. Authorities apprehended some 50 traffickers and patrons of the rape camps but immediately released them, ostensibly because their child-victims refused to identify them as their enslavers.

Officials deported most of the victims to Mexico without authorities providing any victim social services to the children. For years a federally employed Latina physician who provided condoms to the victims was threatened by her supervisors with severe legal sanctions if she spoke out and did not keep quiet about the sexual victimization. What is more, a social worker that investigated the San Diego case reportedly witnessed federal immigration agents having sex with the enslaved girls in exchange for the traffickers' protection. Police believe that several murdered teenage Latinas found in the San Diego area are killings linked to the traffickers, yet prosecutors have failed to indict anyone for the murders. In 2003, authorities convicted one of the trafficking ringleaders, who received only 18 months in jail. Remarkably, a San Diego television news station recently documented that the rape camps continue to exist. While law enforcement agencies recognize that the trafficking of young children to the United States for sexual exploitation is a *crisis,* the child sex slave tragedy has yet to garner the full attention of criminal justice professionals.

Sources: Charles M. Goodsby, Jr., *Dynamics of Prostitution and Sex Trafficking from Latin America into the United States,* September 2003, available at www.libertadlatina.org/LL_LatAm_US_Slavery_Report_01_2003.htm; "The Sex Trafficking of Children in San Diego, California," *El Universal (The Universal Newspaper),* January 9, 10, 11, 2003, available at www.libertadlatina.org/US_Sex_Trafficking_San_Diego_Case_01122003_English.htm; U.S. Senate, 2000, U.S. Senate Foreign Relations Committee on Near Eastern and South Asian Affairs Subcommittee Hearingston International Trafficking of Women and Children, April, 4, 2000, available at www.libertadlatina.org/US_Slavery_Case1_pl.htm; Peter Landesman, "The Girl Next Door," *New York Times,* January 24, 2004; LibertadLatina, "San Diego Sex Trafficking Scandal," available at www.libertadlatina.org/LatAm_US_San_Diego_Crisis_Index.htm.

export; indigenous peoples were moved to plantations or mines; forced work, including slavery, was the rule. Allen explains that "the colonized societies were forcibly brought into the worldwide system of commodity circulation, contributing their economic 'surplus' to the growing capital of Europe."[56] The relations between white Europeans and colonized peoples overseas (generally peoples of color) were highly exploitative because of the economic goals of a rapidly expanding European capitalistic system.

In the United States, the economic exploitation and other social oppression of people of color such as African Americans—sometimes called *internal colonialism*—emerged out of European overseas colonialism, but it soon took on a life of its own. The landed slaveowners of the agricultural South, together with northern shipping and slave trading interests, created a racist social structure and economy early, with African Americans and Native Americans at the bottom. Over time, industrial capital and enterprises in the northern states developed substantially from the merchant capital gained from the great Atlantic trade in enslaved Africans and the agricultural products they produced (for example, cotton and tobacco).[57]

Over several centuries in North America, all social classes of whites have benefited to some degree from the presence of a large group of extremely subordinated African American workers and other workers of color. For example, large employers have historically benefited from the lower wages they imposed on black workers and from the racial divisions they helped to create between black and white workers—divisions that reduce the likelihood of working-class organization to fight capitalistic exploitation of all workers. Even smaller capitalists have had the low-wage workers of color they need to make a profit. Moreover, power–conflict analysts have noted that racial domination has also benefited whites in the working class. The structure of racial discrimination exists not just because the white employer class benefits from its establishment but also because white workers benefit. More than a traditional Marxist analysis is necessary to make sense out of persisting patterns of racial discrimination. In the period from 1830 to 1920 the capitalist system in the northern United States relied heavily on white European immigrants—first the Irish and later southern and eastern Europeans. By the 1840s, free black workers were being displaced by white immigrants, as Irish workers took over skilled manual jobs—such as that of teamster—from free black workers. Opposition from white workers in the North led to exclusion of African Americans from important job categories. This intentional exclusion from better-paying job categories once substantially black in composition is one factor underlying the significant job segregation found today in the U.S. labor market. The history of the white-dominated labor movement is also a history of much discrimination against black and other non-European workers.

Historically, most white workers have not seen the black struggle for freedom and equality as part of their own struggle. The source of racial exploitation has been not only capitalism but also the fact that the white working-class victims of capitalism have had a "primary racial loyalty to their masters" rather than a class loyalty to black workers.[58] Today, white racial domination in the United States still includes much racial discrimination in the workplace, housing, education, politics, and numerous other arenas. Still important from the point of view of business owners is the divisiveness of the racial line within many working-class organizations. Whites in several classes have long benefited from the formal and informal discrimination against black Americans in the workplace, as well as in public accommodations, education, and housing.

In addition, the patterns of racial prejudice and discrimination originally established to enforce the subordination of African Americans have been extended, in whole or in part, to other people of color as they have come within the sphere of the United States. When Asian and Latino workers were brought into the United States by war, labor recruitment, and immigration beginning in the 1840s, they too faced much white hostility and discrimination in areas such as business, employment, and housing. Moreover, their descendants—together with more recent immigrants of color and their families—have continued to face racial discrimination in many areas, even into the early 2000s. For this reason, analysts such as Allen have argued that even radical (for instance, democratic–socialist) societal changes moving away from capitalism will not necessarily do away with major forms of racial domination. Racial discrimination and related oppression will need to be focused on explicitly if the full removal of racist arrangements is to be accomplished.[59]

In conclusion, class, racial, and gender relations are at the heart of U.S. society. Generally speaking, capitalists dominate workers, men dominate women, and whites dominate people of color. Not one of these systems of exploitation and discrimination stands alone, and none can be reduced to another. As we will see, each of these systems of exploitation creates and shapes serious social problems in U.S. society—sometimes independently and, sometimes in conjunction with the others.[60]

SOME WORKING PROPOSITIONS

Traditionally, many social-problems textbooks have adopted a cafeteria approach to the study of U.S. society, taking the reader through a string-of-beads list of topics with little relation to an integrated conceptual framework. In this book, we look at a more modest number of major problems in greater depth. We use an integrated framework for interpreting problems. Drawing on the previously discussed power–conflict perspectives, we suggest the following guiding propositions:

Proposition one

A critical power–conflict perspective provides a more insightful interpretation of major social problems than a conservative order–market perspective or a liberal order–market (corporate–liberal) perspective.

A critical power–conflict approach is more useful than the conservative order–market or corporate–liberal approach in making sense out of many social problems in this modern capitalistic society. The conservative order–market viewpoint tends to blame problems on the victims and to neglect questions of racism, sexism, and class exploitation. The liberal order–market view, with its belief in the validity of the free market system and in government-managed solutions to social problems, usually recognizes some problems, but in a piecemeal fashion. Corporate–liberal analysts do not dig deeply enough into the class, racial, and gender roots of societal problems. Across-the-board social-interest agreements among capitalists and workers, whites and people of color, males and females do not generally exist. A critical power–conflict perspective recognizes that deep inequalities and divisions in U.S. society generate major and continuing conflicts, that mainstream social science has often been allied with corporate capitalism, and that one's approach to the study of society is usually colored by one's class, racial, or gender position. The orientation behind a social-problems analysis should be made explicit and not left hidden behind a veil of alleged neutrality. *All* analyses of society reflect the values of those doing the analyzing. Thus, the perspective emphasized here usually reflects a power–conflict viewpoint oriented to the interests of the oppressed groups of Americans at the bottom of the class, racial, and gender hierarchies.

A power–conflict perspective, however, does not mean that a critical social scientist can change the data to fit her or his needs; all good social scientists should be objective and honest about the data they analyze. Furthermore, this book assumes that social reality is best studied from a unified perspective and that the divisions among social science disciplines (sociology, economics, political science, history, and so on) are artificial. An important difference between the conservative and corporate–liberal approaches and a more critical social science perspective lies in the scale and character of the restructuring of society that is envisaged. Traditional conservative and liberal perspectives vary, but they generally involve a commitment, at best, to piecemeal and moderate social reforms. Power–conflict analysts think in terms of a more substantial restructuring of this society that would solve or lessen social problems in many areas.

Proposition two

Powerful people have power over others because they have greater control over important societal resources, such as private property in offices, factories, and land; more wealth and income; more information and knowledge resources; and more control over police and military forces.

Powerful people, such as the capitalists and top managers who control U.S. factories, stores, and offices, have more of the economic and political resources that are important in maintaining sociopolitical control of society than do much less powerful groups such as the masses of ordinary working people. Men as a group have more power and control over resources than women as a group. White Americans as a group have more economic and political resources to use routinely and to mobilize in times of conflict than do African Americans and most other people of color. The powerful can, if necessary, use force such as that of the police to control the powerless or reduce their resources. Exploitation refers to the ability of the powerful to take for their own use the labor, socioeconomic resources, or even lives of the less powerful. Many laws, such as property laws, protect this fundamental inequality of resources. In addition, large bureaucracies (complex hierarchical organizations) have come to be a major feature of a modern capitalistic society. Private-sector bureaucracies (such as corporations) and government bureaucracies (such as the FBI) are used as instruments of domination by the powerful.

Proposition three
The powerful routinely shape the prevailing beliefs and ideologies that explain and interpret the hierarchical and often troubled social arrangements of U.S. society.

Those with great power and resources have the ability to shape what people believe and think about the economic, political, and social structures around them. Major examples are the ideology of individualism, attitudes of obsessive materialism and consumerism, and negative racial and gender stereotyping. These belief systems are generally taught through such means as parents, peers, schools, advertising, and the media. Such beliefs help to preserve the legitimacy of the existing class, racial, and gender systems.

Proposition four
In U.S. society, several interrelated systems of stratification, of domination and subordination, create or shape major social problems. Among these are the following:
1. A class system in which a very large working class of blue-collar and white-collar workers is dominated by a small capitalist class.
2. A racial system in which non-European groups—such as African Americans, Latinos, Asian Americans, and Native Americans—are generally dominated by white European groups.
3. A gender system in which women are generally dominated by men.

These social-group relations are grounded in major differences in control over basic resources. In the class arrangements, a powerful, profit-oriented capitalist class generally controls the major means of production and distribution of goods and services, while the largest class, the working class, generally sells its labor to the capitalist class. The system of racial stratification predated and shaped industrial capitalism. Today in the United States, as in the past, white Europeans as a group generally dominate people of color in terms of such resources as income, wealth, good jobs, quality housing, and political power. In the gender stratification system—the most ancient of systems of large-scale group subordination—men as a group are the most powerful and play a central role in subordinating women, as a group, in terms of child-rearing responsibilities, housework, wealth and income, political power, and better-paying jobs outside the home.

Recent U.S. federal court decisions, made by mostly white male judges, have weakened or rejected government programs designed to remedy racial discrimination.

The impact and operation of class, racial, and gender domination can be seen in the major societal problems. Numerous problems result from, or are aggravated by, the long-term operation of these class, racial, and gender hierarchies. For example, a range of class-related problems such as excessive hazards in the workplace, depletion of energy sources, serious industrial water and air pollution, toxic waste, corporate crime, and high medical costs are serious for society as a whole because of their scale. Most of the important decisions that create, or dramatically shape, these problems are in the hands of a small group of powerful people—primarily the capitalist class and its managers and professionals—not in the hands of the general working public.

Proposition five

The stress and threat of the societal problems and the built-in conflict between the powerful and the powerless periodically give rise to the mobilization of citizens' movements and organizations aimed at solving problems and redistributing power and resources downward.

Struggle between the powerful and the powerless is a basic feature of this society. The organization and mobilization of subordinate groups (such as blue-collar workers, African Americans, Latinos, and women), who have at least the resource of sheer numbers of people, have had an impact and have forced concessions from the powerful. This impact can be seen in the New Deal unemployment legislation in the 1930s, forced in part by the actions of organized and unionized workers, and in the civil rights legislation of the 1960s, forced in part by the actions of organized African Americans. Actual and threatened protest by, and rebellions of, oppressed class, racial, and gender groups can create a situation in which corporate elites or allied government officials act to repress protest, if they can, or to make political and economic concessions, if they must, to preserve the legitimacy and stability of existing political and economic institutions.

These guiding propositions provide the framework that integrates most of the materials on U.S. social problems presented in the chapters that follow. These propositions suggest insights into the "Why?" and "How?" of our basic economic, political, and social institutions and into the "Why?" and "How?" of major social problems. The set of propositions is simplified here for the purpose of introduction. As we move into more detail, we can add layers of complexity to our understanding. Naturally, these propositions do not help explain all the problems in this society. Rather, they provide a critical power–conflict perspective that makes sense out of much of the trouble and conflict in the society that surrounds us.

SUMMARY

Most Americans know this is a society with major problems. Most know that basic needs are not met for many Americans. Many are aware that their personal and family problems are linked to structural factors and larger societal contexts, but these larger contexts are often seen through a haze of vague explanations and confusing media interpretations. Rationales such as the declining work ethic, lazy individuals, government "welfare," unfair foreign competition, dangerous immigration, "reverse" discrimination, and political corruption are offered to explain, often erroneously, our current societal troubles.

Traditional social science approaches to major societal problems have tended to emphasize order and stability in the society. The dominant viewpoint lying behind much social science reflects more or less of a commitment to the existing social order of corporate capitalism. This social science viewpoint has evolved from a laissez-faire order-market perspective in the nineteenth century to, for many people, some type of liberal order-market view today. Basic to mainstream social science is some type of strain theory of social problems. The breakdown of traditional authority and norms stemming from such realities as urban migration, lax parenting, or "broken homes" is often seen as one major source of social problems. Many mainstream social scientists see government as a more or less neutral judge of competing groups, as the instrument to restore, with a variety of piecemeal reforms, stability within the framework of existing class, racist, and sexist arrangements. Conventional approaches to social problems reject the idea that the problems are rooted so deeply in the society that massive society-wide changes in class, racial, and gender structures will be required to eradicate the problems.

Because mainstream social scientists accept the basic contours of the existing society, they often argue for a value-free "experts" approach to the study of social problems. For this mainline approach, the task of social-problems analysis is to build up a body of empirical facts that can be used by "neutral" policymakers to devise remedies to "fix" existing social problems. Since at least the 1960s, this approach to problems has been strong. Social scientists are often seen as experts who can, apolitically and scientifically, collect data on social problems and provide data on which policymakers can act wisely.

Those who adopt the mainline approach are generally unwilling to explore the implications of a thoroughgoing power–conflict approach for understanding societal problems. This book adopts a critical power–conflict perspective, which gives much greater attention than do mainstream social scientists to the great inequalities of power and resources in society; to inequality along class, racial, and gender (and other) lines; and to how that inequality creates a broad array of problems for most Americans. Most power–conflict theory gives much attention to exploitation of the powerless by the powerful and to deeply rooted conflict between powerless and powerful groups. This approach emphasizes that existing arrangements in this society provide the greatest benefits for those on top. Such a perspective looks critically at the often-hidden roots of social problems in exploitative, discriminatory, and alienating institutions.

Today, power–conflict social scientists are a diverse group, including not only neo-Marxists (who emphasize class) but also feminist scholars (who emphasize gender oppression) and antiracist analysts (who focus on racial and ethnic oppression). Although important differences exist within this critical perspective, most power–conflict analysts analyze vigorously the dominant institutions and ruling ideas of U.S. society and propose major changes for existing societal problems.

This book sorts through a number of major social problems using a multifaceted power–conflict perspective that takes into consideration not only capitalistic social patterns but also racial, gender, and other important types of social stratification and exploitation.

STUDY QUESTIONS

1. Émile Durkheim has provided one of the most influential perspectives in sociology, yet he neglected to analyze several important topics seriously. What are they? What is the significance of these omissions for understanding social problems?

2. What is the critical power–conflict perspective? What are some of its main arguments?

3. A strong case can be made that corporate liberalism remains the dominant ideology in the United States. What is the corporate–liberal view, and how does it contrast with the earlier laissez-faire view?

4. Considering the power–conflict view of the world, how do neo-Marxists differ from feminists and antiracist analysts?

5. In the writings of Harry Braverman, a deskilling thesis about work has emerged to counter the more pervasive job-upgrading thesis. Using examples, describe the major issues involved in this debate.

6. In traditional social-problems texts of the early twentieth century, what was portrayed as the cause of our major social problems?

ENDNOTES

1. See William Ryan, *Blaming the Victim* (New York: Vintage Books, 1976).
2. CBS News Poll, The Economy, Jobs, and the President (August 11–12, 2003), available at www.cbsnews.com/htdocs/CBSNews_polls/economy0813.pdf.
3. Quoted in Steven VanderStaay, *Street Lives: An Oral History of Homeless Americans* (Philadelphia: New Society Publishers, 1992), pp. 49–50.
4. David A. Snow and Leon Anderson, *Down on Their Luck* (Berkeley: University of California Press, 1993), p. 130.
5. Donald D. Stull, Michael J. Broadway, and Ken C. Erickson, "The Price of a Good Steak: Beef Packing and Its Consequences for Garden City, Kansas," in Louise Lamphere, ed., *Structuring Diversity* (Chicago: University of Chicago Press, 1992), p. 57.

6. Quoted in Walli F. Leff and Marilyn G. Haft, *Time Without Work* (Boston: South End Press, 1983), pp. 282–85.
7. Bruce D. Butterfield, "Diminished Jobs, Added Worry," *Boston Globe,* March 21, 1993, p. 1.
8. Ibid.
9. Ibid.
10. Ibid.
11. Kristin Kloberdanz, Consumer Health Interactive, Blueprint for Health, *Special Report: Poultry Workers* (ret. April 8, 2004), available at blueprint.bluecrossmn.com. See also, Barbara Goldoftas, "To Make a Tender Chicken, Poultry Workers Pay the Price," *Dollars & Sense: The Magazine of Economic Justice,* (July/August 2002), available at www.dollarsandsense.org/archives/2002/0702goldoftas.html.
12. Peter T. Kilborn, "For Hispanic Immigrants, a Higher Job-Injury Risk," *New York Times,* February 18, 1992, p. A1.
13. This woman was interviewed as part of a research project conducted by the senior author. See Joe R. Feagin and Melvin P. Sikes, *Living with Racism* (Boston: Beacon Press, 1994).
14. Quoted in Studs Terkel, *Working People Talk about What They Do All Day and How They Feel about What They Do* (New York: Random House, 1972, 1974), pp. 299–301.
15. Nijole Benokraitis and Joe Feagin, *Modern Sexism: Blatant, Subtle, and Covert Discrimination* (Upper Saddle River, N.J.: Prentice Hall, 1995), p. 139.
16. Interview from author's files, used by permission.
17. Quoted in Leff and Haft, *Time Without Work,* pp. 336–38.
18. E. J. Hobsbawm, *Primitive Rebels* (New York: W. W. Norton & Co., Inc., 1959), p. 2.
19. Clifford Cobb, Ted Halstead, and Jonathan Rowe, *The Genuine Progress Indicator: Summary of Data and Methodology* (San Francisco: Redefining Progress, 1995), p. 2.
20. Ibid., p. 43.
21. Clifford Cobb, Mark Glickman, and Craig Cheslog, *The Genuine Progress Indicator, 2000 Update* (December 2001), available at www.redefiningprogress.org/publications/2000_gpi_update.pdf.
22. Redefining Progress, "Nation's Economic Health Overstated By $7 Trillion: Genuine Progress Indicator Tells The Real Story" (April 4, 2004), at www.redefiningprogress.org/media/releases/040311_gpi.html.
23. Cobb, Halstead, and Rowe, *The Genuine Progress Indicator,* p. 45.
24. Bernice Bonillas, Bakersfield, California, letter to senior author, February 1988; Ron Karten, "Grape Wars," *Progressive,* July 1992, p. 14.
25. "Farmworkers file suit to protect workers from being poisoned by two harmful pesticides" (January 13, 2004), available at www.ufw.org/104wapest.htm.
26. Alan R. Gold, "Harvard Concedes Victory of Clerical Workers Demanding a Union," *New York Times,* national ed., November 5, 1988, p. 6; "Harvard University Called Hostile to Unions," *Daily Labor Report,* November 19, 1992, p. A-5.
27. "Harvard, Workers Agree," *AFL-CIO News,* August 14, 1995, p. 4.
28. Muriel H. Cooper, "Perseverance, Campaign Help Win First Contract," *AFL-CIO News,* December 18, 1995, p. 2.
29. "UNITE Airs Dirty Laundry at Life Uniforms: Garment Workers' Union Launches Campaign Against Sweatshop-Produced Uniforms" (January 26, 2004), available at www.uniteunion.org/pressbox/; "Employees Charge Martin Luther King's Dream Is Being Denied at Nation's Largest Uniform Supplier: Bias Against African-Americans and Latinos in Hiring, Promotion and Pay Are Cited as Evidence of Widespread Discrimination," (January 19, 2004), available at www.uniteunion.org/pressbox/release.cfm?ID=97.
30. "Labor and Environmentalists Defeat Plan to Burn Hazardous Waste," *Communities of Resistance,* October 1992, p. 3.
31. "Economy v. the Environment—A False Choice," *Toxic Times,* Fall 1992, p. 5.
32. *Touching Bases: Newsletter of the National Toxics Campaign Funds' Military Toxics Project,* November–December 1992, pp. 1, 4.
33. National Environmental Law Center, "NELC Sues Dow Chemical Company," *NELC Newsletter,* Fall 1995.
34. National Environmental Law Center, "Citizen Groups Reach Settlement with Dow Chemical" (ret. February 3, 2004), available at nelconline.org.
35. James Weinstein, *The Corporate Ideal in the Liberal State, 1900–1918* (Boston: Beacon Press, 1969); Herman Schwendinger and Julia R. Schwendinger, *The Sociologists of the Chair* (New York: Basic Books, 1974), p. xix.

36. Lewis A. Coser, *Masters of Sociological Thought,* 2d ed. (New York: Harcourt Brace Jovanovich, 1977), pp. 130–33, 140–42; Charles Tilly, *From Mobilization to Revolution* (Reading, Mass.: Addison-Wesley, 1978), pp. 16–24; Émile Durkheim, *The Division of Labor in Society,* trans. George Simpson (Glencoe, Ill.: Free Press, 1933).
37. Schwendinger and Schwendinger, *Sociologists of the Chair,* pp. 125–28.
38. Ibid., pp. 123–24.
39. C. Wright Mills, "The Professional Ideology of Social Pathologists," in *Power, Politics, and People,* I. L. Horowitz, ed. (New York: Ballantine Books, 1963), p. 526.
40. Stuart A. Queen and Delbert M. Mann, *Social Pathology* (New York: Thomas Y. Crowell, 1925), p. 17 and passim.
41. Quoted in Mills, "Professional Ideology," p. 532.
42. Ibid., p. 548.
43. Talcott Parsons, *The Social System* (Glencoe, Ill.: Free Press, 1951); Parsons, *The System of Modern Societies* (Upper Saddle River, N.J.: Prentice Hall, 1971), esp. pp. 142–43; Norbert Wiley, "The Rise and Fall of Dominating Theories in American Sociology," in *Contemporary Issues in Theory and Research,* W. E. Snizek, E. R. Fuhrman, and M. K. Miller, eds. (Westport, Conn.: Greenwood Press, 1979), pp. 67–68, 70–73.
44. Robert Nisbet, "The Study of Social Problems," in *Contemporary Social Problems,* Robert Nisbet and Robert K. Merton, eds. (New York: Harcourt Brace Jovanovich, 1971), pp. 1, 21.
45. Robert K. Merton, "Social Problems and Sociological Theory," in ibid., p. 801.
46. This section draws on Karl Marx, *Capital,* 1, Ernest Mandel, trans. (New York: Vintage Books, 1978); Coser, *Masters of Sociological Thought,* pp. 42–52; Tilly, *From Mobilization to Revolution,* pp. 13–14.
47. C. Wright Mills, *The Marxists* (New York: Dell, 1962); Coser, *Masters of Sociological Thought,* pp. 580–81, quotation on p. 580; C. Wright Mills, *The Power Elite* (New York: Oxford University Press, 1959), pp. 20–126; Mills, *White Collar* (New York: Oxford University Press, 1956), pp. 50–73.
48. Mills, *Power Elite,* p. 212; David McLellan, *Marxism After Marx* (New York: Harper and Row, 1979), pp. 319–20.
49. Harry Braverman, *Labor and Monopoly Capital* (New York: Monthly Review Press, 1974), pp. 35, 290–95, 355–445.
50. Lester Thurow, *The Future of Capitalism* (New York: William Morrow & Co., 1995), p. 246.
51. Ibid., p. 254.
52. See Frederick Engels, *The Origin of the Family, Private Property, and the State,* in Karl Marx and Frederick Engels, *Selected Works, 2* (Moscow: Foreign Languages Publishing House, 1962), pp. 185–237; Heidi Hartman, "Capitalism, Patriarchy, and Job Segregation," *Signs* 1 (Spring 1976): 137–69; Erik O. Wright, Class, *Crisis and the State* (London: NLB, 1978), pp. 53, 92.
53. Juliet Mitchell, *Woman's Estate* (New York: Vintage Books, 1973), pp. 144–51; Kate Millett, *Sexual Politics* (New York: Avon Books, 1969), pp. 25–27.
54. Zillah R. Eisenstein, "Developing a Theory of Capitalist Patriarchy and Socialist Feminism," in *Capitalist Patriarchy and the Case for Social Feminism,* Zillah R. Eisenstein, ed. (New York: Monthly Review Press, 1979), pp. 5–40.
55. Ibid., p. 31.
56. Robert L. Allen, *Reluctant Reformers* (Washington, D.C.: Howard University Press, 1974), p. 255.
57. Michael Perelman, *Farming for Profit in a Hungry World* (New York: Universe Books, 1977), p. 26.
58. Selma James et al., *Sex, Race and Class* (Bristol, England: Falling Wall Press, 1975), p. 6.
59. Allen, *Reluctant Reformers,* pp. 6, 224, 247.
60. Other stratification systems are not considered here, such as those involving inequality in bureaucratic (for example, government) power and resources and that of the system of heterosexism that oppresses gay and lesbian Americans.

chapter **2**

Class Relations and the Problem of Inequality

Great differences exist in the power that people have in U.S. society because of great differences in the control of major resources. Some people control far more money than do most others. Some people have far more income than do most others. Some people have far more wealth—in personal possessions, corporate stocks, and real estate—than do most others. Some people have far more organizational and political resources than do most others. Many are relatively powerless and poor because others are too powerful and too rich.

We suggested in Chapter 1 that capitalism in the United States now faces a growing economic crisis as the inflation-adjusted incomes of average American workers oscillate or decline. This is a new experience for many Americans since real incomes increased more or less steadily for a few decades after World War II. Moreover, when capitalism in the United States experienced periods of decline over the last century or so, as in the Great Depression, those who control the U.S. government saw to it that government intervened to help relieve the economic crises. Over the last decade or two, however, we seem to have entered a new political–economic era in which the dominant economic and political elites seem no longer willing to intervene to provide relief for the growing economic inequalities in society.

GOALS OF THIS CHAPTER

In this chapter, we explore inequalities in the distribution of economic, political, and social resources and how these inequalities relate to differences in opportunities and life chances. Differences in the control of major resources result in differences in actual day-to-day power. Small groups of very powerful people shape the lives of large groups of less powerful Americans. If necessary, the very powerful can even use government police and military forces to back up their decisions. To better understand the *why* and *how* of this resource and decision-making inequality, we first examine briefly four snapshots of U.S. society.

SOME REVEALING SOCIETAL SNAPSHOTS

Plant Closings

In 1990, the Levi Strauss Co. announced it was moving its largest Texas plant—the South Zarzamora Street sewing plant in San Antonio—to Costa Rica where it could pay workers a fraction of the wages paid to U.S. workers. The company closed the plant even though the plant's profits had reached a record high. Levi Strauss dismissed 300 of the nonunion plant's 1,150 predominantly Mexican American women workers; the remaining workers were out of work within three months. Since the 1980s, Levi Strauss had been closing many of its manufacturing plants across the country. Paid low wages on a piecework basis ($5 an hour), U.S. workers had to repeat the same movements many times at high speeds. Although at least 10 percent suffered from work-related injuries, workers were "deterred from reporting injuries for fear of being assigned to lower-paying jobs . . . In the fall of 1989, even as managers assured worried workers the plant would stay open, its engineers went around to every sewing machine and added a task that slowed down the operators and thus lowered their pay. When it came time for calculating severance pay, the rate was set on the basis of the average from October to December, reflecting the lower amount after the machines were jigged."[1]

Later, a company spokesperson defended the company's actions, noting that the company did more for the workers "than almost anyone in American industry." Whether this was true in the past is unclear. That Levi Strauss, like other garment manufacturers, was abandoning many U.S. workers for lower-wage workers in other countries was quite clear—the company now contracts with manufacturers in Mexico, the Caribbean, and Asia. Many workers laid off by Levi Strauss became active in the union Fuerza Unida (United Strength), which staged a protest march and boycotts in San Francisco asserting that Levi Strauss closed plants unnecessarily and did not properly compensate abandoned workers in terms of retirement pensions and severance payments.[2] Fuerza Unida sued the company for better severance packages but lost.

Just before Thanksgiving 2003, Levi Straus shut down its remaining plant in San Antonio, leaving another 815 workers without jobs. Almost half of the employees had worked at the plant for more than 20 years, and nearly 300 other workers had been at the plant for more than 10 years. With workers earning between $11 and $12 an hour, San Antonio officials estimated the city economy would lose $19 million in revenue due to the layoffs.[3]

Workplace Hazards

In September 1991, a hydraulic line burst in the Imperial Foods Products Plant in Hamlet, North Carolina, spraying fluid into gas flames used to heat vats of frying oil. In the resulting fire, 25 poultry workers died from smoke inhalation and 54 others suffered injuries because company managers had locked the doors to the plant to prevent workers from "stealing chickens." The plant was in violation of workplace safety codes: It had no evacuation plan, no automatic sprinklers, and only one fire extinguisher. The plant's owner and CEO of Imperial Foods was later convicted of 25 counts of involuntary manslaughter and sentenced to 19 years in prison since it was he that gave the order to lock the doors.[4] No safety inspector had ever visited the plant throughout its 11-year operation because cutbacks in funding for OSHA (Occupational Safety and Health Administration) severely reduced the number of field inspectors. At the time of the fire, North Carolina had only 27 safety inspectors to monitor some 180,000 workers.[5]

Workers later said that they were afraid to protest unsafe conditions for fear of losing jobs. These problems with workplace safety remain serious to the present day. Deborah Berkowitz of the United Food and Commercial Workers International Union later testified before Congress that "[t]here are still many workplaces in this country where workers are fired or discriminated against, [for] reporting injuries or safety hazards."[6]

This fire, plus many other workplace disasters across the country, prompted labor advocates to push for reforms to strengthen OSHA. Even with such major problems with workplace safety, a conservative-controlled U.S. Congress has periodically moved to weaken OSHA.

9 Million "Rolling Fire Bombs"

Between 1973 and 1987, General Motors (GM) marketed a pickup truck designed to go farther on a tank of gasoline than its competitors. GM produced more than 9 million of the popular C/K pickups over this period. According to a GM design engineer, the truck's large-capacity fuel tank was mounted outside the truck's frame because it made the truck easier to sell, even though GM engineers reportedly knew during the truck's design stage, that the fuel tank's location left it exceedingly vulnerable in a side-impact crash. GM also opted not to install a $10 fire-preventing plastic liner inside the trucks. In a series of 22 crash tests from 1981 to 1983, the tanks "split like melons" on impact, even at speeds as low as 25 miles per hour.[7]

GM covered up the truck's hazards by withholding crash test data from the public and from plaintiffs in lawsuits against the company for almost 20 years. GM also insisted on secrecy agreements and gag orders in lawsuits involving the fuel tank design. Between 1973 and 1992, crash fires involving these GM vehicles killed an estimated 300 people—more than ten times the number of burn deaths caused by the highly publicized faulty design of Ford's Pinto (1969–1977). By late 1992, petitioners had filed more than a hundred lawsuits against GM. In some 30 additional cases, the company made confidential settlements with claimants, and it paid more than $100 million in claims to people who were seriously injured or who had died in crashes involving these trucks—victims who GM might have spared had the company designed the truck's gas tank not to burst into flames during side-impact collisions. GM still refused to recall the vehicles. One spokesperson told a media reporter that the company felt it was cheaper to pay claims than to recall the trucks.[8]

In 2001, while researching a story that federal regulators dropped an investigation in 1994 that could have led to a recall of the C/K trucks in exchange for GM earmarking $51 million for safety programs, a *Los Angeles Times* reporter learned that GM has paid out at least $495 million to settle lawsuits brought by crash victims involving the pickup trucks—for an average of more than $1.6 million per case. It seems likely that GM has paid out more money to claimants since 2001.[9]

Toxic Chemicals in the Environment

A few large U.S. corporations dominate the multibillion-dollar world pesticide market. In recent decades, that industry has produced billions of pounds of pesticides annually, most for use in Western countries, although corporations have distributed large quantities of pesticides elsewhere. Further increases in overseas use of pesticides are expected. Corporate executives in the multinationals that manufacture pesticides aggressively defend pesticide use in general and exports overseas. These pesticides, they argue, are required in the world fight against hunger, to increase agricultural production, to modernize poor countries, and to prevent famine.

Yet critics of the chemical industry point out that much food grown in poor countries consists of luxury crops, intended not as food for local people but for shipment to richer industrialized countries. A significant proportion of the pesticide exports are chemicals that the United States has banned, restricted, or not registered for use in the United States. Some are known to cause cancer and birth defects. Many workers in poor countries cannot read the labels of pesticide packages and cans, and therefore cannot follow warnings on labels. At times, growers spray pesticides on fields when workers are laboring there, and some workers and their families live in huts near sprayed fields.

Critics of the sale abroad of unsafe pesticides consider such sales to be unethical "dumping." Company executives argue that it is good business practice to sell a product wherever it is not banned. They argue that if the United States bans the pesticides, they should be able to sell it in other countries where it is legal. This view overlooks the human costs of dumping chemical carcinogens worldwide. Researcher David Pimentel has used data provided by the World Health Organization to estimate that each year pesticide use poisons 1 million persons worldwide, including about 67,000 in the United States. Nearly 20,000 people each year die from pesticide poisoning worldwide.[10] Ironically, researchers have found that when the United States imports food products back into the country from countries that use U.S.-banned pesticides, the "circle of poison" is complete. Some of these foods contain excessive levels of dangerous pesticides. U.S. General Accounting Office data for one specific period found that half of imported coffee beans had testable levels of pesticides banned in the United States.[11]

These societal snapshots reveal much about the problems faced by U.S. society. They suggest, as well, some of the social sources of those costly problems.

How Social Scientists Define "Class": Some Lessons from the Snapshots

These snapshots highlight the importance of class in U.S. society. Class is not simply a matter of prestige or even of income. Rather, power–conflict analysts define class primarily by differential economic power to shape the society. That is, the economic interests of the capitalist class and those of the working people (blue collar and white collar) are often not the same. Members of the propertied, decision-making capitalist class own or control the means of production and distribution—the plants, offices, stores, and warehouses—and the working class usually sells its labor power to that employer class.

Most importantly, the preceding societal snapshots show top corporate executives in control of major investment decisions concerning not only the type of product manufactured by the corporation but also the product's safety features and the workplace conditions of those making the product. Moreover, corporate executives often make important investment and other business decisions without regard to consumers' or workers' concerns. Their fundamental economic interest lies in making investments that bring a good profit, not necessarily investments that put other human or community needs (for example, safety) before profits.

The Levi Strauss case illustrates top corporate executives firmly in control of capital investment and disinvestment decisions. They are capitalists because they have control over major, company-wide, capital investment decisions, including control over plants, equipment, and raw materials. This case also shows that top decision makers have tremendous control over the labor power of ordinary working people. The decision of these executives to abandon a profitable manufacturing plant on short notice, without consulting workers or consumers, created major human and community costs. The profit interests of the top executives and other stockholders were not the same as the family, job security, and community interests of the workers. Similarly, the pesticide "circle of poison" story illustrates the tremendous power of chemical company executives to invest capital in enterprises they choose and thus to affect and sometimes shorten the lives of workers and consumers not only in the United States but also around the world.

A CLOSER LOOK AT CLASS RELATIONS IN U.S. SOCIETY

Hierarchies of social stratification—as in the ladderlike arrangements of large social groups shown in Figure 2.1—play an important part in the everyday life of this society. The groups are arranged roughly in order of their control over basic resources. In the class system, capitalists are at the top, followed by middle-level managers, with workers much farther down. The simplified racial-stratification system in Figure 2.1 is composed of whites (such as white Anglo-Protestants) at the top and non-European groups (such as African Americans and Native Americans) much farther down. In the gender stratification system, males are generally dominant over females. As groups, those at the top of each hierarchical system have higher levels of resources, such as ownership and control of property, income, and various types of wealth, than do groups lower in the hierarchy. We deal with racial and gender stratification in later chapters. In this chapter, we examine the system of class relations and the problem-generating unequal distribution of socioeconomic resources in society.

The Class Structure

In his first annual message to Congress in 1861, President Abraham Lincoln accented a point about the source of capital that many have been forgotten: "Capital is only the fruit of labor, and could never have existed if labor had not first existed. Labor is the superior of capital, and deserves much the higher consideration." In defining labor as the *source* of capital, Lincoln (like Marx) focused attention on the efforts and rights of working people. For the most part, capital is directly or indirectly created by ordinary working people who provide the goods and services that are exchanged in markets and thereby converted into profits. Under the U.S. system of capitalism, a small minority of the population owns and controls the places where goods and services are produced and distributed. These owners have the legal right to use and move these facilities (and the equipment and materials) for their own private profit and in the interest of their social class. A person's class position is determined by position in the means of production. Those who own or control the means of production are capitalists; those who do not are noncapitalists, such as blue-collar and white-collar workers. Many social problems are rooted in the power and resource inequalities of this class system.

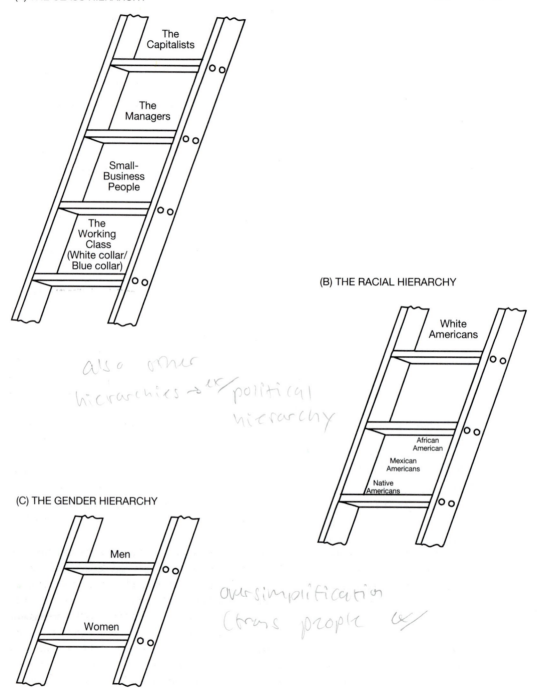

(A) THE CLASS HIERARCHY

The Capitalists

The Managers

Small-Business People

The Working Class (White collar/Blue collar)

(B) THE RACIAL HIERARCHY

White Americans

African American

Mexican Americans

Native Americans

(C) THE GENDER HIERARCHY

Men

Women

also other hierarchies → us/political hierarchy

oversimplification (trans people us/

Figure 2.1   Relations of dominance and subordination

Table 2.1   Class Relations in U.S. Society

Class	Composition	CONTROL OVER CAPITALIST SYSTEM			Major Sources of Income
		Control Over Company-wide Investments and Others Resources	Control Over Plants, Offices, Equipment, and Raw Materials	Control Over Labor Power of Others (Buying Labor)	
Capitalist class	Traditional capitalists, top corporate executives	Great	Great	Great	Profits, interest, high salaries
Managerial class	Managers, top professionals	None to a little	A little to some	Some to much	Salaries, bonuses from profits
Small-business class	Very small entrepreneurs	Great	Great	Minimal	Profits
Working class	Blue-collar and white-collar workers	None	None to a little	None to a little	Wages, salaries

Source: Portions of this table are loosely adapted from Erik O. Wright, *Class Structure and Income Determination* (New York: Academic Press, 1979), pp. 38–42.

In Table 2.1, we suggest the basic shape of the U.S. class system.[12] We distinguish the major classes of (1) capitalists, (2) managers, (3) small-business entrepreneurs, and (4) workers. These classes and their relations regularly shape the everyday lives of all Americans, as do the systems of gender and racial stratification.

Typically, one's class position determines one's food, clothing, housing, educational opportunities, and politics. If we are top corporate capitalists, we own or control property such as factories and offices; have great wealth and power; and, if we wish, live like kings and queens. If we are middle-level managers, we usually have higher-than-average incomes and thus some wealth and power. If we are blue-collar or white-collar workers, we typically have lower incomes and less access to life's goods and services than those in the higher classes, and our lives can become very difficult in times of serious recession, depression, or exporting of jobs overseas.

For some social scientists, *classes* are simply groups of people with common life chances or groups of people at the same position on a status or prestige ladder. Our view is that classes are more than this. Classes generally relate to one another in terms of dependence and exploitation. They are defined in their relations with one another. Classes are seen in the many workplaces of this country: in factories, stores, warehouses, farms, and offices. Classes also have an impact on political and educational institutions. Classes persist beyond the lives of individual people. Individual capitalists and workers die, but the capitalist and working classes have persisted for generations. Looking at this society in terms of its basic contradictions, we see a regular clash between the interests of capitalists and the interests of the broad group of rank-and-file workers.

The Capitalist Class

The top class in terms of power and resources is the capitalist class. Today it is composed not only of traditional capitalists—major corporate owners such as the famous Rockefellers, Hunts, du Ponts, Waltons, Fords, and Bill Gates—but also of top corporate executives whose stock ownership or company investment control gives them substantial power. The capitalist class is a small percentage of the population but has extensive control over the economic system both in the United States and around the world. Families of capitalists, including top corporate executives, directly or indirectly dominate U.S. society. Ownership and control of productive property (such as factories and offices and land) are at the heart of their power. Large or small, capitalists today, as in the past, believe strongly in their right to own and control property to make a privately controlled profit from that property *without* democratic input from workers or other citizens. Employers generally believe that this way of doing business makes for the best political–economic world for all.

Table 2.1 summarizes key differences in control and power among major social classes. Many capitalists serve on the boards of directors of corporations or as top corporate executives; others work behind the scenes as major shareholders. Some own their companies or controlling amounts of stock. Yet many top executives have only partial—even small—legal ownership of the companies or other businesses they control. Like traditional capitalists, though, these top company executives can have substantial "economic ownership" in the sense that they have decisive control over companywide investments, profits, and resources around the globe. Capitalists, alone or as a small group, have decisive control over the physical means of production, distribution, and exchange; over land and buildings; and over the labor power of others. Capitalists have the power to decide what products and services are produced for consumers, how workplaces are structured, and how many workers are hired or fired. Great wealth is concentrated in this class, virtually all of whose members own a significant amount of property, such as a controlling share (a small percentage may suffice) of stock in companies or land and buildings. This group includes industrial capitalists, banking capitalists, real estate capitalists, and high-tech capitalists. As a group, they have great decision-making power in the United States and abroad.[13]

Small capitalists, such as those who own one store or factory, may hire only a few dozen workers. Larger employers control many workplaces with tens of thousands of workers. Profits and incomes of capitalists can thus differ significantly. The investment and other important decisions made by those controlling larger firms can shape the business decisions of those in smaller firms, even setting limits on the latter's business decisions. As we will see later, capitalists in major corporations have a disproportionate ability to create large-scale problems for the entire society, whether the problem is unsafe vehicles, pollution, corporate crime, or the destruction of mass transit.

The Working Class

Most Americans employed outside the home are members of the working class, which does not own or control large amounts of *productive* property. Compared with most members of the capitalist class, members of the working class typically have modest levels of savings and own a modest amount of property, perhaps personal property in the form of a car or a mortgaged home. Many renters have no savings and, obviously, no mortgaged home. Those

Built for Herman Oelrichs in 1902, this huge mansion in an exclusive area of Newport, Rhode Island, was modeled after a palace in Versailles, France. *The Great Gatsby* was filmed here. (The Preservation Society of Newport County, Newport, RI)

workers who do own property often share that ownership with a financial institution. Most workers who are unemployed for a long time must fall back on their modest savings and government aid in the form of unemployment assistance or welfare. Most have little if any wealth, such as stocks and bonds, to fall back on if needed. The working class, as shown in Table 2.1, has no significant control over the important decisions involving company-wide investments; how private profits are spent; or about the crucial decisions regarding the location of plants, stores, and offices, the equipment and machinery used, or the purchasing of raw materials. Most ordinary workers have little control over the labor of other workers; those promoted to first-line supervisors may have some limited control over the labor of workers under their direct supervision.[14]

Ordinary workers routinely follow the orders of others. Most workers must work for 30 to 40 or more hours a week just to feed, clothe, and house themselves and their families. For the most part, the major tasks people do at work, as well as the pace and character of their work, are built into their jobs. While many have some limited control over certain working conditions, most live workaday lives largely structured by those at higher-class levels. In our capitalistic system, most members of the working class are indeed arranged in hierarchies in their workplaces.

The modern working class, today's wage and salary proletariat, is made up of a number of subgroups, which are sometimes called *fractions* of the working class. Broadly viewed, one fraction is called *blue collar.* The blue-collar fraction is also composed of several different groups of workers, some better paid and highly skilled, others poorly paid and unskilled. Some are skilled workers, such as electricians and plumbers. Others are unskilled laborers, laundry workers, and other service workers.[15]

Another fraction, called *white collar,* has sometimes been described as a "new middle class," but this group is really just a fraction of the working class. It includes a range of workers, from secretaries and other clerical workers, to sales workers, to most technicians and engineers. As in the case of blue-collar workers, these workers do not own the means of production and distribution in the U.S. economy. Most are relatively propertyless compared with members of the capitalist class. Much of their work is mechanized and routine. A certain number of white-collar workers, such as well-educated technicians and professionals, emphasize "careers" and professionalism and have higher incomes and prestige than do other members of the working class. These differences have been used by business leaders to get such white-collar workers to think of themselves as so different that they need not join unions to improve working conditions.

Many workers labor hard throughout their lives. Some, however, are very alienated from the work they do. Many dislike their work. They daydream on the job or use drugs and alcohol to get through the week. Much of the time, though, they more or less accept their lot. Many have come to accept the sanctity of corporate ownership and private profit making. Other workers, however, see through the rationalizations of a system run mostly for private profit. Resisting work alienation, they react with such actions as high absenteeism, sabotage, slowdowns, or work stoppages such as strikes. Thus, the U.S. workplace regularly experiences important types of resistance by workers who individually or collectively try to alter some working conditions.

Broadly speaking, it is in the interest of the capitalist class to maintain the existing political–economic system that it substantially controls. It is in the interest of the broadly defined working class to increase workers' control over this same political–economic system and, ultimately, to replace capitalist control of business, industry, and politics with a far more democratic system of worker control. There is thus a fundamental clash of interests between workers and employers, a continuing class struggle. Democratic unions are a major type of organization created by workers to struggle with employers for better working conditions.

The Managerial Class

One of the other important classes is the managerial class. Managerial employees at various management levels make up a growing percentage of workers. Modern capitalism has evolved this intermediate class, to which the capitalist class has delegated substantial control over many workplaces.

In Table 2.1 we see that the managerial class, composed of middle-level and lower-level managers and top professionals, typically has little or no say in company-wide decisions about the overall investment of profits, but middle-level managers typically have a substantial say in how the plants, stores, or offices they supervise are run. They also may have a lot of control over the hiring and firing of ordinary blue-collar and white-collar workers. Lower-level managers have less control over how plants, stores, and offices are structured but usually have some control over hiring and firing of some workers. Top professionals (such as research scientists) often have some control over the structure of their work (for instance, in laboratories) and also may have some people working under them.

Some scholars have noted that the managerial class location is *contradictory* in that middle- and lower-level managers share with capitalists the ability to control the labor of ordinary workers, but they often share with those workers the lack of a controlling ownership of the places in which they work. Because of their higher salaries, however, many managers do have the money to invest in corporate stock, bonds, and real estate from which they may derive significant unearned income. Managers as a group tend to be committed more to the fundamental desires of the capitalist class than to the desires of ordinary workers. Those in the managerial class, sometimes called the *coordinators*, tend to ally themselves with the capitalist class and its basic interests.[16]

Some social science research shows that higher-level employees, such as managers, are more likely to be satisfied with their workaday roles, whereas lower-paid employees are much less satisfied and often want changes in authority and control. Lower-level employees have often been found to want more democracy in their work. While a work hierarchy can solve—often only temporarily—the problem of coordinating the activities of a large number of workers, it can also create major conflicts among people of differing ranks.

The Small-Business Class

Another class has long been important in U.S. society; indeed, it predates the rise of large industrial corporations. This class is composed of self-producers such as mom-and-pop grocery store owners and other small-business people. These individuals usually control the profits from, and structure of work at, their businesses, but as a rule they control little labor of others. They do most of the work at their business. If they do hire other workers, the number is small. Many make modest profits from their businesses, but some, such as doctors and lawyers, receive large incomes from the sale of their services. Moreover, some doctors and lawyers have a large number of employees working for them and have incorporated their businesses, so that they have merged into the capitalist class.

For many rank-and-file workers, the hope that they will own their own businesses someday helps them get through the difficulties of their working day. Many long to become part of the small-business community, which a congressional report described thus: "As a provider of jobs, as a deterrent to high prices and monopoly power, and as the wellspring of the innovation and development that have made our Nation a world leader in technological advances and standard of living, the small business sector's record is unsurpassed."[17] Yet this image of small business as central to the economy and to creativity is exaggerated. Research data suggest that small business plays a modest role in the U.S. economy today. If we look at the truly small businesses, those with ten or fewer workers, we find that they make up more than three-quarters of all companies, yet employ *fewer than one-sixth* of all employees. While very small businesses are highly visible because there are several million of them, they do not control the U.S. economy.

In addition, smaller businesses are not the independent firms that the picture of "being your own boss" suggests. Most small businesses are risky, with long hours and few vacations. Many are heavily dependent on big banks and other large corporations; they have to do business the way their bankers want or they do not get the credit or loans they need. Most new businesses fail in the first few years—and not because of the high wages or poor quality of the workers. A survey by the U.S. Small Business Administration revealed that most small businesses reported that their causes of failure were high interest rates, inflation, competition from big businesses, or taxes. In addition, small businesses that hire workers often pay poorly.[18]

Other Important Groups

What of other groups of Americans, such as retired people, church workers, and government workers? Where do they fit in this system of class relations? These other groups of Americans generally have close ties, in terms of their basic economic and political interests, to one of the four basic classes just discussed. Even though these groups are not currently themselves a part of the productive relations of private enterprise, they share basic class interests with the major classes. For most purposes, they can be grouped together with one of the major classes. In addition, many in these other groups at some point in their lives have worked or will work in private enterprise. Family members who do not work outside the home tend to share the same basic class interests as those who do. For example, female homemakers who do not work outside the home are often linked to working-class male workers and share an interest in expanding workers' wages, fringe benefits, and control of the workplace. Moreover, although they are no longer part of the production process, retired people tend to reflect the class interests of the particular class they were formerly in as members of the workforce.

People holding government jobs are stratified into several levels, ranging from highly paid administrators and elected officials at the top to poorly paid janitors at the bottom. Depending on their level, those in government tend to ally themselves with the political, ideological, and economic interests of the capitalist and managerial forces or the working-class forces. Top government officials are often drawn from the capitalist class and thus mostly ally themselves with the capitalist class. Whatever their origins, top government officials tend to work to help meet the needs of that dominant class, whether those needs are for special tax benefits and loopholes, for a strong military to protect corporate investments overseas, for loans to bail out bankrupt corporations, or for a belief system that legitimates the capitalist system in the eyes of rank-and-file Americans. Periodically, however, top government officials must intervene to meet the protests of working people lest they seriously rock the system.[19]

Most high-level and middle-level federal government officials come from capitalist, managerial, or related professional backgrounds. These officials generally operate, with some exceptions, to maintain the capitalist system and the capitalist class against the threat of a takeover or of massive reform of the political–economic system by the much larger working class. Some corporate–liberal top government officials (such as President Franklin Roosevelt) may bring about modest reforms in the capitalist system with regulative programs and social welfare programs (for example, Social Security), but they, too, usually resist any significant move toward widespread worker control of politics or the workplace.

Lower-level government employees—the millions of clerical and blue-collar employees—play little direct role in top-level decisions about government policy. Employee groups such as typists and janitors have political and ideological interests similar to those of comparable white-collar and blue-collar workers in private-sector businesses. They share a basic interest in increasing the democratic control of workers over the society's major institutions. Today many of these local, state, and federal government workers are organizing themselves into effective unions seeking to improve working conditions.

The Corporate Structure

Over the last century, industrial capitalism has developed from a more competitive system with many competing firms to a near-monopoly system with ever-larger corporations dominating many sectors of business. (In this text, we use the term *corporation* to include a variety of profit-oriented business organizations, firms, and companies, including some that are, legally speaking, unincorporated.) Capitalism as we know it today has both a competitive sphere, composed of many smaller corporations and businesses, and a monopoly (or oligopoly) sphere, characterized by very large corporations such as General Motors, Microsoft, and International Business Machines. Small or large, corporations are central organizations of modern capitalism, characterized by bureaucratic organization of the workplace and a hierarchical work system, in which the top positions are filled by members of the capitalist and managerial classes, including top professionals.

In this and later chapters, we discuss the actions of corporate executives and corporations as they create problems for this society. Much control of labor, property, investment, and resources that rests in the hands of members of the capitalist class and the managerial class is now expressed through the routine operation of small-to-large bureaucratized corporations. Capitalists and their senior managers make the key decisions in corporations, whether they be computer firms, construction companies, oil companies, medical technology companies, or any other. Generally, saying that corporations "do" this or that is a shorthand way to describe the decisions made by top executives and other managers in those corporations.

Most actions of corporate officials reflect the role requirements of the officials' positions in business and industry. Regardless of who occupies the top positions, officials in all positions are under heavy pressure to behave according to the norms, values, and beliefs of capitalism. Old or young, male or female, moderate or conservative, top officials tend to act in accordance with the drive of capitalism for capital accumulation (to expand the rate of profit), for labor control, and for expanding markets.

THE STATE

The structure and character of the U.S. government have long been shaped by the power and resources of corporate America, particularly of top officials in larger corporations, as well as by the racial- and gender-stratification patterns we discuss elsewhere in this text. The legal system protects the property held by the propertied classes, and the federal government is, for the most part, controlled at the top by those with ties to corporate America. Members of presidential cabinets, heads of top congressional committees, many members of Congress, and many presidents have been top executives or senior managers in corporations, professionals (such as lawyers) servicing corporate America, or politicians groomed for political service by corporate interests. For example, Presidents H. W. Bush, Bill Clinton, and George W. Bush were lawyers or corporate executives before becoming president.

Moreover, most top government officials hold values that parallel those of corporate leaders, even where there are no direct ties. Some officials may have liberal attitudes on certain issues, but the coordination of business and government is a major goal of top capitalists and their political allies. Over the last few decades, we have seen a regular presentation of the conservative view that government should be redirected so that it operates ever more effectively to promote business interests. Conservative administrations have sought to reduce regulations on businesses and decrease taxes, such as capital gains taxes for businesses. Most local officials, from state legislators to city council members, also have ties to, or hold values supportive of, capitalistic and small-business interests.

Government is important to corporate capitalism. Many federal, state, and local government programs currently in operation reflect the interests of the propertied class. The state, according to James O'Connor, has had to take over more and more of the *social costs* of modern capitalism, even though the profits of business are still privately controlled.[20] Capitalism increasingly requires that government pay many of the human costs of continuing economic growth. That is the reason why so much government attention is given to toxic waste dumps, to corporate taxes, to Federal Reserve interest rates, and to subsidies or bailouts for ailing corporations, such as banks.

Under modern capitalism, government must try to meet certain goals, including (1) improving the rate of profit and (2) maintaining the legitimacy of the political–economic system in the eyes of the public. Profit accumulation is fostered by government projects and services that increase productivity of labor and the rate of profit, such as government-subsidized industrial development parks, urban development projects, airports, and highway and utility projects built to facilitate business needs. Firms using these facilities, as well as those constructing the facilities, profit greatly from such government expenditures. Moreover, much scientific research and the education of skilled labor power—both major

Wealthy contributors to congressional political compaigns have often received new tax breaks.

needs of business—are paid for by government. Many types of government regulation (such as regulation of stock market trading) have been implemented under capitalists' pressures for government to stabilize a capitalism that is too intensely competitive. Government funds provide many goods and services for which corporations do not have to pay.

Other critical government expenditures help legitimize the capitalistic system. One important category of expenditures, such as those for unemployment assistance and public welfare programs, helps protect the system from distressed workers who might otherwise protest. (These programs often exist because of worker protest in earlier periods.) In addition, some police and military expenditures are necessary to protect a capitalistic system from its unorganized and organized enemies in the working class, such as angry Americans rioting in the cities over unemployment or racial discrimination.

The growth of government intervention in society since the early 1900s reflects both working-class pressure for reform and the fundamental needs of capitalism. The social welfare reforms associated with corporate liberalism, such as unemployment insurance and Social Security programs, have been implemented and shaped by government officials, whose views were close to those of leading capitalists. Such programs respond to and help defuse workers' movements and their protests. Regulatory reforms and antitrust laws have also reflected the desire of some business leaders for a more orderly, less wildly competitive capitalism and a more stable marketplace purged of the most unscrupulous investors. Corporate–liberal capitalists have gradually come to support government benefit programs and expanded police forces to reduce strikes and labor unrest. For the most part, those capitalist leaders who call themselves "conservatives" also accept government intervention on behalf of corporations and other businesses, although they are much less supportive of government action in the form of social welfare programs. Since the 1980s, for example, the Reagan and both Bush administrations have symbolized a movement in this conservative, laissez-faire direction for public health and welfare programs.

The growth of large corporations is usually accompanied by a drive to expand corporate markets overseas. This drive for expansion has periodically been coupled with the deployment of huge U.S. military forces (army, navy, air force), designed in part to expand or protect the overseas markets required by multinational corporations. Moreover, the monopoly sector of capitalism (the big firms) periodically lays off surplus workers, generating serious problems of unemployment and poverty. Pressure from those workers has sometimes required an expansion of such government social programs as unemployment assistance. However, since the 1980s it has become more difficult for U.S. workers to organize, and thus to secure expanded government benefits, because of more effective union busting by corporations and the ease with which corporations can move plants and other facilities overseas.

In many ways government is a battleground for class conflict. Corporations and capitalists want the general public to pay for the industrial development and urban renewal projects they desire. Small businesses want the general public to pay for small-business loans. Many Americans want better social services in the areas of unemployment and health care. All classes want to pay lower taxes. Not surprisingly, periodic government fiscal crises, including huge budget deficits, have occurred. Governments cannot easily meet the needs of corporate America for capital accumulation and worker demands for better services and tax relief at the same time.

Kevin Phillips, a moderate Republican analyst, notes that at three points in U.S. history the Republican party used patriotic themes to gain substantial control over the federal government for a generation. This occurred during the Civil War period, again from 1896 to 1932, and in 1968, when the Republican party came to power and controlled the presidency for most years until 1992. After the 1994 congressional elections, in which Republicans gained control of the U.S. House and Senate, Republican business and political leaders again expressed views and took actions similar to those of Republicans in earlier periods. They strongly favored the interests of businesses and entrepreneurs at the great expense of workers. They encouraged increased financial speculation and mergers of corporations, favored tax-rate cuts, and worked for a greater inequality of income in the United States.[21] This pattern of favoritism for corporations and the rich was repeated with the election of George W. Bush in the years 2000 and 2004.

Phillips argues that conservative Republican actions led to major economic depressions in 1893 and 1929. A similar depression is threatened today, not only by Republicans but also by many Democrats who have tilted heavily in their support for corporate goals and interests, including bailing out troubled financial institutions and cutting federal government social spending in order to please investors. Phillips writes, "Drugstore owners can fail and employees' real wages can erode without a word from Washington. But in our new federal bailout era, big and powerful banks, corporations, and investment firms can no longer fail."[22] The federal government now puts far more money into a variety of corporate welfare programs than into social programs for the poor and working class, yet many in the working class still vote in elections for the Republican party and against their own economic interests.

Capitalism, Large Corporations, and the State: The Example of the Farm Crisis

We now look briefly at an example illustrating the major role of government in the U.S. economy. America's family farm system, historically the most productive in the world, has become the victim of a government farm policy manipulated by the interests of agribusiness (large corporate farms, processors, and wholesalers). One commentator has noted that "The farm crisis is a result of the same corporate attack on the American people that keeps unemployment rising and industrial wages slipping."[23] In the 1930s, the U.S. Congress initiated price supports for farm products to help family farmers, keying prices to production costs. Responding to pressure from agribusiness in the 1960s and seeking to promote U.S. agricultural exports, Congress changed its criteria and began setting prices below production costs and paying farmers a subsidy to make up the difference. In recent years, prices for some products have fallen to much less than farm production costs, yet even the government agricultural subsidies have often been inadequate for the family farmer.[24] Mark Ritchie of the Institute of Agriculture and Trade Policy has pointed out that the real beneficiary of the new price-setting policy "is often the buyer/trader, processor, marketer, all of whom benefit from a low buying price, while the [family] farmer is still unable to cover costs."[25] Agribusiness has also used its power to limit small and medium farmers' access to bank capital (loans) and to markets.

In an attempt to further counteract growing trade deficits during the 1970s, the U.S. government encouraged farmers to expand production for export. As a result, many farmers went heavily into debt. When the easy credit policy toward foreign purchasers of U.S. farm products was later reversed, markets shrank, prices fell, and large numbers of farmers were unable to pay the high-interest loans they had been encouraged to get during the earlier period of expansion. Bankers, who aggressively pursued foreclosures to minimize their

losses, sought federal rescue legislation to save the banking system. Such government legislation protects bankers and investors holding long-term bonds but is of little benefit to
family farmers who are losing their land.[26]

Since 1958, more than 2 million small and medium-sized farms have been forced to
close, many by foreclosures. In contrast, very large corporate farming operations have prospered for a number of reasons. Consolidation in farm production and food processing has resulted in domination of farming by a handful of corporations with diverse operations, so that
losses in one operation can be offset by profits in another. In addition, agribusiness corporations enjoy an economy of scale unavailable to small and medium-sized farmers. The large
corporations frequently buy foreclosed farms at unrealistically low prices. During the farm
crisis of the 1980s, for example, as tens of thousands of farms faced foreclosures, the assets
of ConAgra, a huge corporation whose interests include food processing and merchandising,
agricultural chemicals, and animal feeds, increased by 1,280 percent and its net income increased by 1,730 percent.[27]

The situation of African American farmers today is particularly bleak. Over the last
80 years, denial of fair access to capital (bank loans) and many product markets, often
solely because of racial prejudice and hostility, has played a key role in reducing the number of black farmers by *more than 97 percent*—from 890,000 in 1910 to fewer than 29,145
in 2002. Black-owned farmland also decreased by more than 83 percent—from 15 million
acres to 2.3 million acres.[28]

To stop the discrimination against African American farmers in the farm lending and
benefit programs of the federal government, thousands of black farmers brought a class action suit against the U.S. Department of Agriculture in 1997. Of nearly 22,000 claimants, a
federal facilitator determined that 13,110 were meritous, and as of July 2003, the facilitator had settled 12,831 claims for more than $631 million.[29] Most African Americans who
own small farms, however, still need technical assistance to move their operations from traditional crops to alternative crops that are more suitable to their relatively small acreage.
They need cooperative arrangements to reduce individual risks while enabling members to
expand their marketing and purchasing capabilities. Yet these opportunities are not available to most in these early years of the twenty-first century.[30]

The U.S. farm population has declined by 25 percent since the 1980s. Today, less than
2 percent of the U.S. population live on farms. Thousands of family farms disappear each
year. Owning and operating a farm has become one of the highest-stress occupations. The
rural poverty rate is 14.2 percent, more than 1.5 times the suburban rate (8.9 percent) and
nearly as high as the inner-city rate (16.7 percent).[31] Rural unemployment is much higher
than the national average.[32] Influenced by the far right, some white farmers have blamed a
worldwide Jewish conspiracy for farmers' economic troubles, even though Jews do not
control any of the major lending institutions involved in the farm crisis. A few farmers have
joined far-right organizations such as "The Order," which have engaged in violent crimes
such as armed robbery in futile attempts to overthrow the U.S. government and restore previous farming conditions.[33]

Suicide is the highest cause of preventable death among farmers. Since 1985, several
hundred farm suicides have occurred in Oklahoma alone, where the farm-related suicide rate
of 42 per 100,000 population is almost three times that of the state's population as a whole. In
Montana and Wisconsin the rates are even higher. Because many farm suicides are recorded
as accidents, the actual numbers are probably considerably higher than the official tally.[34]

According to one counselor at Ag-Link—an Oklahoma hotline providing counseling, mediation, and other emergency services to farm families—who has intervened to prevent more than 300 suicides and a half dozen potential homicides, "In most cases in my documentation, these farmers had recently received threats or intentions from lenders to foreclose. Much wrongdoing has occurred by lenders toward farm families—accusations, degradations, insults, legal violations, threats, hammering away at their self-esteem, and choosing directions which would throw farmers out of business, into bankruptcy, foreclosure, auction, or eviction."[35]

Farm advocates support a government farm policy that would "set up a minimum price for farm goods that would give farmers the chance to recoup their production costs. It would also take some land out of cultivation, enhance soil-conservation programs and boost food-stamp benefits."[36] Such a plan faces intense opposition from agribusiness interests, who support deregulation of farm prices and the eradication of subsidies, which they see as barriers to international trade. Yet agribusiness corporations also seek out government subsidies of various kinds; for example, such corporations have received billions in federal subsidies for their export markets in recent years.[37] The farm crisis clearly illustrates how a handful of large corporations with the aid of the U.S. government can gain control of a major economic sector.

CONTRASTING VIEWS OF INEQUALITY

Great inequalities of wealth and income have characterized this society since the 1600s and 1700s, when a great number of poor and yeoman farmers, small merchants, indentured servants, and enslaved workers were ruled by a small group of well-off landowners, merchants, and professionals. The reasons for such inequalities are viewed differently by conventional social science and power–conflict analysts.

Reflecting an order–market perspective, sociologists such as Kingsley Davis have argued that the basic source of wealth and income inequality lies in the functional necessities of society: "Men have always dreamed of a world in which distinctions of rank did not occur. Yet this dream has had to face a hard reality. Any society must distribute its individuals in the positions of its social structure and induce them to perform the duties of these positions."[38] Because some positions are more important or more unpleasant than others, societies develop a hierarchy of significantly different rewards. Income and wealth are among the most valued rewards. Inequality, these social scientists argue, results from the operation of underlying market forces, an "invisible hand" that sees to it that the important positions are "conscientiously filled by the most qualified persons." In this view, persons holding the highest-ranking positions (such as corporate executives) deserve and will generally receive the greatest rewards (such as high salaries and stock options).

Some mainstream social scientists who defend this view recognize that socially created barriers such as racial subordination keep many talented people from rising to the top, yet they still argue that inequality is inevitable. An extreme view appeared in a controversial book, *IQ in the Meritocracy* (1973), in which Harvard professor Richard Herrnstein argued that society's top groups are a hereditary meritocratic elite: The most intelligent and able people inevitably rise to the top in business and politics and pass on, through their genes, their abilities to their children. For a time these views were acclaimed by some newspaper and TV commentators; Americans were being pressured to accept the very questionable argument that psychological science had proven that those holding the highest-ranking positions in U.S. society were indeed the most intelligent. This perspective has reappeared from time to time in the last decade or two.[39]

Indeed, in a 1990s book, *The Bell Curve,* Herrnstein and Charles Murray developed the argument that black and Latino Americans are inferior in intelligence to whites, and this alleged inferiority substantially explains the lower social status of these Americans of color. These arguments, as we show in Chapter 4, misconstrue the skills test (so-called "IQ") data that they utilize and thus are wrongheaded. At the end of their book Herrnstein and Murray go further, viewing the United States as a society in which inequality is a necessary feature. They are skeptical about the ideal that "all men are created equal." This ideology of equality has "done only some good, but most of its effects are bad." Like many antiegalitarian ideologues, they argue that most Americans need to become *content* with patterns of inequality and learn to respect elites who are better than they are.[40] Other influential analysts go even further in criticizing the ideals of democracy and equality. Pulitzer Prize–winning journalist William Henry III argues that the myth of egalitarianism is responsible for the recent "dumbing" of America. In his view, moreover, many democratic notions are hopelessly wrong.[41]

Those adopting a critical power–conflict perspective point out major problems in these conservative theories of inequality. In a highly stratified society, powerful individuals and groups shape the reward structure and are able to take resources and rewards by pressure or force whether or not they deserve them. In capitalistic societies, well-off families can pass major rewards along to their children even if, as is often the case, they have not earned them.

Capitalists, including top corporate executives, who buy labor from white-collar and blue-collar workers, have the power to appropriate for their own use a significant share of the value of the labor of large numbers of ordinary working people. As a rule, the wages received by working people do *not* represent the full worth of the labor they perform at the workplace. Some of their work is *unpaid* labor, and that unpaid labor is translated into the profits and high salaries of members of the capitalist and managerial classes. Evidence that unpaid labor is the basis of profits is seen in the fact that virtually no factory or office can produce goods or services without many rank-and-file workers, but some factories and offices do flourish without profit-taking capitalists owning and controlling them. (Note the worker-owned factories in Chapter 13.)

Income and wealth derived from the unpaid labor of rank-and-file workers enable members of the dominant classes to consume goods and services worth more, often far more, than what they themselves actually produce. Top corporate executives, particularly those in large corporations (for instance, large computer and oil companies), tend to have higher incomes than do those from smaller corporations and much higher incomes than ordinary skilled workers.

THE PERSISTING PROBLEM OF INCOME INEQUALITY

In 2003, William Clay Ford, Jr., the Chairman and Chief Executive Officer of Ford Motor Company, received $14,737,753 in total salary and other compensation. In that same year, the average nonunion janitor working at a Ford plant most likely could not afford to pay the sticker price of Ford's best-selling Taurus model.[42] Similar patterns of income inequality are found in numerous workplaces across the country.

The desire for control over one's work can be seen in the ancient dream that an average person can start his or her own farm or other business and thereby prosper. Opinion polls show that a large proportion of workers would like to go into business for themselves. Fewer than half of all Americans were wage and salary workers in the mid-1800s. Most were self-employed, many on farms. Since that time, the chances of starting a successful small business have fallen sharply. By the 1880s, nearly two-thirds of U.S. workers were wage and salary employees. Today, the proportion of self-employed is less than 5 percent of the labor force.[43]

Today, most workers' incomes derive from the sale of their labor to those who control the workplace. Their incomes vary because of several factors. Racial and gender discrimination has a significant effect on incomes of groups such as African Americans, Latinos, Native Americans, and white women. Workers with greater education and training often earn higher incomes. Workers in the monopoly (oligopoly) corporate sectors of industry, especially those with unions, often receive higher wages than those in smaller, competitive, nonunionized industries.

The earnings of the average worker today barely keep pace with inflation.[44] In 2002 the median annual earnings for full-time, year-round workers was $39,429 for male workers and $30,203 for female workers.[45] However well educated, intelligent, or skilled she or he may be, no ordinary worker's income is as high as that of a top capitalist. In recent years, as numerous companies have laid off large numbers of employees and many Americans have experienced major hardship, considerable media attention has been focused on the exorbitant amounts paid to corporate America's top officials and the disparity between such compensation and the far lower incomes of rank-and-file workers. The pay of top executives is many times that of rank-and-file workers. While top executive pay has decreased somewhat in the last few years, in 2002 the median pay for 365 CEOs of U.S. corporations rose by 5.9 percent to $3.7 million each. (The average pay among the ten highest-paid CEOs was $54.7 million!) Yet, "even with the [modest] declines in executive pay over the last few years, CEOs still earn more than *200 times* as much as the average worker."[46]

The pay for some skilled workers has not even kept pace with inflation. For example, the pay of a coronary-care nurse with 15 years of experience increased by less than 3 percent over a recent 6-year period, resulting in a real earnings loss because of inflation. Yet the salary of the CEO of Columbia/HCA Healthcare, the corporation that owns the hospital where the nurse was employed, more than doubled during much of this period, and Columbia/HCA's profits grew by almost 25 percent.[47] Much of the income inequality in U.S. society reflects the power of those with the greatest resources to routinely garner additional economic resources for themselves.

Patterns of Income Inequality

Income is important to the well-being in this society because most goods and services—food, housing, clothing, medical care, legal aid, a college education—are often rationed according to ability to pay, and for most people, ability to pay depends on income. Many people cannot earn enough income to stay out of poverty: Some 27.5 million Americans earn less that $8.70 an hour.[48] Not surprisingly, those with larger incomes generally get for themselves and their families better food, housing, medical care, and so on than do those with lesser incomes.

Foreign Workers in the United Stat...

Besides native-born workers, the U.S. labor force includes *foreign guest workers* and *undocumented workers*. The Employment Policy Foundation estimates that more than 970,000 foreign guest workers are now in the country. Guest workers represent less than 1 percent of the entire civilian labor force but contribute $82 billion annually to the gross domestic product—or 8 percent of the economy. Many U.S. capitalists depend heavily on these workers.

There are five types of guest worker programs, which are usually referred to by their visa codes. Thus, the H-2 programs include 84,325 seasonal agricultural workers (H-2A) such as farm workers and seasonal crop pickers, and 98,641 seasonal nonagricultural workers (H-2B) employed as tree planters, television camera operators, stage lighting technicians, day laborers, housecleaners, cooks, musicians, and chefs. Despite their low earnings, the main attraction for employers is that H-2 workers contribute about $8.1 billion annually to the U.S. economy. The H-3 program includes 5,236 international trainees in communications, finance, government, transportation, and manufacturing. Since these foreign guests are *trainees* and are not allowed to engage in paid employment, they do not contribute to the economy. Some 217,488 foreign guest workers employed through the L-1 visa program are intra-company transferees working for multinational corporations. These guest workers contribute about $13.9 billion annually to the economy. In the O-1 program, about 21,151 guest workers are experts in the arts, sciences, education, or business and contribute about $1.8 billion annually to the economy. The largest visa category of foreign guest workers is H-1B. These workers total about 543,204 and are highly educated and highly trained persons involved in specialty occupations. H-1B workers alone generate $53.6 billion in economic output annually, nearly two-thirds of the total foreign guest worker output.

The U.S. capitalists who import foreign workers often displace native-born workers of color. One fact rarely discussed in referenc... foreign guest workers is the unwillingness many U.S. capitalists (most of whom are white) t... train and employ native-born African Americans for the same work. Historically, these U.S. employers have regarded black Americans as a residual labor pool to be drawn on only when undocumented workers are in short supply. Indeed, recent poor job growth has had a negative effect on younger and less-educated black workers. The number of young black workers declined significantly in the early 2000s. Failing job markets and substantial use of foreign guest workers by U.S. capitalists have also had a pernicious effect upon older, better-educated, middle-class black workers. In this recent period, many black workers were significantly disadvantaged—with rising job loss rates among black workers in longer-term jobs (those held three years or longer). Employers have displaced 1 in 14 longstanding black workers, compared to 1 in 18 longstanding white workers.

Unlike foreign-born workers, undocumented workers do not enter the United States through official programs. The Census Bureau estimates that 8 to 9 million undocumented (illegal) immigrant workers are in the United States. Most work in low-paying agricultural operations, where they are critical to U.S. food production. Many of them are unaccompanied children that growers hire for farm work, and still others are children of adult farm workers who work alongside their parents. Unaccompanied child workers usually range from 14 to 18 years old, while accompanied children as young as 4 work in fields. These child workers suffer high rates of injuries and deaths every year.

Migrant farm workers constitute one of the country's poorest groups. The average worker earns $7,500 per year (only $1,000 to $2,500 for unaccompanied children), while the agribusinesses for whom they labor hard garner *billions* of dollars in annual profits. Archer Daniels Midland, for example, the world leader in producing soy

continued on next page

meal, corn, wheat, and cocoa, reaped $1.7 billion in profits in 2003 and its CEO received nearly $3 million in compensation. Dole, the world's largest producer of fresh fruit, vegetables, and cut flowers generated nearly $5 billion in revenues in 2003.

Despite the illegality of hiring undocumented migrant workers, U.S. farmers who hire these workers claim that their agricultural operations would have to be closed down if they did not have access to undocumented workers. Many Americans have accepted this claim and the misin-

formed notion that utilizing low-paid farm workers helps to keep U.S. food prices affordable. However, low-wage undocumented farm workers save the average American household *only $50 a year* in their food costs. Economists concede that U.S. agriculture would prosper even without undocumented workers. Moreover, providing all farm workers, whether native born or undocumented, with decent wages and working conditions would increase the typical American family's food bill relatively little.

Sources: Employment Policy Foundation, *National Security and the Economy: The Numbers Behind Foreign Guest Workers* (January 9, 2002), available at www.epf.org/pubs/newsletters/2002/pb20020109.pdf; Philip Martin, *There Is Nothing More Permanent than Temporary Foreign Workers*, Center for Immigration Studies (April 2001), available at www.cis.org/articles/2001/back501.pdf; John Schmitt, *Recent Job Loss Hits the African-American Middle Class Hard*. Center for Economic and Policy Research (October 7, 2004), available at www.cepr.net/publications/job_tenure_report.htm; Human Rights Watch, *Adolescent Farmworkers in the United States: Endangerment and Exploitation*, available at www.hrw.org/reports/2000/frmwrker/frmwrk006–02.htm; Shelly Davis, *Child Labor* (October 2001), National Advisory Council on Migrant Health by the National Center for Farmworker Health, available at www.ncfh.org/docs/00–10%20–%20monograph.pdf.

Table 2.2 reports the percentage of total income received by each fifth of U.S. households for key years since 1929.[49] The distribution of income has changed little since 1929; most changes came during the Great Depression and World War II. The top fifth of all households received half or nearly half of all income in each decade. The proportion received by the top fifth declined from the 1930s to 1970, but increased between 1970 and 2001, in part because of state and federal legislation that favored well-off Americans. Significantly, the lowest fifth of Americans received a disproportionately small share of the total income at every point. Great inequality in income has long been a major fact of life in the United States.

Notice the substantial amount of total income going to the very small group at the top of the income pyramid. In 1929 the top 5 percent of U.S. households, which includes members of the capitalist class and top managers/professionals, received 30 percent of the country's total income. Their share declined significantly until about 1960, then gradually started moving up in the 1980s. Today, the top 5 percent receives *more than four times* its proportionate share of the total income.

The data in Table 2.2 do not include in-kind income, such as tax-supported food in the form of food stamps or medical care in the form of Medicaid (which redistribute income downward from higher-income groups to lower-income groups), or tax-supported subsidies, such as those paid to large agribusiness corporations (which redistribute income upward from the less well off to the rich). In-kind income for the affluent also includes expense accounts and other substantial employee fringe benefits. Various other categories of money income also are not included in the data in Table 2.2, such as income from capital gains. One careful research study of the income shares received by various groups of U.S. households, which added in figures or estimates for most of the in-kind and tax factors for both the rich and the poor, found little change in the basic income distribution from these additions. In-kind and tax benefits to the poor were *offset* by the substantial in-kind and tax benefits to the rich, a much smaller group of Americans.[50]

Table 2.2   Income Distribution for Households (before tax deductions),*
Selected Years: 1929–2001

Population Proportion	1929	1935–36	1941	1950	1960	1970	1980	1990	2002
Lowest 20%	13%	4%	4%	3%	3%	4%	4%	4%	3%
Second 20%		9	10	11	11	11	10	10	9
Third 20%	14	14	15	17	18	17	17	16	15
Fourth 20%	19	21	22	24	25	25	25	24	23
Highest 20%	54	52	49	45	44	43	44	47	50
Total	100%	100%	100%	100%	101%	100%	100%	101%	100%
Top 5%	30%	27%	24%	18%	17%	17%	17%	19%	22%

*Data may not total 100 percent because of rounding.

Sources: U.S. Bureau of the Census, *Historical Statistics of the United States, Colonial Times to 1957* (Washington, D.C.: 1960), p. 166; U.S. Bureau of the Census, *Current Population Reports, Consumer Income,* P60–105 (Washington, D.C.: 1977), p. 57; U.S. Bureau of the Census, *Money Income of Households, Families, and Persons in the United States: 1991,* P60–180 (Washington, D.C.: 1992), p. B11; U.S. Bureau of the Census, *Current Population* Survey, March 1995.; Carmen DeNavas-Walt and Robert Cleveland, U.S. Bureau of the Census, *Current Population Reports, Money Income in the United States: 2001* (Washington, D.C.: September 2002), available at www.census.gov/prod/2002pubs/p60-218.pdf. The data for 1950–2002 include wage and salary income, pensions, Social Security, and welfare but not in-kind or capital gains income; the data prior to 1950 include certain in-kind income.

If one visualizes the income of Americans as a pyramid with the richest at the top and the poorest at the bottom, it is a pyramid with a very broad base and a very high top. To quote economist Paul Samuelson, "If we made an income pyramid out of a child's blocks, with each layer portraying $1,000 of income, the peak would be far higher than the Eiffel Tower, but most of us would be within a yard of the ground."[51]

The typical (median) income for all U.S. households in 2003 was $43,318.[52] The latest data available (2001) measuring incomes for households with different numbers of earners, however, shows that the median income ($34,104) for a one-earner household was far less than the median income for all U.S. households ($42,228). (Approximately 41 percent of all households in the United States had more than one earner in 2001.) The median incomes for households with different numbers of earners are in Table 2.3.[53]

The Very Rich

Government census data focus on broad income groups and pay little attention to the very-high-income capitalists and managers at the top of the income pyramid. Thus, we must turn to business sources to look at higher-level incomes in detail. Top corporate executives are extremely well paid. According to a 2003 issue of *Business Week,* the highest salary plus bonus ($5,530,000) in 2002 went to chief executive officer (CEO) Jeffrey C. Barbakow of Tenet Healthcare, but this was only a modest part of his total compensation of more than $116 million.[54] Including all their corporate income, chief executive earners netted an average of *$35.8 million* in 2002. Sources report very high individual salaries. For example, Oracle paid CEO Lawrence Ellison a record-shattering $706 million in 2001. Salary-and-bonus figures for many corporate executives are the tip of the iceberg;

Table 2.3 Median Incomes by Number of Earners, 2001

Number of Earners	Median Income
0	$15,452
1	34,104
2	64,522
3	77,255
4 or more	94,589

most also receive very substantial income in the form of long-term pay, such as the option to buy their company's stock at a low price, an exercise that can result in a large profit. In addition to salaries, expense accounts, bonuses, stock options, pensions, and profit sharing, a range of other fringe benefits are frequently available to top corporate executives:

> Financial counseling, tax and legal assistance, company automobile and chauffeur services (for business and sometimes personal use), company-provided planes, boats, and apartments (for business and sometimes personal use), company-paid or subsidized travel, recreation facilities, club memberships, liberal expense accounts, personal use of business credit cards, thorough physical examinations, complete medical coverage, including inpatient, outpatient, home health care, dental, and psychiatric care all without any outlays by the executive, "educational benefit trusts," i.e., college expenses for children, "social service sabbaticals," and the best and most complete form of disability, accident and life insurance.[55]

In Table 2.4, we list the top corporate executives according to *Business Week* in order of total compensation for 2002. Their salaries and bonuses range from $5,530,000 for Tenet

Table 2.4 The Pay of Corporate Chief Executives, 2002

The Top Ten	Annual Pay (Salary and Bonus)	Long-Term Pay (Stock Options and Other Compensation)	Total Pay in 2002
1. Tenet Healthcare (CEO)	$5,530,000	$111,050,000	$116,580,000
2. Tyco Intl. (CFO)	2,243,000	72,872,000	75,115,000
3. Tyco Intl. (CEO)	4,047,000	66,991,000	71,038,000
4. Qualcomm (CEO)	1,750,000	61,574,000	63,324,000
5. Activision (Co-Chairman)	500,000	46,317,000	46,817,000
6. Activision (CEO)	500,000	42,793,000	43,293,000
7. Starbucks (CEO)	2,451,000	36,322,000	38,773,000
8. Anheuser-Busch (CEO)	3,641,000	31,021,000	34,662,000
9. Lehman Brothers (Exec. VP)	1,500,000	27,721,000	29,221,000
10. Lehman Brothers (CEO)	1,800,000	26,896,000	28,696,000

Source: Adapted from "Exec Pay: More Pain for CEOs," *Business Week Online* (March 31, 2003).

Healthcare's CEO to $1,800,000 paid to the CEO of Lehman Brothers. Stock options and gains raised total 2002 incomes to more than $116 million for Tenet Healthcare's CEO and to almost $29 million for the "lower-income" CEO at Lehman Brothers.[56]

Individuals with very high salaries, as well as many managers and professionals with incomes above $100,000 or so but well below these stellar salaries, tend to use a portion of their incomes to buy corporate stocks, bonds, and real estate. With time they can realize a substantial unearned income from investments, which raises their total income well above their salary level. In addition, the salaries of top corporate executives are far more than the real worth of their labor in a company. Much of these high salaries represents part of company profits, part of the surplus appropriated from the unpaid portion of lower-level employees' labor. Top executives, as a result, usually are major property owners and an important part of the capitalist class. Many CEOs continue to earn exorbitant compensation packages even in the face of billion-dollar losses in sales and poor stock performances for their corporations. Despite poor corporate performance, for example, Sun Microsystems paid Scott McNealy $53.1 million while the value of Sun's stock declined by 92 percent. Even criminal investigations of corporate fraud appear not to affect CEO earnings. For example, Jeffrey C. Barbakow at Tenet Healthcare Corporation earned $111.1 million in long-term pay in 2002 despite the company facing multiple federal probes involving Medicare billing. Tyco International paid L. Dennis Kozlowski almost $73 million just before his indictment for tax evasion.[57]

Effects of Income Inequality: Length and Quality of Life

A major consequence of income inequality is the control and power that a substantially greater-than-average income can provide. Level of income shapes differences in access to goods and services. Various studies have found that people above the poverty level generally eat more and have better nutrition than do those below the poverty level. Those with lower incomes have more illness days per year and shorter life expectancies than their better-paid counterparts. In addition, the distribution of doctors and medical facilities tends to follow the income distribution, with relatively fewer doctors and medical facilities in rural counties and poorer urban areas than in more affluent areas.

A recent analysis of family expenditures for poor and nonpoor working families (those poor and nonpoor families with at least one member in the labor force) found that poor families had only one-third as much income to spend as nonpoor working families. As is shown in Table 2.5, poor families spent a higher proportion of their incomes for basic necessities (food at home, shelter, utilities) than did their nonpoor counterparts.[58]

Another consequence of income inequality can be seen in access to electronic media and the information superhighway (Internet). About 88 percent of U.S. families with annual incomes over $75,000 or more own at least one personal computer, and 79 percent have Internet access. Yet, only 28 percent of family households with incomes less than $25,000 have access to a computer and just 19 percent have Internet access.[59]

Education and Income Inequality

Most Americans believe strongly in education as a solution for personal and national ills. As a result, educational attainment is considerably more equally distributed in the United States than income or wealth. Thus, in 2001, 84.3 percent of Americans aged 25 to 29 were

Table 2.5 Distribution of Family Expenditures for Working Families, 2001

	Poor	Non-poor
Food at home	10.9%	7.9%
Shelter	21.4	19.0
Utilities	9.2	6.4
Household expenses	7.4	7.2
Food away from home	5.3	5.7
Transportation	16.7	19.0
Health care	7.5	5.3
Apparel	4.7	4.7
Entertainment	4.8	5.1
Pensions and Social Security	1.6	8.2
All other expenses	10.5	11.5
Total	100.0%	100.0%

Source: U.S. Department of Labor, *Overview of Report on the American Workforce 2001* (ret. March 27, 2004).

high school graduates.[60] As shown in Table 2.6, income levels are closely tied to educational opportunities. Census data for 2000 on the median annual incomes of year-round, full-time workers 25 years of age and older by level of education completed and sex indicate a significant relationship between annual income and education.[61]

Table 2.6 Annual Income by Education and Gender, 2000

School Years Finished	Males	Females
Less than 9th grade	$20,466	$15,399
9th to 12th grade (no diploma)	24,437	17,209
High school graduate	32,493	23,719
Some college, no degree	38,652	27,190
Associate's degree	41,069	30,178
Bachelor's degree	53,505	38,208
Master's degree	65,052	47,049
Professional degree	91,324	56,345
Doctorate degree	75,631	55,620

In each gender group, those with higher educational levels have higher median incomes. A cycle lies behind these data. Higher parental incomes tend to increase children's educational possibilities, and more education often increases opportunities for better-paying jobs. Note also that at every educational level, the median incomes of males are substantially higher than those of females. Indeed, the median income for female high school graduates is slightly less than that of males whose educational attainment level is between the ninth and twelfth grades with no diploma. The median income for female college graduates is a little less than that for men with some college but no degree. Gender discrimination targeting women workers is a major reason for this pattern (see Chapter 5).

Impact on Government

Unequal control over politics is another result of income and wealth inequality. Evidence from political campaigns shows how wealth enables many people in the top classes to select or disproportionately influence politicians by large contributions to political campaigns and other financial assistance. Particularly important have been the large contributions made directly and indirectly to presidential and congressional candidates, as well as to members of state legislatures, by corporate officials. To ensure their influence on the political process, many contributors give to both political parties. As people in senior government positions essentially control executive branch appointments and shape legislation passed, control over entry into the senior positions thereby ensures substantial control over government.

In 2002, Congress passed a federal campaign finance law banning unlimited amounts of soft money contributions through state committees to political parties. The law also doubled the amounts of hard money individuals may contribute to federal candidates and political parties. Despite these new limitations, individuals contributed more than a billion dollars to federal candidates, national political parties, and political action committees for the 2004 presidential election. Wealthy individuals and corporate representatives contributed $612 million to the national political campaigns, nearly 25 times the amount contributed by organized labor ($25 million).[62]

Indeed, candidates with strong business appeal have huge coffers to fund their political campaigns, while candidates from citizens' groups have far less financial support. Well-heeled corporate contributors have received presidential appointments (such as ambassadorships), special tax concessions, and weakened regulation of particular industries in return for their large campaign contributions. Campaign reform laws have not significantly reduced the power of big money to shape the corrupted democratic process of the United States. A former Republican senator once told a business meeting the unvarnished truth about the U.S. political system: "I believe in a division of labor. You send us to Congress; we pass laws under . . . which you make money . . . and out of the profits you further contribute to our campaign funds to send us back again to pass more laws to enable you to make more money."[63]

The relationship between money and Medicare illustrates the senator's point. Congress recently passed the Prescription Drug and Medicare Improvement Act. According to the Center for Responsive Politics, pharmaceutical representatives and health maintenance organizations contributed an average of $28,504 to the 204 Republicans and $16,296 to the 16 Democrats who supported the bill. President Bush signed the Medicare bill in December 2003, giving the pharmaceutical industry an estimated $139 billion in profits by preventing the government from negotiating lower prices. Another example of the senator's concerns is that in 2004 Congress was slated to pass a proposed energy bill that would give $20 billion in tax breaks to the oil, gas, coal, and nuclear industries in return for the $71.8 million

Increasingly, the U.S. Congress serves corporate business interests.

in campaign contributions made by the industry. Tracking the payback reveals similar situations in which special interests and corporate money influence political outcomes.[64]

One aspect of this control of the U.S. political process is that most candidates elected to major offices are drawn primarily from the top 10 percent of well-off Americans. Studies of members of Congress have shown that the overwhelming majority of these politicians have business or professional backgrounds, and most are affluent-to-rich business executives or professionals. Very few members of Congress in recent decades have had blue-collar backgrounds, and relatively few have been women or non-European Americans.

People of color are mostly disenfranchised from the political campaign system. In a recent comparison of federal campaign finance figures from U.S. Census data on race and ethnicity, researchers found that the most affluent whites in the United States mostly finance federal election campaigns. Nearly 90 percent of the more than $2 billion contributed by individuals ($200 or more) to the 2000 and 2002 federal election cycles came from neighborhoods comprised mostly of non-Hispanic whites. In comparison, only 1.8 percent of campaign funds came from Latino neighborhoods, 2.8 percent came from African American neighborhoods, and 0.6 percent came from Asian and Pacific American neighborhoods. Wealthy whites contributed *84 times* more dollars than African Americans, *102 times* more than Latinos, and *39 times* more than Asian and Pacific Americans. The inability of persons of color to contribute to political campaigns effectively denies them full democratic participation in the political process because they cannot compete with whites for the attention of policy-makers since they have little input in the money-driven political system. Those who contribute large sums to political campaigns get the attention of elected officials. Essentially, as one of the study's authors explains, the current campaign finance system acts like a modern-day poll tax that effectively blocks low- and moderate-income voters of color from an equal voice in the political process.[65] It is also significant that lower-income persons vote far less in national elections than higher-income persons. In the 2000 presidential election, for example, only 38 percent of eligible voters in households earning under $10,000 a year voted, while 75 percent of eligible voters in households earning more than $75,000 voted.[66]

Workers' Real Incomes

Sharp income inequality is not as hard for ordinary workers to bear if their real incomes are rising year after year. *Real income* refers to the actual buying power of one's income after subtracting the effects of inflation. A household's income can double over a ten-year period in terms of dollars, but it may actually buy less than it did ten years earlier. Actual dollar incomes, as well as real incomes (controlled for inflation), of working families did increase after 1945 and continued to increase significantly until the late 1960s.[67] A 1955 *Fortune* magazine editorial argued, rather prematurely, that "Certainly the day is close at hand when almost everybody with a job can afford to own a house."[68]

During the 1960s and 1970s, *class convergence* theorists emphasized the concrete material achievements of working people since the Great Depression, the substantial improvements in ordinary workers' incomes, and the amounts of consumer goods such as food and clothing these rising incomes could buy. Noting that U.S. capitalism was providing, each year, a better standard of living for ordinary people, they projected a continuing rise in the affluence of workers; some even predicted that workers' incomes would continue to double every generation or so.[69]

However, the actual data on incomes over recent decades have proven this class convergence view to be a myth. In the 1970s, growth in real income was reversed. Living standards began to decline for many workers as housing and other goods became less affordable. By the mid-1990s fewer than half of U.S. families could afford to buy a median-priced home in the area where they lived.[70] The decline in families' purchasing power is a direct result of the declining income of workers. Between 1972 and 1995, real average weekly wages, *in constant 1982 dollars,* declined 19 percent, then increased between 1995 and 2005 by 8 percent:[71]

Table 2.7 Average Weekly Earnings for Selected Years
(in 1982 dollars)

Year	Average Weekly Earnings
1972	$315.44
1995 (December)	255.49
2005 (March)	276.06

However, real average weekly wages in 2005 were still significantly *less* than in 1972! Clearly, our capitalistic system can no longer provide an increasing standard of living for large numbers of workers. Indeed, for many even an adequate standard of living is not possible.

A Two-Tiered Society?

Rather than growing more similar, as class convergence theorists predicted, the economic circumstances of ordinary workers and managers and top executives have become more unequal in recent decades. Controlling for inflation, the average per person income of families in the poorest quintile increased by 5.5 percent between 1979 and 2002, while the average per person income of families in the richest quintile rose by 31.3 percent. The richest one-fifth of U.S. shares of household income grew from 43 percent in 1970 to about 50 percent in 2001, while the household income share going to the bottom fifth dropped from 4 percent to 3 percent and the second-lowest fifth dropped from 10 percent to 9 percent during this period. The rich got richer, and the poor indeed got poorer.[72]

To study income inequality, the Census Bureau has introduced a method of describing income distribution called *relative income*. Relative income adjusts incomes for differences in family size and then measures the distance of each income from the median. *Low relative income* indicates those income values that are less than one-half of the median. *High relative income* indicates values that are at least twice the median. Applying this procedure to data for the period from 1969 to 1996 (the latest data available), the Census Bureau found an overall *increase* in income inequality in the United States. The proportion of Americans whose incomes fell in the middle range had dropped. Almost 39 percent of the total population had either low or high relative income values in 1996, a 6 percent increase in this inequality index over three decades. In 1996, 22.2 percent of the population had low relative incomes and 16.6 percent had high relative incomes. Female-headed households with no spouse had the highest inequality index (55.0 percent) as well as the highest proportion with low relative incomes in 1996.[73]

The deindustrialization of the economy has been an important factor in the declining economic status of many families. Most new jobs created in the U.S. economy over the last few decades have been outside the manufacturing sector. Service-sector jobs, which make up a large share of new jobs, tend to be either high wage or low wage. The decline of manufacturing has reduced the number of workers with middle-level wages and salaries, whereas the increase in jobs in areas such as computers and electronics means a large number of lower-wage assembly and clerical jobs and a modest number of highly paid professional and technical jobs. New jobs being created tend to pay much less than old jobs that are lost. Even working families now often fall below the federal poverty line. As we will see in Chapter 3, about 7 million Americans are now classified as working poor. The total earnings of a third of all workers 25 years old and over are below the poverty level for a four-person family. A substantial proportion of families today *require* two earners to stay above the official poverty level.

A decline in living standards for many ordinary families makes inequality much harder to bear. Class convergence theorists ignore the very high level of income inequality, which, as we have shown previously, has persisted in the United States since 1945. The decline in real incomes undercuts optimism about an ever-prosperous future. Many rank-and-file Americans are very worried about their economic futures, as well as the futures of their children. Family savings are being depleted. Plans for retirement are jeopardized by reduced savings, corruption in pension plans, and a chronically troubled Social Security system. It was once thought by economists that times of high unemployment were times with low inflation, and that times of low unemployment were times with high inflation. Yet recently we have had years with some inflation and a relatively high level of unemployment compared with the low 1 to 3 percent unemployment figures of the 1940s. Many analysts view a current troubled economic situation as temporary, as only a bad moment soon to be followed by better times. But a power–conflict perspective suggests that these troubles reveal a fundamental structural weakness in this capitalistic economy, one that will not disappear. Chronic unemployment, for example, is a permanent feature of many contemporary capitalistic societies.

In the 1990s *Fortune* magazine reported, "The number of people who think society would be better off without any millionaires at all has risen by 11 percentage points, from one in four Americans to about one in three."[74] Reflecting the growing dissatisfaction of ordinary Americans with the extreme income inequality, Share the Wealth, a Boston-based national advocacy group, was created in the 1990s. The group holds workshops to inform the public about how economic inequality has evolved and to explore ways to remedy the problem. In 1995 a bill called the Corporate Responsibility Act, which would cut over $100 billion of direct corporate subsidies and tax loopholes over a 5-year period, was backed by a group of progressive members of Congress, a number of national citizens' organizations, and more than a hundred local groups.[75] Another bill, the Income Equity Act, would limit the executive compensation that a corporation could claim as a tax deduction to no more than 25 times the wages of that corporation's lowest-paid worker. The unlimited executive pay deduction allowed by current law costs taxpayers billions of dollars annually.[76] Some Americans today are taking seriously the words Daniel Webster spoke more than a century ago: "The freest government cannot long endure when the tendency of the law is to create a rapid accumulation of property in the hands of a few."[77]

THE INEQUALITY OF WEALTH

The relationship of the capitalist class to the working class is one of wealth inequality as well as income inequality. Because of a substantial family inheritance, many capitalists come into the world with far more wealth than do workers. Wealth inequality indicates that the class system is alive and flourishing. Wealth includes property such as land, farms, houses, factories, and office buildings, as well as such other assets as corporate stocks, bonds, cash, and life insurance policies.

Wealth in Contemporary America

Wealth, defined as the dollar worth of all personal property and income-producing property, is distributed far more unequally than is annual income. Between the late 1970s and 1998, the share of the country's personal wealth held by the *richest 1 percent* of U.S. families nearly doubled, climbing from 22 percent to 38 percent. The concentration of wealth in the United States is today the greatest among major industrialized nations.[78] Table 2.8 shows the concentration of privately held wealth in the United States among selected assets in the year 2000.[79]

Table 2.8 Concentration of Wealth in the United States for Selected Assets (households, 2000)

Monthly Household Income Quintile	Interest-Earning Assets at Financial Institutions	Other Interest-Earning Assets	Stocks and Mutual Funds	Home Equity	Equity in Business or Profession	IRA or Keogh Accounts	401k and Thrift Saving Plans
Lowest quintile	7.1%	1.6%	3.2%	11.5%	3.9%	5.9%	2.2%
Second quintile	14.7	5.0	9.6	15.9	7.2	13.9	4.2
Third quintile	16.4	10.9	12.1	17.0	12.3	14.9	10.3
Fourth quintile	19.9	16.2	20.3	21.3	17.4	21.1	22.5
Highest quintile	41.9	65.6	54.8	35.4	59.0	44.2	60.8
Total	100.0	100.0	100.0	100.0	100.0	100.0	100.0

The top two fifths of wealthy American households, it is clear, own most of the privately held assets. The share of total wealth controlled by the top 20 percent of Americans is often more than the share of the country's total income that this group receives.

In 1995 it took at least $340 million to qualify for a place among *Forbes* magazine's 400 wealthiest individuals in the United States, up from "only" $150 million a decade before. Today, the last person on the *Forbes* 400 list of America's richest people, Tom Werner, is worth $600 million. The wealthiest person in the United States (and indeed the world) is Bill Gates, cofounder of Microsoft Corporation, the world's largest computer software company. His fortune is estimated to be worth $46.3 billion. In this list of the wealthy, most individuals are white men. A very large proportion have inherited some wealth from parents or grandparents.[80]

Families and Corporations

Wealth statistics generally focus on individuals and relatively small nuclear families, less frequently on large extended families (that is, close relatives and their families). Yet in the United States, extended families whose members no longer have recognizable names hold great amounts of wealth. For example, descendants of John D. Rockefeller (1839–1937), the world's first billionaire, share a multibillion-dollar fortune. *Forbes* estimates the descendants of Pierre-Samuel du Pont (1739–1817) to be worth $27.7 billion. Numerous individual du Pont heirs are wealthy. The widow and children of the late Sam Walton (founder of Wal-Mart Stores, Inc. the largest U.S. retailer), whose combined net worth is estimated to be at least $22.6 billion, comprise one of the wealthiest families. Today, the Wal-Mart stores have about $259 billion in revenues. The original source of wealth for many U.S. families whose fortunes equal or exceed a billion dollars is inheritance.[81] Hard work is not the only means to the top in the United States.

Most top capitalist families make use of institutionalized corporate and financial arrangements, such as holding companies and trust funds, to protect and perpetuate their wealth. Often a large family fortune is no longer administered by one capitalist but is directed by a committee of family members who rely in part on financial experts and lawyers to maintain their fortune. Provision is made—by means of trust and other legal arrangements—so that most wealth can be inherited by subsequent generations without too much going to the tax collector. Family holding companies may own stock in a number of companies on behalf of family members, including children. Through family trusts and holding companies, a top capitalist family can function as one powerful unit. A top family may control a major bank, one or more major industrial corporations, and an important foundation. Much wealth is tied to major corporations; for example, historically the Rockefellers have been tied to Standard Oil (ExxonMobil) and the Fords to Ford Motor Company. In the United States, whose mottos are "liberty and justice for all" and "all men are created equal," *great wealth* is regularly passed along from generation to generation with no consideration or screening for the worthiness of those who inherit that wealth.[82]

One of Wall Street's favorite myths is that capitalists are no longer a dominant elite, since several million Americans now are "owners" of corporations because they own a little, or some, corporate stock. What this view ignores is the fact that a majority of Americans own no stock directly and that those who do, on the average, own only a modest number of shares. One recent study found that only 23 percent of employees in for-profit firms own any stock in their firms, with the median value of that stock being $10,000.[83] Stock market experts do put the number of Americans who own stock directly or through pension plants at some 85 million, or perhaps half of all adult Americans. Yet this figure is misleading since relatively few of those Americans have any control over the buying and selling of that stock, as it is often in pension plans controlled by "experts." Indeed, individual stock ownership is mostly in the hands of well-off Americans, who own the overwhelming majority of privately held corporate stock.[84]

The U.S. House Subcommittee on Banking has noted that a family, individual, or small group of individuals need own only 5 percent (sometimes less) of a corporation's stock to run and control it, when the rest of the stock is widely dispersed. In this way powerful capitalist families can control one or more major corporations. This same capitalist network also controls most of the "institutional investors" (e.g., insurance firms or banks that buy stock). A common pattern is for a controlling block of the stock in a corporation to be held by one or a few financial or insurance companies, many of which are closely tied to or controlled by top families.[85]

The system of wealth holding is interlocking, with certain industrial corporations being closely tied to certain banking and insurance corporations. Even supposed competitors often have indirect interlocks with one another; that is, directors from several "competing" oil companies may sit and operate together on the board of directors for a major bank. Because of interlocking boards of directors, most major industrial, banking, insurance, and miscellaneous other corporations are tied together in the persons of a small number of top corporate officials.[86]

The acquisition of many fortunes of the superrich has, at some point, involved questionable operations, such as conspiracy or bribery of government agents. One example is that of the famous capitalist John D. Rockefeller, who used a variety of means to drive competitors out of business. He made secret and questionable deals with leading railroads to ship his oil and pay him a kickback, reducing his shipping costs compared with his competitors. Rockefeller built such an oil monopoly that he could cease shipments of oil supplies to companies that bought from him, forcing them to go bankrupt and permitting him to add the then bankrupt companies to his Standard Oil trust. Railroads, under pressure from

Rockefeller's monopoly power, were forced to increase freight rates on Rockefeller's competitors, often driving them out of business. According to Matthew Josephson, in at least one documented case, Standard Oil officials working for Rockefeller used violence to destroy the refinery of a vigorous competitor.[87]

Those with greater wealth can afford better houses, vacations, medical care, and consumer goods than can those with little wealth. Wealth is a particular advantage in a major economic crisis like a recession. Those with substantial property and wealth are in a distinctly different position compared with those who have only an income on which to rely. Even a middle-income working-class family, faced with a protracted period of no or poor jobs for its wage earners, is likely to lose savings, house, and car and may go on public welfare. The same does not hold true for those with great wealth.

Wealth buys political power. The wealthy have the power to exert direct and indirect control over society. Wealth can purchase lobbyists and politicians who directly shape domestic and foreign activities of the federal government, as well as much state and local government activity. The wealthy have power to stop political activity contrary to their interests.

TAXATION

In the United States, taxation is often accused of destroying opportunity for Americans to get rich and is credited with supposedly decreasing the inequality of income and wealth. The facts, however, do not support either contention. Many superrich families made their initial fortunes well before the 1930s—before there were *any* significant taxes. Today, the regressive character of local and state taxes and of Social Security, numerous tax loopholes that disproportionately benefit those with high incomes, and the fact that federal income tax rates are not nearly so progressive as many people think combine to place a proportionately heavier total tax burden on middle-income and poor Americans than on the rich.

Tax "reforms" enacted over the last two decades increased taxes on low- and moderate-income families while generally decreasing taxes on the wealthy. For example, because rising Social Security taxes offset cuts in income taxes for those below the level of the wealthy, 95 percent of Americans paid a larger percentage of their incomes in federal taxes in the late 1980s than they had ten years earlier.[88]

Much wealth is passed from generation to generation by avoiding estate taxes. Hundreds of billions of dollars are held in bank trust funds for children of the wealthy. For tax purposes, the beneficiaries may receive only the interest income on the fortune, not the principal, or they may receive the principal only late in life and then establish a new trust for the next generation to circumvent inheritance taxes. Strategies such as giving substantial gifts to relatives, as well as complicated trust arrangements and special foundations, sharply reduce estate taxes. Nominally high estate taxes have seldom significantly reduced the wealth of most wealthy families. Indeed, the richest 1 percent of the U.S. population has seen its share of total personal wealth generally increase since the 1950s.[89]

Most wealthy families are linked to corporations that pay a smaller share of all taxes paid to governments than they did a few decades ago. In the mid-1940s corporations paid 34 percent of all federal taxes, but by the mid-1980s the percentage had dropped to a remarkably low 6.2 percent, in part because of huge tax cuts given to corporations during the Ronald Reagan administration. Individual income taxes now constitute a much larger percentage of

The huge federal budget deficits in recent years have greatly weakened the U.S. economy.

tax revenues than do corporate income taxes. While the proportion of total taxes paid by individuals has increased sharply between the 1940s and the present, a large proportion of the largest companies have paid little or no tax in at least one year since the 1970s.[90] An obvious suggestion for eradicating the federal budget deficit is to increase corporate taxes to earlier levels, yet this suggestion has not been made by any major politicians in recent years, likely because of their close ties to corporate America, especially for campaign funding.

Over the last decade the increasing costs of domestic programs have shifted from the federal government to state and local governments, whose generally regressive tax structures, based substantially on sales and excise taxes, disproportionately burden the poor and the middle class. According to a new study by the Institute of Taxation and Economic Policy (2002), most states tax middle- and low-income families far more heavily than wealthy people. While middle-income families pay about 10 percent of their earnings in state and local taxes and poor families pay about 11 percent, the richest people pay only 5.2 percent of their incomes in state and local taxes. In ten states, poor families pay up to 5.5 *times* a share of their earnings in taxes as do wealthy people, and middle-income families pay up to 3.5 *times* a share of their incomes as do wealthy people.[91] After the federal income tax deduction for state and local income and property taxes is taken into account, the wealthy in all 50 states paid a *lower* net percentage of their income in state and local taxes than did either middle-income or low-income families.[92]

CONSEQUENCES OF INCOME AND WEALTH INEQUALITY

Over the past several decades, many economists and business and political leaders have held the view that economic inequality does not harm this nation's economic well-being. The more money the well-off portion of the population has, so the theory goes, the more they spend and invest—all to the good of the economy as a whole. However, this naive theory has come under attack in recent years as a number of economists have provided evidence that countries with the greatest inequality of income and wealth generally over time have the lowest rates of economic growth.[93] These present-day cautions are reminiscent of the words of the ancient Greek historian Plutarch: "An imbalance between rich and poor is the oldest and most fatal ailment of republics."

The inequality in income and wealth in the United States is now so great that the future of the country is likely threatened with instability as those with less may come to question the growing inequality. Increases in economic inequality of the scale experienced over the last few decades are new for the United States. MIT economist Lester Thurow suggests the danger of the current trend: "In effect, we are conducting an enormous social and political experiment—something like putting a pressure cooker on the stove over a full flame and waiting to see how long it takes to explode. . . . Historically, some very successful societies have existed for millennia with enormous inequalities of wealth and income—ancient Egypt, imperial Rome, classical China. . . . None believed in equality in any sense—not theoretically, not politically, not socially, not economically. Democracies have a problem with rising economic inequality precisely because they believe in political equality— 'one person, one vote.'"[94]

SOURCES OF CAPITALISTS' WEALTH

We have thus far considered the problems of income and wealth inequality and have shown how that inequality is linked to our class-stratified capitalistic system. Now we review how capitalism came to be the dominant system and how it has changed over the last century or two. We can distinguish four periods in the development of U.S. capitalism:

1. Mercantile and plantation capitalism (1700–1850)
2. Industrial capitalism (1850–1890)
3. Early monopoly capitalism (1890–1940)
4. Advanced (late) monopoly capitalism (1940–?)

Mercantile and Plantation Capitalism (1700–1850)

We have previously noted the overseas expansion of capitalism in the fifteenth to nineteenth centuries and the ways European investors, merchants, and colonists exploited indigenous populations by stealing land or by forcing them to labor to create Europeans' wealth. Subordination of non-European peoples began with the colonizing Europeans' often-genocidal attempts to destroy indigenous populations and take their lands. Spanish colonizers stole the wealth (for example, gold) of Native Americans and killed them off with violence or European diseases, from the Caribbean to Central and South America. English settlers often killed Native Americans or drove them off desirable lands. The fur trade and agricultural development eventually brought profits to the European investors who backed a number of the settlement ventures. In the southern area of the American colonies, and later in the United States, Africans and African Americans were enslaved to create great wealth for white plantation owners and the European merchants who bought their agricultural products. Plantation owners brutally exploited enslaved blacks, and most can be viewed as agrarian capitalists attuned to commercial trade and profit. This slave plantation gentry generally dominated the U.S. economy and federal government from 1800 to just before the Civil War.[95]

Kirkpatrick Sale has analyzed the lack of ecological consciousness in the common European view of nature. European investors and colonists saw nature as something to be exploited and destroyed to meet their needs. What Sale calls "Europe's special emphasis on material acquisitiveness" may have grown out of the difficulty Europeans had in surviving in a small land area. The principal cause of their aggressive quest for accumulation, however, was the emerging capitalist system of this period, whose perspective was "more materialist, for sure, than any other economy, more expansionist, more volatile and energetic, more linked to growth and progress, and almost everywhere without the kinds of inhibitions found in the world's other high cultures."[96] The colonizing bearers of European civilization were driven to change the entire world to gain wealth and power. The eventual result of this European attitude has been a revolutionary destruction of many indigenous peoples and much of the world's forests, topsoils, plants, animal species, air, and water.[97]

Industrial Capitalism (1850–1890)

In 1800 the majority of the nonslave, male, working population in the new United States was composed of farmers, artisans, merchants, and a few professionals. A small group of agricultural and commercial capitalists held power in the new nation. Gradually, domination was assumed by urban industrialists, who were often in substantial conflict with elements of preindustrial America, such as the land-owning slaveholders of the South. From the beginning, capital for investment was spread unequally among U.S. families. Prior to the Civil War an estimated 200 capitalist families controlled all major trade and financial organizations, including larger industrial enterprises, as well as much westward expansion and large-scale commercial agriculture.[98]

Geographical and technological expansion across the new country fed capitalistic development in commerce, agriculture, and industry. By the mid-nineteenth century, the steam engine was spreading to all parts of industry, providing a technological base for extensive manufacturing development. Iron and steel production, which fed the growth of railroad and construction industries, was well developed in the United States by the 1870s; indeed, by the 1890s the United States exceeded British production in these areas. This was the era of well-known capitalists, including Andrew Carnegie, Cornelius Vanderbilt, and John D. Rockefeller. By 1890 the new machinery and chemical processes introduced by industrial capitalism had increased not only the productivity of the growing class of industrial workers but also the pace and danger of their work. Class inequality was becoming more conspicuous in the side-by-side poverty and wealth in growing industrial cities.[99]

Early Monopoly Capitalism (1890–1940)

The boom-bust cycles of overproduction and underproduction, with their accompanying cycles of unemployment, were a very serious problem for U.S. capitalists after 1890. Workers, heavily dependent on the capitalists for jobs, often organized and became more militant. The United States became involved overseas in the market-building adventure called *imperialism,* a conspicuous feature of capitalism since this period. Capitalism's drive for profit, which during previous years had emphasized technological innovation to expand productivity, now moved to global competition for new markets. Imperialist expansion has periodically made use of the U.S. military to guarantee access to exploitable labor, materials, and markets in countries around the world.[100]

According to a U.S. House Committee on Foreign Affairs report, uniformed U.S. forces were used *165 times* overseas in military interventions in other countries between 1798 and 1970. Prior to 1941 the U.S. military invaded or intervened in many countries, including the Philippine Islands, China, Colombia, Honduras, the Dominican Republic, Panama, Korea, Nicaragua, Mexico, Haiti, and Cuba. These imperialistic interventions helped to maintain class inequality within the countries invaded and facilitated the expansion of U.S. businesses and access to relatively cheap labor and raw materials in poorer countries.[101]

Prior to 1880 most firms were relatively small, but after 1880 mergers created huge corporations in such areas as oil, sugar, steel, oil, and grains. Industrial concentration accelerated as decentralized capitalism declined. Using legal and illegal means, stronger corporations forced weaker ones out of business; major industries came under control of a few companies. Occasionally a single company monopoly was established, but near-monopoly or oligopolies (control by a few companies) were more common. One example was the formation of the U.S. Steel Corporation, an industrial trust that "in 1901 controlled or acquired 785 plants worth a whopping $1.37 billion."[102] Several hundred major industrial mergers occurred in the 1890s and early 1900s. Industrial wealth was concentrated more and more in a small number of major corporations.

Over the last century the U.S. government has become heavily involved in saving capitalism from serious economic crises, a federal intervention that was accelerated by the Great Depression of the 1930s. Conservative order–market view economists have seen most unemployment as "voluntary," as resulting supposedly from workers' choices, including excessive demands for wages. Yet when Depression-era unemployment exceeded 25 percent, and jobs could not be found *at any wage,* British economist John Maynard Keynes pressed his government-intervention theories, arguing that greatly increased government spending was essential to expand both business profits and consumer incomes, and business and consumer demand, during recurring capitalistic crises of overproduction and underemployment (depressions). At first considered "communistic," by the 1960s the idea of large-scale government intervention to reduce worker protest and help business out of economic recessions was accepted even by formerly conservative business leaders.[103]

The period from 1890 to 1940 saw the rise of significant new organizations among workers, as resistance to inequalities in the capitalist system escalated and working people demanded better wages and working conditions. The number of recorded strikes thus increased from 1,026 in 1896 to 3,495 in 1903. Labor conflict issues included wages, recognition of unions, and reduction of working hours. Workers' movements began to gain strength again during the 1930s; the proportion of workers in unions increased from 11 percent in 1930 to 35 percent in 1954.[104]

Advanced (Late) Monopoly Capitalism (1940–?)

Most characteristics of early monopoly capitalism have persisted into the contemporary period, changing only in scale. Advanced monopoly capitalism has seen increased centralization and mergers of corporations, increased emphasis on consumerism and advertising, and periodic government intervention in the society. Many U.S. corporations have sought overseas outlets for the investment capital they have accumulated from previous profit making, and the number of large U.S. corporations (multinationals) operating in many countries around the globe has grown dramatically.

The increasing concentration of control in major industrial and business sectors has generated a greater centralization of wealth in many industries. On a regular basis, U.S. newspapers detail mergers, acquisitions, and actual or attempted takeovers of corporations. By the 1990s among more than 200,000 industrial corporations, a few dozen firms owned 50 percent of all assets.[105] This pattern continues today. One recent report notes that "Most corporations in the United States have less than $100,000 in assets, and the top .002 percent holds about 83 percent of all corporate assets. The largest 9 percent of all corporations control over 95 percent of all corporate assets."[106] Such asset control directly translates into national economic and political dominance for the larger companies.

In addition, government intervention in the economy, stimulated by the Great Depression and World War II, has become far-reaching in the period since the 1940s, creating a conflict between private profit and public need. Citizen pressures to remedy social problems such as environmental pollution and workplace diseases emphasize the contradiction between the private control of profits, pocketed by corporations that often draw on government loans and other aid, and the social costs of private enterprise, frequently paid for by public taxes. At the heart of the recurring government fiscal crises is the question of how many social costs of capitalism government can pay. How many bankrupt savings and loans, banks, and other corporations can taxpayers bail out? How many tax loopholes for corporations can taxpayers afford to provide? For how much pollution cleanup can taxpayers pay? The government's ability to sustain continued economic and societal growth is limited by the size of government expenditures and by the demands of working people for social programs, such as Social Security and unemployment insurance. Government, increasingly, cannot support corporate needs (for example, for business subsidies) and meet the needs of working people as well.

Since the 1940s, military-related expenditures and arms production have been significant parts of government intervention into the economy. Direct military spending, excluding such items as veterans' benefits and space program spending, increased from 1.5 percent of the gross national product in 1939 to 5.0 percent in 1949, to 9.7 percent in 1959, and then declined a bit to 7.5 percent in the 1960s. Since the 1980s various presidential administrations have increased or maintained high levels of military spending while often reducing commitments to education, housing, and other social programs. The military–industrial complex has grown enormously in the United States since the 1960s, and not just in time of war. Some scholars and a few political leaders, including the late President Dwight D. Eisenhower at the end of his term, have worried about the negative impact of the huge military–industrial complex.[107] A few U.S. historians have recently argued that excessive military expenditures have played a central role in the decline of many nations and societies over past centuries.

A critical feature of late monopoly capitalism is its global character. In recent decades many U.S. corporations have become multinational, investing in South American, African, and Asian countries and in formerly Communist countries. Today, the entire globe is available for capital investments of U.S. corporations, as well as those in other leading industrial countries. U.S. firms have exported large amounts of capital and large numbers of jobs overseas by creating plants that employ manufacturing and white-collar workers at lower wages than those of U.S. workers they replace. Top corporate executives, not world political leaders, have become the major decision-making force in this expanding capitalist system. These executives "want a level playing field in every arena in which they operate, whether it is sourcing parts in Latin America or raising capital in Hong Kong."[108] Typically, they fear strong worker organizations and seek minimal restrictions on their wages and workplace conditions.

Capitalists see global expansion as an indication of the international strength of the United States. Yet international expansion and the success of large multinational corporations have paralleled the *decline* of the U.S. economy's manufacturing base, which once supplied decent-paying jobs to many Americans. Chronically high unemployment and the declining standard of living of many U.S. workers have led many to question whether the United States is becoming a lesser economic power. Possibly this extensive overseas investment will create a multitiered system in which U.S. capitalists do well and the majority of U.S. workers do increasingly poorly.[109]

SUMMARY

Many social problems in this society are deeply rooted in the class system. In this chapter we have emphasized the importance of four major classes, which are defined according to their position in the capitalistic system of production and distribution. The classes are socially related. The top class is the capitalist class, composed of traditional capitalist owners and corporate executives whose economic ownership and control of capital investments worldwide are substantial. Next is a managerial class, an in-between class composed of managers and top professionals, to which the capitalist class has delegated substantial control over the means of production and distribution—over particular plants, warehouses, stores, and offices. The small-business class is composed of entrepreneurs whose incomes derive substantially from their own labor. Finally, the working class is that very large group of blue-collar and white-collar workers who generally have modest property and wealth to fall back on during hard times and who must sell their labor power to those who own and control the means of production, distribution, and exchange.

These class relations regularly shape the everyday lives of all Americans. One's class position largely determines one's privileges, opportunities, and lifestyle. Powerful capitalists, because of their wealth and power, can live like kings and queens, through periods of inflation, depression, or recession, while ordinary workers suffer greatly from the ravages of unemployment and inflation.

Major income inequality has been a basic feature of U.S. society from the beginning of the republic to the present. Official data indicate that the top fifth of households has pulled in half, or nearly half, of all income, and the poorest fifth a very small share, since at least the 1930s. Income is important because, in our society, access to food, clothing, housing, medical care, education, and many other goods and services is determined by a household's income. More important than the money itself is what it can buy, in addition to the control and power a substantially greater-than-average income can provide.

Noting the substantial improvements in ordinary workers' incomes and living standards, many have argued a class convergence theory in regard to the concrete material achievements of working people since the Great Depression. However, although real incomes generally increased from World War II to the early 1970s, they have overall declined, in a down then up movement, since that time. The drop in living standards for many families makes the inequality of income and wealth across class lines even harder to bear. Indeed, such conditions can breed political protest and revolt, as has been seen in a few urban riots since the 1980s.

In the U.S. there is even greater inequality of wealth than of income. The top 1 percent of households control very large shares of the wealth, including cash, bonds, real estate, and corporate stock. In this group are the superrich top capitalist families such as the Rockefellers, Fords, Waltons, Gateses, and du Ponts. Most top capitalist families are tied into important corporations. Through trusts, holding companies, and other institutional arrangements, a top capitalist family can act as a powerful and influential unit, with substantial ownership and control of at least one major corporation.

In the last section of this chapter we briefly reviewed the history of U.S. capitalism since 1700. The expansive period of industrial capitalism, from about 1850 to 1890, saw large-scale industrialization and urbanization in the constant quest by capitalist industrialists for productivity and profits. The next period, early monopoly capitalism (1890–1940), witnessed a growing concentration of power in fewer and fewer monopoly corporations and a continuing series of economic crises, culminating in the Great Depression. Gradually, the federal government became more and more involved in attempts to save capitalism from its periodic crises of overproduction and underproduction. These attempts ranged from military intervention in the form of U.S. imperialism in countries overseas to domestic government programs to assist businesses and provide such assistance as major aid to unemployed workers. Beginning in the 1940s, the United States has moved into a late monopoly capitalism period, with more and more concentration of power in the hands of a few corporations and continuing government intervention to aid businesses and forestall protest from working people. Corporations have increasingly sought new outlets overseas for investment, preferably in countries with lower wages and conservative political climates.

Today the U.S. government is experiencing a recurring financial (deficit) crisis. The federal government's ability to intervene to sustain corporate growth and profitability is limited by the size of government expenditures and by demands of working people for support programs such as Social Security and unemployment compensation. Governments, both federal and local, are having difficulty meeting business needs and the social program needs of rank-and-file working people. This creates the potential for recurring societal crises and class conflict.

STUDY QUESTIONS

1. Using as examples (1) GM truck safety and (2) the Levi Strauss Co. and capital flight, discuss the central features of a definition of classes in U.S. society.

2. Compare and contrast trends in income inequality with those of wealth inequality. Does either show a significant trend toward equality? Which of these two is more equitably distributed?

3. Why is income important? What difference does it make in people's everyday lives?

4. Outline the distinguishing features of industrial capitalism, early monopoly capitalism, and advanced (late) monopoly capitalism.

5. Using illustrations from the text or from contemporary events, compare the effects of regressive taxation with progressive taxation on different classes.

6. On occasion, the United States has engaged in overseas imperialism to guarantee access to exploitable cheap labor, raw materials, and markets in poorer countries. Identify several specific historical and contemporary examples.

ENDNOTES

1. Alexander Cockburn, "Clinton, Labor, and Free Trade," *The Nation,* November 2, 1992, pp. 508–509.
2. Philip Bookman, "Strife Battles Levi's," *Independent Journal,* March 9, 1995, p. C1.
3. L. A. Lorek, "Levi's Shuts Down Remaining U.S. Plants in San Antonio," *San Antonio Express-News,* December 15, 2003.
4. Khalid Elhassan, *The OSHA Mission: Found and Lost, A Public Reminder,* Center for the Study of Responsive Law, February 2000, available at www.csrl.org/reports/OSHA.html#N_26_.
5. "Death in a Poultry Plant," *Dollars & Sense,* November 1991, p. 5.
6. Testimony by Deborah Berkowitz before Joint Hearing of the Senate Small Business Labor and Human Resource Committees, as reported by Federal News Service, December 8, 1995.
7. Letters and documents provided to authors by Clarence M. Ditlow, Executive Director, Center for Auto Safety, Washington, D.C.
8. Ibid.
9. Myron Levin, "GM Paid $495 Million in Suits," *Los Angeles Times* (May 7, 2003), available at www.autosafety.org/article.php?scid=94&did=793. For a comprehensive overview of the history and continuing saga of the C/K pickup truck and GM's denial that the truck is inherently unsafe, see the Center for Auto Safety Web site at www.autosafety.org/index.html.
10. Robert C. Cowen, "Weaning Farmers from Pest Control Strictly by Pesticides," *Christian Science Monitor,* February 28, 1995, p. 12.
11. David Weir and Mark Shapiro, *Circle of Poison* (San Francisco: Institute for Food and Development Policy, 1981), pp. 3–30.
12. Portions of this table are loosely adapted from Eric O. Wright, *Class Structure and Income Determination* (New York: Academic Press, 1979), pp. 38–42.
13. Erik O. Wright, *Class Structure and Income Determination* (New York: Academic Press, 1979), pp. 38–42; Michael Albert and Robin Hahnel, *Unorthodox Marxism* (Boston: South End Press, 1978), pp. 186–98.
14. This section draws on Richard Edwards, *Contested Terrain* (New York: Basic Books, 1979), pp. 184–99; Albert and Hahnel, *Unorthodox Marxism,* pp. 195–99; Charles H. Anderson and Jeffrey R. Gibson, *Toward a New Sociology* (Homewood, Ill.: Dorsey Press, 1978), p. 125.
15. For a review of the social plight of the working poor in the United States, see David K. Shipler, *The Working Poor: Invisible in America* (New York: Alfred A. Knopf, 2004).
16. Wright, *Class Structure*, pp. 88–90.
17. Quoted in Mark Obrinsky, "Facts about Small Businesses," *Economic Notes* 50 (December 1982): 8.
18. "Why Small Businesses Fail," *Economic Notes* 50 (December 1982): 11.

19. This section draws on Erik O. Wright, *Class, Crisis and the State* (London: NLB Books, 1978), pp. 92–96; Albert and Hahnel, *Unorthodox Marxism,* pp. 186–95.

20. This section draws on James O'Connor, *The Fiscal Crisis of the State* (New York: St. Martin's Press, 1973), pp. 5–9 and passim.

21. Kevin Phillips, "Today's 'Gingrichomics' Echoes GOP Eras of Old," *Christian Science Monitor,* December 22, 1995, p. 18.

22. Ibid.

23. Jay Walljasper, "Farmers and the Left," *The Nation,* October 25, 1986, p. 402.

24. Ibid.; Chris Williams, "Farm Policy for Whom?" *Dollars & Sense,* March 1992, p. 10.

25. Quoted in Williams, "Farm Policy for Whom?" p. 10.

26. Heather Ball and Leland Beatty, "Blowing Away the Family Farmer: The Debt Tornado," *The Nation,* November 3, 1984, p. 442; Keith Schneider, "Crisis in Farm Credit Brings a Bitter Harvest," *New York Times,* December 17, 1987, p. 1.

27. Williams, "Farm Policy for Whom?" pp. 10–11, 20; League of Rural Voters, "Rural Vote '92," February 1992, p. 1.

28. U.S. Department of Agriculture, *Preliminary Report: Census of Agriculture 2002* (February 2004), available at www.nass.usda.gov/census/census02/preliminary/cenpre02.pdf.

29. See *Pigford v. Veneman: Consent Decree in Class Action Suit by African American Farmers, Background and Current Status,* U.S. Department of Agriculture, available at www.usda.gov/da/status.htm. See also Jennifer Myers, "Rough Terrain," *Legal Times* (November 18, 2002), p. 1.

30. Ibid.

31. Bernadette D. Proctor and Joseph Dalaker, U.S. Census Bureau, *Current Population Reports, Poverty in the United States: 2002* (September 2003), available at www.census.gov/prod/2003pubs/p60–222.pdf.

32. League of Rural Voters, "Rural Vote '92," August 1992, p. 1; Beth Lilley, "Ag Crisis Hotline Readies for Annual Wave of Phone Calls," *Enid (Okla.) News and Eagle,* January 26, 1992, p. C1; *The Window: Farm Business Issues from a Woman's Point of View,* March 1991, p. 2; Bernadette D. Proctor and Joseph Dalaker, U.S. Census Bureau, Current Population Reports, *Poverty in the United States: 2002.*

33. James Ridgeway, *Blood in the Face* (New York: Thunder's Mouth Press, 1990), p. 187.

34. Letter to authors from Mona Lee Brock of Ag-Link, November 11, 1992; Charlene Finck, "The '80s Are Over, but Farmers Are Still Killing Themselves," *Farm Journal,* October 1990, pp. 36–39; "Mediation Program Sparks Hope for Farmers, Bankers," *Oklahoma Banker,* November 1991, p. 8.

35. Letter to authors from Mona Lee Brock of Ag-Link, November 11, 1992.

36. Walljasper, "Farmers and the Left."

37. Williams, "Farm Policy for Whom?" p. 20; "Bush's Ruling Class," *Common Cause Magazine,* April/May/June 1992, pp. 14–15.

38. Kingsley Davis, *Human Society* (New York: Macmillan, 1949), p. 366; see also p. 367.

39. Richard Herrnstein, *IQ in the Meritocracy* (Boston: Little, Brown, 1973). This section draws generally on Eduardo Del Rio, ed., *Marx for Beginners* (New York: Pantheon Books, 1976), pp. 104–108; Ernest Mandel, *Marxist Economic Theory,* vol. 1 (New York: Monthly Review Press, 1968), pp. 132–60; Wright, *Class Structure,* pp. 92–93.

40. Richard J. Herrnstein and Charles Murray, *The Bell Curve: Intelligence and Class Structure in American Life* (New York: Free Press, 1994), pp. 527–33.

41. William Henry III, *In Defense of Elitism* (New York: Doubleday, 1994).

42. AFL-CIO, *Executive Pay Watch* (ret. April 9, 2004), available at www.aflcio.org/corporateamerica/paywatch/ceou/database.cfm?tkr=F&pg=1; U.S. Bureau of the Census, *Statistical Abstracts of the U.S., 2003* (ret. April 9, 2004), available at www.census.gov/prod/2004pubs/03statab/labor.pdf; "America's Top Trash: The Justice for Janitors Enemies List," *Justice for Janitors Newsletter,* 1992.

43. U.S. Census Bureau, Statistical Abstract of the U.S., 2003, available at www.census.gov/prod/www/statistical-abstract-03.html; Jackson T. Main, *The Social Structure of Revolutionary America* (Princeton, N.J.: Princeton University Press, 1965), pp. 271–73; Michael Reich, "The Development of the Wage-Labor Force," in *The Capitalist System,* 2d ed., R. C. Edwards, Michael Reich, and T. E. Weisskopf, eds. (Upper Saddle River, N.J.: Prentice Hall, 1978), p. 180.

44. Louis Lavelle, "Exec Pay: More Pain for CEOs," *BusinessWeek Online* (March 31, 2003), www.businessweek.com/bwdaily/dnflash/mar2003/nf20030321_1805_db035.htm; Deborah Lutterbeck, "Falling Wages," *Common Cause,* Winter 1995, p. 13.

45. Carmen DeNavas-Walt, Robert Cleveland, and Bruce H. Webster, Jr., U.S. Census Bureau, Current Population Reports, *Money Income in the United States: 2002* (September 2003), available at www.census.gov/prod/2003pubs/p60–221.pdf.
46. Louis Lavelle, Frederick F. Jespersen, Spence Ante, and Jim Kerstetter, "Executive Pay," *BusinessWeek Online* (April 21, 2003), available at www.businessweek.com/magazine/content/03_16/b3829002.htm.
47. Lutterbeck, "Falling Wages," pp. 11, 13.
48. Eileen Appelbaum, Annette Bernhardt, and Richard J. Murnane, *Low-Wage America: How Employers Are Reshaping Opportunity in the Workplace* (New York: Russell Sage, 2003).
49. Households consist of families, unrelated individuals occupying a housing unit, and individuals living alone.
50. Timothy M. Smeeding, "The Trend toward Equality in the Distribution of New Income: A Reexamination of Data and Methodology," in *Institute for Research on Poverty Discussion Papers* (Madison: University of Wisconsin Press, 1977), p. 28.
51. Paul A. Samuelson, *Economics,* 9th ed. (New York: McGraw-Hill, 1973), p. 84.
52. Carmen DeNavas-Walt, Bernadette D. Proctor, and Robert J. Mills, U.S. Census Bureau, Current Population Reports, *Income, Poverty, and Health Coverage in United States: 2003* (August 2004), available at www.census.gov/prod/2004pubs/p60–226.pdf.
53. Carmen DeNavas-Walt and Robert Cleveland, U.S. Census Bureau, Current Population Reports, *Money Income in the United States: 2001* (September 2002), available at www.census.gov/prod/2002pubs/p60–218.pdf.
54. Louis Lavelle, "Exec Pay: More Pain for CEOs," *Business Week* (March 31, 2003), www.businessweek.com/bwdaily/dnflash/mar2003/nf20030321_1805_db035.htm.
55. Paul Blumberg, "Another Day, Another $3,000: Executive Salaries in America," *Dissent* 25 (Spring 1978): 160.
56. Louis Lavelle, "Exec Pay: More Pain for CEOs," *BusinessWeek Online* (March 31, 2003), available at www.businessweek.com/bwdaily/dnflash/mar2003/nf20030321_1805_db035.htm.
57. Louis Lavelle, Frederick F. Jespersen, Spence Ante, and Jim Kerstetter, "Executive Pay," *BusinessWeek Online* (April 21, 2003), available at www.businessweek.com/magazine/content/03_16/b3829002.htm.
58. U.S. Department of Labor, *Overview of Report on the American Workforce 2001* (ret. March 27, 2004), available at stats.bls.gov/opub/rtaw/rtawhome.htm.
59. U.S. Census Bureau, *The Population Profile of the United States: 2000 (Internet Release),* "The PC Generation: Computer Use, 2000" (ret. April 9, 2004), available at www.census.gov/population/pop-profile/2000/profile2000.pdf.
60. National Center for Educational Statistics, *Digest of Education Statistics, 2002* (June 23, 2003), nces.ed.gov/programs/digest/d02/tables/dt008.asp.
61. U.S. Census Bureau, *The Population Profile of the United States: 2000 (Internet Release),* "Money Matters: Money Income, 2000" (ret. April 12, 2004), available at www.census.gov/population/pop-profile/2000/profile2000.pdf.
62. The Center for Responsive Politics, *Political Action Committee Contributions to Federal Candidates,* March 29, 2004, available at www.opensecrets.org/pacs/sector.asp?txt=Q03&cycle=2004.
63. William G. Domhoff, *The Powers That Be:* Processes of Ruling Class Domination in America (New York: Random House, 1978), pp. 145–46.
64. The Center for Responsive Politics, *Money and Medicare,* November 2003, available at www.capitaleye.org/inside.asp?ID=113. See also, Antonio Gonzalez and Stephanie Moore, "Wealthy Campaign Donors Stifle Minority Voices," *USA Today,* December 11, 2003, p. 23A.
65. Public Campaign, the Fannie Lou Hamer Project, and the William C. Velasquez Institute, *Color of Money 2003: Campaign Contributions, Race, Ethnicity, and Neighborhoods,* December 2003, available at www.colorofmoney.org/report/com112103.pdf.
66. David K. Shipler, "Why John Kerry Needs the Needy," *Los Angeles Times,* April 25, 2004, p. M5.
67. U.S. Bureau of Labor Statistics, *Employment and Earnings, U.S., 1909–1978* (Washington, 1979); Paul Blumberg, *Inequality in an Age of Decline.* (New York: Oxford Univ. Press, 1980), p. 68.
68. Quoted in Blumberg, *Inequality in an Age of Decline,* p. 200.
69. Blumberg, *Inequality in an Age of Decline,* pp. 16–18; see also Herman Kahn, *2000 A.D.* (New York: Macmillan, 1967).
70. U.S. Bureau of the Census, *Who Can Afford to Buy a House in 1991* (Washington, 1993), pp. 2–9.
71. *Economic Notes,* 64 (March 1996): 4. See also, U.S. Department of Labor, "Real Earnings in March 2005," (April 20, 2005), available at stats.bls.gov/news.release/pdf/realer.pdf.

72. Carmen DeNavas-Walt, Robert W. Cleveland, and Bruce H. Webster, Jr., *Current Population Reports, Income in the United States: 2002* (September 2003), available at www.census.gov/prod/2003pubs/p60–221.pdf. Proctor and Dalaker, *Current Population Reports, Poverty in the United States: 2002.*

73. U.S. Bureau of the Census, *Current Population Reports, Changes in Median Household Income: 1969 to 1996* (July 1998), available at www.census.gov/prod/3/98pubs/p23–196.pdf.

74. Quoted in *Too Much,* Spring 1995, p. 2.

75. "Pressure Builds to Slice Corporate Welfare Subsidies," *Too Much,* Fall 1995, p. 3.

76. "Sabo Limit on CEO Pay Starts Winning Kudos," *Too Much,* Fall 1995, p. 3.

77. Quoted in *Too Much,* Fall 1995, p. 3.

78. Edward N. Wolff, *Recent Trends in Wealth Ownership, 1983–1998,* Jerome Levy Economics Institute (April 2000), available at www.levy.org/docs/wrkpap/papers/300.html. See also, Edward N. Wolff, "For Most Americans, Economic Pie Is Shrinking," *Baltimore Sun,* September 3, 1995, p. F1; Arthur B. Kennickell and R. Louise Woodburn, *Estimation of Household Net Worth* (Washington, D.C.: 1992), p. 37. See also, Edward N. Wolff, "How the Pie Is Sliced: America's Growing Concentration of Wealth," *The American Prospect* (June 23, 1995), available at www.prospect.org/print-friendly/print/V6/22/wolff-e.html.

79. Shawna Orzechowski and Peter Sepielli, *Net Worth and Asset Ownership of Households: 1998 and 2000,* U.S. Census Bureau, May 2003, available at www.census.gov/prod/2003pubs/p70–88.pdf.

80. "400 Richest Americans," *Forbes,* (ret. March 27, 2004), available at www.forbes.com/400richest/.

81. Ibid.

82. "Who Has the Wealth in America?" *Business Week,* August 5, 1972, pp. 55–57; Thomas R. Dye, *Who's Running America?* 5th ed. (Upper Saddle River, N.J.: Prentice Hall, 1990), pp. 52–62.

83. National Center for Employee Ownership, "New Data Show Employee Ownership to Be Widespread," available at www.nceo.org/library/widespread.html (ret. April 8, 2004).

84. Jamie Chapman, "Grasso and Wall Street's 'Governance' Crisis" September 2003, available at www.wsws.org/articles/2003/sep2003/gras-s30.shtml.

85. See Corporate Data Exchange, *Stock Ownership Directory: Energy* (New York: Corporate Data Exchange, 1980). See the summary of this report by Robert Sherrill, "Where Is the Cry of Protest?" *The Nation,* October 25, 1980, pp. 413–14.

86. Sherrill, "Where Is the Cry of Protest?" p. 414.

87. Matthew Josephson, *The Robber Barons* (New York: Harcourt Brace Jovanovich, 1962), pp. 264–79.

88. Robert S. McIntyre, "The Populist Tax Act of 1989," *The Nation,* April 2, 1988, p. 462; Mark L. Goldstein, "End of the American Dream?" in *Social Problems 89/90,* LeRoy W. Barnes, ed. (Guilford, Conn.: Dushkin, 1989), p. 27; "Get the Little Guy," *Dollars & Sense,* May 1991, p. 4.

89. John A. Brittain, *Inheritance and the Inequality of Material Wealth* (Washington, D.C.: Brookings Institution, 1978), pp. 4–5; Kennickell and Woodburn, *Estimation of Household Net Worth,* p. 37.

90. Robert M. Brandon, Jonathan Rowe, and Thomas H. Stanton, "Tax Politics," in *Crisis in American Institutions,* 4th ed., J. H. Skolnick and E. Currie, eds. (Boston: Little, Brown, 1979), pp. 100–118; Thea Lee, "Closing in on Corporate Freeloaders," *Dollars & Sense,* December 1988, pp. 16–17.

91. These ten states are Washington, Florida, Tennessee, South Dakota, Texas, Illinois, Michigan, Pennsylvania, Nevada, and Alabama. See Institute on Taxation and Economic Policy, *Who Pays? A Distributional Analysis of the Tax Systems in All 50 States,* 2nd ed. (January 2003), available at www.itepnet.org/wp2000/pr.pdf.

92. Citizens for Tax Justice, *A Far Cry from Fair* (Washington, D.C.: Citizens for Tax Justice, 1992), pp. 1–8, 19–69.

93. Torsten Persson and Guido Tabellini, "Is Inequality Harmful for Growth?" *American Economic Review,* June 1994, pp. 600–622, and Andrew Blyn and David Miliband, *Paying for Inequality: The Economic Cost of Social Injustice* (London: Institute for Public Policy Research, 1994).

94. Lester Thurow, "The RICH: Why Their World Might Crumble," *New York Times,* November 19, 1995, sec. 6, p. 78.

95. Joe R. Feagin and Clairece Feagin, *Racial and Ethnic Relations,* 5th ed. (Upper Saddle River, N.J.: Prentice Hall, 1996), pp. 235–40.

96. Kirkpatrick Sale, *The Conquest of Paradise* (New York: Penguin Books, 1991), pp. 90–91.

97. Ibid., p. 363.

98. Samuel Bowles and Herbert Gintis, *Schooling in Capitalist America* (New York: Basic Books, 1976), p. 65.

99. John N. Ingham, *The Iron Barons* (Westport, Conn.: Greenwood Press, 1978), p. xv.

100. Douglas F. Dowd, *The Twisted Dream,* 2nd ed. (Cambridge, Mass.: Winthrop Publishers, 1977), pp. 37–38.

101. Eduardo Galeano, "Guatemala Occupied Country," in *The Capitalist System,* ed. by R. C. Edwards, M. Reich, and T. E. Weisskopf (Upper Saddle River, N.J.: Prentice-Hall, 1978), pp. 33–35.

102. E. K. Hunt and Howard J. Sherman, *Economics,* 3rd ed. (New York: Harper and Row, 1978), p. 87.

103. Dowd, *Twisted Dream,* pp. 22–24.

104. Bruno Ramirez, *When Workers Fight* (Westport, Conn.: Greenwood Press, 1978), pp. 8–11; Philip Taft and Philip Rose, "American Labor Violence: Its Causes, Character, and Outcome," in *Violence in America,* H. D. Graham and T. R. Gurr, eds. (New York: Bantam Books, 1969), pp. 380–82.

105. Dye, *Who's Running America?* pp. 17–18.

106. Linda A. Renzulli, Howard E. Aldrich, and Jeremy Reynolds, "It's Up in the Air, or Is It?" (December 2001), available at www.unc.edu/~healdric/Workpapers/WP138.pdf.

107. Ernest Mandel, *Late Capitalism,* J. DeBres, trans. (London: NLB Verso Books, 1978), pp. 391–94.

108. James Srodes, "The Rule Makers," *Financial World,* March 5, 1991, p. 40.

109. Ibid.

chapter 3

Poverty, Unemployment, and Underemployment

A large central city with more than a quarter of its workers permanently unemployed. Large numbers of young men with no jobs hanging around, playing pool or cards, and collecting welfare. Many unemployed adult children living with unemployed parents. Many local residents with alcohol and drug problems. Large numbers of older men out of work for years. Teenagers with illegitimate children living with their parents in public housing. Most people resigned to their hard lives.

The population described here certainly fits the image of a poor urban "underclass" popular in some mass media and scholarly discussions. Many readers may guess that we are describing a major U.S. urban area—perhaps the central city of Detroit, Newark, or Los Angeles. Some might guess that the residents are black or Latino Americans. Yet the city described above is in fact Liverpool, England, and the residents are overwhelmingly white and British.[1]

Reflection on conditions in Liverpool suggests some serious problems with current discussions of America's urban poor. Few media analysts or scholars would likely describe Liverpool's white families as an entrenched, multigenerational "underclass." Indeed, before the recent industrial decline in northern England, the majority of the families there were middle income, with one or two breadwinners. Explaining the problems and tribulations of these now poor families does not require an ideology of individual pathology and the loss of "family values." The major responsibility for Liverpool's troubles lies in the flight of corporate capital to more profitable locations outside northern Britain. Large-scale unemployment is reproduced from one generation to the next, not primarily because of deficient personal or family values but because of the workings of capital investment markets and the actions of corporate investors to disinvest in an urban economy. Without decent-paying jobs, workers cannot adequately support their families in any city in the world, regardless of their racial group, color, gender, or nationality. In this chapter, we examine the interrelationship of poverty, unemployment, and underemployment in the United States.

Although poverty appears to be a permanent feature of U.S. society, concern with the problems of poverty and unemployment has been a roller-coaster phenomenon, rising and falling with changes in economic conditions and in working people's protest actions. Vacillating concern has characterized the attitudes of not only top business and political officials but also much of the public. The Great Depression of the 1930s—U.S. capitalism's worst depression since 1900—triggered large-scale working-class and union protests that forced new government action on behalf of poor and unemployed Americans. The relief programs that developed out of this political upheaval included federally subsidized unemployment insurance and those public assistance programs now commonly termed "welfare." An emerging confidence that the so-called affluent society had arrived brought a relative decrease in government concern with the poor in the 1940s and 1950s as business leaders, scholars, and government officials emphasized the new wave of prosperity in the United States. In the view of many observers, poverty was all but vanquished, and most citizens would soon be affluent suburbanites—in spite of the fact that more than 22 percent of the population (39.5 million individuals) were below the officially defined poverty level in 1959.[2] John Kenneth Galbraith wrote about this new age in *The Affluent Society* (1962), suggesting that since the United States had achieved the status of an affluent society, poverty could no longer be seen as a major affliction. Common acceptance of this point of view among prominent economic and political leaders caused the poor once again to become invisible.[3]

However, another book published in 1962, Michael Harrington's groundbreaking *The Other America,* focused attention on the more than 50 million Americans who were then in serious economic need.[4] As the decade progressed, and as protests grew, poverty was re-discovered and openly recognized and discussed as a major social problem. Advisers to the Kennedy and Johnson administrations were persuaded that the federal government had to take action. In his War on Poverty, which began in 1964, President Lyndon Johnson imple-mented a number of concrete antipoverty programs, many of which continued to expand during the 1970s. By 1973, the official poverty rate was down to 11.1 percent and remained relatively low throughout the 1970s.[5]

Concern turned away from poverty and the poor again from the 1980s to the 2000s as na-tional politicians imposed large-scale budget cuts on people-oriented social programs. Annual poverty rates again increased, fluctuating between 12 percent and 15 percent.[6] Aid to Families with Dependent Children (AFDC) was the main public welfare program for the poor until 1996 when the federal government reformed welfare in the Personal Responsibility and Work Op-portunity Reconciliation Act (PRWORA). Strikingly, the median *decline* in maximum state AFDC benefits for a three-person family between 1970 and 1994 was nearly 50 percent.[7] In 1979 cash and noncash government programs, including means-tested cash, food, and housing benefits, lifted only 16.5 percent of otherwise poor individuals above the poverty line; by 1983, this figure had dropped to 9.9 percent, and in 1992 it was just over 12 percent.[8] In the 1990s, contrary to common media images, fewer than half of those below the poverty level received cash assistance through a government program. Less than two-thirds of children in poverty re-ceived AFDC benefits.[9] Today, cutbacks in government aid programs continue despite nearly 35 million Americans remaining below the official poverty line.[10]

Today, large numbers of people are homeless and even larger numbers are hungry or malnourished. Nearly 35 million people in the United States experience hunger because they cannot afford enough food. Slightly more than 3 million female-headed households experi-ence the highest rates of hunger among household types, and more than 13 million children are living in households with food shortages. About a fifth of black and Latino households experience hunger. This is much more than the rate for white households (8.0 percent). Hunger is more prevalent in central cities (14.4 percent of the people) and rural areas (11.6 percent) than elsewhere (8.8 percent).[11]

The health consequences of hunger among children are alarming. Hungry children suffer health problems associated with weight loss, retarded growth, anemia, fatigue, headaches, poor concentration, and frequent colds. Hungry children miss more days of school than other children. Medical professionals have linked infant mortality rates to in-adequate diets of prenatal mothers, and this is particularly the case among African Ameri-cans whose infant mortality rate is twice that of whites. Undernourished infants are more likely to have behavioral and learning problems. Poor nutrition among children has detri-mental effects on cognitive development. The effects of hunger among the country's 1.6 million elderly households experiencing hunger worsen diseases among the aged.[12]

What the future holds for poverty-aid programs in the United States is unclear. The poor remain outcasts and out of sight for many affluent Americans, including now most business and political leaders—except when the poor turn to violent crime or rioting in our cities as ways of protesting their oppressive conditions.

GOALS OF THIS CHAPTER

We begin this chapter with a discussion on the extent, character, and distribution of poverty in the United States. Employing a critical analysis of poverty reveals discrepancies in the official poverty counts, variations in the numbers of impoverished corresponding directly to the boom–bust cycles of the U.S. business-centered economy, and an unequal distribution of poverty among the country's various populations. We explain that poverty is significantly connected with unemployment and underemployment in the United States, and that the persistence of poverty is often rationalized, incorrectly, as the result of the character shortcomings of poor people—the "gospel of individualism." We close the chapter with a discussion on the failure of state and federal government entitlement programs to improve the living standards of poor people.

LOW INCOMES AND POVERTY

Who are low-income Americans, and how do the nonpoor view them? The language historically used to describe those with low incomes has had a class bias—that is, it has often been the language of the "overclasses." Historian Michael Katz points out that terms such as the "undeserving poor" and the "underclass" are often terms of malicious distinction and "quickly become unexamined parts of discourse."[13] Even the term *poor* has some of these negative connotations. Such descriptions of less advantaged Americans are assumed by the unthinking to reflect natural qualities of those described. However, these politically constructed categories mostly *do not* reflect the perspectives of those being labeled.

Americans with low incomes do have far fewer *resources* than those with higher incomes. Their lack of resources is seen in low incomes, but their lives are also regularly and severely constrained by a lack of other economic, political, and social resources. "Poverty . . . is a social product."[14] Too many analyses, both liberal and conservative, of low-income Americans ignore questions of inequality and power.

The Extent and Character of Poverty

One international comparison of eight major industrialized countries in 1992 found that the U.S. poverty rate (11 percent) was then *more than 4 points higher* than the next-highest country (Canada) and almost 2.5 times the eight-country average. The U.S. poverty rate for children in one-parent families (54.2 percent) was more than 17 points higher than the next-highest country (Canada) and 27 times as high as Sweden's rate for this group.[15] "Free market" capitalism in the United States has brought a relatively high level of poverty.

In 2002, the U.S. population totaled about 285 million people. Some 12.1 percent of these (about 34.6 million) were poor, according to the federal government's official poverty line ($18,556 for a family of four).[16] A poverty-level income typically prevents a family from buying some of life's basic necessities.* If the family buys adequate food, its housing and cloth-

---

*The official poverty line, devised in 1964, is based on the Department of Agriculture's "economy" food plan, a low-cost food budget on which a family could survive nutritionally on a short-term basis. The poverty line, in most cases, is figured to be about three times the cost of this "economy" food budget. Actually, there are several poverty lines, one for the aged, one for two-person families, one for three-person families, and so on. The official number is calculated using several poverty lines.

ing will be inadequate. In many cases, a poor family must go without some of life's basic requirements; millions of Americans go hungry or are inadequately nourished day after day.

The War on Poverty, with the 1960s' economic expansion, brought a significant reduction in the number of Americans below the poverty line; the number dropped from almost 40 million in 1959 to a low of just under 23 million in 1973. The number rose again during the politically conservative and economically troubled 1980s, reaching a high of nearly 35.3 million in 1983. It declined somewhat by the end of that decade, and then began to rise again in the 1990s. Remarkably, the number of people below the government poverty line in 1994 was the highest number in over 30 years. More recently, the total number of people below the government poverty line has crept back down and now approximates the 1983 figure. Yet, in 2003 it was still *higher* than the *low point* in 1973; the percent poor was also higher than in 1973. As the numbers in Table 3.1 indicate, the United States has not made consistent progress in bringing economic opportunities to its poorest citizens.[17] The boom–bust cycles of our corporate-run, business-centered economy significantly shape the number of poor; that number regularly goes up in times of business-generated unemployment, recession, and depression.

Table 3.2 shows that the risk of poverty varies by subgroup. In 2002, white Americans comprised 68 percent of the poor. African Americans and Latinos, such as Puerto Ricans and Mexican Americans, had the greatest likelihood of being poor, however. African Americans made some civil rights and economic gains during the 1960s and 1970s, but during the 1980s these gains were partially reversed. During the first three years of the Reagan administration, the poverty rate for blacks rose to a high of 35.7 percent. Today, nearly a

Table 3.1 Poverty in the United States, 1959–2003

Year	Number of Poor Individuals	Percent Poor
1959	39,490,000	22.4%
1964	36,055,000	19.0
1967	27,769,000	14.2
1970	25,420,000	12.6
1973	22,973,000	11.0
1978	24,497,000	11.4
1981	31,800,000	14.0
1983	35,266,000	15.2
1985	33,064,000	14.0
1987	32,546,000	13.4
1990	33,585,000	13.5
1994	38,059,000	14.5
2002	34,600,000	12.1
2003	35,900,000	12.5

Source: U.S. Bureau of the Census, *Current Population Survey,* September 2003.

Table 3.2   The Unequal Distribution of Poverty, 2003

Population Group	Percentage of Group Falling Below Official Poverty Line
Total population	12.1%
Racial/ethnic groups	
Whites	8.2
Blacks	24.4
Latinos	22.5
Asians	11.8
Age groups	
Under 18 years	17.6
18 to 64 years	10.8
65 years and over	10.2
Residence	
Inside metropolitan areas	12.1
In central cities	17.5
Outside central cities (suburbs)	9.1
Outside metropolitan areas	17.2
Families	
Married couple	5.4
Female householder, no husband present	28.0
Male householder, no wife present	13.5

Source: U.S. Bureau of the Census, *Current Population Survey,* September 2003.

third of black children live in poor families; the percentage for Latino children is 28.2 percent. The percentages of poor among the young and those living in central cities are considerably above that for the general population.[18]

Since 1960, poverty has become more urban centered. In 1960, most poor Americans lived in rural areas or nonmetropolitan cities and towns. Today, most of those below the poverty line live in metropolitan centers, especially central cities. They make up nearly one-fifth of the population in central cities. In nonmetropolitan areas, mostly rural places beyond the central cities and suburbs, the proportion of people below the poverty line is much higher than in suburban areas.[19]

Questioning the Official Poverty Count

The government's official count of the poor has been questioned by both conservative and power–conflict analysts. Some conservative order–market analysts have talked about an overcount of the poor; critical analysts have pointed to an undercount.

The theme that government in-kind aid programs have abolished poverty has been popular among conservative analysts since the 1970s. Today, some conservatives continue to argue that government statistics exaggerate the number of poor, since in-kind aid such as Medicaid and food stamps is not included when determining poverty status.[20] Indeed, over the last two decades, with some up and down movement, some federal in-kind aid programs have reduced the number of people below the official poverty line. Critical analysts point out, however, that in-kind aid has not brought as great a reduction in the number of poor as claimed. A significant portion of the official (often inflated) estimated dollar value of in-kind aid cannot reasonably be considered an addition to incomes of the poor. For example, Medicaid programs may improve medical care for the poor, but since a significant portion of these expenditures pays often unnecessarily high medical bills, this in-kind aid does not expand poor people's incomes as much as it might appear.[21]

Many social scientists consider the official number of poor to be a serious undercount because of the government's unrealistically low poverty-income level. Molly Orshansky, the government researcher who helped establish the official poverty line, has argued that to be accurate the line must be set higher. The official poverty line is calculated by multiplying the cost of a short-term, emergency, low-cost food budget by three. If, however, one uses a more reasonable assumption that a poverty-line family should spend only 20 percent (not one-third) of its income for food, and if one uses a food budget level that is the bare minimum for a year (not the temporary budget on which the official line is based), then the poverty level would have to be set much higher, and the actual number of poor people might be *double* the official figure. In addition, the Census Bureau admits that population statistics used to determine the number of poor people are an undercount because census forms do not make their way to many poor citizens, including homeless and migrant workers. An estimated 2 million to 5 million poor people are missed by the census for various reasons.[22]

Opinion surveys have also found that the American people place the real poverty (deprivation) line considerably higher than the official line. Since World War II, nationwide samples of Americans have been asked "What is the smallest amount of money a family of four needs to get along in this community?" The average amount mentioned by respondents has ranged from 56 to 75 percent of the actual median income of the relevant U.S. families in the year of the survey. One poll found that the average estimate was a yearly income of $21,800 for a four-person family to meet basic expenses, a bit more than half the median income of four-person families at that time ($39,000). About one-quarter of U.S. families fell below this poverty–deprivation line, far more than the percentage below the official poverty line. A majority of Americans agree with critics that the actual number of the economically deprived is far more than the official count.[23]

Income is not the only resource that the poor lack, for they are also poor in wealth, political power, access to legal aid, and other resources. Raising incomes somewhat by means of in-kind aid such as Medicaid or food stamps usually does not significantly increase access to these other important resources.

UNEMPLOYMENT, UNDEREMPLOYMENT, AND POVERTY

Some people are poor because they are unable to work—because of age, severe disability, or chronic illness. Many others are poor because they are unable to find jobs. If every person seeking work could find a job with a decent wage, poverty would be dramatically decreased.

Sometimes it is said that jobs are plentiful and that the unemployed are too lazy to take them. For example, then-President Ronald Reagan was asked at a press conference why unemployment had gotten so much worse during his administration. In response, he said he had counted 24 pages of classified ads in the last Sunday paper he read. But using want ads in this way is misleading. One *Fortune* magazine study of Sunday paper want ads in Middletown, New York, found 228 separate entries. The *Fortune* researcher found, however, that a large proportion of these were not real jobs but were instead ads for products or franchise opportunities. Other jobs were listed twice, involved limited part-time work, or were out of the city area. Only 142 (62 percent) of the ads were for full-time wage or salary jobs in the Middletown area, enough to lower (if filled) the local unemployment rate a mere 0.2 percent, from 7.4 to 7.2 percent. Indeed, most of the jobs advertised were eagerly sought and quickly filled.[24] Today, as in the past, millions of workers find it difficult or impossible to find work—particularly full-time, permanent jobs with decent wages, benefits, and security—as more companies restructure their workforces, replacing many permanent workers with temporary workers or with lower-wage workers in corporate facilities now located overseas.

Official Unemployment Statistics

Table 3.3 presents official data on the number and percentage of the unemployed since 1929.[25] The official unemployment rate has varied considerably with the ups and downs in the U.S. economy. In the Great Depression of the 1930s, one-quarter of the labor force officially had no job. Moreover, in some metropolitan areas the jobless rate reached 60 percent for black males and 75 percent for black females during this period.[26] The proportion of unemployed dropped sharply during World War II—to a low of just 1.2 percent—and then hovered in the 4 to 6 percent range until the major 1974–1976 recession. (The 1.2 percent figure demonstrates what the U.S. economy can supply in jobs if necessary.) In 1983 official unemployment was close to 10 percent, the highest since the Great Depression. The rate has oscillated between 5 and 8 percent since the mid-1980s. Note that since the 1940s, whatever the rate, it has been much higher than is desired by most workers.

Unemployment does not hurt all equally. Certain groups of workers—especially Latinos, African Americans, Native Americans, those in declining cities, and teenagers—typically have higher rates of unemployment than others. The unemployment rate for African Americans has consistently been two to three times the national average as long as records have been kept. Table 3.4 shows unemployment rates for various worker groups.[27] African Americans suffer much higher unemployment rates than whites. Significantly, moreover, some analysts have suggested revising the official government definition of the unemployed to exclude teenagers and women, whose unemployment rates are higher than average.[28] Adult males, whose unemployment rate is usually lower than aver-

Table 3.3 Unemployment in the United States, 1929–2002

Year	Number of People Unemployed	Percentage of Labor Force Unemployed
1929	1,550,000	3.2%
1933	12,830,000	24.9
1944	670,000	1.2
1947	2,311,000	3.9
1957	2,859,000	4.3
1967	2,975,000	3.8
1975	7,929,000	8.5
1979	6,137,000	5.8
1980	7,637,000	7.1
1983	10,717,000	9.6
1985	8,312,000	7.2
1988	6,701,000	5.5
1991	8,426,000	6.7
1995	7,404,000	5.6
2002	8,378,000	5.8
2003	8,774,000	6.0
2004	8,149,000	5.5

Source: U.S. Bureau of Labor Statistics, *Employment and Earnings,* January 2004.

age, are apparently considered to be the "real" workforce. Such an orientation intentionally minimizes the impact of a high unemployment rate on society as a whole and trivializes employment needs of women and teenagers. As Table 3.4 reveals, modest differences

Table 3.4 Unemployment Rates for Specific Groups, 2002

Adult white men	5.3%
Adult white women	4.9
White teenagers	14.5
Adult black men	10.7
Adult black women	9.8
Black teenagers	29.8
Adult Latino men	7.2
Adult Latino women	8.0
Latino teenagers	20.1

Source: U.S. Bureau of Labor Statistics, unpublished data, January 2004.

exist between unemployment rates for males and females within each racial group. We usually associate higher levels of educational attainment with employment security. Although less educated persons suffer disproportionately during periods of economic crisis, long-term unemployment has begun to affect more educated persons as well. In a recent report by the Economic Policy Institute, the percentage increase in numbers of the long-term unemployed between 2000 and 2003 was *156 percent* for persons with high school diplomas or less, *259 percent* for persons with some college, and *299 percent* for persons with bachelor's degrees or more.[29] While the rates of unemployment for better-educated workers are less than for the least well educated, they are increasing more rapidly than for the latter workers.

What is the minimum unemployment rate that a society can tolerate? In the 1950s, British economist A. W. Phillips argued that because wage rates regularly decrease when the unemployment rate increases, an unemployment rate of about 5.5 percent was "necessary" to keep wage rates from rising. According to Phillips, higher employment should bring higher inflation, and rising unemployment should mean low or no inflation.[30] Following this theory, mainstream U.S. economists began talking about "tolerating" higher unemployment (not their own, of course) to keep inflation in check. Yet economic events from the 1970s to the present have refuted the Phillips curve and the views of many prominent economists on this matter. Significant inflation and high unemployment have periodically occurred at the same time. Even those business and political leaders committed to government intervention to save capitalism have been baffled. When inflation is a problem, according to some postwar economic (Keynesian) theory, government should tax more and spend less; when unemployment is high, it should tax less and spend more. The federal government cannot do both at the same time, however.[31]

Full employment literally means that everyone who can and wants to work has a job, but the official (that is to say, the political) definition of full employment has varied depending on the economic conditions. Prior to the Great Depression and during World War II, unemployment was 2 percent or less of the U.S. civilian labor force. In spite of the obvious contradiction, this situation of low unemployment was then considered to be "full employment." Moreover, higher unemployment rates since 1945 have encouraged many government officials and citizens to more willingly accept ever-higher rates of unemployment as "normal." By the 1960s, most economists began to see a 4 to 5 percent unemployment rate as "full employment" and have since continued to alter their definitions of "healthy" unemployment levels to higher percentages as actual unemployment has risen.[32] Significantly, over the last few decades the United States has often had a higher unemployment rate than other Western industrial countries.[33]

Questioning Official Unemployment Statistics

The publicized unemployment rate, compiled by the federal Bureau of Labor Statistics (BLS), seriously underestimates the extent of unemployment in the United States. The BLS's official definition of the unemployed excludes "discouraged workers"—those who have given up looking for work—and the *underemployed*—part-time workers who want but cannot find full-time work, and full-time, year-round workers who make very low wages. (The percentage of people working part-time because they *cannot* find a full-time job has ranged from 5.6 percent in 1993 to 3.6 percent in 2003.[34]) Including these various groups raises the *real* unemployment–underemployment rate to much higher than the official unemployment rate. In some black, Latino, and Native American communities, more than half of all workers are unemployed or underemployed. The BLS emphasis on monthly unemployment rates distorts the extent of unemployment. An annual rate that showed the proportion of the labor force that was unemployed at some time during the year would show a much more serious problem. Contrary to its official claim, the BLS does not "measure precisely and objectively the extent of unemployment in the U.S."[35]

Another interesting "jobless" statistic is the percentage of the adult population that economists usually define as "out of the labor force"—those persons who are not working and do not want to work—such as students, married women with young children, retirees, and millionaires. This category of jobless persons also includes many non-elderly disabled adults, whose numbers have increased from 3.8 million in 1983 to 7.7 million in 2000. Economists estimate that considering all these persons in the unemployment figures would also increase the official jobless rate another two-thirds of a point.[36]

The Unemployment Link to Poverty

Available jobs rise and fall in number with business cycles. In boom times employment expands, more workers find jobs, and unemployment decreases. In recessions, when capitalists "go on strike" and reduce investments in jobs, working people lose jobs and unemployment increases. Poverty increases when unemployment increases. Those with the fewest resources and those who live nearest the poverty level are vulnerable. One study of single mothers who relied on a combination of work and public assistance programs to support their families found the respondents' probability of being poor increased 31 percent for every 1 percentage point increase in their state's unemployment rate.[37]

Work experience data for householders indicate the critical significance of unemployment for most poor families.[38] Without full-time work, a typical U.S. family is likely to face serious economic problems. Poor families are much more likely than nonpoor families to have workers who cannot find full-time work. Women of color and women from low-income backgrounds have an especially difficult time finding full-time, well-paid work. In addition, most of the unemployed receive no unemployment compensation. Recent data indicate that fewer than one-third of all U.S. unemployed workers qualified for unemployment insurance benefits, and the national dollar average for these unemployment benefits was only a bit more than one-third of workers' former average weekly wages. Contrary to some public images, most unemployed workers *do not* have a safety net to keep them from falling into severe economic deprivation.[39]

In addition, the low wages received by many of those who work full-time now in effect guarantee a poverty standard of living. The federal minimum wage during the 1960s to 1970s was about enough to keep a family of three above the poverty level, since the poverty level for a family of three was roughly equal to the yearly earnings of a full-time, year-round worker earning the minimum wage. Since then, however, the minimum wage has fallen significantly in real dollars (that is, adjusting for inflation). In 1990 the federal minimum wage ($3.35 per hour) was the same as it had been in 1981, but its buying power had declined 30 percent over the decade of the 1980s.[40] In the mid-1990s, full-time employment (50 weeks) at the then-current minimum wage of $4.25 per hour totaled only $8,500 annually before taxes, a figure well *below* the official poverty line for an urban family of two. Today, a full-time, year-round worker has to earn about $7.83 an hour ($2.68 more than the current minimum wage) for a family of three to stay above the current official $15,670 poverty level.[41] Note that the federal minimum wage established by the Fair Labor Standards Act a few years back is $5.15. In real dollars (adjusting for inflation), the minimum wage is today worth just $4.82—only slightly more than the wage guaranteed workers in the mid-1990s and lower than in almost all years between 1955 and the mid-1990s.[42] Despite increases in the minimum wage, that level of earnings still leaves a family of three about 34 percent below the official poverty line. Undeniably, the U.S. capitalistic system guarantees poverty even for its full-time, minimum-wage employees.

Unemployment's Impact

The connection between unemployment and poverty means that those unemployed for a significant period of time usually pay a heavy price. The costs of unemployment are primarily borne by workers and their families. Even those who qualify for unemployment benefits usually experience a sharp loss in income, with a corresponding loss in purchasing power. The majority of long-term unemployed workers are unable to support their families at a decent level. People who cannot support themselves or their families become demoralized; families break apart, suicides occur, and property loss and crime increase.

Studies of the severe personal and family impact of unemployment were conducted during the Great Depression of the 1930s. Recent studies have confirmed these early findings, which are still relevant during periodic recessionary conditions today. During the Great Depression, purchases of basic necessities such as clothing declined sharply, and many families doubled up in housing with relatives. For many, the Depression meant ragged clothing, dilapidated or no housing, and inadequate nourishment. Neighborly visits and evenings with friends declined. Homeless men wandered through the country and cities, sleeping in subways, parks, and empty factories. People became sick or died of starvation; malnutrition brought an increase in rickets and scurvy. Eating garbage became common. One 1932 Chicago report noted, "Around the truck which was unloading garbage and other refuse were about thirty-five men, women and children. As soon as the truck pulled away from the pile, all of them started digging with sticks, some with their hands, grabbing bits of food and vegetables."[43] Field studies of Depression-era workers showed the severe emotional impact of unemployment.

> Bewilderment, hesitation, apathy, loss of self-confidence were the commonest marks of protracted unemployment. A man no longer cared how he looked. Unkempt hair and swarthy stubble, shoulders-a-droop, a slow dragging walk, were external signs of inner defeat, often aggravated by malnutrition. Joblessness proved a wasting disease.[44]

The Great Depression also saw a considerable explosion of xenophobia (hatred of foreigners), anti-Semitism (hatred of Jews), and antiblack prejudice. Today, as in the 1930s, innocent people of color have often become convenient scapegoats (for example, in hate crimes) for societal problems such as unemployment.

Worker protest increased in the 1930s, with rent strikes, union strikes, demonstrations, and food marches. In one people's movement in 1932, some 1,500 homeless World

War I veterans, called the Bonus Army, marched on Washington, D.C., and camped out, seeking to pressure Congress for bonus money promised to veterans. The marchers were driven out of their ragged camp by the police and federal troops with bayonets. Many workers became radicalized during the Depression; in one survey, one-quarter of the unemployed agreed that "a revolution might be a good thing for this country." But a majority of the demoralized workers did not participate in organized movements, most likely because of the individualistic ethic (with its self-blame aspect), the numbing effects of poverty, the absence of an industrial democracy movement with a clear ideology for change, and the international character of the Depression.[45]

Unemployment and underemployment continue to have a severe impact on individuals, families, and communities today. Unemployment often causes serious health problems and a loss of self-esteem. One French study found that 80 percent of workers were in good health before they were laid off from work. After layoffs, a majority experienced anxiety, depression, nervous troubles, and insomnia even though they received unemployment benefits. Nearly one-third experienced problems with heart disease. Such an impact is likely for U.S. workers as well. Some U.S. researchers have found that personal levels of depression and anxiety and stomach diseases increase with upsurges in joblessness. Even the infant mortality rate, associated with inadequate nutrition and health care for mothers, has been found to increase during economic recessions. Research at Johns Hopkins University concluded that for every 1 percent increase in unemployment sustained over a six-year period, an additional 36,800 Americans die from increased rates of heart disease, suicides, and alcoholism. Yale University researchers discovered increased blood pressure and other heart problems among unemployed workers; they found a suicide rate 30 times the national average. Studies of unemployed aircraft workers in New England found increases in psychiatric disorders, clinical depression, and alcoholism, especially among middle-aged male breadwinners with dependent children. Other research has suggested a continuing linkage between the high infant mortality rates and unemployment in large, job-starved urban poverty areas.[46]

Property crime is often correlated with unemployment and underemployment. During one Christmas season a hungry unemployed man was sentenced to three days in jail for stealing sweet rolls from a supermarket. Store officials insisted on prosecuting the man, even though a bystander offered to pay for the food. One earlier *Manpower Report to the President,* citing research studies of poor youngsters who wanted education, a successful career, and responsible work but had no means to secure them, concluded that many poor people see crime as an alternative to low-wage, no-future jobs. Meaningless, part-time, low-wage jobs seemed less attractive to some of them than did higher "wages" from gambling, drugs, and property crime.[47] In addition, poor or underemployed African American rioters from Detroit and Newark in the 1960s to Miami and Chattanooga in the 1980s to Miami and Los Angeles in the 1990s have often attacked and looted white-owned and other non–black-owned businesses. Indeed, poor Americans of all racial and ethnic backgrounds have engaged in the drug business, or on occasion have rioted, in substantial part out of frustration in their quest for better-paying jobs, housing, and other basic material needs that other Americans take for granted. A society that tolerates high underemployment and unemployment in its cities will likely have much property and violent crime.

Unemployment has more than an individual or family impact, for it also has devastating effects on moderate- and low-income communities, particularly certain communities of color. Often large proportions of low-income communities are unemployed for long periods, both annually and over their lifetimes. This can create a sense of injustice, frustration, despair, and rage across large areas—in direct contradiction to the pledge made daily by millions of U.S. schoolchildren, "one nation . . . with liberty and justice for all."

CAPITALISM, UNEMPLOYMENT, AND POVERTY

Capitalism and the Poor

How does our capitalist system relate to unemployment, underemployment, and poverty? Whether one is poor or unemployed depends on a number of factors:

1. Certain personal characteristics such as racial group, gender, and age, over which a person has no control.
2. Characteristics such as health and education, over which a person has some control.
3. Characteristics of the larger capitalistic society such as profit rates, private control of profit accumulation, and capital flight.[48]

Let us look first at some characteristics of capitalism that often generate unemployment and poverty in the U.S. today.

The Intense Quest for Private Profit

On occasion, business leaders and politicians talk about the persisting U.S. unemployment problem as an inevitable and necessary sacrifice to reduce inflation and to improve the health of a periodically troubled economy. Yet these same leaders have often intentionally engineered these sacrifices, which are primarily borne by people *other than themselves.* Investment decisions by members of the capitalist and managerial classes are based substantially on profit considerations, short term or long term. These decisions play a major role in the boom–bust cycle of modern capitalism. The causes of most unemployment, underemployment, and poverty lie not in personality characteristics but in the economic and political structure of U.S. society.

Decisions about levels of profit, investment, and industrial development, about where to locate new facilities, and about automation are made by a few powerful people in the capitalist and managerial classes, generally without consulting those working people most affected by these decisions. If profit levels are unsatisfactory, elite investors may refuse to make new investments. For example, in peak periods factories operate at 90 percent or more of their capacities, while in recession–depression periods they may operate at far less capacity. In both periods the unused capacity could be used to employ many unemployed workers and to make more and cheaper products, particularly to meet the basic housing, transportation, clothing, and food needs of millions of Americans. But since this redirected production—perhaps for needed products that would yield small profit margins—might well mean lower profits for the employer class, it is not undertaken, even though major human needs in our society are substantially unfulfilled. Under capitalism, business profits are ordinarily elevated over broader human and societal needs.

Corporate investment decisions create unemployment. For example, in 1950 U.S. steel firms had half the world market in steel. By 1980, following sharp increases in steel production in countries such as Japan, Korea, and Brazil, the U.S. world market share had dropped to 14 percent. Many Americans were then, and are now, aware of the great increase in steel imports to the United States. Steel companies have denounced foreign competition as unfair (because of foreign government subsidies to steel industries) and have cited the lower cost of imports as the reason for the decline of the U.S. steel industry. Steel company executives have also blamed federal pollution controls and the high wages of U.S. steel-workers for their problems.

To some extent these complaints have been valid. Foreign steelmaking has been sub-sidized by foreign governments. However, an important reason for the decline of the U.S. steel industry was the decision of U.S. executives *not* to invest heavily in new steelmaking technologies in the 1950s (such as the basic oxygen furnace) but rather to stay with older technologies (such as the open-hearth furnace). When the error in these decisions became obvious, many U.S. steel executives decided not to cut heavily enough into current profits to quickly retool their plants. Changes to new technologies were made too slowly to com-pete effectively with overseas steelmakers. Some plants were modernized, but others were allowed to deteriorate. Many steel companies became conglomerates, such as U.S. Steel (later USX), investing in chemicals, real estate, financial services, oil, and other sectors of the world economy.[49]

In the recent past and in the present, many American workers and their families have paid a heavy price for these business investment decisions. For example, the closing of the U.S. steel mill in the 1980s in Braddock, Pennsylvania, the birthplace of big steel, created major problems for workers. Many were unable to find work elsewhere and barely man-aged on unemployment benefits or their spouse's (usually) low-wage job.[50] This pattern of unemployment has been created in many cities of the industrial heartland of the United States, as well as more recently in Sunbelt cities and in all city areas with high levels of white-collar employment. For mainstream workers, including growing numbers of former white-collar workers, serious deprivation is a new experience. Many thousands have even-tually found themselves seeking what they once regarded as "charity" or "government handouts."

Indeed, one significant aspect of this new unemployment-driven poverty and hunger in middle America is a growing understanding of what it's like to be poor among those once unconcerned or hostile to the poor. People who once cursed "welfare chiselers" and the "lazy poor" now find themselves in line for groceries or becoming "dependent" on welfare offices. Many talk of the humiliation of taking these handouts. Some drown their humilia-tion in alcohol. Many face the real prospect of never holding another full-time, decent-paying job in their lives.

Pursuing business profits, many U.S. corporations have expanded blue-collar and white-collar production in cheap labor areas in other countries over the last decade, thereby reducing the number of employees needed in the United States. This export and investment of U.S. capital overseas is usually called *capital flight*. A number of U.S. corporations have increasingly shifted white-collar work to overseas areas. American Airlines, for example, has employed data processors in Barbados, where low wages save the company millions of dollars. One large insurance company, New York Life, transported some of its U.S. claims to be processed by lower-wage white-collar workers in Ireland. Government agencies have promoted export of U.S. capital and jobs overseas. For example, the government-run Over-seas Private Investment Corporation provides insurance for U.S. corporate assets overseas.

In addition, the U.S.-dominated International Monetary Fund (IMF) has pressured numerous poverty-stricken countries to develop "austerity programs" (for example, tripling the price of bread and other basic necessities) that improve the local profit-making climate for U.S. multinationals and for the U.S. banks that hold much of the debt of poorer countries.[51]

Unemployment helps the interests of the capitalist and managerial classes by making it more difficult for ordinary workers to press for higher wages and better working conditions. The underemployed and the unemployed are essential to the operation of the capitalist system because they put downward pressure on wages and provide a reserve labor force that can be drawn into employment when investment conditions require it. Not only the officially unemployed but also other groups make up this reserve labor force: discouraged workers, part-time workers, and immigrant laborers. Workers who protest in times of a glutted labor market may well find themselves replaced by people from the great pool of unemployed.

Moving to the Sunbelt and Overseas

A fundamental concern for profits leads many corporate executives to relocate facilities and other investments, including manufacturing plants and an increasing number of white-collar service jobs, from one geographical region in the United States to another, or from the United States to foreign countries. One of the major profit-oriented relocations in recent decades has been to the South and Southwest. Even more significant of late is movement of U.S. jobs overseas. For example, more than 264 U.S. corporations exported roughly *2.8 million* manufacturing jobs overseas in the years 2002 to 2004.[52] This exporting of (often decent-paying) jobs throws thousands of U.S. employees out of work, often on short notice. Capital moved overseas would once have been invested in plants, offices, and other facilities in the United States.

Significantly, the in-migration of business has typically done little to improve the lot of the Sunbelt's poor. Relocating industries have often brought managers and skilled workers with them from the North. The large numbers of unskilled workers in Sunbelt cities have more than met the low-paid "dirty work" needs of relocated and new industries. Indeed, the poverty of southern and southwestern cities is a major attraction for northern capital. Lower wages and lower taxes there have meant higher profits than are often possible in the North, where unions are generally stronger and taxes are often higher.[53]

James O'Connor has summed up the ways in which capitalism regularly creates poverty in particular regions:

> Capitalism is in part the history of peasants and farmers, home-workers, petty craftsmen and tradesmen, and others forced into poverty by the advance of capitalist agriculture, factory production, mass retailing, and so on; in part the history of industries and entire regions becoming economically impoverished as a result of changes in technology and market forces; in part the history of poverty generated by recessions and depressions and by particular industrial and occupational structures that confine some people to low-income, unstable employment.[54]

Unemployment and poverty do not result primarily from the psychological characteristics of workers but are a by-product of the routine operation of basic institutions in this society—the ups and downs of the business cycle and corporate decisions about automation and relocation. Problems of low incomes, hunger, poor health, and dilapidated housing are symptoms rooted in the tendency of the capitalist system to throw people out of work when they are no longer needed. In addition, the routine operation of capitalism creates poverty by disabling some workers (for instance, as a result of unsafe working conditions), by retiring many able workers on small (or no) pensions, and by opposing adequate social support programs for the disabled and the retired.

The Working Poor

The working class is a diverse group. One important fraction of that class is the *working poor.* The Department of Labor defines the "working poor" as individuals who spend at least 27 weeks in the labor force in a year and whose incomes fall below the poverty line.[55] About 6.8 million people were classified as working poor in 2001, representing nearly 5 percent of all workers. The total earnings of a fifth of all workers 25 years old and older were below the poverty level for a two-person family; and one-third earned less than the poverty level for a four-person family. Nearly 3.5 million workers who fell below the government's official poverty line worked *full-time* for the entire year. African Americans and Latinos are disproportionately represented among the country's working poor—roughly 10.1 percent of all black workers are working poor, and 13 percent of Latino workers, but only 7.7 percent of white workers. A major reason for the high incidence of poverty among African Americans and Latinos is low pay, often in full-time jobs. In practice, individual characteristics, such as racial or gender group, over which people have no control, are screening characteristics for many jobs. Capitalism's tendency to create and maintain separate labor markets with distinctive job characteristics and mobility chances, for different groups of people, is a major factor shaping the life experiences of the poor.

The U.S. economy has two diverse labor markets: a *primary labor market* and a *secondary labor market.* The primary labor market—characterized by better wages, more unionization, profitable firms, internal mobility opportunities, lower unemployment, and better benefits—is at the core of the economy. The primary labor market is composed disproportionately of white male workers. The secondary labor market—typically characterized by low wages, modest profits, small- and medium-sized employers, firms with low market power, more job turnover, little internal mobility, higher unemployment, and no (or weak) unemployment benefits—employs large numbers of people of color and white women. Secondary labor market workers include laborers, janitors, waitresses, lower-level sales clerks, typists and file clerks, migrant laborers, and workers in sweatshops. Most jobs in the secondary market provide little employment security. Wage levels are typically 60 to 80 percent of the average wages of workers in the primary market.[56]

One explanation for the two market divisions suggests that they were a corporate strategy to counter the threat posed to corporate domination by the rise of labor unions from the 1930s to the 1960s. By focusing on the status differences and rewards available to skilled workers, corporate leaders sought to minimize the extent to which these skilled workers and the unskilled workers could feel kindred to one another. The segregation of workers effectively accomplished this goal. Secondary jobs could be offered to women, people of color, and young people without fear that primary sector groups would identify with secondary groups. Credentials, job titles, and variations in pay and privileges intensify job segregation within the working class. However, this is only a partial explanation of the segregation of workers. Racial and gender discrimination also channel workers into segregated job categories.[57]

Research indicates that the working poor are generally employed "for fewer weeks per year and hours per week than higher-wage workers" and that "even if the former group

Corporate Cultures: Wal-Mart and Costco Stores

Betty Dukes is a 54-year-old woman working for Wal-Mart. For 10 years, Betty worked as a cashier with aspirations for a career in management until carpal tunnel injuries forced her demotion to a "people greeter" earning less than $8.00 an hour. Three years later, Wal-Mart increased her wages to $12.53 an hour after she became one of six named plaintiffs and one of more than 1.6 million current and former female employees who filed the largest class action employment lawsuit in the history of U.S. litigation. As the country's largest corporation and the world's largest retailer (reported sales in excess of $256 billion in a recent fiscal year), Wal-Mart employs over 1.2 million workers in 3,566 stores across the United States.

The suit claims that Wal-Mart Stores, Inc., including Wal-Mart discount stores, super centers, neighborhood stores, and Sam's Clubs (a division of Wal-Mart), systematically discriminate against women workers in wages and promotions and engage in other mistreatment of women workers. Reportedly, two-thirds of Wal-Mart's employees are female, yet they are underrepresented in store management positions and overrepresented in sales associate and cashier positions. According to the lawsuit, female Wal-Mart employees earn considerably less than male counterparts in every major job category despite their longer employment, higher performance ratings, and lower rates of worker turnover.

Besides the salary and wage discrimination and the denial of equal promotion opportunities, senior managers are alleged to engage in other forms of insulting conduct toward their female workers that suggest a hostile corporate culture. Male managers are said to refer to female employees as "little Janie Q's" and "girls," and approved corporate policy requires female managers to go to Hooters sports bars and strip clubs for store meetings. One store manager allegedly remarked to a room full of employees that "the only reason Wal-Mart needed female assistant managers was to ensure that women associates had someone with whom they could discuss their periods."

The evidence of gender discrimination at Wal-Mart seems overwhelming. Plaintiffs' attorneys say they have 110 sworn statements from women at 184 different Wal-Mart stores in 30 states asserting that they faced maltreatment, as well as testimony and exhibits from more than 100 deposed Wal-Mart managers and executives, data from Wal-Mart's electronic payroll data file, and 1.2 million pages of documents from corporate files. According to the federal judge that ordered Wal-Mart to stand trial for company wide discrimination, "plaintiffs present largely uncontested descriptive statistics which show that women working at Wal-Mart stores are paid less than men in every region, that pay disparities exist in most job categories, that the salary gap widens over time, that women take longer to enter management positions, and that the higher one looks in the organization the lower the percentage of women." Most recently, the Ninth Circuit Court of Appeals has agreed to hear an appeal by Wal-Mart contesting the federal judicial order demanding that Wal-Mart stand trial.

The earnings data in the following table are from a *Los Angeles Times* story on the lawsuit.

continued on next page

Wal-Mart Workers' Average Yearly Earnings by Gender, 2001

Position at Wal-Mart	Men	Women	Women's Earnings as Percentage of Men's Earnings	Percentage of Women in the Jobs
Regional vice president	$419,435	$279,772	66.7%	10.3%
District manager	239,519	177,149	73.9	9.8
Store manager	105,682	89,280	84.5	14.3
Comanager (large stores)	59,535	56,317	94.6	23.0
Assistant manager	39,790	37,322	93.8	35.7
Management trainee	23,175	22,371	96.5	41.3
Department head	23,518	21,709	92.3	78.3
Sales associate	16,526	15,067	91.2	67.8
Cashier	14,525	13,831	95.2	92.5

In another context, nine (undocumented) Mexican immigrants that worked as janitors at Wal-Mart and were paid lower wages with fewer benefits than legal workers have filed a lawsuit against the company for this employment discrimination. They are among 250 people arrested in a federal immigration crackdown at 60 Wal-Mart stores in many states in 2003. Federal prosecutors have sent Wal-Mart a letter warning the company of a grand jury investigation into its hiring of undocumented immigrants.

Moreover, in August 2004, lawyers in San Francisco filed a class action lawsuit against Costco Wholesale Corporation claiming that Costco also operates a "glass ceiling" at the store-management level that slows or stops women from promotion to assistant managers and general managers. The corporation allegedly promotes female managers at a much lower rate than male managers. Costco's senior management is virtually all male, and fewer than 12 percent of Costco's general managers are female. Allegedly, too, the company has no application procedure for assistant and general manager job openings; it promotes males to managerial positions using a "tap on the shoulder" approach. The suit specifically asserts that Costco has pursued policies and practices that deny equal opportunities to qualified women. The suit not only seeks a federal injunction ordering Costco to stop its discriminatory practices but also to pay damages to the women denied promotions, including lost pay and benefits.

Sources: "Women Present Evidence of Widespread Discrimination at Wal-Mart," Wal-Mart Class Website, Case Developments (April 28, 2003), available at www.walmartclass.com/walmartclass94.pl?wsi=0&websys_screen=all_press_release_view&websys_id=11; Nancy Cleeland, "Women Recount Pervasive Inequality at Wal-Mart," *Los Angeles Times,* June 23, 2004, pp. C1, C11; *Dukes* v. *Wal-Mart Stores, Inc.* N. D. Cal. No C-01–2252, available at www.walmartclass.com/staticdata/walmartclass/classcert.pdf; "Federal Judge Orders Wal-Mart Stores, Inc., the Nation's Largest Private Employer, to Stand Trial for Company-Wide Sex Discrimination: Class Certification Creates Largest Civil Rights Class Action Ever," June 22, 2004, available at www.walmartclass.com/walmartclass94.pl?wsi=0&websys_screen=all_press_release_view&websys_id=14; "Illegal Immigrant Workers Sue Wal-Mart," *NewsMax.com Wires* (November 10, 2003), available at www.newsmax.com/archives/articles/2003/11/9/123605.shtml; "Profile of the Costco Gender Discrimination Class Action Lawsuit," Costco Class Website, available at genderclassactionagainstcostco.com/costco94.pl?wsi=0&websys_screen=public_case_developments.

worked full-time, full-year at their present wages, many of them would still not earn enough to bring their families out of poverty."[58] Typically, the heads of families among the working poor are in secondary market jobs paying low wages. For the most part, these workers are prevented from moving into better-paying primary market jobs by such barriers as lack of training and educational credentials and racial or gender discrimination. Many workers in the secondary market—often Native Americans, African Americans, Latinos, white women, and teenagers—are likely to be poor.

Those who rely on public assistance have long been the target of hostility from non-poor Americans, many of whom believe that large numbers of people who do not want to work are supported lavishly by the taxes of those who work. But the facts do not support this myth.[59] First, it is important to note that public assistance benefits generally do not even bring family incomes up to the poverty level. Second, many studies have documented that work and public assistance are intimately interrelated for many of the poor. For example, four out of ten aid recipients in a sample of mothers on assistance worked at least part of the year, either simultaneously while receiving benefits or alternating periods of work and welfare. Even so, their incomes remained below the poverty level for more than half the months during the two-year study.[60]

Today, most public aid recipients move in and out of the secondary labor market. They work for awhile, until their nonunion, low-wage jobs end or they are laid off in a recession. Then they go on public aid for awhile. Later on they may move off welfare and take another low-wage, perhaps part-time, job. In 1998, two-thirds of the 14 million individuals receiving benefits through the (now ended) AFDC program were children; most of the rest were mothers. Contrary to public stereotypes, the typical AFDC family then was a *white mother between the ages of 30 and 39 with two children.* Significantly, the median state maximum AFDC benefit in 1998 was *only 38 percent* of the federal poverty level.[61] Substantial, if not extreme, poverty is the lot of most public assistance recipients.

Because public aid recipients are generally unable to find jobs that pay above poverty-level wages, it is very difficult for them to break the cycle of work and need for public assistance. The most realistic way for them to bring their families out of poverty is to combine work and assistance. Yet, no matter what they do, and no matter how hard they work, most still remain very poor.[62] Indeed, large numbers of the working poor endure unsafe conditions—sometimes behind locked fire doors—in factories located in old buildings and converted storefronts.[63] Thousands of women work 10- to 12-hour days for garment manufacturers in cities like New York and Los Angeles, often earning well below the minimum wage. One writer observes that "except for their fluorescent lighting, these factories are not that different from the sweatshops that Jacob Riis uncovered a century ago."[64]

Thousands of sweatshops can be found from New Jersey to Texas to California. Many workers are immigrants from such countries as Haiti, Mexico, China, Korea, and Puerto Rico. Some are undocumented immigrants and completely at the mercy of owners. If they are cheated out of wages, they cannot easily complain because employers report them to the U.S. Immigration and Naturalization Service. Sweatshops operate illegally and do not pay fringe benefits. Nonunionized sweatshops produce greater profits, while unionized shops force employers to pay better wages and provide fringe benefits.

A commonplace misconception in the United States sees all paid work as ennobling: Any job is better than no job at all. Yet this notion ignores the fact that many jobs are very poorly paid, dangerous, degrading, or otherwise unsatisfying. A worker's wages may be de-

termined in part by level of skill and other factors that shape productivity, but the
greater power of employers over employees enables employers to set wages indepe...
of skill. Some employers pay wages too low to support a family at a level above the poverty
line. Many modest-wage jobs, such as the garment trades and agricultural labor, pay wages
that may be temporarily sufficient for a college student or a single person, but for the head
of a family such work and its wages may literally be life threatening.[65] Clearly, the living
standards of the working poor are a betrayal of this country's ideals of fairness and equity.[66]

A Reform Initiative

Periodically, some members of the U.S. Congress have argued for a Fair Labor Standards
Amendment, a bill designed to reduce the typical work week from 40 to 32 hours with the
same pay. This would create millions of jobs, and something close to full employment. Supporters have pointed to research findings that those who work shorter hours are more productive. The current costs of unemployment, the billions of dollars in unemployment
compensation and public assistance costs paid by governments (that is, taxpayers), and the
physical and mental health costs to unemployed workers are far greater than the costs of a
shorter work week and full employment.[67]

These reformers have noted that the 40-hour week is not sacred. In the 1880s a "normal" work week for U.S. workers was 60 to 80 hours. The Fair Labor Standards Act (1938),
which made a 40-hour week the legal limit and required overtime pay for additional hours,
was passed only after a long and militant struggle led by unionized workers. Since 1938,
numerous worker groups and sympathetic members of Congress have pressed for a shorter
work week, arguing that fewer hours of work for the same pay along with higher rates of
employment would increase consumer demand, particularly for necessities such as food,
clothing, and housing, and thus improve the health and the standard of living for many
Americans. Increased employment and demand would stimulate the economy, increase tax
revenue, and reduce federal deficits.[68]

THE IDEOLOGY OF INDIVIDUALISM AND THE POOR

Poor Americans have suffered not only the indignities of unemployment, underemployment, low incomes, inadequate food, and rundown housing but also considerable hostility
directed at them by better-off Americans. The *gospel of individualism* is central to the dominant value system in the United States. The following beliefs are widely accepted:

1. Each person should work hard and strive to succeed in material terms.
2. Those who work hard will in fact succeed.
3. Those who do not succeed (for example, the poor) have only themselves to blame—their laziness, immorality, or other character defects.

Ideas linked to private property and the so-called "free market" or "free enterprise" are
closely related to these individualistic beliefs. Emphasis on the ideology of individualism has
fostered a positive view of successful people as virtuous and a negative view of poverty as
punishment for the nonvirtuous. One of North America's most distinctive folk myths praises
the self-made, rags-to-riches Horatio Alger–type hero and vilifies the lazy and immoral poor
person. Attacks on the poor have commonly focused on public assistance recipients, who are

often seen as the most serious violators of the work ethic. While significant numbers of Americans have regularly challenged these hyperindividualistic beliefs, many still accept them. Challenging this hyperindividualistic value system is a countering value system that accents greater interpersonal cooperation, mutual support, and group-oriented values.

Some Historical Background

The gospel of individualism is rooted in nineteenth-century thought. Rapid capitalist expansion in the United States during the last half of the nineteenth century brought about an unprecedented exploitation of natural and human resources along with development of new industries. The main themes of the evolutionary perspective called *social Darwinism* were compatible with this aggressive expansion: the "struggle for survival" and the "survival of the fittest." Adopting this harsh viewpoint, many intellectuals and business leaders considered society and the economy as by nature life-and-death struggles in which the best competitors both should and would win out. The hierarchical structure of this capitalistic society and its class divisions were viewed as the result of the operation of basic laws of nature.

Social Darwinist thinking about the natural character of (often ruthless) social and economic competition, the inevitability of poverty, and the perils of government reform spread in the United States, heavily influencing capitalist entrepreneurs, the clergy, and other leaders. Utilizing the language of social Darwinism to justify railroad monopolies, James J. Hill, a railroad entrepreneur, argued that "the fortunes of railroad companies are determined by the law of the survival of the fittest." John D. Rockefeller, one of the wealthiest capitalists of his day, identified aggressive competition—an example of which was his Standard Oil Trust—with the enduring laws of nature and of God:

> The growth of a large business is merely a survival of the fittest . . . . The American Beauty rose can be produced in the splendor and fragrance which bring cheer to its beholder only by sacrificing the early buds which grow up around it. This is not an evil tendency in business. It is merely the working-out of a law of nature and a law of God.[69]

Views on the Poor: The 1960s Accent on Structural Issues

Moral rationalizations for poverty have persisted in the United States, subscribed to not only by powerful business and political leaders but also by many ordinary working people. Individualistic views have solidified into a basic value system that is still very much alive. Numerous state and national leaders have commented negatively on poverty and welfare issues. For example, in newspaper columns and telecasts from the 1960s through the 1980s, Ronald Reagan, formerly governor of the nation's most populous state and later U.S. president, played up the image of undeserving masses of public welfare aid recipients. In media broadcasts he stereotyped the poor as lazy and argued for new work requirements for the poor, as though they did not already seek to work.[70]

Periodically, other national figures have taken the view that the problem of poverty is often more than an individual matter and that government intervention is needed. In the 1960s, thus, President John F. Kennedy generated government programs directed toward services and work-oriented counseling for the poor. In his message to Congress on the 1962 social services amendments, Kennedy emphasized the importance of noneconomic factors in the problems of the poor and called for more than a "relief check"; he stressed the need for "positive services and solutions. . . to help our less fortunate citizens help themselves."[71]

Not long thereafter, President Lyndon Johnson adopted a similar approach in about his War on Poverty in the 1960s: "We are not trying to give people more re want to give people more opportunity."[72]

In actual practice, however, by utilizing a negative image of the poor and tʜᴇɪʀ sub-culture, President Johnson's 1960s War on Poverty tended to reinforce the traditional an-tipoor orientation. The lives of poor families were often seen as contradictory to traditional middle-class values of hard work and a stable family life. By means of greater government involvement, the War on Poverty aimed (1) to relieve the suffering of the poor through ex-panded social work, education, and training programs and (2) at the same time reform the morals and values of the poor in line with the individualistic ethic. Still, for some Ameri-cans, the War on Poverty helped to foster a structural interpretation of poverty alongside the persisting individualist view.

Public Opinion

Rationalizations of poverty and negative views of welfare aid have long been held by many rank-and-file Americans. Two national surveys (1969 and 1980) have explored pub-lic opinion on poverty and the poor. The first survey, conducted by Joe R. Feagin, polled 1,017 adults from all regions of the United States, randomly selected to represent a cross-section.[73] A decade later James R. Kluegel and Eliot R. Smith conducted a second national poll using the same questions.[74] The results of these surveys provide a profile of beliefs about the poor and poverty.

To determine whether the individualistic ideology was still prevalent, respondents were asked to evaluate the importance of a list of "reasons some people give to explain why there are poor people in this country." The reasons mentioned in the survey questions, which are paraphrases of explanations common in public discussions of poverty, fall into three cat-egories: (1) individualistic explanations—placing the responsibility for poverty primarily on the poor themselves; (2) structural explanations—blaming external social and economic forces; and (3) fatalistic explanations—citing such factors as bad luck, illness, and the like.

Individualistic explanations for poverty received the greatest emphasis by respon-dents in both survey years. In 1969 and in 1980, about half the sample evaluated lack of thrift, laziness, and loose morals—individualistic factors—as very important reasons for poverty. In both years, significantly less emphasis, on the average, was given to structural factors, such as low wages, the failure of private industry to provide enough jobs, and labor exploitation by the rich. Fatalistic explanations such as bad luck were given little emphasis in general, but explanations emphasizing specific types of bad luck, such as illness, received substantial emphasis. Explanations that cite lack of ability and talent as causes of poverty are similar in some ways to individualistic explanations because they minimize emphasis on social and economic conditions and concentrate on personal qualities. They differ from structural interpretations in that the blame for poverty is not charged to flaws in the society.

These opinion surveys also asked the respondents a list of questions on public welfare programs. In general, respondents' views of public welfare recipients (such as their honesty or their lack of effort to find a job) were stereotyped and negative. People who held an indi-vidualistic view of poverty were also quite negative about welfare recipients, even though most of their beliefs about welfare recipients actually contradicted known facts. On the whole, the views of Americans about the causes of poverty and the characteristics of the poor, including the welfare poor, were still as negative in 1980 as they were a decade earlier.

No systematic studies of antipoor and antiwelfare attitudes have been done since the 1980 survey. However, recent national opinion surveys have on occasion asked a question or two about attitudes toward the poor and welfare recipients. These more recent surveys continue to find the same general pattern as in the earlier surveys. Two-thirds of the respondents in one recent poll felt that the government was spending too little to aid the "poor." However, when the word *welfare* was substituted for "the poor," only 23 percent of the respondents felt that too little was being spent. Three-quarters of the respondents in another 1990s poll felt that public welfare fostered dependency in recipients and encouraged them to have larger families than they otherwise would.[75] While support for structural views of poverty has increased in some groups of the U.S. population since the 1960s, it is clear that an individualistic, blaming-the-victim view is still widely and strongly held in the United States.

Current government public assistance programs, with their limited funding, are ineffective in remedying the basic conditions that cause most poverty. Instead of developing programs to offer recipients job training and other economic opportunities, attempts to reform public "welfare" programs have focused primarily on ways to reduce the number helped by government or ways to control recipients, who are usually stereotyped as lazy.[76] Such strategies have strong elements of social coercion and antipoor prejudices at their core. In addition, many proposals ignore the central fact that U.S. society does not today create enough jobs at decent wages for all those who want to work.

Consequences of the Rationalizations for Poverty

Given the strength and pervasiveness of views about the poor and welfare, certain questions arise as to the functions or consequences of both the traditional view of the poor and the traditional antiwelfare view embedded in the individualistic ethic. What do these harsh beliefs accomplish? What have been their past—and present—consequences for this society? It is likely that antiwelfare and antipoor attitudes among large numbers of Americans, particularly in the working class, signal a lack of awareness of their own basic socioeconomic interests.

As we have shown, much poverty results from structural conditions, particularly underemployment, unemployment, and racial or gender discrimination. Antipoor and related individualistic views, which have long buttressed the structure of capitalism, offer a distorted picture of this social and economic world.

Culturally ingrained exhortations to work hard—with hard work seen as leading toward material success—have been important in stimulating the work effort of workers under Western capitalism. Strong acceptance of the individualistic focus on personal success among many U.S. workers indicates a poorly developed awareness of class exploitation and membership. Workers' attention has been focused on signs of individual success—which often take the form of private consumption—rather than on their *lack of democratic control* over their workplaces. Moreover, the view of poverty as reflecting laziness and immorality has served as a strong motivating force behind the work of the average worker in capitalist countries. The fear of falling into poverty was twice buttressed, once by the specter of economic deprivation itself and again by the shame that such deprivation would bring.

A second consequence of antipoor perspectives among middle-income workers has been a focusing of hostility on poor workers. Accusations of immorality and improper work attitudes directed at the poor have diverted attention away from middle-income workers' own economic exploitation. Alvin Schorr argues that harsh public attacks on public assistance (welfare) recipients can be explained thus: Under tension, particularly recurrent economic tension, many nonpoor Americans have selected this disadvantaged group to receive their concentrated hostility. By turning attention away from the economic and political status quo—away from the class inequality that is detrimental to the lives of both poor and middle-income workers but beneficial to the capitalist class—antipoor attitudes help legitimize the existing inegalitarian class structure. Welfare and other government expenditures for the "immoral" poor and the high taxes they allegedly require are seen as a conspicuous public burden, whereas the much higher proportion of taxes that finances unnecessary military expenditures, huge business subsidies, and many benefits to middle-income workers receives little or no consideration as a "societal problem." Antipoor views help depoliticize the society and forestall conflict by concentrating the attention of middle-income workers on those at the bottom, shifting the hostility of most workers downward rather than upward.[77]

The emphasis on individual success and antipoor views operates to separate workers from one another by reinforcing status lines between workers. Such views retard workers' joint action, such as unionization, aimed at major social change. By focusing better-off workers' attention on status differences between themselves and the poor, the antipoor ideology causes better-off workers to lose sight of their own inequality and reduces the likelihood of their joining with the working poor in protest efforts.[78]

Ideological Socialization

What is the origin of antipoor views among average Americans? Why do many workers continue to hold conservative views on matters of poverty and welfare? Who benefits the most from the acceptance of this individualism? The individualistic ethic has been carefully taught to most Americans over the course of their lives. With the growth of capitalism in the nineteenth century, dominant elites intentionally reinforced the ideology of individualism and associated beliefs—about welfare, private property, and "free" enterprise. U.S. employers and their political allies aggressively propagated this ideology throughout the population through the media and schools. As beliefs justifying this ideology became ruling ideas, they came to appear as part of the natural order of things. While the spread of the individualistic ideology was supported most vigorously by members of the most advantaged classes, majorities in other classes have long been persuaded by much of it as well. Once the beliefs became dominant, they developed a forward momentum of their own.[79]

Advertising agencies and the media have reinforced prevailing ideologies. A major function of advertising is to maintain, directly or indirectly, allegiance to the capitalistic system and its core values. Strategies of media influence include advertising campaigns on productivity and the need for greater work effort, as well as routine accents on individualism and consumerism. From an early age, most Americans learn these values through television and radio programs and media advertising.[80]

Top government officials have reinforced the individualistic ethic. Since the 1980s the generally negative views of conservative presidents and of many congressional leaders in regard to the poor and public assistance have reflected the old ideology of individualism in new conservative dress. Conservative officials at various levels of government have circulated misinformation about "free" markets, individualism and competition,

In recent years, some conservative business and political leaders have tried to weaken or eliminate programs for the poor and the elderly.

public welfare programs, and the poor through news releases, news conferences, speeches, and media articles.

GOVERNMENT INTERVENTION: THE BROAD SUBSIDY SYSTEM

Citing Social Security, unemployment insurance, and related programs for workers and public assistance and health programs for the poor, some analysts of U.S. society feel that the United States has made "dramatic progress" since the 1930s in "redistributional" reform. Other analysts express concern over the slow pace of remedying inequalities. Harold Wilensky and Charles Lebeaux have described the United States as the "most reluctant welfare state."[81] Numerous power–conflict analysts and researchers view the much-touted U.S. Social Security and other social welfare programs as no more than a meager substitute for significant changes in the distribution of economic opportunities, privileges, and wealth. They argue that the rhetoric of freedom and equality has not been matched by the wealth, resources, or organizational shifts necessary to bring about a significant decrease in economic and other inequalities.

The Context of Aid for the Poor

The current public assistance ("welfare") system for the poor began in earnest with President Franklin Roosevelt's Social Security Act (1935), which was a modest step taken against great opposition. Conservative business and government officials feared that such legislation would destroy individual initiative. White southern legislators in particular were concerned with protecting the low-wage structure of the South against generous government assistance levels. They also wanted to ensure that local officials would have more to say about how programs were operated than would federal officials, who they suspected might be more sympathetic to needy African Americans.

The 1930s program that became AFDC was created not to help the poor move out of poverty but as "a minimum income support program for impoverished women and their children." AFDC and other family support programs were patterned after an earlier Mother's Aid program, which was designed to help working-class widows keep their children out of orphanages.[82] Based on the assumption that relief had to be restricted and that the major causes of poverty with which government should be concerned were blindness, old age, and dependent children, cash assistance to certain categories of the poor was withheld. The original legislation established aid programs for only three groups: Aid to the Blind, Old Age Assistance, and Aid to Dependent Children (ADC).

Since 1950, programs to aid the disabled and adults caring for dependent children have been developed, although the desire to maintain a supply of low-wage workers and keep public aid expenditures low made some state legislatures reluctant to implement these programs. Moreover, every few years members of Congress and state legislators have initiated attacks on "welfare" recipients at the low-income levels (but not on corporations or well-off Americans who receive much larger governmental "handouts," such as corporate farmers who get paid huge sums *not* to grow certain crops). For example, after one of these antiwelfare campaigns, the Family Support Act of 1988 (FSA) required all able-bodied adult welfare recipients whose youngest child was at least three years old to participate in a Job Opportunity and Basic Skills (JOBS) training program, which included education, job training, job search, or work for up to 20 hours a week. However, the FSA's intention was primarily to reduce welfare rolls, not to improve the lives of the least-advantaged Americans. Thus, the JOBS program did not improve the earning capacity of most of its participants or even find jobs for most of them. As a result of FSA and similar legislation, actual benefits to the working poor have been drastically reduced.[83]

Moreover, in 1996, the federal government again reformed welfare with the Personal Responsibility and Work Opportunity Reconciliation Act (PRWORA), which replaced the old Aid to Families with Dependent Children (AFDC) program with the Temporary Assistance for Needy Families (TANF) program of block grants to states, which has new limitations on eligibility. Among its major provisions are requirements for recipients to work or lose benefits, and it limits aid to five years over a person's lifetime, lowers federal food stamp assistance, eliminates cash assistance for children, and encourages unwed mothers to identify the fathers of their children to enhance child support enforcement as well as to stay in school and live with their parents.[84] Since its passage, the numbers of persons officially "on welfare" have dropped and numerous former welfare recipients are working. However, as Heather Boushey, an economist with the Economic Policy Institute, has noted, these are poor measures of "the disturbing realities for millions of current and former welfare recipients." In testimony before a Congressional committee in September 2001 on the effects of PRWORA on working families, Boushey noted that while most former public welfare recipients are working, most are not working full-time or year-round and usually cannot earn enough wages to provide for their families—especially when women (who often face sex discrimination in the workplace) are the sole heads of their households. For these families, poverty has deepened and the economic hardships associated with poverty have not lessened—such as food insecurity, inadequate child care, access to health care, and housing costs.[85]

Low funding of family support programs also has resulted in a decline in the real value of low-income assistance payments. Between 1970 and January 2000, the real (adjusted for inflation) *maximum* AFDC/TANF benefit for a three-person family declined for all states. The median state percentage decline was an incredible 47 percent. In all states, the 2000 AFDC/TANF benefits were below the government's poverty threshold; and in eight states they were less than half. The lowest *maximum* monthly AFDC/TANF benefits for a family of three were in Mississippi ($170), Alabama ($164), Texas ($201), Tennessee ($185), and Louisiana ($190)—all southern states that had once had high levels of slavery and legal segregation. These figures are *near the level of starvation* for families. The combined value of food stamps and AFDC/TANF payments left recipients in 15 states at less than two-thirds of the poverty threshold.[86]

Some recent political campaigns, as well as the mass media, have given the impression that the poor are the major recipients of government dollars. This is *not* the case. Federal, state, and local governments provide a vast array of subsidies for groups above the poverty line, aid that has aptly been termed "welfare for the rich" or "wealthfare." The irony of this type of aid can be seen in the case of an Idaho rancher with a net worth of more than $500 million who leased federal grazing lands for one-quarter the rate charged by private landowners. The taxpayers' subsidy for this rancher's lease for one year would have paid the welfare costs of about 60 families. The costs of wealthfare, which in addition to the subsidized use of public resources includes corporate tax reductions and loopholes, tax breaks for wealthy individuals, direct grants, and publicly funded research and development, total hundreds of billions of dollars each year. The Office of Management and Budget estimates that the cost of tax credits, deductions, and exemptions for corporations and wealthy individuals in just one recent year amounted to an estimated $440 billion. This was 27.5 times as much as the annual cost of federal child support programs for that same year.[87]

Even most of government's extensive aid for educational and health care programs benefits the nonpoor. The 1960s and 1970s saw a dramatic increase in federal expenditures for social programs and income transfer programs, including grants to local governments for education and training, health, cash assistance, and food stamps. Expenditures for middle-income and upper-income Americans have remained very substantial since that era. Most of these government expenditures have *not* gone to the poor.

Conservatives such as Charles Murray have attacked many government antipoverty programs as doing more damage than good.[88] He has asserted that poverty does not grow out of economic conditions. Even though the data presented in this chapter demonstrate that this view is wrong, commentators like Murray have become widely influential, in part because of the substantial backing they have received from powerful conservative foundations and think tanks. Media attention to their discredited ideas has helped to create a conservative climate in which governmental social programs are considered wasteful, ineffective, or dangerous.

In recent years conservatives in Congress have replaced much federal spending for the poor with block grants administered by state governments. Support by political leaders in many states for strict measures to reduce welfare rolls—denying benefits to children born to mothers on public assistance, mandatory workfare for recipients, short time limits for benefits—have created harsh circumstances for poor recipients with little or no education or salable job skills and those whose earnings are inadequate to support families.

Significantly, in fiscal 2003 the largest items in the federal government budget were Social Security ($471 billion), military-defense expenditures ($405 billion), discretionary domestic expenditures ($421 billion), the interest on the federal debt ($153 billion), and Medicare ($274 billion).[89] These are programs that mostly benefit middle-income Americans and corporations, including banks. In comparison, the U.S. government spent significantly smaller sums on income-support programs for poor Americans: It spent $195 billion on all public welfare and food stamps programs and $161 billion for Medicaid. Programs for the poor receive, relatively speaking, *small amounts* of federal dollars—including unemployment compensation ($55 billion), supplemental security income ($33 billion), earned income tax credit ($38 billion), food stamps ($25 billion), family support ($26 billion—includes Temporary Assistance for Needy Families and various programs that involve payments to states for child support enforcement and family support, child care entitlements, and research to benefit children), child nutrition ($12 billion), and foster care and adoption assistance ($6 billion). Head Start programs, for example, received only $6.6 billion.[90] Defense expenditures are much greater than the combined total spent for income, social, and health programs for poor Americans. The United States has had no major political (state-level) enemies since the end of the Cold War, yet it spends three times more on its military establishment than any other country around the globe. Indeed, the United States spends almost as much as *all other countries* put together. And the United States has also become the world's major supplier of military hardware.[91]

The real growth rates (adjusted for inflation) for entitlement programs for the poor and elderly have been modest over the last few decades. Income support programs such as food stamps, family support, child nutrition, and foster care grew on average 1.2 percent annually over the last decade, while Social Security and Medicare, programs benefiting mostly middle-income and upper-middle-income Americans, grew faster annually, at 4.4 percent and 2.4 percent respectively over the period.[92] Contrary to the assertions of many commentators, an "explosion" in the growth of programs for the poor in this period never occurred.

Commentary abounds, especially from conservative analysts, about the great increases in the federal government's budget in recent years. Indeed, the federal budget did grow from a now modest $118 billion in 1965 to a huge $2.3 trillion in 2004. Interestingly, however, the biggest share of this growth occurred *during the conservative administrations* of Ronald Reagan and the first George Bush. During this period the federal military budget more than doubled. Interestingly, too, the U.S. government's budget as a percentage of the gross domestic product was less in fiscal 2003 (19.9 percent) than it was 20 years earlier in 1975 (21.3 percent) and only slightly higher than it was in 1970 (19.3 percent).[93]

Today, the United States has a broad subsidy-for-many government funding system. One part of the system, government aid for rich and middle-income Americans, is seldom thought of as a questionable subsidy or welfare program and is usually seen as worthwhile. Yet, it is indeed a "welfare for the affluent" program. Another part of the system, public assistance for the poor, is disparagingly called "welfare" and is often viewed as wholly or

Welfare subsidies for the affluent and for corporations far exceed those for the poor.

partially illegitimate. The less egalitarian subsidy programs, aid for business and industry, and even Social Security, have historically been the most favored; the most truly egalitarian programs, such as direct cash assistance to poor families, have been relatively starved.[94]

SUMMARY

Poverty has been a fundamental and persisting feature of U.S. society, both in the past and in the midst of today's relative affluence. Government concern with poverty tends to rise and fall with changes in economic conditions and shifts in poor people's movements. In this twenty-first century, about one American in every eight is officially regarded as poor, and judging from surveys perhaps one-quarter seem to be regarded by the American people as seriously deprived in terms of income and related socioeconomic conditions.

The poor have far fewer resources than anyone else; they not only have low incomes but also lack significant political power and access to adequate housing and legal aid. Although many low-income Americans are unable to work because of age, disability, or chronic illness, many other people are poor because of recurring unemployment and underemployment. In each year since the early 1970s, between 6 million and 10 million Americans have been officially unemployed. In addition to this official unemployment, however, the very serious problem of widespread underemployment is a fact.

Unemployment and underemployment are related to decisions made by corporate executives and investors—with profit accumulation and control of the workforce as corporate goals. Decisions by the economically powerful play a major role in shaping the boom–bust cycles of capitalism. Decisions about profit, location of new enterprises, and automation are made without significant democratic consultation with employees affected, yet such decisions have profound effects on working people and their families. The unemployed and underemployed are essential to the operation of the economy because they put downward pressure on wages and provide a reserve labor force. In recent years, many U.S. corporations have created serious unemployment problems by profit-oriented decisions that do not take worker costs into account. A concern for profits and a docile labor force has motivated decisions by many corporations to relocate operations in countries overseas, particularly those with many low-wage workers.

Poor Americans not only suffer indignities of unemployment and low incomes but also endure considerable hostility aimed at them by middle- and upper-income people. The ideology of individualism includes beliefs about hard work for success and about the character defects and laziness of those who do not succeed, including the poor. The ideology of individualism and the view of the poor as villains have developed with the growth of the economy and have been fostered by capitalists and allied politicians from the nineteenth century to the present.

Such an ideology helps to legitimate the many inequalities in U.S. society. Culturally ingrained exhortations to work hard have been important in stimulating the effort of workers to do the jobs provided by our capitalistic system. One indication of a poorly developed awareness of economic exploitation among many workers is their strong acceptance of the individualistic views on poverty and unemployment as reflecting immorality. A major consequence of intense antipoor views among ordinary workers is to direct attention away from their own economic exploitation.

Government aid for the poor is the focus of much political attention. Many affluent Americans complain about the high costs of welfare, but far larger than government subsidies for the poor are subsidies for middle-income and upper-income Americans, as well as corporations. The United States has a broad subsidy system. Government subsidies for the affluent and the rich are usually viewed as legitimate and are not considered welfare; subsidies for the poor are considered to be illegitimate and are viewed, often with hostility, as only "handouts." The United States still lives by a hypocritical and abstract ethic of "justice for all," which is still far from implemented in everyday social realities.

STUDY QUESTIONS

1. What are the major trends in the incidence of poverty? Which groups are most likely to fall into the poverty category? Which groups are least likely to be found there?

2. The Bureau of Labor Statistics (BLS) presents an "official" picture of unemployment each month. Contrast this official unemployment rate with the "true" rate by identifying several categories important to measuring underemployment.

3. What is the social impact of unemployment? Give examples of individual and community harm.

4. How has the ideology of individualism shaped our perceptions about the causes of poverty, welfare, unemployment, and underemployment in the United States?

5. Given the option, most workers would probably choose to work at a job in the primary labor market rather than the secondary labor market. What conditions make these jobs relatively attractive?

ENDNOTES

1. This description is based on unpublished research done by Joe Feagin on Liverpool, England.
2. Committee on Ways and Means, U.S. House of Representatives, *Overview of Entitlement Programs: 1992 Green Book* (Washington, D.C.: 1992), pp. 1,273–75.
3. John Kenneth Galbraith, *The Affluent Society* (London: Penguin Books, 1962), p. 260; Joe R. Feagin, *Subordinating the Poor* (Upper Saddle River, N.J.: Prentice Hall, 1975), pp. 1–2.
4. Michael Harrington, *The Other America* (New York: Macmillan, 1962).
5. Committee on Ways and Means, U.S. House of Representatives, *Overview of Entitlement Programs: 1992 Green Book,* p. 1,275.
6. Ibid.
7. Committee on Ways and Means, U.S. House of Representatives, *Overview of Entitlement Programs: 1994 Green Book* (Washington, D.C.: 1994), p. 377.
8. Ibid., p. 1,171.
9. Ibid., p. 399.
10. Bernadette D. Proctor and Joseph Dalaker, U.S. Census Bureau, *Current Population Reports, Poverty in the United States: 2002* (September 2003), available at www.bls.gov/cps/=cpswp2001.pdf; U.S. Bureau of the Census, Current Population Survey, March 1995.
11. Mark Nord, Margaret Andrews, and Steven Carlson, U.S. Department of Agriculture, *Houshold Food Insecurity in the U.S.: 2002* (October 2003), Tables 1 and 2, available at www.ers.usda.gov/publications/fanrr35.
12. Food Research and Action Center, Hunger in the U.S., *Health Consequences of Hunger* (ret. February 12, 2004), available at www.frac.org/html/hunger_in_the_us/health.html.
13. Michael B. Katz, *The Undeserving Poor* (New York: Pantheon Books, 1989), p. 5.
14. Ibid., p. 7.
15. Committee on Ways and Means, U.S. House of Representatives, *Overview of Entitlement Programs: 1992 Green Book,* p. 1,289. The countries surveyed were Canada, Australia, Sweden, West Germany, the Netherlands, France, the United Kingdom, and the United States.
16. Bernadette D. Proctor and Joseph Dalaker, U.S. Census Bureau, *Current Population Reports, Poverty in the United States: 2002* (September 2003), available at www.bls.gov/cps/cpswp2001.pdf. See also, Federal Register, *Annual Update of the HHS Poverty Guidelines* (February 13, 2004), available at aspe.os.dhhs.gov/poverty/o4fedreg.html.
17. The statistics in this section and in Table 3.1 are drawn from U.S. Bureau of the Census, *Current Population Survey,* March 1995 and from Bernadette D. Proctor and Joseph Dalaker, U.S. Census Bureau, *Current Population Reports, Poverty in the United States* (September 2003), available at www.bls.gov/cps/cpswp2001.pdf.
18. Ibid.
19. Ibid.; U.S. Bureau of the Census, *Income, Poverty, and Valuation of Noncash Benefits: 1993,* Current Population Reports, P60–188 (Washington, D.C.: 1995), p. xvi.
20. Michael Harrington, *Decade of Decision* (New York: Simon & Schuster, 1980), pp. 235–36; Carleton Bryant, "More Americans Are Poor, According to Census Bureau: But Critics Say Stats Are Loaded," *The Washington Times,* September 4, 1992, p. A1.
21. Harrington, *Decade of Decision,* pp. 236–39.
22. Ibid., pp. 237–38.
23. William O'Hare, "What Does It Take to Get Along? Local Differences in the Cost of Living Can Have a Big Impact on a Market's Spending Potential," *American Demographics,* May 1990, p. 36.
24. "Help Wanted Ads Don't Add Up," *Dollars & Sense,* January 1984, pp. 12–13; Michael J. Mandel, "No Help Wanted," *Business Week,* September 21, 1992, p. 26.
25. U.S. Bureau of Labor Statistics, *Current Population Survey* (ret. January 23, 2004), available at ftp.bls.gov/pub/special.requests/lf/aat5.txt; U.S. Bureau of Labor Statistics, *Employment and Earnings,* January 1992, p. 162; U.S. Bureau of Labor Statistics, unpublished data, January 1996.
26. Francis D. Adams and Barry Sanders, *Alienable Rights: The Exclusion of African Americans in a White Man's Land, 1619–2000* (New York: HarperCollins 2003), p. 256.

27. U.S. Bureau of Labor Statistics, *Current Population Survey* (ret. January 23, 2004), available at ftp.bls.gov/pub/special.requests/lf/aat5.txt.

28. *Economic Report of the President: 1980* (Washington, D.C.: 1980), pp. 238–39.

29. Sylvia Allegretto, Economic Policy Institute, "The Highly Educated Are the Latest Victims of the Weak Recovery" (February 11, 2004), available at www.epinet.org/content.cfm/webfeatures_snapshots_archive_02112004.

30. For a discussion of the Phillips curve of business cycles between 1861 to 1957 and published in 1958, see Kevin D. Hoover, *Philips Curve,* in *The Concise Encyclopedia of Economics,* available at www.econlib.org/library/Enc/PhillipsCurve.html.

31. John A. Garraty, *Unemployment in History* (New York: Harper and Row, 1978), pp. 167, 241–47.

32. U.S. Bureau of the Census, *Statistical Abstract of the U.S.: 1995* (Washington, D.C.: 1995), p. 862.

33. Ibid.

34. David Streitfeld, "Jobless Count Skips Millions," *Los Angeles Times* (December 29, 2003), pp. A1, A16, A17.

35. Thomas Vietorisz, Robert Mier, and Bennett Harrison, "Full Employment at Living Wages," *Annals of the American Academy of Political and Social Science* 418 (March 1975): 104.

36. David Streitfeld, "Jobless Count Skips Millions," *Los Angeles Times* (December 29, 2003), pp. A1, A16, A17.

37. Roberta M. Spalter-Roth, Heidi I. Hartmann, and Linda Andrews, *Combining Work and Welfare: An Alternative Anti-Poverty Strategy* (Washington, D.C.: Institute for Women's Policy Research, 1992), p. iv.

38. U.S. Bureau of the Census, *Current Population Survey,* March 1995.

39. U.S. Census Bureau, *Statistical Abstract of the U.S.: 2002* (ret. February 24, 2004), available at www.census.gov/prod/2003pubs/02statab/labor.pdf; Paul Sherrer, "The shredding of the US 'safety net': most laid-off workers denied unemployment benefits" (April 2, 2001), World Socialist Web Site, available at wsws.org/articles/2001/apr2001/unem-a02_prn.shtml.

40. *Economic Notes* 56 (January–February 1988): 14; "Trends in the Minimum Wage," *Economic Notes* 56 (March–April 1988): 12–13, 16; Susan F. Rasky, "Minimum Wage Rise Wins Final Senate Vote," *New York Times,* November 9, 1989, p. A27.

41. Federal Register, *Annual Update of the HHS Poverty Guidelines* (February 13, 2004), available at aspe.os.dhhs.gov/poverty/o4fedreg.html.

42. AFL-CIO, "The Realities Behind the Myths: Minimum Wage" (ret. February 11, 2004), available at www.aflcio.org/yourjobeconomy/minimumwage/myths/index.cfm.

43. Dixon Wecter, *The Age of the Great Depression: 1929–1941* (Chicago: Quadrangle Books, 1971), pp. 39–40; see also pp. 28–33.

44. Ibid., p. 32.

45. Ibid., pp. 36–38; Garraty, *Unemployment in History,* pp. 181–83.

46. Garraty, *Unemployment in History,* pp. 181–83; William Kapp, "Socioeconomic Effects of Low and High Employment," *Annals of the American Academy of Political and Social Science* 418 (March 1975): 65–66; "Unemployed Workers Lose More than Jobs," *Dollars & Sense,* November 1980, p. 19; Ralph Catzlano and C. D. Dooley, "Economic Predictors of Depressed Mood and Stressful Life Events in a Metropolitan Community," *Journal of Health and Social Behavior* 18 (September 1977): 292–307; M. H. Brenner, *Mental Illness and the Economy* (Cambridge, Mass.: Harvard University Press, 1973); Susan Newell, "Michigan Unemployment Sends Infant Death Rate Soaring," *Labor Notes,* January 27, 1983, p. 7; George Tucker, "Unemployment Kills," *Economic Notes* 51 (October 1983): 6.

47. *The 1971 Manpower Report to the President,* quoted in Harrel R. Rodgers, Jr., *Poverty Amid Plenty* (Reading, Mass.: Addison-Wesley, 1979), p. 154; see also Joe R. Feagin and Harlan Hahn, *Ghetto Revolts* (New York: Macmillan, 1973).

48. Howard W. Wachtel, "Looking at Poverty from a Radical Perspective," in *Problems in Political Economy,* 2nd ed., D. M. Gordon, ed. (Lexington, Mass.: D. C. Heath, 1977), p. 310.

49. "Steel: Too Little, Too Late," *Dollars & Sense,* October 1982, pp. 8–9, 12.

50. "Left Out," *Newsweek,* March 21, 1983, p. 32.

51. "Offshore Office Work," *Global Electronics Information Newsletter,* March 1984, p. 1; David Eisenhower, "Government and Unemployment," *Economic Notes* 51 (October 1983): 5.

52. Cable News Network, *Lou Dobbs Tonight* (February 10, 2004), Transcript #021001cb.110, interview with U.S. Chamber of Commerce CEO Tom Donohue on outsourcing of jobs by U.S. corporations.

53. Steve Babson and Nancy Brigham, *What's Happening to Our Jobs* (Sommerville, Mass.: Popular Economics Press, 1978), p. 608.

54. James O'Connor, *The Fiscal Crisis of the State* (New York: St. Martin's Press, 1973), p. 158.

55. Abraham Moisa, Division of Labor Force Statistics, Bureau of Labor Statistics, *A Profile of the Working Poor, 2001* (June 2003), available at www.bls.gov/cps/cpswp2001.pdf.
56. Richard Edwards, *Contested Terrain* (New York: Basic Books, 1979), pp. 165–68, 184–88.
57. Bennett Harrison, *Education, Training, and the Urban Ghetto* (Baltimore: Johns Hopkins University Press, 1972), pp. 123–43; David M. Gordon, *Theories of Poverty and Underemployment* (Lexington, Mass.: D. C. Heath, 1972), pp. 68–74.
58. Spalter-Roth et al., *Combining Work and Welfare*, p. 4.
59. See, for example, Heather Boushey, Economic Policy Institute, *The Needs of the Working Poor* (February 14, 2002) [Testimony presented before the U.S. Senate, Committee on Health, Education, Labor and Pensions], available at www.epinet.org/content.cfm/webfeatures_viewpoints_boushey_testimony_2002021; Heather Boushey and Bethney Gundersen, Economic Policy Institute, *When Work Just Isn't Enough: Measuring Hardships Faced by Families after Moving from Welfare to Work* (June 2001), available at www.epinet.org/content.cfm/briefingpapers_hardships.
60. Spalter-Roth et al., *Combining Work and Welfare*, pp. iii, 15.
61. Committee on Ways and Means, U.S. House of Representatives, *Overview of Entitlement Programs: 1994 Green Book,* pp. 10–11, 325, 401–402.
62. See Christopher Jencks and Kathryn Edin, "The Real Welfare Problem," *The American Prospect* 1 (1990), reported in Spalter-Roth et al., *Combining Work and Welfare*, p. 5.
63. Gina Kolata, "More Children Are Employed, Often Perilously," *New York Times,* June 21, 1992, p. 1.
64. Sam Roberts, "New York in the Nineties," *New York Times,* September 29, 1991, sec. 6, p. 35. See also Muriel H. Cooper, "Unions Rally in Garment District," *AFL-CIO News,* November 6, 1995, p. 16.
65. James O'Toole, "Planning for Total Employment," *Annals of the American Academy of Political and Social Science* 418 (March 1975): 72–79.
66. Julian Brookes, "Witness to the Betrayal," *Mother Jones* (February 23, 2004), available at www.motherjones.com/news/update/2004/02/02_403.html.
67. "History of Struggle for a Shorter Work Week," *Economic Notes* 52 (March 1984): 4–5.
68. Ibid.
69. Both are quoted in Richard Hofstadter, *Social Darwinism in American Thought,* rev. ed. (Boston: Beacon Press, 1955), p. 45.
70. Ronald Reagan, speech printed in *New York Times,* September 10, 1966, p. 13; Ronald Reagan, gubernatorial address printed in *New York Times,* January 6, 1967, p. 18. See also 1980 and 1984 presidential campaign speeches and advertisements.
71. Quoted in Edgar May, *Wasted Americans* (New York: Signet Books, 1965), p. 187.
72. Quoted in Donald G. Howard, *Social Welfare* (New York: Random House, 1969), p. 108.
73. Feagin, *Subordinating the Poor,* pp. 93–105.
74. Data from the James R. Kluegel and Eliot Smith poll are reported in James R. Kluegel, "Inflation, Unemployment, and Attitudes toward the Poor and Welfare," paper presented at the meeting of the American Sociological Association, San Antonio, Texas, August 1984.
75. Robin Toner, "New Politics of Welfare Focuses on Its Flaws," *New York Times,* July 5, 1992, p. 1; see also, National Opinion Research Center, General Social Survey, 1988–1991, available at www.norc.uchicago.edu/projects/gensoc.asp.
76. Griffen, "Poor Relations," pp. 6–8; Dorothy Miller, *Women and Social Welfare: A Feminist Analysis* (New York: Praeger, 1990), pp. 29–43.
77. Alvin L. Schorr, "Problems in the ADC Program," unpublished paper, n.d.; Richard C. Edwards, "Who Fares Well in the Welfare State?" in *The Capitalist System,* Richard C. Edwards et al., eds. (Upper Saddle River, N.J.: Prentice Hall, 1972), p. 250.
78. Alan Wolfe, *The Seamy Side of Democracy* (New York: David McKay, 1973), pp. 136–37.
79. Charles H. Anderson, *The Political Economy of Social Class* (Englewood Cliffs, N.J.: Prentice Hall, 1974), p. 60.
80. Wolfe, *The Seamy Side of Democracy,* p. 133.
81. Harold L. Wilensky and Charles N. Lebeaux, *Industrial Society and Social Welfare* (New York: Free Press, 1965), pp. xvi–xvii.
82. Spalter-Roth et al., *Combining Work and Welfare,* pp. 1–2; quotation from p. 2; Miller, *Women and Social Welfare,* pp. 29–46.
83. Ibid., pp. 2–3.
84. Committee on Ways and Means, U.S. House of Representatives, *The 2000 Green Book: Background Material and Data on Programs within the Jurisdiction of the Committee on Ways*

and Means (October 6, 2000), Section 7, available at www.utdallas.edu/~jargo/green2000/contents.html.

85. Heather Boushey, *The Effects of the Personal Responsibility and Work Opportunity Reconciliation Act on Working Families* (ret. February 21, 2004), available at www.epinet.org/content.cfm/webfeatures_viewpoints_tanf_testimony. See also, Heather Boushey and Bethney Gundersen, *When Work Just Isn't Enough: Measuring Hardships Faced by Families after Moving from Welfare to Work* (June 2001), available at www.epinet.org/content.cfm/briefingpapers_hardships; Heather Boushey, *Former Welfare Families Need More Help: Harships Await Those Making Transition to Workforce* (March 2002), available at www.epinet.org/content.cfm/briefingpapers_bp123.

86. Committee on Ways and Means, U.S. House of Representatives, *The 2000 Green Book: Background Material and Data on Programs within the Jurisdictrion of the Committee on Ways and Means* (October 6, 2000), Section 7, available at www.utdallas.edu/~jargo/green2000/contents.html.

87. Chuck Collins, "Aid to Dependent Corporations: Exposing Federal Handouts to the Wealthy," *Dollars & Sense,* May/June 1995, pp. 15–17, 40; Edward A. Chadd, "Manifest Subsidy," *Common Cause,* Fall 1995, p. 18. See also Donald Barlett and James Steele, *America: Who Really Pays the Taxes?* (New York: Simon and Schuster, 1994).

88. Charles Murray, *Losing Ground* (New York: Basic Books, 1984). See also John L. Palmer and Isabell V. Sawhil, eds., *The Reagan Record* (Cambridge, Mass.: Ballinger, 1984), pp. 183–87.

89. Congressional Budget Office, *The Budget and Economic Outlook: Fiscal Years 2005 to 2014* (January 2004), Table 3–6, available at www.cbo.gov/showdoc.cfm?index54985&sequence54.

90. See Kay Mills, "Don't Mess with Head Start's Success," *Los Angeles Times* (February 22, 2004), p. M2.

91. Committee on Ways and Means, U.S. House of Representatives, *Overview of Entitlement Programs: 1994 Green Book,* pp. 1,255, 1,267.

92. Congressional Budget Office, *The Budget and Economic Outlook: Fiscal Years 2005 to 2014* (January 2004), available at www.cbo.gov/showdoc.cfm?index54985&sequence511.

93. Congressional Budget Office, *The Budget and Economic Outlook: Fiscal Years 2005 to 2014* (January 2004), available at www.cbo.gov/showdoc.cfm?index54985&sequence511.

94. A. Dale Tussing, "The Dual Welfare System," *Society* 11 (January–February 1974): 53.

chapter 4

Problems of Racism and Racial Inequality

The last few decades have seen recurring protests by African Americans and other Americans of color against racial discrimination and other mistreatment, in cities such as Miami, Philadelphia, and Los Angeles. Veterans of the civil rights era of the 1960s see familiar issues in these protests: police brutality, violence by white supremacist groups, unemployment, poverty, and widespread discrimination. Signs of retreat from civil rights progress that spur protests include recurring hate crimes and white supremacy groups and the many attempts by whites to eliminate affirmative action and other programs established to quell racial and ethnic discrimination. Another antagonizing force is recurring pressure from white officials in the courts or Congress to revise or repeal civil rights acts such as the 1965 Voting Rights Act, a law that helped bring African Americans back into U.S. politics in a major way after centuries of exclusion.

Such actions confirm the continuing importance of racist thinking and racial stratification in the United States. In several chapters in this book, we consider the importance of racial groupings and institutionalized racism concerning specific societal problems. Because racial discrimination and conflict remain fundamental to this society, this chapter focuses on these matters.

GOALS OF THIS CHAPTER

An underlying thesis of this chapter is this: Contemporary racial relations in U.S. society are deeply rooted in long-term economic and political developments historically linked to racial oppression. We begin the chapter with an overview of how racist thinking has justified the inherent contradiction between civil rights reserved for white Americans and the suppression of those rights for people of color. We explain here that one should view patterns of immigration, and the subsequent adaptation of different racial and ethnic groups, not just from an assimilation perspective but, more accurately, from a power–conflict perspective. The historical data indicate that the ancestors of many people of color were brought to the United States through coercion or violence, often to serve white employers' labor needs. Using the power–conflict framework, we see clearly why and how Americans of color have long been racially subordinated—and thus we see the development of society as racially stratified to the present day. Institutionalized forms of racial discrimination continue to affect Americans of color in economic, political, and other societal institutions. We will see too that white reactions to equal opportunity and other change efforts have brought new problems for Americans of color. We close with a discussion of important issues surrounding recent immigration.

THE REVOLUTIONARY BACKGROUND

Historians have long characterized North America's early days as an era of dedication to freedom and equality. Yet this new society had a very negative side. In its founding period and unfolding history, the new white-governed republic embedded much racial and ethnic oppression and conflict. Thus, government policies brought about the intentional killing of Native Americans or their forced removal from long-occupied lands. By the mid-seventeenth century, enslavement of Africans was basic to the economy of the colonies, and revolts by those enslaved were a constant "problem" for whites. Other peoples of color, such as Chinese Americans, Japanese Americans, and Mexican Americans, would later suffer similar yokes of racial oppression. Discrimination, less severe overall, against later white immigrant groups was also part of the now forgotten history of the nineteenth and early twentieth centuries.[1]

The basic documents of our republic show the existence of patterns of racial subordination. An early draft of the Declaration of Independence, prepared by Thomas Jefferson, accused King George III of pursuing slavery, of waging "cruel war against human nature itself, violating its most sacred rights of life and liberty in the persons of a distant people who never offended him, captivating them and carrying them into slavery in another hemisphere, or to incur miserable death in the transportation thither." Jefferson, who was himself a major slaveholder, further said that King George had not attempted to prohibit the slave trade and had encouraged those slaved to "rise in arms" against white colonists.[2] Under pressure from southern slave-holding interests and northern slave-trading interests, however, the white male signatories to the Declaration deleted this critique of slavery from the final version. Even in this revolutionary period, the country's white founders did not extend the ideals of liberty and equality to the African American population.

The U.S. Constitution recognized the racial subordination of African Americans in three major sections: First, because of a compromise between northern and southern representatives to the Constitutional Convention, Article I required that each enslaved American be counted as three-fifths of a person for the purposes of determining (whites') legislative representation and taxes. In this case, southern slave owners pressed for full inclusion of those enslaved in the population count, which northern interests opposed. Second, a section in Article II permitted the bloody slave trade to continue for two more decades. The Constitution also incorporated a fugitive slave provision, requiring the return of freedom-seeking runaways to their white owners.[3] Neither the Declaration of Independence, with its great "all men are created equal" phrase, nor the Constitution, with its revolutionary Bill of Rights, was seen by its white framers as applying to a large proportion of the population: residents of African and Native American descent. Indeed, because of the constitution enslavement of black Americans would last much longer in the United States than in Great Britain.[4]

Inequality in life opportunities along racial and ethnic lines was a fundamental fact of this new country's institutions. In the 1700s and early 1800s, substantial liberty existed only for northern European men. Over the next two centuries, new European and non-European immigrant groups (men and women) trying to move up within economic and political institutions challenged this established group. The new groups were forced to adapt to the dominant Anglo-American culture and society, with some gaining significant power and status. Yet, certain groups—especially people of color—have remained disproportionately in lowly social, political, and economic positions in U.S. society.

From the beginning, racial subordination and inequality have been basic facts of American life. The racial hierarchy, with white European-origin groups at the top and groups of non-European origin down the ladder in terms of access to resources and power, is a central feature of society today, as it has been for centuries. As Figure 4.1 suggests, whites as a group generally predominate over non-European groups such as African Americans, Mexican Americans, and Native Americans (among others) in terms of such resources as wealth, income, jobs, housing, and political power. A variety of blatant, subtle, and covert discrimination mechanisms in institutional sectors such as the economy, education, and politics guarantee the continuing racial domination of white Americans. The taproot of contemporary racial patterns goes deep into the country's history. One can view this racial stratification as an overlay on other social stratification, such as that of class and gender. Over time, racial stratification has grown, together with other types of oppression, thereby thickening the societal texture.

Figure 4.1 The Racial Ladder of Dominance (selected groups)

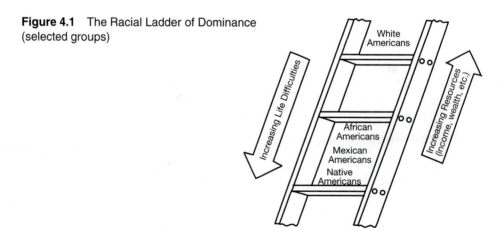

RACIALIZED THINKING

Racial Groups and Racism

Social science researchers and popular writers have used the term *racial group* and the common term *race* in different senses. Popular phrases like *human race, Jewish race,* and *white race* suggest a range of meanings. The earliest use of *race* in sixteenth-century Europe referred to descendants of a common ancestor, thus emphasizing kinship linkages.[5] In the late eighteenth century, *race* came to mean a distinct category of human beings with *physical* characteristics transmitted by descent.[6] This increasingly prevalent view among whites saw supposedly distinctive physical and genetic characteristics of groups as the basis of the social hierarchy of racial groups.[7] In this context *ideological racism* emerged. Ideological racism is a broad viewpoint that (1) sees certain physical characteristics, such as skin color, as unchangeable and linked in a causal way to cultural or intellectual characteristics and that (2) on this basis distinguishes between superior and inferior racial groups for the purposes of subordination and discrimination.[8]

The *scientific racism* of writers such as Europe's Count de Gobineau in the nineteenth century rationalized the colonialism and imperialism of European countries in Asia, Africa, and the Americas by emphasizing the alleged racial superiority of white Europeans. A long line of "scientific" racists followed de Gobineau's example, from Madison Grant in the United States and Adolf Hitler in Germany to today's advocates of racial inferiority and white supremacy. In the United States, the ideology of racial inferiority was even in the early 1900s applied to culturally distinct groups such as Jewish and Italian immigrants, who initially were *not* seen as "white." Later, they too would be classified as "white."

Racist thinking believes that physical differences such as skin color are closely tied to group differences in intelligence and culture. Since no scientific support for this assumed linkage exists, almost all social scientists have come to reject attempts at constructing biological–racial typologies with inferior and superior categories. The lack of scientific support, however, has not prevented racist ideologies from continuing to have a tremendous negative impact. Nazi officials based their killing of millions of European Jews and Gypsies in the 1940s on a racist ideology. As we will see, white racist ideologies, if less often publicly expressed, still underlie much discrimination against Americans of color in the twenty-first century.

Social Definition of Racial Groups

Characteristics such as skin color and hair texture, which racist ideologies and popular thinking about "race" often single out, have no unique biological meaning. The primary meaning of these characteristics is social.[9] A *racial group* is not something that the natural order of the physical universe generates; it is a social category that persons outside the set-apart group have decided is important to single out based on real or alleged, subjectively selected physical traits. Over the history of the United States, a number of distinct social groups, including Italian and Jewish Americans, have at times been categorized as different "races" and have been considered by north-European American journalists, political leaders, and scientists to be *biologically* inferior. For example, Kenneth Roberts, a prominent journalist of the early 1900s, wrote of the dangers of the new immigrants from southern and eastern Europe:

> Races cannot be crossbred without mongrelization, any more than breeds of dogs can be cross-bred without mongrelization. The American nation was founded and developed by the Nordic race, but if a few more million members of the Alpine, Mediterranean and Semitic races are poured among us, the result must inevitably be a hybrid race of people as worthless and futile as the good-for-nothing mongrels of Central America and Southeastern Europe.[10]

The phrase "Mediterranean and Semitic races" generally referred to Italian and Jewish immigrants of the late 1800s and early 1900s.

Significantly, for much of the country's history, most "white" Americans have defined Americans of color—such as African, Native, Latino, and Asian Americans—as racially different because of physical characteristics, such as skin color and hair type, presumed to be unchangeable. History, not biology, answers the question of why white Americans have used certain physical characteristics to single out particular groups. Historically, differences in military organization and firepower between European and African peoples played a major role in the subordination of Africans who were enslaved and transported to the Americas. Soon, Africans' darker skin color and certain other physical differences became identifying traits for whites that indicated differences in privileges and power. Social definition of racial groups moves us away from a biological determinism that views racial groups as genetically fixed with unchanging physical or mental characteristics. Human beings themselves, outside and inside a given group, determine whether, and which, physical or cultural characteristics are important enough to single out for the purposes of discrimination and subordination.

EXPLAINING RACIAL DOMINATION

Patterns of immigration and subsequent adaptation to the receiving society are a major focus of social science theories that seek to explain relations between different racial or ethnic groups. Such theories fall roughly into two categories: assimilation theories and power–conflict theories. Assimilation theorists are often concerned with voluntary migration of European and other immigrants to the United States. Most assimilation theorists emphasize the orderly adaptation of a migrating group (such as Italian or Russian immigrants) to the ways of an established host group (white Anglo-Protestants). They accent the social process of one group becoming similar to another. In general, assimilation analysts have not been centrally concerned with how and why a racial hierarchy of social groups, such as whites dominating blacks and Latinos, has maintained its basic structure in the United States for a long period.[11]

Power–conflict models have developed because traditional assimilation perspectives do not fit well the experience of racially subordinated groups. It is generally inaccurate to view African Americans and many other people of color as successfully assimilating into all major institutions of U.S. society. For much of its history, the U.S. political–economic system brought in certain people of color, such as Africans, Native Americans, and early Mexicans, through white coercion and violence. Later adaptation by these groups was usually along inegalitarian lines, with a continuing element of actual or threatened force and much discrimination at the hands of whites.

Recall that, at its peak in the early twentieth century, European colonialism extended into Africa, Asia, the Middle East, Latin America, and the islands of the oceans. Moreover, modern "racial" relations actually began in the late 1400s, with Pope Alexander VI's bill of demarcation and the Treaty of Tordesillas between Spain and Portugal. These diplomatic instruments put all of the world's peoples and their resources at the disposal of particular European nations.[12]

Wherever European invaders, colonists, and investors went, indigenous populations were increasingly reorganized into capitalist labor systems, as a subordinated workforce. European invaders stole land and wealth of all kinds, shifted local agriculture to agriculture for export, and forced workers onto plantations or into mines. Colonized peoples were brought by violence "into the worldwide system of commodity circulation, contributing their economic 'surplus' to the growing capital of Europe."[13] European colonization of the Americas began with genocidal violence and exploitation directed against the Native Americans. Relations between whites and other Americans were exploitative, not just because of white prejudices but also because of the economic needs of an expanding capitalist system. Non-Europeans' land and labor became the major source of *new wealth* for European colonizers everywhere.[14] Let us now turn to the archetypal example of racial exploitation and oppression in U.S. history—that of African Americans.

Although racial segregation such as this has been illegal since the 1960s, there is still much racial discrimination directed against black and other minority Americans. (Russell Lee/FSA/Library of Congress)

THE CASE OF AFRICAN AMERICANS

Today the U.S. population includes about 35 million African Americans, whose history in this country goes back nearly 400 years to shortly after the first white immigration.[15] We examine here certain features of this black experience, past and present. We focus on labor, employment, and income since these are at the heart of institutionalized inequality. A more thorough review than we have space for here would also include a detailed discussion of educational discrimination, political inequality, and patterns of protest, some of which we will examine in later chapters.

The Chains of Slavery

Initially, white colonists forcibly imported Africans to fill the growing labor demands of the North American colonies. Enslavement ensured this source of labor by preventing African American workers from moving up into better socioeconomic conditions. The Africans bought by whites from a Dutch ship at Jamestown in 1619 were part of an international slave trade then dominated by the Dutch.[16] *Ideological racism* directed at African Americans initially arose because white merchants and planters sought to keep enslaved Americans fully subordinated and exploitable. The white ideology of racial inferiority legitimized in white eyes the brutal enslavement of African Americans.[17]

Southern slave owners, together with northern merchant, insurance, and banking interests, created a racial hierarchy, with whites at the top and African Americans and Native Americans at the bottom. Capital for new industrial development in the North came in part from the capital gained from northern trade in enslaved human beings and in slave-produced products, such as cotton and tobacco, from southern plantations. One scholar notes that "by transferring the profits skimmed off the cotton and tobacco trade into manufacturing investments, the northern bankers were able to transform the sweat of slaves into the vital fluids of industry."[18] Robert Allen notes that slavery-generated capital accumulation stimulated technological development: "The development of the steam engine, heavy industry, shipbuilding, and many modern financial institutions, for example, were all underwritten directly or indirectly by the colonial slave trade and other forms of colonial exploitation."[19] This massive theft of the fruits of black labor became the foundation of economic prosperity for many whites at the time, and thus for many of their descendants to the present day.

The Labor Market: A Racial Split

In the 1800s the growing northern industrial system relied on European immigrants: first the Irish and later southern and eastern Europeans. Many new white workers, as well as employers, benefited from racial subordination of African Americans. By the 1840s, white immigrants were replacing free black workers in cities. Irish workers took over skilled manual occupations, such as teamsters' jobs, from free blacks. The hostility of white workers brought exclusion of black workers from various job categories and often forced the latter into menial jobs. White workers strove to keep black workers racially subordinate.[20]

A great urban trek to the North for African Americans began in earnest around World War I, and the percentage of the black population living outside the South continued to increase in subsequent years. By the mid-twentieth century, millions had moved from the South—where slavery had placed them and their ancestors—to what they often saw as the "promised land" of the North and West. They again faced widespread job, school, and housing discrimination in these regions.[21]

During this period of informal legal segregations black workers provided low-wage labor for a variety of southern and northern businesses. Dominant whites maintained a racial division of labor by force and law and channeled growing numbers of black workers moving out of farm occupations into low-wage urban jobs characterized by little mobility and high unemployment. Assimilation theorists have viewed this urban migration as the source of great opportunities for social and economic mobility. Indeed, they often see African Americans as just another immigrant group in a long line of immigrant groups, such as the Irish and Italians, successfully seeking their fortunes in the cities.

However, the reality of urban economics has been different for black and white Americans. For generations, widespread and blatant discrimination, with consequent low-paying jobs or unemployment, were the lot of most African Americans moving to northern cities. White employers benefited from the lower wages these workers had to accept. In addition, middle-income white workers, as well as white capitalists and top managers, thereby had a supply of low-wage domestic labor for their homes.[22] When black workers entered the northern industry, they generally got the poorest jobs, in part because of the organized actions of white workers. Fear of competition from black workers led to numerous *white-dominated* riots between 1890 and 1930.

Many unions excluded or segregated black workers until the 1950s and 1960s, and after that some unions persisted in using informal discrimination against black workers. At first receptive to black workers, the Congress of Industrial Organizations (CIO), created in the 1930s, soon moved toward the exclusionary racist stance of the older American Federation of Labor (AFL).[23] Historically, most white workers have not seen the clear linkage between the black struggle for freedom and equality and their own struggle for better working conditions. Then, as now, many white workers have preferred to accept what W. E. B. Du Bois once called the "psychological wage of whiteness"[24] (a sense of racial superiority) instead of working together equally with black workers to get better wages and employment conditions for all workers. Black Americans have often noted that the source of black workers' subordination was not only capitalist employers but also many white workers who, as Selma James puts it, "had a primary racial loyalty to their masters as opposed to a class loyalty to us."[25]

Recent Gains and Losses in Employment and Income

After World War II, black employment and income conditions improved in absolute terms, but similar absolute improvements for white Americans left African Americans facing continuing economic inequality. Today, significant racial inequalities remain in the U.S. economy, as can be seen in the unemployment rate. The jobless rate for black Americans has remained much higher than that for white Americans (see Table 4.1).[26]

In hard times or in good times, the black unemployment rate has stayed about twice that of whites. During recent decades, African Americans have suffered relatively greater

Table 4.1   Annual Black-White Unemployment Rates for Selected Years

	Black (or Nonwhite)	White	Black/White Ratio
1949	8.9%	5.6%	1.6
1959	10.7	4.8	2.2
1964	9.6	4.6	2.1
1969	6.4	3.1	2.1
1975	13.8	7.8	1.8
1980	14.3	6.3	2.3
1982	18.9	8.6	2.2
1985	15.1	6.2	2.4
1989	11.4	4.5	2.5
1995	10.4	4.9	2.1
2002	10.2	5.1	2.0
2005	10.6	4.4	2.4

unemployment, compared with whites, than they did even in the 1940s. The black–white unemployment ratio reached a record high of 2.5 in 1989, and in 2005 it was still at 2.4. Black workers have lost jobs at twice the rate of white workers in recent economic recessions, and employers have generally recalled them at a much slower rate. One key reason for the continuing inequality in employment opportunities is the movement of investment capital and jobs *from* central cities, by mostly white capitalists, *to* white-dominated suburbs or low-wage countries overseas (see Chapter 10).

The data in Table 4.2 show some variations in recent unemployment rates by level of educational attainment:[27]

Table 4.2   Black-White Unemployment Rates by Educational Level, 2004

Level of Education	Black	White	Black/White Ratio
No high school diploma	15.5%	7.5%	2.0
High school diploma only	8.7	4.4	1.9
Some college, no degree	8.3	3.8	2.2
Associate degree	5.8	3.3	1.7
Bachelor's degree and higher	4.3	2.5	1.7

Clearly, a college degree reduces the likelihood of unemployment for both groups and narrows the white–black unemployment gap to some, albeit modest, degree. Yet, African Americans with college degrees still have higher unemployment rates than whites with much less in the way of education, such as those with only a year or two of college.

In addition, the *underemployment* rate for African Americans—which includes those with no jobs, those working part-time, and those making poverty wages—is *much* higher than their unemployment rate. A large proportion of black workers receive very low wages, have part-time work but want full-time work, or are discouraged workers (have given up looking for work). If underemployed workers are included, the actual jobless rate is far higher than the official rate.

African Americans have made significant occupational gains since the 1960s when the near-slavery of legal segregation finally ended. However, the greatest gains came just after liberation from legal segregation. Government data for "nonwhite" (mostly black) employed workers in 1955 and 1972 show increases in the nonwhite proportions in professional, managerial, sales, clerical, crafts, and operatives categories, as well as decreases in unskilled and service categories. Growth in the proportion of black employees in better-paid categories was most rapid in the 1960s, yet slowed by the 1980s and 1990s. Indeed, in 2003 black men were still *much less likely* than white men to be in the top-five better-paying job categories for males: managerial, professional, technical, sales, and crafts. The proportion of black men in managerial and professional jobs was about half that of white men. In contrast, black men were more than twice as likely as white men to be in blue-collar service jobs and 1.5 times as likely to be in the job category of operators and laborers. Black women have made more occupational progress than have black men, although they too have a less favorable job distribution than their white counterparts. In 2003, black women were less likely to be employed in managerial and professional jobs than were white women and were more likely to be in service jobs.[28]

Black workers within the government's broad white-collar categories tend to be in subcategories with lower pay and status. Within the professional–technical category, black employees today are most commonly found in such fields as social work, kindergarten teaching, vocational counseling, personnel, dietetics, and health care. One is far less likely to find blacks serving as lawyers and judges, dentists, artists, engineers, and professors at historically white universities.

Since the 1950s, black family income as a percentage of that of whites has oscillated a little but has remained in the 52 to 62 percent range. Black (or nonwhite) family income as a percentage of white family income fluctuated a little during the 1950s, rose significantly by the late 1960s to 61 percent, and then dropped substantially over the period from the 1970s to the early 1990s. As Table 4.3 shows, it was not until 2002 that the black–white income differential again rose to a level a little above that of 1969 (62 percent).[29]

As in the past, societal conditions continue to force African American families into poverty at much higher rates than their white counterparts. Today, nearly a quarter of black families, and nearly one third of black children, live below the official poverty line. In contrast, less than 8 percent of non-Latino white families live below the poverty line.[30] The poverty rate for black families is much higher than that of comparable white families—regardless of the educational level or work experience of family heads. In addition, families headed only by single, separated, or divorced mothers tend to be poorer than those with both parents present. In 2001, women were sole parents in 48 percent of black families, and half of these lived in poverty.[31] And the median income for these black female-headed families was just over half that of white female-headed families.[32] Direct

Table 4.3 Black (or Nonwhite) Income as a Percentage of White Income

1950	54%
1954	56
1959	52
1964	54
1969	61
1974	58
1980	58
1985	58
1990	58
1993	55
1994	60
2002	62
2003	62

employment discrimination (both racial and gender discrimination) and indirect discrimination (for example, inadequate educational and job training programs in central cities) are major causes of the unemployment and low incomes often faced by single black mothers.

Issues of Wealth

Income is only one measure of economic well-being. Accumulated wealth, measured here in terms of net worth (financial assets minus liabilities), is in some ways a more meaningful basis for determining economic security and power. In the year 2000, the median net worth of white households ($67,000) was *eleven* times that of black households ($6,166). In addition, median net worth of white households is roughly *ten* times that of Latino households ($6,766). The figures in Table 4.4 are the most recent available and document the continuing, greatly unequal distribution of wealth.[33]

About 29 percent of black households had *zero* or *negative* net worth, a condition in which debts exceed assets. Nearly two-thirds had a net worth of less than $25,000. A majority of whites, in contrast, had assets above $50,000, with nearly 45 percent having assets above $100,000. Today, for African Americans, this lack of substantial economic assets—which is often combined with lower wages for family earners than comparably educated white earners—gives many black families little margin of security when faced with serious economic setbacks such as job loss, prolonged illness, or other family troubles. It also gives black families fewer resources to help their children get college and graduate school educations. Even black middle-income families have significantly less wealth, on the average, than white middle-income families.

Table 4.4 Percentage Distribution of Households by Net Worth

Net Worth	Blacks	Whites
Zero or negative	29.1%	11.3%
$1–$4,999	16.0	7.2
$5,000–$24,999	18.9	12.4
$25,000–$49,999	12.7	9.8
$50,000–$99,999	12.6	14.8
$100,000–$499,999	10.1	34.4
$500,000 and over	0.6	10.0
Percent Totals	100.0%	99.9%

This current lack of significant assets for most black families demonstrates the long-term impact of four centuries of white discrimination and related oppression greatly favoring whites over African Americans and many other Americans of color. Historically, whites have benefitted greatly from an array of government programs designed for whites (only or principally). Some readers may remember that President Abraham Lincoln and other prominent Republicans promised freed black families the famous "40 acres and a mule," yet most never received such land. Instead, in the 1860s the U.S. Congress passed the Homestead Act, which provided huge amounts of federal government land as farms to homesteading families—some 99.5 percent of whom were white. From the 1860s to the 1930s, some 246 million acres were provided, at no cost or low cost, to 1.5 million (overwhelmingly white) homesteading households. Social scientist Trina Williams has estimated that some 46 million Americans, virtually all white, are likely the current beneficiaries of this large wealth-generating program.[34] In addition, many other federal government resource giveaways (for example, radio and television frequencies, airline routes, timber and oil leases, and business contracts) were provided *only* to earlier generations of whites living in a legally segregated society.[35] Such gross racial favoritism for whites in earlier generations, in effect massive *unjust enrichment,* has continued as unjustly gained wealth that is passed down quietly to subsequent generations of whites—indeed, to tens of millions of whites today.

PATTERNS OF DISCRIMINATION: EMPLOYMENT AND HOUSING

Racial Discrimination: Some Dimensions

A common perspective on racial discrimination focuses only on the individual discrimination generated by personal prejudices or ill will. The negative impact of white prejudices directed at groups such as African Americans, Latinos, Native Americans, and Asian Americans is certainly conspicuous in U.S. history. However, we must move beyond this traditional emphasis on individual prejudices and consider other types of discrimination. Some social scientists have developed privilege theories that examine discrimination's deep institutionalized roots. Charles Hamilton and Kwame Ture were among the first to probe the concept of *institutional racism.* They contrasted *individual racism,* exemplified by the actions of a few white terrorists bombing a black church, with *institutional racism,* illustrated by inadequate food and medical facilities that lead to the deaths of many black children in urban and rural areas each year.[36]

What is *discrimination?* The following is a working definition: *Discrimination* refers to actions or practices carried out by members of a dominant group, or their representatives, that have a differential and harmful impact on members of a subordinate group. Racial discrimination involves actions, actors (discriminators), and targets. Such actions can be obvious or subtle, and they vary in the degree to which they involve large-scale organizations.[37]

Drawing on these dimensions, one can describe four types of discriminatory practices.

Type A: *Isolate discrimination*
Type B: *Small group discrimination*
Type C: *Direct institutionalized discrimination*
Type D: *Indirect institutionalized discrimination*

Type A, *isolate discrimination,* refers to harmful action taken intentionally by a dominant group individual against members of a subordinate racial group, without that action's being supported by his or her organizational or community context. An example of this type of discrimination would be a white police officer acting out hostility to blacks by beating black prisoners at every opportunity, even though police department regulations and procedures actually prohibit and punish such actions. If a substantial proportion of officers in that department behaved in this fashion, however, these beatings would no longer fall in the Type A category; they would then be part of the informal normative consensus of a large-scale organization. (The word *isolate* does not mean that Type A discrimination is unusual in the United States, for it is commonplace.)

Type B, *small group discrimination,* refers to harmful actions taken intentionally by a small group of dominant racial group individuals acting in concert against members of a subordinate racial group, without the support of the norms or rules of a large organizational or community context. The recent burning of black churches and the burning of crosses in front of the homes of black families by whites in small white supremacy groups are often examples of this type of racial discrimination.

Type C, *direct institutionalized discrimination,* refers to organizationally prescribed or community-prescribed actions of white Americans that by intention have a negative impact on members of subordinated racial groups. Typically, a large number of individuals guided by the norms of a large-scale organization or community routinely carry out these actions. Historical examples include the legal segregation of African Americans in inferior schools, public accommodations, and housing. Today, this category includes a broad array of informal practices carried out by large numbers of whites in particular organizations or institutions. These would include the discriminatory actions of numerous white real estate agents who routinely steer black and Latino families away from white housing areas and the many white employers who reject well-qualified black, Native American, Latino, or Asian American applicants for good-paying job opportunities or job promotions.

Type D, *indirect institutionalized discrimination,* refers to current actions an tices of white Americans that have a negative impact on members of subordinate groups even though the organizationally prescribed or community-prescribed norms or rules guiding those actions were established, and are carried out, with no intent to harm the members of those subordinate groups. For example, white employers' hiring and promotion standards that require certain educational credentials may handicap some African Americans today, even though these procedures are not now intentionally discriminatory. Some African Americans lack the necessary education credentials that would allow them to compete with dominant whites for better-paying jobs through no fault of their own, but because of the racially inferior educational opportunities—direct (intentional) institutionalized discrimination—that they encountered in the past as they were growing up. Intentional discrimination by whites against people of color in one sphere of life often has negative consequences for the targets of that discrimination in yet other spheres, and at later periods, of their lives.

Various combinations of these types of discrimination coexist in particular organizational and community settings, at the same time. African Americans, as well as other Americans of color, often suffer from institutionalized practices that are intended to harm and those not now intended to harm, as well as from the acts of white bigots who openly focus their racist hostility on human targets within their reach.

Research indicates that black and white Americans often disagree significantly about the extent and character of racial discrimination today. Opinion polls show that the majority of black respondents report that substantial discrimination still exists, while a majority of whites generally disagree. In one survey, more than half the black respondents agreed that black workers generally faced discrimination in getting skilled jobs; and 61 percent replied in a similar way concerning managerial jobs.[38] A Los Angeles survey of more than 1,000 black workers found that six in ten reported having faced workplace discrimination, such as being refused a job because of their skin color. Just under half of those with less than a high school diploma reported recent job discrimination, while eight in ten of those with a college degree, and *almost all* of those with postgraduate work, reported discrimination at work. Majorities of well-educated Asian American and Latino workers also reported discrimination in employment.[39]

Today, a majority of whites refuse to view racial discrimination as a major barrier for people of color. In recent surveys, more than six in ten whites believed that discrimination was not the main reason that blacks today, on the average, have worse jobs, income, and housing than white people. A majority of the white respondents believed that most blacks "just don't have the motivation or will power to pull themselves up out of poverty."[40]

One persisting reason that whites refuse to see racial discrimination, even though it remains pervasive, lies in persisting white stereotypes and prejudices. For example, one major national survey found that most whites admit to holding one or more antiblack stereotypes. Nearly six in ten of the whites surveyed agreed with one or more of these traits as applicable to black Americans: lazy, aggressive or violent, prefer to live on welfare, or always complaining. (A third agreed with two or more.)[41] In another survey, whites were asked to evaluate on a scale of 1 to 7 how work-oriented blacks are. A small percentage (16 percent) ranked blacks at the hardworking end; just under half chose the lazy end of the spectrum. In contrast, the majority of these white respondents ranked whites as hardworking; few placed whites in the lazy ranks.[42] Numerous opinion surveys have presented similar findings: A majority of white respondents hold to antiblack stereotypes.[43] These surveys likely underestimate the level of racial stereotyping and prejudice among white Americans, for some number likely give more socially acceptable answers when responding to a pollster, who is a stranger. These racial stereotypes and prejudices, in their turn, are major generating motivations for continuing discrimination against African Americans by many whites.[44]

Most white Americans today also view black Americans as having generally achieved substantial equality of opportunity, if not parity with whites, in employment, education, and housing.[45] Yet, in contrast, most black Americans do not see this supposed equality in their everyday lives.

Persisting Discrimination in Recruitment and Hiring

Research studies and federal court cases dealing with employment practices document all four types of discrimination we have identified. Indirect institutionalized discrimination can be seen in employers' use of word-of-mouth recruitment networks. Traditionally, word-of-mouth recruiting has served a positive function for employers, providing inexpensive advertising and solicitation; it is probably the most widely used method of recruitment in many areas of employment. Studies have found that most workers find jobs through informal networks of friends or relatives. When an existing workforce is mostly or entirely white, word-of-mouth recruitment practices usually bring in few workers of color. Information networks are shaped by widespread discrimination in housing (see the following section) and by past discrimination in employment, and thus are an example of indirect institutionalized discrimination. Suburbanization of industries and retail trade has had a significant effect on black employment. African Americans and other people of color, many of whom live in central cities, have little opportunity to enter suburban word-of-mouth recruitment networks. Coupled with the still widespread prejudices of white employers and workers, conventional recruitment practices limit employment opportunities for Americans of color in major ways.[46]

Today, discrimination is institutionalized in hiring and screening practices in both public and private employment areas. White prejudice and stereotyping still play a role in discriminatory practices. Urban Institute researchers conducted an urban study in which they sent comparable white and black applicants to the same employers to apply for jobs. A significant proportion of black applicants suffered discrimination at this entry stage.[47]

The Hostile Racial Climate and the Glass Ceiling

Once one is hired, the problems with racial hostility and discrimination do not end. For example, several thousand African American personnel in the U.S. military were recently interviewed in some detail; nearly half, or more, had encountered in their workplaces in the last year racist jokes, offensive racial discussions, or racial condescension. Substantial numbers also reported serious racist comments and an array of other racial barriers concerning their careers.[48] Like workers in the civilian sector, they often face a hostile racial climate at work.

Promotion, job progression, and transfer practices by white employers and managers have had a negative impact on workers of color. In a recent nationwide survey, more than a third of the black respondents reported they had faced discrimination in their jobs or promotions.[49] Reluctant to tear down traditional exclusion barriers, many white officials and administrators have retreated to a second line of defense—subtle and covert practices that are sometimes difficult to prove. One interview study of black managers and professionals found a number of these examples. One older black manager at a federal agency summed up his experiences: "I don't think that I have been given the same chances. . . . There have been whites that were promoted over me, and around me and everything else, with less education and no experience. . . . When I went to work, I had nine years' experience in the type of work that I was doing, and they brought in this young white fellow and put him as my supervisor, and he had no experience and no formal education."[50]

In many such situations, one might speak of "second-generation" discrimination, since *internal* employment barriers only become significant for large numbers after people of color are actually hired. Getting a nontraditional entry job, thus, does not guarantee such employees equal access to higher-level jobs in the organization, whether it is in business, government, or education. Some refer to promotion barriers as the "glass ceiling" because opportunities to move up are not what they at first seem. Promotion procedures, which often involve subjective judgments of white supervisors and operate in relative secrecy, are difficult to observe from the outside. While most companies and government agencies have written regulations for evaluators in the promotion procedure, informal and unwritten rules often have a greater impact. Employers may pass over a person of color for promotion for supposed "lack of initiative or aggressiveness" or because he or she is alleged to "not be a good team player," when the real reason is the employee's racial identity. Subjective criteria for promotion are sometimes applied to blacks but not to whites, such as requiring that black employees must get along well with white employees (but not vice versa).[51]

Making official pronouncements about "equal opportunity" while actually doing the least possible to promote people of color within an organization is another way some whites hide intentional discrimination. Research studies reveal that white executives in industry and government tend to move slowly in making nontraditional employment opportunities at middle- and higher-management levels available to workers of color. Foot dragging often represents an intentional decision (or no decision) to keep most employees of color from moving up into nontraditional jobs, particularly at higher salary levels. One 1980s study examined U.S. economic, political, and educational institutions and discovered just 20 black people and 318 nonblack women in the 7,314 most powerful positions at the top of these institutions.[52] White men still dominate at the very top of larger businesses. As of 2003, only 3 black males and 11 females (4 white, 4 African American, and 3 Asian American) are top executives of *Fortune* 500 corporations.[53] A federal study found that white men, who make up about 38 percent of the adult population, account for 95 percent of all senior corporate executives at vice president and above.[54]

Tokenism, a sophisticated type of discrimination now widespread in U.S. workplaces, is another way white employers slow down the process of dismantling institutionalized racial and gender discrimination. People of color and white women are hired for nontraditional jobs and put in conspicuous or powerless positions. Drawing on his work as a management consultant, psychologist Kenneth Clark once noted that blacks moving into nontraditional jobs in corporate America are often tracked into "ghettos" within organizations, such as a department of "community affairs" or of "special markets."[55] Recent research has confirmed his observations. For example, Sharon Collins has found that many professional and managerial blacks end up in selected staff jobs such as equal opportunity officer, rather than in line managerial jobs. In 76 interviews with top black executives in major corporations in Chicago, she found that most of these black executives had been ghettoized by senior white executives, and placed in dead-end staff jobs dealing with such things as affirmative action or special markets in black communities. In spite of high qualifications, they had little chance to move up corporate ladders.[56] Thus, black "tokens" in managerial and professional jobs are frequently placed in staff jobs with little power.

Isolated and alone, unable to draw on white networks for routine assistance, workers of color who are ghettoized or presented as tokens must often cope with a high level of job-related stress. Serious illness and rage over discrimination may increase as the discrimination by whites persists over long periods of time.[57] Later on, ironically, white managers and supervisors may even cite the stress-related problems of these token employees as a reason not to promote them or to pursue more aggressive equal opportunity programs.

Discrimination in Public Places and in Business

African Americans and other Americans of color face much discrimination in public accommodations. For example, one *Washington Post* survey found that more than eight in ten black citizens who enter public accommodations face discrimination at the hands of whites—differentially poor service, racial slurs, defensive acts, and a lack of respect.[58] Another report that examined the experiences of more than a hundred African American tourists discovered that most had faced discrimination while dining, shopping, or securing a room in a hotel.[59] Many Americans of color also face discrimination in the business sector. Frustrated over discrimination in large corporations, some Americans seek their fortunes in small businesses. One successful owner of a small consulting firm in the Southwest described her experiences in this business world:

> I have a contract right now with a city government; and I practically gave my services away. I had to become very creative, you know. I wanted the contract because I know I could do the work, and I have the background and the track record to do it. However, in negotiating the contract, they wanted to give it to all these other people who never had any experience . . . simply because they're a big eight accounting firm, or they're some big-time institution. So, I had to compete against those people.

She explained a barrier that was thrown up even after a professional panel evaluating the bids gave her the highest rating because of her record of accomplishment.

> The director of their department made a very racial statement, that "they were very sick and tired of these niggers and these other minorities because what they think is that they can come in here and run a business. None of them are qualified to run a business, especially the niggers." (Now, a white person, female, heard this statement, and because they had some confrontational problems—I think the only reason she really told me was because of that.) He was going to use that, not overtly, but in his mind that was going to be his reason for rejection.[60]

The discrimination here took the form of a white man's blatant attempt to restrict a talented black person's advancement. This woman was unusual in having proof of the man's attempt at exclusion. Blatant discrimination grounded in prejudices has not disappeared from the economy. The surveys cited previously indicate that discrimination is widespread.

Housing Discrimination

Americans of color face large-scale discrimination in areas other than public accommodations and employment. For example, one national poll found that half the black respondents agreed that there was serious discrimination against black home seekers.[61] Discrimination in housing works to bypass the fair housing laws and often relies on the difficulty of proving intent to discriminate to prevent remedial action by its targets. Discrimination can be seen in the persisting practice of *steering* black, Latino, or Asian American customers to segregated or mixed areas and discouraging them from considering predominantly white housing areas, while steering white customers only to those predominantly white areas.

Millions of cases of housing discrimination against Americans of color occur annually. Such discrimination not only creates barriers to the American dream of home ownership but also acts to perpetuate racial segregation. The most comprehensive study on housing discrimination to date shows that persons of color suffer severe forms of racial discrimination as home seekers. A major Urban Institute study involved 4,600 paired tests in 23 metropolitan areas in the summer and fall of 2000. These paired tests involve two individuals—one is a person of color and the other white—posing as home seekers as they visit real estate or rental agents and inquire about advertised housing. While the overall rates of housing discrimination have decreased somewhat since 1989, people of color still experience substantial levels of discrimination in seeking rental housing and homes for sale.

According to this report, rental agents in metropolitan rental markets are less likely to give people of color information about available housing or an opportunity to inspect available housing than they are for whites. Nationally, rental agents subject African Americans and Asian Americans to discrimination about 22 percent of the time; Latinos, 26 percent of the time; and Native Americans, in three states where they are most numerous, 29 percent of the time. In metropolitan home sales markets, real estate agents are less likely to give home buyers of color an opportunity to inquire about or inspect available homes in predominantly white neighborhoods. Agents are also less likely to give home buyers of color assistance with financing and more likely to keep home buyers of color from purchasing homes. African Americans home buyers are discriminated against 17 percent of the time, and Latino home buyers are discriminated against about 20 percent of the time, with Asian American and Pacific Islander home buyers experiencing discrimination about 20 percent of the time and Native American home buyers (in New Mexico) facing discrimination 17 percent of the time.[62]

If we were to go beyond this initial-stage (one-visit) discrimination and examine later-stage housing discrimination, such as in multiple searches or in mortgage lending, and if we extrapolated these data to all people of color searching for housing across the country over a year, we could reasonably estimate that several *million* cases of housing discrimination are carried out by whites each year. Indeed, Roberta Achtenberg, assistant secretary at the U.S. Department of Housing and Urban Development in the 1990s, noted that the actual number could be as high as 10 million cases of housing discrimination annually.[63]

Racial discrimination in mortgage lending substantially lessens the availability of home ownership among Americans of color, as well as for all poorer Americans.[64] A 2001 Association of Community Organizations for Reform Now (ACORN) study collected from 68 metropolitan areas found that financial institutions are *more than twice* as likely to reject black applicants as white applicants for conventional mortgages. Lenders reject Latino home buyers at a rate more than 1.5 times the rate for whites. They also deny home mortgages to residents of all racial groups in low-income neighborhoods 3.14 times more often than to residents of high-income neighborhoods. If families of color owned homes at the same rate as whites, the United States would have an additional 5.7 million minority home-owners. In 2003, while 76 percent of white families owned a home, only 48 percent of black families and 46 percent of Latinos owned one.[65] One reason why discrimination in lending continues is that federal examiners scrutinize the lending practices of credit unions and in-dependent mortgage banks far less than they do other financial institutions. Yet, these or-ganizations are the fastest-growing segments of the mortgage-finance industry.[66]

Persons of color often pay more for home mortgages than whites. A study by the Cen-ter for Community Change found that, despite comparable household income levels, black and Latino home buyers pay much higher interest rates on mortgage loans than whites. Higher mortgage rates for home buyers of color result from the fact that they, regardless of income, are targets for unscrupulous lending predators, and that outreach efforts from con-ventional bank lenders fail to offer significant alternatives to abusive lenders. The report calls for much stronger enforcement of fair lending laws, improved consumer protection, and education to inform borrowers about eligibility for conventional home loans.[67]

Manipulation of white fears by white real estate agents complicates the housing pic-ture. Once a residential neighborhood develops some natural integration—that is, once a few families of color have moved in—real estate salespeople, using the technique of "blockbusting," can act to destroy that natural integration, while at the same time signifi-cantly increasing the price of available housing for families of color. Real estate agents have numerous techniques for exploiting the fears of whites in neighborhoods that have begun to experience racial change, including telephone, mail, and face-to-face solicitations for property listings. In this manner, some real estate agents today fuel the property value de-cline and other stereotypes that help to sustain discrimination in housing.

The attitudes of white homeowners perpetuate discriminatory housing patterns. Over the last few decades, North and South, ever more whites have told interviewers they would be willing to accept a black family if one moved into their neighborhood. Many observers have taken their statements as a sign of a sharp decline in white prejudice. Still, a recent na-tionwide survey found that roughly a third of all whites still believe that a white homeowner should have the *legal right to refuse* to sell their home to a black person, which is contrary to federal law.[68] Older surveys suggest that the overwhelming majority of white respon-dents oppose having a significant number of blacks as neighbors, while blacks' ideal choice is a blended neighborhood, about half white.[69] Research data suggest that most whites are unwilling to accept residential integration beyond the level of a modest number of black families in their neighborhoods. Deeply embedded racial prejudices and stereotypes still play a significant role in housing discrimination by white Americans.

Persisting Residential Segregation

Residential segregation remains high in most cities. Housing segregation is mostly invol-untary for African Americans and some other Americans of color because white stereotyp-ing and discrimination have historically shaped the housing choices of Americans of color. In an examination of housing data for 30 northern and southern metropolitan areas, re-searchers Douglas Massey and Nancy Denton discovered little change between 1980 and 1990 in the high levels of residential segregation along racial lines. The very small declines in housing segregation from 1980 to 1990 were less than for the period from 1970 to 1980.[70] Their research also indicated that while housing segregation decreases for most racial–ethnic groups as education and income increase, it does not do so for African Americans.[71] Many middle-class African Americans still live in substantially black areas, often adjacent to poorer black neighborhoods, in large part because of persisting patterns of white discrimination in the area of housing. This residential segregation has many negative consequences. Sociologist Robert Bullard has shown how segregated African American communities are much more likely to have garbage and industrial dumps nearby than are white communities.[72]

Recent research in metropolitan areas shows a continuing, but slow, decrease in levels of segregation of whites and blacks between 1990 and 2000. Most of the modest decrease in patterns of still high residential segregation for African Americans occurred in cities in the West and South, although residential segregation actually increased in several southern metropolitan areas. Less residential desegregation took place in cities in the Northeast and Midwest. This research shows that among all Americans of color, African Americans still experience the highest levels of residential segregation from whites. Significantly, Asian and Latino Americans have experienced *increased* residential segregation from whites over the last two decades. Residential segregation generally increases for Asian Americans (and Pacific Islanders) and Latinos in areas where they are becoming more numerous. For Latinos, residential segregation over this period has declined in some southern metropolitan areas, yet increased in most western metropolitan areas. New York continues to be the most residentially segregated city for Latinos. Residential segregation patterns for Native Americans is a complicated picture, with some measures indicating increases and others indicating decreases in residential segregation in southwestern cities.[73]

Many white scholars and media commentators discuss the problems faced by darker-skinned Americans as though discrimination by whites had little to do with their difficult housing conditions, higher-than-average unemployment, and lower family incomes. These analysts say that these problems are mostly "their own fault" and not the result of whites' actions. If this notion of the irrelevance of discrimination were true, then blue-collar black workers and their families should face roughly the same social, economic, political, and housing conditions as similar blue-collar whites. This is definitely *not* the case, however. Because of past and present racial discrimination, blue-collar black families as a rule do not live in integrated neighborhoods with comparable white families. Blue-collar black workers are less likely than comparable white workers to receive unemployment compensation when unemployed. They tend to hold lower-paying and less secure jobs than otherwise comparable whites. They face much more discrimination at the hands of the police and other white officials than do comparable whites. Past discrimination, coupled with blatant, subtle, and covert discrimination today, is the demonstrable reason for much of the unemployment, underemployment, and housing difficulties faced by darker-skinned Americans today.[74]

WHITE REACTIONS TO EFFORTS TO REDUCE DISCRIMINATION

Negative White Attitudes

A majority of African Americans in surveys report experiencing discrimination in various sectors of society. Most sense a hypocrisy in white commitments to "liberty and justice for all" and to equal rights and opportunities, which they view accurately as a long way from being achieved. One survey of young Americans discovered that the majority of black youth thought racial relations in this country were "generally bad," and they were more likely than whites to see racial relations as getting worse.[75]

In contrast, many whites, including corporate, government, and academic leaders, view racial discrimination as no longer serious. In an influential book, the conservative George Gilder made common arguments that there is no need for government action to assist Americans of color today for two reasons: (1) It is virtually impossible to find in a position of power a seriously racist white person; and (2) Discrimination has already been effectively abolished in this country.[76] Similarly, in a 1990s book, *The End of Racism,* Dinesh D'Souza, an Asian Indian immigrant whose career has been fostered by white-run conservative organizations, argues that discrimination no longer creates widespread barriers for most African Americans. Echoing white conservatives, D'Souza calls for dismantling antidiscrimination efforts in the United States.[77]

Recent opinion surveys find that most whites are not sympathetic to aggressive government or private-sector programs designed to eradicate racial discrimination and inequalities. While there is majority support for mild or reduced affirmative action, more than half of the white respondents in one major survey said that the equal rights struggle had been pushed too far.[78] Other surveys show that the majority believe black Americans have fully equal opportunities. In a survey for the National Conference of Christians and Jews, 69 percent of whites felt that black Americans currently have an equal opportunity for a quality education, 63 percent believed black Americans have equal opportunities for skilled jobs, and a majority felt blacks have an equal chance to get decent housing.[79] Indeed, most white Americans believe that there is "reverse discrimination." A 1998 survey found that about two-thirds of whites said it was "very" or "somewhat" likely that "a white person won't get a job or promotion while an equally or less qualified black person gets one instead."[80]

White Supremacists and Hate Crimes

The Ku Klux Klan (KKK), racist "skinheads," and other white supremacists have increased in number in recent years and have been involved in deaths of people of color. Many are white men who suffer unemployment because of technological innovations or corporate downsizing, yet they blame people of color, Jews, or immigrants of color. In 1982, two unemployed white autoworkers beat to death a Chinese American engineer, Vincent Chin. They accused Chin of being Japanese and responsible for unemployment of U.S. autoworkers. Recently, white supremacists have engaged in hate crimes against Arabs and Muslims in retaliation for terrorist attacks on September 11, 2001. Anti-Muslim incidents increased by nearly 70 percent in 2003.[81] This violence has included physical assaults, arson, vandalism of places of worship and other property damage, death threats, and public harassment. Violence directed at Middle Eastern people has claimed at least three lives, and police investigators suspect white supremacists have murdered other people because of anti-Muslim prejudices.[82]

Openly racist groups often believe in Nazi-type doctrines of racial superiority. Some have secret camps where members are put through paramilitary training for what they term "survival." One speaker at an Aryan World Congress urged his listeners to stockpile weapons in preparation for "race war."[83] Some 708 white supremacist and other hate groups operate now in the United States.[84] The extremism of these groups may be escalating with the use of "lone wolf" activities (small cells or individuals acting alone), use of the Internet to disseminate information, and utilization of "white power" music as a recruiting tool.[85] Attacks on people of color by terroristic white supremacists (like Ku Klux Klan members) have occurred since the Civil War, but whites still refuse to officially end such terrorist organizations or recognize their long-term effects on black communities. The worst racial terrorism by whites, many of them KKK members since 1900, took place in Tulsa, Oklahoma, in May 1921. An Oklahoma Commission (2001) report revealed that at least 300 black Tulsans were killed by whites and buried in an unmarked grave. More than a thousand black homes, businesses, churches, and schools were destroyed. Thousands were left homeless. In 2005, the Supreme Court dismissed a class-action suit by surviving black victims seeking compensation from the city of Tulsa and the state of Oklahoma. The high court's dismissal let stand a lower court ruling that a two-year statute of limitations on claims expired in 1923, even though most white judges on the segregated courts of Oklahoma were then white supremacists. One of the plaintiffs' lawyers concluded: "If these victims were white . . . no one would be arguing that they be denied an opportunity to have their case heard."[86]

The first conviction of KKK members for racial violence did not occur until the late 1980s. In 1981 in Mobile, Alabama, Klan members lynched Michael Donald. Donald's family sued the United Klans of America and won a $7 million award. Texas authorities convicted Shawn Allen Berry, John William King, and Russell Brewer, Jr., of capital murder in the killing of James Byrd, Jr., a father of three living on a pension. On June 7, 1998, Byrd accepted a ride with these white men, who took him to the outskirts of Jasper, Texas, beat him, and harnessed him to a truck and dragged him three miles. Police found Byrd's head and right arm a mile away from his shoes. Media reports point out that white supremacist culture had influenced King and Brewer while they were in a Texas prison. After Byrd's death, members of the KKK marched in Jasper and stated that the town "is part of the invisible empire. Make no mistake about it, this is Klan country."[87]

Members of hate groups carry out racial crimes. Victims of hate-inspired crimes reported 7,462 incidents to police in 2002, including 11 hate-motivated murders. White attackers targeting Americans of color or Jewish Americans carried out most crimes. Bias-motivated acts against black Americans make up more than two-thirds of hate crimes against people of color, and hate crimes against Jewish Americans are two-thirds of anti-religious crimes. Nearly half of all violent hate incidents take place in California, New York, New Jersey, Massachusetts, and Michigan. About one in ten hate crimes occurs in schools and colleges. Some 12 percent of all students ages 12 to 18, including many students of color, report that someone at school has used hate words against them.[88] The Simon Wiesenthal Center has found that of the 4,000 online hate sites, more than 200 involve online games that allow children to "shoot" illegal immigrants, Jews, and blacks.[89]

The number of hate-motivated incidents in 2002 represented a decrease in hate crimes over the record figure of 9,726 in 2001. However, official figures are undercounts. While the Hate Crimes Statistics Act authorizes the FBI to collect hate crime data from police agencies, agency compliance is voluntary.[90] Many other jurisdictions consistently report no, or few, hate crimes.[91] Of the 17,784 state and local law enforcement agencies in the United States, only 68 percent participated in the hate crime data

collection program as of 2002, and of those participating only 15.5 percent actually submitted hate crime incident reports to the FBI. It is likely that the actual number of hate crimes is *several times* the officially reported number.

These bias-motivated crimes may be encouraged, at least indirectly, by some police agencies' insensitivity to criminal activity directed at racial and ethnic groups. As one scholar points out, "[t]oo frequently . . . victims of bias-motivated vandalism, hateful graffiti, threats, or assaults do not receive the police attention they merit."[92] Many victims of bias-motivated crimes fail to report hate crime incidents to police agencies because the victims fear reprisals from the police institutions designed to protect people against those very crimes. Because the criminal justice system has not fully institutionalized an antihate orientation within its judicial ranks, antihate efforts have often been ineffective in bringing justice to most victims of hate crimes. For example, undocumented immigrants are unlikely to report hate crimes out of fear that an investigation would reveal that they are in the country illegally and that local police agencies would turn them over for deportation. Another problem with reporting hate crimes is that many police officers do not understand what constitutes a hate crime, particularly white line officers who tend to be cynical about bias-motivated crimes. For example, when a black gay man reported to officers of the Los Angeles Police Department that white skinheads had beaten and stabbed him, white officers actually ridiculed him by calling him names, pulled on his earrings, and told him the attack was his fault.[93]

Prosecutors, who are overwhelmingly white, are extremely selective in choosing which hate crimes to prosecute.[94] In 1997, the U.S. Justice Department prosecuted only 22 of the 8,049 reported hate crimes that year.[95] The next year, law enforcement officia ecuted just six cases involving 13 defendants belonging to KKK and other organized hate groups. This weak enforcement of bias crimes laws likely results from the exclusion of disfavored groups in law enforcement, prosecutorial discretion, and overt or unconscious racial prejudice.[96] Judicial bias also underscores the problem of accountability for hate crimes. In the case of the murder of Vincent Chin, the County Circuit Judge, Charles Kaufman, sentenced the murderers only to *three years probation* and fines for each of $3,000 (plus modest legal fees), after only hearing arguments from defense attorneys and not from the state prosecutor. Kaufman allowed the defendants to "repay their debt" to society in small monthly payments. The judge justified the lenient sentence this way: "These [aren't] the kind of men you send to jail. We're talking here about a man who's held down a responsible job with the same company for seventeen or eighteen years and his son who is employed and is a part-time student. . . . These men are not going to go out and harm somebody else. I just [don't] think that putting them in prison [will] do any good for them or for society. . . . You don't make the punishment fit the crime; you make the punishment fit the criminal."[97] Also, in the recording and enforcement of bias crimes, persons of color seem to be more likely to be reported, arrested, convicted, and punished as bias-criminals than whites—the problem of "disproportionate-enforcement."[98] Black Americans, who are about 12 percent of the population, are overrepresented in relation to their representation in the U.S. population, and non-Hispanic whites are underrepresented, as reported hate crime offenders.[99]

Regarding racist speech, the U.S. Supreme Court made it more difficult to enforce hate crime laws in its 1992 decision, *R.A.V. v. St. Paul.*[100] The case stemmed from the conviction of several white skinheads who burned a cross inside the fenced yard of a black family. A local ordinance prohibited display of any symbol, such as a burning cross, that is known to arouse significant anger, alarm, or resentment because of race, color, creed, religion, or gender. The court rejected the ordinance because it prohibited both protected and unprotected speech. A year later, in *Wisconsin v. Mitchell,* however, the court did uphold the constitutionality of enhancing penalties for crimes in which perpetrators intentionally target victims because of race, religion, sexual orientation, gender, or ethnicity.[101]

Contexts of White Supremacist Groups

Across the United States, white supremacist groups rise and fall depending on the support or indifference they receive from the rest of whites in particular communities. Influential whites, such as those in business or government, who talk strongly about the need to dismantle equal opportunity and affirmative action programs often thereby give some legitimacy to the more extreme racism of white supremacist groups. In this atmosphere, whites often label the modest government affirmative action and equal opportunity efforts that still exist as *reverse discrimination.* Yet the phrase is inaccurate and oxymoronic. Think for a moment about the nearly four-centuries-old patterns of well-institutionalized discrimination against African Americans, first in slavery, then in brutal legal segregation, and now in extensive patterns of informal racial discrimination. Antiblack discrimination has meant—and still means—*widespread* blatant, subtle, and covert discrimination directed by many whites against many black Americans in most organizations in all the major institutional areas of this society—in

Vindicating Civil Rights–Era Cases: Retrying Segregationists for Decades-Old Murders

Since the late 1980s, prosecutors in southern states have revisited old cases involving racial killings of civil rights leaders and activists by white segregationists during the civil rights struggles of the 1950s and 1960s. In some cases, the prosecutions of these decades-old murders have resulted in convictions and prison sentences for white segregationists.

Most recently, the U.S. Department of Justice reopened the investigation of the murder of Emmett Louis Till, a 14-year-old black teenager murdered by white men in 1955 for allegedly whistling at a white girl in a store in Money, Mississippi, while visiting from Chicago. Till was not a civil rights activist, but his murder became an early catalyst for the civil rights movement. Authorities charged Roy Bryant and his half brother J.W. Miliam for Till's murder, but an all-white jury acquitted both men. After his acquittal, Miliam admitted to a *Look* magazine reporter in 1956 to beating Till, shooting him in the head, and then tying a heavy metal fan to the body and dumping it in the Tallahatchie River. Both men are now deceased, but the Justice Department claims others still living may have been involved in the killing.

In 2001, an Alabama jury convicted Thomas Blanton, Jr., after prosecutors reopened a case involving the 1963 dynamite bombing of the 16th Street Baptist Church in Birmingham, Alabama, that killed four young black girls, ages 11 to 14: Denise McNair, Carole Robertson, Cynthia Wesley, and Addie Mae Collins. The church had been the center of civil rights activities in Birmingham. An FBI investigation of the young girls' deaths found Robert E. Chambliss had ordered the bombing in response to a school desegregation order. In 1971, Alabama prosecutors reopened the case and a state court convicted Chambliss in 1977 for

his part in the bombing and sentenced him to prison, where he died in 1985. Investigators reexamined the case again in 1980 and 1988 but made no arrests. In response to community pressure, the FBI reopened the case a third time in 1995 and indicted Blanton and accomplice Bobby Frank Cherry in 2000. An Alabama court declared Cherry incompetent to stand trial but convicted Blanton of first-degree murder. Blanton is presently serving a life sentence with the possibility of parole at a state correctional facility. In January 2002, a circuit court judge reversed the order that held Cherry incompetent, and in May 2002 an Alabama jury convicted Cherry for his role in the killings.

In 1994, Hinds County district attorney Bobby DeLaughter in Jackson, Mississippi, finally won a conviction against Byron De La Beckwith for the 1963 murder of NAACP Field Secretary Medgar Evers. As an outspoken proponent of desegregation in Mississippi, Evers had become a target of white supremacists. Two all-white jury trials in 1964 ended in hung juries, and the case lay dormant for 25 years until newspaper reporters researched the activities of a now-disbanded secret organization known as the Mississippi State Sovereignty Commission. The researchers discovered documents showing jury tampering and official misconduct in Beckwith's second trial. Officials reindicted Beckwith in 1990, and he received a life sentence in prison where he died in 2001.

One night in 1966, the Imperial Wizard of the White Knights of the Ku Klux Klan, Sam Bowers, along with accomplices, firebombed the home of Vernon Dahmer, president of the Harrisburg, Mississippi, NAACP. Dahmer was a grocery store owner who encouraged blacks to vote and let

continued on next page

them pay their "poll taxes" at the store. Dahmer died when he stayed in the burning house and engaged in a shootout with the Klansmen while his family escaped to safety out a back window. Prosecutors indicted Bowers for Dahmer's murder, but Mississippi juries acquitted him twice. Then, in August 1998, prosecutors reindicted Bowers and a Forrest County trial court convicted him and sentenced him to life imprisonment. Bowers is an inmate at the Central Mississippi Correctional Facility in Pearl, Mississippi.

In 1964 civil rights workers Michael Schwerner, Andrew Goodman, and James Chaney were involved in a black voter registration drive in Mississippi. While driving to Meridian in Neshoba County one evening, a local deputy stopped and arrested the three. Released a short time later, some 22 Klansmen stopped the car again and shot and killed all three. The Klansmen buried their bodies beneath an earthen dam in Philadelphia, Mississippi. FBI agents found the bodies about a month later. Federal prosecutors eventually charged 19 of the Klansmen with conspiracy and civil rights violations after state prosecutors refused to move on the case for lack of evidence. Although there were three mistrials in state courts, a federal district court in Mississippi convicted seven of the Klansmen. The longest sentence im-posed on any of the Klansmen was six years. In 2000, Mississippi Attorney General Mike Moore announced his plan to reopen the case and prosecute those responsible for the murders. As yet, Mississippi officials have not formally reopened the case.

One of the earliest cases reopened by state investigators involved the killing of civil rights activists Harry and Harriette Moore in Mims, Florida. In 1934, Harry Moore founded the Brevard County chapter of the NAACP, and in March 1938 he filed the first lawsuit in the Deep South to bring parity pay to black public school teachers who were paid half the salaries of white teachers. Moore was active in organizing black voters, and in 1944 he investigated the lynching of 15-year-old Willie James Howard who had sent a Christmas card to the daughter of a white former state legislator. In 1951, Klansmen active in Florida bombed the Moore home, killing Harry Moore instantly and seriously injuring his wife Harriette, who died eight days later. A federal grand jury in Miami handed down perjury indictments in 1953 against seven Klansmen after an initial investigation in 1951 and 1952, but officials never made any arrests in the case. State prosecutors reopened the case in 1978 and again in 1991, but they finally closed the case in 1992 for lack of evidence.

Sources: Eric Lichtblau and Andrew Jacobs, "U.S. Reopens '55 Murder Case, Flashpoint of Civil Rights Era," *New York Times,* May 11, 2004, p. 1; "Justice for Four Little Girls," *The Washington Post,* May 24, 2002, p. A34; "Byron De La Beckwith, 80, Dies; Assassinated Medgar Evers in '63," *The Washington Post,* January 23, 2001, p. B6; "Chances Dimming for Trials in Civil Rights-Era Slayings," *The Houston Chronicle,* January 22, 2002, p. 1; *Freedom Never Dies, The Legacy of Harry T. Moore* (visited on May 19, 2004), available at www.pbs.org/harrymoore/harry/mbio.html.

workplaces, residential neighborhoods, housing, schools, health institutions, and the legal system. For nearly four centuries now, many *millions* of whites have participated directly or indirectly in discrimination against millions of black Americans, including the often routinized discrimination imbedded in the large-scale organizations that dominate this society.

Think, in turn, about what the *reverse* of this well-institutionalized, antiblack discrimination would look like. The reverse would mean something like the following: For several hundred years, massive institutionalized discrimination and segregation would be directed by most African Americans against most white Americans. Many traditionally white organizations in key institutional areas such as housing, education, and employment would be run at the top by a disproportionate number of black Americans; and middle- and lower-level decision makers in most major organizations would be disproportionately black. These black decision makers would aim much everyday discrimination at whites, who would be disproportionately in lower-status positions. As a result, many millions of whites would have suffered billions upon billions of dollars in economic losses, lower wages, unemployment, political exclusion, housing segregation, inferior school facilities, and many violent lynchings. That societal condition would be something one could reasonably call a condition of real "reverse discrimination." It does not exist, nor is it likely ever to exist in the United States.

Black Protests against Racial Discrimination and Poverty

Many African Americans, not surprisingly, have periodically expressed anger about the pace of racial change. In the 1960s and 1970s, many nonviolent protests and numerous revolts and riots occurred across the United States, as a new generation of proud African Americans became more willing to engage in aggressive protest against systemic racism. The underlying socioeconomic problems that generate demonstrations, revolts, and riots persist to the present day. In major riots in Miami in 1980, black residents lashed out against the police and the larger white society with extensive burning and looting of stores. Three days of angry rioting took 16 lives, injured 400, and caused more than $100 million in property damage.[102] More black revolts occurred in Miami between 1982 and 1991, all triggered by incidents involving white police officers shooting to death an African American or being acquitted for such a killing. More recently, racial riots generated by police actions in neighborhoods plagued by poverty, high unemployment, and racial discrimination occurred in Cincinnati. There, in 2001, many black citizens protested nonviolently and violently after a white police officer killed an unarmed black man fleeing to avoid arrest on misdemeanor charges. One underlying reason for the protests was that Cincinnati police had killed 14 other African Americans in encounters over the previous six years. Since the 2001 killing, police have killed four more black men.[103] In addition, in 2003 strong protests erupted in Benton Harbor, Michigan, after a black man lost control of his speeding motorcycle and crashed into a building while being chased by a white officer. Black citizens had long complained about police harassment in white communities nearby.[104]

In Los Angeles in the spring of 1992, the acquittal on charges of police brutality of four officers who had been videotaped in the process of beating an unarmed black man, Rodney King, triggered the most serious urban rebellion of the twentieth century. After several days of rioting, police arrested more than 10,000 blacks and Latinos, and more than 50 people had been killed. Property damage exceeded $1 billion dollars. The events in Los Angeles triggered nonviolent protests and rioting in other cities. As in the 1960s' rebellions against racism, underlying conditions triggering this L.A. uprising included serious unemployment and severely inadequate housing conditions.[105]

Police malpractice, especially commonplace brutality against black (and Latino) men and women, has precipitated or accelerated many protests and riots. Police malpractice and brutality targeting African Americans remain a major problem. In one nationwide poll, nearly 80 percent of the black respondents said that in most cities the police did not treat black residents as fairly as white residents.[106] Numerous black communities have reported instances of serious police malpractice and brutality. In 1997, some New York police officers were involved in torturing Abner Louima, a Haitian immigrant, who was handcuffed in a police station restroom. One police witness said another officer thrust a stick into Louima's rectum, causing severe damage to his body.[107] Several officers were tried for aiding in the torture and cover-up. Then, in 1999 another unarmed black man, Amadou Diallo, was riddled with 19 bullets by New York City officers as he tried to show them his wallet. The officers claimed they thought he was reaching for a gun in his back pocket.[108] In a subsequent trial, the officers were found not guilty, yet many observers wondered would the officers have been so quick to shoot at Diallo as he reached for his wallet if he had been white. This shooting of an unarmed black man led to numerous civil rights demonstrations in several East Coast cities.[109]

Given this historical background of commonplace police brutality and other malpractice, the majority of black men and women see white police officers as a possible source of danger and death. In contrast, most whites see the police as protectors of personal safety.[110]

Since the 1954 *Brown* decision the tree of racial justice and equality has grown much too slowly.

THE ISSUE OF CONTEMPORARY IMMIGRATION

If current population trends continue, by the middle of the twenty-first century the typical resident of the United States will not be a European American but rather a Native American or a person who traces her or his ancestry mainly to Asia, Latin America, Africa, or the Middle East. Already, a majority of the residents of many major cities, such as Miami, New York, and Los Angeles, are Americans of color, and majorities of the populations of California and Texas (the largest states in population) are now black, Latino, and Asian American. Unfortunately, much discussion of these demographic changes among white Americans has an alarmist tone, perhaps because many whites fear a loss of power and privilege to people of color.

Millions of immigrants, most of them from Asian and Latin American countries, have entered the United States in the last two decades. The 2000 U.S. Census counted nearly 29 million immigrants living in metropolitan regions throughout the United States, up by 10 million since 1990. Many U.S. citizens vigorously oppose these new immigrants: nativists such as members of the Ku Klux Klan, many political conservatives, some unions, and even some political liberals. Some union leaders fear that immigrants are taking away jobs from native-born Americans. Political conservatives and nativists often express fears that immigrants are destroying the values and moral fiber of the "real America."

Ironically, in the early decades of the twentieth century the hated immigrants were white people from southern and eastern European countries. Indeed, the 1924 Immigration Act established discriminatory quotas that curtailed the number of immigrants from southern and eastern Europe and excluded Asian immigrants. It wasn't until 1965 that these explicitly racist quotas were eliminated. Recent immigration acts passed in 1965, 1986, and 1990 have no exclusionary national-origin quotas but do limit the number of new immigrants who can come to the United States from any one country. The 1986 Immigration Reform and Control Act was intended to restrict the flow of immigrants from south of the border. The 1990 Immigration Act set the annual limit of all immigrants at 675,000 after 1994. This limit most affects immigrants from those countries, such as certain Asian countries, in which many people now wish to come to the United States. This limited immigration also contrasts with the generally unlimited immigration allowed from Europe before the 1910s.[111]

Many native-born Americans are concerned about whether the country can successfully take in large numbers of immigrants. Anti-immigrant activists worry about the impact of this immigration on public schools, public social programs, and workplaces. Advocates of immigration restriction have suggested that new immigrants are a major threat to the jobs of many of those already here or that they are likely to become public charges.[112] Interestingly, these were arguments made against European immigrants in the early twentieth century by earlier anti-immigrant activists.

Immigration from Asia and Latin America is not creating a dramatic population expansion like that created by white European immigrants in the early twentieth century. The ratio of immigrants to native-born population is *much lower* today than in the early twentieth century. Given this country's long history of successful absorption of immigrants and its great geographical size, new immigrants are not likely to overwhelm the United States. In contrast to opponents of current immigration levels, one prominent demographer has argued that immigrants make mostly positive contributions: As a group, immigrants are "upwardly mobile, ambitious, saving; they have traditional values, care about their children. . . .

They've done something very dramatic to upgrade themselves."[113] Immigrants are mostly hardworking and seek to make a good life for themselves.

Implicit or explicit in discussions by many whites of immigration is a basically racist concern that immigrants from Asia and Latin America are somehow not compatible with the image of a substantially white, European American core culture and society that the nativists wish to protect. (Few white critics of immigration ever condemn continuing immigration from Europe!) Popular magazines have run major stories asking "What will America be like when whites are no longer the majority?" *Forbes* editor Peter Brimelow, a U.S. business leader and himself an immigrant from Britain, has articulated this anti-immigrant perspective. In his book *Alien Nation,* he argues for the exclusion of immigrants, contending that "The American nation has always had a specific ethnic core. And that core has been white." As late as 1950, most Americans "looked like me. That is, they were of European stock. And in those days, they had another name for this thing dismissed so contemptuously as 'the racial hegemony of white Americans.' They called it 'America.'"[114] Some white business and political leaders now openly assert that the country is becoming too non-European and must return to the earlier situation of encouraging only or mostly whites to immigrate. In the view of many anti-immigrant advocates, indeed, it is time that the long era of immigration to the United States ended. However, significant opposition to nativist and racist views of immigration exists in all regions of the United States, and it is unlikely that the great American experiment as a "nation of immigrants" will be ended in the near future.

SUMMARY

From the beginning, *racial stratification* and racial exploitation have been fundamental features of U.S. society. Racial stratification, with groups of white European origin at the top and groups of African, Latino, or Native American descent farther down the ladder of power and resources, is a central feature today, just as it has been for centuries.

Ideological racism, with its view of physical characteristics being linked to cultural characteristics and its emphasis on superior and inferior racial groups, has developed extensively in the United States and overseas since the nineteenth century. The lack of scientific support for racist ideologies has not prevented them from having a substantial impact. Today, almost all social scientists see a *racial group* not as a part of the natural order of the universe but as a social category that persons outside the set-apart group have decided is important to single out on the basis of subjectively selected physical traits. Even white immigrant groups, such as Italian and Polish Americans, were singled out as inferior racial groups in the early twentieth century. Today, moreover, Americans of color are still defined by whites as racially different and are singled out for a range of acts of *discrimination,* which have often been institutionalized.

Most new European colonies in the Americas had their origins in violence, and from the beginning the relations between whites and people of color were exploitative, in substantial part because of the goals of the growing agricultural and commercial capitalist system. Today's racial relations have roots in an early history when Native Americans were driven off desirable lands and Africans were enslaved to provide a source of labor for capital accumulation by agricultural and commercial capitalists in the new country.

Today, African Americans are still a racially subordinated group in the United States. From the days of slavery to the present, they have suffered from routine and extensive discrimination in the workplace, housing, education, health care, politics, and other institutional areas. In recent decades black gains in occupational advancement have been offset by the continuing white gains in occupational advancement, by the high black unemployment rate relative to that of whites, by the persisting differential in family wealth favoring whites over blacks, and by an extensive array of discriminatory practices in areas such as employment and housing.

Other Americans of color, such as Latino, Asian, and Native Americans (and, most recently, Middle Eastern Americans), have also faced exploitation and discrimination at the hands of white Americans, both ordinary whites and those in the elites. Like African Americans, they too have often endured problems of poverty, low-wage jobs, high unemployment rates, low incomes, and discrimination in housing. Over the next several decades, the numbers of Americans of Asian and Latin American descent will likely continue to grow, to the point that together with other Americans of color they will likely become a majority of the U.S. population by the 2050s.

Some changes came in the patterns of institutional racism with the civil rights movement and civil rights laws of the 1960s, yet since the 1970s there has been a decrease in the commitment of a majority of whites to reducing racial discrimination and racial inequalities for Americans of color. In recent years most white policymakers and corporate officials have turned away from aggressive equal opportunity efforts, and many have even denied that white-generated racism is still a serious problem. Significantly, a century ago the expansion of opportunities for African Americans during the Reconstruction period after the Civil War was followed by a dramatic resurgence of racist organizations, racial conservatism, and legal segregation for most African Americans. While there are major differences between that reactionary period and the present era of backtracking, today we are indeed in an era when most white political and economic leaders have lost interest in guaranteeing or expanding truly equal opportunities for African Americans and other Americans of color in employment, education, housing, and politics.

This situation of continuing great inequalities along racial lines, and of white denial, is not stable. Many Americans of color are angry about the mistreatment they still face at the hands of white Americans, and some continue to protest, often aggressively, against the racial discrimination and oppression they continue to encounter. The future will likely bring greater, and organized, protests against racial and ethnic discrimination across the United States.

STUDY QUESTIONS

1. In what specific ways did the U.S. Constitution recognize racial subordination?
2. Explain the idea of ideological racism, and describe the social and intellectual climate in which it emerged.
3. Throughout most of the nineteenth century, there was a distinct split in the labor markets between the North and the South. What produced this split, and what did it mean for the workers in each regional market?

4. Compare rates of unemployment, poverty, and income levels for black Americans with those of white Americans.

5. Discrimination in the United States has taken several identifiably distinct forms. Using illustrations, describe the several types presented in the text.

6. What are some of the specific mechanisms that have led to housing discrimination and segregation for blacks in the United States?

ENDNOTES

1. Leonard Dinnerstein and Frederic C. Jaher, eds., Introduction to *The Aliens* (New York: Appleton-Century-Crofts, 1970), p. 4. Portions of this chapter have been adapted from Joe R. Feagin, *Racial and Ethnic Relations,* 5th ed. (Upper Saddle River, N.J.: Prentice Hall, 1996), pp. 1–58, 234–328.

2. Quoted in Peter M. Bergman, *The Chronological History of the Negro in America* (New York: Harper and Row, 1969), p. 52.

3. John Hope Franklin, *From Slavery to Freedom,* 2nd ed. (New York: Alfred A. Knopf, 1963), pp. 141–143.

4. Ibid., p. 143. For discussions on more implicit recognitions of slavery in the U.S. Constitution, see A. Leon Higginbotham, Jr., *Shades of Freedom: Racial Politics and Presumptions of the American Legal Process* (New York: Oxford University Press, 1996), pp. 220–21, note 30; William M. Wiecek, *The Sources of Antislavery Constitutionalism in America, 1760–1848* (New York: Cornell University Press, 1977), pp. 62–63.

5. Wilton M. Krogman, "The Concept of Race," in *The Science of Man in the World of Crisis,* Ralph Linton, ed. (New York: Columbia University Press, 1945), p. 38.

6. *The Oxford International Dictionary of the English Language* (Toronto: Leland, 1957), p. 1,646.

7. Thomas F. Gossett, *Race* (New York: Schocken Books, 1965), p. 3.

8. Pierre L. Van den Berghe, *Race and Racism* (New York: John Wiley, 1967), p. 11.

9. Oliver C. Cox, *Caste, Class, and Race* (Garden City, N.Y.: Doubleday, 1948), p. 402. See also Van den Berghe, *Race and Racism,* p. 9.

10. Kenneth L. Roberts, "Why Europe Leaves Home," reprinted in "Kenneth L. Roberts and the Threat of Mongrelization in America, 1922," *In This Place,* Lewis H. Carlson and George A. Colburn, eds. (New York: John Wiley, 1972), p. 312.

11. See Milton M. Gordon, *Assimilation in American Life* (New York: Oxford University Press, 1964), pp. 71–108.

12. Cox, *Caste, Class, and Race,* p. 332.

13. Robert L. Allen, *Reluctant Reformers* (Washington, D.C.: Howard University Press, 1974), p. 225. This paragraph draws heavily on Allen.

14. Cox, *Caste, Class, and Race,* pp. 333–44.

15. U.S. Bureau of the Census, *Overview of Race Hispanic Origin* (March 2001), available at www.census.gov/prod/2001pubs/c2kbr01-1.pdf.

16. Apparently some of the early Africans forcibly imported were treated more like indentured servants than the slaves all would soon become. See William M. Wieneck, "The Origins of the Law of Slavery in British North America," *Cardozo Law Review* 17 (1996), pp. 1,711–92.

17. Ibid., p. 354; Cox, *Caste, Class, and Race,* p. 475.

18. Michael Perelman, *Farming for Profit in a Hungry World* (New York: Universe Books, 1977), p. 26.

19. Allen, *Reluctant Reformers,* p. 254.

20. Ibid., pp. 170–71.

21. Ibid., p. 264.

22. U.S. Bureau of the Census, *Negroes in the U.S., 1920–1932* (Washington, D.C.: 1935), p. 289; also Gunnar Myrdal, *An American Dilemma* (New York: McGraw-Hill, 1964), pp. 1, 340–42.

23. Joe R. Feagin and Harlan Hahn, *Ghetto Revolts* (New York: Macmillan, 1973), pp. 6–50; also Allen, *Reluctant Reformers,* pp. 166–67.

24. W. E. B. Du Bois, *Black Reconstruction in America 1860–1880* (New York: Atheneum, 1992 [1935]).

25. Selma James et al., *Sex, Race and Class* (Bristol, England: Falling Wall Press, 1975), p. 6.

26. U.S. Bureau of the Census, *The Social and Economic Status of the Black Population in the U.S., 1971* (Washington, D.C.: 1972), p. 52; Andrew F. Brimmer, *The Economic Position of Black*

Americans, 1976 (Washington, D.C.: National Commission for Manpower Policy, 1976), p. 13; U.S. Bureau of the Census, *Statistical Abstract of the U.S.: 1991* (Washington, D.C.: 1992), p. 402; U.S. Bureau of Labor Statistics, *Employment and Earnings,* January 1996, p. 164.; U.S. Bureau of Labor Statistics, *Labor Force Statistics for Current Population Reports,* 2002, available at data.bls.gov/cgi-bin/surveymost?ln.

27. U.S. Bureau of Labor Statistics, *Current Population Survey* (October 2003), available at ftp.bls.gov/pub/suppl/empsit.cpseea17.txt.

28. U.S. Bureau of the Census, *The Black Population in the U.S.: March 1994 and 1993, Current Population Reports,* P20–480 (Washington, D.C.: 1995), p. 19.

29. U.S. Bureau of the Census, *The Social and Economic Status of the Black Population in the U.S., 1971,* p. 29; U.S. Bureau of the Census, *Statistical Abstract of the United States: 1991,* p. 454; U.S. Bureau of the Census, *Statistical Abstract of the United States: 1995* (Washington, D.C.: 1995), p. 474; U.S. Bureau of the Census, *Household Income by Race and Hispanic Origin and Income Definition* (September 2003), available at www.census.gov/prod/2003pubs/p60–221.pdf. The census category *nonwhite* consists mostly of blacks.

30. Bernadette D. Porter and Joseph Daleker, U.S. Bureau of the Census, *Current Population Reports,* P60–219, *Poverty in the United States: 2001* (Washington, D.C: U.S. Government Printing Office, September 2002), available at www.census.gov/prod/2002pubs/p60–219.pdf.

31. U.S. Bureau, Census of the *Current Population Reports* (March 2002), available at ferret.bls.census.gov/macro/032002/pov/new01_006.htm.

32. U.S. Bureau of the Census, *The Black Population in the United States: March 1994 and 1993,* pp. 11, 21, 25, 76; U.S. Bureau of the Census, *Statistical Abstract of the U.S., 1995,* p. 484.

33. White category includes "Whites Not of Hispanic Origin." Percentage totals for white households probably do not add up to 100 percent due to rounding. See U.S. Bureau of the Census, *Percent Distribution of Household Net Worth, by Amount of Net Worth and Selected Characteristics: 2000,* Table 4 (last revised June 4, 2003), available at www.census.gov/hhes/www/wealth/1998_2000/wlth00-4.html.

34. This is her middle-level estimate. See Trina Williams, "The Homestead Act—Our Earliest National Asset Policy," paper presented at the Center for Social Development's symposium, Inclusion in Asset Building, St. Louis, Missouri, September 21–23, 2000.

35. See Joe R. Feagin, *Racist America* (New York: Routledge, 2000), pp. 181–184.

36. Charles Hamilton and Kwame Ture (Stokely Carmichael), *Black Power* (New York: Random House, 1967), p. 4; see also Anthony Downs, *Racism in America and How to Combat It* (Washington, D.C.: U.S. Commission on Civil Rights, 1970), pp. 5–7; cf. Thomas Pettigrew, "Racism and the Mental Health of White Americans: A Social Psychological View," in *Racism in Mental Health,* C. V. Willie, B. S. Brown, and B. M. Kramer, eds. (Pittsburgh: University of Pittsburgh Press, 1973), p. 271.

37. Joe R. Feagin and Clairece Booher Feagin, *Discrimination American Style* (Englewood Cliffs, N.J.: Prentice Hall, 1978), pp. 1–40.

38. Lee Sigelman and Susan Welch, *Black Americans' Views of Racial Inequality* (Cambridge: Cambridge University Press, 1991), pp. 55–57.

39. Lawrence Bobo and Susan A. Suh, "Surveying Racial Discrimination: Analyses from a Multiethnic Labor Market," unpublished research report, Department of Sociology, University of California, Los Angeles, August 1, 1995.

40. National Opinion Research Center, *General Social Survey, 1994, 1998,* available at www.icpsr.umich.edu:8080/GSS/homepage.htm.

41. Lawrence Bobo, "Inequalities that Endure? Racial Ideology, American Politics, and the Peculiar Role of Social Sciences," paper presented at conference on "The Changing Terrain of Race and Ethnicity," University of Illinois, Chicago, Illinois, October 26, 2001.

42. National Opinion Research Center, *General Social Survey, 1998,* available at www.icpsr.umich.edu:8080/GSS/homepage.htm.

43. Anti-Defamation League, *Highlights from an Anti-Defamation League Survey on Racial Attitudes in America* (New York: ADL, 1993), pp. 18–25.

44. On social acceptability and prejudice generating discrimination, see Feagin, *Racist America,* Chapters 4–5.

45. See Joe R. Feagin and Karyn D. McKinney, *The Many Costs of Racism* (Lanham, Md.: Rowman & Littlefield, 2003), pp. 10–11.

46. See Feagin, *Racist America,* Chapter 5.

47. Margery Austin Turner, Michael Fix, and Raymond J. Struyk, *Opportunities Denied: Discrimination in Hiring* (Washington, D.C.: Urban Institute, 1991). Statistics of racial disparities, but not gender disparities, have helped to establish legal claims of employment discrimination. Katharine T. Bartlett, Angela P. Harris, and Deborah L. Rhode, *Gender and the Law: Theory, Doctrine, Commentary* (New York: Aspen Law and Business, 2002), p. 165.
48. Jacquelyn Scarville et al., *Armed Forces Equal Opportunity Survey* (Arlington, Va.: Defense Manpower Data Center, 1999), pp. 46–78; Office of the Under Secretary of Defense Personnel and Readiness, *Career Progression of Minority and Women Officers* (Washington, D.C.: Department of Defense, 1999), pp. 46–85.
49. Richard Morin and Michael H. Cottman, "Discrimination's Lingering Sting," *Washington Post,* June 22, 2001, p. A1.
50. Joe R. Feagin, "Black Americans Research Study," unpublished research manuscript, University of Texas, March 1989; *see also* Joe R. Feagin and Melvin P. Sikes, *Living with Racism: The Black Middle Class Experience* (Boston: Beacon Press, 1994), Chapters 4–5; and Yanick St. Jean and Joe R. Feagin, *Double Burden: Black Women and Everyday Racism* (New York: M. E. Sharpe, 1998).
51. See Feagin and Sikes, *Living with Racism,* Chapters 4–5.
52. Thomas Dye, *Who's Running America?* 4th ed. (Englewood Cliffs, N.J.: Prentice Hall, 1986), pp. 190–205.
53. "Most Powerful Black Executives: Fortune 500 Executives," *Fortune* (July 22, 2002), available at www.fortune.com/fortune/careers/articles/0,15114,368860,00.html.
54. Federal Glass Ceiling Commission, *Good for Business: Making Full Use of the Nation's Human Capital* (Washington, D.C.: March 1995), pp. 12, 60–61.
55. Kenneth B. Clark, "The Role of Race," *New York Times Magazine,* October 5, 1980, p. 30. See also Rosabeth M. Kanter, *Men and Women of the Corporation* (New York: Basic Books, 1977), pp. 186–87, 206–207, 238, 242.
56. Sharon Collins, "Blacks on the Bubble: The Vulnerability of Black Executives in White Corporations," *Sociologial Quarterly* 34 (August 1993): 429–447, see also Feagin and McKinney, *The Many Costs of Racism.*
57. See, Feagin and McKinney, *The Many Costs of Racism,* Chapters 2–4.
58. Richard Morin and Michael H. Cottman, "Discriminaiton's Lingering Sting," *Washington Post,* June 22, 2001, p. A1.
59. Kathy Ciotola, "Black Tourists Report Discrimination in Study," *Gainesville Sun,* October 2, 2001, pp. B1, B3.
60. See Feagin and Sikes, *Living with Racism, Passim.*
61. Sigelman and Welch, *Black Americans' Views of Racial Inequality,* pp. 57–59.
62. Margery Austin Turner, Stephen L. Ross, George C. Galster, and John Yinger, *Discrimination in Metropolitan Housing Markets,* The Urban Institute Metropolitan Housing and Communities Policy Center (November 2002), available at www.huduser.org/publications/hsgfin/hds.html.
63. "Civil Wrongs; As Blacks Go House Hunting, Too Often the Door Is Closed," *Chicago Tribune,* November 14, 1993, p. C1.
64. U.S. Department of Housing and Urban Development, Office of Policy Development and Research, *All Other Things Being Equal: A Paired Testing Study of Mortgage Lending Institutions* (April 2002), available at www.huduser.org/Publications/PDF/aotbe.pdf.
65. The "other" category includes Asian, Native Hawaiian or Pacific Islander, American Indian or Alaska Native (only one race reported), and two or more races. See U.S. Department of Commerce, Bureau of the Census, *Census Bureau Reports on Residential Vacancies and Homeownership,* Table 7: Homeownership Rates by Race and Ethnicity of Householder: 2001 to 2003, available at www.census.gov/hhes/www/housing/hvs/q303prss.pdf.
66. Brian Skoloff, "ACORN Study Says Racial Disparity in Lending Improving in PB," *Associated Press,* October 2, 2002.
67. "Mortgage Gouging: Blacks, Hispanics Pay Higher Rates," *The Dallas Morning News,* May 22, 2002.
68. National Opinion Research Center, *General Social Survey, 1998,* available at www.icpsr.umich.edu:8080/GSS/homepage.htm.
69. See discussion of older surveys in Gerald D. Jaynes and Robin Williams, Jr., eds., *A Common Destiny: Blacks and American Society* (Washington, D.C.: National Academy Press, 1989), pp. 144–46.

70. Douglas S. Massey and Nancy A. Denton, *American Apartheid: Segregation and the Making of the Underclass* (Cambridge: Harvard University Press, 1993), pp. 221–23.

71. Douglas S. Massey and Nancy A. Denton, "Trends in Segregation of Blacks, Hispanics and Asians, 1970–1980," *American Sociological Review* 52 (1987): 802–25.

72. Robert D. Bullard, *Dumping in Dixie: Race, Class and Environmental Quality* (Boulder, Colo.: Westview Press, 1990). See also Robert D. Bullard, "The Legacy of American Apartheid and Environmental Racism," *Saint John's Journal of Legal Commentary* 9 (1994): 445–474.

73. U.S. Bureau of the Census, "Racial and Ethnic Residential Segregation in the United States: 1980–2000" (August 2002), available at www.census.gov/hhes/www/housing/resseg/pdftoc.html; see also John R. Logan, *Separate and Unequal: The Neighborhood Gap for Blacks and Hispanics in Metropolitan America* (October 13, 2002), Lewis Mumford Center for Comparative Urban and Regional Research, University of Albany, available at mumford1.dyndns.org/cen2000/SepUneq/SUReport/SURepPage1.htm.

74. Joe R. Feagin and Clairece Booher Feagin, *Racial and Ethnic Relations,* 5th ed. (Upper Saddle River, N.J.: Prentice Hall, 1996), pp. 234–83.

75. People for the American Way, *Democracy's Next Generation II* (Washington, D.C.: People for the American Way, 1992), p. 63.

76. George Gilder, *Wealth and Poverty* (New York: Basic Books, 1981); see also George Gilder, "The Myths of Racial and Sexual Discrimination," *National Review* 3 (November 14, 1980): 1, 381–90.

77. Dinesh D'Souza, *The End of Racism* (New York: Free Press, 1995), pp. 177–81.

78. Richard L. Berke, "The 1994 Campaign; Survey Finds Voters in U.S. Rootless and Self-Absorbed," *New York Times,* September 21, 1994, p. A21.

79. "Survey Finds Minorities Resent Whites and Each Other," *Jet,* March 28, 1994, p. 14.

80. National Opinion Research Center, *General Social Survey, 1998,* available at www.icpsr.umich.edu:8080/GSS/homepage.htm.

81. "Anti-Muslim Incidents Rise, Study Finds," *Los Angeles Times,* May 3, 2004, pp. B1, B8.

82. Human Rights Watch, *We Are Not the Enemy: Hate Crimes Against Arabs, Muslims, and Those Perceived to Be Arab or Muslim after September 11* (November 2002), available at hrw.org/reports/2002/usahate/usa1102.pdf.

83. Klanwatch Intelligence Report, August 1995, pp. 1–2.

84. Southern Poverty Law Center Intelligence Project, "Active U.S. Hate Groups in 2002" (last visited January 2, 2004), available at www.splcenter.org/intel/map/hate.jsp.

85. Anti-Defamation League, *Extremism in America: Introduction* (last visited January 2, 2004), available at www.adl.org/learn/ext_us/default.asp.

86. Darryl Fears, "In Tulsa, Keeping Alive 1921's Painful Memory: Recognition, Reparations Sought for Race Riot, *The Washington Post* (May 31, 2005), p. A03.

87. John Turner, *The Ku Klux Klan: A History of Racism and Violence* (Montgomery, Ala.: Southern Poverty Law Center, 1982), pp. 48–56; "Blacks Face Off with Klan Marchers in Jasper, TX, Town where Black Man Was Dragged to Death," *Jet Magazine,* July 13, 1998, p. 14. See also Dina Temple-Raston, *A Death in Texas: A Story of Race, Murder, and a Small Town's Struggle for Redemption* (New York: Henry Holt and Company, 2002).

88. Federal Bureau of Investigation, *Crimes in the U.S., Section II* (last visited January 2, 2004), available at www.fbi.gov/ucr/cius_02/pdf/2sectiontwo.pdf; National Center for Educational Statistics, *Indicators of School Crime and Safety, 2003* (October 2003), available at nces.ed.gov/pubs2004/2004004.pdf. See also Robin Parker, "Bias Crime in Schools—An Uncivil Education," *The New Jersey Lawyer,* October 1998; "Reported Hate Crimes Decline in 1994," *Race Relations Reporter,* December 15, 1995, p. 1; "Reported Hate Crimes Rise in 1995," *Race Relations Reporter,* January 15, 1996, p. 1.

89. The Associated Press, "Report: Surge in Hate Web Sites Targeting Young," available at www.cnn.com/2004/TECH/internet/04/20/online.hate.ap/index.html.

90. In September 1994, Congress amended the 1990 Hate Crimes Statistics Act with the Violent Crime Control and Law Enforcement Act to include both physical and mental abilities, and gender-motivated violence, as factors in bias crimes. The 1996 Church Arson Prevention Act also mandated that the collection of hate crime data become a permanent part of the Uniform Crime Reports. The Hate Crimes Prevention Act of 1999 prohibits persons from interfering with another person's federal right by violence or threat of violence due to their race, color, religion, or national origin. This also extends the federal government's authority to investigate and prosecute hate crime offenders who committed their crimes because of perceived sexual orientation, gen-

der, or disability of the victim. See Federal Bureau of Investigation, *Crime in the U.S., Section II* (last visited January 2, 2004), available at www.fbi.gov/ucr/cius_02/pdf/2sectiontwo.pdf.

91. Southern Poverty Law Center, *Intelligence Project* (last visited January 2, 2004), available at www.splcenter.org/intel/hatewatch/fortherecord.jsp?s=AL.

92. Terry Maroney, "The Struggle Against Hate Crime: Movement at a Crossroads, *New York University Law Review* 73 (1998): 564–620.

93. "It's Time to Handcuff the Police," *Los Angeles Times,* April 26, 1995.

94. Kwei Yung Lee, "Race and Self-Defense: Toward a Normative Conception of Reasonableness," *Minnesota Law Review* 81 (1996): 367–500; Angela A. Davis, "Prosecution and Race: The Power and Privilege of Discretion," *Fordham Law Review* 67 (1998): 13–67; Sheri Lynn Johnson, "Racial Imagery in Criminal Cases," *Tulane Law Review* 67 (1993): 1,739–1,805; Anthony V. Alfieri, "Defending Racial Violence, *Columbia Law Review* 95 (1995): 1,301–1,342; Anthony V. Alfieri, "Race Trial," *Texas Law Review* 76 (1998): 1,293–1,369.

95. Michael Lieberman, "Statement of the Anti-Defamation League on Bias-Motivated Crime and the Hate Crimes Prevention Act," *Chicano–Latino Law Review* 21 (2000): 53–77.

96. Tanya Kateri Hernandez, "Bias Crimes: Unconscious Racism in the Prosecution of 'Racially Motivated Violence'," *Yale Law Journal* 99 (1990): 845–864.

97. Rhonda J. Yen, "Racial Stereotyping of Asians and Asian Americans and Its Effect on Criminal Justice: A Reflection on the Wayne Lo Case," *Asian Law Journal* 7 (2000): 1–28, at p. 11.

98. Frederick M. Lawrence, "Enforcing Bias-Crime Laws Without Bias: Evaluating the Disproportionate-Enforcement Critique," *Law and Contemporary Problems* 66 (Summer 2003), pp. 49–69; see also Jeannine Bell, *Policing Hatred: Law Enforcement, Civil Rights, and Hate Crime* (New York: New York University Press, 2002), pp. 7–8.

99. U.S. Department of Justice, *Sourcebook of Criminal Justice Statistics Online,* Table 3.124 (last visited January 2, 2004), available at www.albany.edu/sourcebook/1995/pdf/t3124.pdf.

100. *R.A.V. v. St. Paul,* 505 U.S. 377 (1992). See Terry Maroney, "The Struggle Against Hate Crime: Movement at a Crossroads," *New York University Law Review* 73 (1998): 564–620, at p. 592.

101. *Wisconsin v. Mitchell,* 508 U.S. 476 (1993).

102. "The Mood of Ghetto America," *Newsweek,* June 1, 1980, pp. 32–34.

103. Stephanie Simon, "City Tense after Death in Arrest," *Los Angeles Times,* December 2, 2003.

104. Robert Tait, "Riots after Youth Shot Dead in Cincinnati," *The Scotsman,* April 12, 2001; "Violence in Mich. City; Motorcyclist's Death Spurs Two Nights of Race Riots," *Newsday,* June, 19, 2003.

105. Lara Parker, "Violence after Police Shooting Exposes Miami Racial Tensions," *Washington Post,* June 29, 1991, p. A2.

106. James E. Blackwell, *The Black Community* (New York: HarperCollins, 1991), pp. 456–57.

107. Joseph Fried, "Louima Jury Hears Officer Describe Bloody Gloves," *New York Times,* May 18, 1999, p. B8.

108. Amy Waldman, "The Diallo Shooting: The Overview: 4 Officers Enter Not-Guilty Pleas to Murder Counts in Diallo Case," *New York Times,* April 1, 1999, p. A1.

109. Joe R. Feagin, Hernan Vera, and Pinar Batur, *White Racism: The Basics,* 2nd ed. (New York: Routledge, 2001), pp. 145–146.

110. Charles Leerhsen, "L.A.'s Violent New Video," *Newsweek,* March 18, 1991, pp. 35, 53.

111. Wendy Lin, "Stakes Are High in Lottery for U.S. Green Cards," *Newsday,* October 13, 1991, p. 19.

112. Transcript of press conference with Dan Stein held by the National Press Club, Federal News Service, January 7, 1992.

113. Quoted in Keith Henderson, "Immigration as an Economic Engine," *Christian Science Monitor,* March 27, 1992, p. 9; see also Ben Wattenberg, *The First Universal Nation* (New York: Free Press, 1990).

114. Peter Brimelow, *Alien Nation: Common Sense about America's Immigration Disaster* (New York: Random House, 1995), pp. 10, 59.

chapter 5

Problems of Gender Roles and Sex Discrimination

Hillary Rodham Clinton, a lawyer and later a U.S. senator, was the first professional to become America's First Lady. In spite of her many accomplishments and changes in women's roles in recent decades, during her husband Bill Clinton's first presidential campaign many Americans expected Ms. Clinton to conform to the image of a traditional wife who bakes cookies, takes care of the home, and keeps political opinions to herself.

Gender discrimination against women is deeply rooted in our male-dominated society. For more than a century, women's movements have vigorously protested discriminatory barriers in society. In 1848, the Seneca Falls Declaration pressed for legal rights, the vote, and the opening of employment in education and the professions to women. Between the 1890s and the 1920s, a number of women's organizations worked vigorously to secure the vote. Since the 1960s, such organizations as the National Organization for Women, the Women's Equity Action League, the National Black Feminist Organization, and Working Women have carried forward the tradition of early movements and used protest tactics such as lawsuits, sit-ins, strikes, and civil disobedience. Ranging from moderately reformist to radical, women's organizations today continue to address problems of gender subordination and inequality. For example, a recent report from the National Women's Law Center in Washington, D.C., documents the George W. Bush administration's record of eroding the hard fought progress of women in the areas of work, school, child care, tax and budget policies, retirement, health and reproductive rights, violence against women, women in the military, judicial nominations, and government agencies charged with protecting women's rights and interests in U.S. society.[1]

We discuss in detail three major forms of stratification and oppression in this book: class stratification, racial stratification, and gender stratification. Gender stratification is equal in importance to the others, though until the 1960s inequality and discrimination along gender lines received little attention from social scientists or the media. Today, many men discriminate against this "minority of women"—which is actually a statistical majority of the population—at work, at school, at home, in the media, and in politics, with discrimination in one area reinforcing that in another. Juliet Mitchell has underscored several dimensions of women's position in society: production in the form of work in the outside economy and at home, the reproduction and mothering of children, and subordination as sex objects.[2]

GOALS OF THIS CHAPTER

We begin our discussion on the problems of gender roles and sex discrimination with an emphasis on the patriarchal structure of this capitalistic society. While the neo-Marxist perspective stresses the importance of class in shaping the lives of women, other feminist views remind us that all classes of women share similar oppressive experiences in childbearing, sexuality, and male violence. Gender role stereotyping in family settings, schools, and the media undergirds and generates discrimination against women in contemporary U.S. society. The patterns of discrimination and oppression can be seen in family decision-making practices, childbearing and child rearing, sexuality, housework and shopping work, domestic violence, and child abuse. Oppression targeting women remains the broad framework for our understanding of sexual assault both outside and inside the home, particularly as it concerns spousal rape, date rape, rape and law enforcement, and the horrors of sexual terrorism in our country's penal system. Despite the commonplace public rhetoric about increased gender equality in recent decades, social science research and legal research make it clear that the occupational segregation of women workers, the male–female occupational gap, unequal pay for comparable work, hiring discrimination, discrimination in recruitment and promotion practices, and sexual harassment in the workplace have continuing and disabling effects on women today. Women also continue to face blatant discrimination in housing, law, and politics. We close this chapter with a brief discussion of how the U.S. system of gender subordination has an impact on men.

IDEAS ABOUT STRATIFICATION BY GENDER

Power–Conflict Ideas: A Class Emphasis

Some social scientists have accented the ways in which capitalistic economies such as that of the United States shape the experiences of women. In earlier U.S. and European history, the concentration of day-to-day subsistence activities in farm households and the absence of much private property made the work of women more important than in later industrial periods. Marxist scholars have argued that the subordinate position of women became much worse with the emergence of capitalism in the nineteenth century, as most women's everyday tasks became more male-controlled in the urban household than they had been in feudalism's agricultural household. With industrialization, the factory system replaced home-based activities in which women had more control over work.[3] A rigid gender division of labor developed, with women working specifically for husbands rather than for the extended family group as they usually had on the farm. A man's home was now his castle.[4]

Power–conflict analysts often emphasize the importance of class in shaping the lives of contemporary women. Thus, many poor women see well-off women, who are indeed sometimes their employers, as their class "enemies"—that is, poor women tend to speak of their class or racial experiences more often than of their experiences as women subordinated to husbands and fathers. As Rollins has demonstrated in research on black domestic workers and their white female employers, for women in the poorly paid sectors of the working class, their class and racial experiences are often more overwhelming sources of oppression consciousness than their gender experiences.[5]

SOME FEMINIST VIEWS

Because women of all classes often share similar experiences in regard to childbearing, sexuality, and male violence, some feminist analysts take issue with too much emphasis on class. They note that male oppression of women predates Western capitalism. These analysts locate the source of male–female inequality primarily in women's reproductive and sexual roles. Examining the current scene, Kate Millett has noted that "what goes largely unexamined, often even unacknowledged (yet is institutionalized nonetheless) in our social order, is the birthright priority whereby males rule females. . . . Through this system a most ingenious form of 'interior colonization' has been achieved."[6] An entrenched form of gender "colonialism," the commonplace patriarchal (male-dominant) family structure, has characterized this country from its earliest decades.

Critical feminists note that the age-old, preexisting patriarchal structure and ideology shaped the capitalist system as it spread after the fifteenth century in Europe and North America. Indeed, some class-centered analysts have been slow to recognize that getting rid of class exploitation of workers by employers will not necessarily free women from gender discrimination. Thus, as Zillah R. Eisenstein suggests, "The destruction of capitalism and capitalist exploitation by itself does not insure species [fully human] existence, i.e., creative work, social community, and critical consciousness for women."[7]

The male–female division of household labor is ancient; men have long profited from the subordinate gender-role position of women in the home. However well husbands may treat wives, societal pressures have forced the majority of wives to do a disproportionate share of domestic work, such as child care and food preparation. Unpaid domestic work is necessary to the survival of the patriarchal family, as well as to a capitalistic society.

In the industrialization process over the last century or so, male employers and male workers have also participated in the oppression of women working outside the home by using workplace organization, such as job channeling and job segregation, to keep many female employees in lower-status jobs. Research by Ruth Milkman and Alice Kessler-Harris underscores the contradictions faced by women workers in industry for decades now. Because U.S. institutions relegate most women to the lion's share of domestic work and childbearing, when they enter the labor market outside the home they usually retain these household responsibilities. As a result, they cannot easily compete with male workers who are less occupied with domestic responsibilities. Historically, too, male-dominated workers' movements and unions have discriminated against women.[8]

GENDER AND RACIAL SUBORDINATION

Gender subordination is similar in some ways to racial subordination, discussed in Chapter 4, for both involve discrimination and oppression defined by birth, not by personal achievement. In both cases, the relationship is one of institutionalized dominance by the group with generally greater social, economic, and political power. In the everyday world, today as in the past, gender and racial stratification have a *material* foundation, the former in the gendered division of labor in family and workplace and the latter in the racial division of labor in the workplace and economy. A large proportion of all adult women, whatever their racial–ethnic group, are still engaged in substantial domestic work at home. Outside the home, most women workers are still in positions that confer modest status or pay compared to that of male workers.

Still, the systems of sexism and racism are different in important ways. For example, the economic situation of white women as a group is much better than that of women of color as a group. Indeed, the major gendered burdens of white women—patriarchalism in the family and exploitation in the workplace and media—are partially offset by the closeness many enjoy to white male power and the privileges (such as better incomes, on the average) such closeness provides. Yet, one must not exaggerate the closeness of white women to male power. Marriage can often mean for white women little more than intimacy and a household division of labor; it need not mean equality of wealth, equality in decision making, or equality in communication.

GENDER STEREOTYPING

Socialization practices at home and school still frequently stereotype girls and women as by nature lovable, emotional, and suited to marriage and raising a family.[9] Girls are taught these model characteristics and behaviors associated with them by parents, friends, and teachers. Having grown up under the pressure of such stereotypes, many women come into a family or employment arrangement with the cards stacked against them. The view that a woman should be more or less a "servant" to her "master" at home is still common in the male population. A U.S. senator once defended his vote for a tax break designed to keep wives *out* of the labor market this way: "The guy likes to come home and get supper and a couple of martinis from a woman who is reasonably rested."[10]

Boys also learn gender-role stereotypes at an early age. Little boys learn that they are not to play with girls or to act like girls. If they do, they are "sissies." One analyst noted that in the 1970s there was "a 'girls ugh' line" in television comedies involving young boys, a type of reaction that is *still* present in contemporary movies and television shows.[11] Many boys and men find this line of comedy appealing.

Differential treatment of boys and girls begins at birth; hospital personnel or family members often treat babies differently—for example, boys get blue blankets and girls get pink. One study of male and female babies who were similar in average length, weight, color, heart rate, reflex irritability, and muscle tone found that their parents, when interviewed, saw the babies quite differently: "Both parents described daughters as softer, finer featured, weaker, smaller, prettier, more inattentive, more awkward, and more delicate than sons. Sons were characterized as firmer, larger featured, better coordinated, more alert,

At an early age girls are encouraged to adopt the female gender role, which includes preparing for marriage and childbearing. (Shirley Zeiberg/Simon & Schuster/PH College)

stronger, and hardier."[12] Accompanying much gender typing that begins in infancy is an unequal treatment that has negative effects. Thus, the differential treatment that children experience before they are aware of their gender identity makes later discrimination seem more "normal."

Schools

Schools have traditionally channeled girls and women into subordinate gender roles by such means as the discriminatory treatment of girls by teachers and principals and by stereotyping in teaching and reading materials. Until recently, textbooks used by school-children to learn and perfect reading skills typically presented males as industrious actors, experimenting and making things, showing initiative and overcoming barriers, while girls mostly watched. Books often characterized girls who did dare to take the initiative as unfeminine or aggressive. A survey of elementary-school reading books in the late 1970s found that males were the main characters in 61 percent of stories. Since then, publishers have made some significant changes. A more recent inspection of popular basal reading texts noted that males were main characters in 18 percent of the stories and females were main characters in 17 percent. The remainder had shared main-character

roles or used neutral characters (such as a talking tree or an animal without gender identification). Also changed was the number of occupations of female characters. Contemporary reading books included 37 female occupations compared with only 5 for older
books, and stories in contemporary books did not feature such stereotypically female occupations as nurse or flight attendant. Newer books present children with a more bal-
anced emphasis on male and female characters, although many of today's adult women
and men learned to read using the sexist readers published before 1980. Nonetheless, despite the changes, recent research has found that even texts specifically designed to meet
gender equity guidelines often show a "subtle language bias, neglect of scholarship on
women, omission of women as developers of history and initiators of events, and absence
of women from accounts of technological developments."[13]

Stereotyping of women carries over into college education. Reports on classroom
conditions at law schools in Midwest and East Coast cities have found that fellow male students sometimes put down female students for questions in class, and sometimes call them
"femi-Nazis."[14] In addition, female students often report that their professors ignore or mar-
ginalize them in class, and even occasionally sexually harass them. According to one *New
York Times* report, a "male professor in Chicago told students in a discussion of a Supreme
Court opinion written by Justice Sandra Day O'Connor that it was written by a woman and
'women always change their minds.'"[15]

In the United States, most college and university professors are still male. A recent
report shows that even though women comprise nearly 60 percent of the 13 million college
undergraduates and earn more doctorates than men, they remain highly marginalized as
tenured faculty and administrators in U.S. colleges and universities. Women are slightly
more than one-third of the tenured or tenure-track faculty, 40 percent of the provosts and
deans, and just 30 percent of the chief executives on U.S. college campuses. As Leslie An-
nexstein of the American Association of University Women explains, "higher education has
traditionally been the playground of male academics. It's their turf. And sharing that turf is
difficult for many of them."[16]

The Mass Media

Another sign of stereotyping at the societal level is the treatment of women in the mass media. Essential to modern capitalism is the multibillion-dollar industry of advertising; sexist
ads are commonplace in magazines, in newspapers, on billboards, and on television.
Women often appear in ads for food, home, beauty, and clothing, and the ads frequently accent beauty (modeling, fashion, cosmetics, beauty aids) and homemaker (parenting, cleaning aids, cooking) themes. Mirroring attitudes of the larger society, which lead many
women to base their self-esteem on their looks, ads tend to portray women with much concern for their attractiveness. That is what advertisers think readers want. On the other hand,
readers are expected to judge men primarily on accomplishments, not appearance. The
widespread acceptance of this differential focus is clear, for example, in the Miss America
Pageant's decision to market trading cards picturing Miss America contestants as a counterpart to the football and baseball cards popular with boys.[17]

Recent analyses have found some improvement in television programming and its
portrayal of (white) women 20 to 40 years of age, as compared with 1960s images. In the

last decade or two a few top-rated television programs, such as *Roseanne,* have featured strong, independent women who expressed an "I've-just-about-had-it-with-you-bozos dismay at male behavior."[18] Although such shows are atypical (less than 10 percent of programming), participants at a forum on the portrayal of women cited them as good news amid pervasive sexism in the media.

The treatment of older women, teenagers, and women of color in the media, however, has changed little even in recent years. Analyzing 80 prime-time programs, Sally Steenland found that female adolescent characters were "either budding bimbos or aspiring librarians." The programs portrayed the majority of girls as man hunters interested primarily in clothes and boys. "The messages are very clear: you cannot be both smart and pretty. And boys don't like smart girls."[19] Jennifer Daves of the Center for Population Options notes that television has considerable influence on teenagers' attitudes and behaviors. "They take those characters' actions as advice from friends."[20] Latino women are rare in prime-time roles, and one often finds African American women in comedy formats that reflect the perceptions of mostly white writers and producers. "The problems raised in these comedies are individual problems brought about because of ineptness or corruption or silliness. They are seen as outside the control of the viewers. Therefore, there is no responsibility felt about the African-American experience in our society."[21]

Moreover, as analyst Elayne Rapping notes for films in the last decade, filmmakers rarely allow the heroines to express as full a range of attitudes and emotions as male lead actors. Women are much less often the central characters in movies than are men, and when they are central, a central male actor is usually there to "balance" them. Occasional film heroines are often pop-culture or television "figures whose actions and situations are presented in terms of action/adventure genre stereotypes rather than as realistic social dramas. . . . The happy [film] endings are for those women who betray themselves and play the old Hollywood games. Those who are too honest about their feelings don't last any longer . . . than they did in the 1940s."[22]

Stereotyping in Biologically Oriented Accounts

Over the centuries, elites and other mythmakers have sometimes rationalized discrimination against women in biological terms, in a fashion not unlike the biological racism directed at people of color. More recently, efforts to free women to pursue a broader range of jobs and other social positions have led a few conservative scholars to ground societal gender-role differences primarily in biological (genetic) characteristics. The biological facts that only women can bear children, that childbearing "weakens" women physically (although temporarily), and that women, on the average, are smaller in stature than men are cited as evidence that male domination of the female—patriarchy—is natural and inevitable. Analysts such as Lionel Tiger, Steven Goldberg, and George Gilder have even suggested that attempts to change gender roles are futile. Goldberg, for example, argues that the hormonal differences between men and women render men more aggressive and this "alone would explain patriarchy, male dominance, and male attainment of high-status roles."[23]

Of course, biological differences exist between men and women, but biological determinism arguments put excessive emphasis on hormonal differences, sexuality, and childbearing. Childbearing can periodically disrupt a woman's career outside the home, but contraceptives allow women to schedule or avoid this temporary incapacitation. We must remember, too, that military service, or male stress and male diseases, temporarily handicap many working men. In the modern world, these and other male–female physical characteristics typically have little impact on a person's ability to do well-paid, skilled, or prestigious work, such as being a U.S. senator, a manager, a physician, a lawyer, or an electrician.

FAMILY AND HOME: MORE PATTERNS OF OPPRESSION

Because most adults get married at some point, the marital combination of man and woman is commonplace in the United States. Indeed, most people's closeness to their current family or the family of their childhood clouds their recognition of the gender-role inequality surrounding them. It is difficult to be objective about social organization when one is intimately a part of that organization. All family systems involve critical roles—sets of rights and duties tied to specific positions in families. Gendered roles such as wife and husband, or mother and father, have specific expectations. In most heterosexual families, societal norms dictate that the woman as wife should act in certain ways; she has certain traditional duties and rights. The same is generally true for the role of husband. These specific family roles are part of society's general roles, often called the "woman's role" and the "man's role." Yet, increasing numbers of women now fill nontraditional roles as well, such as college professor and telephone repair person, although most women still must play out traditional gender roles in some areas of their lives. We should note that most families do *not* take the form of what has been called the "Ozzie and Harriet" ideal: a mother at home taking care of children and a father working outside the home. Most families today have dual earners, or single women workers head the families. Many families are same-sex partnerships.

Family Decisions

Decision making in husband-wife families, while still typically patriarchal, may be evolving in a more democratic direction. An early study of family decision making showed that husbands' desires prevail concerning many families' most important decision: the character and location of the husband's job, which often determines the family's location and lifestyle. In addition, husbands' desires tend to prevail more often than wives' in decisions about the family car, whereas decisions about food or choosing a doctor are more likely to reflect the wives' desires.[24] This pattern is still often the case.

Today, all marriages are set within the larger society with conventional female and male roles still largely stratified in terms of power, resources, and benefits. Most women come to marriage with substantially fewer economic and political resources than do their husbands. A husband's power typically derives, to a substantial extent, from his job and income position in the outside world.[25] For the most part, the greater a husband's occupational and income position, the greater his decision-making power within his family. Married women who work full time outside the home tend to increase their decision-making power vis-à-vis their husbands, and their numbers have increased in recent decades. One survey found that almost half of the married women who worked outside the home contributed at least half of their family's total income.[26] Some researchers have suggested that until all women have equal,

In recent decades increasing numbers of women with preschool children have entered the workplace. Most still bear a disproportionate share of the child-care responsibilities. (Ken Karp/Simon & Schuster/PH College)

nondiscriminatory access to the better-paying jobs in the outside-the-home world, many women will not have the resources for an egalitarian position within their marriages.

Childbearing and Child Rearing

The ideology of having children as a woman's principal vocation is still central in many parts of this society. A woman's role in human reproduction has become the idealized counterpart to a man's role in production outside the home. A wife's social position often changes during the childbearing cycle. Dair Gillespie notes that "many women stop working [outside the home] during this stage and, in doing so, become isolated and almost totally dependent socially, economically, and emotionally upon their husbands, further eroding any strength they may have gained due to earning power (as workers outside the home) or participation in organizations."[27] Having to quit work usually reduces wives' resources, and thus their leverage.

Traditional families delegate child rearing primarily to the wife–mother role. Child care originally came under the auspices of the wife because of her biological role in bearing and breast-feeding infants. Today, breast-feeding seldom persists beyond a child's second year, however, and bottle feeding now makes it possible for men to assume the primary care of infants, although very few do so. Today, child care is still a major aspect of the prevailing societal definition of a woman's role.

Much social thought during the last century has emphasized the importance of parental training and care during infancy for the health and intelligence of the child. In the

United States this perspective has led to what has been called the "cult of motherhood," rather than to an emphasis on full participation by mother *and* father in parenting. In recent years, we have seen more discussion of fathers taking greater responsibility in child rearing. Whereas fathers spent half as much time in child rearing as mothers in the 1980s, the figure in more recent years has increased to about two-thirds.[28] Still, parity is not in sight. Even with the decline in birth rates in Western industrial countries over recent decades, pressures persist for women to remain at home—at least for a substantial period—as the primary trainers of the fewer children now at home. Intensive socialization of children becomes a mystique that operates as another way to keep women from engaging in activities outside the home. Some analysts have suggested that possibilities for fuller development for women, such as a wider range of nontraditional career choices, require serious consideration of collective child care, which is common in western European countries.

We Americans often boast that our children are important to us, yet our day-to-day practices suggest that we accord only a medium to low priority to children and child rearing. Neither business nor government officials have shown a strong desire to reward women who spend their lives raising children, or to alter work arrangements so that men can share in major ways in child rearing. If society really cares about child rearing, Laurel Walum notes, why has it not provided "programs such as the GI bill with its attendant benefits of medical care, advanced education, occupational hiring preference, early retirement, and loan benefits, for women who have served their countries in the capacity of mothers?"[29] Men as a group benefit from women performing these child-rearing tasks, because child care consumes so many hours that it is often not possible for a child-care provider to pursue a high-demand professional or technical career at the same time. Of course, individual men can also suffer losses from existing gender-role arrangements. For example, an overemphasis on the male's workplace role can result in emotional isolation from his children.

The majority of women who become wives and partners with men generally are psychologically conditioned to accept much or all of the traditional gender role. U.S. customs pressure a wife to live at her husband's domicile and to serve her husband by doing many of the domestic chores such as cooking and laundering, while he must by custom or law provide her necessities insofar as his income permits. The husband has traditionally had the right to decide the family's residence, and the law has generally regarded the husband as the "head" of household. Even where the law is changing in a much more egalitarian direction, strong informal customs often continue the traditionally inegalitarian practices.[30]

Sexuality

The most taboo-ridden dimension of the traditional woman's role is sexuality. Historically, husbands have had a legal or traditional "right" to insist on sexual intercourse and a wife has had a duty to submit. Even today, in many states it is not likely, because of the traditional view of the husband's sexual rights, that a husband will be convicted and sent to prison for forcibly raping his wife.

Many men still view and treat women as sex objects. The commodity character of women can be seen in the language many men use. Advertising has long presented women as commodities. (Less frequently, advertisers present men as sex commodities for sale to "liberated" middle-income women.) Many women "sell" their bodies for money as prostitutes or advertising models or for their upkeep as dependent wives. Television programs, media advertising, and the cosmetics industry frequently present females as (usually young) sex objects, whom men are encouraged to manipulate for their pleasure, support, or profit.[31]

Housework and Consumption Work

Virtually all adult women work. Unpaid work by homemakers contributes an enormous amount to the goods and services generated in society; the worth of that work is estimated at one-quarter of the gross national product (GNP). Millions of women serve as volunteers for charitable, service, and other civic organizations, work worth billions of dollars were it to be paid. Yet government calculations do not include housework or volunteer work in the GNP. Deckard has suggested that this omission reflects the sexist attitude that women's work at home is less important than other work and also the notion that goods and services are not worth much unless sold as commodities for money in the market.[32]

Societal norms also press women to do consumption work since most food, housing, and clothing are commodities no longer produced at home. To survive, women and men become consumers, but women do much of this necessary work. Society expects homemakers to shop; this activity is not wage work. Beginning in the 1920s, the movement of capitalistic enterprises into its mass-market consumerism phase reshaped this dimension of a typical woman's life. Market capitalism cannot survive unless people consume whatever goods it produces. The ultimate force behind a consumerist society like the United States is corporations' need to expand production for profit into the consumer-goods sector. Research has shown, however, that even the development of consumer appliances, gadgets, and mechanical aids has *not* reduced the time most women devote to housework. Conventional housework responsibilities now include much of this consumption work.[33]

Sociologist Arlie Hochschild has underscored the fact that most women employed outside the home still do the majority of housework and child care. One study of couples by economists found that for men the median amount of housework per week was about five hours, while the figure for women was four times as much. Although surveys suggest that men may be doing more housework than in the past, the inequality in housework is striking. Other research has shown that the total work week for women, including work outside the home, averages one-fifth longer than that of employed men.[34]

Professional women with children often find the demands of maintaining a career and running a household difficult, and thus many leave high-profile jobs at the pinnacle of their careers. Karen Hughes, for example, resigned her position as communications chief at the White House in 2002 because of her family responsibilities. (She came back in 2005 in another position.) Some speculate that Brenda Barnes resigned as chief executive of Pepsi-Cola for similar reasons. Women make up 40 percent of lawyers who leave the largest firms in Massachusetts each year, and 25 percent of women with children who earned Harvard MBAs in the 1970s had left their jobs by the 1990s. Demands of work and home do not affect men nearly as much. A national parenting association study found that half of working mothers leave work to care for sick kids, while *only 9 percent* of working fathers do so.[35] Moreover, many career women have chosen to postpone child rearing until midlife—half of American women with incomes of at least $100,000 are childless at the age of 40, compared to just 10 percent of men.[36] Clearly, U.S. society is a long way from providing gender equity in families or workplaces.

The Abuse of Domestic Workers

Anita Ortega was a 33-year-old Guatemalan brought to the United States in September 1995 to live as a domestic worker in Maryland for a high-ranking diplomat for the Organization of American States. Anita's employer promised to pay her $300 per month with periodic raises and to provide room and board in return for her domestic labor and her providing child care for his three sons. Her household chores actually included preparing meals, washing clothes, ironing, washing floors, washing dishes, washing the car, shoveling snow, raking leaves, and caring for the children. Anita worked 14-hour days, six days a week, and when the family had guests her workday extended to the early morning hours of the next day. Sunday was her day off, but Anita was still required to prepare the family's meals and to care for the children. Anita's employer deducted her room and board from her monthly pay. As a result, Anita earned an hourly wage of $1.74—far below the federal minimum wage. Her employer confiscated her passport when she arrived in the United States, and as a result Anita rarely left the house except to pick up the children at the school bus stop or to accompany the family to church. Anita's employer sexually assaulted her on three separate occasions. She returned to Guatemala in 1997.

A recent report on the abuse of domestic workers by Human Rights Watch shows that Anita Ortega's experience is typical of thousands of women entering the United States on special visas every year as live-in domestic workers for diplomats, officials of international organizations, foreign businesspeople, and U.S. citizens who temporarily return to the United States from homes abroad. Many live-in domestic workers are severely mistreated by their wealthy employers, who require them to work long hours as care-givers and housekeepers. Workers often suffer physical and sexual violence perpetrated by their employers. Domestic workers often stay in unhealthy sleeping quarters in unheated basements or utility rooms next to gas furnaces emitting noxious fumes. Their working conditions are sometimes unsafe. Employers regularly fail to provide medical insurance for domestic workers, and in many cases employers deny workers medical attention for injuries suffered while working. Many live-in domestic workers experience verbal abuse and gross defamation from employers and suffer cultural and social isolation. According to Human Rights Watch, "Often these employers come from a powerful, elite class, and they are abusing the rights of some of the most powerless. This is a serious human rights abuse in the United States, but it has remained largely hidden from public view. This has to stop."

The trafficking of persons into forced labor violates U.S. law. Still, live-in domestic workers are unprotected by the overtime provisions of the Fair Labor Standards Act and do not have the protection of workers' rights to unionization under the National Labor Relations Act. Domestic workers entering the United States under special visas are also unprotected under the Occupational Safety and Health Act mandating safe and healthful working conditions. For all practical purposes, Title VII provisions against sexual harassment in the workplace fail to protect migrant domestic workers. What is more, their often foreign employers usually have diplomatic immunity and are not subject to the criminal, civil, or administrative jurisdiction of U.S. courts. Because of the legal protections of employers, it is virtually impossible for domestic workers to seek legal remedies in U.S. courts for their exploitation and oppression by their employers.

Sources: Human Rights Watch, "Migrant Domestic Workers Face Abuse in the U.S.," June 14, 2001, available at www.hrw.org/press/2001/06/usdom-0614.htm; Human Rights Watch, "Hidden in the Home: Abuse of Domestic Workers with Special Visas in the United States," June 2001, available at www.hrw.org/reports/2001/usadom/index.htm#TopOfPage.

Domestic Violence

Illinois Senator Paul Simon reported that a *lawyer* once said to him, "You have to beat up your wife every once in a while if you're going to have a good domestic situation."[37] Battering by men is the most common cause of injury to women today. Domestic violence injures more women than are hurt in auto accidents, rapes, or muggings. One in six relationships involves domestic violence, and mates or partners batter several million women annually. A government study revealed that about 85 percent of victimizations by intimate partners are against women, with spouses or boyfriends killing about 33 percent of all female homicide victims.[38] Battering of females accounts for 20 percent of women's medical visits and 30 percent of women's emergency room visits.[39] Although intimate violence exists in all racial and ethnic groups and at *all* socioeconomic levels, higher rates of intimate partner victimization occur among women who are young, divorced or separated, earning lower incomes, and living in an urban area. Besides violent assault, rape, and murder, abusive male behavior can also include psychological intimidation, threats of violence, stalking, uncontrolled jealousy, and limiting a woman's physical or economic freedom.

Although men as well as women can be victims of violence, wife battering tends to be more severe on the average than attacks by wives on their spouses. For example, one study found that a third of Pennsylvania's homeless shelter residents were female victims of domestic violence.[40] Moreover, the U.S. Department of Justice has demonstrated that many more cases of wife battering occur than women report to government agencies. Minneapolis opened the first battered women's shelter in 1974; today more than 1,400 shelters operate throughout the country. These shelters for battered women typically have 24-hour hotlines and offer emergency residence as well as counseling, legal assistance, and other support to battered women. Women still do not report the majority of battering they endure, but the growing presence of shelters for women is increasing their likelihood of reporting.[41]

One study found that domestic violence is the chief source of injuries for women in the 15- to 44-year-old age bracket.[42] And a survey of almost 2,000 women seeking treatment at a health care facility linked domestic violence to a list of 20 health problems that often failed to respond to treatment. Interestingly, only one woman in the survey initially cited domestic violence as the reason for her visit to the doctor's office. The findings led researchers to create a treatment model to help doctors identify domestic abuse victims and provide more effective treatment by focusing on the patient's psychological state, as well as on physical issues.[43]

Until recently, prevailing male attitudes have viewed husband–wife relations as a private matter beyond the law. In the past and in the present, police agencies have often denied help to wives who are victims of violence because these attacks are "only domestic assaults." Male police officers have sometimes overlooked battering, especially by affluent men, and have generally given wife battering a low priority in "crime fighting." Largely because of the battered women's movement in recent decades, domestic violence is now a criminal act in every state. Police officers are more likely to arrest batterers. In some areas, officers are required to arrest the batterer even if the victim refuses to press charges. Arrest is the most effective deterrent to men who batter, for it seems to shock them into a realization that what they are doing is a crime.[44]

Still, one can find examples of official acceptance of a husband's right to the power of life or death over his wife. One Baltimore judge gave an 18-month prison sentence to a man who pleaded guilty to killing his wife for infidelity, even though the state's sentencing guidelines called for a three- to eight-year prison term. The judge justified the man's actions: "I seriously wonder how many men married five, four years would have the strength to walk away without inflicting some corporal punishment."[45]

Child Sexual Abuse

Child sexual abuse and other forms of child maltreatment are very common today. Research indicates that many boys and girls are sexually abused. Young girls are the typical victims of sexual abuse, while men are mostly the perpetrators. Today, indeed, the Internet is creating for children yet more risks of sexual victimization by pornographers and pedophiles.[46]

Studies of adult women who as children were victims of sexual abuse have found victimization rates ranging from *22 percent* to *45 percent.*[47] Extrapolating from survey data on physical discipline and sexual abuse, researchers estimate each year some 3 million children suffer physical abuse and 1 million suffer sexual abuse. These figures are much higher than those reported by government agencies.[48] For example, a recent government report on child maltreatment estimates that some 3 million children are the subjects of child protective services investigations or assessments, and 30 percent—or 903,000 children—have experienced or are at risk of experiencing abuse or neglect. Of these children, 59.2 percent are victims of neglect, 18.6 percent are physically abused, 9.6 percent are sexually abused, nearly 6.8 percent are psychologically maltreated, and another 19.5 percent are victims of other maltreatment. (The percentages total more than 100 percent because children are sometimes victims of more than one type of maltreatment.) The actual number of those abused is likely to be much higher. As can be seen from recent developments exposing widespread child victimization by clergy in the Catholic Church, as well as in other religious denominations, official government child abuse figures seriously underestimate the severity of child sexual abuse in the United States.[49]

While parents are 81 percent of all perpetrators of this child maltreatment, many perpetrators are "other relatives." Finkelhor reports that men abuse 94 percent of sexually abused girls and 84 percent of sexually abused boys.[50] According to one report, about half of the abused children are aged 6 to 12, and many are victims of repeated abuse.[51]

As children and as adults, victims are shamed into silence about their abuse because U.S. culture has no comfortable way of framing the experience. Sociologist Carol Rambo has pointed out that this societal reaction perpetuates the problem and in effect perpetuates the continued abuse of victims. The approach of some therapists who counsel victims just to "deal with it—horrible things happen to everyone" and the efforts of some experts to quantify levels of trauma (for example, a child victim who was a recipient of oral sex is thought to have suffered less than a victim of vaginal sex) serve to abuse victims *again* because they shift the focus away from the problem of dominance and male supremacy and fail to address what the abuse experience means to the individuals involved and the larger society.[52]

The effects of child sexual abuse are long-lasting: physical pain, humiliation, terror, grief, helplessness, and, if the perpetrator is a relative, the emotional pain of betrayal by someone with whom the child is supposed to have a bond of love. The effects of abuse follow victims into adulthood, causing problems in relationships, family life, and the workplace. Some research has likened the psychological disorders associated with child sexual abuse to combat-related post-traumatic stress disorders suffered by returning war veterans.[53] One national survey found that adult female respondents who were sexually abused when younger often manifested a "negative self-image, involvement in interpersonal aggression, increased use of intoxicants and higher levels of dating a larger number of different people."[54]

Society often stigmatizes victims, causing them to feel guilt and shame because of their experiences. Rambo, herself a victim of child sexual abuse, writes, "What I thought I was, was something unnameable, sexual, and aberrant."[55] When victims do talk about experiences, listeners often discount the victims themselves as deviant and consider what they say as irrelevant to the experience of "normal" people. Rambo reports being treated as "tainted and discounted by virtue of the stigma that is attached to me once I reveal that I was sexually abused as a child." After she escaped the severe sexual abuse of her father and was able to speak with relatives, she "was still required not to talk about it, to keep it a secret, because it was such a disgrace that it happened, and maybe, just maybe if we don't talk about it, the damage done would go away."[56] Rambo further explains, "The abuse confused me because, for much of my life, I was not taken care of, I did not know what it meant to protect myself because others had never protected me. I had no boundaries or models for how I should allow myself to be treated."[57]

An additional danger of child abuse is that it trains others to abuse. Groth reports that most pedophiles were sexually abused as children.[58] Hyde notes that breaking the cycle of abuse must involve a society-wide change in the definition of appropriate male behavior along with a redistribution of power between the sexes: "If we are to prevent sexual problems, we must prevent sexism by finding effective ways to redistribute power."[59] Abuse grows out of the deep hurt individuals often must endure from the violence of being socialized: "It is perpetuated by a code of silence that says we are not supposed to talk about it, but keep a stiff upper lip and quit complaining. . . . When it becomes an acceptable cultural norm to talk about it, people begin to heal themselves and help others to heal. Only when it becomes public and we all develop class consciousness and become a class in itself for itself can we throw off the shackles of a society that tells us to get even instead of finding out why our neighbors hurt so much that they want to hurt us."[60]

SEXUAL ASSAULT INSIDE AND OUTSIDE THE HOME

The United States seems to be the world's most rape-prone society. We have a much higher rape rate per 100,000 people than European countries. While the U.S. rape rate is 33.0 per 100,000 population, international data show that Poland (5.9), Switzerland (6.3), England (6.7), France (8), Germany (8.2), and Holland (8.9) have *much* lower rape rates.[61]

State laws generally define forcible rape as sexual intercourse forced by a man upon a woman against her will. The annual number of *reported* rapes has climbed steadily over the last few decades, from 28,000 in 1967 to 95,136 in 2002. Still, actual rape figures are much higher than police-report figures. National victimization surveys estimate that at least

366,460 women are victims of rape or attempted rape each year.[62] This figure is much higher than the number shown in official statistics for rapes and attempted rapes reported to police departments across the country. This indicates that women are *not reporting* most rapes and attempted rapes to the police. Some research studies put the actual figure for rapes and attempted rapes even higher. For instance, one study concluded from telephone interviews and rape crisis center data that 683,000 women are victims of rape and rape attempts each year.[63] Females do not report rapes to police for several reasons. For instance, according to one survey 23.3 percent believe the rape is a personal matter, and 16.3 percent fear reprisal from assailants. Rapists can sometimes be strangers, but victims usually know their assailants, who are often boyfriends or husbands. One analysis found that boyfriends, husbands, or ex-husbands perpetrate 26 percent of rapes, attempted rapes, and other sexual assaults. Acquaintances of various kinds carry out about half of all rapes, and strangers commit only one-fifth.[64] Victimization data show that the closer the relationship between female victims and offenders, the greater the likelihood a woman will not report the rape. When the rapist is a current or former husband or boyfriend, about three-fourths of all sexual victimizations go unreported. Also noted is a connection between child sexual abuse and becoming a rapist. One FBI study of repeat rapists found that about three-quarters had themselves been victims of child sexual abuse.[65]

Many influential men (and some women), including many lawyers, judges, and professionals who deal with rape crimes and related offenses, believe widely held myths about rape. Testifying before the U.S. Senate Judiciary Committee in the 1990s, the Illinois attorney general reported that a judge had recently thrown out a rape charge because the woman said that it took place in mid-morning. The judge did not believe a rapist "would break into an apartment and attack a woman in broad daylight with the window shades open."[66]

The common view that male and female gender roles "naturally" mean female sexual submission leads easily to the view, often found in law enforcement and the rest of the judicial system, that an assailant cannot rape a woman against her will. Romanticized views of rape suggest that rape is something women secretly want. Major novels by prominent authors, such as Ayn Rand and John Updike, present this view that women desire rape. Psychoanalytic writers compose rape fantasies and masochistic daydreams as normal female imaginings, and some films, such as *A Clockwork Orange* and *Straw Dogs,* glorify rape and brutalization of women in the guise of art. This attitude is prevalent in the male-oriented pornographic magazine and movie industry, which often portrays women as dehumanized sex objects who often become targets of cruelty, violence, or sex-oriented murder.[67]

At least 18 million women have been victims of rape or attempted rape during their lifetimes. Rape can happen to any female. One five-year study found that the ages of those treated for rape in regional hospitals ranged from 15 months to 82 years. Many rape victims are young children.[68] Roughly *44 percent* of reported rape victims are younger than 18 years of age, and 15 percent are 12 years of age or younger.[69] Most raped women are of the same racial group and income level as the rapist; teenage females and women who live in low-income areas run the greatest risk.[70] The lifetime rate of rape or attempted rape for women overall is about 18 percent. Most rape victims are white, but women of color are more likely to suffer rape. The lifetime rate of rape and attempted rape is nearly 18 percent for white women, about 19 percent for black women, almost 7 percent for Asian and Pacific Islander women, almost 15 percent for Latinas, and over 34 percent for Indian women.[71]

Force and violence are commonplace in rape cases. One research study found that assailants threaten about half of rape victims with a weapon and that many others victims suffer physical coercion in some other way. The reaction of most women to rape is fear for their lives.[72] Note the brutality and violence of rape; indeed, assailants murder hundreds of rape victims each year.

Spousal Rape

Researchers are showing that spousal rape is a common type of rape and is often reported in victimization surveys. One nationally recognized rape researcher interviewed over 900 randomly selected women and found that *one in seven* married women reported a completed or attempted rape by a husband or ex-husband. Studying 300 Boston women, other researchers found that 10 percent of married women there reported sexual assaults by a husband or ex-husband. Surveys of battered women in shelters reveal higher rates for these women: Between one-third and three-quarters report sexual assaults by husbands or partners. And a national survey found that 10 percent of all sexual assault cases reported by women involved a husband or ex-husband attacker.[73] In all cases, the percentages indicate a significant and continuing problem for women with male partners.

One can see the lack of seriousness in prosecuting spousal rape in the attitude of many prosecutors, judges, and juries in the criminal justice system. Wives have brought some lawsuits against their husbands in recent years, but as yet, no nationwide effort is in place to expand protection of wives from rape by husbands, including estranged husbands.[74] Marital rape exemption laws are prevalent in many states and signal a law-imbedded indifference to spousal rape. Marital rape exemption laws indicate the old common law doctrine that prohibits the prosecution of husbands who rape wives under the sexist notion of *coverture*—that is, a wife is the property of her husband and he can do what he wants to her. While reformers have been successful in abolishing marital immunity for sexual offenses in at least 24 states and the District of Columbia, various forms of the marital rape exemption still remain in the other states.[75] Here, too, a man's home is often his patriarchal castle—yet another sign of gender oppression in the United States.

Date Rape

Media coverage surrounding the trials of William Kennedy Smith and Mike Tyson periodically put date rape into the public spotlight. Many people fail to recognize the pervasiveness of date rape. One major survey of 3,187 women and 2,972 men on numerous college campuses found that one-quarter of women students were victims of rape or attempted rape and that 57 percent of these rapes happened on dates. The average age of the women at the time of the rape was 18.5 years. The women also reported more than 2,000 experiences of unwanted sexual contact, such as fondling against their will. One in 12 of the male students admitted committing acts that met the legal definition of rape or attempted rape.[76]

Another survey of 749 students on 50 college campuses found that almost all said they could define what date rape is, and the majority felt this type of rape was underreported. Some 2 percent of the men said they might have committed date rape, and a little more than 10 percent admitted they pressured a partner to have sex after a refusal. More than one-fifth of the women in the survey said they had been victims of date rape.[77] One date-rape victim has recounted her experiences this way: "The whole time I'm thinking, 'I don't believe this is happening to me.' I didn't even have time to walk fully out of the bathroom door when he grabbed me and threw me on the bed and started taking my clothes off. I'm yelling and hitting and pushing him, and he just liked that. He says, 'I know you must like this because a lot of women like this kind of thing.'"[78]

Rape and Law Enforcement

Research on sexual violence consistently shows that a major reason why women fail to report victimization is a belief that police are indifferent toward victims. Women fear that police officers are biased against rape victims, that they will be treated with hostility by police, or that the police will not believe the incident is serious.[79] To some scholars, the failure of women to report their rapes strongly indicates the malfunction of rape laws and related enforcement mechanisms.[80] A former New York City assistant district attorney has suggested that many officials in the criminal justice system are thus "rape collaborators." There are many police officers, prosecutors, and judges who, because of stereotypes and prejudices, do not take aggressive action to bring rapists to justice.[81]

Many male officers harbor common social stereotypes about women and rape, yet it is to these officers that a woman must often go to report a rape. The general approach to rape in law enforcement is changing slowly, because the number of women there is growing and most police departments are providing better training for male officers. Once a woman gets to court, she may find that she is on trial. State laws generally prohibit presenting information about a rape victim's sexual history to juries, yet in more than 90 percent of rape cases surveyed in one study, rape shield laws were not able to prevent juries from hearing testimony on the victim's nontraditional gender-role behavior.[82] In contrast, prosecuting attorneys usually cannot bring up a defendant's prior sexual or rape history unless the defendant takes the stand. Some courts even require extensive corroboration of a victim's story along with evidence that the defendant used force in the rape. Former New York City prosecutor Alice S. Vachss has criticized the criminal justice system in general, and prosecuting attorneys in particular, for allowing rapists to get *more* justice than the women victims: "Sex crimes are the toughest to prosecute. It's the only area of crime where we have standards for the victims while the bad guys get breaks."[83]

The U.S. Senate's Judiciary Committee has estimated that "98 percent of rape victims never see any justice: no arrest, no prosecution, no conviction."[84] Indeed, even for reported rapes the conviction rate is very low—accordingly, "a rape survivor may have as little as a five percent chance of having her rapist convicted."[85] Many rape survivors lack confidence in law enforcement, and this attitude contributes to underreporting. Women in one study said they did not report rape to police because they felt nothing would be done or that they did not have proof. Ironically, the excessive evidence requirements for many rape prosecutions are justified by the common stereotype that women rush to falsely accuse men of rape. Significantly, a male victim of assault or robbery does not, under the law, have to prove that he resisted or that the act involved physical force. Indeed, juries often weigh the victim's testimony in such cases more heavily than they do in rape cases. One scholar found, for instance, that jurors tend to absolve defendants of guilt where the victim violated

[handwritten margin note: yes just like all other victims of rape — similar to a college campus?!]

jurors' notions of proper female behavior such as drinking, using drugs, or being sexually active outside marriage.[86] Research also rejects the notion of many men that "unsatisfied" women freely make false rape accusations.[87]

Several studies have demonstrated that rape is not primarily a crime of sexual passion but rather a crime of violence directed against women. Such violent actions are an extreme extension of the values of a sexist culture that encourages in males an orientation toward subordinating women sexually. The fear engendered in women by threat of rape is similar to the fear of wife beating. Both fears have broader social consequences in pressuring women to accept subordination and degradation across numerous institutional areas. Both fears reduce the likelihood of individual women resisting or protesting the actions of a man.[88]

Sexual Terrorism in Prisons

Prison rape is so pervasive in this country that one commentator characterizes the crisis as "the most tolerated act of terrorism in the U.S."[89] Estimates are that sexual predators assault one in five of the more than 2.2 million prisoners in the United States. Victims of prison rape often endure severe physical and emotional injury, severe depression, and post-traumatic stress disorders. Many experience repeated attacks; in one case, a gang of prisoners sodomized an inmate more than 60 times over a two-day period. Juvenile and mentally ill inmates are particularly vulnerable to rape, and given the high incidence of HIV/AIDS in the prison population, some experts assail prison sentences as death sentences because of these commonplace prison rapes.

Sexual violence persists because many prison officials deliberately ignore the problem or actively participate in creating a brutally oppressive, sexualized environment in prison facilities. Prison personnel often promote inmate victimization by using the threat of rape to control prisoners. Prisoner-on-prisoner violence accounts for most male inmate rapes, but it is the male correctional officers, staff, and prison wardens who pose the greatest risk of sexual violence against female inmates. Female prisoners are subjected to rape, sexual assault, and unlawful invasions of privacy, including prurient viewing during showering and while dressing by those men responsible for safety and security in prison. In one California facility, female inmates reported that it is common for male officers to touch inmates' breasts and genitals when conducting searches. Male officers have vaginally, anally, and orally raped female prisoners, and they often use physical force to compel female inmates to submit.[90] "A climate of sexual terror" characterizes prison life for many female inmates.[91]

Prison rape is indeed "cruel and unusual punishment," but the U.S. legal system has proven totally inadequate in holding officials accountable for their failure to control violent behavior of custodial predators. The seminal case is *Farmer v. Brennan.* There the U.S. Supreme Court devised a legal standard for prison rape victims, that requires victims to demonstrate not only that the conditions under which they were incarcerated "posed a substantial risk of serious harm" but also that prison officials exhibited a "deliberate indifference" toward their safety by allowing the conditions to persist. This legal standard has proven mostly unfavorable to prison rape survivors since inmates often cannot prove these conditions.[92] Congress, however, has moved to stop this sexual terrorism by passing the Prison Rape Reduction Act, which authorizes financial grants to state and local officials to prevent rape and orders the U.S. attorney general to provide assistance and training for federal, state, and local authorities to prevent and punish prison rape. The new law requires the Department of Justice to conduct annual surveys to determine the prevalence of rape in correctional facilities and adopts a national zero-tolerance standard for eliminating rape. Prison officials must also report incidents of rape directly to the Bureau of Justice Statistics.[93]

EMPLOYMENT OUTSIDE THE HOME

For reasons of economic necessity as well as because of women's desire for economic independence from men, the proportion of women in the workforce has risen steadily for several decades. Women make up nearly half the paid civilian labor force; about three-quarters of women between the ages of 25 and 55, and two-thirds of mothers, are in this labor force.[94]

White women first entered the paid workforce in large numbers in response to labor recruitment campaigns during World War II. Significantly, African American women and many other women of color have long been in the outside labor force. When male soldiers returned home at the war's end, aggressive campaigns by the government and private sector were launched to convince employed women that their proper place was again at home doing unpaid household and child-care work. Most women complied with these pressures, often under protest. The next large influx of women into the outside labor market occurred during the 1970s. Throughout these various eras, men have frequently trivialized women's reasons for going into the paid labor force. Many men feel that women, particularly married women, work mainly or only for "extra (pin) money" or other unimportant reasons. Even successes accompanying the women's movement since the 1960s have been unable to eradicate society's negative attitudes toward women's outside work, attitudes that support the patriarchal system and negatively influence jobs available to women, the pay women receive, the way in which women are treated on the job, the rate at which they are promoted, and the benefits provided by pension systems.[95]

Recent data indicate that full-time, year-round–employed female workers as a group earned only 77 percent as much as full-time, year-round male workers.[96] Comparing this with the 59 percent female–male wage ratio of the 1970s suggests a substantial improvement in women's earnings relative to those of men. However, only half of the improvement since 1979 was because of a real increase in women's wages; the other half was the result of a *decline* in men's wages. Today, large numbers of women bear sole responsibility for supporting their families, and the economic importance of these women's earnings is seen in the fact that the poverty rate for single-mother families is much higher than for two-parent families. "Nearly all of the increase in the number of poor families over the past 20 years has been in families headed by women. And one in four older women lives at or near poverty."[97]

Today, paid work is a necessity for the majority of women, including mothers who have substantial responsibilities for work at home. Yet for the most part the business world has not adjusted to the needs of families in which all adults are in the paid labor force. The Family Medical Leave Act (signed in 1993) requires companies with at least 50 employees to allow workers to take up to 12 weeks of unpaid leave per year for childbirth, adoption, illness, or caring for a sick child or parent. While this legislation marked the beginning of government recognition of family obligations of workers, it offers no relief for those workers who cannot afford to take *unpaid* leave for family emergencies and for those in workplaces with fewer than 50 employees.[98]

Occupational Segregation of Women Workers

Most women in the paid labor force are still employed in traditional women's occupations. Most U.S. occupations are gender typed—that is, they are predominantly male or female in composition. To a substantial degree, this gender segregation of job categories reflects institutionalized patterns of discrimination. For example, in a typical corporate business setting, workers mostly fall into the following broad categories:

1. *Managers,* predominantly male
2. *Clerical staff,* mostly female
3. *Technical staff,* mixed-gender, with better-paying positions dominated by males
4. *Janitorial staff,* dominated by men and women of color

Gender and racial segregation is so commonplace in many organizations that it appears to most people to be the "natural order of things." Yet it is not a natural order but one that reflects the historical and contemporary institutionalization of gender and racial discrimination. For example, in 1920 the majority of clerical work was actually done by male workers; even in 1950, some 40 percent of clerical employees were male. Today, only about one in five clerical employees is male, and less than 5 percent of key clerical positions such as secretary are filled by men.[99] This intentional change in the gender composition of clerical jobs resulted in a decline in wages paid to (now women) clerical employees. Men work in many more different types of occupations than do women, who are heavily concentrated in just a few dozen of the several hundred major job categories in the United States.

The Occupational Gap

We can see evidence of this segregation in contemporary occupational data. Table 5.1 shows that women workers make up varying percentages of selected occupational categories charted by the U.S. Bureau of Labor Statistics among employed persons.[100]

While the proportion of women in certain nontraditional job categories has increased in recent decades (for example, engineers, physicians, and lawyers), many job segregation changes are modest.[101] The occupational gap between men and women is closing slowly, in part because the movement of women into traditionally male jobs has often been exceeded by the movement of new women workers into traditionally female jobs. The majority of women workers are still in predominantly female job categories: clerical, retail sales, and service.[102] The proportions of females remain low among engineers, dentists, corporate managers, craft workers, and transport workers. Women are scarce in many traditionally male occupations. For example, Christine Williams underscores the fact that it is rare to find a woman in any police department's most senior positions and that women who do make it to the top usually get extra scrutiny because they are now in what most people see as a "man's job."[103]

Various studies have shown that women hold very few top-level management positions and directorships of corporations. The latest report of the federal Glass Ceiling Commission, a bipartisan group set up by the 1991 Civil Rights Act, found an invisible "ceiling" that restricts advancement for women in corporations. The study found that 95 percent of

Table 5.1   Occupational Categories and Percentage of Women

Occupational Category	Percentage of Women
Engineers	10.4%
Lawyers and Judges	29.3
Librarians	85.7
Physicians	29.3
Dentists	19.9
Registered Nurses	93.1
Elementary School Teachers	82.5
Executives, Managers, Administrators	46.0
Sales Workers, Retail, Personal Services	63.1
Secretaries, Stenographers, and Typists	97.7
Receptionists	97.0
Precision Production, Craft, Repair	8.7
Transportation and Material Moving	10.4
Food Service Workers	57.0
Private Households (maids, servants)	96.2

senior managers and executives in the major companies were male (almost all white men). Women reportedly hold only one-tenth or so of important middle-level executive positions in corporations.[104]

Regarding corporate directorships, a recent report shows that only 13.6 percent of *Fortune 500* board seats were occupied by women in 2003, increasing only slightly from 12.4 percent in 2001. The number of corporate board seats held by women of color increased far less, however, from 2.5 percent in 1999 to 3.0 percent in 2003.[105] Another study of 353 *Fortune 500* corporations between 1996 and 2000 reveals, however, that companies with higher percentages of women in senior management positions have appreciably higher corporate performance ratings. Apparently male corporate leaders in most firms have yet to recognize that increasing gender diversity likely has a substantial impact on corporate performance.[106]

Research shows that women in top-level corporate positions as a group earn less than their male counterparts as a group in ten major industries (those employing 71 percent of U.S. women workers and 73 percent of U.S. women managers). In some private industries (entertainment and recreation, communications, finance, insurance and real estate, business and repair services, other professional services, retail trade, and medical services) women's salaries actually declined between 1995 and 2000, while in more regulated, public sector industries (education, hospitals and medical services, and public administration), the gender salary gap narrowed somewhat. In only half of these major industries do women hold a proportionate share of the management positions. The report also indicates that women managers with children are less valued by high-level employers than childless women—60 percent of women managers do not have children at home.[107]

Because of segregation and discrimination in employment patterns, women as a group still receive much less pay than do men. According to the Labor Department, 70 percent of minimum-wage workers are now women. In 2001 the median income of all females in the paid labor force ($16,614) was barely more than *half* that of their male counterparts ($29,101). The median incomes for white women ($17,229), Asian American women ($18,525), Latinas ($12,853), and African Americans ($16,282) were all considerably lower than the median income for men.[108] In spite of women's gains in education and employment opportunities in recent years, the differential in income has decreased rather modestly. As Miller points out, examples of successful women "serve to mystify the reality of the majority of women, leading many to think that women are doing better than they are and others to aspire to goals that are achievable only for the very few."[109]

Comparable Pay for Comparable Work?

Many business analysts argue that the "market" pays people what they are worth, yet job evaluation studies examining skill, effort, responsibility, and productivity of jobs indicate that this is a myth. Regardless of actual worth in terms of objective job evaluations, women's jobs generally are paid less than comparable men's jobs, Studies in Minnesota, California, and Washington have noted that women in jobs with similar or higher skill and responsibility levels than men still made less than the male workers.[110]

Census data suggest that gender differentials persist. One 1990s study found that the median weekly earnings of jobs that are filled 90 percent or more by women, such as receptionists ($429) and secretaries ($496), are substantially lower than jobs that are filled 90 percent or more by men, such as truck drivers ($604) and auto mechanics ($637). Even within traditionally male or female jobs, women workers make less than male workers. The median weekly earnings for women truck drivers is only $443. Moreover, Nebraska state and community college officials interviewed for a report on the issue of getting women off welfare into jobs noted that traditionally female jobs, such as many in restaurants and child care, typically do not have good pay or health benefits. In contrast, traditionally male jobs, such as in welding and auto parts, typically pay more and include better fringe benefits.[111] Jobs requiring comparable skills often do *not* have comparable pay and benefits.

In a study on gender pay inequity, researchers estimate that the failure of working women to receive wages equal to those of comparably skilled men annually costs working families some $200 billion in lost income, with an average loss of more than $4,000 per family. The study also indicates that, if employers paid married working women the same as men in comparable jobs, annual family incomes would not only increase by $4,205 but the poverty rates for married-couple families would fall substantially. If single working mothers were paid the same amount as comparably skilled men, annual family incomes would increase by an average of $4,459, and the poverty rates for these families would decrease sharply, from 25.3 percent to 12.6 percent.[112]

At all job levels, women workers have had to fight for fair compensation. It is often difficult for women workers to win comparable pay cases in courts because employers will usually argue that they are just following the (discriminatory) wage levels set in local job markets, and thus far most courts (those that allow statistical evidence) have bought into this argument. One journalist's report notes that most federal courts "have ruled against female workers in comparable worth suits, but the threat of lawsuits has often resulted in legal settlements before trials that have granted female workers higher pay. New York City settled a suit claiming that female police dispatchers were being paid less than male fire dispatchers."[113]

Defending inequality in pay, employers argue that they pay women less because they are "less qualified" in terms of education and experience. However, using control variables such as skills and training, sociologist Paula England has examined the relationship of women's earnings to a variety of factors said to account for the gender wage differential, including training, education, and physical demands. Her data on mean incomes for 403 occupational categories showed that 5 to 10 percent of the male–female pay differential stems from gender discrimination and another 2 to 9 percent is rooted in indirect gender bias.[114]

Educational and income data show that, for the most part, women workers average lower earnings than do *less educated* men. Recent (2003) data show the pattern for all full-time and part-time workers over 24 years of age:[115]

Table 5.2   Education by Income by Gender

Education	Median Income for Men	Median Income for Women	Women's Percentage of Men's Income
Less than 9th grade	$ 18,710	$12,987	69%
High school			
9th to 12th grade	22,196	13,695	62
High school graduate	1,411	20,755	66
College			
Some college, no degree	6,887	4,018	65
Associate degree	40,454	5,109	68
Bachelor's degree	1,507	5,109	68
Bachelor's degree or more	7,123	7,839	66
Master's degree	2,495	2,466	68
Professional degree	100,000	6,143	56
Doctorate degree	7,525	6,182	72

In no case do women workers earn more than *72 percent* of men's earnings, and that percentage is at the highest level of education. In the last few decades, the only significant changes in these data have come at the college and postgraduate levels. And these percentages are mostly *lower* than comparable government figures for the early 1990s! Even today, a high level of education does not place women on a par with men in terms of income.

In one court case, a federal judge ruled that Washington State officials had discriminated against women employees by paying lower wages and salaries in female-type job categories than they paid men in male-type jobs with similar skill and knowledge levels. This ruling began a controversy across the country over "comparable pay for comparable work" (often called "comparable worth"). Finding that women were paid 20 to 30 percent less than men in comparable jobs, the judge ordered $828 million in back pay and raises for the women workers.[116]

Differential pay for similar work is by definition gender-related discrimination, and discrimination of the most overt and harmful type. This discrimination is so apparent and overt that (mostly male) employers refuse to accept it as discrimination that they must remedy. Indeed, a major argument against changing pay differentials is that it would be too costly to pay women a fair wage equal to comparable male-type jobs. A new employer or an employer expanding operations usually accepts the prevailing "market wage rates" for women and the prevailing "market segregation" of jobs. In other words, employers accept and perpetuate the gender discrimination long institutionalized in U.S. job markets.

The Institute for Women's Policy Research recently looked at data for women workers aged 16 and older and found that the earnings ratio comparing most women of color and white men is lower than for white women. Researchers found the earnings for employed year-round and full-time white women workers were 70 percent of those of white men, while African American women earned only 63 percent of those of white men (53 percent for Latino women). The earnings ratio is highest for Asian American women, who earn 75 percent of what white men earn. The report estimates that if closing the earnings ratio gap between men and women continues at the same rate as it has over the last decade, women will not achieve wage parity with men for more than 50 years.[117]

Employment Discrimination

The types of discrimination discussed in Chapter 4 apply to discriminatory actions endured by women in all racial-ethnic groups. Remember that *isolate discrimination* refers to intentionally harmful action taken by a dominant group individual (for instance, a white male) against members of subordinate groups (white women and people of color) without being supported by a large-scale organizational context. An example would be an industrial firm's male personnel officer who expresses his personal prejudice against women by defying his company's personnel regulations and repeatedly hiring less-qualified men over better-qualified women. *Small group discrimination* refers to intentionally harmful actions taken by a small group of dominant individuals acting against members of subordinate groups without the support of the norms of the larger organizational context, such as small-scale conspiracies by male managers to subvert company regulations requiring promotion on a merit basis because those disliked are women employees.

Direct institutionalized discrimination refers to organizationally prescribed actions that have an intentionally negative impact on members of subordinate groups such as women. Typically, these actions are not carried out on an episodic basis but are undertaken routinely by a large number of male decision makers in employing organizations. An example would be the gender-segregated job categories in an industry that is resisting gender integration. *Indirect institutionalized discrimination* refers to practices having a negative and differential impact on women even though the organizationally or community-prescribed norms or regulations guiding those actions were established, and are carried out, with no immediate prejudice. For example, some types of past-in-present discrimination have a negative impact because current rules and practices reflect the physical characteristics possessed by those dominant group members (say, white males) who have in the past routinely filled positions in a particular organization. Current height or weight regulations, thus, can have a built-in physical or appearance bias that might not exist if nondiscriminatory access had earlier been provided to women workers. For example, the height and weight requirements for positions in some police or fire departments, positions traditionally filled by white men, can unnecessarily screen out large numbers of women (and some men of color) who are well qualified to hold such positions.

Recruitment Practices

Numerous barriers face women in the area of recruitment. Word-of-mouth job recruitment networks, when used by employers with a predominantly male employee population, can result in indirect institutionalized discrimination against women. Those male employers who rule in most organizations, private or governmental, often prefer to perpetuate their own kind. Diana Kendall has suggested that there may be a weird

> sociobiology of organizations where a person wants to foster another person who will assist him while he is still in the organization and will carry on just as he did when he retires, dies, etc. This may be a way in which people leave their "mark" on an organization—by leaving someone else there who is very much like themselves. The woman and/or minority group member does not fit this model that rules organizations.[118]

Today, this male bonding and modeling pattern remains strong in many business sectors.

Women and men of color often do not have access to critical old-boy job and information networks. These social networks function during work as well as after hours, when (usually white) men who hold the better-paying jobs may drink together in a bar or go on a golf outing. At these times, important advice is often passed along to rising young (male) employees about how organizations operate and promote. Since women are often not part of these informal networks, they frequently miss critical information necessary for regular advancement within the employing organization.[119]

Screening and Tracking Practices

As we have seen in the case of African Americans (Chapter 4), discrimination is commonly institutionalized in screening practices in public and private employment. Openly sexist prejudice still plays a role in shaping discriminatory hiring standards and procedures in U.S. workplaces. Employment interviews are a particularly important part of the job-screening process. Since screening criteria are often subjective—including impressions of potential workers' "intelligence," "appearance," and "emotional makeup"—a personnel evaluator's stereotyped notions may lead to rejection of a job candidate. Stereotyping often operates against women workers. Notions that "they lie about their age" or "have high absenteeism" frequently shape informal norms dictating the rejection of a woman applicant who "doesn't look quite right."[120]

Stereotyped views of a woman's family responsibilities, once routinely used to disqualify women from employment, are now unlawful. The U.S. Equal Employment Opportunity Commission (EEOC) found one employer guilty of gender-based discrimination in refusing to hire a woman because her husband's long-term illness involved family responsibilities that might interfere with job performance.[121] Denial of employment to unwed mothers has been ruled discriminatory. These women were differentially excluded because of employers' views of family or marital responsibilities, even though men with similar situations were hired. Despite court decisions, discriminatory practices still persist.[122] Stereotypical attitudes are especially likely to lead to subtle discriminatory actions when held by personnel interviewers in situations in which the screening interview plays an important role in hiring.

Title VII of the 1964 Civil Rights Act, perhaps the country's most important civil rights act, permits exceptions to the prohibition on gender discrimination in cases where gender is a considered a "bona fide occupational qualification." Some employers, when challenged, have defended discrimination against women in such terms. Jobs such as commercial sales representative and railroad telegrapher, for example, have sometimes been defended as "male jobs," whereas airlines once defended women as "best qualified" for flight attendants. Stereotyped notions of female "liabilities" and male "virtues" underlie such patterns of discrimination. In reality, most jobs, with a few exceptions such as wet nurse, do not necessitate that gender be an occupational qualification.

Discrimination does not cease once women are hired. Internal labor markets contribute to the system of segregated male and female jobs. Today, significant informal tracking of women into lower-paid positions and males into better-paying positions continues throughout business and government. Jobs requiring physical strength are often labeled "for men only," whereas secretarial jobs are generally reserved for women. The separation of women into less-well-paying clerical jobs and men into higher-paying white-collar jobs is well-documented in the worlds of finance, manufacturing, and government—even though women in office occupations often have the same or greater education levels as men in the same office. For decades women office workers have suffered from an institutionalized sexism in which the jobs they often must take, both because of early discriminatory socializing patterns that shape their aspirations and because of employer discrimination, pay less, have lower status, and frequently include a personal component (making coffee) not spelled out in job descriptions.[123]

Promotion Practices

Today women hold nearly half the "managerial" positions at all levels, yet they hold less than 2 percent of top management positions in corporations.[124] Numerous studies have documented a "glass ceiling" phenomenon in which intentional discrimination, including salary inequalities and differential promotion criteria, have blocked women's progression up corporate and other employment ladders.

A management publication surveyed 704 women managers in the field of accounting. More than 90 percent felt they were at least as well prepared as men for accounting jobs, and more than half thought they worked harder than comparable men. Yet only 36 percent felt they had the same chance as their male counterparts to be promoted up the career line. Unequal pay for the same work was a common complaint. One senior manager noted, "I am paid at least $10,000 less than a man would be paid, and I know I am more efficient, cost saving, and more accurate than most men would be."[125] A survey of more than 2,000 *Fortune* magazine subscribers found that more than half of women managers and professionals were dissatisfied with women's overall progress. The majority thought that to succeed in the workplace women had to work harder than men and needed more experience or better educational qualifications than male competitors. These women thought the glass ceiling was one of the most serious barriers to job success.[126]

Women workers in various studies have reported that they have to be "superwomen" or "water walkers" to advance into many higher administrative or management levels. Indeed, a major survey of 461 top female executives found that they got ahead by working harder than male colleagues. The chief reason for success was "that they consistently exceeded performance expectations."[127] In addition, stereotyped views harbored by male executives that male workers would not work under women supervisors and that women workers were supposed to "serve" men have hindered women's promotion possibilities. In many areas, qualified women have been denied promotions based on such rationalizations as "She's likely to quit and get married" and "She has children and her family responsibilities will interfere with a higher-level job."

An example of subtle gender discrimination can be seen in the tendency of many male managers to promote to higher-level positions women who "don't rock the boat." Women employees whom higher management perceives to be "troublemakers" do not do well in modern corporations. A majority of top women executives interviewed in the *Fortune* magazine study previously cited said that the second most important reason they have done well in their corporations is that they conduct themselves in a way that is unthreatening to men. One executive put it this way: "Don't be attractive. Don't be too smart. Don't be assertive. Pretend you're not a woman. Don't be single. Don't be a mom."[128] Ironically, the top executives who are looking for more aggressive senior managers may pass over less aggressive women. At different levels of promotion, both aggressive and nonaggressive women have encountered significant discrimination in what continues to be a "man's world."

In most traditionally male workplaces, the men who decide who will be promoted often take employees' interpersonal training for granted. Yet much crucial information is circulated within the aforementioned informal (old boys) networks. A common problem for women trying to break into traditionally male occupations is the preexisting male information and support network. This remains a problem once women are hired. For example, only relatively recently have women workers broken into traditionally male-dominated sectors of the auto industry. While women have made progress, one industry study noted that "You still have the old boys' network."[129] Moreover, a survey of women managers in accounting found some of them complaining about barriers created by these traditional old boys networks.[130]

Similarly, a recent American Bar Association (ABA) report found that while women now constitute almost 30 percent of the law profession, they total only 15 percent of law firm partners and only 5 percent of managing partners in large firms. Gender discrimination, often rooted in the old boys network, substantially accounts for this small percentage of women at the top of the legal profession.[131] Old boys networks have an impact. For example, one female law partner at a major firm directed a leasing effort for a real estate company successfully, yet the firm's leadership decided to honor the success by taking only some of the firm's male lawyers to a topless bar. Female lawyers have difficulty doing their jobs when excluded from such informal networks.[132]

The ABA study found discriminatory differences in earnings for experienced lawyers, with women earning 73 percent of what comparable male lawyers earn. The chair of the ABA Commission on Women in the Profession recently stated, "Neither the sheer number of female law student graduates, nor the passage of time, nor even the elevation of

In recent years the U.S. Senate has been weak in dealing with gender discrimination in government programs and agencies, including military agencies.

individual women to positions of prominence has dramatically enhanced opportunities for women partners, law professors or judges."[133]

Getting a good promotion often involves being asked to travel on business. Yet one research report found that male workers are much more likely to be asked to take business trips than are women workers, even if they are of the same age or in the same employment positions. One of the research study's authors, Harriet Presser, suggested that the reason for this lies in the fact that employers do not offer women travel opportunities. Without such travel, women employees are less likely to build up experience that makes them prime candidates for job promotion.[134]

If white women seeking promotions encounter a glass ceiling, barriers confronting women of color may be described as a *concrete wall*. One black management consultant noted that "Women of color are ten years behind white women in terms of promotion and upward mobility."[135] Very few people in higher-level management positions are black women. In Bell and Nkomo's study of women's experiences in management, black women reported receiving less support for career advancement from their superiors and less acceptance by colleagues, and they felt they had less control and authority in their jobs, than did their white counterparts. Black women also perceived greater gender discrimination, as compared with white women, and were less optimistic about the commitment of their companies to improving racial and gender relations.[136]

Sexual Harassment

Sexual harassment in workplaces is the widespread and intentional discrimination that reinforces other types of discrimination directed at women. In the eyes of some men, work is a prize men will give to women if they permit harassment. Like rape, sexual harassment is pervaded with stereotypes of women as sex objects, including the notion that most intentionally invite the discriminatory male behavior. Farley defines sexual harassment as "unsolicited nonreciprocal male behavior that asserts a woman's sex role over her function as a worker."[137] Sexual harassment includes touching, including repeated "accidental" contacts, staring at or making jokes about a woman's body, nonreciprocated requests for sexual intercourse, and rape.

Catherine MacKinnon identifies two types of harassment. Some harassing actions are a routine feature of workplaces. The woman employee "may be constantly felt or pinched, visually undressed and stared at, surreptitiously kissed, commented upon, manipulated into being found alone, and generally taken advantage of at work."[138] Other sexually harassing behaviors—sometimes called *quid pro quo actions*—involve rewards or punishments. Sexual favors are demanded in exchange for some employment benefit. Rejection may result in retaliation in the form of unfavorable evaluations, demotions, salary cuts, or pressure to resign. Many women workers must tolerate some sexual harassment just to work.

Numerous surveys have indicated that sexual harassment is common in workplaces. One celebrated case of harassment involved U.S. Senator Robert Packwood, who resigned his seat to avoid being expelled. The U.S. Senate Ethics Committee had unanimously recommended his removal because of his alleged sexual misconduct and because he had altered evidence. The Senate committee's resolution listed "18 specific instances of alleged sexual misconduct on Packwood's part. The harassment included the senator's forcibly kissing, embracing and pawing a number of women, several of whom were on his Senate or campaign staffs."[139]

Women in the military face high rates of assault. A survey by the Minneapolis Veterans Affairs Medical Center questioned 333 women in the military and found that 90 percent reported sexual harassment. One-quarter of the women below age 50 reported being the victim of rape or attempted rape. The perpetrators were usually other military personnel.[140]

Professionals are also plagued by sexual harassment. One survey of 553 female lawyers across the country found six in ten reporting harassment from clients.[141] The ABA report noted above reveals that three-quarters of women lawyers believe sexual harassment is still a problem in their workplace, even though most law firms now have policies prohibiting offensive work environments. Moreover, women lawyers who complain of sexual harassment "are often dismissed as humorless and hypersensitive."[142] And in a study of 8,000 federal government workers, 44 percent of women employees had suffered sexual harassment, including such things as sexual gestures and requests for sexual favors.[143]

At least half of all women will experience sexual harassment during their school or working lives, making harassment "the most widespread of all forms of sexual victimization studied to date."[144] Such harassment is designed to insult, exploit, and degrade and is experienced as offensive, humiliating, and frightening. Some researchers have suggested that the degree of harassment is associated with the proportion of women in a workplace; less harassment has been found in workplaces in which women have achieved numerical parity with male workers.[145] Harassment has devastating psychological effects and may produce harmful physical health symptoms as well. Victims report feelings of fear, anger, depression, self-doubt, guilt, and alienation. Physical symptoms include headaches, sleep and eating disturbances, and gastrointestinal disorders.[146]

The televised testimony of law professor Anita Hill at the U.S. Senate confirmation hearings for Supreme Court nominee Clarence Thomas, in which she alleged sexual harassment by Thomas a decade earlier when he was her employer at the EEOC, forced the issue of sexual harassment to public attention for a time.[147] Following the hearings, sexual harassment—in public schools and institutions of higher education as well as in the workplace—was discussed more openly and taken more seriously.[148]

Charges of sexual harassment have also come from schoolchildren in grades from kindergarten through high school. A recent national survey of students in eighth through the eleventh grades reveals that four out of five have experienced some sexual harassment in school, despite most students knowing sexual harassment is prohibited. Nearly one-third of students who had been harassed reported that they first experienced it in *elementary school.* The researcher had this to say:

> The findings of our report cannot and should not be shrugged off with the attitude that this is just normal pre-teen and teenage behavior. Nor should we assume that 'zero tolerance' for all offenders will help teach children the difference between 'flirting and hurting.' Lines can be drawn, for example, between flirting that is wanted and flirting that is unwanted and other behaviors that are meant to hurt and harass.[149]

Earlier surveys in Minnesota and Massachusetts report that at least half of all female primary and secondary school students have experienced sexual harassment, primarily from male students, but also in a significant number of cases from male teachers. A number of sufferers of harassment have successfully sued public school systems that refused to deal with harassment complaints.[150]

Sexual harassment complaints to the EEOC have risen in recent years. Growing numbers of companies have begun offering sensitivity training to male employees. In one opinion poll a large majority of women respondents said that men, including their employers, had become more sensitive to sexual harassment, yet more than two-thirds felt that most men still did not understand the issues of harassment that concerned women most.[151]

Other Discrimination in the Workplace

Women face other forms of discrimination. Even in the workplace, women are often treated like children. They may be called "baby," "little girl," or other terms used to address children. Like children, they are often not expected to be able to handle responsibility or to take part in important decisions. Women are punished or threatened with punishment like children. The following example was reported by a woman faculty member in a university political science department:

> When I was chair of our department, one of the senior male faculty was very unhappy about the woman faculty member we had just hired. Apparently, she challenged him, talked back to him, and contradicted him in public. As we talked, he got more and more angry about her behavior. Finally, he exploded, "What that young lady needs is a good spanking!"[152]

In some states conservative political groups have censored and weakened the content of sex education courses in schools, thereby fostering ignorance about women's health issues.

Sometimes women employees suffer because of the way they look. One investigative report by an NBC news program sent out two teams of women actors, with one team member of normal weight and the other overweight. The members of each team had similar job stories and employment histories. Seeking jobs at nine employers, sometimes "the women of average weight were offered opportunities while the larger women were not."[153]

Moreover, the movement of women into formerly male-dominated employment areas has led to covert discriminatory acts such as manipulation and sabotage techniques by male workers in an effort to discourage women's participation and success. A female mail carrier recalled, "I've been in this job nine years and I still have problems with the guys. About a year ago, whenever I returned from my route, I'd find a bunch of mail that I hadn't picked up. The district manager said I wasn't doing my job and gave me an undesirable [high crime] route. I found out later that the district manager gave my route to a new guy who was a friend of the family."[154]

Discrimination in benefits also occurs. Part-time workers, a disproportionately large number of whom are women workers or male workers of color, receive fewer fringe benefits than full-time workers at the same workplaces, workers who are more likely to be white men. Clerical employees (mostly women) frequently receive fewer benefits than do their professional and managerial supervisors (mostly men). Even Social Security and private pension systems, which are based on work patterns that are more typical of white men, frequently provide poorer benefits to women than men.[155] Women workers also face more problems in getting work leave because of particular health needs. In 2002, for example, women workers made 4,714 charges to the EEOC of pregnancy-based discrimination by their employers and recovered an estimated $10 million in damages.[156]

Federal government enforcement efforts against employment discrimination fall *far short* of the need. For example, companies doing business with the federal government are supposed to implement an effective affirmative action plan that brings more women and people of color into jobs once reserved for white men. Yet in one year in the 1990s, the Department of Labor Federal Contract Compliance Programs examined just 4,179 companies among the many thousands of U.S. firms. Of these, three-quarters were found to be violating federal regulations by not having an affirmative action plan, by not recruiting widely, or by open discrimination in hiring.[157]

Despite a low compliance rate of U.S. corporations with affirmative action mandates, there have been limited successes in enforcing corporate compliance in recent years. Women employees have won illegal pay and promotion practices claims against a few of the country's most prestigious firms: Home Depot, Kmart, Texaco, Nordstrom, West Publishing Company, Pepsi-Cola, and Albertson's. Noncompliance with federal contract programs resulted in Coca-Cola being forced to settle an $8.1 million claim of gender inequity involving 2,000 female employees. (In addition, a federal judge approved a $192.5 million settlement in a class-action racial discrimination case involving African American employees.) Similarly, Ford Motor Company had to pay some $3.8 million in a settlement with the government over allegations of gender and racial discrimination against women employees and employees of color at seven plants. Lawsuits alleging widespread sexual harassment resulted in a $34 million award against Mitsubishi Motor Company and a $10 million settlement against Astra, the U.S. subsidiary of a Swedish drug maker.[158] Once again, these recent victories for women employees and employees of color signal how pervasive gender discrimination and racial discrimination remain in the United States today.

Double Jeopardy: The Situation of Women of Color

Psychologist Philomena Essed has suggested the term "gendered racism" for the distinctive discrimination often faced by women of color.[159] Gendered racism is found in a variety of settings, from the neighborhood, to the school, to the workplace. In interviews with middle-class African Americans, Feagin and Sikes found that both black men and black women cited the problem of gendered racism, as in the case of this male executive:

> I think a black woman would have it really tough to get through because they have two obstacles to overcome, being a woman, trying to prove that they can do as good as a man, and then trying to prove that they can do as [good as] any white person, a white man in particular. So, that's a lot for a woman to overcome. And I think that's more stressful than what a black male would have to do, because he's just fighting against racism, and a woman is fighting against racism and sexism.[160]

Gendered racism is embedded in U.S. society. To take one important example, women of color suffer much from the dominant culture's image of female beauty. In advertising and the media, a certain type of white female, often thin and blond, is the typical beauty standard. African American models and actors have been underrepresented in the movies and advertising, and those who do appear are often lighter-skinned. This white standard has victimized other women of color, whom we find seldom in ads and the media. They suffer in other ways as well. In the 1990s, Japanese American Kristi Yamaguchi became the center of public attention after she won a gold medal in figure skating at the Olympics. Previous gold-medal winners—European Americans—soon became household names as advertisers flocked to them for endorsements. Yet, at the time, some prominent marketing professionals expressed the view that it would be unwise for advertisers to use a woman who looked so Japanese because of the strong anti-Japanese feeling among non-Asian workers in the United States.[161]

DISCRIMINATION IN HOUSING, LAW, AND POLITICS

Housing

Although federal law prohibits housing discrimination based on race, color, national origin, religion, sex, family status, or disability, women still face significant discrimination in housing. Of the more than 25,000 housing discrimination complaints to federal housing authorities in 2002, some 15 percent involved family status and 6 percent concerned gender discrimination in housing.[162] While gender discrimination complaints are not as frequent as those asserting racial discrimination, they do indicate a serious problem, especially given the fact that most victims of discrimination do not have the time, or are reluctant, to make official housing complaints.

Single women, with or without children, seeking to rent apartments or to buy homes are frequent victims of discrimination, especially if they are women of color. Civil-rights enforcement agencies report many discrimination complaints by women. Many people in the real estate industry hold the misconception that unmarried women have a negative effect on other renters or, in the case of homes, on property values. Single women are considered poor credit risks. Generally, women are commonly stereotyped as having less business sense than men, and women's incomes are thought to be unstable by lenders who fear that women will become pregnant and lose their jobs. In the mortgage loan screening process, real estate agents or bankers, who are reluctant to present a client whose eligibility for a loan appears to be "questionable" in conventional terms, may discourage potential female buyers from pursuing purchase of a home.[163]

In one interview, a Florida home buyer with a high income reported being closely scrutinized by lenders when she applied for home loans: "They wanted every check stub—I had to prove everything over and over. I never knew if it was part of the regular lending process, or if it was because I was a single woman."[164] She felt she had to secure much more documentation than a comparable male applicant. She applied to several lenders before being successful. One Dallas real estate agent noted how she reduces discrimination for women home buyers: "I always try to steer my single women buyers to young loan officers, who have a bit more sensitivity. The over-fifty-year-olds still can be quite misogynistic."[165] Although discrimination against women today is not as overt and blatant as it formerly was, covert and subtle discrimination, as in the "runaround" type of barriers to home buying noted above, remains common.

Many single women, including mothers who are separated or divorced, depend on rental property because of lower incomes and difficulties they experience obtaining home loans. Discriminatory practices in the rental market are rationalized as protecting the interests of the landlords. Single women may be told that a unit is not for rent to a single woman or that a man is needed to "keep up the property." They may be quoted a higher price than a single man or married couple. Landlords have required a male cosigner for a lease, regardless of the individual woman's financial circumstances. Landlords may refuse to consider income from alimony, child care, or welfare payments when assessing a woman's ability to pay rent.[166]

Some landlords exclude all separated or divorced persons or single parents with children. Some women face discrimination in rental housing because they have children. In many cases, landlords charge families with children and women who are pregnant higher rents and deposits; segregate them into separate floors, buildings, or complexes; or deny families because of the number, age, or sex of the children.[167] One Virginia landlord agreed in a consent decree in district court to provide $250,000 in compensation as settlement for a court suit brought by two mothers under an antidiscrimination law. The landlord agreed to have a local fair housing council monitor his rental agreements. The rental company had refused to rent an apartment to two women because their two children exceeded the landlord's limit for two-bedroom units. This is a problem throughout the country. Practices excluding or limiting the presence of children disproportionately affect women, since more women than men fall in this category. Moreover, state and federal laws attempting to restrict antifemale housing practices tend to be ineffective because of weak enforcement. In addition, many women who suffer discrimination do not report, or do not know how to report, the maltreatment to housing authorities—"[t]heir silence only serves to encourage perpetrators of discrimination in our society because they can act without fear of punishment."[168]

Moreover, as housing costs have risen over the last few decades, low-income women, especially single mothers, have found adequate housing more difficult to afford. In many cases, they must pay a huge share of their income for housing. Unable to keep up with rent and utility bills, many families become homeless. Nationwide, families with children make up an estimated one-fifth of the homeless population; many of these are headed by a single mother.[169]

Law and Politics

The subordinate position of women is well illustrated in the history of women's rights. In legitimizing slavery and the slave trade, the U.S. Constitution recognized this type of racial subordination, which remained part of U.S. law until the Thirteenth, Fourteenth, and Fifteenth Amendments were passed after the Civil War. The sexist nature of the legal system became quite explicit when the Fourteenth Amendment gave the right to vote only to "male citizens," making it clear that no woman, whatever her racial or ethnic background, had the right to vote.

Women were finally guaranteed the right to vote in all federal and state elections in the Nineteenth Amendment (1920):

> The right of citizens of the U.S. to vote shall not be denied or abridged by the U.S. or by any State on account of sex. Congress shall have the power to enforce this article by appropriate legislation.

A proposed constitutional amendment to give women equal rights with men (called the Equal Rights Amendment) is strikingly similar to that which expanded black (male) civil rights in the Fourteenth Amendment:

> The equality of rights under the law shall not be denied or abridged by the U.S. or by any State on account of sex. The Congress shall have power to enforce, by appropriate legislation, the provisions of this Article.[170]

While at one point this amendment was supported by 35 state legislatures, this statement extending full civil rights to women has not yet been added to the Constitution, to a substantial degree because of strong opposition by legislators (mostly male) who believe that the amendment will erode women's traditional gender-role requirements. Interestingly, opinion polls have shown that a popular *majority* approves of passage of this amendment.[171]

Between the Civil War and the present, the Supreme Court has dealt with a series of cases belatedly expanding the civil rights of African Americans. Not until 1971, however, did the same high court rule against a legislatively drawn gender-discrimination barrier.[172] In recent years progress toward women's equality in the federal system has slowed. One U.S. Commission on Civil Rights report found 800 sections of the U.S. legal code containing gender bias or gender-based terminology that conflicted with the ideal of equal rights for women. Many state laws are similarly gender biased. The commission report argued that the failure to incorporate an Equal Rights Amendment into the Constitution perpetuates gender bias in law. In recent years, an increasingly conservative Supreme Court has demonstrated a halting move away from equal rights for women. For example, the court has ruled that even if a college receives major federal aid for one of its programs, the entire college is not subject to federal civil rights laws protecting women.[173]

Not surprisingly, women's legal subordination is reflected in concrete political attainments. Women are seriously underrepresented among officeholders in the United States. Although women make up half the population, and 93 percent of respondents in a national poll stated that they would vote for a qualified woman candidate for president, no woman has *ever* served as president, vice president, or Speaker of the House. Between 1940 and 1990, few women served in the U.S. senate and only a small handful in the U.S. house.[174] (In addition, only two women have *ever* served on the U.S. Supreme Court, the two currently on that court.)

Women have been elected to many local, state, and federal offices in more significant numbers since 1990. In 2003, women held 25 percent (79) of the 316 statewide elective executive positions across the country. Additionally, women have increased their percentages in state and local elected offices. In 2003, women were about 22 percent of the 7,382 state legislators. Women now hold 401 (20 percent) of 1,984 state senate seats and 1,244 (23 percent) of 5,411 state house seats. At the federal level, the number of women in the U.S. house and senate has increased steadily, although women still make up only 14 percent of senators and 13.6 percent of representatives. Women also serve as delegates to the House of Representatives from Guam, the Virgin Islands, and Washington, D.C. One reason for these improvements in political representation is that women's voter turnout rate usually equals or betters the rate for men. Furthermore, women's organizations, such as the fundraising group Emily's List, have become top money-raising groups.[175] Nonetheless, even these gains indicate that women are still severely underrepresented in most state and federal legislative assemblies. At the national level, women are far less numerous than in most major European countries, where women generally have more political clout. In this regard, the United States remains one of the more backward industrialized countries.

Interestingly, there is a *major* gender gap in regard to how women and men view numerous social and political issues. In national surveys, thus, women are more likely than men to oppose the death penalty and support social programs. Because of differences in views, women—who once voted more Republican than men (for example, in the 1956 and 1960 national presidential elections)—now are more likely than men to vote for the Democratic Party. In numerous states since 1980, women voters have made the difference in elections of Democratic senators and representatives, and in the 2000 presidential election women voters made up the deficit in male voters and made it possible for Al Gore to win 12 of 19 states that he won. (Gore actually won more total votes than George W. Bush in that election because of women voters.)[176] Susan Carroll, a Rutgers researcher, notes that "Women bring their life experiences with them and, because their life experiences are still somewhat different than men's, that is reflected in public policy."[177] Significantly, after one election, women in Congress identified four legislative priorities for them: "fully funding Head Start, passing family-leave legislation, codifying legal abortion, and rescinding Congress's immunity to sexual-harassment laws."[178] Women's presence in state and federal legislatures is beginning to make a difference in debates there.

The Resurgence of Femininity

In recent years, we have seen a renewed emphasis on femininity among many U.S. women, a trend that may stem, some experts argue, from many women's inability to get good jobs or from intensified competition for "available men." The resurgence of excessive concern with feminine clothing, which is by definition "not designed to project a serious demeanor,"[179] seems symbolic of retreat from progress toward equality for women. One major newspaper report has asserted that new clothing lines for women reject the dress-for-success look of previous decades and are "representative of a resurgence of unabashed femininity."[180] One prominent women's clothing designer has a renewed accent on femininity in his clothing line: "There is a resurgence of femininity today. A woman knows she doesn't have to dress like a man to compete in the workplace, but she still wants to wear clothes that make sense."[181] However, as Brownmiller notes, "To care about feminine fashion, and do it well, is to be obsessively involved in inconsequential details on a serious basis. . . . Functional clothing is a masculine privilege and practicality is a masculine virtue. To be truly feminine is to accept the handicap of restraint and restriction, and to come to adore it."[182] Clothing reinforces gender divisions: Who is who is clear from grouping men in pants and women in skirts.

Women moving into traditionally male activities often feel pressure to be more feminine, at least as many men define that. For example, female bodybuilders once went for extreme muscle development, just like men, but now, as one prominent bodybuilder has noted, judges at bodybuilding contests have "tried to steer it back the other way, rewarding a woman who's got muscularity and a feminine shape. They wanted the women to look like women. The ideal is to have some muscularity but not to the degree where they look like men or unnatural."[183] In recent years, we see a strong, renewed emphasis on women's "grace and poise" and on feminity in many areas of U.S. society.

SOME HAZARDS TO BEING MALE

Gender-Role Problems

The gender system has an impact on men as well as women. Since the 1970s a number of male authors have argued that men pay a heavy price for the system of masculine power and prestige in which they are generally dominant. In *The Hazards of Being Male* (1976), Herb Goldberg argued that men's high death rate compared with that for women of the same age was evidence of the high price men pay for being "top dogs." In *The Liberated Man* (1975), Warren Farrell discussed men's psychological burdens, including pressure to conform to the masculine mystique. From childhood through adulthood the male is pressured to be "masculine," to suppress emotions such as crying and fear. Men are pressured to compete with other men, make more money, and climb the ladder to success. These and more recent books note the societal pressures on men to be sexually dominant over women, which can lead to fears of sexual inadequacy in men who cannot live up to the image, as well as to gestures of gallantry, sexual jokes about women, and displays of wanting to "make" every attractive woman they see.[184]

These masculine-analysis books have proposed solutions. Goldberg argued that the individual man should liberate himself psychologically, opening up his emotions. Goldberg focused on freeing men from adverse pressures of gender stratification.[185] Other authors, such as Marc Feigen Fasteau, adopted a broader view, but even they tended to focus on issues of personality and sexuality. Fasteau has called for the development of new androgynous personalities that would allow for the expression of both "masculine" and "feminine" characteristics, for greater freedom in sexual matters, for less interpersonal dominance, and for more mutual communication. Boys and men should be socialized from childhood onward to understand that they do not have to be tough, violent, and in control of the female. Fasteau has noted the need for new societal sex roles, institutionalized patterns, and personality traits—for girls to be allowed to play baseball and boys to play with dolls without stigmas; for women to be lawyers, engineers, and surgeons, and for men to get involved in child care.[186]

It is true that in societal stratification systems dominant group members pay some psychological price for the subordination they impose on others. Discussion of costs of being members of a dominant group can identify what the privileged group has to gain from dismantling an oppressive system. Still, books like those noted previously have served to minimize the *much* higher psychological and social costs of being female. Few such books on male problems explore this society's institutionalized, patriarchal structure. They ignore the broader social costs of sexism for the society. They seldom discuss the loss to society of the intelligence, ability, creativity, and effort of the many millions of women who lack equal employment or equal education and political opportunities—or the general impact of gender discrimination on civil liberties and democracy. In addition, some "hazards" attributed to being male are actually hazards attached to being workers—male or female, white-collar or blue-collar—in capitalistic, hierarchical workplaces. competitiveness

Since the 1980s, some male scholars have developed critiques of the older research and asserted a profeminist perspective. Clyde Franklin, for example, argues that masculinity researchers must reject the antifeminist viewpoint and "recognize that women have been oppressed by men; that men have gained privilege from this oppression; that men have reaped numerous disadvantages from patriarchy; and that society as a whole has suffered greatly from sex and gender inequality."[187]

Since the 1980s a new men's movement has developed. Some of these are openly religious. In recent years hundreds of thousands of men from a variety of racial and ethnic groups have gone to weekend rallies, such as those of the group called Promise Keepers, to recommit themselves to wives and children and boost their sense of masculinity. However, these rallies have sometimes been protested by women's organizations because Promise Keepers and other groups are trying to remake families into the traditional patriarchal ideal.[188] Ellen Goodman, a syndicated columnist, has put the criticism this way:

> The mass men's movement in this country now carries all these texts [of being better fathers, etc.] to men. Under the tutelage of anti-abortion, anti-gay leaders, it also carries a subtext: female submissiveness. As Marcia Gillespie, the editor of *Ms.* magazine and an African American, describes it, "They are telling men, 'We've been bad masters. Let's now become better masters.'"[189]

Many groups emphasize male bonding and rituals. Influenced by the books of authors like the poet Robert Bly, these groups emphasize putting men in touch with deeper emotions and making men masculine by putting "softer men" in touch with "primitive roots" and removing them from domination of mothers. Many groups have retreated to the woods to pound drums, make masks, and live in primitive conditions to get in touch with the "man within." Male counseling centers and "spirituality groups" have developed across the country. Some analysts interpret the men's movement as reflecting a desire to develop strong father–son bonds allegedly lost over decades of industrialization and urbanization. Indeed, some conservative analysts explain the movement as a reaction to an alleged "psychological castration" of men by the feminist movement.[190]

Research on local men's groups shows that participants in these ritual-oriented groups are mostly white and middle class. Local groups' ceremonies, which include dancing and drumming, provide male bonding and fellowship. Men often come from troubled families with weak male models and seek to develop a positive image of masculinity. While sympathetic to these attempts, researcher Michael Schwalbe suggests that the orientations of these groups reinforce patriarchy because they show little understanding of male domination of women in society.[191] The white men who dominate the men's movement are part of the dominant group. Unlike the women's movement, this men's movement cannot claim to be redressing serious grievances such as gender discrimination. In her book *Backlash,* Susan Faludi argues that while "the New Age masculinists claimed to bear no ill-will toward the women's movement," in their retreats the true subject is "power—how to wrest it from women and how to mobilize it for men."[192]

Some profeminist men's organizations, such as the National Organization for Men against Sexism, have developed workshops at which men deal with issues of sexism, homophobia, and sexual assault. Yet these groups are a minority among men's organizations.[193] In addition, even analysts such as Bly have developed a nuanced view of gender roles. Bly argues that masculinity for men must not mean a "fossilized patriarchy" and thus must be disconnected from notions of male dominance. Bly is very concerned about the roles of father and mother. In U.S. society, "the destruction of . . . the father's authority is almost complete." He cites such data that indicate a third of families have no effective father, but he also argues that forces are undermining the mother role, such as the constant attack by conservative groups on single mothers. Increasingly, children are raised by siblings and peers, not parents. Bly prefers what he sees as the better morality of the past: "But the Sixties were also a time when the ideas of genuine adults like Thoreau and Gandhi were being considered seriously; it was a time of adult moral energy. Right wingers forget that."[194]

Men Moving into Traditionally Female Jobs

Researcher Christine Williams studied men who have moved into traditionally female occupations, such as male nurses, and women who have moved into traditionally male occupations, such as women marines. She has found that male nurses, although they often suffered negative stereotyping by other men, generally prospered in nursing and advanced up the career ladder. They suffered no discrimination by female nurses, who encouraged them. Male nurses did not adopt aspects of the traditionally "feminine" stereotype. Indeed, the fact that they were male gave them an edge over female competitors in the traditionally female occupation of nursing.

In sharp contrast, women marines were expected by male superiors and peers to be "superfeminine." A cosmetics course was added to their basic training, and male colleagues generally expected them to conform to traditionally "feminine" stereotypes. Women marines suffered significant discrimination in this traditionally male occupation,

including the legally prescribed prohibition on women serving in many combat-likely positions—and denial of access to promotions based on such service. Research by Williams
and others suggests that the access of men and women to all occupational categories has
in many cases benefited men more than women. Male workers retain male privileges in
nontraditional jobs, whereas women continue to suffer traditional female liabilities in nontraditional jobs.[195]

SUMMARY

Gender stratification and sexist ideologies are deeply rooted in this society. European settlers to North America brought patriarchal arrangements with them. Most men have long
benefited from the subordinate position of women in home and workplace. In the capitalistic industrialization process of the last century, male employers and male workers shaped
gender segregation and discrimination in the labor market outside the home using patriarchal control techniques.

Gender-role stereotypes are still widespread. Girls and women grow up under the intensive pressure of life-shaping stereotypes. At home, at school, in the workplace, and in
the media, girls and women are frequently stereotyped as emotionally unstable, lovable,
sexy, or best suited to marriage and raising a family.

Traditional expectations about the wife-mother role emphasize domestic work, childbearing and child rearing, and submission to husbands. Husbands have had a traditional
"right" to insist on intercourse, and a wife has had a duty to submit. Today it is difficult in
some states for a husband to be convicted of forcibly raping his wife because of this traditional view.

Violence against wives and other women is now coming "out of the closet." Wife
abuse and violence against all women in the form of rape and assault are major national
problems. Police departments are gradually becoming sensitive to the problem of violence
against women, but sexism remains institutionalized in the justice system.

Most women workers remain concentrated in relatively few occupations, such as domestic worker, food service worker, nurse, secretary, sales worker, and school teacher, while
men dominate a larger array of occupational categories. In many job situations, women face
a variety of discriminatory barriers relating to hiring, promotions, and life on the job. In numerous business sectors, many of the best-paid jobs are still labeled informally "for men
only." In many worlds of business and government the separation of women into less-well-
paying clerical jobs and men into higher-paying white-collar jobs is well documented, even
though women and men in office occupations often have the same educational levels.

Institutionalized sexism places women in occupational roles that often have lower
status than male occupational roles. Many such jobs have a personal service component.
Sexual harassment on the job is another problem. It takes the form of unacceptable staring
at or touching a woman worker's body, nonreciprocated requests for intercourse, and rape.
A key aspect of harassment is that it reinforces other types of antifemale discrimination.

Discrimination in education, housing, and politics still confronts women. Women
have not yet been guaranteed equal rights under the law. The legal difficulties for women
are reflected in the lack of large-scale political advances in Congress, the executive branch,
state legislatures, local government offices, and court systems.

STUDY QUESTIONS

1. Sexual harassment is a broad concept. Define it and discuss several examples. Construct a continuum of possibilities from less to more severe forms of harassment.

2. Compare men's annual incomes with those of women. What effect does education appear to have on the income disparity between the sexes?

3. What kinds of formal and informal mechanisms are responsible for the concentration of women into relatively few occupational categories?

4. What are some of the principal reasons women fail to report (a) all incidents of rape and (b) all incidents of wife abuse?

5. How do the views of orthodox Marxists differ from those of many feminists in explaining patterns of female oppression and exploitation?

6. From what sources do our most common gender stereotypes emanate? How are stereotypical images perpetuated?

7. What is a *profeminist* perspective on masculinity and male sex roles?

ENDNOTES

1. See, for example, A Report by the National Women's Law Center, *Slip-Sliding Away: The Erosion of Hard-Won Gains for Women Under the Bush Administration and an Agenda for Moving Forward,* April 2004, available at www.nwlc.org/pdf/AdminRecordOnWomen2004.pdf.

2. Juliet Mitchell, *Woman's Estate* (New York: Vintage Books, 1973), pp. 99–120.

3. Joyce McCarl Nielsen, *Sex in Society* (Belmont, Calif.: Wadsworth, 1978), p. 42.

4. See Friedrich Engels, *The Origin of the Family, Private Property, and the State,* in Karl Marx and Friedrich Engels, *Selected Works,* vol. 2 (Moscow: Foreign Languages Publishing House, 1962), pp. 185–237; Karen Sacks, "Engels Revisited: Women, the Organization of Production, and Private Property," in *Woman, Culture and Society,* M. Z. Rosaldo and L. Lamphere, eds. (Stanford, Calif.: Stanford University Press, 1974), pp. 209–21.

5. Judith Rollins, *Between Women* (Philadelphia: Temple University Press, 1985).

6. Kate Millett, *Sexual Politics* (New York: Avon Books, 1969), p. 25.

7. Zillah R. Eisenstein, "Developing a Theory of Capitalist Patriarchy and Socialist Feminism, in *Capitalist Patriarchy and the Case for Socialist Feminism,* Zillah R. Eisenstein, ed. (New York: Monthly Review Press, 1979), pp. 5–40; see also Kirsten Amundsen, *A New Look at the Silenced Majority* (Upper Saddle River, N.J.: Prentice Hall, 1977); Joe R. Feagin and Clairece Booher Feagin, *Discrimination American Style* (Upper Saddle River, N.J.: Prentice Hall, 1978), pp. 9–15, 37–39.

8. Ruth Milkman, *Gender at Work* (Urbana: University of Illinois Press, 1987); Alice Kessler-Harris, *Out to Work* (New York: Oxford University Press, 1982); see also Heidi Hartman, "Capitalism, Patriarchy, and Job Segregation," *Signs* 1 (Spring 1976): 137–69.

9. For more on gender as socially constructed and created, see Nancy L. Marshall, ed., "The Social Construction of Gender in Childhood and Adolescence," *American Behavioral Scientist* 46 (June 2003).

10. Quoted in "Bits and Pieces," *Dollars & Sense,* February 1984, p. 11.

11. Marc Feigen Fasteau, *The Male Machine* (New York: Delta Books, 1975), p. 37.

12. Lenore J. Weitzman, "Sex Role Socialization," in *Women,* Jo Freeman, ed. (Palo Alto, Calif.: Mayfield, 1984), p. 160.

13. American Association of University Women, *How Schools Shortchange Girls* (Washington, D.C.: American Association of University Women, 1992), pp. 61–66, quotation on p. 63; see also Mary E. Hitchcock and Gail E. Tompkins, "Are Basal Reading Textbooks Still Sexist?" *Education Digest* 53 (May 1988): 38–39.

14. Nina Bernstein, "Study Says Equality Eludes Most Women in Law Firms," *New York Times,* January 8, 1996, p. 9.

15. Ibid.

16. Associated Press, *Women a Minority of Tenured Faculty and Administrators* (ret. February 17, 2004), available at www.cnn.com/2004/EDUCATION/02/17/women.on.campus.ap/index.html.

17. "No Comment," *The Progressive,* October 1992, p. 12.
18. Elayne Rapping, "Gender Politics on the Big Screen," *The Progressive,* October 1992, p. 36.
19. Denise Barricklow, "Women in the Media: With Few Exceptions, Sexist Stereotypes Endure," *The Ford Foundation Report,* Summer 1992, pp. 17–19, quotation on p. 18.
20. Ibid., p. 19.
21. Ibid., p. 18.
22. Rapping, "Gender Politics on the Big Screen," p. 37.
23. Steven Goldberg, *The Inevitability of Patriarchy* (New York: William Morrow, 1973), pp. 104–107; Fasteau, *Male Machine,* pp. 44–49; Lionel Tiger, *Men in Groups* (New York: Vintage Books, 1970), pp. 203–61; and George Gilder, *Sexual Suicide* (New York: Quadrangle Books, 1973).
24. Robert O. Blood and Donald M. Wolfe, *Husbands and Wives* (New York: Free Press, 1960), pp. 20–22; Lillian Rubin, *Intimate Strangers* (New York: Harper and Row, 1983).
25. Dair L. Gillespie, "Who Has the Power? The Marital Struggle," in J. Freeman, ed., *Women: A Feminist Perspective* (Palo Alto, Calif.: Mayfield, 1975), pp. 65–86.
26. The survey was conducted by the Families and Work Institute and others. Cited in Sue Schellenbarger, "'Incompetence Defense' Doesn't Wash, So Men Do More Housework," *Orange County Register,* March 4, 1996, p. D10.
27. Gillespie, "Who Has the Power?" p. 84.
28. Research is cited in Schellenbarger, "'Incompetence Defense' Doesn't Wash," p. D10.
29. Laurel Richardson Walum, *The Dynamics of Sex and Gender: A Sociological Perspective* (Chicago: Rand McNally, 1977), p. 182; see also pp. 181–83.
30. Gillespie, "Who Has the Power?" p. 84.
31. Ibid., p. 171; Mitchell, *Woman's Estate,* pp. 110–14.
32. Barbara Sinclair Deckard, *The Women's Movement,* 2nd ed. (New York: Harper and Row, 1979), p. 87.
33. Batya Weinbaum and Amy Bridges, "The Other Side of the Paycheck: Monopoly Capital and the Structure of Consumption," in *Capitalist Patriarchy,* pp. 194–96; Ruth Schwartz Cowan, *More Work for Mother* (New York: Basic Books, 1983).
34. Arlie Hochschild, *The Second Shift* (New York: Viking, 1989); the study by Peter von Allmen and Michael Leeds is cited in Marilyn K. Melia, "Sharing Housework an Uneven Bargain," *Cleveland Plain Dealer,* September 9, 1995, p. E5; Fawn Vrazo, "The Breakup of the Family Is Worldwide," *The Phoenix Gazette,* May 30, 1995, p. A1.
35. Emily Bazelon and Judith Resnick, "At Home and Work, Still a Man's World," *Los Angeles Times* (January 2, 2004), p. B13; "Karen Hughes to Leave White House Post," *The Bulletin's Frontrunner* (April 24, 2002).
36. Sylvia Ann Hewlett, *Creating a Life: Professional Women and the Quest for Children* (New York: Talk Miramax Books, 2002).
37. Quoted in Linda P. Campbell, "Burris Backs U.S. Bill for Battered Women," *Chicago Tribune,* April 10, 1991, p. 5.
38. Callie Marie Rennison, *Intimate Partner Violence, 1993–2001,* U.S. Department of Justice, Bureau of Justice Statistics (February 2003), available at http://www.ojp.usdoj.gov/bjs/pub/pdf/ipv01.pdf.
39. Patricia Horn, "Beating Back the Revolution," *Dollars & Sense,* December 1992, pp. 12–13, 21–22.
40. Ibid., pp. 12–13.
41. Ibid., p. 22; See also Anastasia Toufexis, "Home Is Where the Hurt Is," *Time,* December 21, 1987, p. 68; George Colt, "Stop! For God's Sake Stop!" *Life,* October 1988, pp. 121–31.
42. Cited in David Bauman, "Lautenberg, Torricelli Want to Link Domestic Abuse to Gun Control," *Gannett News Service,* March 20, 1996.
43. Jeanne McCauley, "The 'Battering Syndrome': Prevalence and Clinical Characteristics of Domestic Violence in Primary Care Internal Medicine Practices," *Annals of Internal Medicine* 123 (November 15, 1995): 737–46.
44. Del Martin, *Battered Wives* (New York: Pocket Books, 1976), pp. 88–119; Colt, "Stop! For God's Sake Stop!" p. 130; Toufexis, "Home Is Where the Hurt Is," p. 68; "Spouse Beaters: The Handcuff Cure," *U.S. News & World Report,* March 2, 1987, p. 12; Horn, "Beating Back the Revolution," p. 22.
45. "Man Who Got 18 Months in Wife's Killing Is Released," *Washington Post,* October 31, 1995, p. C6.
46. Julia Whealin, *Child Sexual Abuse,* National Center for Post-Traumatic Stress Disorder (ret. January 13, 2004), available at www.ncptsd.org/facts/specific/fs_child_sexual_abuse.html.

47. "The Career Price of Sexual Abuse," *Harvard Magazine,* May–June 1994, p. 20; David Finkelhor, *Sexually Victimized Children* (New York: Free Press, 1979); Mary Ellen Fromuth, "The Relationship of Childhood Sexual Abuse with Later Psychological and Sexual Adjustment in a Sample of College Women," *Child Abuse and Neglect* 10 (1986): 5–15; Christopher Bagley and L. Young, "Depression, Self-Esteem, and Suicidal Behavior as Sequels of Sexual Abuse in Childhood: Research and Therapy," in Michael Rothery and Gary Cameron, eds., *Child Maltreatment: Expanded Concepts of Helping* (Hillsdale, N.J.: Lawrence Erlbaum, 1988); Diana Russell, "The Incidence and Prevalence of Intrafamilial and Extrafamilial Sexual Assault of Female Children," *Child Abuse and Neglect* 7 (1983): 143–46.
48. Bruce Frankel, "Report: Child Abuse Estimates Low: Federal Data Understate Problem, Gallup Group Says," *USA Today,* December 7, 1995, p. A3.
49. U.S. Department of Health and Human Services, Administration on Children, Youth and Families, *Child Maltreatment 2001* (Washington, D.C.: U.S. Government Printing Office, 2003), available at www.acf.dhhs.gov/programs/cb/publications/cm01/cm01.pdf.
50. Finkelhor, *Sexually Victimized Children;* David Finkelhor and Gerald T. Hotaling, "Sexual Abuse in the National Incidence Study of Child Abuse and Neglect: An Appraisal," *Child Abuse and Neglect* 18 (1984): 23–33, quotation on p. 27.
51. Mary Gibbons and E. Chris Vincent, "Childhood Sexual Abuse," *American Family Physician* 49 (January 1994): 125.
52. Carol Rambo, "Multiple Reflections of Child Sex Abuse: An Argument for a Layered Account," unpublished manuscript, 1993.
53. J. Douglas Bremner, Steven M. Southwick, David R. Johnson, Rachel Yehuda, and Dennis S. Charney, "Childhood Physical Abuse and Combat-Related Posttraumatic Stress Disorder in Vietnam Veterans," *American Journal of Psychiatry,* 150 (February 1993): 235–239; and P. Ackerman, J. Newton, W. McPherson, J. Jones, and R. Dykman, "Prevalence of Post Traumatic Stress Disorder and Other Psychiatric Diagnoses in Three Groups of Abused Children (Sexual, Physical, and Both)," *Child Abuse & Neglect* 22 (1998): 759–774.
54. Quoted in Bill Hendrick, "Study: Sexual Abuse as Child Puts Young Women at Risk," *Austin American-Statesman,* May 13, 1994, p. A10.
55. Rambo, "Multiple Reflections of Child Sex Abuse."
56. Ibid.
57. Ibid.
58. A. N. Groth, "Patterns of Sexual Assault Against Children and Adolescents," in Ann Wolpert Burgess, ed., *Sexual Assault of Children and Adolescents* (Lexington, Mass.: Lexington Books, 1978).
59. Margaret O. Hyde, *Sexual Abuse: Let's Talk About It* (Philadelphia: Westminster Press, 1987), p. 79.
60. Rambo, "Multiple Reflections of Child Sex Abuse."
61. U.S. Department of Justice, *Crime in the U.S., 2002* (ret. January 2, 2004), available at www.fbi.gov/ucr/cius_02/html/web/offreported/02-nforciblerape04.html; S. Linnet Myers, "U.S. Ahead in Incidence of Rape, Too: Europe Has Less Child Abuse as Well," *Chicago Tribune,* November 22, 1995, p. 14; see also U.S. Department of Justice, *The World Factbook of Criminal Justice Systems* (ret. January 2, 2004), available at www.ojp.usdoj.gov/bjs/abstract/wfcj.htm.
62. Callie Marie Rennison, *Rape and Sexual Assault: Reporting to Police and Medical Attention, 1992–2000* (August 2002), available at blackstone.ojp.usdoj.gov/bjs/pub/pdf/rsarp00.pdf.
63. "Survey Questioning Change, F.B.I. Doubles Its Estimates of Rape," *New York Times,* August 17, 1995, p. A18.
64. Dawn M. Baskerville, "Safe AND Secure," *Essence,* January 1996, p. 104.
65. Cited in Myers, "U.S. Ahead in Incidence of Rape, Too," p. 14.
66. Campbell, "Burris Backs U.S. Bill for Battered Women," p. 5.
67. Susan Brownmiller, *Against Our Will* (New York: Bantam Books, 1975), pp. 346–49; Martin, *Battered Wives,* pp. 90–99.
68. Cited in Brownmiller, *Against Our Will,* p. 388.
69. Lawrence A. Greenfeld, *Sex Offenses and Offenders: An Analysis of Data on Rape and Sexual Assault* (February 1997), available at www.rainn.org/Linked%20files/soo.pdf.
70. M. Joan McDermott, *Rape Victimization in 26 American Cities: Application of Victimization Survey Results Project* (Washington, D.C.: 1979), p. xi.
71. Patricia Tjaden and Nancy Thoennes, *Full Report of the Prevalence, Incidence, and Consequences of Violence against Women: Findings From the National Violence against Women Survey,* U.S. Department of Justice (November 2000), available at www.rainn.org/fullnvawsurvey.pdf.

72. Cited in Brownmiller, *Against Our Will,* p. 396. See also Ann Wolpert Burgess and Lynda Ly-tle Holmstrom, "The Rape Victim in the Emergency Ward," *American Journal of Nursing* 73 (October 1973): 1,740–45.

73. Diana E. H. Russell, *Rape in Marriage* (Indianapolis, Ind.: Indiana University Press, 1990); David Findelhor and Kersti Yllo, *License to Rape: Sexual Abuse of Wives* (New York: Holt, Rinehart, and Winston, 1985).

74. Brownmiller, *Against Our Will* (New York: Bantam Books, 1975), pp. 346–49; Martin, *Battered Wives,* pp. 90–91.

75. Michelle J. Anderson, "Marital Immunity, Intimate Relationships, and Improper Inferences: A New Law on Sexual Offenses by Intimates," *Hastings Law Review,* 54 (2003): 1,465–1,574.

76. Robin Warshaw, *I Never Called It Rape* (New York: Harper and Row, 1988), pp. 3–16.

77. Survey done by *Playboy,* cited in Chip Rowe, "The Safe Generation: Campus Survey Results," *Playboy,* June 1995, p. 74.

78. Warshaw, *I Never Called It Rape,* p. 16.

79. See Patricia Tjaden and Nancy Thoennes, *Full Report of the Prevalence, Incidence, and Conse-quences of Violence against Women: Findings from the National Violence against Women Survey,* U.S. Department of Justice (November 2000), available at www.rainn.org/fullnvawsurvey.pdf; also see Callie Marie Rennison, *Rape and Sexual Assault: Reporting to Police and Medical Atten-tion, 1992–2000* (August 2002), available at blackstone.ojp.usdoj.gov/bjs/pub/pdf/rsarp00.pdf.

80. Jennifer K. Trucano, "Force Consent and Victims' Rights: How State of New Jersey in *Re M.T.S.* Reinterprets Rape Statutes," *South Dakota Law Review* 38 (1993): 203–225 at 203 fn6.

81. Marcia Froelke Coburn, "Sex Crimes Prosecutor's War against Offenders Hits System as Well," *Chicago Tribune,* August 15, 1993, p. 3.

82. Gary LaFree, *Rape and Criminal Justice* (Belmont, Calif.: Wadsworth, 1989), p. 204.

83. Quoted in Coburn, "Sex Crimes Prosecutor's War against Offenders Hits System as Well." See also Alice S. Vachss, *Sex Crimes* (New York: Random House, 1993).

84. Coburn, "Sex Crimes Prosecutor's War against Offenders Hits System as Well."

85. *The Violence against Women Act of 1991: The Civil Rights Remedy: A National Call for Pro-tection against Violent Gender-Based Discrimination,* S. REP. No. 197, 102d Cong., 1st Sess. 33–34 (1991).

86. Gary D. LaFree, "Jurors' Responses to Victims' Behavior and Legal Issues in Sexual Assault Trials," *Social Problems,* 32 (1985): 389–407 at 401.

87. McDermott, *Rape Victimization in 26 American Cities,* p. 49. The New York study is reported in Brownmiller, *Against Our Will,* p. 435; see also Susan A. Basow, *Sex-Role Stereotypes* (Mon-terey, Calif.: Brooks/Cole, 1980), p. 286.

88. Basow, *Sex-Role Stereotypes,* pp. 277–78.

89. James E. Robertson, "A Clean Heart and an Empty Head: The Supreme Court and Sexual Ter-rorism in Prison," *North Carolina Law Review* 81 (2003): 433–481, at 433.

90. Anthea Dinos, "Custodial Sexual Abuse: Enforcing Long-Awaited Policies Designed to Pro-tect Female Prisoners," *New York Law School Law Review* 45 (2000–2001): 281–296, at 283. See also *Human Rights Watch All Too Familiar: Sexual Abuse of Women in U.S. State Prisons* (1996) available at hrw.org/reports/1996/Us1.htm.

91. Human Rights Watch, *All Too Familiar: Sexual Abuse of Women in U.S. State Prisons;* see also Human Rights Watch, *Sexual Abuse of Women in U.S. State Prisons: A National Pattern of Mis-conduct and Impunity* (1996) available at hrw.org/press/1996/12/usprisons.htm; Human Rights Watch, *Nowhere to Hide: Retaliation against Women in Michigan State Prison* (1998), avail-able at www.hrw.org/reports98/women/; Human Rights Watch, *Women Raped in Prisons Face Retaliation. Michigan Failing to Protect Inmates, Says Rights Group* (1998) available at www.hrw.org/press98/sept/women921.htm; Human Rights Watch, *Human Rights Watch Chal-lenges Michigan's Subpoena to Reveal Confidential Information* (1998) available at www.hrw.org/press98/oct/michig1015.htm; Human Rights Watch, *U.S. Department of Justice Bargains Away Rights of Women Prisoners: Settlement Agreement Lacks Adequate Protections for Female Inmates Sexually Abused by Prison Staff* (1999) available at www.hrw.org/press/ 1999/jun/reno611.htm; Human Rights Watch, *Doing Something about Prison Rape (2003),* available at www.hrw.org/editorials/2003/prison092603.htm.

92. *Farmer v. Brennan,* 511 U.S. 825 (1994). See also, Katherine C. Parker, "Female Inmates Liv-ing in Fear: Sexual Abuse by Correctional Officers in the District of Columbia," *American Uni-versity Journal of Gender, Social Policy and the Law* 10 (2003): 443–477; Anthea Dinos, "Custodial Sexual Abuse: Enforcing Long-Awaited Policies Designed to Protect Female Pris-oners," *New York Law School Law Review* 45 (2001): 281–296; Amy E. Laderberg, "The 'Dirty Little Secret': Why Class Actions Have Emerged as the Only Viable Option for Women Inmates

Attempting to Satisfy the Subjective Prong of the Eighth Amendment in Suits for Custodial Abuse," *William and Mary Law Review* 40 (1998): 323–63.

93. "Victims of Prison Rape Rally for Legislation," *Corrections Professional* 8(20) July 25, 2003.

94. Institute for Women's Policy Research, "Research-in-Brief: Are Mommies Dropping Out of the Labor Force? *No!*" April 1992, pp. 1–2; U.S. Bureau of Labor Statistics, *Employment and Earnings* (Washington, D.C.: January 1992), p. 162.

95. See Nancy C. M. Hartsock, *Money, Sex, and Power: Toward a Feminist Historical Materialism* (New York: Longman, 1983), and Dorothy Miller, *Women and Social Welfare: A Feminist Analysis* (New York: Praeger, 1990), pp. 66–67, 128–30, 135–48.

96. Carmen DeNavas-Walt, Robert W. Cleveland, and Bruce H. Webster, Jr., *Income in the United States: 2002, Current Population Reports,* U.S. Bureau of the Census (September 2003), available at www.census.gov/prod/2003pubs/p60–221.pdf; see also, U.S. General Accounting Office, *Women's Earnings: Work Patterns Partially Explain Difference between Men's and Women's Earnings* (October 2003), available at www.house.gov/maloney/issues/womenscaucus/2003EarningsReport.pdf.

97. Diana Kunde, "Women at Work: A March Through Time," *Dallas Morning News,* July 4, 1995, p. D1.

98. "Know Who You're Pulling For," *Star Tribune,* October 11, 1992, p. 22A.

99. Evelyn Nanko Glenn and Roslyn L. Feldberg, "Clerical Work," in Freeman, ed., *Women,* pp. 317–20; U.S. Bureau of the Census, *Current Population Survey,* March 1995.

100. U.S. Bureau of the Census, *Statistical Abstract of the U.S., 2001,* No. 588 (ret. January 3, 2004), available at www.census.gov/prod/2003pubs/02statab/labor.pdf.

101. U.S. Department of Labor, Bureau of Labor Statistics, *Nontraditional Occupations for Women in 2002* (ret. January 16, 2004), available at www.dol.gov/wb/factsheets/nontra2002.pdf.

102. U.S. Department of Labor, Bureau of Labor Statistics, *Twenty Leading Occupations of Employed Women Full-Time Wage and Salary Workers 2002 Annual Averages* (ret. January 16, 2004), available at www.dol.gov/wb/factsheets/20lead2002.pdf.

103. Quoted in Leigh Hopper and Zeke MacCormack, "Confidence Poll Doesn't Rattle Watson; Chief of Police Says She Won't Resign No Matter the Results of the Survey," *Austin American-Statesman,* August 9, 1995, p. B1.

104. Frank Swoboda, "Law, Education Failing to Break Glass Ceiling: Panel Reports Boardrooms Remain 'Overwhelmingly' White, Male," *Washington Post,* November 25, 1995, p. C1.

105. Catalyst, *2003 Catalyst Census of Women Board Directors of the Fortune 500* (December 2003), news release available at www.catalystwomen.org/press_room/press_releases/WBD_03_PR.pdf.

106. Catalyst, *The Bottom Line: Connecting Corporate Performance and Gender Diversity* (January 2004), news release available at www.catalystwomen.org/press_room/press_releases/2004Fin_Per.pdf.

107. *A New Look Through the Glass Ceiling: Where Are the Women? The Status of Women in Management in Ten Selected Industries* (January 2002), report sponsored by Congressional Representatives John D. Dingell (D–MI) and Carolyn B. Maloney (D–NY) using data compiled by the U.S. General Accounting Office, available at www.house.gov/maloney/issues/womenscaucus/glassceiling.pdf; see also Robert E. Robertson, *Women in Management: Analysis of Current Population Survey Data,* U.S. General Accounting Office (April 2002), available at www.gao.gov.

108. U.S. Bureau of the Census, *Current Population Reports,* Table P-2 (ret. January 13, 2004), available at www.census.gov/hhes/income/histinc/p02.html.

109. Miller, *Women and Social Welfare,* p. 67.

110. "Desperately Seeking Nurses," *Dollars & Sense,* March 1988, p. 9.

111. U.S. Bureau of the Census, *Current Population Survey,* March 1995, available at www.bls.gov/cps/cpsaat39.pdf; see also, Paul Hammel, "With Good Jobs, They Leave Welfare: Women Train for Traditionally Male Work," *Omaha World Herald,* December 17, 1995, p. B1.

112. Institute for Women's Policy Research, *Equal Pay for Working Families* (June 1999), available at www.iwpr.org.

113. Robert E. Kessler, "Nassau a Victor in Sex-Bias Lawsuit," *Newsday,* August 26, 1992, p. 7; see also Laura M. Padilla, "Gendered Shades of Property: A Status Check on Gender, Race & Property," *Journal of Gender, Race and Justice* 5 (2002): 361–409.

114. Paula England, *Comparable Worth: Theories and Evidence* (New York: Aldine de Gruyter, 1992), as cited in Lois Yachetta, "Comparable Worth: Theories and Evidence," *Industrial and Labor Relations Review* 47 (January 1994): 335.

115. U.S. Bureau of the Census, *Current Population Survey* (March 2001), available at www.census.gov/hhes/income/histinc/p20.html.

116. "Washington Women Win Raises in Wage Suit," *Austin American-Statesman,* December 2, 1983, p. A5.
117. Amy Caiazza, April Shaw, and Misha Werschkul, *Women's Economic Status in the States: Wide Disparities by Race, Ethnicity, and Region,* Institute for Women's Policy Research (ret. June 31, 2004), available at www.iwpr.org/pdf/R260.pdf; see also Marianne Sullivan, "Mind the Gap," *Women's eNews,* April 26, 2004, available at www.alternet.org.
118. Diana E. Kendall, letter to author, March 1984, used by permission; see also Diana Kendall, *Sociology in Our Times* (Belmont, Calif.: Wadsworth, 1996), pp. 346–85.
119. Felix Lopez, "The Bell System's Non-Management Personnel Selection Strategy," in *Equal Employment Opportunity and the AT&T Case,* Phyllis A. Wallace, ed. (Cambridge, Mass.: MIT Press, 1976), pp. 226–27.
120. See Joe R. Feagin and Nikitah Imani, "Racial Barriers to African American Entrepreneurship: An Exploratory Study," *Social Problems* 41 (November 1994): 562–84.
121. EEOC Decision No. 71–2613, 4 FEP Cases 22 (1971).
122. See Joe R. Feagin and Melvin P. Sikes, *Living with Racism* (Boston: Beacon Press, 1994), pp. 182–83.
123. Jean Tepperman, *Not Servants, Not Machines* (Boston: Beacon Press, 1976), p. 49.
124. U.S. Department of Labor, Bureau of Labor Statistics, "Employed Persons by Occupation, Sex, and Age" (2002), available at www.bls.gov/cps/cpsaat9.pdf; see also J. A. Jacobs, "Women's Entry into Management," *Administrative Science Quarterly* 37 (1992): 282–301.
125. Karen S. Bell, Robert F. Randall, and Kathy Williams, "Women in Management Accounting: Determined to Succeed," *Management Accounting* 77 (November 1995): 20.
126. "How Well Are Women Doing in the Workplace? Fine, Say the Men. Not So, Say the Women," *PR Newswire,* February 14, 1996 available at www.prnewswise.com/.
127. Kirstin Downey Grimsley, "From the Top: The Women's View: Long Hours, Small Numbers, and Flexibility Characterize Female Executives," *Washington Post,* February 28, 1996, p. C1.
128. Ibid., p. C1.
129. Betsy Folks, a researcher at the Office for the Study of Automotive Transportation at the University of Michigan, quoted in Mike Casey, "Women Step into Driver's Seat of Auto Industry, Offering Service," *Crain's Detroit Business,* March 25, 1996, p. 12.
130. Bell, Randall, and Williams, "Women in Management Accounting."
131. Deborah L. Rhode, ABA Commission on Women in the Profession, *The Unfinished Agenda: Women and the Legal Profession* (2001), available at www.abanet.org/ftp/pub/women/unfinishedagenda.pdf; see also Bernstein, "Study Says Equality Eludes Most Women in Law Firms," p. 9.
132. Brian Gott, "Bar Says Female Attorneys Still Face Discrimination," *Charlotte Business Journal,* February 12, 1996, p. 1.
133. Gott, "Bar Says Female Attorneys Still Face Discrimination," p. 1.
134. Cited in Stuart Silverstein, "Work & Careers," *Los Angeles Times,* March 24, 1996, p. D13.
135. Dawn M. Baskerville, et al., "Women of Power and Influence in Corporate America," *Black Enterprise,* August 1991, p. 43; see also Ella Louise Bell and Stella M. Nkomo, "The Glass Ceiling vs. the Concrete Wall: Career Perceptions of White and African American Women Managers," unpublished paper, October 1992.
136. Bell and Nkomo, "The Glass Ceiling vs. the Concrete Wall," pp. 16–25.
137. Lin Farley, *Sexual Shakedown* (New York: McGraw-Hill, 1978), p. 14.
138. Catherine A. MacKinnon, *Sexual Harassment of Working Women* (New Haven, Conn.: Yale University Press, 1979), p. 40.
139. "Packwood Has Himself to Blame," *State-Times/Morning Advocate,* September 9, 1995, p. B10.
140. Alison Bass, "Military Remains Lair of Sexual Harassment," *Boston Globe,* May 18, 1995, p. 3.
141. Eric Matusewitch, "Sexual Harassment: Employers Can Be Liable for Customers' Actions," *New Jersey Lawyer,* December 4, 1995, p. 14.
142. Rhode, *The Unfinished Agenda,* p. 20.
143. Ruth Larson, "Sex-Harassment Report Critical," *Washington Times,* November 25, 1995, p. A4.
144. Louise F. Fitzgerald and Alayne J. Ormerod, "Breaking the Silence: The Sexual Harassment of Women in Academia and the Workplace," in F. Denmark and M. Paludi, eds., *Psychology of Women: A Handbook of Issues and Theories* (Westport, Conn.: Greenwood Press, 1993); see also Louise F. Fitzgerald, Sandra Shullman, et al., "The Incidence and Dimensions of Sexual Harassment in Academia and the Workplace," *Journal of Vocational Behavior* 32 (1988): 152–75.
145. N. L. Baker, *Sexual Harassment and Job Satisfaction in Traditional and Nontraditional Industrial Occupations,* unpublished doctoral dissertation, California School of Professional Psychology, Los Angeles, 1989, cited in Fitzgerald and Ormerod, "Breaking the Silence."

146. See M. P. Koss, "Changed Lives: The Psychological Impact of Sexual Harassment," in M. Paludi, ed., *Ivory Power: Sex and Gender Harassment in the Academy* (New York: SUNY Press, 1990); also see Fitzgerald and Ormerod, "Breaking the Silence."

147. Adam Clymer, "Parade of Witnesses Support Hill's Story, Thomas's Integrity," *New York Times,* October 14, 1991, pp. A1, A10–14.

148. Quoted in Eloise Salholz, "Did America 'Get It'?" *Newsweek,* December 28, 1992, p. 22.

149. American Association of University Women, *Hostile Hallways: Bullying, Teasing, and Sexual Harassment in Schools* (2001), available at www.aauw.org/research/girls_education/hostile.cfm.

150. John M. Leighty, "When Teasing Goes Over the Line," *San Francisco Chronicle,* November 8, 1992, p. 12; see also *Franklin v. Gwinnett County Public Schools,* 112 S.Ct. 1028, 1992.

151. Salholz, "Did America 'Get It'?" p. 22.

152. Nijole Benokraitis and Joe R. Feagin, *Modern Sexism* (Englewood Cliffs, N.J.: Prentice Hall, 1986), p. 78.

153. The study is summarized in Sue Morem, "Too Much Weight Is Given to Appearance," *Chicago Sun-Times,* January 15, 1996, p. 44.

154. Nijole Benokraitis and Joe Feagin, *Modern Sexism,* 2nd ed. (Upper Saddle River, N.J.: Prentice Hall, 1995), p. 135.

155. Camille Colatosti, "A Job without a Future," *Dollars & Sense,* May 1992, pp. 9–11, 21; also see Miller, *Women and Social Welfare,* pp. 135–48.

156. U.S. Equal Employment Opportunity Commission, *Pregnancy Discrimination Charges EEOC and FEPAs Combined: 1992–2002* (February 6, 2003), available at www.eeoc.gov/stats/pregnanc.html.

157. Pamela Mendels, "Up for Evaluation: Is Affirmative Action Still Working after 30 Years on the Job?" *Newsday,* June 13, 1995, p. 6.

158. Scott Leith, "Coke Settles Gender Inequity Lawsuit," *The Atlantic Journal-Constitution* (May 25, 2002), p. 1A; also see Nikki Tait, "Ford to Pay $3.8 Million in U.S. Discrimination Suit," *The Financial Times Limited* (February 21, 2000), p. 8; and Fay Hansen, "Pay and Promotion Lawsuits Surge and Judgments Get More Costly," *Business and Management Practices* (September 1998).

159. Philomena Essed, *Understanding Everyday Racism* (Newbury Park, Calif.: Sage, 1991), pp. 30–32.

160. For more on this issue, see Feagin and Sikes, *Living with Racism.*

161. See John Jeansonne, "Though Tremendously Popular after the Olympics, on the Marketing Front There's No Gold for Kristi," *Newsday,* April 16, 1992, p. 160. This section draws on Benokraitis and Feagin, *Modern Sexism,* 2nd ed., pp. 146–47.

162. Juan Andrade, "Bias Can't Go Unopposed," *Chicago-Sun Times* (June 21, 2002), p. 43; also see National Fair Housing Alliance, *2003 Fair Housing Trends Report* (ret. January 17, 2004), available at www.nationalfairhousing.org.

163. See, for example, Jennifer L. Money, "Rights Law Aids 4 People," *Chapel Hill Herald,* October 28, 1995, p. 1.

164. June Fletcher, "Single Women Face Bias in Home-Buying," *Newsday,* March 15, 1996, p. D1.

165. Ibid.

166. National Fair Housing Alliance, *2003 Fair Housing Trends Report* (ret. January 30, 3004), available at www.nationalfairhousing.org; U.S. Department of Housing and Urban Development, *Women and Housing: A Report on Sex Discrimination in Five American Cities* (Washington, 1975), pp. 54–58.

167. Shanna Smith, *Women and Housing Discrimination,* McAuley Institute (September 2000), available at www.mcauley.org/discrimination.pdf.

168. Juan Andrade, "Bias Can't Go Unopposed," *Chicago Sun Times* (June 21, 2002), p. 43; also see National Fair Housing Alliance, *2003 Fair Housing Trends Report* (ret. January 30, 3004), available at www.nationalfairhousing.org.

169. *Priority: Home!* (Washington, D.C.: Interagency Council on the Homeless, 1995), p. 23.

170. See James M. Burns, J. W. Peltason, and Thomas E. Cronin, *Government by the People,* 10th ed. (Upper Saddle River, N.J.: Prentice Hall, 1978).

171. Basow, *Sex-Role Stereotypes,* p. 280.

172. Kenneth M. Davidson, Ruth Bader Ginsburg, and Helma Hill Kay, *Text, Cases, and Materials on Sex-Based Discrimination* (St. Paul, Minn.: West Publishing, 1974), p. 3.

173. Tristam Coffin, "Women's Lib: The Revolution at the Gates," *Washington Spectator,* March 1, 1983, p. 2.

174. National Opinion Research Center, *General Social Survey, 1998.* Analysis by authors.

175. The National Foundation for Women Legislators, *Facts about Women Legislators: Women in Elective Office 2003* (ret. January 21, 2004), available at www.womenlegislators.org/facts/; see also Deborah Shanahan, "Force to Be Reckoned with Vote: Anniversary Sees an Increase in Women's Clout," *Omaha World Herald* (August 20, 1995), p. A1.

176. John B. Judi, *The Emerging Democratic Majority* (New York: Scribner's, 2002), pp. 49–50.

177. Shanahan, "Force to Be Reckoned with Vote," p. A1.

178. Salholz, "Did America 'Get It'?" pp. 20–22; quote on p. 22.

179. Susan Brownmiller, *Femininity* (New York: Simon & Schuster, 1983), pp. 14–19, 79–102; quotation on p. 101.

180. Elizabeth Snead, "Stylish Dresses Are Suitable for the Office Again," *USA Today,* January 17, 1991, p. D5.

181. Dianne M. Pogoda, "Oscar Plays Bridge: Oscar de la Renta's Clothing Collection," *Women's Wear Daily,* October 3, 1995, p. 8.

182. Brownmiller, *Femininity,* pp. 81, 86.

183. Bill Morri, "The Definition of Beauty," *Greensboro, N.C., News & Record,* January 19, 1996, p. D1.

184. Herb Goldberg, *The Hazards of Being Male* (New York: Signet Books, 1976), pp. 172–79; Warren Farrell, *The Liberated Man* (New York: Bantam Books, 1975), pp. 29–77; and Fasteau, *Male Machine,* pp. 20–23.

185. Goldberg, *Hazards of Being Male,* p. 172; see also pp. 172–83.

186. Fasteau, *Male Machine,* pp. 196–98.

187. Clyde W. Franklin III, *Men and Society* (Chicago: Nelson-Hall, 1988), p. 16; see also Harry Brod, ed., *The Making of Masculinities* (Boston: Allen and Unwin, 1987).

188. Ben Winton, "Gathering Their Faith: Upheaval Spawns Men's Movement," *Arizona Republic,* October 29, 1995, p. A1.

189. Ellen Goodman, "Two Men's Movements Expressing a Single Desire," *Newsday,* October 24, 1995, p. A36.

190. Stephen Randall, "Media Men's Movement," *Playboy,* January 1992, p. 24.

191. Michael Schwalbe, *The Men's Movement, Gender Politics, and American Culture* (Oxford: Oxford University Press, 1996). We draw in part on the summary in "Unlocking the Iron Cage: The Men's Movement, Gender Politics, and the American Culture," *Kirkus Reviews,* November 1, 1995.

192. Susan Faludi, *Backlash* (New York: Crown, 1991), pp. 307, 310.

193. See, for example, the list of groups in Bob Summer, "Male Spirituality on the Move," *Publishers Weekly,* March 11, 1996, p. 28.

194. Interview with Robert Bly in Neil Spencer, "Men Behaving Buddily," *Guardian,* December 17, 1995, p. 7.

195. Christine L. Williams, *Gender Differences at Work* (Berkeley: University of California Press, 1989).

chapter 6

Problems in Education

Today the troubled state of public education in the United States is widely commented upon. International comparisons—whether of student achievement or spending for public education—consistently find the United States below numerous other major countries. Conservative analysts call for a return to the "better days" of the past, although an examination of historical facts indicates that in terms of standards, availability, and attainment, the educational system, for all its troubles, is far better today than in earlier decades.[1]

Problems in education have broad implications for the future. Virtually all Americans see the education of children as an extraordinarily important aspect of society. Poorer Americans have traditionally looked to education as a way out of misery. The current educational system is helping to perpetuate poverty, however. Poor students are less likely than affluent students to complete high school or college, and black and Latino students are less likely than whites to complete either high school or college. Today, more than one in ten young people aged 16 to 24 is a high school dropout. The dropout percentage for black youth (10.9 percent) is slightly higher than the national percentage (10.7 percent). Strikingly, the percentage for Latino youth (27.0 percent) is almost *three times* the national percentage.[2] Young people from poor families are three to four times more likely to drop out of school than are youth from affluent families.[3] The reasons include having to work at an early age and the lack of a clear link in the economy between getting more education and getting better jobs.

From the 1800s forward, as cities developed, most children came to be educated outside the home—in school and other institutional settings—where they acquired knowledge about how to function as citizens, workers, and consumers. Many people assume that public education's major purpose is to maximize each child's skills and opportunities for mobility in society and that individual effort, not family background, accounts for personal success.

All is not well with the important public schools, however. Learning problems, illiteracy, biased "IQ" testing, discrimination, student protests, dropouts, boredom, violence—the list of publicly discussed issues in education is long. For decades, critics of public education have repeatedly called for more emphasis on basic skills, improved professionalization of teachers, dismantling of centralized bureaucracies, and greater parent and community involvement. Some have noted the increasing educational impact of commercial interests, especially television and advertising that move education away from the public interest toward these commercial interests. Others argue that lack of co-ordination in the curriculum limits classroom effectiveness. More than two-thirds of adult respondents in one nationwide opinion poll took the view that the public school system has failed. More than 80 percent of respondents in another poll felt that the controllers of education have made little progress toward the officially proclaimed goals of increasing the high school graduation rate, freeing schools of drugs and violence, or improving students' competency in regard to challenging subject matter. Innovations, while sometimes successful, have been too modest, short-lived, or limited to a few schools.[4]

Many problems in education are related to the inadequate funding of public schools by federal, state, and local governments. One often hears conservative arguments that the United States spends more dollars than any other country on public schools, yet this statement is misleading. The United States is clearly *not* the world's leader in spending on education, for it ranks only ninth among the 16 most industrialized countries of the world in annual per student spending, and it maintains only a middle ranking among these countries in terms of the percent of gross domestic product spent on schools.[5] State governments now spend more on *correctional systems* than on major education programs.

GOALS OF THIS CHAPTER

We begin this chapter with the observation that the bureaucratization of U.S. schools in the early nineteenth century reflected the goal of industrial capitalism to create submissive, disciplined workers rather than just literate ones. Formal schooling successfully indoctrinated diverse workers to the market demands of the economy. The market-oriented curriculum of most schools continues to ensure the teaching of dominant American values and conventional beliefs favorable to consumer-oriented capitalism. Intelligence tests, college entrance tests, academic credentialing, and racial, ethnic, gender, and class subordination in U.S. education act to justify the social privileges of whites, men, and the capitalist and managerial classes. We suggest that the many problems identified in this chapter that persist in U.S. education are best understood by looking carefully at the way in which these problems are rooted in the class, racial, and gender stratification patterns of the larger society. We survey the struggle for school desegregation and the damaging effects of classism, racism, and sexism in education. Beginning with this chapter on schools, then, we explore the varying impact of class, racial, and gender realities in a variety of institutional sectors of U.S. society.

THE GROWING SCOPE OF EDUCATION

Educational attendance and attainment levels have increased greatly since the nineteenth century. In 1870, just half of children 5 to 17 years old were in a public school; by 2002, the proportion had grown to over 96 percent. Public school enrollments increased from about 7 million students in 1870 to 47.7 million in 2002. Today, 91,380 public schools are operating in the United States.[6] Private elementary and secondary schools also enroll sizeable student populations. Today, more than one-quarter of the total U.S. population spends a significant amount of time annually in school. Educational attainments have also risen: Of those 25 years old and over, 84 percent have completed high school, 26 percent have completed four or more years of college, 6 percent have earned master's degrees, 1 percent hold professional degrees, and 1 percent hold doctorates.[7]

The number of institutions of higher education has increased in recent decades, reaching 4,182 in 2001; interestingly, 41 percent of these are local community colleges.[8] Enrollment in colleges and universities grew from 52,000 in 1870 to an estimated 16.1 million for the year 2005.[9] Community college enrollments increased from 451,000 in 1960 to an estimated 6.1 million in 2004. As a result, the proportion of Americans with college degrees has grown.[10]

ROOTS: THE DEVELOPMENT OF PUBLIC SCHOOLS

Public Schools in Urban Areas

Public elementary schools in urban areas began in the early 1800s with the "common" schools of New England, which taught the basics of reading and writing. Support for expansion of these schools came from native-born industrialists, merchants, and educators who shared a concern about the growing numbers of urban workers coming from rural areas of the United States and of immigrant workers from Europe. These leading industrialists thought that the morals ("immorality") of the rural and immigrant poor were mostly responsible for their poverty and misery. This individualistic perspective, discussed in Chapter 3, was then, as now, widespread.

Public education grew hand in hand with ever-expanding industrial capitalism in the late nineteenth and early twentieth centuries. Thus, Homer Bartlett, a representative of the Massachusetts Cotton Mills, often argued that the "owners of manufacturing property have a deep pecuniary interest in the education and morals of their help." He believed that because of competition the "best educated and most moral help will give the greatest production at the least cost per pound." For many of these industrialists one of education's basic goals was teaching discipline, obedience, and respect for authority. One urban school committee in 1851 complained that many of the city's youngsters "have to receive their first lessons of subordination and obedience in the school room." In the mid-1800s George Boutwell, head of the Massachusetts Board of Education, wrote of the role of the schools in preparing workers for industry: "When workers are well-educated and employers are disposed to deal justly, controversies and strikes can never occur, nor can the minds of the masses be prejudiced by demagogues and controlled by temporary and factious

These immigrant children are saluting the flag in an early New York school. (Library of Congress)

considerations."[11] Thus, business leaders saw schools as useful in reducing the pressure for worker organizations, such as unions, and in limiting protests against substandard work conditions.

These powerful reformers of education also thought in terms of the improved skills and literacy of potential workers. Yet literacy was not their only concern, since only one-fifth of their jobs actually required literacy. Business leaders and their allies were at least equally interested in the disciplinary aspects of schooling.[12]

High Schools

Another big push in education came after 1900, with the great expansion in junior high schools and comprehensive high schools. Vocational counseling and tracking systems were added to this system. So were extracurricular activities, such as athletics, which business leaders saw as grooming more cooperative workers. Large-scale, complex bureaucratic organizations, both private companies and government agencies, were for the first time beginning to dominate national life during this period. Many considered large corporations and government agencies to be more productive than smaller organizations. They could be run efficiently using ideas of "scientific management" (such as carefully timing work activities of employees). Many educational reformers were corporate liberals committed to an efficient and corporate-centered society.[13]

Corporate liberals believed that large corporations, allied governments, and "responsible" (not militant) unions should work together. In 1900 the National Civic Federation was formed as a meeting place for corporate leaders and union leaders who accepted the corporate view. Fear of unions and democratic socialist movements motivated this new organization to press for business and government cooperation to make the capitalistic system operate from the corporate viewpoint in a more orderly manner. Corporate liberals hoped that a moderate amount of government regulation could reign in excesses of a few "evil" capitalists, who might unfairly monopolize industrial sectors, as well as rising demands of workers, millions of whom were participating in strikes.[14] Public schools were seen as important in providing support for corporate liberalism by training students in the skills and discipline necessary to hold jobs in an increasingly specialized industrial system and by fostering in them the Anglo-Protestant, obedience values prized by business leaders.

Beginning around 1900, the National Association of Manufacturers (NAM), a leading business group, pushed for more public high schools and trade schools and for foreign-language courses and commercial subjects in those schools. The NAM saw development of trade schools as a way to take apprenticeship-training programs for workers out of worker-controlled unions.[15] By 1900, most public colleges and universities also felt the impact of business leaders' pressures as they expanded their academic courses to include such areas as business, engineering, journalism, and veterinary medicine.[16]

In the early twentieth century, an alliance of corporate executives and professional educators, with the help of Anglo-Protestant–dominated state legislatures, managed to replace many locally controlled school boards with more centralized school boards, central administrations, and professional educators. Local community control over schools declined as major business interests gained more control over school boards. Research studies from 1915 to 1925 by Scott Nearing and George Counts demonstrated that business leaders heavily dominated these new urban school boards, and these board members clearly did not represent a cross-section of the general population. This undemocratic pattern was also true for college boards of trustees. One consequence of this dominance was a string of firings of liberal teachers by business-oriented boards.[17] From then to now, most public school systems have been under the direct or indirect influence of business interests, while the interests of working-class citizens are often ignored.

In contrast, early twentieth-century educational reformers, such as John Dewey, viewed the social control function of education as important but tried to moderate the oppressiveness of much schooling by emphasizing the importance of humanistic concerns. In their view, democracy required that schooling promote intellectual development and produce an educated citizenry. Progressive terms such as *personality development, the whole child,* and *social and emotional growth,* which have dominated much educational policy over the decades, reflect the changes in educational policy that these reformers supported. In recent years, however, many conservatives have attacked the innovations of Dewey-type educational progressivism as providing too little discipline for students. Conservative thinking about education now predominates in many areas, and today concern with discipline, obedience, and productivity has often won out over more humanistic, whole-child values.[18]

Labor Movement Resistance

Since the early 1900s, many business and other influential leaders have supported a stratified school system, with a vocational track for many working-class children and an academic (college) track for children of business and professional families. However, many workers, viewing schools as critical to building a fairer society, have opposed these leaders' attempts to make schools into educational "factories" with several segregated tracks. In the past and the present, and across the country, labor unions have fought efforts to limit the scope of worker education, such as by accenting a strictly vocational, job-skills educational program. Labor groups have supported expansion of schooling and have pressed for more adequate funding, a broader curriculum, and greater democracy in schools.

In 1923, for example, the Chicago Federation of Labor challenged an attempt to change the Chicago school system into a duplicate of an automobile plant. Labor leaders condemned the local system's class bias and "threw their political resources into battles over changing the content and the direction of the public schools."[19] The federation was able to mobilize its followers to restrain business proposals to increase the vocational emphasis of public schools serving working-class neighborhoods.

Early working-class reaction to business-dominated public schools included creation of alternative schools. For example, the Modern School at Stelton, New Jersey, pioneered in nonauthoritarian approaches to education. There, educators permitted children greater freedom to learn without rigid discipline and to explore a diversity of classical and modern books and ideas. Moreover, since the civil rights movements of the 1960s, citizens in numerous cities and towns have created many progressive schools designed to break away from an overly structured status-quo orientation. To varying degrees, these alternative schools reflect values critical of the discipline-and-punishment emphasis in many public schools.[20]

School Choice and Schools-for-Profit

In recent years, many political and business leaders have placed an increased emphasis on making public schools fit the demands of the market economy and, thus, on running schools "like a business." School officials have implemented various forms of school choice as part of a "free market" approach to education. Some plans allow students to attend public schools outside their own districts, with each former school paying tuition to each receiving school. Other plans use "tuition vouchers" from public funds to pay students' tuition at private schools. Advocates for this market competition among schools argue that subsidizing student choice will force improvements in poor-quality schools. However, many educational researchers point out that taking funds from public schools to fund transfers to private schools only makes the troubled public schools even more underfunded and inadequate than they were. At best, so-called "choice" plans are available to a limited number of children, and they often favor those families who are better able to pay transportation and other costs related to sending youngsters to other schools. Educator Robert Lowe has commented that "A market system of education is merely an extension of deregulation that promises to compound social inequities. The consequences will be a more drastic maldistribution of opportunity than exists today."[21] While most affluent students become more privileged, most students from low-income families suffer even more.

Many educational critics object to providing public funds to private (especially religious) schools, which have no public accountability regarding the students they accept or the values they emphasize. Indeed, public subsidies for private religious schools seem to clearly violate the First Amendment to the Constitution.

The business approach to schools is often narrow-minded. Jonathan Kozol has pointed out that "when business enters education . . . it sells a way of looking at the world and at oneself. It sells predictability instead of critical capacities. It sells a circumscribed, job-specific utility." As a case in point, Kozol quotes the principal of one of Chicago's corporate-sponsored high schools, who stated, "I'm in the business of developing minds to meet a market demand."[22]

A number of educational entrepreneurs have advocated restructuring the educational system in ways that would remove some schools from government or community-based control. As a former CEO of Xerox Corporation stated, business should now "take ownership of the schools."[23] Yet the same leaders often strongly support publicly funded vouchers to help families pay the costs of private education. The latest tactic in attempting to privatize public education is the *corporate* tax credit voucher program. Pennsylvania and Florida, for example, recently passed tax credit programs allowing businesses to take a dollar-for-dollar tax credit for contributions made to nonprofit school-funding organizations. These nonprofit organizations supposedly provide low-income students "scholarships" or tuition vouchers that they can use at private schools. However, such voucher programs are currently diverting some $224 million in what would have been public tax funds to private (including religious) schools, with little to no accountability for how the funds are spent. Even though these and other tuition voucher programs are often touted as benefiting mostly poor children, most private schools that get tuition tax credit vouchers are in middle-class and affluent areas, not in poor districts. Another problem with these public-to-private programs is that public schools are accountable for student academic performance, and government officials regularly sanction them for failing to meet state academic standards; in contrast, private schools are not held accountable for their academic standards like the public schools.[24]

Numerous recent experiments in shifting public schools to private corporate control have proven unsuccessful. For example, Whittle Communications, which announced a plan to open 1,000 for-profit schools, abandoned this plan and instead entered into contracts to manage existing public schools, promising to improve academic records while still making a profit. During this same period, another private corporation, Educational Alternatives, Inc. (EAI), lost its contracts with public school systems in Miami, Florida; Hartford, Connecticut; and Baltimore, Maryland. The nine EAI-run inner-city schools in Baltimore had received 11 percent more money than the city's other schools, and although the company improved the schools' physical appearance and introduced up-to-date technology, it failed to improve students' academic performance.[25] EAI's performance makes clear the need to look beyond management efficiency in addressing the educational needs of children from families destabilized by poverty. As one educator has stated, "The truth is that nobody has yet found a way to operate a good public

[handwritten note in left margin: Solution to the Poor]

school system in places where most of the students come from poor, troubled families."[26] The way to turn around failing public schools is relatively easy to see—that is, provide much greater economic and human resources, smaller classes, better teachers, much less segregation and discrimination, and access to meaningful jobs after schooling—but it is quite hard to implement politically in a society still riddled by racial and class inequalities.

TRACKING SYSTEMS AND THE CURRICULUM

Tracking systems are commonplace: Students from higher-income backgrounds tend to be placed by school officials in academic, college-oriented tracks. In contrast, school officials tend to offer vocational programs that teach such things as clerical skills, the use of machinery, or home economics to students from low- to moderate-income working-class backgrounds. High schools vary in their emphasis on vocational and academic programs depending on geographical location, with central city and rural schools that are disproportionately composed of working-class students or students of color stressing vocational education and predominantly white suburban schools emphasizing academic programs. In desegregated schools, school officials are three times more likely to place black and Latino students than white students in vocational education or in classes for the mentally retarded.[27] While many working-class students manage to move into academic tracks, this is often difficult to do. Tracking and ability grouping within schools have by no means been absolute, but these segregating programs remain fundamental features of educational systems.

Researcher Vincent Roscigno has noted that "the preponderance of evidence suggests that tracking operates to widen the gap between high and low achievers."[28] The typical tracking system assigns students of color "unjustifiably and disproportionately to lower tracks and almost excludes them from the accelerated tracks; it offers them inferior opportunities to learn and is responsible, in part, for their lower achievement."[29] Recent research shows that African American students with ability comparable to white students often get put into tracks lower than their abilities indicate. Not surprisingly, those students in "higher" tracks get more attention and better resources, including better-qualified teachers and more rigorous instruction. This, in turn, enables the students to perform better in later schooling and in after-schooling jobs. White children disproportionately populate "gifted" tracks and students of color disproportionately populate special education tracks, in both cases in proportions often not justifiable in terms of children's test scores.[30] Indeed, school systems that have eliminated or reduced ability tracking generally have had better achievement results for students than those that maintained or increased such tracking.[31]

Significantly, debate continues on whether tracking is a good educational strategy for *any* students, much less for those who need extra help in learning certain educational skills. Tracking has negative effects on all children in that they are much less likely to learn the effective ways of interacting with people of different backgrounds when they socialize mostly with children of their own racial and class backgrounds. Such homogeneous socializing limits the breakdown of stereotyping and reinforces inegalitarian divisions within society.[33] Indeed, a growing body of social psychological literature indicates that the more diverse and stimulating the learning milieu, the more likely children are to go beyond traditional ways of thinking to critical and innovative thinking.[33]

Two-Tiered Schooling

Great disparities in the distribution of educational resources have produced a two-tiered educational system: Students in affluent, predominantly white suburban communities usually attend well-equipped schools that provide almost unlimited learning opportunities. Students in poor communities—who often face larger classes, outdated books or equipment, and inferior facilities—have less incentive to study. At one poorly lit school with aging, half-painted walls and graffiti-covered doors, students have talked about the "prison vibes" of their environment.[34]

Most states have huge disparities in funding from one school district to the next because large portions of educational funding come from local property taxes. In 1995 in New York, the highest-spending public district spent $32,792 per pupil, as compared to only $5,066 for the lowest-spending district. In Texas, the range was from $40,505 to $2,570; in California, from $20,000 to $2,808; and in Massachusetts, from $21,000 to $2,846.[35] Then as now, those communities with moderate-income populations cannot spend nearly as much on schools as more affluent communities. The major reason for this is that the poorer districts do not have as much high-priced property to tax as affluent districts. Property is very unequally distributed in the United States, and when school systems depend heavily on local property taxes to support schools, those districts with less high-priced property inevitably have less adequate school systems.[36]

While money is not the only factor affecting the quality of schools, it is the major factor shaping resources available to students and teachers. Schools with few resources cannot provide equality of educational opportunity. In *Savage Inequalities: Children in America's Schools,* Jonathan Kozol has described students he observed while researching his famous book:

> The real little kids seem so hopeful—first- and second-graders. Kindergarteners are so full of hope, cheerfulness, high expectations. By the time they get into fourth grade, many begin to lose heart. They see the score, understand they're not getting what others are getting . . . . They see suburban schools on television. . . . They begin to get the point that they are not valued much in our society. By the time they are in junior high, they understand it. In Morris High School in the Bronx, one child said to me, and I'll never forget it, "We have eyes and we can see; we have hearts and we can feel." He said, "We know the difference."[37]

When asked recently if anything had changed since he wrote *Savage Inequalities,* Kozol replied:

> Not much. . . . I get the sense that the press is bored with "equity" in general, along with racial segregation. Therefore, it tends to focus on mechanistic solutions—various types or restructuring, downsizing this and upsizing that, centralizing this and decentralizing that. There's an enormous faith in slogans. . . . We certainly can't accept this bizarre idea that money and race and a great deal of racial hatred are not at the heart of the school problem in the cities of America. Because those are the ultimate issues.[38]

Many schools today graduate large numbers of students without the well-developed job skills needed to succeed in the economy. During and after high school, they often feel like failures and are not motivated to excel. Yet it is not students tracked into poorly funded schools who have failed but the officials (and affluent citizens) who control local school systems who have *failed them*.[39] Significantly, recent lawsuits filed in several states have sought to force a more equitable distribution of tax resources among school districts. A number of these suits have charged that local and state governments have not met the requirements of their constitutions, which often promise "adequate" school systems for all.[40]

The tracking systems and dramatically unequal resources of the central city, rural, and suburban schools are not random conditions but reflect the *intent* on the part of many business and political leaders and school officials, at the national, state, and local levels, to structure schools according to the same class–race–gender framework that exists in the larger society. Inequality of educational opportunity is still the norm in the United States.

The Content of Schooling

Business-oriented concerns have shaped both the content and the structure of schooling, particularly at the high school level. Teachers are important socializers of children since what they teach in schools generally communicates and reinforces society's basic values and conventional beliefs. Many teachers, directly or indirectly, teach the ideology of individualism, prevailing stereotypes about the poor, an uncritical view of market capitalism, and various stereotypes about women or people of color. For example, we have previously noted some stereotypes of girls and women in school textbooks (Chapter 5). Conventional stereotypes and unexamined beliefs about society are passed along informally in the ways teachers act toward students, in stories they tell, and in comments on current events. Often, the formal curriculum communicates beliefs supporting the status quo; little information is presented on racism or sexism in U.S. history or on progressive people's movements that have challenged the oppressive status quo over the course of U.S. history, movements that have periodically increased democracy in the country.

Teachers, principals, and school boards decide what materials students read. U.S. schools are generally oriented toward reproducing the status quo. In the last decade, major groups of corporate leaders have renewed their commitment to expanding the business-oriented curriculum materials used in U.S. classrooms. Business leaders, fearing that public criticisms of big business may grow in scale and significance, push political officials and school administrators to provide even more thorough and uncritical training in so-called "free enterprise." Major business groups have funded programs to develop free-enterprise materials and have pressured state legislatures and local school systems to require more uncritical free-enterprise courses. Most states have responded to these pressures in concrete ways. Typically, however, such business-oriented education does not involve critical thinking about an inegalitarian capitalism.

The Educational Needs of American Indian Schoolchildren

Federal government officials have historically viewed education as a way to assimilate American Indian children to European American customs and culture—"to convert young Native Americans into 'white men,' with future generations naturally following their lead since Western European–based society was 'inherently superior' to tribal society." Government-enforced isolation of American Indian children in boarding and mission schools located great distances from their families and friends furthered their assimilation into European American culture and society. In these government schools, such as the Carlisle Indian School in Pennsylvania, the usually white administrators forced Indian children to abandon home traditions and customs, to wear uniforms, and, for boys, to wear short hair. Children were greatly pressured to give up their indigenous religions and adopt Christianity, to speak only English, and to adopt non-Indian names. Educational opportunity for these children entailed learning vocational trades rather than preparing for advanced education. Not until the 1960s did the federal government and its educational establishment provide Indian children with a better-quality education. Even then, Indian leaders had to force the federal government to act responsibly in regard to Indian education.

Cultural assimilation pressures still persist in Indian education today. Because of the large number of non-Indian teachers educating Indian children, much about American Indian education lacks an indigenous perspective. One recent research study shows that in tribal schools only a third of the teachers are Indian, while in public schools with high Indian enrollments only 15 percent of the teachers are Indian. Educational researchers stress the importance of language and cultural similarity among teachers and students to academic success for Native American schoolchildren. Among other benefits, when teachers and students share a cultural identity that enhances children's learning, it creates stronger student–community bonds and increases children's desires to stay in school. Otherwise, cultural identity is at risk in a white-controlled educational environment. In such environments students "experience difficulty maintaining rapport with teachers and establishing relationships with other students; feelings of isolation; racist threats; and frequent suspension." One researcher's visit to an elementary school on a Chippewa Indian reservation exposed the cultural imperialism of Indian education. He observed students in a sixth-grade English class working on a composition for Thanksgiving, which was entitled "Why We Are Happy the Pilgrims Came." Yet, the early English colonists who are celebrated uncritically by whites were responsible for killing many Indian men, women, and children and stealing most of their land.

Interestingly, almost all respondents in a recent survey of teachers in Indian teacher preparation programs nationwide believed Indian languages and cultures should be included in the schooling of Indian children; yet only 26 percent of them reported that they were prepared to teach a curriculum incorporating such languages and cultures.

The continued miseducation and marginalization of Native American students explain why they as a group score below national averages on math, reading, and history tests. Their high school dropout rate is nearly *four times* the rate for white students, and their dropout rate at grades seven and eight is *five times* the rate for white students. Moreover, reforming Indian education itself would not directly address the other serious problems facing Indian children and their families. For example, the poverty rate for American Indians is 23.2 percent, well above the white percentage.

continued on next page

As part of his No Child Left Behind education policy, President George W. Bush signed an executive order mandating an assessment of the role of Indian languages and culture in educational strategies to improve Indian children's academic achievement. However, it is not *assessment* of the importance of languages and culture that educational institutions require but rather the *implementation* of Indian languages and cultures in existing Indian education. For a long time, the research record has shown unmistakably the importance of language and cultural integration to the educational success of Indian schoolchildren.

One researcher examining the importance of building an Indian teaching force has put it this way: "American public education still does not seem to recognize diversity as an asset, which raises the strong possibility that unique heritages, dialects, and values of particular cultural groups will be excluded with the implementation of the No Child Left Behind legislation, state standards, and high-stakes testing." Many scholars fear that contemporary Indian education is becoming as white-assimilationist as the Indian boarding and missions schools of the past.

Sources: D. Michael Pavel, "Schools Principals and Teachers Serving American Indian and Alaska Native Students," *ERIC Digest* (January 1999), available at www.ael.org/page.htm?&pd=1&scope=ai&index=217&pub=x; Kathryn D. Manuelito, "Building a Native Teaching Force: Important Considerations," *ERIC Digest* (December 2003), available at www.ael.org/page.htm?&pd=1&scope=ai&index=755&pub=x; Richard Schaefer, *Race and Ethnic Groups* (New York: Prentice Hall, 2004), p. 191; Angela A. Willeto, "Navajo Culture and Female Influences on Academic Success: Traditional Is Not a Signficant Predictor of Achievement among Young Navajos," *Journal of American Indian Education,* 38(2), pp. 1–24 (Winter 1999); U.S. Commission on Civil Rights, *A Quiet Crisis: Federal Funding and Unmet Needs in Indian Country* (July 2003), available at www.tedna.org/usccr/quietcrisis.pdf.

TESTING AND PUBLIC SCHOOLING

"Intelligence" Tests

Stereotyping of subordinate racial and class groups has long been commonplace in the United States. Racial and class stereotypes were—and are—based in part on misreading the results of a variety of psychological tests, including those labeled "intelligence" or "IQ" (intelligence quotient) tests. To begin with, the term *intelligence test* is inaccurate because these conventional tests measure only *selected* verbal and quantitative skills, and not broad intelligence. Most questions on paper-and-pencil tests involve reading English, English vocabulary, math, and symbol manipulation. Human intelligence involves far more than these limited skills. The Carnegie and Rockefeller Foundations once poured millions of dollars into development of such tests. Writing in 1916, the leading psychologist Lewis Terman voiced the dominant view of links between social class and the new IQ testing: "Preliminary investigations indicate that an IQ below 70 rarely permits anything better than unskilled labor; that the range from 70 to 80 is preeminently that of semiskilled labor, from 80 to 100 that of the skilled ordinary clerical labor, from 100 to 110 or 115 that of the semiprofessional pursuits; and that above all these are the grades of intelligence which permit one to enter the professions or the larger fields of business."[41]

Terman argued that IQ-test information would help in devising different school tracks for students; following his advice, since the 1920s many school systems have used psychometric tests to screen and separate students into curriculum tracks or other educational programs. In recent decades, in response to researchers' criticisms of IQ tests and of the uncritical use of test scores to channel students, many school systems have become more cautious in their use of tests for pupil sorting, ability grouping, and tracking. Still, today one can find Terman's class-biased legacy in the various psychometric tests used for sorting purposes in schools—from public elementary schools to graduate schools at universities. For example, the Scholastic Aptitude Test (SAT), which is used to screen students for college admission, is one of the most widely used paper-and-pencil tests in use today, yet it has long been known from research that such tests contain a built-in racial and class bias greatly favoring students from white and middle-class family backgrounds.[42]

Some influential educators and writers have used scores on these class-biased "IQ" tests to justify the greater wealth, income, and other privileges of the employer and managerial classes. For example, the late Harvard psychologist Richard Herrnstein argued aggressively (and naively) that upper-income groups must have greater intelligence because they have higher IQ test scores than most other Americans, whereas lower-income, working-class groups must have less general intelligence because they score lower on existing IQ tests.[43]

Yet another problem with so-called IQ testing is language bias. For example, Latino students on average perform less well than non-Latino whites on certain academic achievement tests given in English. Not surprisingly, the predictive validity (for college grades and college success) of the tests used for college and graduate school entrance (SAT and GRE) is considerably lower for Latinos than for whites. One psychologist has commented on the inaccuracy of English-language test scores: "In my clinic, the average underestimation of IQ for a Puerto Rican kid is 20 points. We go through this again and again. When we test in Spanish, there is a 20 point leap immediately—20 higher than when he's tested in English."[44] Some Spanish-language achievement tests have been developed in recent years, yet since most are translations of English-language tests, they usually pass along whatever cultural and class bias existed in the original tests.[45]

Racial Issues

In the early twentieth century, prominent white scientists used differential scores on the new IQ tests to defend the common racist views of non-British European immigrants then entering the United States in large numbers. Using verbal and performance measures, white psychologists associated with the American Psychological Association conducted large-scale testing of World War I draftees. Their statistical analyses were published in the 1920s and gained public and congressional attention, mainly because of the racial-inferiority interpretation placed on test results for the southern and eastern Europeans among the draftees.[46]

In the 1920s Carl Brigham, a Princeton psychologist who would later help develop today's college entrance tests, wrote a book on the intellectual and racial inferiority of these (later seen as white) immigrant groups, drawing on the army tests. Average scores for foreign-born draftees ranged from a high of 14.87 for English draftees to lows of 10.74 for Polish American draftees and 11.01 for Italian American draftees. Brigham—who later recanted—considered those white groups with lower scores to be *inferior racial stocks*.

Numerous prominent scholars interpreted these "scientific" results to support the then-prevalent ideology of northern European (racial) superiority over immigrants from southern and eastern Europe, who were there regarded as members of inferior (not Nordic) racial groups.[47]

For much of the twentieth century, few researchers, educators, and test givers considered the possibility that the linguistic (English), cultural (Anglo-Protestant), and other biases in these relatively short tests accounted for differences among European groups. They assumed, naively, that these tests measured real differences in intelligence rather than differences in learned skills. Today, debates over the inferiority of these white "racial" groups are a historical curiosity. Virtually no physical or social scientist today would advance arguments for racial or biological inferiority among white groups based on such test data.

However, some popular and scholarly analysts now use similar arguments to explain IQ and other test-score differences between white and black (or Latino) Americans. This theme of "intellectual inferiority" between racial groups has periodically received renewed attention since the 1960s, partially in response to court orders desegregating school systems. White social scientists Arthur Jensen and Richard Herrnstein, among others, have alleged that differences in IQ test scores are not just environmentally determined but reflect genetic differences between whites and blacks. In their view, lower test scores are evidence that groups at the lower socioeconomic levels are intellectually and genetically inferior to

Some court and board of regents' decisions have rejected admissions programs designed to increase the number of black and Latino students at traditionally white universities.

those at higher levels and that whites and blacks have different types of intelligence requiring different educational techniques. Jensen has also expressed concern about black birth rates, which he believed might result in a lowering of national IQ.[48] Although many social scientists have successfully critiqued the reactionary racial views of Jensen and Herrnstein, especially for omitting major educational and environmental variables, such notions about black (or Latino) group intelligence are still advocated by a small handful of academics and politicians.[49]

As early as the 1930s, some psychologists questioned whether "IQ test" results were evidence of genetic differentials. Citing data on extremely oppressive conditions suffered by black Americans, they cogently argued that white–black differences in test scores reflected education and income differences. Research studies showed that IQ test scores of black children improved with better economic and learning environments, such as when children in segregated southern schools moved to integrated northern schools. Moreover, results from large-scale IQ testing showed black children and adults in some northern states scoring *higher* than whites in some southern states.[50] Using the racist logic of analysts such as Jensen, one would conclude that white southerners are thus mentally and "racially" inferior to black northerners! These white analysts would of course avoid this interpretation; as defenders of black inferiority, they would not argue that IQ test data show black intellectual superiority. Rather, they would likely accept the *environmental* explanation for uncomplimentary regional IQ-score differentials for whites versus blacks. Differentials *favoring* whites are also most reasonably interpreted as reflecting environmental factors, including pervasive racial discrimination against most Americans of color.

Some analysts have focused on the white middle-class bias inherent in virtually all achievement and psychometric tests (including "IQ tests"). Most such tests are created by middle-class whites and measure only learned skills and acquired knowledge (such as linguistic, literary, or geographic knowledge)—skills and knowledge not equally available to all U.S. income and racial groups because of discrimination and inadequate educational facilities. Researchers have found that achievement test taking is a skill white middle-class children are more likely to possess because their parents have more socioeconomic resources and are most familiar with such testing. White middle-class children take many such tests and by doing so enjoy a built-in advantage over other children.[51] They usually have parents who can pay expensive fees charged by organizations that tutor children to do better on such tests.

Why do many Americans still accept a biological or genetic view not only concerning IQ differences but also other racial, class, and gender differences? Perhaps this happens because schools often accent a biological view of the world. The "biological" is often seen as more real than the "social" or the "cultural." Explanations of persisting racial and gender differences in terms of biological differences are often more easily accepted than are more complicated explanations of institutionalized racial roles or patriarchal gender roles. As a result, in discussions of roles, *biological, genetic,* and *inherited* can become code words used to justify racial and gender subordination and discrimination. Because biological views of the world often receive more attention in schools than do sociological and structural views, it is not surprising that many students come to accept biologically grounded explanations of racial, class, or gender inequality.[52]

HIGH SCHOOLS TODAY

Restlessness in Suburbia

Today's suburban high schools often resemble the troubled environment that Ralph Larkin found in a field study of an affluent suburban high school: "The most serious complaint among Utopia High School students is boredom. They are restless. They complain of having nothing to do. They want to leave town, but they have no idea of where to go. They are forced to compete with each other for grades, sexual attractiveness, hipness, and all the other minutiae that are involved in the status race."[53] At this school, the youth culture was split along racial, gender, and occupational lines. Sex and drugs had become routine, part of the weekly experiences for most of these relatively affluent high school students.[54]

Many relieved parents are glad to see the complacent, unprotesting, patriotic youth of recent decades. These students are less likely to protest school and political authorities than were students of the 1960s. Today, students tend to be more introspective, and despair and restlessness are common complaints. Larkin interprets this boredom as "the result of the repression of the impulse to rebel."[55] Most of these students have adjusted to a routine way of life. Affluent parents tell their children to postpone their work lives in the outside world. They must stay in their academic track where they are constantly told to work hard so they can go to a good college.[56]

Learning Consumerism

Seeking profits and maintaining low labor costs, as well as control of ordinary workers, are goals driving the corporate capitalists who control the economy. Today, just a few thousand capitalists, mostly top corporate executives, have much control over an economy in which many millions of Americans work. To maintain the legitimacy of this highly inegalitarian system in the eyes of workers, modern capitalism must promise good jobs and material rewards. By the 1920s, increased investment of capital in consumer manufacturing and rising demand from workers for a better way of life had created a new consumer society. For decades, a large sector of the economy has centered in production of consumer commodities. Parents, friends, media and other advertising, and schools teach youth the need for expansive consumerism. Under capitalism, almost anything can become "commodified" and "consumerized." Things that were once signs of youth protest against the adult world—casual dress, rap music, and freer sexuality—have become commodities pushed by advertising aimed especially at the young.[57]

Television and other media, peer groups, and schools teach students that needs can be satisfied by a growing list of often unnecessary commodities. Many advertised goods are not accessible equally; only those in the top social classes and the affluent fraction of the working class are able to participate extensively in consumerism. Many working-class Americans are unable to participate much beyond necessities and other inexpensive consumer items. Moreover, even when the material and commodity needs of more affluent people, young and old, have been met or exceeded, other important needs often remain unfulfilled. A hyperconsumerist society tends to ignore human needs that cannot be "commodified" for profit—needs such as a healthy environment, creativity, meaningful lives, self-mastery, esteem, and love.[58]

In 1989, Whittle Communications began offering school systems "Channel One," a free televised news program with commercials for junk food and other products. In exchange for television sets and satellite dishes, Whittle's contracts require schools to show the program uninterrupted and in its entirety to 90 percent of the school's students. By 2001, 12,000 schools had contracted to show Channel One. Eight million schoolchildren are a captive audience to such programs.[59] A coalition of educators, parents, and children's advocates have voiced harsh disapproval, calling Channel One a "perversion of the education process" and a tool to teach consumerism that offers an illusion of news. Students have voiced their own disapproval of the program, and some teachers have risked their jobs by not showing it. New York was the first to ban Channel One, and other states have brought legal action to remove the program from schools.[60]

A study by the University of Wisconsin's Center of the Analysis of Commercialism in Education found that an increase in the already high levels of commercialism in public schools occurred for the academic year 2002–03. One reason is that many school systems have tight budgets and need revenue. Some schools have even had fund-raising telethons or hired fund-raisers. Using a mass media database, the center found 1,206 mentions of corporate sponsorship of school programs, 252 accounts of agreements with companies giving them rights to sell products on school grounds, 326 accounts of schools selling naming rights or advertising on school property, and 310 mentions of schools using corporate-sponsored educational materials. The same report also found 1,570 references to the private or for-profit management of public schools or school programs.[61] The author of this major report concluded "that schoolhouse commercialism is a reflection of larger economic, social, cultural, and political forces. Whether or not schools and their students are subordinated to the market place will depend in large measure on society's understanding of childhood and its assessment of the proper relationship between adults and children."[62]

Corporate concern for profit also brings much mindless television fare for U.S. children. Mindless (and often violent) television programs for children reduce the level of literacy in society. Barry Sanders, an English professor, has shown how the large amount of time children spend watching television is having a negative effect on their welfare. Sanders's key point is not about the damage that TV does to children in terms of increasing their insensitivity to violence, a point documented in other research studies. Rather, he shows the damage TV does to their literacy. Children spend so many hours sitting before electronic images that they lose some of their abilities to communicate orally and accurately. Absorbing messages from TV over many hours, children spend less time communicating with other people. Passive, less oral, less literate, and less creative citizens are the result of children spending excessively large amounts of time with TV, movies, and recorded music.[63]

Corporations provide schools with a wide variety of free teaching materials. After examining 200 examples of classroom materials produced by commercial interests, Consumers Union reports that more than two-thirds "contained biased or incomplete information, promoting a viewpoint that favors consumption of the sponsor's product or service or a position that favors the company or its economic agenda."[64]

Teen Sitting and Discipline Problems

In addition to tracking, job training, and value socialization, schools often play another role in society. Harry Braverman has argued that "the postponement of school leaving to an average age of eighteen has become indispensable for keeping unemployment within reasonable bounds."[65] Social stability would be in jeopardy without these large teen-sitting organizations. Teachers and administrators sometimes refer to this function of schools as keeping students "off the street" or "out of trouble."

Problems of discipline and drug use in high schools, as well as in junior high and elementary schools, are at the heart of national discussion of the crisis in schools. Although drug use among teens has fallen since the mid-1990s, the rate of illicit drug use among elementary, middle school, and high school students remains alarming: In 2002, some 24 percent of eighth-graders, 45 percent of tenth-graders, and 53 percent of twelfth-graders reported that they had used illegal drugs.[66] And even though school-related violence has also decreased over the last decade, students still suffer about 2 million nonfatal crimes of violence every year in the United States, including rape, sexual assault, other physical attacks and threats of attack, and robbery. In addition, 400 school-related deaths occurred on elementary and secondary school campuses between 1992 and 2004.[67]

Responding to the recent incidents of school shootings across the country, nearly all public schools in the United States have implemented "zero-tolerance" policies prohibiting weapons and firearms, fighting, alcohol, illegal drugs, and tobacco. Some public school systems have so expanded their zero-tolerance policies that many offenses have little to do with school safety.[68] Schools often deal with student infractions of these policies and other disciplinary problems through suspensions and expulsions. Public schools have nearly doubled the rate of student suspensions over the last few decades—from 1.7 million student suspensions in 1974 to 3.2 million in 1998. It is interesting, however, that while suburban, middle-class, white students have perpetrated most of the well-publicized incidents of school violence giving rise to zero-tolerance policies, school officials have directed these restrictive policies primarily at urban, low-income students of color, as evidenced by the alarming racial disparities in student suspension and expulsion rates. U.S. public schools are *three times* more likely to suspend black and Latino students from school than white students. It is noteworthy that public schools have suspended roughly 25 percent of all black male students at least once over a four-year period. Yet these suspensions and expulsions often do more harm than good, for suspended students are much more likely than other students to engage in violent conduct and use alcohol or illicit drugs. Suspended students are also three times more likely to drop out of school than are other students.[69]

Central city schools, with less in the way of resources than suburban schools, often have a very difficult time with working-class boys. This is especially true when teachers and administrators are mostly or disproportionately white and the male students are disproportionately black and Latino. These central city schools clearly need more resources to deal with all their students—male and female—and they particularly need resources to deal with the educational and related problems of working-class boys. As one black man, a former troubled schoolboy, who now teaches psychology at the Pacifica Graduate Institute has put it, schools need to take aggressive action to support boys who face racism, classism, and lack of support in schools and society: "Recruit 'bad-boy literate' young men, from groups overrepresented by school failure and underrepresented by educators, for teacher training programs. Stop kicking salvageable boys out of school and onto the streets. Instead, provide in-school suspension programs with boy-friendly curricula and teachers/counselors well trained to work with noncompliant boys." He adds, "Given the right opportunity, most troubled boys are fully capable of learning and changing their lives in a positive direction."[70]

We cannot fully understand school discipline and drug problems without understanding the traditional indoctrination role of schools. Schools teach obedience to authority and highly individualistic values. The curriculum is divided into fragmented subjects, many with a vocational or career orientation. Generally, the structure of the classroom places a teacher at the front of a room giving a large number of students history, science, or math facts for students to memorize. Critical thinking, open debate, and cooperative learning are not commonly encouraged. This is not "education" in an idealistic sense but rather a utilitarian training-oriented approach that has, argues George Leonard, "made possible colonialism, the production line . . . and the H bomb."[71] Critics of this uncritical, often authoritarian style of education note that it has not necessarily made people better, happier, or more creative human beings.

Given the typical classroom structure and the job market outside, we should not be surprised that significant numbers of students rebel. All but one state require that students be in school until age 16. Many students are aware that school may not help them get a secure, well-paid job and, as a result, some students may lose their commitment to learning. Compulsory participation in an environment perceived as meaningless makes life miserable for large numbers of students and their teachers, who typically suffer from relatively low status and pay. It is *not individual failings but the structure of education* that lies behind a broad range of school problems—dropouts, discipline, violence. A progressive educational viewpoint, such as that of John Dewey, cannot be fully implemented in most schools because of the neglect of critical thinking and learning. Classes are generally too large; some students become discipline problems; others rebel by moving into drugs. Many drift along, engaging in lesser forms of resistance such as daydreaming or absenteeism. In addition, unsupportive parents and homes stressed by unemployment and a lack of resources often generate troubled students.[72]

There is no simple solution to problems such as discipline and drugs. The periodic move toward more repression—a tightening of discipline and surveillance of students—is not likely to solve them. While personality can cause discipline and drug problems, this is frequently less important than underlying societal causes of student discontent growing out of the authoritarian structure of the classroom, large classes and lack of resources, an educational value system emphasizing memorization rather than critical thinking, and an outside job world with unemployment and alienating workplaces.

COLLEGES AND UNIVERSITIES

Since World War II, the number of young people in college has increased dramatically, and now a majority of high school students expect to go to college. Yet today colleges and universities face serious funding problems, and many students may in the near future be unable to obtain higher education because of the high costs. In most states, legislators and policymakers must try to balance the fiscal needs of colleges against the burgeoning costs of state government, especially of state corrections systems.

In recent years the costs of jails and prisons have *exceeded* the costs of higher education. From 1952 to 1980 state government spending on colleges and universities increased from 3 percent to 8 percent of state budgets while corrections spending remained relatively unchanged from 1.5 percent to 2 percent. Over the last two decades, though, the prison population has quadrupled (from 500,000 in 1980 to more than 2 million in 2004),

[margin handwriting: more on Prison than Education]

and state governments are now spending *more* on building prisons and jails than colleges and universities. (For example, California built 23 new prisons, but only one university, over this period.) While state spending on higher education increased by 24 percent over this period, corrections spending increased, incredibly, by 166 percent. Most states have either doubled or tripled their corrections spending since 1985, yet Nevada is the only state that has doubled its overall higher education spending. Indeed, state governments have shifted much of the costs of higher education to students through increased tuition and fees, as many readers of this book know. Since the 1980s, the percentage change in state funding per student has been about 13 percent, while the percentage change in tuition and fees per student has been far more at 107 percent. In addition, these sharply rising costs in higher education affect most working-class students and many students of color very disproportionately—thereby further accentuating class and racial inequality in the society.[73]

Tracking in Higher Education

Many states have established hundreds of community and other two-year colleges in recent decades to meet the needs of students from less affluent backgrounds. Policymakers have written explicitly of channeling the demand for education away from universities to these community colleges. The result is that state legislatures have stratified higher education in the United States much like the primary and secondary school systems. A rough outline of this system looks like this:

	Emphasis on Rules, Scheduled Course Work	Emphasis on "Job" Training	Emphasis on Independence Training and "Careers"	Percentage White
1. Junior college, community college	Decreases	Decreases	Increases	Increases
2. Four-year state college				
3. State university				
4. Elite university, elite college				

Students in category 1 tend to come disproportionately from blue-collar and lower-middle-income families, and are often tracked through vocational lines in high schools and community colleges into skilled blue-collar and low- to mid-level white-collar jobs. Students in categories 2 and 3 come disproportionately from middle-income families and tend to move into middle-level and upper-level white-collar jobs (sales, professional, technical). Many students in the elite colleges and universities (category 4) go on to occupy society's higher-level capitalist, managerial, and professional positions. First-year students in private universities typically come from families with much larger annual incomes, on the average, than do first-year students in two- and four-year colleges. Even with the numerous exceptions in each category, the general inclination of higher education to reinforce existing social stratification is clear.

Government subsidies to higher education, paid for by the taxes of all, go disproportionately to support students from higher-income families. High school students who do not go to college receive no direct benefits from these government subsidies, though their parents have helped pay for them through taxes.

Some 1.4 million high school students take the Scholastic Aptitude Test (SAT) annually, and a majority of four-year colleges and universities still use this or similar tests to screen students into or out of undergraduate and graduate programs. Researchers have found, however, that such tests are biased in overt and subtle ways against students from working-class backgrounds, especially those who are African American, Latino, and Native American. The language and numerous items in these tests favor students from white, upper-middle-income families. White students from higher-income households tend to perform better on these tests because, for one, their families can better afford costly test preparation programs than less affluent students. Moreover, the mostly white, upper-middle-income creators and administrators of such tests resist efforts to significantly reduce this class and racial testing bias. Such tests play a critical role in the stratification of higher education. In addition, the disadvantages of these tests are far reaching, for numerous employers use biased SAT-type tests to screen job applicants, thereby creating unnecessary class and racial barriers for jobs.[74]

Government, Corporations, and Universities

In his farewell address, President Dwight Eisenhower warned about the dangers of a huge military–industrial complex and its associated government-sponsored university research: "The free university, historically the fountainhead of free ideas and scientific discovery, has experienced a revolution in the conduct of research. Partly because of the huge costs involved, a government contract becomes virtually a substitute for intellectual curiosity."[75] Since the 1940s, the federal government has become even more closely linked to corporations in the military–industrial complex and to major university research programs.

Over the last few decades, large corporations have received many lucrative federal contracts for military supplies and services and for military-related research. Most military-oriented funding has gone directly to industry, but a substantial amount has flowed to researchers at universities. New technologies generated in this government-funded university research often contribute to private industry's profits. As a result, the major research universities have generally become less teaching oriented and more oriented to securing government-funded research.

Many people see the close corporate relationship with universities as a positive way to support international competitiveness for U.S. corporations and to help students gain skills leading to jobs. Yet many scholars find the relationship between universities, business, and government inherently problematic, resulting in major disadvantages for the university.[76] Critics often refer to this relationship as "the Academic-Industrial Complex" or the "Market-Model University."[77] Increased funding for high-tech–related education programs has often meant reduced funding for liberal arts and humanities programs. Greater corporate penetration of universities has had an impact on curriculum and faculty research agendas. Many universities are moving away from studying critical societal issues, such as industrial pollution and hazards in the workplace, and refocusing billions of dollars into biotechnology and other types of research that universities can patent and thus use to generate new sources of funding. In this regard, universities are acting much like for-profit corporations and drastically reshaping their educational purpose and academic ideals alongside those of the business corporation.[78] Another outgrowth of the "business of education" is an increased marketing of academic courses through the Internet with many colleges and universities now offering entire academic programs online.

Student Protests

Student protests have periodically signaled that all is not well in colleges and universities. There have been antiwar and antinuclear demonstrations, protests against companies doing military business and university military-oriented research, environmental protests, and civil rights and women's liberation demonstrations. The most widespread student action—in the 1960s and 1970s against the war in Vietnam—reached half of all colleges. Scholars like David Westby have linked the development of student protests to the surrounding political–economic system.[79] They suggest that college protests have most often developed in liberal-arts colleges or in social science and humanities departments of various colleges and universities where faculty and students are more likely to analyze critically the social stratification systems of modern capitalism.

Ever since the Vietnam era of the 1960s and 1970s, student protests have periodically focused on racism and civil rights, women's issues, gay and lesbian rights, environmental questions, international agreements (like NAFTA), U.S. military involvement in areas such as Latin America and the Middle East, and local campus problems such as rising tuition. Numerous protests have focused on incidents of bigotry and animosity toward Jewish and Middle Eastern students, or students of color, that have taken place on many campuses across the country.

DIPLOMAS, CREDENTIALS, AND "HUMAN CAPITAL"

One must understand student alienation, boredom, and protests in high schools and colleges in relation to the broader societal context. In recent decades many business and political leaders have viewed schooling as a good "investment" for individuals. In this common view, youth should invest their "human capital" in education for higher returns later. Statistics have been circulated that suggest each year of education is worth thousands of dollars in later income.[80]

Yet recessions and various job problems such as unemployment, capital flight, and the restructuring of the U.S. economy have brought into serious question some of these human capital arguments about education, particularly the argument that a good education guarantees an individual a better-paying job. Many better-educated Americans, including the college educated, have had difficulty in recent years in finding the promised good employment. Some college graduates are unemployed, and increasing numbers are employed in jobs below their levels of education. Indeed, many corporations are increasingly exporting white-collar jobs to areas (such as India and southeast Asia) where college graduates there will work for much lower wages than will workers in the United States.

Qualifications and Credentialism

Ever-increasing numbers of U.S. workers are overqualified for jobs they hold. With millions more workers than good jobs, the use of educational credentials can provide employers a way of excluding many with capability but not credentials. Many jobs only require tenth- or eleventh-grade skills for competent performance, yet these factory and clerical jobs usually have a screening requirement of a high school diploma or, in some clerical cases, college work. Thus, educational requirements are often unrelated to actual job needs. Research studies have suggested that in performing routinized jobs the better educated may be less competent and more frustrated. Existing data strongly suggest that, beyond a certain point, formal educational attainment does not predict level of performance in many types of employment.[81]

According to government predictions, only a modest percentage of new wage and salary jobs created over the next few decades will be in high-tech or other better-paying job categories. In terms of absolute numbers, four of the five fastest-growing job categories are now, and likely will continue to be, in low- to moderate-wage service sectors—jobs such as cashiers, janitors and cleaners, retail salespersons, waitpersons, and nurses. Only one of these categories (nursing) actually requires a college degree. And these occupations, whether requiring vocational or academic credentials, will account for a much larger proportion of the job growth in 2010 (42 percent) than in 2000 (29 percent).[82] Moreover, four of the five fastest-growing categories in *rate* of growth are relatively low-wage: home health aides, physicians' aides, medical assistants, and human services assistants.

Since World War II large numbers of college-trained people have been needed for the increasingly complex corporations to function effectively. Millions of youth have been encouraged to train for white-collar careers in such companies, but today well-paid career jobs are available for perhaps half of those so educated. Many others face temporary jobs without benefits. Some have found that the jobs they secured do not require the education they achieved. Even many middle-level managerial, professional, and technical jobs have become fragmented, repetitive, less creative, and more controlled.[83] This situation generates alienation from unsatisfying jobs and feeds back into college settings, creating both a growing sense of alienation from higher education or, for many, periodic shifting to those disciplines such as accounting, law, or computer science that, for a while at least, seem to promise better-paying jobs.

New Concerns for "Human Capital"

Nonetheless, for many young workers the problem is not over- but rather underqualification for jobs. Many business analysts of the future consider "building a qualified workforce" to be the most important challenge facing U.S. companies in the decades ahead. Large numbers of poorly educated students are coming out of many of our rural and city high schools—the underfunded and troubled schools previously cited. Many newer jobs, such as jobs in high-tech industries, require problem-solving skills and a grasp of math and communications skills that exceed those of most high school dropouts, and indeed of many high school graduates. For example, 84 percent of the almost 23,000 applicants tested recently for entry-level jobs at the New York Telephone

Many government officials say they want to improve education but are unwilling to raise taxes for that purpose.

Company failed. Some companies keep a database of retirees to fill gaps when they cannot find qualified new employees. One corporate executive has estimated that remedial training to prepare students to think and create on the job may cost many businesses a minimum of $200,000 per employee over time. Today, public school systems as a whole spend approximately $7,376 per year per student; as we have already noted, some spend much less.[84]

Without recognizing the irony in his statement, one business leader has compared today's schools to nineteenth-century factories: In U.S. education, large impersonal groups of students proceed from room to room where "each teacher puts a part on the kid." Graduates of public schools possess "the forbearance needed for unskilled manual labor, but [are] devoid of the problem-solving skills necessary for today's globally competitive workplace." This commentary recognizes that competition from corporations in Japan and Europe seems to be forcing some breakdown in U.S. business's support for a conformity-oriented public school classroom. Indeed, a few business-funded experimental educational programs have produced interesting results. For example, 135 of the 2,100 students in a Fort Worth high school participated in a "school within a school." Classes of 20 students remained with the same teachers for four years. Learning was more personalized, with teachers functioning as coaches rather than lecturers. Students were actually encouraged to develop thinking and reasoning skills.[85] Still, such schooling experiences as yet are available to just a handful of students.

DISCRIMINATION AND RELATED PROBLEMS

Racial discrimination has long been a feature of the U.S. educational system. In earlier decades, white southern and eastern European immigrants—many of them Catholics and Jewish Americans—were actually viewed and treated as "inferior races" by the Anglo-Protestant teachers and administrators who then ran the public schools. Today, racial segregation and discrimination in schooling are still significant problems for the United States. Now they are mostly problems for students of color, especially African, Latino, and Native American students. After long years of legal segregation, school desegregation was finally begun in earnest in the 1960s. In recent years, however, whites in the Supreme Court and Congress have largely abandoned these attempts to bring meaningful racial desegregation to public schools. Not even half the country's black children are today in schools that are majority white, and increasingly few white children are in public schools in any of the large central cities.[86]

Schools for Children of Color

Children of color have long faced inferior educational facilities across the United States. Thus, in the early 1900s overt institutionalized discrimination was conspicuously evident in the grossly inferior educational facilities provided for black Americans, north and south. Indeed, all southern states had *legally* segregated schools operating under a "separate but equal" doctrine. Yet, the *quality* of black schools was far from equal to those of white schools. One 1930s study of school systems in southern states found the average per-pupil expenditure was $49.30 for white children but only $17.04 for black children.[87]

In many areas, a racial discrepancy in local school expenditures and resources has persisted to the present day, though this discrepancy no longer involves legal segregation but broad patterns of de facto institutionalized racism. Indeed, a variety of educational resources, including extracurricular programs, better and more experienced teachers, and foreign languages, are less available for children of color than for white children. Children of color are also more likely to attend schools with poorer physical facilities.[88] Children attending schools in troubled urban school systems frequently receive inferior educations and consequently often perform at poor academic levels. The 2003 National Assessment of Educational Progress tests in math and reading reveal that significant percentages of low-income African American and Latino students cannot read at even a basic level and many score at a "below basic" level in math.[89]

Historically, relatively few black adults have had educational attainment levels comparable to those of white adults. Today, however, the educational gap between whites and blacks has closed appreciably at least in secondary education. The latest census data show that about 79 percent of black Americans 25 or more years old have completed high school or higher compared with 88 percent of white Americans. This reflects great efforts by black children and parents. The postsecondary educational differential between blacks and whites still persists—most likely because of the high cost of college attendance and the inferior quality of education that blacks have received historically. Whites (29.4 percent) are still much more likely than blacks (17.2 percent) to complete four years or more of college or university work.[90] The narrowing black–white educational gap also stands in sharp contrast to the persisting income gap we noted in Chapter 4. Securing a good education does not necessarily bring access to a good-paying job, again in part because of persisting discrimination.

The Struggle for Desegregation

The African American struggle for more and better education has created a significant body of civil rights law. Early civil rights activists directed their attention toward improving the quality of segregated education. One of the first objectives of the National Association for the Advancement of Colored People (NAACP), for example, was the inauguration of a drive to equalize opportunity. The slow movement toward breaking down the wall of school segregation began in earnest in the 1930s, with an NAACP legal attack. In 1954, with NAACP help, black parents won a famous school desegregation case, *Brown et al. v. Board of Education of Topeka*. Nonetheless, school desegregation came very slowly, with most white-controlled school systems ignoring the *Brown* decision. Whites established private schools to avoid desegregation, and some used collective resistance to forestall desegregation. The NAACP was able to sustain its slow legal struggle because of the commitment of rank-and-file black parents to improved education for their children.[91]

As a result, by the early 1970s many formerly all-white schools had at least a few black students, and by the 1980s many black children were in schools with whites. School desegregation, for a time, was spreading across many cities, large and small, and especially in the South.

However, after two decades of desegregation efforts, an ever more conservative Supreme Court began backing off on the national commitment to school desegregation. In the 1974 *Milliken v. Bradley* decision, the majority (all white men) blocked a metropolitan-wide school desegregation plan combining a northern city, Detroit, and its suburbs.[92] In his dissent in *Milliken*, Thurgood Marshall, the great civil rights lawyer and Supreme Court justice, noted that after two decades of desegregation, the justices had abandoned the interests of African Americans in eliminating the "badges" of slavery: "Our precedents . . . firmly establish that where, as here, state-imposed segregation has been demonstrated, it becomes the duty of the State to eliminate root and branch all vestiges of racial discrimination and to achieve the greatest possible degree of actual desegregation."[93] Moreover, between the year of *Milliken* (1974) and the present, the Supreme Court and numerous other federal courts have gradually retreated on the national commitment to desegregate the schools, as an earlier decision put it, "root and branch." Thus, in a series of 1990s and early 2000s cases, such as *Board of Education of Oklahoma v. Dowell* (1991) and *Freeman v. Pitts* (1992), the Court has decided to allow white officials to resegregate their public schools so long as there is no legal and official segregation.[94] Covert and subtle discrimination that leads to resegregation is now permissible. White interests are again regularly taking precedence over the interests of parents of color in bringing real desegregation to the public schools.

Today, in the North and South, many elementary and secondary schools remain highly segregated, with white children in mostly white schools and black and Latino children in schools whose substantial majorities are children of color. Current national data reveal that the average white child attends a school that is over 78 percent white, and the average black child attends a school where black children are 57 percent of the student population. One study shows that over the last 15 years the trend in U.S. school segregation has reached levels experienced in 1969.[95] Moreover, two-thirds of the black children are from families below or near the official government poverty line. To achieve real desegregation of all schools, two-thirds of white children would have to transfer to a different school—an action most white parents would resist strongly. Less than a century and a half since the freeing of enslaved African Americans, one can still see the vestiges and badges of slavery in this great isolation and segregation of children in public schools.[96] The reality of systemic racism in U.S. society is that the white majority—including most white decision makers in local, state, and federal governments—has *never* been strongly committed to a comprehensive desegregation of major institutions, including the public schools.

Does More Education Bring Higher Incomes?

Among the population in general, those with higher levels of education have generally had higher incomes. Looking at the general population over the age of 21, a recent Census Bureau report showed that those Americans with a professional education average nearly $5,524 in monthly income, compared with $3,573 for those with a bachelor's degree and $2,279 for those with a high school diploma.[97] This pattern holds true for both black and white Americans. For this reason, numerous analysts of U.S. racial relations—especially those with a conservative perspective—have suggested that greater educational attainment will solve the problem of racial inequality in the United States.

However, much evidence indicates that this is not now the case—and will not likely be the case in the future. Thus, one analyst notes that "it is simply daydreaming to hope that equalizing educational opportunity among children can undo the natural and normal effects of a social system."[98] Of the spheres of life where significant changes in institutionalized racism in the United States would bring great benefits to African Americans—the areas of housing, employment, and education—changes in education can probably bring the fewest material benefits. The main reason is that schools are set within a society that is still pervaded by racial discrimination in all its other institutions (see Chapter 4).

In the not-so-distant past, employers have excluded many African American workers from many jobs because they lacked an adequate education—largely because of the blatant racial discrimination in schooling under legal segregation. Since the breakdown of this legal segregation, most African Americans have worked hard to secure more education and, remarkably, have raised their median educational attainment to a level only a little less than that of whites. Yet while increases in educational attainment have resulted in occupational and earnings benefits for many black Americans, the median earnings for blacks still remain *substantially below* those of *comparably educated* whites. Among men 25 or more years old who worked full-time and year-round, black high school graduates earned just 77 percent as much as whites in this category. Significantly, black college graduates earned even less: only 75 percent as much as their white counterparts.[99] Education is clearly not a panacea for problems of U.S. racism.

Dropouts or "Pushouts"?

The number of school dropouts is a major problem in U.S. education today; the problem is most severe in poor rural and central city areas. The job opportunities and general life chances for dropouts are significantly lower than for high school graduates. The unemployment rate for high school dropouts is nearly 36 percent.[100] Although the dropout rate for black youth has been consistently higher than that for white youth, poverty is the major determining factor for most students dropping out. Students from poor families, regardless of racial or ethnic group, are much more likely to drop out than are students from affluent families. Researchers have linked the grinding poverty for many black, Latino, and Native American students to the long-term employment and housing problems of their parents and grandparents. Poverty makes it hard for poor students to cope with and stay in school.[101] While most poor parents of color are usually committed to more education for their children, they may face the difficult choice of taking the child out of school to help with younger children or to put them to work to help support the family.

Some critical analysts have raised questions about the term *dropout.* Indeed, the term *pushout* is more accurate in many cases. For many poor students, the school is an irrelevant bureaucratized environment that is unsupportive of personal development. In addition, poor children are commonly malnourished and not adequately supplied with school clothes and supplies. They often come to first grade unprepared for reading and writing, are placed in large classes with little personalized attention, are given teachers who do not expect them to achieve, and are faced with a curriculum with modest relevance to their real world. School boards and administrators either do not, or cannot because of limited budgets, provide an adequate response to these problems. Not surprisingly, many children from rural and central city families decide that the public school is not for them.

Racial Inequality in College Environments

For its first 170 years the U.S. had a system of higher education in which most of its historically white colleges and universities openly excluded, or severely limited the number of, black applicants—and often other students of color. Only since the 1960s have most historically white institutions attempted to have a significant diversity of students on their campuses. Yet, just a decade after most historically white colleges and universities began to admit significant numbers of students of color, in the 1970s, white students and parents began to challenge the positive action (affirmative action) programs designed to desegregate these white institutions. For example, in a 1978 decision, called the *Bakke* case, the Supreme Court ruled that admissions programs open only to applicants of color at a University of California school of medicine violated the rights of white applicants—even though the number of students of color admitted under this program was small and some white students had been admitted to the school with lower scores than the student who protested. In *Bakke,* white judges on a divided Supreme Court held that colleges and universities can use "race" as one factor in seeking student diversity but cannot use it as the *only* factor—as in preferential admissions for students of color. According to this decision, colleges must use an array of admissions criteria in addition to race, such as "exceptional personal talents, unique work or service experience, leadership potential, maturity, demonstrated compassion, a history of overcoming disadvantage, [and] ability to communicate with the poor."[102]

In 2003, the Supreme Court again dealt twice with the issue of affirmative action in admissions at state universities. It heard challenges to the University of Michigan's undergraduate and law school admissions policies. In *Gratz v. Bollinger,* the court invalidated an undergraduate admissions plan because it gave admission points to applicants for being persons of color as part of the University of Michigan's efforts to try to overcome the effects of past and present racial discrimination.[103] In its naive reasoning about racial matters in the United States, the court majority ignored the fact that the university also gave points to applicants who were the children of alumni and to those from rural areas, applicants who were virtually all white. Indeed, the university admissions process had a number of other point awards that went to groups of applicants that were virtually all white. The mostly white and conservative Supreme Court did *not* decide that almost all of an historically white major university's alumni being white is a problem of racial discrimination for which a few years of remedial programs in admissions would be a reasonable solution.

Analysts Charles Murray and Richard Herrnstein published a book arguing that "IQ" tests demonstrate racial inferiority in intelligence for some groups, an old theme in white supremacist groups.

Interestingly, in the University of Michigan law school case, *Grutter v. Bollinger,* the court upheld the school's affirmative action policy in admissions because it did not have the point award system used for undergraduates but "considered a range of qualities and experiences in addition to race."[104] That is, each candidate was evaluated subjectively by the admissions committee. The justices viewed the law school admissions policy as evaluating candidates as individuals, and not in such a way that an applicant's race or ethnicity was a defining feature of her or his application. In both cases, the court did restate its long-standing principle that achieving racial and ethnic diversity in college populations is a legitimate government interest. It just did not have a clear vision of why this should be done and how it might be accomplished. Indeed, in both cases the judges in the majority indicated that they were poorly informed on U.S. racial history. In neither case did the majority take into serious consideration the century and a half of racial segregation and overt discrimination that most historically white educational institutions had participated in up until the 1960s. Given the past and current data discussed in Chapter 4, it will take more than a few years of modest remedial programs—such as most affirmative action programs in admissions—to overcome the heavy legacy of well-institutionalized racism.

The increasing numbers of students of color on campuses in recent decades has not lessened the national problem of racist incidents on campuses. Since the 1960s, students of color, especially African American students, have frequently had to endure racist graffiti, have watched white fraternity parties accent antiblack themes, have seen Ku Klux Klan and other racist literature passed out on campus, and have endured violent attacks. Research studies have recorded hundreds of such racist incidents in recent years, many involving assaults on students of color.[105] Many such studies rely on student reports, but researchers suggest that the incidence of bias-motivated events on campuses is significantly higher than what students report.[106] Colleges and universities across the country continue to experience an alarming number of racist acts. At one college, for example, white students dressed in sheets and hoods like Klan members threatened a black student with a burnt cross.[107] Racist graffiti was scrawled in public places at a number of colleges and universities across the country, including Yale Law School, Swarthmore College, Harvard University, the University of Colorado, the University of Wisconsin (River Falls), Antioch University, the University of West Virginia, Central Missouri State University, the Southern College of Technology, and Heidelberg College, to mention just a few places. Racist flyers were posted or handed out at Indiana University, the University of Northern Colorado, and the University of California Law School. Racist effigies were found at the University of Minnesota.[108] Most recently, a black student at the University of Washington found a racist note posted to her dormitory room door. The note read, "I will kill you," and it was signed "KKK."[109] And at the University of Wisconsin (Madison), police arrested three skinheads for trying to break into the Eagle Heights housing complex for students of color, while yelling, "We are going to get these people, we are going to kill them." The men had illegal weapons and were dressed in paramilitary clothing with swastika patches and a patch that read, "I'm proud to be white."[110]

Blatant instances of racism have very negative effects on students of color, sometimes making them consider leaving campus. One black student interviewed in a research study reported a serious incident involving a white fraternity:

> In my freshman year at a university student parade there was a group of us standing there, not knowing that this was not an event that a lot of black people went to! . . . our dorm was going, and this was something we were going to go to because we were students too! And we were standing out there and [there was] a group of white fraternity boys—I remember the southern flag— and a group of us, five or six of us, and they went past by us, before the parade had actually gotten underway. And one of them pointed and said, "Look at that bunch of niggers!" I remember thinking, "Surely he's not talking to us!" We didn't even use the word nigger in my house. . . . [How did you feel?] I think I wanted to cry. And my friends—they were from a southwestern city— they were ready to curse them, and I was just standing there with my mouth open.[111]

This perceptive student reveals the pain that racist comments caused. Note too that the Confederate battle flag carried by whites in the parade is a symbol that for many African Americans recalls painful memories of antiblack violence by white supremacy groups. Indeed, the widespread use of this battle flag began with white resistance to racial desegregation in the 1950s and 1960s.

Students of color also face subtle forms of discrimination. One research study interviewed African American students about experiences on a predominantly white campus in the North. One student noted stereotyped remarks:

> One time she was taking attendance, and there were these two Asian kids. One was like Japanese and the other was like Vietnamese, right. So she . . . said the one kid's name wrong. And she was like, "Oh well, it doesn't matter because like you guys all look alike." She said that . . . I mean she said that. [No one said anything to her?] Well, most of the people were white people, so they were just like, whatever? But we—the black people just connected right there. One of these kids dropped the course. I don't know if that's why, but I'd have dropped it if she said that to me.[112]

It is unclear whether the professor was joking, but whatever her intention the remark had a negative impact—not only on Asian students but also on other students of color. Such faculty insensitivity suggests that conservative critics of college settings, such as right-wing analysts Allan Bloom and Dinesh D'Souza, are wrongheaded in their view of these university settings as "too tolerant and liberal."

Latinos and Issues of Language

Mexican American, Puerto Rican, Cuban American, and other Latino children, whose home language is frequently not English, have faced difficulties in the one-language, often anti-Spanish, environment of many school systems. Recall the earlier discussion of language bias in the "IQ" and other skills tests used in schools. Not long ago southwestern schools with high percentages of Mexican American students rigidly prohibited manifestations of Mexican subculture. Anglo teachers anglicized children's names and otherwise downgraded the Mexican cultural heritage. More subtle forms of this discrimination still persist. For example, for many years to the present day, school curricula have often neglected Latino history.[113]

Nationwide, Latino students are even less likely than black students to attend desegregated schools. Indeed, the segregation of Latino schoolchildren has increased in numerous areas in recent decades. Mexican American students make up more than one-fifth of students in the Southwest, and in most cities, north and south, they attend schools in which students of color predominate. This de facto segregated schooling often has negative implications for students of color: low retention rates, many students who read below grade level, high teacher–student ratios, less-qualified teachers, and low teacher expectations. Researchers have established a strong correlation between expectations and academic achievement. Students whose teachers expect them to achieve are much more likely to succeed. Many predominantly Latino schools have inferior educational resources and lower per-student expenditures. Latinos also remain significantly underrepresented among teachers, administrators, and school board members in most school systems.[114]

From the beginning, the United States has been "a land of many different languages and cultures," yet in the last two decades bilingual education has been made more difficult by many state governments banning major bilingual programs or establishing "English-as-official language" laws.[115] The main motivation for these laws is whites' concern with growth in Latino populations and the spread of Spanish. Xenophobic nativists praise English-only antibilingual policies as a means to unify the diverse groups within U.S. society and to promote shared values. On the contrary, writes Catherine Walsh, "Such efforts toward linguistic cohesion resonate with a kind of colonial domination, a hegemony that threatens to silence the less powerful [and attempts] to render invisible the complex, abstract, socio-ideological nature of language."[116] Language is one of the ways in which people define themselves. Far from simply a set of neutral symbols, language shapes thought and is inseparable from identity. In her years as a teacher, Walsh documented the struggle faced by language-minority students over *whose* language and perspectives are accepted and whose are belittled. She quotes a young bilingual student: "Sometimes I two-times think," she said. "I think like in my family and in my house. And then I think like in school and other places. Then I talk. They aren't the same, you know." Realizing that the language context of her home was not only different but also less acceptable than that of the school, this child often told her teacher, "It makes me feel funny, all alone ... . different."[117]

Placed in classrooms in which instruction is in English, children with limited English proficiency frequently become discouraged, develop low self-confidence, and fail to keep pace with English-speaking peers. Schools often assign them to low-ability groups, "language-disabled" classes, or lower grades. This condition affects many Latino students because most schools are not structured to deal with large numbers of non–English-speaking students. Research in high schools has found that students in good quality bilingual programs have higher attendance and completion rates and that such programs contribute to more positive self-concepts for students.[118] Yet good quality bilingual programs are seldom part of the mainstream curricula. Those programs in operation often devalue biculturalism and teach English as a replacement language rather than valuing the strength of Latino cultures and recognizing the importance of the Spanish language.[119]

Estimates of the dropout rate for Latino children range from two to more than three times that of non-Latinos.[120] Poverty and the need to earn money to help support their families are major obstacles. School counselors often advise those who have fallen behind to drop out. The educational level of Mexican Americans and Puerto Ricans is far below that of the general population.[121] Yet the determination of many Latinos to get more education remains high. Milga Morales-Nadal writes about the struggles of Latino women: "It is not uncommon for some mothers to take their children with them to class in some public colleges." At all levels of higher education, teaching that respects the nonmainstream language, culture, and identity are vital to the empowerment of Latino youth.[122]

Critiquing conventional explanations offered for poor school performance by students of color, Walsh explains that to attribute school problems to individual or cultural inadequacies is to blame the victim. To understand the problem of underachievement, we must look instead mainly to the surrounding social system. Mainstream school curricula are built on the dominant European American culture and English language and equates success with slavishly adopting that dominant culture and language. Since the dominant group views non-European cultures as negative environments from which students of color need to escape, the school curriculum typically ignores non-European history, culture, and experiences. Thus, poor school performance is often a response to alienating school and other society conditions that have robbed students of color of their dignity and voice.[123]

In spite of often-unsupportive school settings, Latino parents and children remain strongly committed to education. Indeed, when asked in a Harvard study if they agreed with the statement "To me, school is the most important thing," 84 percent of Mexican immigrant children agreed, as compared with only 40 percent of non-Latino American students. Student responses to other questions about school showed a similar pattern of strong immigrant commitment to education. The problem of education for Latino children appears to lie primarily in the discriminatory structure and operation of public schools, and the larger society, not in Latino children or their parents.[124]

Stereotyping and Asian Americans

Since the relaxation in the 1960s of immigration laws discriminating against Asians, their increased immigration has produced an expansion of Asian American populations—including Chinese Americans, Asian-Indian Americans, Korean Americans, Filipino Americans, and Vietnamese Americans. Together with Japanese Americans, who have not immigrated recently in significant numbers, these groups make up much of the Asian American population. Many immigrants have come to the United States with modest economic resources and a strong commitment to education. Indeed, Asian American students have often won major student awards, especially in the physical sciences.[125] The periodic dominance of such awards by students from a small segment of the population tends to reinforce popular stereotypes of Asian Americans as "naturally" gifted in science and as a "model minority." Such stereotypes have appeared in the mass media and in protests by prejudiced non-Asian Americans against Asian American recipients of awards. While it is true that many Asian Americans excel in science, many also do well in other areas of educational achievement, including the arts. Focusing only on high-achieving students also diverts attention from the educational needs of the many Asian Americans who are poor or uneducated. Moreover, the accent by *white* commentators, from the 1960s to the present day, on Asian Americans as special "model minorities" (a term invented by whites, not Asian Americans) who should be imitated by other groups of color, such as African Americans or Latinos, not only involves racial stereotyping but also neglects the substantially different histories of immigration of Asian Americans and groups such as African Americans.[126]

Today, many white Americans see Asian American students at all levels of education as a "problem." Whites often complain now that Asian American students "work too hard" and are "grade grabbers." Yet, in spite of their often remarkable educational achievements, Asian American students have been victims of discrimination. White children often mock the "look" of Asian American children. And in recent decades numerous major colleges (including Harvard, Brown, Princeton, Yale, Stanford, and the University of California) have periodically imposed hidden ceilings to limit to some degree the percentage of Asian American students on their campuses.[127]

PERSISTING GENDER DISCRIMINATION

Elementary and Secondary Schools

In the U.S. school system, girls and women encounter many problems similar to those discussed in regard to racial discrimination. Widespread occupational segregation in elementary and secondary schools signals deeply embedded discrimination. Most teachers are female, yet fewer are school principals, especially at the high school level, and fewer still are school superintendents. This pattern attests to the continuing pattern of gender discrimination in schools.[128] One can see the discriminatory practices reflecting gender stereotypes in the construction of curriculum materials that play down the woman's role in society and history or suggest that women are best suited for homemaking or female-typed jobs such as nursing. In Chapter 5, we noted the prevalence of traditional male–female stereotypes in school texts and teaching materials. Until recently, the typical boy has been seen as active, industrious, and clever; the typical girl has been portrayed as passive, emotional, and dependent. These stereotyped portraits are still sometimes reflected in discriminatory practices affecting girls and women in schools today.

Other forms of gender bias in the classroom, identified by the National Education Association, include double standards for males and females, condescension, tokenism, denial

Most elementary school teachers are women, and they work for relatively low salaries.
(Ken Karp/Simon & Schuster/PH College)

of achieved status or authority, backlash against women who succeed, and praise of individuals as better than others in their gender group (divide-and-conquer strategies).[129] A report by the American Association of University Women (AAUW) concluded the following:

> Whether one looks at achievement scores, curriculum design, self-esteem levels, or staffing patterns, . . . there is clear evidence that the educational system is not meeting girls' needs. Girls and boys enter school roughly equal in measured ability. On some measures of school readiness, such as fine motor control, girls are ahead of boys. Twelve years later, girls have fallen behind their male classmates in key areas such as higher-level mathematics and measures of self-esteem.[130]

Recent studies show some gains in girls' achievement in math and science relative to boys, but scholars are concerned that these gaps still persist—and that new gender gaps are being created in computer science, biotechnology, and environmental science.[131]

The AAUW researchers also point out that, by focusing on abstract "students," most studies in education ignore girls' needs. Reviewing the work of 35 recent school-reform task forces and commissions, the AAUW researchers note that few included women as either members or leaders, that most neither investigated the issue of gender equity nor included gender data as a separate category, and that few made recommendations specifically addressed to gender issues.[132] Moreover, being black *and* female can compound a teacher's or student's sense of invisibility in schools. As one female African American high school student has stated, "In twelve years of school, I never studied anything about myself."[133] School curricula often omit the histories of women of color. Discrimination also takes subtle forms, such as lower teacher expectations for female students, often beginning in elementary school. Nancy Frazier and Myra Sadker state, "The lowered expectations that teachers and counselors hold for female students do not even have to be stated to have their effect. In countless nonverbal ways they are transmitted, almost intangibly, and the impact they have on the student is devastating."[134] Numerous research studies focusing on the classroom treatment of boys and girls have found that boys receive more attention, both approval and disapproval, from teachers than do girls.[135] Periodic studies have also found that, among elementary school students with equivalent abilities, the girls downgrade their mental abilities more than do the boys.[136]

Higher Education

The percentage of young women who are college educated has quadrupled since 1940. Today, more women than men earn undergraduate and graduate degrees, and the number of women earning college degrees has increased at a much higher rate than men. Yet, inequalities remain, for a *large* proportion of female college graduates still earn degrees in traditionally female fields, such as education and nursing.[137]

The absence or scarcity of women faculty in many college departments, especially in science and math and in major research universities, leaves many female students with few female role models. Some older research shows that female college students are much less likely to participate in classroom discussions when the teacher is male than when the teacher is female.[138] In fact, the continuing dominance of male faculty in many disciplines today has consequences that reach beyond the realm of academic employment to influence the broader career aspirations of female students. They might infer, for example, that not only do women not become professors of mathematics, but they also do not become mathematicians. In addition, the male professor's worldview can consciously and unconsciously shape and interpret educational materials and course presentations in gender-biased ways.

Title IX of the 1972 Education Amendments of the 1964 civil rights act was a milestone for gender equality. Prior to it, schools were free to make different standards for male and female students in areas ranging from occupational counseling to athletic scholarships to college acceptance rates. Because of Title IX, the federal government prohibits gender discrimination in institutions receiving federal funds. The percentage of high school and college women participating in interscholastic sports increased dramatically as a result. In addition, previously male-dominated graduate schools began admitting women in record numbers. In 1985, moreover, the U.S. Congress passed the Civil Rights Restoration Act, which made it clear that discrimination in one program meant a cutoff of federal assistance to an entire college or university.[139]

The clear mandate of Title IX is still unrealized at many of the country's colleges and universities, however. In the mid-1990s a federal judge ruled that Brown University's athletics program violated Title IX because it had cut two women's athletic programs and reduced the percentage of women among athletes below the percentage of women among undergraduates. Yet many schools continue to legally challenge the Title IX legislation. In 1999, California State University at Bakersfield, for example, lost a claim that capping the number of athletes on men's teams is "reverse discrimination." In June 2003, a federal judge dismissed a suit against the U.S. Department of Education by the National Wrestling Coaches Association challenging the underlying regulations of Title IX, claiming it has resulted in colleges cutting more than 400 men's teams.[140] Many women athletes and activists today are actively pressing for much greater equality for women in college athletic programs since men's athletic programs still get a disproportionate share of scholarships and budgets in collect sports. Today, only 9 percent of the NCAA universities have substantially complied with Title IX, and male athletic programs still receive about twice the college athletic budgets as female programs.[141] One study also found that while women coached more than 90 percent of women's teams in 1972, today women coach only 44 percent of women's teams. Indeed, 90 percent of new head-coaching jobs in women's athletics now go to men because the number and prestige of women's teams have increased at colleges and universities.[142]

SUMMARY

Public schools have long been critical to the process of socializing children and adults. Commitment to ever-increasing education has held an important place in the U.S. value system for nearly two centuries. Public elementary schools began to proliferate in the nineteenth century, nurtured by professional educators and entrepreneurs who recognized the usefulness of schools in providing skills and fostering the legitimacy of the established system by instilling in children the individualistic ethic and a positive view of a class-stratified, ineqalitarian social system. Comprehensive high schools spread after 1900, with vocational and tracking systems. Again, socializing and disciplining children for work in a class-structured economy were central concerns of leaders who pressed for public high schools. A more progressive emphasis on the whole child and on broad educational development often took second place.

Clearly, schools have multiple purposes and outcomes. Most children learn to read and write and do math. These and other basic skills are part of developing as a complete human being. Much information learned in schooling is useful, but numerous contemporary observers and researchers have underscored the alienating and unpleasant character of much schooling. Too often, schools are grim places, particularly for the many students in underfunded schools in rural areas and central cities.

From the beginning, public school systems have been under the control of business interests and allied groups of political leaders and professionals committed to legitimating the so-called free-enterprise system. Public schools reflect the structure and needs of a class-, race-, and gender-stratified society. Thus, they vary greatly in the socioeconomic resources provided to students. There are major differences by racial group and class. Today, no equality of educational opportunity exists. Schools have varied in their emphasis on vocational and academic programs, depending on where they are located. The course content, "IQ" and related testing, academic tracking systems, and the varying character of poor and suburban schools are not random arrangements but often reflect the intent on the part of business leaders, political leaders, school board members, and administrators to structure schools along the same problematical class–race–gender lines as those of the larger society.

Higher education is also stratified by class, racial group, and gender. Students from blue-collar families, especially students of color, are tracked disproportionately into two-year colleges, while white students from professional and managerial backgrounds tend to be tracked into the elite colleges and universities. In spite of affirmative action programs in admissions, which are now being cut back, the enrollments of black and Latino students in numerous public and private universities have remained modest in recent years. Moreover, major universities are often dependent on corporate and federal government funding, and such linkages tend to reduce the inclination of faculty members and students to critically analyze the class, racial, and gender stratification of U.S. society.

One important problem today is the growing number of college-educated young people who have much college-related debt or cannot find jobs that make full use of their educations. Millions have trained themselves for white-collar careers but perhaps half of those so educated have found no good jobs. This employment situation generates discontent inside and outside educational settings. Moreover, in recent years a new concern has arisen among many critics that U.S. high schools are not educating their graduates well enough for the new jobs emerging in high-tech and other expanding employment settings.

Discrimination based on racial group and gender has long been part of public and private school systems. Racial discrimination has ranged from the legal segregation of schools, which lasted in many places into the late 1960s, to the informal patterns of racial segregation and other discrimination today, seen in such matters as within-school tracking more or less along racial lines. Overt and subtle racism and protest against that racism regularly appear on high school and college campuses. Gender discrimination ranges from stereotype-motivated sorting of male and female students into traditional roles, such as woodshop or sports for boys and home economics or cheerleading for girls in high schools, to the informal channeling of girls and young women into traditional female-type jobs and professions by high school and college teachers and counselors. In the United States, education has yet to live up to its highest ideals of equal opportunity and "liberty and justice for all."

STUDY QUESTIONS

1. In what specific ways have public schools enhanced the profitability and stability of business enterprise in the United States?

2. What do the "IQ" tests really measure?

 3. Some of the major aspects or functions of the public school system today result in student boredom and restlessness. What are these school functions?

4. Characterize the current debate over Title IX in public schools and colleges. What kinds of issues have been raised by women athletes and activists?

5. In what specific ways do school tracking systems guide students into certain occupations and not others?

6. How has educational segregation (legal and informal) inhibited the development and prosperity of U.S. society?

7. What is the problem with regarding Asian Americans as "model minorities" in the area of education?

8. In what ways do racism and sexism in education (at all levels) reflect and reinforce racism and sexism in the broader society?

ENDNOTES

1. National Center for Educational Statistics, *Digest of Educational Statistics: 1995* (Washington, D.C.: 1995), pp. 15, 17.
2. National Center for Educational Statistics, *Digest of Educational Statistics: 2001,* Table 108, available at nces.ed.gov/programs/digest/d01/dt108.asp.
3. Ibid., Table 109, available at nces.ed.gov/programs/digest/d02/tables/dt109.asp.
4. "The Education Business," *The Polling Report,* July 6, 1992, p. 2; "Report Card on the Nation's Schools," *The Polling Report,* September 7, 1992, pp. 1, 7; See also Howard Gardner, "Beyond the Walls of School," *Newsweek,* September 21, 1992, pp. A4–5; Theodore R. Sizer, "The Activist Library: A Symposium," *The Nation,* September 21, 1992, p. 293.
5. Gerald Bracey, "Debunking the Myth That the U.S. Spends More on Schools," *Rethinking Schools,* 9, Summer 1995, p. 7.
6. U.S. Bureau of the Census, *Historical Statistics of the U.S., Colonial Times to 1957* (Washington, D.C.: 1960), p. 207; National Center for Educational Statistics, *Digest of Educational Statistics: 1995,* p. 12; National Center for Educational Statistics, *Overview of Public Elementary and Secondary School Districts: School Year 2001–2002* (May 2003), available at nces.ed.gov/pubs2003/overview03/#d.
7. National Center for Educational Statistics, *Digest of Educational Statistics: 2002,* Tables 8 and 9, available at nces.ed.gov/programs/digest/d02/ch_1.asp#1.
8. National Center for Educational Statistics, *Digest of Educational Statistics: 2002,* Table 5, available at nces.ed.gov/programs/digest/d02/tables/dt005.asp.
9. National Center for Educational Statists, *Digest of Educational Statistics: 2002,* Table 2, available at nces.ed.gov/programs/digest/d02/tables/dt005.asp.
10. National Center for Educational Statistics, "Participation in Education," available at nces.ed.gov/programs/coe/2003/section1/index.asp.
11. The quotations here are from Samuel Bowles and Herbert Gintis, *Schooling in Capitalist America* (New York: Basic Books, 1976), p. 162.
12. Joe R. Feagin and Clairece Feagin, *Racial and Ethnic Relations,* 5th ed. (Englewood Cliffs, N.J.: Prentice Hall, 1996), pp. 84–85, 120, 147–48; David Nasaw, *Schooled to Order* (New York: Oxford University Press, 1979), pp. 83–84.
13. Joel H. Spring, *Education and the Rise of the Corporate State* (Boston: Beacon Press, 1972), pp. xii, 21.
14. Ibid., pp. 9–20.
15. Ibid., pp. 41–42.
16. Beverly H. Burris and Wolf V. Heydebrand, in *New Directions for Higher Education,* 35, J. Wilson, ed. (San Francisco: Jossey-Bass, 1981), p. 11.

17. Bowles and Gintis, *Schooling in Capitalist America,* pp. 194–95; Scott Nearing, "Who's Who on Our Boards of Education," *Schooling and Society* 5 (January 1917): 89–90; George S. Counts, *The Social Composition of Boards of Education* (Chicago: University of Chicago Press, 1927), as discussed in Spring, *Education and the Rise of the Corporate State,* p. 128.
18. Bowles and Gintis, *Schooling in Capitalist America,* pp. 18–48.
19. Julia Wrigley, *Class Politics and Public Schools* (New Brunswick, N.J.: Rutgers University Press, 1982), pp. 14, 261–66.
20. Allan Graubard, "Radical School Reform: Some Ambiguities," in *Innovations in Education,* 3rd ed., John M. Rich, ed. (Boston: Allyn & Bacon, 1981), pp. 284–89.
21. Anthony A. Parker, "Choosing Sides on School Choice," *Dollars & Sense,* January–February 1992, p. 8; see also pp. 6–8.
22. Jonathan Kozol, "Whittle and the Privateers," *The Nation,* September 21, 1992, pp. 272–74, quotations on p. 277.
23. Ibid., pp. 274–78, quotation on p. 278.
24. People for the American Way, *Unaccountability by Design: Corporate Tuition Tax Credit Schemes Drain Millions from States,* September 2003, available at www.pfaw.org/pfaw/dfiles/file_264.pdf.
25. Quoted in Peter Maurer, "Has School Privatization Failed? Yes: Private Firms Can't Better Public Schools," *Detroit News,* February 18, 1996, p. 7; see also Bruce Shapiro, "Privateers Flunk School Privatization," *The Nation,* February 19, 1996, p. 4.
26. Maurer, "Has School Privatization Failed? Yes," p. 7.
27. "Separate and Unequal," *Minority Trendsetter* 1 (Summer 1988): 4; Nasaw, *Schooled to Order,* pp. 136–39.
28. Vincent J. Roscigno, "The Social Embeddedness of Racial Educational Inequality: The Black-White Gap and the Impact of Racial and Local Political-Economic Contexts," in *Research in Social Stratification and Mobility* (New York: JAI Press, 1995), pp. 135–65.
29. Roslyn A. Mickelson, "The Academic Consequences of Desegregation and Segregation: Evidence from the Charlotte-Mecklenburg Schools," *North Carolina Law Review* 81 (2003): 1,531.
30. Ibid.
31. We draw here on Joe R. Feagin, "Heeding Black Voices: The Court, *Brown,* and Challenges in Building a Multiracial Democracy," *University of Pittsburgh Law Review* 66 (Fall 2004): 57–81.
32. Ibid.
33. Patricia Gurin et al., "Diversity in Higher Education: Theory and Impact on Educational Outcomes, *Harvard Educational Review* 72 (2002): 330–66.
34. Kelvin Powell, "Two Schools," *Essence,* August 1992, pp. 62, 110; see also "Learning in America: Upstairs/Downstairs," Public Broadcasting System, April 3, 1989; Jonathan Kozol, *Savage Inequalities: Children in America's Schools* (New York: Harper-Perennial, 1991).
35. Stan Karp, "Equity Suits Clog the Courts," *Rethinking Schools* 9 (Summer 1995): 18–19.
36. Stan Karp, "Money, Schools and Justice," *Rethinking Schools* 18 (Fall 2003), available at www.rethinkingschools.org/archive/18_01/just181.shtml.
37. Nick Chiles, "Separate and Savagely Unequal," *Essence,* August 1992, pp. 61–62, 106–110.
38. "Savage Inequalities Four Years Later," *Rethinking Schools* 9 (Summer 1995): 5.
39. Amy Ambrosio, "Unacceptable: My School and My Students Are Labeled as Failures," *Rethinking Schools* 18 (Fall 2003), available at www.rethinkingschools.org/archive/18_01/unac181.shtml.
40. See Karp, "Money, Schools and Justice."
41. Lewis Terman, *The Measurement of Intelligence* (Boston: Houghton Mifflin, 1916), pp. 27–28, quoted in Bowles and Gintis, *Schooling in Capitalist America,* p. 197.
42. See Allan Nairn, *The Reign of ETS: The Corporation That Makes Up Minds* (Washington, D.C.: Allan Nairn and Associates, 1980).
43. Richard J. Herrnstein, *IQ in the Meritocracy* (Boston: Little, Brown, 1973). see also the discussion in Chapter 2 of this text.
44. Quoted in U.S. Commission on Civil Rights, *Puerto Ricans in the Continental U.S.: An Uncertain Future* (Washington, D.C.: 1976), p. 99.
45. Clara E. Rodríguez, *Puerto Ricans: Born in the U.S.A.* (Boston: Unwin Hyman, 1989), p. 126.
46. Leon J. Kamin, *The Science and Politics of I.Q.* (New York: John Wiley, 1974), pp. 15–19.
47. Carl C. Brigham, *A Study of American Intelligence* (Princeton, N.J.: Princeton University Press, 1923), pp. 124–25, 177–210.
48. Herrnstein, *IQ in the Meritocracy;* Arthur R. Jensen, "How Much Can We Boost IQ and Scholastic Achievement?" *Harvard Education Review* 39 (1969): 1–123; Tom Wilkie, "The American Association for the Advancement of Science: Research Revives Dispute over IQ,"

Independent, February 19, 1991, p. 7; Charles Murray and Richard Herrnstein. *The Bell Curve* (New York: Free Press, 1994).

49. Cited in Richard Brookhiser, "Fear and Loathing at City College," *National Review,* June 11, 1990, p. 20.

50. See, for example, data gathered by Otto Klinberg as cited in I. A. Newby, *Challenge to the Court* (Baton Rouge: Louisiana State University Press, 1967), p. 74; see also Thomas F. Pettigrew, *A Profile of the Negro American* (Princeton, N.J.: D. Van Nostrand, 1964), pp. 123–26.

51. Kamin, *The Science and Politics of IQ,* pp. 175–78; N. J. Block and Gerald Dworkin, "IQ, Heritability, and Inequality," in N. J. Block and Gerald Dworkin, eds., *The IQ Controversy* (New York: Random House, 1976), pp. 410–540.

52. The authors are indebted to Teresa A. Sullivan for suggesting this point.

53. Ralph W. Larkin, *Suburban Youth in Cultural Crisis* (New York: Oxford University Press, 1979), p. 60.

54. Ibid., pp. 107–109, 120–23.

55. Ibid., p. 131.

56. Ibid., pp. 128–30, 141, 160–62.

57. Stuart Ewen, *Captains of Consciousness* (New York: McGraw-Hill, 1976), pp. 17–20; Larkin, *Suburban Youth,* pp. 38–39.

58. Larkin, *Suburban Youth,* pp. 207–120.

59. Jim Metrock, "Group Launches New Campaign to Turn Off Channel One," *Education Reporter* 186 (July 2001), available at www.eagleforum.org/educate/2001/july01/channel-one.shtml.

60. Quoted in "Selling School," *Delaney Report,* December 18, 1995, n.p.; see also S. C. Gwynne, "Hot News in Class: Channel One Has Drawn Fire for Bringing Commercials into School," *Time,* December 18, 1995, p. 79; David Streitfeld, "The News on Channel One," *Washington Post,* April 20, 1992, p. B5; Cyndee Miller, "Teachers Fight Channel One; Two Advertisers Drop Out," *Marketing News,* August 17, 1992, p. 1.

61. Alex Molnar, "No Student Left Unsold," Sixth Annual Report on Schoolhouse Commercialism Trends, 2002–2003, Commercialism in Education Research Unit, Arizona State University, October 2003 (ret. January 2, 2004), available at www.asu.edu/educ/epsl/CERU/Annual%20reports/EPSL-0309–107-CERU.doc.

62. Ibid.

63. Barry Sanders, *A Is for OX: Violence, the Electronic Media, and the Silencing of the Written Word* (New York: Pantheon, 1995). We draw on the summary in James Daly, "Losing Literacy in the Glow of TV," *San Francisco Chronicle,* January 15, 1995, p. 5.

64. Consumers Union, "Captive Kids: Commercial Pressures on Kids at School," cited in Bruce Shapiro, "Privateers Flunk School Privatization," *The Nation,* February 19, 1996, p. 4.

65. Harry Braverman, *Labor and Monopoly Capital* (New York: Monthly Review Press, 1974), p. 439; see also p. 440.

66. L. D. Johnson, P. M. O'Malley, and J. G. Bachman, *Monitoring the Future: National Survey Results on Drug Use, 1975–2002. Volume I: Secondary School Students.* National Institute of Drug Use, August 2003, available at www.monitoringthefuture.org/pubs/monographs/vol1_2002.pdf.

67. National Center for Educational Statistics, *Indicators of School Crime and Safety: 2003,* available at www.ojp.usdoj.gov/bjs/pub/pdf/iscs03.pdf.

68. Applied Research Center, ERASE Initiative, *Profiled and Punished: How San Diego Schools Undermine Latino and African American Student Achievement* (December 5, 2002), available at www.arc.org/erase/profiled.html.

69. See Tammy Johnson, Jennifer Emiko Boyden, and William J. Pittz, *Racial Profiling and Punishment in U.S. Public Schools: How Zero Tolerance Policies and High Stakes Testing Subvert Academic Excellence and Racial Equity* (October 3, 2001), available at www.arc.org/erase/profiling_nr.html; Vincent Schiraldi and Jason Ziedenberg, *Schools and Suspension: Self-Reported Crime and the Growing Use of Suspension,* The Justice Police Institute (September 2001), available at www.justicepolicy.org/article.php?id=49; Rebecca Gordon, Liberto Della Piana, and Terry Kelecher, *Facing the Consequences: An Examination of Racial Discrimination in U.S. Public Schools* (March 1, 2000), available at www.arc.org/erase/FTC1intro.html.

70. Anonymous, "Slipping through the Cracks at School," static.pacifica.weblogger.com/gems/kipnis/1AYMCh3.pdf (ret. January 2, 2004).

71. George B. Leonard, "How School Stunts Your Child," in D. Gottlied, ed., *Children's Liberation* (Upper Saddle River, N.J.: Prentice Hall, 1973), p. 151; see also pp. 149–56.

72. David. F. Labaree, "Academic Excellence in an Early U.S. High School," *Social Problems* 31 (June 1984): 565.

73. Jason Ziedenberg and Vincent Schiraldi, *Cellblocks or Classrooms? The Funding of Higher Education and Corrections and Its Impact on African American Men,* The Justice Policy Institute, August 2002, available at www.justicepolicy.org/article.php?id=3. See also, Bruce Western, Vincent Schiraldi and Jason Ziedenberg, *Education and Incarceration,* Justice Policy Institute, August 2003, available at www.justicepolicy.org/downloads/EducationandIncarceration1.pdf.

74. See Mark Franek, "Reveal the Racial Data on SAT Scores," *The Christian Science Monitor* (December 17, 2003), available at www.csmonitor.com/2003/1217/p09s02-coop.html; Roy O. Freedle, "Correcting the SAT's Ethnic and Social-Class Bias: A Method for Reestimating SAT Scores," *Harvard Educational Review,* 73 (Spring 2003): 1–43; "Misuse of the SAT." *The Journal of Blacks in Higher Education Newsletter,* November 27, 2003; and Nairn, *The Reign of ETS.*

75. Quoted in Edgar B. Gumbert and Joel H. Spring, *The Superschool and the Superstate: American Education in the Twentieth Century* (New York: John Wiley, 1974), p. 52.

76. Bill Readings, *The University in Ruins* (Cambridge, Mass, Harvard University Press, 1996). See also, David Harvey, "Univerity, Inc.," *The Atlantic Online* (October 1998), available at www.theatlantic.com/issues/98oct/ruins.htm.

77. Nasaw, *Schooled to Order,* pp. 187–94. For a critique of the relationship between corporations, government, and universities, see Eyal Press and Jennifer Washburn, "The Kept University," *The Atlantic Online* (March 2000), available at www.theatlantic.com/issues/2000/03/index.htm.

78. Frank H. W. Edler, "Campus Accreditation: Here Come's the Corporate Model," *Thought & Action* (Winter 2004): 91–104.

79. David L. Westby, *The Clouded Vision* (Lewisburg, Penn.: Bucknell University Press, 1976), pp. 25–39.

80. George Caffentzis, "Throwing Away the Ladder," *Zerowork* 1 (December 1975): 131.

81. Irar E. Berg, *Education and Jobs: The Great Training Robbery* (New York: Praeger Publishers, 1970), pp. 87–96.

82. Daniel E. Hecker, "Occupational Employment Projections to 2010," *Monthly Labor Review* (November 2001), available at www.bls.gov/opub/mlr/2001/11/art4full.pdf.

83. Braverman, *Labor and Monopoly Capital,* p. 438.

84. National Center for Educational Statistics, *Revenues and Expenditures for Public Elementary and Secondary Education: School Year 2000–01* (May 2003), available at nces.ed.gov/pubs2003/2003362.pdf.

85. Nancy J. Perry, "Saving the Schools: How Business Can Help," *Fortune,* November 7, 1988, p. 44.

86. Peter Irons, *Jim Crow's Children: The Broken Promise of the Brown Decision* (New York: Viking, 2002), p. 338.

87. Henry A. Bullock, *A History of Negro Education in the South* (New York: Praeger, 1967), pp. 1–99, 170–86; John H. Franklin, *From Slavery to Freedom,* 4th ed. (New York: Alfred A. Knopf, 1974), pp. 284–86.

88. R. Sutton, "Equity and Computers in the Schools," *Review of Educational Research* 61 (Spring–Summer 1991): 475–503; Roscigno, "The Social Embeddedness of Racial Educational Inequality," pp. 143–44.

89. National Center for Educational Statistics, National Assessment of Educational Progress, *The Nation's Report Card* (ret. January 12, 2004), available at nces.ed.gov/nationsreportcard; see also Gary Blasi, "Far Along Yet Far from Equal," *Los Angeles Times* (January 11, 2004), p. M3.

90. U.S. Bureau of the Census, *Educational Attainment in the U.S.* (March 2002), available at www.census.gov/population/socdemo/education/ppl-169/tab01a.txt.

91. T. R. Dye and L. H. Zeigler, *The Irony of Democracy,* 4th ed. (North Scituate, Mass.: Duxbury Press, 1978), p. 345; U.S. Commission on Civil Rights, *Twenty Years after Brown* (Washington, D.C.: 1975), pp. 11–41.

92. *Milliken v. Bradley,* 418 U.S. 717 (1974).

93. Ibid., p. 782.

94. *Board of Education of Oklahoma v. Dowell* 498 U.S. 237 (1991); *Freeman v. Pitts,* 503 U.S. 467 (1992).

95. Gary Orfield and Chungmei Lee, *Brown at 50: King's Dream or Plessy's Nightmare,* Harvard Civil Rights Project (January 2004), available at www.civilrightsproject.harvard.edu/research/reseg04/brown50.pdf.

96. John R. Logan, *Choosing Segregation: Racial Imbalance in American Public Schools, 1990–2000* (March 29, 2002), The Lewis Mumford Center for Comparative Urban and Regional Research, available at mumford1.dyndns.org/cen2000/SchoolPop/SPReport/SPReport.doc.

97. U.S. Bureau of the Census, *Earnings by Occupation and Education,* Table 1, available at www.census.gov/hhes/income/earnings/call1usboth.html.

98. R. Aronson, "Is Busing the Real Issue?" *Dissent* 25 (Fall 1978): 413.
99. U.S. Bureau of the Census, *Current Population Survey,* March 1995.
100. National Center for Educational Statistics, *Digest of Educational Statistics: 2002,* Table 384, available at nces.ed.gov/programs/digest/d02/tables/dt384.asp.
101. Marian Wright Edelman, "Black Children in America," in *The State of Black America: 1989,* Janet Dewart, ed. (New York: Urban League, 1989), p. 74.
102. *University of California v. Bakke,* 438 U.S. 265 at 314, 317 (1978); see also *Hopwood v. University of Texas,* 78 F.3d 932 (5th Cir. 1996), cert. denied, 518 U.S. 1033 (1996); *Smith v. University of Washington,* 233 F. 3d. 1188 (9th Cir. 2000), cert. denied, 532 U.S. 1051 (2001); *Johnson v. University of Georgia,* 263 F.3d 1234 (11th Cir. 2001).
103. *Gratz v. Bollinger,* 123 S.Ct. 2411, U.S., 2003; decided June 23, 2003.
104. *Grutter v. Bollinger,* 123 S.Ct. 2325, U.S., 2003; decided June 23, 2003.
105. Howard J. Ehrlich, *Campus Ethnoviolence and the Policy Options* (Baltimore: National Institute against Prejudice and Violence, 1990), p. iii.
106. Nadine Recker Rayburn, Mitchell Earleywine, and Gerald C. Davison, "Base Rates of Hate Crime Victimization among College Students," *The Journal of Interpersonal Violence 18* (October 2003).
107. Denise K. Magner, "Blacks and Whites on the Campuses: Behind Ugly Racist Incidents, Student Isolation and Insensitivity," *Chronicle of Higher Education,* April 26, 1989, pp. A27–29.
108. This paragraph draws on Joe R. Feagin, Hernan Vera, and Nikitah Imani, *The Agony of Education* (New York: Routledge, 1996), pp. 60–61. The data are mostly from 1993–2000 issues of *Race Relations Reporter.*
109. "Racial Incident at the University of Washington," *The Journal of Blacks in Higher Education, Race Relations Reporter, Weekly Bulletin,* December 25, 2003, available at www.jbhe.com.
110. *The Journal of Blacks in Higher Education, The Race Relations Reporter,* Weekly Bulletin, November 3, 2003, available at www.jbhe.com/rrr/rrr.html.
111. Joe R. Feagin and Melvin P. Sikes, *Living with Racism* (Boston: Beacon Press, 1994), pp. 60–61.
112. Feagin et al., *The Agony of Education,* p. 88.
113. Tom Carter, *Mexican Americans in Schools* (New York: College Entrance Board, 1970), pp. 97–102; U.S. Commission on Civil Rights, *Ethnic Isolation of Mexican Americans in the Public Schools of the Southwest* (Washington, D.C.: 1971), pp. 21–25, 41–51; Charles W. Hall, "In Arlington, School Plan Stirs Diverse Anxieties," *Washington Post,* January 25, 1994, p. B1.
114. Alan Lupo, "Crosstown Express; One Step at a Time," *Boston Globe,* January 30, 1994, p. 2; Rodríguez, *Puerto Ricans,* pp. 122–23, 149–50.
115. Juan F. Perea, "Demography and Distrust: An Essay on American Languages, Cultural Pluralism, and Official English," *Minnesota Law Review* 77 (December 1992): 269–373; quotation on p. 273.
116. Catherine E. Walsh, *Pedagogy and the Struggle for Voice* (New York: Bergin & Garvey, 1991), p. ix; see also pp. 100–101, 127; See also Henry Giroux, *Border Crossings* (New York: Routledge, 1992), pp. 166–70.
117. Walsh, *Pedagogy and the struggle for Voice,* pp. vii–xi, 1–27, 65–68; quotations from p. vii.
118. Rodríguez, *Puerto Ricans,* pp. 147–48.
119. Ibid., pp. 139–40.
120. Ibid., pp. 122–23, 127; National Center for Educational Statistics, *Digest of Educational Statistics: 2002,* Table 105, available at nces.ed.gov/programs/digest/d02/tables/dt105.asp.
121. Barbara Kantrowitz with Lourdes Rosado, "Falling Further Behind," *Newsweek,* August 19, 1991, p. 60; Robert Lee Maril, *Poorest of Americans* (South Bend, Ind.: University of Notre Dame Press, 1989), pp. 117–18; U.S. Bureau of the Census, *We the Americans: Our Education,* available at www.census.gov/apsd/wepeople/we-11.pdf.
122. Milga Morales-Nadal, "Puerto Rican/Latino(a) Vistas on Culture and Education" (paper, 1991), n.p.; see also Antonia Darder, *Culture and Power in the Classroom* (New York: Bergin & Garvey, 1991).
123. Walsh, *Pedagogy and the Struggle for Voice,* pp. 95–113.
124. The research was done by Marcelo Suarez-Orozco and Carola Suarez-Orozco at the Harvard Graduate School of Education; cited in Georgie Ann Geyer, "The Disaffected Immigrants," *Tulsa World,* April 25, 1996, p. A17.
125. Guy Halverson, "Indicators of U.S. Prospects," *Christian Science Monitor,* January 31, 1991, p. 13.
126. Feagin and Feagin, *Racial and Ethnic Relations,* pp. 404–44.

127. Ibid., pp. 440–41. See John H. Bunzel, "The Diversity Dialogues in Higher Education," *Fordham Urban Law Journal* 29 (2001): 489–512, 495; Michael W. Lynch, "Affirmative Action at the University of California," *Notre Dame Journal of Law, Ethics and Public Policy* 11 (1997): 139–158; Haeryung Shin, "Safety in Numbers? Equal Protection, Desegregation, and Discrimination: School Desegregation in a Multi-Cultural Society," *Cornell Law Review* 82 (1996): 182–224, 219.

128. American Association of University Women, *How Schools Shortchange Girls* (Washington, D.C.: American Association of University Women, 1992), p. 7 (executive summary available online at www.aauw.org/research/hssg.pdf); the AAUW has updated its 1992 report in *Gender Gaps: Where Schools Still Fail Our Children* (1998); an overview with selected findings, tables, bibliography, and recommendations for educators and policymakers is available online at www.aauw.org/research/GGES.pdf; see also Betty Lindsey, "Schools Still Have a Gap in the Area of Gender Equality," *Courier Journal,* October 3, 1993, p. 1E.

129. K. Bogart, *Solutions that Work: Identification and Elimination of Barriers to the Participation of Female and Minority Students in Academic Educational Programs,* vol. 3 (Washington, D.C.: National Education Association, 1992), cited in ibid., p. 63.

130. American Association of University Women, *How Schools Shortchange Girls,* p. 2.

131. American Association of University Women, *Gender Gaps: Where School Still Fail Our Children* (1998) available at www.aauw.org/research/GGES.pdf; American Association of University Women, *Tech Savy: Educating Girls in the New Computer Age* (2000), available at www.aauw.org/research/techexecsumm.cfm.

132. Ibid., pp. 6, 8.

133. Ibid., p. 61.

134. Nancy Frazier and Myra Sadker, *Sexism in School and Society* (New York: Harper and Row, 1973), p. 139.

135. David Sadker and Myra Sadker, *Year 3: Final Report, Promoting Effectiveness in Classroom Instruction* (Washington, D.C.: National Institute of Education, 1984); American Association of University Women, *How Schools Shortchange Girls,* pp. 68–71.

136. American Association of University Women, *Gender Gaps: Where Schools Still Fail Our Children;* American Association of University Women, *How Schools Shortchange Girls,* p. 70; Pauline Sears, *The Effect of Classroom Conditions on the Strength of Achievement Motive and Work Output of Elementary School Children,* U.S. Department of Health, (Washington, D.C.: 1963); James Patterson, "Rivalry Yielding Results," *Indianapolis Star,* November 4, 1995, p. A12.

137. U.S. Department of Education, National Center for Education Statistics, *Post Secondary Education,* Table 246, Table 255, available at nces.ed.gov/programs/digest/d02/list_tables3.asp#c3a_5.

138. David Karp and William Yoels, "The College Classroom," in H. Robboy, S. L. Greenblatt, and C. Clark, eds., *Social Interaction* (New York: St. Martin's Press, 1979), pp. 106–108.

139. National Organization for Women, "NOW Reports on Equity in Education," 1987, p. 1.

140. Erik Bradley, "Time Fails to Lessen Title IX Furor," *USA Today* (June 19, 2002).

141. National Collegiate Athletic Association, *NCAA 2001–2002 NCAA Gender-Equity Report,* available at www.ncaa.org/library/research/gender_equity_study/2001–02/2001–02GenderEquityReport.pdf; National Women's Sports Foundation, *Gender Equity, Creative Solutions—A Case Study in Compliance* (July 28, 2000), available at www.womenssportsfoundation.org/cgi-bin/iowa/issues/rights/article.html?record=109.

142. Sara Steindorf, "Women Make the Team, but Less Often Coach It," *Christian Science Monitor,* March 12, 2002, p. 13.

chapter 7

Problems in Health and Medical Care

The very large number of Americans who have no health insurance (43.6 million) and the sharply rising costs of medical care ($1.7 trillion) are at the core of a widely recognized health care crisis.[1] Many patients who cannot afford regular or timely outpatient care rely on the much more costly services of hospital emergency rooms, and many others go without any care altogether. In the 1990s, addressing these issues was a priority of President Bill Clinton, who said that without solving its health care financing problem, the United States could not hope to solve its other economic problems. Clinton was the first American president to focus centrally on health care issues. Yet his health care proposals were vigorously attacked by members of Congress (mostly by Republicans), and they were not implemented. Many health and health care issues continue to plague the United States, including the continuing struggle against heart disease and cancer, the impersonality of much of the medical establishment, unnecessary operations, medical malpractice lawsuits, fraud and poor-quality care by physicians, and toxic pesticides and other cancer-causing additives found in food and manufactured consumer goods.

GOALS OF THIS CHAPTER

In this chapter, we examine numerous U.S. health issues. We begin by looking at health statistics showing that, although major death and illness rates have generally declined over the decades, mortality rates remain relatively high in U.S. society. One reason for the poor performance of the country's health care institutions is the unequal distribution of income and wealth. As in other sectors of the society, racial, ethnic, and gender inequalities in medical care significantly shape health problems affecting the country's residents, especially the poor, Americans of color, and women. We also examine how and why health care has become a major U.S. industry—in part the result of the dramatic growth and increasing complexity of the *medical-industrial complex.* Here we explore the underlying political–economic causes of health and health care problems. In the last sections, we focus on government intervention in health care and some issues affecting the nursing home industry.

HEALTH STATISTICS

Government statistics indicate that Americans are not as healthy as people in numerous other industrialized nations. Health statistics show the effects of life in the United States, but they usually only hint at the causes of problems. These root causes may lie in the type and quality of the medical care system, in food and nutrition, in dangers in the workplace, in environmental pollution, or in certain inherited characteristics.

Death and Illness Rates

Infant mortality rates in the United States have declined sharply since 1900—from 162 deaths for every 1,000 live births around 1900 to 6.8 deaths per 1,000 live births today. Yet the United States has not led the world in this regard. Significantly, the U.S. infant mortality rate is higher than that of most other industrialized countries. Indeed, the United States is not among the world's 20 countries with the lowest infant mortality rate.[2] The United States has a higher percentage of low-birth-weight babies than most other Western countries.[3] Thousands of children die unnecessarily each year because of inadequate infant and maternal health care. Death rates for U.S. adults in certain age categories, such as the cardiovascular death rate for middle-aged men, are also relatively high. As a result, the life expectancy for Americans is lower than in many other Western countries.[4]

Health Care Services

The number of health care workers has increased dramatically since 1940, from just over 1 million to almost 10.3 million in 2001. More than 825,000 of these are physicians. In recent decades, the proportion of primary care physicians—that is, family doctors and general practitioners—among physicians as a group has dropped sharply, from almost two-thirds at mid-century to about 11 percent today. Today the vast majority of physicians are specialists. The shift to specialization is related in part to the development of a high-technology medical care system centered on diagnosing illnesses and the use of drugs and expensive equipment. This high-tech practice is very costly. For example, more than $60 billion of the country's annual medical bill is spent on radiology tests. Yet one radiology expert has asserted that most radiology tests ordered by doctors are unnecessary. Some experts believe physicians could reduce the number of such procedures if they proceeded more thoughtfully in their diagnoses and did not worry about lawsuits.[5]

Today preventive care is still the weakest part of the health care system. Public health programs account for less than 4 percent of all health care expenditures.[6] Serious expansions in preventive health care would encompass not only expanded public health programs but also serious discussions of preventive action in schools, colleges, and the media. Some physicians have recently argued for Americans to pay greater attention to their eating habits, particularly eating habits that result from aggressive advertising by various food corporations of products (such as high-sugar and high-fat foods) contributing to health problems. A report by the Physicians' Committee for Responsible Medicine estimates that at least $28 billion (and perhaps $61 billion) in annual medical costs could be saved if Americans consumed less meat. Comparing the costs of illnesses suffered by meat eaters with the costs of illnesses of vegetarians, the study estimated that the country's medical expenditures to treat high blood pressure, heart disease, some cancers, and certain other illnesses could be reduced sharply if more Americans were to significantly reduce their meat consumption or become (vegan) vegetarians. Not surprisingly, such arguments are considered "too radical" by meat-oriented firms, which have played a role in suppressing serious public discussion of these food-oriented issues.[7] Still, concern in the public about the health impact of the food we eat seems to be growing in the twenty-first century, especially about the food consumed in fast-food restaurants.

Health care facilities and personnel are unevenly distributed. Industrial and highly urbanized areas have a higher concentration of doctors than do less industrialized and rural areas. This unequal distribution holds for hospital beds, nurses, and other health care workers. Across the United States, numerous counties, especially less populated ones, are without physicians or hospitals. In recent decades, many rural hospitals have closed because of

financial troubles. Rural areas face shortages of health care workers and mental health services, even though the number of rural elderly, poor, and medically uninsured people remains substantial.

The High Cost of Health Care

Health care is a major U.S. industry, and its cost is now very high. National health expenditures increased from $2.9 billion in 1935 to an estimated $1.7 trillion in 2003, or $5,650 per person in the United States. Health care industry analysts expect national expenditures to exceed $3.1 trillion by 2012. Health care expenditures have increased at a much faster rate than those for food or housing. Per capita health care expenditures are the highest in the world and account for a significant percentage of gross national product (GNP). They constituted approximately 15 percent of GNP in 2003, up from 5.3 percent in 1960. Although the proportion of federal government expenditures for health care has increased—from 4 percent in 1950 to nearly 13.2 percent in the early 2000s—the United States is the only major industrialized country in the world that does not have a government-coordinated national health care system. Such government systems generally are more egalitarian in the provision of health care and also reduce medical and other health care costs substantially.[8]

Medical costs can be overwhelming. One news story reported about a man whose two-hour visit to a hospital emergency room for the removal of a small bone lodged in his throat cost almost $4,000. A hospital administrator explained that in addition to the cost of removing the bone, additional charges included a small percentage of the cost of marketing and running the hospital.[9] Hospital expenditures constitute the largest portion of health care expenditures—31.3 percent in 2002; home health care accounted for only 2.3 percent. Expenses in short-stay hospitals increase more than 10 percent per year.[10] The cost of a major operation and a week or two in a hospital can often wipe out the savings of poor and middle-income families, even if they have health insurance. Hospital fees pay for expensive equipment and often cover some care for nonpaying patients. But the largest expense incurred by hospitals is their highly trained and highly paid personnel. (Most doctors' salaries, for example, are many times the wages of average workers, including some other well-educated workers.)

Most hospitals make a profit. This quest for greater profitability is often cited as a major reason for cutbacks in the nursing staff in many hospitals. More than two-thirds of nurses in one survey reported cuts in the number of registered nurses at their workplaces. More than 93 percent of them said that the cuts had reduced the quality of patient care. Hospital managements cited profit-related reasons to justify the cuts.[11]

Many hospitals use their profits to employ large marketing staffs and purchase high-tech equipment to compete for physicians. The director of UCLA Medical Center's hospital described this competition as a "medical arms race." Such competition leads to unnecessary and costly duplication of equipment at more than one hospital in a geographic area. Possession of high-tech equipment can mean overuse. Medical ethicist Lawrence Schneiderman has noted that heroic but futile lifesaving efforts are painful and invasive for the patient and expensive for society, easily running to $100,000 a week. Often, it is when medical care is most futile that so many dollars are spent.[12] Meanwhile, more basic health care needs of many Americans are seriously underfunded.

Many people rely on private insurance to protect themselves financially from medical catastrophes. Private health insurance is a highly profitable industry. Yet, as Table 7.1 reveals, 15.2 percent of Americans have *no* medical insurance, and nearly 8.5 million of them are children. More than 30 percent of those below the federal poverty line have no insurance, and many others are underinsured. Nearly 92 percent of those in families with incomes of $75,000 or more are covered by insurance, but the proportion drops to 77 percent for those in families with incomes of less than $25,000, and to nearly 70 percent for those below the poverty line. Racial group, ethnicity, and country of origin remain significant factors influencing insurance coverage. African Americans are *twice* as likely as whites are to be without insurance, and Latinos are *three times* as likely to have no insurance coverage. The foreign born and noncitizens are more likely to be without insurance than native-born persons and naturalized citizens.[13]

Some 61 percent of workers have employment-based health insurance, and nearly 26 percent are covered by a government health plan such as Medicare (13.4 percent), Medicaid (11.6 percent), or military insurance (3.5 percent). The unemployed and many part-time employees have no such employer-paid coverage. Nearly half of the working poor have no coverage. Moreover, sick people or those at high risk of becoming sick may be excluded from employer-paid coverage and may find it impossible or extremely expensive to buy private insurance. Also, insurance coverage seldom applies to preventive medical care. Significantly, *less than half* of U.S. consumers' total medical care costs are covered by insurance plans.[14]

HIGH-TECHNOLOGY MEDICINE

The Bureaucratization of Medicine

The large U.S. medical-industrial complex absorbs many consumer dollars. High-technology medicine emphasizes specialized physicians, expensive equipment, and extensive use of expensive drugs. Devotion to high technology has encouraged growth of bureaucratized medicine and large medical organizations. More than half of all physicians are in group practices, hospitals, and other institutions. The last decade or two have seen an explosion in the growth of health maintenance organizations (HMOs), which are groups of doctors whose patients pay monthly premiums for HMO services.

Large medical institutions are often the only places that can afford to purchase expensive technology, which is often beyond the reach of individual doctors and smaller hospitals. Large profit-seeking medical-technology corporations reinforce the trend toward large centralized medical institutions. The growing involvement of the federal government in medical care since the 1960s has facilitated the growth of large complexes of hospitals and medical colleges. In cities from New York to Houston to Los Angeles, bureaucratized health care empires centered around large hospitals and medical schools receive most government money for medical research and control most city hospital beds and medical care resources.[15]

High-tech medicine is so prestigious that many prominent doctors and other hospital board members want expensive equipment and facilities whether or not they unnecessarily duplicate those of nearby hospitals. In larger cities, hospitals sometimes even compete for doctors by adding expensive medical equipment. Many hospitals do not use this high-tech equipment often enough to justify the expense or to maintain the skills of the units. The acquisition and upkeep costs of these expensive machines are partially responsible for rising health care costs.

Table 7.1   People without Health Insurance by Selected Characteristics: 2002

Characteristics	All People (% without Health Insurance)	Persons in Poverty (% without Health Insurance)
Total	15.2	30.4
Age		
Under 18 years	11.6	20.1
18 to 24 years	29.6	43.9
25 to 34 years	24.9	48.6
35 to 44 years	17.7	46.0
45 to 64 years	13.5	33.1
65 years and over	0.8	1.9
Race		
White	10.7	25.4
Black	20.2	26.4
Asian	18.4	38.7
Latino	32.4	42.8
Nativity		
Native	12.8	25.6
Foreign born	33.4	55.3
Naturalized citizen	17.5	35.0
Not a citizen	43.3	61.4
Household Income		
Less than $25,000	23.5	n/a
$25,000 to $49,999	19.3	n/a
$50,000 to $74,999	11.8	n/a
$75,000 or more	8.2	n/a
Education		
No high school diploma	28.0	37.9
High school graduate only	18.8	36.4
Some college, no degree	15.0	33.5
Associate's degree	12.1	32.3
Bachelor's degree or higher	8.4	32.3
Work Experience		
Worked during year	18.0	47.4
Worked full-time	16.8	49.3
Worked part-time	23.5	44.4
Did not work	25.7	38.1

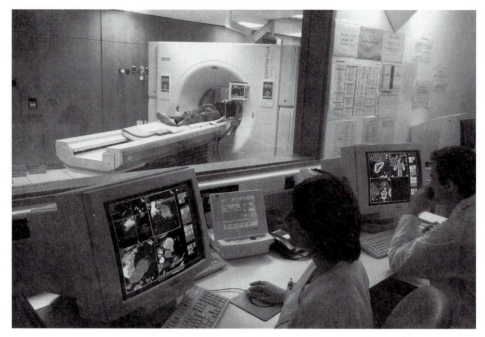

High-tech devices like this CT scanner are one reason for the escalating costs of medical care. (Edwige/Phototake NYC)

Technology or Corporate Decisions?

High-technology modern medicine is generally the result of a series of decisions made by key officials in large corporations, medical societies, government agencies, and corporate foundations. Their decisions help explain not only the technological, drug-oriented, and often impersonal character of much modern medicine but also its very high costs. Particular societal problems are sometimes blamed on technology and industrialization. Much sociological analysis of medicine emphasizes that technological advance creates health care problems. But technology does not originate on its own, nor does it usually determine the path of development.[16] The decisions of corporate capitalists, corporate managers, and chief government officials have substantially determined which technologies are developed and how they are used. Consider, for example, the technology of nuclear power. The citizenry was not directly consulted about the character, pace, or development of nuclear power; the technology was implemented by a few large corporations working closely with the federal government. Between 1946 and 1970, no significant public debate took place on alternative nuclear power strategies or safety. Less dangerous conservation or alternative technologies, such as solar power, were not considered seriously, at least in part because large energy corporations could not make as much profit with alternative technologies.

Similarly, a prevention- and nutrition-centered health care system would likely mean much less profit for large corporations that produce medical equipment and drugs, as well

Since the 1980s, conservative politicians and business leaders have succeeded in reducing regulations protecting the health of Americans.

as for for-profit hospitals. Little public debate has occurred on the development of a prevention- and nutrition-oriented alternative to replace the existing disease-oriented, high-tech system, which is becoming too expensive for this society to maintain without sacrificing other major societal needs.

The High-Tech Focus

Beginning just after 1900, medicine in the United States came to be increasingly focused on the cure-oriented, complex technological approach of today. Victor and Ruth Sidel discuss the dimensions of this approach: (1) an emphasis on a specific-agent theory of disease and quick-fix (drug) cures, rather than a multifaceted approach looking at broader environmental factors, (2) the strong development of medical technology versus the weak development of public health and prevention approaches to health, and (3) reforms in medical education leading to an emphasis on hospitals, offices, and laboratories rather than on home settings for study and care.[17] The emphasis on a specific-agent theory of disease and on extensive use of drugs for quick-fix cures has prevailed to the present day in much of U.S. medicine, as a trip to a nearby physician will usually reveal.

   Nowhere is the high-technology orientation toward cure of illnesses more clear than in the case of cancer, a major cause of death. An estimated one-third of Americans now living will get cancer, and more than half of those will probably die from it. The traditional medical care and research approach to the cancer epidemic has emphasized surgery, chemotherapy, and radiation. Huge sums are spent on this expensive high-technology treatment and research each year, while far less is spent on environmental analysis, nutrition, and disease prevention.[18]

What has the expensive high-tech research effort brought the American people? In the 1990s, Dr. Samuel Epstein, author of major books on cancer and health care, argued that organizations like the National Cancer Institute (NCI) and the American Cancer Society "have misled and confused the public and Congress by repeated claims that we are winning the war against cancer," a conclusion endorsed by some 70 scientists.[19] Changes in the five-year survival rates for most cancers since the mid-1970s have been marginal, and improvements that have occurred in the five-year survival rate for some forms of cancer are likely the result of increased early detection.[20] Epstein and numerous other experts believe that most cancers are *environmentally caused.* Yet removal of environmental carcinogens (cancer-causing agents) has not been a high government priority. For example, widespread action to reduce the public health hazards of tobacco smoke came slowly to the United States, even though it has been known for decades that such smoking is responsible for many cancer deaths annually. (Secondhand smoke from smokers is still a debated issue.) In addition, most carcinogenic chemicals used in the workplace and most of the pesticide residues on food have not been targeted for aggressive removal action by corporate officials or government regulators.

Rather than undertake extensive studies of environmental carcinogens, U.S. medical researchers usually study genetic or other biological causes and suggest drug cures for diseases. Most physicians and medical researchers have traditionally been interested in containing disease agents but much less interested in preventing critical causal conditions of disease, such as poverty and dangerous living and working conditions. Most corporate executives would not approve of *aggressive and large-scale* health research programs that examine unsafe chemical food additives, unsafe working conditions, or serious air and water pollution in home, community, and work environments that corporations have created or shaped. For decades, U.S. courts have upheld the rights of employers to maintain certain dangerous workplace and community environments (see Chapter 10). In the view of many corporate officials, the public must not be allowed to view disease as substantially the result of workplace hazards or other corporate actions.

Medical Education: The Move to Hospitals and Offices

Beginning in the twentieth century, members of the corporate capitalist class, working in part through their charitable foundations, helped to shape a high-technology medical care system to meet what they saw as the needs of a modern society. They felt their goals for modern medicine would bring benefits to everyone. Linked to these top executives were science-oriented professional groups and organizations of physicians and hospitals.[21]

At the beginning of the twentieth century, U.S. health care was still diverse, with numerous types of practitioners and competing theories about causes and cures for disease. The medical profession was divided into groups centered around different theories or medical procedures. Scientific reformers of this diverse system sought to improve it according to their values and also to control the character of the medical profession, thereby attempting to exclude competing health care groups. Until World War I, medical research was centered in Europe, and many U.S. physicians went to study there. A few elite U.S. medical schools modeled themselves after European schools, and graduates of these schools practiced a scientifically based, and increasingly prestigious, medicine, with strong support from corporate capitalists.[22]

Both basic and applied sciences have long been a central commitment of industrial capitalism. Scientific medicine, with its microbiological (germ) theory of disease and specific drug cures, was attractive to leading corporate executives. Here was an opportunity to cure society of diseases with high-tech engineering applied to the human body, a strategy that could be profitable for certain corporations. Moreover, a few spectacular successes by scientific medical researchers, for diseases such as diphtheria, received press attention. This new medical science brought anesthetics, insulin, antibiotics, and other "wonder drugs," which gave the science-oriented medical schools and physicians great prestige. However, for all their dramatic and important successes, these new cures were coupled with a special-agent theory of disease and helped to establish a medicine focused on *diseases* rather than on the health of the whole person and the prevention of disease. Unlike older folk medicine practitioners and traditional family practice physicians, most new scientist–specialist physicians paid less attention to the contributions of family, community, and work settings in generating both illness and "wellness" for Americans.[23]

Competing types of folk medicine, including the beneficial and the harmful, had to be driven out, so medical reformers used political pressure to persuade state legislators to require special licensing for medical practitioners. Thus the dramatic benefits of the new scientific medicine were partially offset by health care losses. Poorer working-class people especially suffered losses from the new dominance of scientific medicine, since existing working-class, black, and female practitioners (such as herbalists and midwives) in local communities were often driven out of practice by new state licensing requirements increasingly under the control of new (white-male) medical societies. This trend reduced the availability of care. With the rise of scientific medicine, medical treatment became much more expensive and geographically inaccessible for many people of modest means. Certain types of important medical care, such as that provided by midwives, were prohibited for several decades.[24]

The science-oriented medical faculties at schools such as Johns Hopkins University became dominant in the American Medical Association (AMA), as well as in medical education. In 1910 a Carnegie Commission study underscored deficiencies in many existing medical schools. Soon many medical schools were closed—closings usually (but not always) necessary to protect the public. Entrance (educational) requirements were raised for the remaining schools—requirements often excluding students from modest-income families. One intended result of these closings was to enhance the prominence of the science-oriented university medical schools and to cut the total number of trained medical doctors, thus reducing competition and raising the incomes of physicians substantially.[25]

Medical research, medical schools, and thousands of new hospital facilities cost a lot of money. Local small-business owners and working people contributed to the building of hospitals, but medical research increasingly came to depend on large corporations. From 1910 to the 1930s corporate foundations contributed $300 million to the development of medical schools, including research facilities. Massive contributions to research have brought not only medical breakthroughs but also tax and other benefits to the corporations involved. One benefit of this research involvement was a better image for corporations, which were increasingly under fire from workers critical of corporate exploitation of employees. Corporate officials believed that scientific medicine would build support among working-class people for an expanding scientific-industrial capitalism and would persuade employees that their misery and other problems could be solved by a greater dependency on technical experts for solutions. Expanded reliance on medical technology has been very profitable for several sectors of corporate America, including pharmaceutical firms and for-profit hospital companies.[26]

By the 1920s the AMA came to be dominated by fee-for-service physicians in private practice; among other things, these physicians have used the AMA to control the growth of medical schools and to oppose, to the present, much government intervention in medical care, including an effective national government-fostered health service.

Benefits and Problems

High-technology medicine has, of course, brought numerous major benefits to residents of the United States, as well as to other people throughout the world. While recognizing the significant contributions of the health sciences—such as penicillin, antibiotics, the polio vaccine, prenatal health care, and many types of surgery—some critical scholars have argued that the positive impact of this high-tech medical system—the specialists, the expensive equipment, and the costly hospital care and drugs—on the health of both Americans and Europeans has been greatly exaggerated. They note that many major gains in public health have resulted *not* from the high-tech medical care system but from public health measures such as improvements in food quality, nutrition, sanitation, safe water sources, and safety at work. Historically, tuberculosis, cholera, dysentery, and typhoid declined significantly *before* the new scientific physicians and drugs entered the scene in a major way; it has been estimated that 90 percent of the declining death rates for numerous children's diseases occurred before the widespread use of immunization, antibiotics, and other drugs. Better nutrition, housing, water, and sanitation are likely the major causes of these declines, factors that remain critical to future health improvements throughout the world today.[27]

Since the nineteenth century, courageous doctors, nurses, and public health workers have played an important role in pressing for sanitary treatment of sewage, for improved nutrition, for the use of soap by midwives and doctors, and for other antimicrobial procedures. The spread of sanitary techniques to the general population has played a major role in the decline of many traditional diseases.

Most such advances in human health have not required, and still do not require, expensive high-tech medicine. Moreover, high-tech medicine has also brought its own diseases and illnesses, sometimes called *iatrogenic* problems, to people around the world. A number of perceptive analysts, such as Ivan Illich, have pointed to the evidence of problems generated by modern medicine itself: unnecessary surgery and other medical treatments, the excessive use of drugs with serious side effects, the significant number of doctor- and hospital-caused diseases and accidents, the decline of self-care, and the rising dependency of medical consumers on medical experts. Thereby, many thousands of patients are killed or injured each year. These trends indicate that the health care system itself can sometimes be dangerous to one's health.

Iatrogenic problems refer to harm brought to patients by hospitals, doctors, and other health care personnel, as well as by the bureaucratic organization of medicine. Examples of iatrogenic problems include the negative side effects of doctor-prescribed medications taken regularly by a large proportion of Americans. Some are taking contaminated drugs; others are taking drugs that are dangerous when combined with other medications. Some medications are habit-forming or have destructive side effects. Excessive use of certain diagnostic procedures has also created iatrogenic problems. In one study of 30,195 patient records at 51 hospitals, researchers found some 1,278 injuries caused just by medical treatment.[28]

Some critical analysts criticize the heavy dependence of ordinary people on the medical technology engineered by expert technological manipulation of the medical system. Ivan Illich, for example, emphasizes the importance of a return to self-care and a preventive system of health maintenance. From this perspective, individuals should learn more about, and take a more direct role in, their health care. The suggestion of expanded self-awareness and self-care is excellent as far as it goes, but an overemphasis on the individual citizen's responsibility can take the blame for health problems off the political–economic system. People can often improve their health and life chances by giving up a too-heavy dependence on doctor-prescribed medications. Yet this action does not answer the larger question of why and how this dependence became widespread in the United States, or the question of what to do to change this often harmful drug dependency system.

The dependency of consumers on fee-for-service, high-tech medicine was not created by the medical system alone. This medical system is part of the larger economy. Vincente Navarro has underlined the fact that this economic system commonly prefers a dependent, unquestioning consumer for generating profits. The established medical system reinforces the society-generated consumption tendencies that are already there: the "need" for a new car, for a new detergent product, or for the latest in high-tech medications. In the capitalistic mode of for-profit production and distribution, most workers' labor and the products and services they produce are largely controlled by capitalistic decision makers, and people's consumption is manipulated by a variety of procedures, including often misleading advertising. Consumer "needs" are often the creations of this profit-oriented system and do not represent real needs. Aggressive advertising and publicity by pharmaceutical companies and other medically oriented corporations reinforce consumption desires for medical products, some of which can be dangerous to consumers' health. From this perspective, consumer dependency and lack of questioning in the medical sphere stem from the "consumerist" society.[29]

HEALTH CARE: PRIVATE CONTROL AND PRIVATE PROFIT

The Medical-Industrial Complex Today

Figure 7.1 diagrams six of the major components of what some have called the *medical-industrial complex:* physicians, medical schools, pharmacies, drug companies, medical-technology firms, and hospitals. Each of these components is tied in critical ways to other components of the system; some of these (usually reciprocal) relationships are suggested by the arrow-headed lines. The dramatic growth and increasing complexity of this medical-industrial complex have been evident over the last several decades.

Profits

Our high-technology health care system is part of an economic system that emphasizes control of consumption by a business elite and the continuing demand for profit. In the mass media and in Congress, many discussions of reforms for this medical care system see its problems in the "nonsystem" of inefficient, separated, fee-for-service physicians and

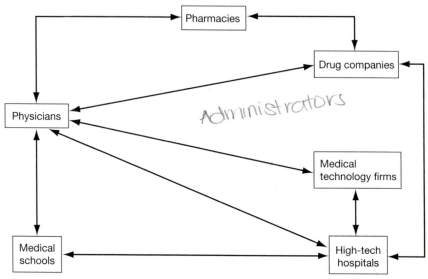

Figure 7.1   The Medical-Industrial Complex

duplicative hospital equipment. One argument is that U.S. health care is not as rationally organized as it could be. Some critics seem to assume that the only intent of today's medical care is to improve the health of people. Yet health care is not the only major function of the medical care system. Elite control, money accumulation, and rate of profit are very important for many decision makers in the medical-industrial complex.

For example, one means by which pharmaceutical companies and other manufacturers of health care products, health insurance companies, health service companies and HMOs, hospital systems and nursing homes, and other health interests assure enormous corporate profits and industry control is by maintaining a powerful lobby in Washington, D.C. In its analysis of health industry lobbying records, the Center for Public Integrity recently learned that since 1998 the industry has spent $1.79 billion in lobbying efforts. The pharmaceutical and health products industry alone spent $759 million to support nearly 3,000 professional lobbyists on more than 1,400 congressional bills. The legion of industry lobbyists translates into four and a half pharmaceutical lobbyists for every member of Congress—more than any other corporate interest group—and includes some 805 former federal officials, 48 former members of the U.S. House of Representatives, and 15 former members of the U.S. Senate. Passage of the Medicare Prescription Drug, Improvement, and Modernization Act of 2003 that goes into effect in 2006 is one result of the industry's lobbying efforts. Under the Act, the federal government must purchase at least $40 billion in drugs every year from drug companies, and it prohibits the federal government from negotiating drug prices. Lobbying campaigns have weakened federal regulation of pharmaceutical interests, strengthened patent protections on drugs, extended patents, won tax credits, and gained government protection of foreign markets. Also, the health care industry has been able to gain substantial influence over the Food and Drug Administration (FDA) and its drug approval process. Under an extension of the Prescription Drug User Fee Act, the

FDA will earn more than $284 million in users fees that, according to one industry analyst, means that the pharmaceutical industry is contributing substantial sums to the agency's overall budget and thereby creating potential conflicts of interest.[30]

Fee-for-Service Physicians

The centrality of the profit concern is seen in many small medical businesses, such as those of many private practice physicians, as well as in large drug and medical equipment corporations. The fee-for-service system for physicians has meant relatively high incomes for the majority. At some points in its history, the AMA has worked to limit the number of physicians. Until the 1960s, the AMA played a role in sharply restricting the number of medical schools and the number of new physicians, reportedly to keep quality high, but this action also had the effect of reducing competition and keeping physicians' incomes high.

The number of physicians in the United States is now more than 825,000. The number of doctors per 100,000 population changed very little from 1950 to 1965 but has slowly increased from that time to the present. After 1970, the AMA finally agreed that there was a critical shortage of doctors. As a result, the number of medical schools increased from 103 to 146 between 1970 and 2001, and during this same period the number of students graduating from medical schools each year more than doubled.[31] Nonetheless, the absolute number of new physicians graduated annually is still relatively modest—about 16,000 in 2003. Since 1996, moreover, the number of applicants to medical schools has generally declined, probably because of "the plummeting prestige of doctors, the specter of enormous medical school debt, the rise of managed care and the lure of other careers perceived as less difficult or more promising."[32] And if most new physicians become specialists, the family doctor shortage—especially in poor or rural areas, small towns, and some southern states—will not be significantly relieved in the future. We might note that foreign medical schools have trained a significant proportion of physicians now practicing in the United States.[33] In this way other countries, including poor countries that often pay dearly for the privilege (for example, in loss of medical care), subsidize the medical educations of U.S. physicians.

Private practice physicians typically charge a fee for their medical services, and many such fees are not significantly affected by competition, although this may change in the future. Today, the average income of physicians in private practice is among the highest of any professional category. The average net income for all U.S. doctors in 2002 was $202,442—many times the income of ordinary workers and more than that of most other professional groups with comparable education and skills.[34]

The fee-for-service system of paying doctors can be abused. Dr. Charles E. Lewis, a professor of public health at the University of California, has suggested that "Medicine as currently structured is one of the few fields where if a wife really wants a new coat, all you have to do is maybe a couple more hysterectomies this week and you can buy it."[35] Many unnecessary surgeries are indeed performed each year. On a per capita basis, Americans undergo many more surgeries than the British. Since most British physicians work on salaries, they have little incentive to perform unnecessary surgeries. Even in the United States today, members in prepaid health care plans with salaried doctors often undergo fewer surgeries than do those who have conventional health insurance and use private, fee-for-service physicians. Each year an estimated 15 to 25 percent of all surgical operations in the United States are unnecessary.[36]

One of the most common operations in the United States is the caesarean surgical procedure for childbirth. Over the last several decades, caesarean procedures have increased from about 5 percent to about 26 percent of all births. This shift is costly for the country's health care bill since the operation and related hospital charges cost 2.3 times more than a vaginal delivery in a hospital. A significant number of these operations, according to the Public Citizen's Health Research Group, are unnecessary.[37] One study found that some of the increase in caesarean sections is because of mothers' choice, which is likely influenced by discussions with physicians.[38]

One *Consumer Reports* study noted that "Hysterectomy is the second most common major surgical procedure in the United States. One in three women have one—often for no good reason."[39] The report cites a research study that examined hysterectomies performed under managed-care plans. Its medical experts judged one in six to have been unnecessary. Since these surgeries were conducted under a managed-care plan that paid attention to cost issues, the report suggests that nationally the proportion of unnecessary hysterectomies is likely to be higher.

Perhaps a thousand people die each year from unnecessary surgery.[40] While the desire of a surgeon for a large income is by no means the only motive for unnecessary surgery, it does appear to be one reason. For example, in 2003 federal prosecutors claimed a $54 million settlement with Tenet Healthcare Corporation as part of an investigation into two cardiologists who allegedly performed 167 unnecessary heart procedures where patients died. The physicians allegedly funneled millions of dollars to Tenet by means of unnecessary surgeries and kickbacks rewarding certain physicians for patient referrals. Physicians and patients complained to Tenet's hospital administrators, but the peer-review programs used to scrutinize medical care at hospitals failed and disregarded complaints.[41] The private, fee-for-service payment arrangement does not always serve patients well.

In a related context, the Public Citizen organization has revealed that some 6,700 physicians across the country that medical boards and agencies have disciplined for serious offenses are still practicing, and patients are generally unaware of their offenses. The majority of these doctors have been disciplined for sexual abuse or sexual misconduct; substandard care, incompetence, or negligence; criminal convictions; misprescribing or overprescribing drugs; and substance abuse. In one egregious case, a California physician delayed a caesarean section so long that the baby was born in a vegetative state and died. Nationally, only a tiny fraction of physicians face disciplinary actions—only 3.36 serious disciplinary actions are taken for every 1,000 physicians. Some knowledgeable commentators suggest that state governments need to do far more to protect the public.[42]

Corporate Profits

The current high-technology medical care system provides substantial profits for a variety of corporations. We have noted the role of corporations and corporate foundations in shifting the U.S. health care system in the direction of disease-oriented, high-tech medicine. Today large hospital firms, insurance companies, drug companies, medical technology companies, and commercial blood banks seek substantial profits from services provided to medical consumers. Insurance companies derive profits from investing the premiums paid to them by millions of Americans, including premiums for health insurance. Some privately owned nursing homes have made large profits by taking money from patients or the government Medicaid program while failing to provide the quality of services such payments should ensure. A profit-centered system can mean that many health care decisions serve corporate profit desires instead of real human needs.

Private For-Profit Hospitals

A major trend in U.S. health care is in the direction of hospitals run for profit. Since the 1920s, most hospitals have been nonprofit operations run by churches, universities, and local governments. In 1965, the federal government took over much responsibility for paying for the health care of the aged and poor through Medicare and Medicaid programs. This legislation, together with the large increase in private insurance, kindled a new interest among investors in for-profit hospitals that rely on the government or insurance companies to cover most bills. A number of profit-oriented chains have emerged. In the early twenty-first century, roughly 13 percent of the country's 5,801 hospitals are now investor owned.[43]

For-profit hospitals tend to receive high rankings for their return on investment. A major reason that for-profit hospitals prosper is that they often take more affluent patients, employ fewer people per patient, and charge more. They tend to prefer patients with private insurance programs, since government programs such as Medicare and Medicaid frequently do not pay the full amount billed for treating patients. These hospitals also prefer younger patients and those needing lab or X-ray services. Some hospital executives call this "buyer selection." But critics argue that it too frequently means segregating poor patients in public hospitals from better-off patients in private hospitals.[44] New locations for private hospitals tend to be in areas of high population growth, with younger, more affluent families, and in (usually nonunion) Sunbelt areas. In some cases people without insurance or cash have been turned away from emergency rooms at private hospitals and sent to public hospitals. As Paul Starr wrote in his Pulitzer Prize–winning analysis, which explores the "corporatization" of medicine:

> Humana's [a hospital chain's] policy is to treat all emergency cases. However, if a wallet biopsy—one of the procedures in which American hospitals specialize—discloses that victims are uninsured, it transfers them to public institutions; as a Humana official explained, in regard to a patient who died after being transferred within one day of suffering a heart attack, "These freebies cost $2,000 or $3,000 a day. Who's going to pay for them?" The chains certainly aren't.[45]

For-profit hospitals do have some advantages. Because they often keep better records than many nonprofit hospitals, they can keep inventories down. But superior record keeping can make it easier to put pressure on employees to cut costs, accept closer surveillance, and—sometimes—go part-time. Large private chains often pay less for supplies because they order in bulk. These chains can often borrow more easily from banks and have greater access to capital markets.

Nonprofit community hospitals were once committed to serving all patients in need without regard to ability to pay. One serious consequence of private hospital expansion is pressure on nonprofit hospitals to imitate for-profit hospitals in advertising, offering incentives for physicians, limiting the number of poor patients, and charging more for services. Many nonprofit hospitals now operate much like for-profit hospitals.

Blood Banks and Profits

Blood transfusions are a good example of major technological advancement in contemporary medicine; transfusions provide a way to save lives that otherwise would be lost. Blood drives have become commonplace in many communities. This lifesaving practice of modern medicine is widely accepted.

The United States has thousands of blood banks. For example, nearly 2,000 institutions (community and hospital blood banks, hospital transfusion services, and laboratories) and about 8,000 individuals are members of the American Association of Blood Banks, including physicians, scientists, administrators, medical technologists, blood donor recruiters, and public relations personnel.[46] Commercial blood banks collect, store, process, and sell blood for private profit. Substantial profits can be made from blood plasma, which is separated from the rest of the blood and converted into its various fractions, such as gamma globulin. Commercial operations account for a significant share of the whole blood and most plasma and fractionated blood products in the United States. In addition, large quantities of blood fractions are sold to other countries.[47]

Corporations that buy blood plasma often rely on populations that desperately need some income. In some prisons, for example, officials allow inmates to sell blood plasma to outside corporations. A substantial proportion of those who sell blood plasma are poor urbanites. Until 1972, when stricter federal licensing went into effect, the number of commercial blood centers in central cities grew rapidly. Licensing forced some to close, but many are still located in or near impoverished areas. Corporations transfer the plasma from some of America's least healthy people to recipients throughout this country and around the world. A variety of diseases are transferred in blood plasma. Screening is a problem for commercial blood banks, both because of profit pressures and because many donors may not be truthful about diseases they have because of fear of losing necessary income. Comparison studies have found that blood from commercial blood banks that use paid donors is more likely to carry diseases than blood from voluntary donors. Public health problems caused by inadequate screening techniques are illustrated in a tragic incident of the 1980s. The first person diagnosed with AIDS in one city was a frequent seller of blood plasma. By the time health officials discovered this, the seller's plasma had been combined with vast amounts of plasma and fractionated products shipped across the world. Later, after it was learned that AIDS can be transmitted through blood products, screening procedures were significantly improved.[48]

The value of the global market in blood plasma is now estimated at $4 billion and is expected to reach $15 billion by the year 2006.[49] In the last decade or two, some companies have imported blood plasma from poor countries, redistributing blood products from poor to more affluent countries. Yet most donors in poor countries cannot afford, in terms of their health, to give up blood plasma. Blood has become a commodity in the United States and across the globe, and the growth of a commercial-corporate blood distribution system means that the profit-oriented laws of the capitalistic market will prevail. Corporations argue that private competition for blood protects pharmaceutical companies and other business interests seeking a fair profit, but critics ask this: Who is to protect the general public from the dangers of a profit-oriented, worldwide market in blood?

Drugs and Profits

High-tech medicine is oriented to drug therapy. With the development of sulfa drugs in the 1930s, penicillin in the 1940s, and other drugs in later decades came an explosion in both drug therapy and drug manufacturing. Drugs have helped to decrease death rates associated with pneumonia, rheumatic fever, syphilis, and heart disease; they have helped to control epilepsy, asthma, hypertensive heart disease, and thyroid disease. Today, pills are often the preferred solution to both physical and emotional ailments. Physicians can choose from thousands of medications, many of which are unnecessary duplications put on the market primarily to make a profit. In addition, many drugs are now widely available without prescriptions.[50]

Americans spent nearly $216 billion for prescription drugs in 2003, an increase of nearly 11.5 percent over the previous year and nearly *three times* the expenditure in the mid-1990s.[51] Drug expenditures are the fastest-growing component of health care costs, with drug prices rising faster than the consumer price index. Much of this growth is concentrated in only four categories of drugs: oral antihistamines (such as Claritin, Zyrtex, Allegra), antidepressants (such as Prozac, Zoloft, Paxil), cholesterol-reducing drugs (such as Lipitor, Zocor, Pravachol), and anti-ulcerant drugs (such as Prilosec, Prevacid, Pepcid). The average price for a prescription for drugs ($71.49) has more than doubled since the early 1990s.[52]

More than half of all Americans over the age of 45 are regularly taking prescription drugs. Indeed, one medical research study found that eight in every ten elderly Americans were taking some type of prescription drug. One-fourth of these were taking inappropriate drugs, that is, medication not recommended for older patients.[53] An estimated one in five Americans takes a nonprescription over-the-counter medication daily. Since the 1950s the drug industry has usually ranked high in profit rates. Most drugs are developed by scientists in the laboratories of pharmaceutical companies, although even drugs that are developed through taxpayer-funded research, such as the AIDS drug AZT, may later be the source of huge profits for private drug companies.

Drug companies' large contributions to congressional candidates and the huge sums they spend on lobbyists have given them a great deal of influence over federal and state legislation relating to drug pricing and cost controls. The citizens' advocacy group Common Cause reports that in European countries with price regulations, drug costs are 54 percent less than in the United States. U.S. pharmaceutical companies have secured tax breaks and monopoly marketing rights for certain medications, which have resulted in large profits. As Common Cause has noted, "Drug firms . . . don't operate in a pure free-market environment."[54]

Some drug companies have increased their profits by moving plants out of the continental United States to take advantage of low-wage workers and reduced taxes. In addition, monopoly patents and extensive advertising keep many brand-name drug prices high—sometimes many times the price of a generic counterpart. Sharp differentials have also been found in drug prices from one pharmacy to another, and prices are often higher in low-income communities.

Negative reactions to drugs are a major cause of hospitalization in the United States and are estimated to kill more people each year than breast cancer. Patients hospitalized for other reasons run a serious risk of a negative drug reaction even while they are hospitalized. Many other drug users are left blind, deaf, or with damaged organs. The growth in the number of yearly prescriptions from fewer than three per capita in the 1950s to six per capita in recent years greatly increases the possibility of adverse drug reactions. At the same time, the Food and Drug Administration (FDA) has reported that many prescription and over-the-counter medicines and medicinal preparations are not effective. In one report, 84 percent of new drugs were found to have little or no potential for improving patient care. Other health care products are often worthless. For example, research has found that mouthwashes do not kill bacteria as they claim. A study of 800 nonprescription remedies for coughs found that only three of the many listed ingredients had an effect on coughs.[55]

Why have legal drugs and drug use had such a negative impact? Who is to blame? Some analyses of health problems blame the victims—the patients—for problems because many patients either pressure doctors to give them drugs or shop for physicians who will give them certain drugs. Other observers ask "Who taught these patients to look to expensive drugs for solutions to their problems?" They suggest that the primary responsibility rests not with the patients but with the companies that have vigorously sold the drugs by means of advertising to doctors and patients, including subtle advertising to doctors and media stories about new "wonder cure" drugs. Government surveys have found that millions of Americans believe that drug advertising cannot be false because of government regulation. Traditionally, most Americans have had faith in the science of a high-tech society, a science whose benefits were vigorously sold to the citizenry by corporate interests and their professional allies in medicine and in the universities without an adequate presentation of the significant dangers of such technologies.[56]

Consumers, Drugs, and Advertising

A business fable goes like this: Manufacturers mostly make products that consumers demand, and that consumer demand creates markets and thus new profits that encourage firms to come up with innovative, reasonably priced products. Some truth can be found in this fable, as in the case of electronic calculators and personal computers, where demand has played a major role in the expansion of production. Yet many demands are being made by consumers that are *not* being met in the marketplace. Surveys have shown that many women are dissatisfied with available contraceptives. A safer contraceptive would be no doubt profitable. Yet, following a controversy over the health hazards of contraceptives, and a subsequent reduction in their sales, for many years most of the pharmaceutical companies that manufacture the most popular form of birth control (the "Pill") turned to new, more highly profitable areas, such as cosmetics and biosynthetics.[57]

Advertising is vital for the promotion of new drugs. The pharmaceutical industry spends $13.8 billion annually on advertising. Pharmaceutical corporations spend about $12 billion on "professional spending" such as contacting doctors ($3.6 billion) and hospitals ($712 million), advertising in professional journals ($470 million), and giving samples to physicians for patient use ($7.2 billion). A new type of aggressive advertising in recent years is the direct appeal to consumers to use drugs available by prescription only. This "direct-to-consumer" advertising has increased sharply, from $35.2 million in 1987 to $4.2 billion in 2004. Drug companies spend 60 percent of direct-to-consumer advertising on television advertising, 37 percent on print ads, and 3 percent on billboards and other forms of advertising. The Internet is one such alternative form of advertising. Some 25 percent of online information is health related; more than 50 percent of all adults using the Internet seek health care information; and 26 percent of adults using a disease-oriented Web site request a specific brand of medicine from their doctors.[58]

Health care policy experts warn that direct-to-consumer advertising by pharmaceutical companies creates a number of new or aggravated problems in the existing health care system such as misinforming consumers, encouraging drug consumption, increasing health care costs, straining the doctor–patient relationship, and undermining the quality of patient care. To other commentators, however, direct-to-consumer advertising by pharmaceutical companies is indicative of a health care system in transition—from a physician-directed system to a patient-directed system where patients have far more information about a medical condition and any options available to them for treatment. Patients are making more office visits to physicians for heavily advertised conditions, and physicians are accommodating their patients' requests for specific drugs. This indicates that the direct-to-consumer advertising is effective and that patients are taking on more control in the management of health care.[59] Moreover, surveys demonstrate that many physicians choose the drugs they prescribe to patients on the basis of advertising or presentations by drug company representatives rather than on the basis of medical journal research articles. A professor at Harvard Medical School has noted that "drug companies spend more on advertising and marketing to doctors than is spent on medical education. Most of what many doctors learn comes from drug companies and their interest is in selling drugs."[60]

Profits from Poor Countries

The U.S. health care system has drawn off resources from poorer countries. A significant number of physicians practicing in the United States are immigrants from these countries. Even blood and human organs for transplants have been shipped from poorer countries to U.S. medical centers. At one point, Colombian officials even banned the shipment of human organs to the United States.

Drug and medical equipment companies draw large amounts of capital from poorer countries in the form of excessive profits from overpricing. Until 1986, U.S. law prohibited drug manufacturers from exporting medications not approved for sale in the United States. Some companies ignored this law, however, because there was little chance that they would be caught. Other companies bypassed the law by building production facilities overseas. One of many examples is Upjohn's Depo-Provera, a contraceptive administered by injection into a woman's arm. Adverse side effects of this drug include profuse menstrual bleeding and reduction of the body's resistance to infection. Depo-Provera is banned in the United States. However, Upjohn moved production of this drug to Belgium and made it available without prescription in 80 countries. Pressure from drug companies resulted in a weaker U.S. law in 1986, allowing drugs not approved in the United States to be exported to 21 countries.[61] The overseas sale of drugs considered unsafe for use in the United States is called "dumping." Warnings on the adverse reactions of drugs are often removed in countries that do not require warnings, and claims for drugs can be greatly exaggerated in countries with no regulations on advertising.

The corporate emphasis on exporting high-tech medicine to poorer countries to increase profits may indirectly cost many thousands of lives. Chilean economist Jorge de Ahumada has suggested that every dollar spent on high-tech hospitals, doctors, and drugs in South American countries *costs* a hundred lives that could have been saved if that money had been invested instead in safe water supplies.[62] Although the size of this estimate is debatable, the point is clear.

One example of the concern for profits can be seen in the small amount of research that targets the health problems of the less-developed countries that contain a majority of the world's people. No more than about 3 percent of the world pharmaceutical industry's research expenditures target the health needs of these countries.[63] As one reporter has summarized the evidence, "The annual combined sales of all disease-preventing vaccines in the world, for example, do not equal the annual sales of one 'blockbuster' ulcer drug." Yet millions of children in poor countries might be saved if such vaccines were improved.[64] Most poor countries are likely to see the same dramatic health improvements from relatively modest monetary investments in improved water, sewage, and preventive health procedures such as vaccinations as did Europe and the United States in earlier decades, yet such health investments are usually considered unprofitable by both local capitalists and multinational corporations.

INCOME AND HEALTH

Numerous health problems result from the way in which this class-stratified society of ours rations income. The unequal distribution of income and wealth is a major contributor to health problems. Studies of variations in illness rates have demonstrated the important role of income and racial group. Preschool children in poverty areas are less likely to be immunized against major childhood diseases and thus have higher illness rates than those in nonpoverty areas. Poor adults typically receive less preventive care than the affluent population. Most communicable disease and accident rates are higher in low-income areas. Today, members of low-

income families are much more likely to report fair or poor health and much more likely to be significantly limited by a chronic health problem than members of high-income families.[65]

Interestingly, visits to both doctors and dentists are more frequent for members of higher-income families. The wealthy can buy the services of the best surgeons and physicians anywhere in the world. The poor receive fragmented care, if they have care at all. Much medical care for poor working people is provided by overburdened city hospitals. In many areas such medical facilities are scarce, with long waiting lines, poorly paid staff, or degrading income tests for patients. Poor Americans often cannot seek necessary medical help because of cost or distance to a medical facility.

RACIAL AND GENDER DISCRIMINATION

Racial Discrimination

The problems of medical care can become more severe if one is a person of color. Racial discrimination in health care, subtle and blatant, includes certain well-institutionalized practices of the medical establishment of doctors, clinics, and hospitals. Indeed, differential racial treatment in the routine operation of medical facilities was cited by Kwame Ture and Charles Hamilton in their pioneering discussion of institutional racism in the 1960s:

> When white terrorists bomb a black church and kill five black children, that is an act of individual racism, widely deplored by most segments of the society. But when in that same city—Birmingham, Alabama—five hundred black babies die each year because of the lack of proper food, shelter and medical facilities, that is a function of institutional racism.[66]

Today, as then, inequality in medical care and hospital facilities has a serious impact on the health and well-being of many Americans of color. Black Americans have higher death and disease rates and a shorter life expectancy than white Americans. The black infant mortality rate (14.0 per 1,000) is nearly 2.5 times the white rate (5.7 per 1,000), and the maternal death rate of black mothers (24.7 per 100,000) is *more than three times as high* as the maternal death rate of white mothers (7.2 per 100,000). Moreover, the life expectancy of black males is 6.6 years less than white males, and for black females it is 4.9 years less than white females.[67] The mortality rates in the poorest black communities in U.S. cities are often as high as those of the poorest countries overseas.

Historically and in the present, some of this negative impact on the lives of African Americans stems from racial discrimination by whites. Following the belated desegregation of many hospital facilities just in the 1960s, institutionalized discrimination became more covert, subtle, and indirect. In the North and South, black Americans have sometimes received impersonal, condescending, or rough treatment from prejudiced white personnel, particularly in facilities without significant numbers of black nurses and physicians. Numerous studies have documented the discriminatory treatment that patients of color receive at the hands of prejudiced white doctors and nurses in clinics and emergency rooms. Often the discriminatory treatment suffered by patients of color involves "unconscious, implicit negative racial attitudes and stereotypes" of medical professionals.[68] Thus, in one research study actors portrayed black and white patients with certain disease symptoms. Some 720 physicians were asked to look at the taped interviews and other patient data to assess the likelihood of coronary artery disease. Black patients, especially women, were less likely to be recommended for cardiac catheterization, compared to whites with similar occupations and medical histories. Yet another study found that black patients with lung cancer were less likely to receive the best surgical treatment than whites, and thus they died sooner than whites.[69]

In addition, African American physicians have long faced discrimination in the health care system. The American Medical Association excluded African American doctors from its organization until the 1950s. As a result, black professionals organized separate medical societies, including the National Medical Association. These organizations are still important in facilitating the professional exchange and networking needed for success. Today, medicine remains substantially segregated, with many black physicians serving mostly black clienteles and few white doctors locating in or near black communities. Although many blacks are patients of white doctors, others prefer black doctors because they do not have to fear unfair treatment.[70]

In research conducted by Feagin and Sikes, black health care professionals reported discrimination by white practitioners. A physician in one East Coast city described the racial problems faced by her husband:

> My husband has faced discrimination. And he's a neurologist. And his problem has been because he's black, and because the hospitals that we practice in, it's very cliquish, WASP-ish. They are very threatened by him, because of course they feel that he will take their black clientele. And so they have put barriers in his way to try to hold him back—as far as monitoring his charts, holding him up for the operating room so that he's late for his case.[71]

Black physicians also face discrimination from patients. An article in the *Journal of the American Medical Association* noted a black woman physician in a hospital who was mistaken for a cleaning person by a white patient. This is likely gendered racism, since the white stereotype of black women comes into play.[72]

Blacks comprise only 3 percent of all faculties in U.S. medical schools, and a recent study shows that racial prejudice continues to limit their professional advancement in academic medicine. Conducted by researchers at Vanderbilt University School of Medicine, the survey of thousands of medical school faculty at 24 randomly selected medical schools found that while 63 percent of the black medical school faculty reported that they perceived racial bias in their academic environment, only 29 percent of the white medical school faculty believed racial bias existed at their medical school. More than one half of the black faculty also stated that they had been victimized personally by racial bias in advancement, and a substantial majority said they had suffered racially insensitive remarks and inadequate recognition for their work.[73]

The rationing of health care by income is an example of indirect institutionalized discrimination (see Chapter 4). The scarcity of physicians and the lower quality of hospital care in low-income residential areas, as well as difficulties in access to medical care caused by lack of income, disproportionately affect people of color because of the higher incidence of poverty among them. The location of hospitals, mostly outside low-income communities, is often the result of institutionalized discrimination.

Relatively few African Americans, Latino Americans, or Native Americans have the chance to become physicians because of direct and indirect institutionalized discrimination in the educational system. African Americans are about 12 percent of the population, yet are only 5 percent of physicians, 4 percent of dentists, 8 percent of pharmacists, and 10 percent of registered nurses. Many working in health care jobs are at the less well-paid levels of the job hierarchy, such as practical nurses or health care aides. Similarly, Latinos constitute about the same proportion of the population as blacks, but they are even less represented in some major health professions. Latinos are 5.8 percent of physicians, 3.3 percent of dentists, 2.5 percent of pharmacists, and 3.3 percent of registered nurses.[74] In a recent report the Institute of Medicine points out that, despite the United States becoming a diverse society, little is being done actively to increase racial diversity among health care professionals.[75]

Health care corporations that overcharge persons of color also perpetuate racial discrimination in the health care industry. A group representing Latino patients in California has recently filed a lawsuit against the giant for-profit hospital owner Tenet Health Care Corporation. Tenet operates 111 hospitals in 17 states. According to the plaintiffs, Tenet charged uninsured Latino patients rates that were *four to seven times higher* than those charged to insured patients. In turn, Tenet allegedly collected inflated reimbursement charges from the government through the Disproportionate Share Reimbursement program designed to reimburse hospitals for costs incurred from patients who cannot afford to pay hospital bills. Tenet acknowledges that it charges self-paying patients a higher rate than it does insured patients.[76]

Sexism in Health Care

Today, roughly one-third of physicians are women. Until recently, medical schools limited female applicants. However, since the 1970s the proportion of women in schools for health professionals traditionally dominated by men has increased sharply. By 2000 women were 40 percent of the total enrollment in schools of medicine and in schools of dentistry. By fall 2003, women made up 51 percent of Harvard Medical School's first-year class.[77] Once admitted to medical schools, women still suffer some gender discrimination. Some of the predominantly white and male medical school administrators have accepted more women students grudgingly. Important informal networks that facilitate professional grooming have often been less accessible to white women students and students of color. In addition, the still predominantly white and male faculty members often steer women into less prestigious areas of medical practice and away from such areas as surgery and academic research.

Today, women make up 31 percent of medical school faculties, which is a significant increase in recent decades.[78] Despite this influx, research shows that women faculty still receive unequal treatment.[79] They earn less than men in comparable positions, spend more time at lower ranks, and are promoted more slowly than men. Although women are now more represented in academic departments, they still constitute less than 15 percent of senior (full) professors in medical schools.[80] Women faculty are often given less institutional support, including research funding and secretarial support than men—this is particularly true of female faculty with children.[81] As a result, women faculty with children have fewer publications and lower career satisfaction than male counterparts with children. A recent study on the prevalence of gender-based discrimination among female faculty found that 77 percent of women faculty experienced some form of sexual harassment during their careers, including not only discriminatory actions but also official policies resulting in disparate treatment or creating an intimidating environment.[82] One study found that sexism in women's professional environments constitutes a formidable barrier to advancement in academic medicine.[83]

Research over the last decade or two has shown that women students in medical schools have faced considerable sex stereotyping and joking in some male teachers' lectures. One study found that six in ten women students reported facing gender discrimination, including sexual harassment. They were five times more likely than male students to be quizzed about their commitment to medical careers. Women students are still asked how they plan to relate the roles of wife, mother, and doctor, although male students are not pressured to explain their competing roles of husband, father, and doctor.[84] Discrimination also comes from some patients. One woman medical student has noted that her problem of sexism has been "with the patient who, when I walk into the room, calls out 'Nurse!'—or sometimes [with] the private-practice physician. I can see once we get out and we're not as protected, it will become more an issue."[85]

In the decades before and after 1900, skilled women midwives were largely displaced by male physicians. In recent years, the majority of obstetricians and gynecologists have been male, and most women must use male obstetrician-gynecologists for their medical care. Also, since the early twentieth century, the view of women's health care has gradually changed, so that an emphasis on technical care in the physician's office and on childbirth in the hospital has generally replaced the earlier emphasis on in-home care. Many male gynecologists share some prevailing male stereotypes about the character and bodies of women, and gender stereotypes frequently shape day-to-day medical practice. Male gynecologists sometimes stress that the biology of women creates unusual problems, as in this comment from a hospital physician: "Premenstrual tension produces an oppressive, cyclic cloud which prevents women from functioning in a smooth, logical male fashion."[86] Such stereotyping typically fails to address the role of regular male hormonal changes in men's routine functioning. Indeed, is there really such a common pattern as "logical male fashion"?

Numerous decisions affecting women's health have been made with little attention to women's safety and well-being and virtually no input from women themselves. One example is the use of foam-covered silicone breast implants, which in recent decades have been surgically implanted in millions of women. Breast implant surgery is lucrative for plastic surgeons. For many years recipients were told that the implants were safe, although the devices had never been adequately tested, nor were they required by law to be approved for safety. One should also ask why so many implants are needed, since most such operations are done for cosmetic reasons. The answer likely lies both in the pressures on women in the larger society to develop a certain body type, as well as in pressures from some medical practitioners. Thus, the American Society of Plastic and Reconstructive Surgeons (mostly male physicians) once sent a memo to the Federal Drug Administrator (FDA) asserting that small breasts were "deformities . . . really a disease . . . [causing] a total lack of well-being . . . in most patients."[87]

An early 1990s study linked the polyurethane-coated silicone implants to cancer—the foam may disintegrate inside the body, adhering to breast tissue and producing a chemical that causes cancer in animals and is a suspected human carcinogen. Still, the FDA waited for months before publicly acknowledging the findings. Although recent research studies have shown no link between breast implants and certain types of disease, there are still no comprehensive, long-term safety data on breast implants.[88]

A Houston plastic surgeon once ran a newspaper ad stating that the "cultural influence is such in this city that for a woman to feel attractive usually includes a Mercedes, a gold Rolex, and three or four operations—nose, breasts, liposuctions. It's just part of living in this city in a certain way, in a certain socioeconomic strata. . . . The Texas woman is a combination of many things, not the least of which is a surgeon's scalpel."[89] Arthur Caplan, of the University of Minnesota's Center for Biomedical Ethics, has argued that "what women need to feel more secure is counseling, not surgery. And what men need is an eyeball and brain transplant."[90] The point of course is that it is sexism that pressures many women to try to change their bodies to fit the male ideal of "attractiveness." We should also note that many injury suits have been filed against companies making breast implants. Leaking silicone has seeped into women's bodies, causing pain and infection; it has eroded ribs and caused severe headaches and fatigue. At least one researcher believes that a large percentage of breast implants will eventually fail and cause wearers very serious problems.[91]

Female patients encounter a variety of sexist practices and attitudes from male doctors. Women are more likely than men to be diagnosed as mentally ill, and depression is often called the "female malady." A study of the responses of doctors to male and female patients with symptoms of heart trouble found that doctors were more likely to label women's abnormal heart symptoms as psychological or something other than heart disease. Moreover, treatments for cardiovascular disease are based on information derived from studies mostly on men, although this disease is a leading cause of death for both men and women.[92]

Many doctors are apparently threatened by critical questions; they tend to take a paternalistic or autocratic position toward their patients. This paternalistic orientation is accentuated in male doctor–female patient relationships. Male physicians may assume that women cannot understand complex medical diagnoses or proposed cures, and thus they may hide important information from their patients about their health. In one study, male obstetrician-gynecologist physicians reported that they preferred women patients who would trust their authority and not question their instructions.[93] In addition, blatant sex exploitation is present in some medical care. For example, some male psychologists and psychiatrists have taken advantage of the doctor–patient relationship to exploit their female patients sexually.

The profit-oriented fee-for-service arrangement in medicine is given credit for many unnecessary operations in this country each year. Perhaps because the paternalistic doctor–patient relationship is most excessive in male doctor–female patient situations, hysterectomies are high on the list of all operations. The large number of these unnecessary operations reflects professional norms, not deviance from norms, for arguments supporting the prophylactic hysterectomies that can be found in medical textbooks and journals.[94]

Abortion and Control

A woman's right to an abortion was legal in every state in 1800. By the end of the 1800s, however, every state had abolished this right, and abortion was outlawed except to save a woman's life. The situation changed again in the 1970s. The *Roe v. Wade* decision handed down by the U.S. Supreme Court in 1973 gave women the right to safe abortion procedures. Before *Roe,* "between 200,000 and 1.2 million illegally induced abortions occur[red] annually in the U.S. . . . and as many as 5,000 to 10,000 women died per year following illegal abortions and many others suffered severe physical and psychological injury."[95] These figures speak to the moral significance of *Roe*—it took abortions out of the back alleyways of America. Although numerous polls have shown that a majority of Americans support *Roe v. Wade,* the decision has been challenged, sometimes violently, by antiabortion groups.[96] In recent decades, protests against women's reproductive liberties have taken the form of sit-ins, invasions and harassment at abortion clinics, violent attacks on clinics, and terror-ist actions against medical personnel.[97] Arguments by antiabortion groups that children's welfare is their primary concern have been betrayed by the failure of most such groups to strongly support expanded and substantial government services for poor pregnant women and to adopt unwanted children. Interestingly, most major antiabortion groups have histor-ically been headed by men.

Although a majority of the population continues to support legal abortion, a number of states have passed laws severely restricting abortions, leading to fears that the conser-vative majority on the current Supreme Court will eventually overturn the *Roe v. Wade* de-cision. Much debate over abortion has implicitly or explicitly focused on the traditional role of women as child bearers and mothers. Most antiabortion laws and regulations, par-ticularly those requiring women to sign fetal death certificates or preventing access of vic-tims of rape or incest to safe abortions, reveal institutionalized sexism. In general, recent antiabortion legislation reinforces the subordinate position of women in society, a subor-dination that means that women do not have full control over their own bodies.[98]

GOVERNMENT INTERVENTION IN HEALTH CARE

A Shift in the 1930s

Government-sponsored health care insurance was spreading in Europe by the early 1900s. Under pressure from unions and other working-class organizations, business leaders there agreed to some government health insurance systems. In contrast, national health insurance did not spread to the United States, probably because U.S. working-class organizations were weaker than those in Europe. Not until the 1930s was there enough pressure from working people in the United States to bring a few changes. Then government began to take action to create public welfare, Social Security, unemployment, and some medical care pro-grams. The Emergency Relief Administration provided federal aid for states for unem-ployment relief, including medical care in some cases. The 1935 Social Security Act provided some federal aid to states for child and maternal care programs. Hospital con-struction was also subsidized by the government.

However, proposals for national health insurance were defeated then, as they have been since. Instead, private insurance companies were developed to provide insurance for medical care. Profit-oriented companies and nonprofit insurance companies such as Blue Cross/Blue Shield have provided plans that pay some bills from doctors and hospitals. Membership in these plans is often not available to many workers, however.

New Programs in the 1960s

The civil rights and other protest movements of the 1960s helped to generate new social programs, one of which was the neighborhood medical care demonstration project in low-income areas. These centers demonstrated that neighborhood-run medical care centers worked. But as conflict developed between community residents and medical school physi-cians at the centers over who should run the centers, decreases in federal funding for pub-lic health centers reduced the number of poor who could get aid. In the late 1960s, President

Richard Nixon committed himself to reducing or eliminating many public health programs in favor of private health interests.[99]

Although vigorously opposed by the AMA, federal government Medicare and Medicaid programs were finally passed in the 1960s under pressure from American workers and their unions. Medicare provides health care coverage for people receiving Social Security payments from the federal government; Medicaid provides some federally subsidized health care coverage for low- and moderate-income Americans. These government-financed programs provide medical services and hospital care mostly for the elderly, the poor, and the infirm—groups that private insurers shun. While Medicaid has expanded access to health care to millions, not all of the poor are covered by the program. Medicaid is state controlled, and the range of benefits varies greatly from one state to another. Numerous states do not provide benefits for all their poor residents. Care for the poor is often impersonal, episodic, and fragmented. In addition, many office-based physicians have refused to accept Medicaid patients because of such factors as limits on physicians' fees and the high-risk nature of many in the Medicaid population. Limited physician participation affects the range of services available for low-income families.[100]

Although the majority of physicians in the AMA initially opposed Medicare and Medicaid programs, the high cost of medical care has made such government involvement inevitable. Ironically, physicians have generally prospered under these federal programs. Physicians' fees and incomes have grown faster since the legislation was passed than before.

A small number of physicians have made fraudulent profits from Medicare or Medicaid, by requesting unnecessary tests, performing unnecessary surgeries, or billing for care never provided. One surgeon was sent to prison for 11 years for billing private companies and Medicare for $20 million worth of unnecessary surgeries. Professional fraud is the reverse of the usual welfare fraud stereotype, but it is much more costly. All types of health care fraud account for perhaps 10 percent of total medical care costs in the United States.[101] Nonetheless, because of lobbying from the AMA and other medical care organizations, government intervention in and surveillance over medical care have for the most part left the private profit-making character of corporate medicine and fee-for-service physician care unchanged.

Alternative Health Care

In the last two decades the number of alternative or holistic health care practitioners has grown. Americans spend billions of dollars annually on these practitioners, much of it out of their own pockets because of lack of insurance coverage. Some traditional medical practitioners have made a comeback. Finally, in 1971, the profession of midwife was again recognized as legitimate by the American College of Obstetrics and Gynecology. By the late 1990s the number of nurse-midwives in practice nationwide had climbed to several thousand, and dozens of accredited educational programs for midwives had been approved.[102]

Numerous patients have experienced healing from therapies such as chiropractic care, acupuncture, biofeedback, meditation, herbal medicine, massage, and megavitamins. Many people credit the various alternative health care practices—which often focus on treating the whole person and on changing the conditions that cause disease—with enriching or extending their lives. These therapies are not taught at most medical schools and are not generally available at hospitals. They are defined as "unconventional, alternative, or unorthodox" by many in the medical establishment, which tends to ignore or scorn some or all of these treatment choices. Nonetheless, many Americans use at least one alternative health care technique each year. One study estimated that Americans make more visits to alternative health practitioners than to primary care medical doctors, yet this alternative care costs a tiny percentage of the country's total health care expenditures.[103] In the 1990s the director of the National Institutes of Health's newly created Office of Alternative Medicine linked the popularity of alternative medicine to the public's desire for more humane and less invasive treatment.[104]

HEALTH CARE FINANCING

Over the last two decades, the U.S. health financing crisis has grown steadily worse. Many health insurers have failed or reorganized. Others have raised premium rates and canceled policies, even as they have paid millions of dollars to their top executives in salaries, benefits, and allowances, spent millions more for lobbying and contributions to political candidates, and lost billions in risky investments and fraud. An investigation by Common Cause revealed that many insurance failures were caused by underpriced premiums, investment losses, and alleged fraud. Thousands of policyholders have been stranded with unpaid medical claims or lost or reduced coverage.[105]

Opinion polls have found that most Americans believe the health care financing system is in need of fundamental change.[106] One uninsured former coal miner stated, "I don't know what I'd do if I got sick. It would depend on how sick. It might be better, cheaper, and easier to just stay home and die." According to one union spokesperson, "Eighty percent of U.S. labor conflicts in the last few years have been over medical benefits. Health care happens to be one issue people are willing to go out on the street for. They know they could be destroyed financially, and they want to be able to take care of their families."[107] Yet in recent decades health care financing reform legislation has remained stalled in Congress, largely because of the opposition of the powerful medical industry lobby, which has contributed tens of millions of dollars to congressional candidates. Medical-oriented companies make large political contributions to members of Congress to help pass legislation that protects their profits and stalls a substantial expansion of public health and medical care.[108]

Various proposals for health care restructuring have been debated. Numerous citizens' groups and some political leaders have supported a national health service, sometimes called a "single-payer plan," which would provide tax-financed, comprehensive coverage to all Americans. Patients would be free to choose their own private doctors and hospitals, and fees for medical services would be regulated by the independent government agency running the program, thus eliminating profiteering. A similar plan is successful in Canada. Since the 1990s many state legislatures have considered Canadian-style single-payer plans that have widespread public support. Indeed, two-thirds of the respondents in two separate nationwide polls favored a single-payer plan. A single-payer plan would save billions of dollars a year in administrative costs. In the 1990s Common Cause reported that administrative costs relative to benefits paid were 1.4 percent for Medicare (a single-payer plan for a specific group), as compared to the much higher 17 percent for private health insurance companies. According to a General Accounting Office report, administrative savings in such a government supported plan would pay the health care costs of *all* uninsured Americans.[109]

Physicians tend to favor government programs requiring employers to provide health insurance to employees or pay a tax into a public fund for the uninsured workers. However, such programs do not control escalating medical fees nor do they cover individuals without jobs. The medical insurance industry, which would be largely out of business under a single-payer plan, supports a proposal called "managed competition," under which most insurers and health maintenance organizations (HMOs) would compete for contracts to represent large groups of Americans, particularly workers. Certain regional health coverage groups would accommodate those without jobs and those working part-time or in small businesses. However, HMOs have faced substantial public criticism and resistance because participants are not free to choose their own physicians and hospitals. Moreover, some critical analysts point out that under such plans the still largely uncontrolled quest for private profit in the medical system would compromise the quality of care and that provisions allowing affluent individuals to pay more for higher levels of coverage would generate a two-tiered health system—with the most vulnerable Americans, such as low-income individuals, likely receiving lower-quality care.[110]

WAREHOUSES FOR THE AGED AND DISABLED: THE NURSING HOME INDUSTRY

Numbers and Private Homes

The complex relationships between private profit and government intervention can be seen clearly in the nursing home industry. The many problems of this industry fall hardest on older Americans. Old age has been called the "last segregation," because at the end of life many people are living alone in houses, apartments, and nursing homes. During the 1970s, one Kansas newspaper carried the story of militant revolt by the aged in a Topeka nursing home in which a group of the aged locked the nurse in charge in a closet and staged a protest for more self-management over their day-to-day lives. Police were called, and three of the 80-year-old leaders were arrested![111] For several decades now, nursing home residents and their relatives across the country have protested the often poor care, callous treatment, and exploitative overcharging in their facilities.

Today, nearly 1.5 million older or disabled Americans, including just over 4 percent of those 65 or more years of age, live in the country's approximately 14,841 nursing homes. National expenditures for this nursing home care totaled nearly $100 billion in 2001. The average monthly cost for nursing home care is nearly $4,000, and many residents pay far more than that for still-modest care.[112] Still, government reports periodically indicate that many nursing homes do not meet minimum government standards. Since the 1970s, nursing home scandals—involving major fires, drug experimentation, violence against patients, fraud and kickbacks, contaminated food, and neglect—in many states, from New York to Texas to California, have revealed poor patient care and profiteering. Although many abuses have been corrected, some of the country's nursing homes remain warehouses with minimal-to-modest patient care and great use of drugs and television to keep patients tranquil.[113]

A common belief is that many aged are in nursing homes because their children do not care or because of the breakdown of the family in the United States. The evidence shows that this is not true. Most growth in the number of nursing home residents is because people are living longer. The typical resident of a nursing home is a widow aged 75 or older, with chronic diseases and a modest income of several thousand dollars a year. Most go to nursing homes either because they no longer have a close family member who can care for them or because their extreme mental or physical deterioration requires constant care beyond the capabilities of most family members.[114]

Nursing for Profit

The number of privately owned nursing homes has grown in recent decades. The expansion of government-funded Medicare and Medicaid programs for the elderly and physically disabled poor—an expansion brought about by pressure from working-class Americans—became an opportunity for substantial private profit. A majority of nursing homes are privately owned by individual entrepreneurs, partnerships, or corporations.[115] Total annual revenues for all nursing homes are in the billions of dollars. Directly or indirectly, Medicaid, Medicare, and Social Security programs provide much revenue for owners of nursing homes.

Many nursing home problems stem from the contradiction between for-profit goals and the health of patients. A *Labor Notes* analysis of one major nursing home firm illustrates this point. Adopting a vertical integration policy, the company, which had nursing homes in most states, developed retirement living centers and home health services and was tied to a hospital corporation that owned a controlling interest in the nursing home company. Over a period of just a few years, the firm's profits rose more than *1,900 percent.* Yet some of the firm's nursing homes were charged with seriously inadequate conditions by state health department reports.[116] High profits and high-quality nursing home care frequently do not go together. Some entrepreneurs enter the nursing home business with no prior experience in health care or geriatrics. In some cases, nursing homes are bought and sold by speculators interested in short-term profit and tax shelters. After a few years, rather than repair or improve the homes, they sell the properties to other investors looking for a tax shelter.[117]

In states across the United States, nursing home complaints have increased significantly in recent years—from roughly 145,000 complaints in 1996 to about 186,000 complaints in 2000.[118] Today as in the recent past, most complaints about nursing homes involve slow assistance for residents in need, unnecessary accidents, the type of care plans, poor treatment from staff, problems in hygiene, and staff shortages. Of the 15,010 complaints a year involving abuse or neglect in nursing homes, physical abuse was the most common type of problem reported—followed by resident-to-resident abuse, verbal and mental abuse from staff, gross neglect by staff, financial exploitation, and sexual abuse by staff.

Many culprits in the complaints are the relatively low-paid and poorly trained nursing home aides. One-third of the respondents in two surveys of nursing home workers said that within the last year they had seen nursing home residents physically abused by other workers. In one two-year period, the Louisiana attorney general's office obtained convictions of nursing home workers who had held pillows over residents' faces to quiet them, hit residents to get them to obey orders, whipped residents with electrical cords, and stolen residents' possessions.[119] An attorney general in Oklahoma noted that the state gets more nursing home complaints than it can investigate: "What we keep finding time and again is nursing homes cutting corners to save money . . . people are profiting . . . making more money by cutting overhead which results in added risk."[120] The Oklahoma attorney general's office has sought new laws making owners and others legally accountable for elder abuse and neglect.[121]

The state of Florida has hundreds of nursing homes, many of which offer good conditions for residents. However, some repeatedly abuse residents and violate their rights. The corporations that own the majority of homes are so large that the modest state penalties for poor conditions do not provide a deterrent. One investigative report by a Tampa, Florida, newspaper concluded that "The state . . . sets minimum staffing levels, and the nursing home industry says they're fine; labor is their highest expense. Advocates for the elderly say they're obscenely low and the source of most nursing home problems."[122] A major problem is the typically low pay (a little above the minimum wage) for many nursing assistants. Additional problems involve the supervision of nursing home workers and the poor quality of communication that exists between the facility's management and residents' families.[123] Understaffed homes lead to serious neglect of patients, and underpaid workers can sometimes mean a lack of commitment to the residents. Understaffing contributes to workplace injuries. Each year an estimated 200,000 nursing home workers are hurt on the job, often as a result of injuries from trying to lift patients.[124] In addition, the poorest conditions are often found in homes with a high percentage of low-income Medicaid patients.[125]

One of the largest nursing home chains is Beverly Enterprises, a health care corporation that owns businesses in such areas as medical supplies and drugs. Beverly owns hundreds of nursing homes that house many thousands of residents in cities and towns across the country. As with many large health care corporations, a very large share of company revenues—in the billions of dollars—comes from government programs such as Medicare and Medicaid.[126] One study of Beverly homes by the Food and Allied Service Trades Department of the AFL-CIO, which examined the firm's own studies and state inspection reports, cited a "pattern of violations" that raised the issue of whether the firm has the "ability to provide even basic care."[127] Particular problems cited in the report included inadequate staffing and high employee turnover.

Government action and inaction, particularly at state and local levels, have contributed to nursing home problems and abuses. State governments must pay a significant share of Medicaid costs. Because strong political pressures are exerted to control state budgets, owners of nursing homes are sometimes pressured by government agencies to keep costs low. In addition, conservative representatives in state legislatures are often unwilling to increase government supervision of businesses, no matter how many scandals may have occurred in an industry. This political pressure reinforces the profit-oriented approach to the creation of substandard and minimally adequate homes. Government regulation of the nursing home industry has traditionally been weak, and sanctions against substandard homes have traditionally been modest or weakly enforced.[128]

Many people with physical or mental disabilities who live in nursing homes, including many requiring skilled nursing, could enjoy a better quality of life and retain more control of their lives by living at home if personal attendant services were available. A representative of American Disabled for Attendant Programs Today (ADAPT), an advocacy group in 26 states, has explained the sentiments of millions of people who need such support services: "Whether a child is born with a disability, an adult has a traumatic injury, or a person becomes disabled through the aging process, people overwhelmingly want attendant services provided in their own homes, not nursing homes or other institutions."[129]

Another recent ADAPT report states, "According to information from the [federal] HHS Center for Medicare and Medicaid Services (CMS), between 1989 and 2001 payments to nursing homes increased by 625%, or $35.9 billion dollars, while the number of people in nursing homes increased only incrementally. During the same period CMS reports that community based services, which operate at roughly a quarter of the nursing home budget, have gone up by only $18.9 billion dollars while serving approximately 500,000 more people."[130]

Living at home is not an option for most of the physically disabled who rely on Medicaid benefits. Under the current system, regulations heavily favor institutional care. States are required to provide nursing home care for people with disabilities who

Here, 200 wheelchair-bound Americans conduct an organized protest over failed government policies for the disabled. (Paul J. Richards/Getty Images)

qualify for Medicaid, although no such entitlement is available for community-based attendant services. This means that what Medicaid funds are available for long-term care are used for institutional services, thereby leaving little for community-based services. Pressure from the influential nursing home industry has maintained this institutional bias even though, on average, community-based services are less costly than nursing home care. Even in states that do have some type of attendant care program, most Medicaid clients who require long-term care have still been forced into nursing homes because the state refuses to fund such attendant care. A group of Pennsylvania nursing home residents took this issue to court and won the right to receive services that allow them to live in the least restrictive setting appropriate to their needs—their own community. Citing this decision as a major victory, an ADAPT leader explained, "States that have attendant care programs will likely no longer be able to force people into nursing homes with the excuse that there is no money for community-based services. The money which now is spent on individuals in nursing homes must follow those individuals into the community."[131]

Long-term health care problems will continue to increase in coming decades as the U.S. population ages substantially. The total number of patients in nursing homes is now moving rapidly toward 2 million persons. More than a million Americans are already working in the country's nursing home industry, and by the end of the first decade of the twenty-first century the nursing home industry will add perhaps another million workers.[132]

Eugenics in the United States

In May 2002, Rose Brooks and Raymond Hudlow helped Virginia state officials to unveil a plaque commemorating the thousands of persons who had suffered *forced sterilization* for eugenics (literally, "good breeding") purposes in the state of Virginia some decades earlier. After giving birth to twin boys at 17 years old, Rose Brooks was taken by Virginia authorities to the Virginia Colony for Epileptics and Feeble-Minded, where physicians surgically removed her fallopian tubes without her consent. Medical officials had diagnosed her as "feebleminded" and as unable to care for her children. Authorities put her twins up for adoption and incarcerated her for 11 years following her sterilization. It was 33 years before she saw her children again. Virginia officials also victimized Raymond Hudlow. At the age of 16, Hudlow underwent forcible sterilization ostensibly because he was a "runaway" and incorrigible. At the unveiling, the state officials also awarded Hudlow with a Purple Heart, a Bronze Star, and a Prisoner of War Medal for his service during the second World War.

The state government atrocities committed against Americans like Rose Brooks and Raymond Hudlow in Virginia resulted from the classist and racist thinking that was fostered by the eugenics movement that gripped the United States in the early decades of the twentieth century. The movement began in Indiana in 1907 and ended in North Carolina in 1974. During this period, some 30 state legislatures enacted compulsory sterilization laws that resulted in the forced sterilization of some 70,000 persons stigmatized often wrongly as "feebleminded," thereby depriving them of their human right to bear and raise children. Virginia performed more than 2,000 sterilizations, and Oregon forcibly sterilized 2,600 people. California eugenically sterilized more than 20,000 people. North Carolina sterilized more than 7,600 people, many of whom were children.

The U.S. government allowed states to use federal funds for this eugenic sterilization of children until 1978. In fact, more than 300 of the 16,000 women and 8,000 men sterilized using federal government funds were under the age of 21. Compulsory sterilization laws remain in effect in seven states, including Arkansas, Delaware, Georgia, Idaho, Mississippi, Vermont, and Virginia. In Arkansas, for example, a state statute allows guardians of persons with mental retardation, mental illness, or other mental incapacity to solicit sterilization petitions. Mississippi law allows for involuntary sterilization of those with "hereditary forms of insanity."

One support for the eugenics movement in the United States came from the U.S. Supreme Court, which ruled in favor of such involuntary sterilization in the famous *Buck v. Bell* (1927) case. This amazing case of state oppression involved a county court decision ordering the sterilization of Carrie Buck, an unmarried 18-year-old mother who had been raped and then institutionalized at the Virginia State Colony for Epileptics and Feeble-Minded. In upholding the county court decision against Carrie Buck, the Supreme Court legitimated compulsory sterilization in the United States as a lawful practice for those ruled by authorities to be "mental incompetents." Writing for the court's majority, Justice Oliver Wendell Holmes argued, "It is better for all the world, if instead of waiting to execute degenerate offspring for crime, or to let them starve for their imbecility, society can prevent those who are manifestly unfit from continuing their kind." In reference to Carrie Buck specifically, Justice Holmes said, "Three generations of imbeciles are enough." Indeed, not until 1942 in *Skinner v. Oklahoma ex rel. Williamson* did the U.S. Supreme Court recognize a person's fundamental right to procreate. In that decision, the court rejected the Oklahoma Habitual Criminal Sterilization Act, which had forced a habitual criminal to undergo a vasectomy.

The more that scholars investigate the history of eugenic sterilization, the more a picture of malevolent government activities in regard to communities of color emerges. For African Americans, the history of eugenic intervention in the lives of Americans of color began during slavery with white planters castrating rebellious men they had enslaved. White slave holders also punished enslaved women who did not have children, and they frequently forced enslaved women to become pregnant by raping them. Female slaves suffered brutal medical experimentation by white physicians. Physicians often practiced new surgical techniques on enslaved black women, usually without anesthesia, before performing the same procedures on white women. The most notorious of these was James Marion Sims, a founder of modern gynecology, who purchased enslaved women expressly for the purpose of perfecting his surgical techniques. Sims operated on one woman 30 times in four years without anesthesia.

During the eugenics movement in the early twentieth century, this racist orientation continued. More than 60 percent of those sterilized in North Carolina were black, virtually all girls and women. To lower black birthrates, many southern states actually funded birth control clinics in the 1930s. As late as the 1970s, white physicians regularly conditioned the delivering of babies and the performing of abortions for black women only upon the latter's consent to sterilization. In 1974 an Alabama federal district court discovered that federally funded state programs in Alabama had forced the sterilization of 100,000 to 150,000 poor women annually as a condition of maintaining their public assistance. In California, the eugenics program was purposely "designed to strengthen the Aryan gene pool," and forced sterilization kept many Mexican and Asian immigrants and other persons of color from having families. Thus, in 1977 ten Mexican American women sued a Los Angeles County hospital for attempting to obtain their consent in English to sterilization while the women, who did not speak English, were in labor.

Eugenics views, and their associated racist views, still have their impact today. A Texas judge recently imposed surgical castration as punishment on a black man convicted of rape. Recently, white judges have ordered sterilization as a condition for probation in criminal cases for poor women of color who come before them. (Whites do not face such judicial action.) Also, some conservative policymakers still call for compulsory birth control measures for poor people. In the last two decades, more than ten states have proposed legislation requiring women on welfare to use Norplant, a birth control measure. Although these measures have mostly been unsuccessful, some human rights advocates fear that the health care and anti-poverty programs of the U.S. Department of Health, Education, and Welfare are secretly implementing compulsory birth control and sterilization for some women.

One of the chilling aspects of the early twentieth century U.S. attempts at eugenics—at "good breeding" and state government sterilization and experimentation programs—is that no less a figure than Adolph Hitler admired U.S. eugenics. Hitler indicated in his writings that U.S. eugenics efforts had influenced his thinking—thinking that led to his crimes against humanity in Germany and its occupied territories during World War II.

Sources: Michael G. Silver, "Eugenics and Compulsory Sterilization Laws: Providing Redress for the Victims of a Shameful Era in United States History," *George Washington Law Review* 72, pp. 862–891 (April 2004); Chris Ayres, "Liberal California Confronts Years of Forced Sterilization," *The Times* (London), July 11, 2003; "Nation in Brief," *The Atlanta Journal and Constitution,* February 15, 2001; Matthew Engel, "State Says Sorry for Forced Sterilizations," *The Guardian* (London), May 4, 2002; Laura Briggs, "Discourses of 'Forced Sterilization' in Puerto Rico," *Contemporary Women's Issues* 10, Summer 1998, pp. 34–37; Naomi Schaefer, "The Legacy of Nazi Medicine," *The New Atlantic* 5, Spring 2004; pp. 54–60; Dorothy Roberts, "Crime, Race and Reproduction," *Tulane Law Review* 67, June 1993, pp. 1945–77; Barron H. Lerner, "Scholars Argue Over Legacy of Surgeon Who Was Lionized, Then Vilified," *New York Times* (October 28, 2003), p. F7.

SUMMARY

Statistics on U.S. health are often not what one might expect, given the sophisticated technology and high cost of the medical and health care system. Over the last hundred years that system has come to emphasize specialized physicians, expensive medical equipment, large medical organizations, institutionalization, and a drug-oriented approach to disease. Large, profit-seeking medical corporations have accelerated the trend toward the bureaucratization and high cost of medicine. High-tech medicine is the result of a long series of decisions disproportionately made by officials in large corporations, professional medical societies, and corporate foundations—decisions often resulting in an impersonal, highly technological, drug-oriented medicine pervaded by the drive for profit and private control over the system. A prevention- and nutrition-oriented self-care health system might mean greater power and better health for most Americans, as well as lower costs, but it would also mean less power and lower profits for corporations, hospitals, and those doctors excessively committed to high-technology medicine.

Most top corporate executives and their middle-level managers would not support an environmentally oriented, publicly controlled health research and health care system that regularly and aggressively examined home and work environments for unsafe chemical additives and working conditions and serious air and water pollution in communities. Although high-tech medicine has certainly made important contributions in the cure of diseases, historically widespread improvements in people's health have often come from major improvements in nutrition, sanitation, and water sources.

The dependency of consumers on a privately controlled, profit-centered, drug-oriented, high-tech medicine was not created by the medical system alone. The broader capitalist system of for-profit production and distribution has created a situation in which most people do not control their own work and where workers for many decades have been manipulated in their consumption by advertising techniques. Consumer dependency in medicine is linked to a more general worker and consumer dependency under our class-stratified political–economic system.

The medical care industry is highly organized and very profitable. Physicians and dentists are among the highest-paid small-business people, and drug corporations have been highly profitable. Patient care is not the only goal of the medical system, for private control and profits are at the top of the list. This profit-oriented system slights the needs of many Americans, particularly those living on low incomes and those in rural areas. Medical care is rationed in the United States according to income despite the development of government programs such as Medicaid and Medicare. The problems of adequate medical care can become more severe if one is not white, for institutionalized racial discrimination can still be seen in such areas as the distribution of health care personnel and facilities and in basic health statistics.

Gender discrimination, blatant and subtle, is part of the medical system, ranging from the discriminatory treatment of female students in medical schools to paternalistic treatment of female patients by some male physicians. The private profit-oriented, fee-for-service arrangement in medicine is a major reason for the many unnecessary operations each year. This feature of medicine, together with the paternalistic approach of many male doctors to women patients, may well explain the excessive number of certain types of operations.

The complex relationships between private control and profit in health care and government intervention in health care can be seen in the nursing home industry, where major scandals have occurred over the last few decades involving understaffing, safety violations, patient abuse, and profiteering. The expansion of government aid programs such as Medicaid and Medicare has become an opportunity for substantial private profit. Large corporations now own chains of nursing homes across the country. In some of its current problems, the nursing home industry reveals the general contradiction between capitalists operating privately for their own profit and the meeting of broader human and social needs.

STUDY QUESTIONS

1. The practice of high-technology medicine has many problematic consequences. Using illustrations, explain the concept of iatrogenesis as it relates to high-tech medicine.

2. The infant mortality rate is generally viewed as one of the best indicators of a country's ability to deliver quality health care. Using historical and international comparisons, evaluate this rate for the United States.

3. Pressure to control the escalation of health care expenses has produced some strange political bedfellows. Who is behind the current cost-control initiatives and health care reforms, and what seems to be the motivation?

4. Identify three specific examples of institutionalized racial discrimination in the delivery of health care in the United States.

5. In what ways does our fee-for-service health care system undermine good patient care?

ENDNOTES

1. Julie Appleby, "43.6 Million Don't Have Health Insurance," *USA Today* (September 30, 2003), available at www.usatoday.com/money/industries/health/2003-09-30-insurance_x.htm; Julie Appleby, "Almost $1.7 Trillion Spent on Health Care in '03," *USA Today* (February 12, 2004), available at www.usatoday.com/money/industries/health/2004-02-12-healthcosts_x.htm.

2. "Countries with the Lowest Infant Mortality Rates," *Aneki.com* (2003), available at www.aneki.com/lowest_mortality.html.

3. National Center for Health Statistics, *Health, U.S., 1994* (Hyattsville, Md.: U.S. Public Health Service, 1995), p. 2; U.S. Bureau of the Census, *Children's Well-Being: An International Comparison,* International Population Reports, P95–80 (Washington, D.C.: 1990), pp. 13–14, 33.

4. "Countries with the Lowest Death Rates," *Aneki.com* (2003), available at www.aneki.com/lowest_death.html.

5. Alex Pham, "Radiology at Your Service: Natick Network Aims to Cut Health Costs," *Boston Globe,* March 27, 1995, p. 17.

6. U.S. Bureau of the Census, *Statistical Abstract of the U.S., 2003,* available at www.census.gov/prod/2004pubs/03statab/health.pdf.

7. N. D. Barnard, A. Nicholson, and J. L. Howard, "The Medical Costs Attributable to Meat Consumption," *Preventative Medicine* 24 (1995): 646–55; see Physicians Committee for Responsible Medicine, available at www.pcrm.org/index.html.

8. National Center for Health Statistics, *Health, U.S., 1994* (Hyattsville, Md.: U.S. Public Health Service, 1995) p. 5, available at www.cdc.gov/nchs/data/hus/hus94.pdf.

9. Patricia Neighmond, *National Public Radio, Morning Edition,* January 11, 1993.

10. National Center for Health Statistics, *Health, U.S. 1994* (Hyattsville, Md.: U.S. Public Health Service, 1995) p. 7, available at www.cdc.gov/nchs/data/hus/hus94.pdf.

11. "Nurse Cuts Hurt Patients," *Economic Notes,* April 1995, p. 6.

12. Neighmond, *National Public Radio, Morning Edition,* January 11, 1993; Patricia Neighmond, *National Public Radio, Morning Edition,* January 13, 1993.

13. Robert J. Mills and Shailesh Bhandari, "Health Insurance Coverage in the United States: 2002," U.S. Bureau of the Census, *Current Population Reports* (September 2003), available at www.census.gov/prod/2003pubs/p60-223.pdf.

14. Ibid; see also, U.S. Census Bureau, *Population Profile of the United States: 2000* (Internet release), *People at Risk: Health Insurance Coverage, 2000,* available at www.census.gov/population/pop-profile/2000/profile2000.pdf; U.S. Census Bureau, *Statistical Abstracts of the United States, 2002,* available at www.census.gov/prod/2004pubs/03statab/health.pdf.

15. Barbara Ehrenreich and John Ehrenreich, *The American Health Empire* (New York: Vintage Books, 1971), pp. 32–35.

16. E. Richard Brown, *Rockefeller Medicine Men* (Berkeley: University of California Press, 1979), p. 34.

17. Victor W. Sidel and Ruth Sidel, *Healthy State* (New York: Pantheon Books, 1977), pp. 231–33.

18. Bill Thomson, "Surviving Cancer," *Natural Health* 23, no. 2 (March–April 1993): 75.

19. Quoted in Thomson, "Surviving Cancer," p. 76; see also Samuel S. Epstein, *The Politics of Cancer* (San Francisco: Sierra Club Books, 1978), pp. 24, 34, 322–24, 327–29.

20. Quoted in Thomson, "Surviving Cancer," p. 76.

21. Brown, *Rockefeller Medicine Men,* pp. 4–5.

22. Ibid., pp. 69–73.

23. Sidel and Sidel, *Healthy State,* p. 234; Brown, *Rockefeller Medicine Men,* pp. 79–80.

24. Brown, *Rockefeller Medicine Men,* pp. 79–80, 96.

25. Ibid.; Sidel and Sidel, *Healthy State,* pp. 236–37.

26. Brown, *Rockefeller Medicine Men,* pp. 132–34, 193.

27. This and the following three paragraphs draw in part on Ivan Illich, *Medical Nemesis* (New York: Pantheon Books, 1976), pp. 15–20.

28. Helen R. Burstin, Stuart R. Lipsitz, and Troyen A. Brennan, "Socioeconomic Status and Risk for Substandard Medical Care," *Journal of the American Medical Association* 268 (November 4, 1992): 2,383–87.

29. Vincente Navarro, *Medicine Under Capitalism* (New York: Prodist Books, 1976), pp. 103–34.

30. M. Asif Ismail, *Prescription for Power: Drug Makers' Lobbying Army Ensures Their Legislative Dominance,* The Center for Public Integrity (April 28, 2005), available at www.publicintegrity.org/lobby/report.aspx?aid=685&sid=200; we also draw in this section on Ehrenreich and Ehrenreich, *American Health Empire,* pp. 21–22.

31. Bureau of Labor Statistics, U.S. Department of Labor, *Occupational Outlook Handbook, 2004–05 Edition, Physicians and Surgeons,* (ret. March 3, 2004) available at www.bls.gov/oco/ocos074.htm.

32. Douglas J. Barrett, "Health Care at Risk," *Tampa Tribune* (March 22, 2003), p. 19; "Medical Schools Losing Allure," *Los Angeles Times* (September 5, 2003); "Med School Applicants Fall 22% since 1997," *USA Today* (September 3, 2003); Barbara Barzansky and Sylvia I. Etzel, "Educational Programs in U.S. Medical Schools," *Journal of the American Medical Association* 290 (September 3, 2003): 1,190–96 and Appendix 1A.

33. U.S. Bureau of the Census, *Statistical Abstract of the U.S., 1995,* p. 121.

34. Medical Group Management Association, *Physician Compensation and Production Report, 2003;* see also U.S. Department of Labor, Bureau of Labor Statistics, *Physicians and Surgeons* (ret. March 3, 2004), available at stats.bls.gov/oco/ocos074.htm.

35. Quoted in Spencer Klaw, *The Great American Medicine Show* (New York: Viking Press, 1975), p. 4.

36. Spencer Klaw, *The Great American Medicine Show* (New York: Viking Press, 1975), pp. 7–9; Robert Spero, "The Progressive Interview: Sidney Wolfe," *Progressive,* March 1992, pp. 32, 34.

37. Virginia Linn, "The Other Way May Be the Only Way," *Pittsburgh Post-Gazette,* December 25, 1994, p. F1.

38. HealthGrades Quality Study, *First-Time Preplanned and "Parental Choice" Caesarean Section Rate in the United States* (July 2003), available at www.healthgrades.com/media/english/pdf/Patient_Choice_Csection_Study_July_2003.pdf.

39. "Office Visit; Hysterectomy: When to Say No," *Consumer Reports on Health,* January 1996, p. 11.

40. Spero, "The Progressive Interview: Sidney Wolfe," pp. 32, 34.

41. Mark Taylor, "Storm Warning: Rainmaker Doctors Bring in Big Bucks for Hospitals, but When Oversight Goes Awry, They Also Can Bring a Deluge of Legal Problems," *Modern Healthcare* (November 17, 2003), p. 26; see also Jessica Brice, "Tenet Settles with Feds Over Unnecessary Surgeries at Redding Hospital," *San Francisco Chronicle* (August 6, 2003).

42. Public Citizen, "Public Citizen Releases Database with Names of 6,700 'Questionable Doctors' in 12 States—Most Still Practicing" (June 5, 2002), available at www.citizen.org/pressroom/release.cfm?ID=1123.

43. U.S. Bureau of the Census, *Statistical Abstracts of the U.S.: 2003,* available at www.census.gov/prod/2004pubs/03statab/health.pdf.
44. "Hospitals for Profit," *Dollars & Sense,* September 1983, p. 7.
45. Paul Starr, *Social Transformation of American Medicine* (New York: Basic Books, 1982), p. 436.
46. American Association of Blood Banks, *ASBB Annual Report 2002,* available at www.aabb.org/About_the_AABB/Org_Overview/ar2002.htm.
47. Richard M. Titmuss, *The Gift Relationship* (London: George Allen & Unwin, Ltd., 1970), pp. 110–19, 140–50; George M. Anderson, "Selling the Blood of the Poor," *America,* April 28, 1979, pp. 353–54.
48. Titmuss, *The Gift Relationship,* pp. 147–49; Anderson, "Selling the Blood of the Poor," pp. 353–54; Erik Larson, "First Blood: How the Red Cross Wounded a Resume," *Time,* July 1, 1996, p. 36.
49. "Behringwerke and Armour in Plasma Protein Venture," *Pharmaceutical Business News,* March 1, 1995, n.p.
50. Morton Mintz, *By Prescription Only* (Boston: Beacon Press, 1967), pp. 2–42; Milton Silverman and Philip R. Lee, *Pills, Profits, and Politics* (Berkeley: University of California Press, 1974), p. 6.
51. "Drug Sales Grew 11.5 Percent in 2003," *Washington Drug Letter* 36(8), (February 23, 2004).
52. The National Institute for Health Care Management Research and Education Foundation, *Factors Affecting the Growth of Prescription Drug Expenditures* (July 1999), available at www.nihcm.org/FinalText3.PDF.
53. The study is summarized in Michael Lasalandra, "Docs Giving Many Seniors Wrong Drugs, Study Finds," *Boston Herald,* July 27, 1994, p. 1.
54. Cited in "Health Care Reform," *Economic Notes,* January–February 1993, p. 13.
55. Silverman and Lee, *Pills, Profits, and Politics,* pp. 17, 260–61; "We're Spending More for Cures That May Not Do the Job," *USA Today,* March 15, 1983, p. 1; "Health Care Reform," p. 13.
56. Mintz, *By Prescription Only,* pp. 56–70.
57. "The Contraceptive Industry," *Dollars & Sense,* January 1983, pp. 6–7.
58. Merrill Matthews, Jr., *Whose Afraid of Pharmeucetical Advertising? A Response to a Changing Health Care System,* National Institute for Policy Innovation (May 2001), available at www.ipi.org/ipi/IPIPublications.nsf/PublicationLookupFullTextPDF/5760149884B984D686256A4F0024DBD2/$File/PR155-PharmAdvertising-FINAL..pdf?OpenElement; see also Christopher Rowland, "Unfazed by Attacks, Marketers Plan More Aggressive Strategies," *The Boston Globe* (March 2, 2005), p. C1.
59. Ibid; see also the National Institute for Health Care Management Research and Education Foundation, *Factors Affecting the Growth of Prescription Drug Expenditures* (July 1999), available at www.nihcm.org/FinalText3.PDF.
60. Quoted in Michael Lasalandra, "Docs Giving Many Seniors Wrong Drugs, Study Finds," *Boston Herald,* July 27, 1994, p. 1.
61. Russell Mokhiber, *Corporate Crime and Violence* (San Francisco: Sierra Club Books, 1988), pp. 188–89.
62. Richard J. Barnet and Ronald E. Muller, *Global Reach* (New York: Simon & Schuster, 1974), p. 165.
63. Donald Drake and Marian Uhlman, *Making Medicine, Making Money* (Kansas City: Andrews and McMeel, 1993).
64. Paul Nyden, "Unhealthy Conditions: Medicine, Money Stall Health Reform," *Charleston Gazette,* February 1, 1995, p. P5.
65. U.S. Department of Health and Human Services, *Health Status of Minorities and Low-Income Groups: Third Edition* (Washington, D.C.: 1991), pp. 37–49; National Center for Health Statistics, *Health, U.S., 1994,* p. 4.
66. Charles Hamilton and Kwame Ture (Stokely Carmichael), *Black Power* (New York: Random House, 1967), p. 4.
67. U.S. Bureau of the Census, *Statistical Abstracts of the United States: 2003* (ret. March 5, 2004), available at www.census.gov/prod/2004pubs/03statab/vitstat.pdf.
68. Institute of Medicine, *Unequal Treatment: Confronting Racial and Ethnic Disparities in Health Care* 10(2002): 172, 177 , available at www.nap.edu/books/030908265X/html; see also Louise G. Trubek and Maya Das, "Achieving Equality: Healthcare Governance in Transition," *American Journal of Law and Medicine* 29 (2003): 395–421; Gwendolyn Roberts Majette, "Access to Health Care: What a Difference Shades of Color Make," *Annals of Health Law* 12 (2003): 121–42.
69. Kevin A. Schulman et al., "The Effect of Race and Sex on Physicians=Recommendations for Cardiac Catherization," *New England Journal of Medicine* (February 25, 1999): 618–26; Peter

B. Bach et al., "Racial Differences in the Treatment of Early-Stage Lung Cancer," *New England Journal of Medicine* (October 14, 1999): 1,198–1,205.

70. Joe R. Feagin and Melvin P. Sikes, *Living with Racism: The Black Middle Class Experience* (Boston: Beacon Press, 1994), pp. 204–205.

71. Ibid., pp. 206–207.

72. Richard E. Peschel, "The Empathic Practitioner: Empathy, Gender and Medicine," *Journal of the American Medical Association* 273 (June 21, 1995): 1,881.

73. "Survey Shows Racial Bias Persists in Academic Medicine," *The Journal of Blacks in Higher Education Weekly Bulletin,* April 29, 2004.

74. U.S. Bureau of the Census, *Statistical Abstract of the U.S., 2003,* available at www.census.gov/prod/2004pubs/03statab/labor.pdf.

75. Institute of Medicine, *In the Nation's Compelling Interest: Ensuring Diversity in the Health Care Workforce* (February 2004), available at www.iom.edu/report.asp?id=18287.

76. David S. Broder, "California Hospital Chain Sued: Anti-Latino Bias Alleged," *The Washington Post* (February 7, 2002), p. E02; see also, Simon Avery, "Lawsuit Accuses Tenet Health Care of Overcharging Hispanic Patients," *San Francisco Chronicle* (February 8, 2002), p. 17.

77. Harvard Medical School, Basic Facts 2003–2004 (ret. February 27, 2004), available at www.hms.harvard.edu/about/facts.html; U.S. Bureau of the Census, *Statistical Abstract of the U.S., 2003,* available at www.census.gov/prod/2004pubs/03statab/labor.pdf; "0 to 54 Percent—in 50 Years," *Harvard Magazine,* January–February 1996, p. 23.

78. Association of American Medical Colleges, "U.S. Medical School Faculty," Table 9 (ret. February 27, 2004), available at www.aamc.org/data/facultyroster/usmsf03/03table9.pdf.

79. Anne L. Wright, Leslie A. Schwindt, Tamsen L. Bassford, Valerie F. Reyna, Chaterine M. Shisslak, Patricia A. St. Germain, and Kathryn L. Reed, "Gender Differences in Academic Advancement: Patterns, Causes, and Potential Solutions in One U.S. College of Medicine," *Academic Medicine,* 78 (May 2003): 500–508.

80. Association of American Medical Colleges, "U.S. Medical School Faculty," Table 13 (ret. February 27, 2004), available at www.aamc.org/data/facultyroster/usmsf03/03table13.pdf.

81. Phyllis L. Carr, Arlene S. Ash, Robert H. Friedman, Laura Szalacha, Rosalind C. Barnett, Anita Palepu, and Mark M. Moskowitz, "Relation of Family Responsibilities and Gender to the Productivity and Career Satisfaction of Medical Faculty," *Annals of Internal Medicine* 129 (October 1998): 532–38; see also Bonnie J. Tesch, Helen M. Wood, Amy L. Helwig, and Ann Butler Nattinger, "Promotion of Women Physicians in Academic Medicine: Glass Ceiling or Sticky Floor," *Journal of the American Medical Association* 273 (April 5, 1995): 1,022.

82. Phyllis L. Carr, Arlene S. Ash, Robert H. Friedman, Laura Szalacha, Rosalind C. Barnett, Anita Palepu, and Mark M. Moskowitz, "Faculty Perceptions of Gender Discrimination and Sexual Harassment in Academic Medicine," *Annals of Internal Medicine* 132 (2000): 889–96.

83. M. Yedidia and J. Bickel, "Why Aren't There More Women Leaders in Academic Medicine? The Views of Clinical Department Chairs," *Academic Medicine* 76 (2001): 453–65.

84. The study is cited in Peschel, "The Empathic Practitioner"; see also Diana E. Kendall, "Square Pegs in Round Holes: Nontraditional Students in Medical Schools" (Ph.D. dissertation, University of Texas at Austin, 1980).

85. Quoted in "Mommy Doctors: Female Influx Gives Medicine New Life and Its Practice a New Perspective," *Chicago Tribune,* August 6, 1995, p. 10.

86. Quoted in Diana Scully, *Men Who Control Women's Health* (Boston: Houghton Mifflin, 1980), p. 20.

87. Nicholas Regush, "Toxic Breasts," *Mother Jones,* January–February 1992, pp. 24–31; Jan Gehorsam, "Women Feeling Pressured to Sculpt a Perfect Body," *Atlanta Journal and Constitution,* March 29, 1992, p. A1.

88. Ibid; "The Hazards of Silicone," *Newsweek,* April 29, 1992, p. 56; Nicholas Regush, "Backtalk," *Mother Jones,* March–April 1992, p. 6.

89. Regush, "Toxic Breasts," p. 26.

90. Gehorsam, "Women Feeling Pressured to Sculpt a Perfect Body," p. A1.

91. Regush, "Toxic Breasts," pp. 26–31.

92. "The Female Heart," *U.S. News & World Report,* August 3, 1987, p. 6; "Medicine: Male Bias?" *Vogue,* October 1988, p. 343.

93. Scully, *Men Who Control Women's Health,* pp. 20, 79.

94. Ibid., pp. 141–44, 234–35.

95. The Center for Reproductive Rights, *Roe v. Wade and the Right to Privacy,* 3rd ed. (2003), p. 5, available at www.reproductiverights.org/pdf/roeprivacy.pdf.

96. Deborah Zabarenko, "Activists Rally on Abortion Rights Anniversay," *Reuters* (January 22, 2003, available at www.reuters.com.
97. See Susan Faludi, *Backlash* (New York: Crown, 1991), pp. 413–14.
98. For a constitutional history of women's right to privacy as it regards abortion, see the Center for Reproductive Rights, *Roe v. Wade and the Right to Privacy,* 3rd ed.
99. Sidel and Sidel, *Healthy State,* pp. 244–45.
100. U.S. Department of Health and Human Services, *Health Status of Minorities and Low-Income Groups,* 3rd ed., pp. 349–52, 367.
101. Helen Lippman, "New Ways to Fight Fraud," *Business & Health,* August 1995, p. 40.
102. Mary Anne Wentworth, "The Rebirth of a Profession: Midwifery Has Claimed a Special Place in Women's Health Care," *Rochester Business Journal,* January 12, 1996, p. 13.
103. David M. Eisenberg, Ronald C. Kessler, Cindy Foster, Frances E. Norlock, David R. Calkins, and Thomas L. Delbanco, "Unconventional Medicine in the U.S.: Prevalence, Costs, and Patterns of Use," *New England Journal of Medicine* 328 (January 28, 1993): 246–52.
104. Natalie Angier, "Patients Rushing to Alternatives," *New York Times,* January 28, 1993, p. A12; David Barron, "Study Shows Alternative Medicine Use Surprisingly High," *National Public Radio, Morning Edition,* January 28, 1993.
105. Jeffrey Denny, "Risky Business," *Common Cause,* Spring 1993, pp. 9–15.
106. Vicki Kemper and Viveca Novak, "What's Blocking Health Care Reform?" *Common Cause,* January, February, March 1992, p. 8.
107. Peg Byron, "The Health Insurance Conspiracy," Ms., September/October 1992, pp. 40, 43–44.
108. See Drake and Uhlman, *Making Medicine, Making Money.*
109. Denny, "Risky Business," p. 10; Constance Matthiessen, "Code Blue," *Mother Jones,* November–December 1992, p. 30; Glen Boatman, "Polls Show Overwhelming Support for 'Single-Payer' Alternative," *Labor Notes,* May 1993, p. 14.
110. Kemper and Novak, "What's Blocking Health Care Reform?" pp. 8–13, 25; Matthiessen, "Code Blue," pp. 26–32, 62.
111. Claire Townsend, *Old Age* (New York: Grossman, 1971); Frank E. Moss and Val J. Halamandaris, *Too Old, Too Sick, Too Bad* (Germantown, Md.: Aspen Systems Corporation, 1977), p. xiii.
112. U.S. Bureau of the Census, *Statistical Abstract of the U.S., 2003,* available at www.census.gov/prod/2004pubs/03statab/health.pdf.
113. Bruce C. Vladeck, *Unloving Care* (New York: Basic Books, 1980), p. 4.
114. Ibid., pp. 13–16.
115. U.S. Bureau of the Census, *Statistical Abstract of the U.S., 1995,* p. 134.
116. Joe Montuori, "Two Unions Stress Patient Care in Joint Organizing Drive at Beverly Nursing Home," *Labor Notes,* February 23, 1984, p. 10.
117. See Vladeck, *Unloving Care,* pp. 175–84, and Moss and Halamandaris, *Too Old, Too Sick, Too Bad,* pp. 113–16.
118. Department of Health and Human Services, Office of Inspector General, *State Ombusdman Data: Nursing Home Complaints* (July 2003), available at www.oig.hhs.gov/oei/reports/oei-09-02-00160.pdf
119. John C. Hill, "Claims of Nursing Home Abuse Rise," *Times-Picayune,* March 21, 1993, p. A1.
120. Jerry Fink, "Elder Care a Major Problem, Says Prosecutor," *Tulsa World,* January 28, 1996, p. D1.
121. Ibid.
122. Lindsay Peterson, "Nursing Homes: A State of Uncertainty," *Tampa Tribune,* November 12, 1995, p. 1.
123. See Anthony Moser, "Nursing Homes," *Arkansas Democrat-Gazette,* February 16, 1996, p. E1.
124. Kathleen Doheny, "Injuries Grow among Nursing Home Workers," *Los Angeles Times,* July 5, 1995, p. D1.
125. Peterson, "Nursing Homes," p. 1.
126. "Patient Care at Beverly Enterprises, Nation's Largest Nursing Home Chain, Is 'Shockingly Deficient,' New Analysis Shows," *PR Newswire,* January 11, 1995.
127. This study is cited in Ibid.
128. See Hill, "Claims of Nursing Home Abuse Rise," pp. 77, 162–96; Moss and Halamandaris, *Too Old, Too Sick, Too Bad,* pp. 153–70.
129. "Capitol Confrontations," *Incitement* 11 (July 1995): 2.
130. "ADAPT to Confront Health Care Lobby in New Orleans, 'Our Homes Not Nursing Homes,'" (March 18, 2004), www.adapt.org/adaptpr/cgi/getlink.cgi?82R.
131. Bob Kafka, "Major ADA Victory," *Incitement* 11 (July 1995): 7; the case was *Idell S. et al. v. Karen F. Snider,* 46 F.3d 325, 1995 U.S. App.
132. Doheny, "Injuries Grow among Nursing Home Workers," p. D1.

chapter 8

Problems of Crime and Criminal Justice

In the 1830s, a lawyer named Abraham Lincoln made a speech in Illinois condemning "the increasing disregard for law which pervades the country."[1] *Century Magazine* complained in the early 1900s about an "epidemic of crime" in the United States, citing gambling houses, prostitution, and bars.[2] Contemporary Americans continue to worry about crime. In a recent public opinion poll, for example, over a third of the respondents answered yes to the question "Is there any area right around here—that is, within a mile—where you would be afraid to walk alone at night?"[3] Responding to decades of an increasing concern about crime, state legislatures and the federal government have adopted "three strikes" laws requiring mandatory life sentences for defendants convicted of three felony offenses where the victim suffers injury.[4] Even so, 56 percent of the respondents nationwide think that the government spends far too little to "halt the rising crime rate."[5]

In the past and the present, people have frequently associated fears about crime with the poor and alleged criminal predispositions of particular racial–ethnic groups. A common notion among white colonial Virginians, for example, was slaves' "proclivity to steal whatever they could."[6] A hundred years ago, native-born Americans believed strongly that immigrants from southern and eastern Europe, such as Italian Americans, were a major cause of crime. Today, many citizens, especially whites, believe that the major cause for concern is African Americans, Mexican Americans, or Puerto Ricans.

Yet citizens and researchers alike are becoming increasingly more aware that "street crime" does not constitute the totality of criminal activity. Beyond street crime is "corporate crime" and "political crime," which include offenses committed by the affluent such as tax fraud and insider trading. Fraud is now one of the most common crimes—accounting for roughly one-fifth of all property crimes in the United States.[7] White-collar and corporate crimes have become commonplace, yet their perpetrators frequently go unpunished— and if judges do assess penalties, they are seldom of the same magnitude as the offenses.

GOALS OF THIS CHAPTER

In the first section, we categorize crime relating to dominance, control, and oppression, on the one hand, and crimes of accommodation and resistance to oppression, on the other hand. By adopting a critical power–conflict perspective, we distinguish "crimes in the streets" from "crimes in the suites." While street crimes relate to the difficult conditions under which U.S. society forces poor citizens to live their lives, crimes in suites are actions specifically designed to ensure corporate profits at any expense, sometimes including the lives of our country's people. We explore the relationship between organized crime, government, and legitimate business enterprises in the United States in this section. Our goal in the second section to this chapter is to expose the strong class and racial bias entrenched within the administration of the laws in the United States. Here we show that racism and classism are established features of U.S. justice administration—which features substantially serve the interest of the ruling class in protecting itself against the struggles of those resisting racial and class oppression.

TYPES OF LAW VIOLATIONS

Each of us is born into a society with a system of law and order that we generally accept as valid. Our socialization teaches us that the existing laws and legal system are in place to protect us from crime and criminals. Local, state, and federal governments, by way of their respective police, regulatory, and judicial agencies, are the organizational enforcers of our legal system. The U.S. system defines violations of criminal laws as acts against the state, and not just as difficulties among individuals. These violations are generally punishable by monetary fines and jail or prison sentences. Violations of civil, administrative, or regulatory laws usually are punishable by monetary fines.

  While there has long been consensus among Americans on the criminality of certain actions, such as killing innocent people and stealing personal property, what our legal system officially defines as a crime or law violation varies over time and from one area to another. For example, cocaine use was once legal but now criminal justice authorities punish its use, often severely. (Use of even more addictive drugs like alcohol and tobacco, interestingly, is not punished in this way.) Opium dens frequented often by white middle-class homemakers were common in the late nineteenth and early twentieth centuries.[8] And half the 100,000 people arrested by Chicago police in 1912 had violated laws that did *not* exist 25 years earlier.[9] Acts once officially defined as illegal are now legal. Gambling is legal in most states, and legalized gambling now constitutes a multibillion-dollar industry. Small-scale marijuana use is legal in some areas; in several states, its use is legally limited to medical purposes. When looking at official statistics for a particular period, one must keep in mind changing societal and legal definitions of law violations.

  The social sciences and popular analyses use the word "crime" in a narrow and a broad sense. Some prefer limiting the word to violations of criminal laws, while others use it broadly for acts that violate criminal laws, civil laws, and important governmental regulations. In this chapter, we use the word "crime" in the broad sense. One power–conflict criminologist has suggested two major categories of crime: one related primarily to dominance, control, and oppression by the ruling class (the wealthy and powerful), and another covering crimes linked primarily to the actions, accommodation, and resistance to oppression by the unemployed and underemployed.[10] The first broad category consists of crimes of control, crimes of economic domination, and other crimes by government officials. The second broad category consists of predatory crimes, personal crimes, and political resistance crimes.

Crimes of control include illegal burglary and wiretapping by government officials (for example, Central Intelligence Agency and Federal Bureau of Investigation personnel) seeking to prevent dissent. This category also includes police brutality directed at Americans of color. Crimes of economic domination include corporate price fixing, bribery, and allowing unsafe working conditions. Crimes by government officials, other than those tied to control of dissenting Americans, include crimes committed to keep officials in office or to run secret political operations, such as those illegal acts committed by assistants to presidents Richard Nixon and Ronald Reagan in major political scandals.

Although television news programs and crime dramas have typically focused on crimes disproportionately committed by working-class people, such as robbery, burglary, and theft, serious corporate violations are a much more significant threat to the life and safety of millions of citizens than street crime. Our criminal law's definition of theft excludes many types of robbery and theft, such as advertisers' intentional misrepresentation of products. Criminal justice authorities usually do not define fraudulent overcharges for weapons produced by large military-industrial corporations as thefts deserving of serious prison terms.

Crimes in the second category of accommodation and resistance include predatory crimes that disproportionately involve crimes by the unemployed and underemployed against other working-class people and higher-income people. This category includes the majority of property offenses such as burglary and robbery. Aggressive drug "pushing" in poor communities fits this category. Personal crimes include murder and assault, crimes disproportionately committed by working-class people against other working-class people. For the most part, the actions of these often-violent criminals are the product of growing up with problems of serious racism, unemployment, poverty, drugs, and alcoholism. Many violent crimes reflect a striking out by the poor against the brutality of life in a social system that tolerates large communities of poverty, unemployment, and poor housing. As some power–conflict criminologists have noted, however, most predatory criminal offenders have little consciousness of class conflict. Instead of rebelling against the oppressiveness of the established political–economic order, they prey on other working-class people as well as on higher-income people.

The third type of crime that poor people disproportionately commit encompasses crimes of resistance, such as riots and civil disobedience—violations that are part of the periodic eruption of open class and racial conflict in U.S. society. Although labeled as crimes by the established legal system, these actions often involve conduct aimed at changing what the actors see as an oppressive and exploitative "law and order." Sometimes, those who are oppressed, but not poor, will participate in crimes of resistance, as in the case of civil disobedience by middle-class African Americans during the civil rights movement and the unrest that took place in South Central Los Angeles in the aftermath of the Rodney King beating there in 1991.

In addition to these two broad categories of law violations, there is the category of so-called "victimless" crimes, crimes of "public morality," which usually do not involve the use of force against other people by law violators. Examples include violations of laws on prostitution and personal drug use. These violations differ from acts of domination and resistance. Some violations, such as much of the illegal drug use in the United

In April 1995, an antigovernment terrorist's bomb exploded at a federal building in Oklahoma City, killing many people.

States, are tranquilizing and reflect users' attempts to forget harsh conditions of everyday life in their communities.

STREET CRIME

Of the several major categories of law violations, only certain categories and certain types of crimes within these categories—"conventional" street crimes—receive sustained attention in the media and among police officials, researchers, and the public. (We use the term *conventional street crime* here as a descriptive category, but the reader should remember that much conventional street crime occurs in places other than the street.) Conventional street crime, as defined by police and the public, includes interpersonal crimes such as murder and assault, property crimes such as burglary and theft, and "morals" crimes such as prostitution and illegal drug sales and use.

Official Statistics: An Inadequate Measure of Crime

Official government statistics provide estimates of certain types of conventional street crime. The Federal Bureau of Investigation (FBI) publishes the Uniform Crime Reports (UCR), which it bases on data collected from local police agencies. Part I of the UCR, called the "Index," includes data on seven felony (serious) offenses: murder and nonnegligent manslaughter, forcible rape, robbery, aggravated assault, burglary, larceny–theft, and motor-vehicle theft.[11] Although the Index is widely used as a measure of the number of crimes committed in the United States, it shows only those occurrences that persons report to the police. Part II of the UCR tabulates the total number of arrests reported by law enforcement agencies.

The annual number of crimes reported by the UCR Index has increased from less than 3.4 million to 14 million over the decades since 1960.[12] This increase corresponds to public perceptions that this country's streets and homes are not as safe as they once were. However, the crime index shows only those crimes that people report to law enforcement. A change in the index means a change in crimes reported, not necessarily a change in number of crimes committed. Many factors influence level of reporting: number of police, the aggressiveness of policing, the confidence victims have in police, and whether property is insured. A modest percentage of most crimes come to attention of police, although the crime-reporting rate has increased over the last decade. According to one important survey, victims reported only about 49 percent of all violent crimes and 40 percent of all property crimes in a recent year.[13]

The National Crime Victimization Survey (NCVS) is an alternative method of collecting statistics. These data, which include crimes that victims did not report to police, show a dramatic *decrease* in victimization rates over the last several decades—thereby disproving the common belief in a rapidly increasing crime rate. Today, the overall violent victimization and property crime rates are the *lowest* recorded since the inception of the NCVS in 1973.[14] Since then, personal crimes dropped from 124 to 26 per 1,000 households, and property crimes dropped from 218 to 167 per 1,000 households.[15] Given these very large reductions in rate of crime reported in victimization surveys, one might ask why they have received so little attention from the media or policymakers. One likely answer is that it is in the *political interest* of many police and other government officials to keep the public obsessed with problems of street crime.[16]

Dimensions of Street Crime

Guns, particularly handguns that people can conceal, play an important role in violent crime. Some 41 percent of Americans in surveys report owning a firearm.[17] Significantly, a large proportion of guns used by criminals are weapons stolen from households. Two-thirds of all homicides involve firearms, and about half are committed with handguns.[18] Police organizations support laws restricting sale of handguns since a significant proportion of officers killed die from handguns; thus 43 percent of the 142 law enforcement officers feloniously killed in 2001 died by firearms, mostly handguns.[19] Opinion polls reveal that most Americans favor the registration of handguns and *requiring* a police permit prior to gun purchase.[20] Americans favor banning handguns except for police and other authorized persons, and most favor a ban on the manufacture, sale, and possession of assault rifles. Gun lobbies, however, have kept the wishes of the majority of Americans from becoming a political reality.[21]

Of the nearly 16,503 murders and nonnegligent homicides reported by the FBI for the most recent year available (2003), roughly 43 percent of the victims were relatives, friends, or acquaintances of assailants, 12.5 percent of the victims were strangers to the assailants, and about 44.5 percent involved unknown victim–offender relationships.[22] These figures suggest that a person is *less* likely to be killed by a stranger than by a relative, friend, acquaintance, or neighbor. The personalized aspect of crime is not unique to cases involving murder and manslaughter. Victimization surveys report that relatives, friends, or acquaintances of victims commit 51.2 percent of the 4.9 million violent crimes committed annually in the United States, including 66.6 percent of rapes and attempted rapes.[23] These findings help explain why victims do not report many of the more serious crimes to police, and why many crimes that victims do report to police go unpunished. When victims know the assailant, they may refuse to cooperate in prosecutions. This may also explain why such a small proportion of rapes result in convictions.[24]

Perpetrators of most conventional violent crimes and major property crimes are disproportionately male, young, poor, and from groups that suffer discrimination in this society. Victimization surveys show that one-third of the perpetrators of violent crime are between the ages of 12 and 20, and an additional 26 percent are between 21 and 29 years old. Males perpetrate 80 percent of all single-offender victimizations, and they are involved in 74 percent of multiple-offender victimizations.[25]

Explaining Street Crime

Early approaches to explaining conventional crime emphasized biological and psychological factors. Individualistic, psychological explanations of crime, such as Freudian and other psychoanalytic theories, have been commonplace.[26] These perspectives view criminal acts as a way for individuals to solve internal psychological problems such as repressed hatred of parents. Yet research has found few psychological differences between conventional criminals and noncriminals.[27] Early work by Edwin Sutherland emphasized the broader social context of conventional crime. He emphasized the role of *differential association* in causing crime. Individuals learn criminal behavior, like other behavior, in interaction with others in small groups in which they live their lives. Through interaction in communities or even prison, individuals learn techniques for crime and an orientation toward crime as a way to make a living.[28]

Since the 1950s, much criminology literature has focused on youth crime and offered a number of explanatory theories. One group of theories emphasizes that criminal behavior is learned and that learning to take advantage of criminal opportunities involves normal learning processes. In the 1950s, Albert Cohen, among others, popularized a *subcultural theory,* suggesting that juvenile delinquency flows primarily out of delinquent subcultures, particularly out of youth gangs in poorer working-class areas. The delinquent subculture is a way of dealing with the status problems of poorer young males who are unable to achieve status in the ways available to middle-income youth.[29] Also stressing the crimes of poor young people, Richard Cloward and Lloyd Ohlin have argued for a *strain theory* of criminal behavior, suggesting that juvenile delinquency occurs not because gang members fail to meet conventional standards but because they have insufficient legitimate means to achieve those standards. Therefore, they use illegitimate means—crime—to achieve material and status standards to which they aspire. The material standards are often those aggressively advertised in the mass media.[30]

Another group of theories about crime, *social control theories,* suggests that most people would commit crimes if there were no social barriers. These theories seek to explain why most people do *not* commit crimes. Travis Hirschi argues that people in tightly bounded groups such as families, schools, and churches are less likely to commit criminal acts than persons who are less socially integrated. Hirschi's research on high school students found that poor students were only slightly more likely than affluent students to report engaging in delinquent and criminal acts. He found little racial difference in self-reports, although like other researchers he did find wide racial differences in police arrest rates. That is, police are much more likely to arrest poor or black youngsters for delinquent acts than they are to arrest affluent or white youngsters for similar delinquent acts. The important factors distinguishing less delinquent youth from more delinquent youth were a close attachment to parents, good verbal abilities, and doing well in school.[31]

This social control perspective emphasizes the important role of families and social integration in blocking certain aggressive and criminal behavior. Since many control theorists have focused on relatively minor types of offenses, a number of critics have suggested that this approach assumes too uncritically that an innately aggressive human inclination, one that social networks must restrain, is the underlying reason for crime. Control theories do not focus enough on the larger societal context of crime. In looking at such things as youth crime, these scholars may be discovering some of the negative consequences of our capitalist society's highly individualistic, often inegalitarian, value system rather than fundamentals of human nature.

A Power–Conflict Perspective: Low Wages and Unemployment

We must consider the broader economic context in making sense out of property crimes and many crimes of personal violence. A power–conflict perspective on youth and adult crime puts much less emphasis on a supposedly aggressive human nature, psychological factors, or subcultural factors, with more emphasis on society's large-scale class and racial inequalities. Judith Blau and Peter Blau's examination of crime in 125 U.S. cities illustrates the relationship between crime and social inequality. The Blaus found that cities with higher violent crime rates tended to have greater economic inequality and suggested that "high rates of criminal violence are apparently the price of racial and economic inequalities."[32]

People from low-income backgrounds commit a disproportionate number of street crimes. Lack of material resources, lack of education, and a bleak future of low-wage, dead-end jobs play a very significant part in crimes of poor Americans. Income data on street criminals are not available separately, but general prison data indicate that large proportions of federal inmates (35 percent) and state prisoners (44 percent) did not have full-time jobs at the time of their arrests. Most worked in low-wage jobs and earned less than $15,000 per year before arrest.[33] Criminal justice data also show that nearly one-third of all state and federal prisoners do not have high school diplomas.[34] A majority of criminals come from communities with relatively few socioeconomic resources.

Most middle- and upper-income youth grow up in a consumers' world and have access to a wide variety of goods and opportunities to get the education and jobs necessary to buy these goods. Low-income youth grow up lacking access to many basic goods and necessities; most attractive consumer goods are beyond their reach. They do not inherit significant property, nor do most have the educational and job opportunities necessary to secure many material goods and services as they become adults. Society provides poor youth and adults with values highlighting the importance of material success, but it usually does not provide the means to that success. *Strain theories* have accented the point that socially generated forces drive people to commit crimes. Influenced in part by the work of sociologist Robert K. Merton, numerous analysts have emphasized that young people without access to the material goods celebrated in a consumerist society feel great pressures to secure material goods by illegitimate means if they cannot get them legitimately.[35]

Many Americans find themselves locked into the secondary labor market, where jobs usually provide low wages, weak benefits, and few chances for mobility. Poor workers, young workers, and workers of color disproportionately populate this low-wage labor market. A high percentage of jobs are in the service sector—in laundries, restaurants, garages, and car washes; high underemployment and unemployment often characterize this labor market. An alternative to participation in the precarious secondary labor market is the "hustle" economy—robbery, burglary, numbers running, selling drugs—which becomes an avenue for some youth and adults to add to low family incomes or to satisfy the desire for much advertised consumer goods.

The quest for growth and profits by corporate executives often creates large low-wage job markets in cities, a high level of permanent but oscillating unemployment, and a boom–bust cycle of regular recessions and depressions that throw many people out of work, particularly young and low-income workers. Underemployment and unemployment are major factors in most poverty, and poverty is a major factor in street crime. Conventional street crime appears inevitable in a society in which many people are unemployed, underemployed, and seriously discontented with their economic circumstances, especially in a society with massive wealth and income inequalities. In contrast, numerous European countries with what are called "social welfare states" have far fewer street crimes and much less poverty.

The Structural Solution

Many social scientists, including criminologists, suggest that the way to reduce street crime sharply is to reduce or eradicate unemployment, poverty, and discrimination. Historically, this approach to understanding street crime has proven effective for many groups in the United States. In the early 1900s, for example, such white ethnic (mostly immigrant) groups as Italian, Polish, and Russian Americans perpetrated much street crime. Social and political conservatives of that period, as today, blamed that crime on the immoral values, drunkenness, and animal-like natures of poor (white ethnic) criminals. However, given economic opportunity and declining discrimination over several generations, most in these white ethnic groups moved away from street crime as they moved into better-paying jobs. Drawing on this research, researchers like the authors have suggested that the same would be true today for most poor Americans and most Americans of color if this society provided sufficient and meaningful education and the opportunity for better-paying jobs for them and their children. Such a solution would have to be long-term, not just temporary. Seen from the power–conflict perspective, such a solution would have to be built into the structure of society so that all Americans, whatever their background, would be guaranteed a job with wages enough to provide a decent standard of living.

Crimes of Personal Violence

People of low-income or working-class backgrounds commit a disproportionate number of personal crimes such as murder and assault. They commit these crimes most often against people with similar social characteristics. Yet personal crimes are frequently the predictable outcome of poor living conditions. Personal crimes often reflect the actions of people brutalized by the unemployment, low incomes, and discrimination of our highly unequal social system. Property crimes by the poor against the poor are often misdirected attempts to survive under conditions of low income, lack of education, and underemployment. Crowded living conditions contribute to the escalation of hostility. The rich can move into another room or take a vacation. The poor have less opportunity to escape from conflict; their forced togetherness can sometimes be abrasive.

Not all violent crimes grow out of socioeconomic inequality. Violence often results from quarrels between friends, lovers, and relatives in all social classes. Yet we must understand personal violence in the broader societal context of violence. Tradition has long legitimized violence as a way to solve problems. A "frontier ethic" says that it is all right to carry weapons, including handguns, and to use them if people "cross" you. Many people possess guns to protect themselves from their acquaintances. The mass media contribute to the problem by pushing violent crime as major news and entertainment fare. Local news programs feature brutal crimes. Brutal crimes, such as gory murders, are more likely to be reported than nonviolent burglaries, even though the latter are far more common (in the millions) than the former (in the thousands). While most Americans may not accept the media's distortion of crime as necessarily a representation of the real world, a significant number may grow up believing violent crime is "normal" and that violence is an acceptable way to solve problems.[36]

Some researchers have found that violence on television likely contributes to high levels of violent crime. Murder is the most common crime in television shows, although it is actually one of the least common crimes. Another factor contributing to high levels of violent crime may be glorification of wars or invasions by the U.S. military in countries from Panama to Iraq. One research study examined effects of wars and found that most combatant nations experience increases in postwar homicide rates, whether they are victorious or defeated. Authorized killing during wars often has the unfortunate effect of *legitimizing* violence in peacetime.[37]

The increase in violence suffered by or observed by children in recent years—one of the accurate predictors of later violent behavior—is likely to result in increases in violence in the future. The number of child abuse cases has increased in recent years.[38] Moreover, in some urban neighborhoods "a lot of 13- and 14-year-olds have buried more of their own friends than their grandparents have. . . . [and] attending funerals of their classmates has become for them more a social event than a ritual of mourning, a foreshadowing more than a warning."[39]

CRIMES BY THE POWERFUL

Most Americans focus their concern with law violations on the street crime disproportionately committed by the poor and powerless. Street crime is more widely discussed in the media, news, and films than is corporate crime. Yet the affluent have been involved in many law violations. Edwin Sutherland argued in *White Collar Crime* (1949) that street crimes have received disproportionate attention. Using neglected data, he supported his thesis that "persons in the upper socioeconomic class engage in much criminal behavior."[40] His conclusions still hold true today.

Crimes of the rich and powerful fall into two general categories: *corporate* and *occupational*. Corporate crime involves a number of individuals who violate laws in the larger company interest. An example is corporate officials' aiding their company by setting artificially high prices in collusion with executives of competing corporations. Individuals in bureaucratic settings often carry out such illegal actions, but they do not act in isolation; the operating norms of their organizations may support or require these actions. In contrast, occupational crime is committed for personal benefits by people acting in their occupational roles. Politicians stealing public monies or corporate executives embezzling company funds are examples.[41]

Corporate Crime

Violations of criminal laws are committed not only by criminals "in the streets" but also by criminals "in the suites." Many of the crimes committed by members of the corporate class reflect the motivation suggested by railroad capitalist Cornelius Vanderbilt when he said, "You don't suppose you can run a railway in accordance with the statutes, do you?" Law violations have been committed to help start a business. For example, prior to founding Sears, Roebuck and Company, entrepreneur Richard Sears raised capital by buying $2 watches, putting $20 price tags on them, and mailing them to bogus addresses. When the packages came back, he sold returned watches for $10 to unsuspecting employees where he worked.[42] Interestingly, decades later in the 1990s consumers and state regulators nationwide brought 19 class action suits against the Sears Corporation, charging that its auto repair shops had defrauded customers nationwide by making unnecessary repairs. In the largest settlement in the history of customer fraud to that point, Sears agreed to pay $46.6 million to affected customers.[43]

Corporate crime is well organized and has many victims: consumers, stockholders, employees, and competing businesses. An early opinion survey revealed that most corporate managers believed their competitors "would not refuse to market off-standard and possibly dangerous products."[44] The evidence suggests that this is still true today. Such views underlie much unethical behavior and crime carried out in the quest for better profits.

Corporate crimes remain commonplace and involve the country's best-known corporations. General Electric and Westinghouse top executives in the 1960s were among those fined or jailed for serious law violations, including price-fixing and submission of identical sealed bids to potential purchasers of equipment.[45] Studying law violations of the 500 largest manufacturing corporations and 105 large retail, wholesale, and service corporations, Marshall Clinard and Peter Yeager found that prosecutors had charged 60 percent with at least one violation of federal law in a short period. These included violations of environmental laws (large-scale chemical dumping), financial laws (illegal campaign contributions and tax fraud), and labor laws (employment discrimination), as well as unfair trade practices (price-fixing, bid rigging), administrative violations (hindering federal investigations), and manufacturing violations (making products with safety hazards). They concluded that corporate capitalism frequently operates in ways that violate laws.[46]

In the late 1980s, the Securities and Exchange Commission (SEC) charged the large investment firm of Drexel Burnham Lambert and some employees with insider trading, rigging takeovers of corporations, and falsifying or destroying records. A federal court convicted one leading executive of securities fraud, fined him $1.1 billion, and sentenced him to ten years in prison.[47] In 1995, a federal judge fined Consolidated Edison, a major utilities company, $2 million for conspiracy, deception, and making fraudulent statements when it unlawfully concealed information about the release of asbestos that the company knew had contaminated dwellings and businesses following a pipe explosion.[48]

Companies charged with law violations often lose more from bad publicity than they suffer in monetary fines. One study of 83 companies indicted for price-fixing, collusion, and other illegal practices found these companies' average loss in stock market equity because of indictments was more than double the potential fines imposed.[49]

Massive financial fraud cases involving such corporate giants as Enron, WorldCom, Global Crossing, Adelphia, ImClone, and other major corporations have dominated the headlines and court dockets in recent years. Prosecutors indicted Martha Stewart, chief executive officer of Martha Stewart Living Omnimedia, and her Merrill Lynch securities broker for conspiracy to obstruct justice, making false statements, and perjury regarding insider trading.[50] In the Enron case, prosecutors charged a dozen executives with taking part in a multibillion-dollar fraud designed to cover up Enron's financial problems as an energy broker. WorldCom, one of the largest telecommunication companies, filed for bankruptcy protection after disclosing that its chief financial officer improperly booked billions of dollars in expenses. Investigators accused Adelphia executives of defrauding investors and using corporate assets as a source of billions in family loans. The chief executive officer of ImClone pleaded guilty to insider trading when he allegedly tipped off family members to sell stock just before the Federal Food and Drug Administration rejected approval of a key drug manufactured by the firm.[51]

Although prosecutors continue to investigate many cases of corporate and other business collusion, insider trading, tax evasion, and kickbacks, the number of trials of corporate executives has declined over the past decade. Legal experts attribute this drop to law enforcement's renewed absorption with terrorism and illegal drugs. Other observers have pointed out that sentencing guidelines mandating lengthy jail sentences provide an incentive for white-collar defendants to plead guilty and accept reduced penalties rather than risk a trial.[52] Some commentators are hopeful that legal actions brought against corporate executives in recent scandals are signaling a substantive change in attitudes and laws governing white-collar crime. For Caroline Said, however, "it's too soon to tell. Yes, the cases represent a new wave of increased vigilance, but legal experts are divided about whether they represent a sustainable change or are just window dressing."[53]

Who Pays?

People tend to brush off corporate crime as "not hurting anybody." The truth is that corporate crime hurts many people. Street crime may be more physically threatening, but in many ways illegal acts by corporate officials are more serious for society. Such acts often defraud many people in numerous social classes.

Corporate crimes cost Americans far more money than do conventional street crimes. In some cases, millions of people are hurt a little; in other cases, hundreds or thousands may suffer heavy financial and other losses. The Equity Funding Corporation fraud, for example, in which some company executives manipulated accounts and faked assets to drive up the price of Equity stock, cost clients, investors, and creditors an estimated $1 billion to $2 billion—far more than the amount of *all* losses from robbery and burglary in that same year. The annual economic loss to victims of conventional property crimes totals about $18 billion.[54] Estimates of the annual loss from corporate crimes, including consumer fraud, price-fixing, and deceptive practices, run to 20 to 25 times the cost of conventional property crime. The total cost of white-collar crime is at least $360 billion annually. Health care fraud alone costs roughly $100 billion, and antitrust and other trade violation costs $250 billion annually.[55]

One multibillion-dollar price-fixing conspiracy costs consumers far more than the annual cost of all home burglaries. Reduced supervision of corporations over the last decade or two has made it even easier for companies to get away with such anticompetitive practices. Fraudulent advertising is another frequent economic crime victimizing many consumers. The bailout of major banks and the bailout of the savings and loan industry—which nearly collapsed in the late 1980s primarily because of imprudent or fraudulent practices on the part of officers of numerous savings and loan institutions—ultimately cost taxpayers hundreds of billions of dollars.[56] One commentator has estimated the cost of the Enron scandal to investors, pensioners, and employees at $60 billion.[57]

The cost of corporate and other business crime—and of other unethical and harmful practices that are legal—involves more than just money. Deaths, illnesses, and injuries from serious industrial air and water pollution, defective products, and unsafe foods and drugs far exceed the number of homicides each year. Dangerous consumer products are responsible for many deaths and serious injuries each year. For instance, one report indicated that hundreds of thousands of infants worldwide died because their mothers—rather than breast-feeding—fed their babies infant formula preparations sold by infant formula companies. The dangers of the infant formulas, widely acknowledged for decades, include their use in areas without safe water to mix with the formula and their sole use by mothers too poor to purchase adequate quantities.[58]

Testifying before a congressional committee, the chair of the independent Consumer Product Safety Commission (CPSC) summarized the problem with unsafe consumer products: "Each year there are 21,700 deaths and 28.6 million injuries related to consumer products under Commission jurisdiction. The deaths, injuries, and property damage associated with consumer products cost the nation about $200 billion annually."[59] Reflecting on the country's high health care costs, Brown revealed that "consumer product injuries account for one out of every six hospital days in this country." She further noted the many lives and the money CPSC actions have saved. In the four major areas of fire safety, electrocutions, poisonings, and power mowers, CPSC efforts have saved some $2.5 billion in property damages, medical expenditures, and related costs. In the late 1990s, the CPSC targeted the fire hazards posed by upholstered furniture and bedding; fires in connection with these products cause about 1,200 deaths each year. The CPSC also focused on the 2 million Americans injured each year in sports accidents, with a special emphasis on injury-minimizing equipment.[60]

Sometimes small businesses and large corporations are involved in practices that inflict physical injuries on their workers. At least 40,000 workers die annually from exposure to toxic chemicals and other hazards. Another 10,000 die at workplaces each year, many because of inadequate safety procedures or equipment. Over one recent five-year period, some 11 million workplace injuries occurred, with 340,000 workers suffering permanent disability.[61]

Occasionally, local district attorneys prosecute work-related deaths as "reckless homicides." A member of the Rhode Island Committee on Occupational Safety and Health has noted that "In just this half-decade [1990–1995] alone, 250,000 deaths can be attributed to occupational diseases like brain and bladder cancer, asbestos-related diseases, diseases of the nerves and lungs and of the blood-forming organs."[62] In addition, the workplace exposes millions of workers to potential carcinogens. Many textile workers have suffered and died from brown lung disease; black lung disease has killed thousands of miners and disabled many others.[63]

Another cost of corporate crime is its effect on society's moral climate. A *Fortune* magazine editor once asked, "How much crime in the streets is connected with the widespread judgment that the business economy itself is a gigantic rip-off?"[64] Poor street criminals may justify their crimes by pointing to costly crimes by people in higher-level classes. Corporate actions in Central America, Chile, and Japan have helped to topple existing governments. Huge corporate bribes to the shah of Iran, through the conduit of his officials, eventually contributed to the Iranian revolution and the taking of American hostages in the 1979–1981 U.S.–Iran crisis. Corporation conduct abroad, both that which is illegal and that which is unethical, has affected U.S. foreign policy in many ways.[65]

Punishment

In some cases, such as burglary and robbery, taking property is a crime for which our laws impose severe punishments. In other instances, however, justice officials do not consider the taking of property criminal (a bank taking working people's homes through mortgage

Numerous big corporations have used their money to greatly influence government officials.

foreclosures and employers underpaying employees), even though the takings result in considerable harm to victims. Retail merchants do not hesitate to call the police to arrest shoplifters, but the police would be very unlikely to come if a customer complained about a fraudulent auto repair. While the justice system often treats shoplifting severely, a merchant who intentionally double-bills on a credit card would almost never be prosecuted if the customer complained. Such examples raise the question of how certain behaviors are defined as criminal matters and made punishable by severe penalties, while other actions are at most violations of civil law typically punishable by a token fine. Yet other unethical and harmful actions escape the justice system altogether.

The "Golden Rule" of crime and punishment is that *those who have the gold make the rules.* In U.S. society, the powerful construct criminal laws. Some laws, such as those against murder and assault, relate to criminal infractions. The justice system does not consider all illegal behaviors resulting in bodily injury equally serious. Jurisdictions define only certain avoidable killings as criminal acts of murder. Deaths resulting from employers knowingly cheating on safety standards; deaths from intentional pollution of streams and groundwater by toxic waste dumping by corporate executives; deaths from unsafe drugs or other products rushed into production by executives who know they are dangerous; or deaths from defective motor vehicles that executives were unwilling to recall are not usually defined as murder.[66]

Within the structure of our system, a variety of practices work "to conceal the crimes of the powerful against the powerless, but to reveal and exaggerate crimes of the powerless against 'everyone.'"[67] Techniques to play down the crimes of the powerful include the following:

1. *Differential policing and investigation*—for example, more police assigned to low-income communities than to Wall Street offices and practices.
2. *Differential arrests*—for example, excessive arrests of Americans of color for conventional street crime.
3. *Biased judicial decisions*—for example, greater leniency for the sons and daughters of the well off than for the sons and daughters of the poor concerning similar crimes.

Jurisdictions only occasionally punish corporations and executives in a serious way for corporate crimes. In many cases, serious violations have received only modest fines or forced promises not to commit crime in the future.[68] One survey noted that, while the prosecution of executives had increased, "only a fraction are charged with crime, and of those charged and convicted, even fewer go to prison."[69] The 1988 conviction of and $2 million fine against Beech-Nut Nutrition Corporation and some of its top executives for marketing adulterated and mislabeled juice for babies signaled that major violations of the law by corporate executives were being taken more seriously by the criminal justice system—and by most Americans—than in the past.[70]

Punishments for corporate crimes are far from uniform. For example, a printing company plant manager and employee received 27-month prison sentences for illegally disposing of a toxic chemical in a dumpster that resulted in the deaths of two boys. The firm's lawyers pleaded "no contest" to other charges against the firm, which was assessed a fine. As one legal commentator stated, "Did not these two nine-year-old boys die violent deaths? Where is Attorney General Reno's outraged rhetoric condemning corporate crime and violence? Of course, most corporate and white-collar violent crime goes unprosecuted."[71]

Fines for corporate crimes have increased in recent years, although these fines are typically a very small percentage of profits. Between the early 1980s and the present, the level of fines sought for environmental crimes by corporations has increased. In 1983, some 40 indictments of corporate officials for environmental crimes involved only $341,000 in possible penalties. In contrast, by 1992 the 191 federal indictments entailed some $163 million in possible penalties for the corporations involved. Under 1991 federal sentencing guidelines, authorities can hold corporate executives accountable by imprisoning them for corporate crimes.[72]

While environmental crimes are receiving increasing penalties, the executives involved have received variable penalties. For example, state attorneys charged a California firm with illegally dumping more than 100,000 gallons of waste into Oakland's sewers. Authorities sentenced the head of the firm to two years in prison for violation of federal law. In contrast, however, when Unocal Corporation's refinery managers illegally permitted tons of a toxic chemical to leak into the air, top executives reassigned the managers to another city. The company's $3 million fine was a tiny percentage of its $8 billion revenues. The leak was so serious that it coated a nearby working-class residential area with brown goo, and some residents became ill. Local officials defended their actions not to prosecute the managers with the comment that, while the incident was very serious, it was too hard to determine exactly who was at fault, given the "multiple failures, from top to bottom."[73]

Occupational and Small-Business Crime

Well-off individuals who abuse their occupational roles commit other crimes. Some managerial and professional people pad their expense accounts, and some embezzle money from their companies. Many steal to keep up a high standard of living. Cressey's study of people convicted of embezzlement or similar crimes violating financial trust suggests that some trusted persons become criminals when they cannot solve personal financial problems. They develop rationalizations for "borrowing" other people's money to solve their problems.[74] Lower-level white-collar employees also participate in crime. An estimated 70 percent of retail store losses come from theft by employees, while only 30 percent of the losses come from shoplifting.[75]

Many white-collar crimes go unreported. As the head of the Chicago Crime Commission has stated, "Corporations either fire the perpetrators and take no further action to avoid negative publicity, or write off the loss assuming the government is more concerned with violent crime than white-collar crime."[76] Crimes by white-collar employees have major societal costs, for many firms pass along their crime costs to the consumer.[77]

Small-business people also commit crimes. Many people skim profits to hide income from the Internal Revenue Service. During natural disasters or riots, individuals, usually the poor, who engage in looting are arrested for theft, yet merchants who charge exorbitant prices for food and other necessities during similar circumstances are usually not arrested for price gouging. Unlawful acts by merchants are less publicized and less frequently punished compared with street crimes.

White-collar workers and other employees are sometimes victims of crimes at the hands of clients, other members of the public, and other employees. According to the National Institute for Occupational Safety and Health (NIOSH), an average of 1.7 million persons are victims of workplace violence in the United States annually. While most of these incidents are simple assaults, nearly 20 percent of them constitute more aggravated incidents that cause serious physical and emotional injuries to workers.[78] Besides the physical injuries, workplace violence can have extremely negative effects upon worker morale and worker stress, resulting in increased rates of worker turnover and mistrust of management and co-workers. It can also intensify employee awareness of a hostile working environment.[79]

Occupational statistics are particularly troubling for workplace homicides. Roughly 18,000 workplace homicides involving shootings and other violent acts occurred in workplaces between 1982 and 2001.[80] A significant proportion of workplace homicides occur in technical, sales, and administrative occupations in the trade and service industries. In New York, one-fourth of all job-related injuries for state employees in the early 1990s came from assaults by clients or others in workplaces. A man at an unemployment office in California killed two employees and injured others.[81] The summer of 2003 was a particularly violent period when 12 workplace incidents resulted in 38 killings. The deadliest incident involved a worker armed with a shotgun and a rifle who went on a rampage at a Mississippi aircraft plant and killed five co-workers.[82] Besides inflicting severe physical injury and death on workers, the annual costs of workplace violence to U.S. industries exceed $36 billion.[83]

CRIMES BY GOVERNMENT OFFICIALS

The President's Men

Serious crime occurs in government settings. Top public officials, both elected and administrative, have the power to carry out illegal activities on a major scale by virtue of the government (and often corporate) resources they control. They can often conceal what they are doing.

One illustration of crime by officials was the Watergate burglary carried out in the 1970s by President Richard Nixon's reelection campaign organization. With the cooperation of the president, officials concealed much high-level crime from the public long enough for the American people to reelect a crime-committing president. At the same time Nixon and his assistants, many with ties to corporate America, were calling for stiff punishments for ordinary criminals, for "law and order." Also, during this corrupt political administration, a White House investigative operation called the "Plumbers" forged diplomatic cables and paid people to break up political rallies. Most of Nixon's aides who were involved served only short prison sentences. President Gerald Ford quickly pardoned Nixon to preclude the former president's prosecution for felonies, such as covering up a burglary and income tax fraud, or for the illegal use of the Central Intelligence Agency (CIA) and Federal Bureau of Investigation (FBI).[84]

A number of top political officials in the Ronald Reagan presidential administration, including CIA Director William Casey, National Security Council advisers Robert McFarlane and John Poindexter, and National Security Council official Lt. Colonel Oliver North, were involved in a similar scandal in the 1980s, known as "Iran-Contra." These men allegedly engaged in a variety of questionable or illegal activities aimed at fostering a secret guerrilla war against the legal government of Nicaragua. They were involved in a secret arms sale to the government of Iran, the proceeds from which they used to support the Contra guerrillas' war. Once these activities became public, Reagan claimed that members of his administration had diverted the funds without his knowledge. In 1988, McFarlane pleaded guilty to withholding information from Congress, and a grand jury indicted North and Poindexter for conspiracy to defraud, obstruction of justice, and destruction of documents. Federal authorities convicted North on several counts, but an appellate court overturned the convictions because of a congressional promise of immunity. U.S. Senators William S. Cohen and George J. Mitchell concluded, "Twice in the past fifteen years our government has been virtually paralyzed because rules were stretched, laws broken, and policies twisted in an effort to avoid complying with restrictions thought by presidents to be either unwise or unconstitutional."[85] The fact that the "big fish," such as high government criminals, often get off with modest or no punishment helps to create distrust of the political and judicial systems.

During the Reagan administration and the first George Bush administration (1981–1992), other major political scandals developed. By the end of the period, many allegations of malfeasance and obstruction of justice had been directed at the Department of Justice (DOJ)—failure to investigate criminal conduct by the Bank of Credit and Commerce International, covering up the illegal diversion of U.S.-taxpayer-guaranteed loans to build up Iraq's military, and a list of lesser-known cases. The "trail of suspicion" reached to other executive departments and to the White House itself. The scandal discredited Edmond Meese, the first attorney general in the Reagan administration, who resigned. One longtime congressional investigator described the DOJ as a "totally dishonest organization, riddled with political fixes."[86]

Illegal campaign activities, including illegal contributions, have been a regular part of U.S. politics. In the mid-1990s, authorities ordered two Korean corporations to pay $850,000 as a fine for illegal contributions to the campaign of a Republican member of Congress.[87] In March of the following year, a Utah congressional representative, Enid Waldholtz, declined to run for reelection because of a scandal involving alleged illegal campaign contributions in her campaign for Congress. One press report noted that "she blamed the scandal on her husband, Joe Waldholtz, who was heavily involved in her 1994 campaign. Joe Waldholtz disappeared for six days before turning himself in to federal prosecutors."[88] Later that same year, Arkansas Lieutenant Governor Mike Huckabee, a candidate for senator, publicly admitted having accepted illegal campaign contributions from two corporations.[89]

In 2002, the Federal Election Commission (FEC) imposed a $719,000 fine against participants in the 1996 Democratic Party fund-raising scandal involving contributions from China, Korea, and other foreign sources. Foreign nationals made campaign contributions to the Democratic Party in return for meetings with then-President Bill Clinton and Vice President Al Gore in violation of federal laws prohibiting foreign nationals and corporations from contributing to federal elections. The FEC fined the Democratic National Committee, the Clinton–Gore campaign, a Buddhist temple where Gore appeared in return for a $100,000 contribution, and two dozen other people and corporations that acted as conduits for illegal contributions.[90]

In election year 2002, some 31 corporate criminals gave more than $9 million to the Democratic and Republican parties. According to one report, corporate criminals gave $7.2 million to the Republicans and $2.1 million to Democrats. The corporate law violators making the largest contributions to the political parties included Archer Daniels Midland ($1.7 million), Pfizer ($1.1 million), Chevron ($875,400), Northrop Grumman ($741,250), and American Airlines ($655,593). In recent years, courts have imposed heavy criminal and civil fines on these corporations for a large range of activities including antitrust, price-fixing, falsifying testimony, and environmental-impact crimes. Yet, unlike what happens to ordinary Americans who commit crimes, the corporate criminals rarely get a negative public image for their deeds, and their political privileges are not curtailed.[91]

The FBI and the CIA

Just as serious have been the law violations of many officials in top police agencies. Between the 1950s and the early 2000s, several government agencies, including the FBI, conducted covert actions against U.S. citizens in the name of national security. These were not legitimate investigative activities aimed at known criminals but politically motivated activities aimed at limiting political dissent. For centuries, government officials have periodically carried out antidemocratic activities to protect the existing political system. In 1798, for example, the Alien and Sedition Acts made public criticism of the government a crime; in the 1860s President Abraham Lincoln suspended the writ of habeas corpus; in 1942 President Roosevelt authorized General DeWitt of the Western Defense Command to place more than 100,000 Japanese Americans in concentration camps because of white prejudice; and in the 1950s Senator Joseph McCarthy and his associates conducted a wide-ranging witch hunt for alleged subversives, destroying the lives of many innocent and loyal Americans.

The criminal activities of the FBI and CIA were extensive under both Democratic and Republican administrations during the 1960s and 1970s. Numerous illegal and questionable FBI and CIA activities designed to reduce the rights of free speech and free assembly among American citizens—such as illegal wiretapping, the illegal opening and photographing of first-class letters, the infiltration of spies into women's liberation organizations, and attempted blackmail and other efforts to discredit the civil rights leader Dr. Martin Luther King, Jr.—have been well-documented. The government spent millions of dollars in these spying campaigns. With revelations about these activities came a decline in CIA and FBI prestige.[92]

In 1981, President Ronald Reagan pardoned two top FBI officials, whom the justice department had convicted of illegal activities, praising them for their actions in illegally monitoring protest groups. In 1988, the Center for Constitutional Rights obtained FBI documents disclosing an extensive FBI "campaign of political intimidation" from 1981 to 1985 that violated dissenters' civil rights. The FBI later disciplined six of its agents and four supervisors for their activities. Three received the modest penalty of a two-week suspension without pay, an extraordinarily mild punishment for violating the civil rights of Americans who were exercising their constitutional right to disagree with their government.[93]

Corporations and Government

Corporate and government officials sometimes participate together in criminal or ethically questionable activities. Selective law enforcement allows for continuation of actions that government agencies know are dangerous or unlawful. For example, General Motors (GM) began marketing a pickup truck in 1973 whose engineers knew that the fuel tank design was dangerous well before the truck went into production. This fault allegedly caused an estimated 300 deaths. The West Virginia Highway Safety Office first alerted the National Highway Traffic Safety Administration (NHTSA), the agency with authority to investigate and recall hazardous vehicles, to the truck's danger in 1974. Even though various sources continued to put NHTSA on notice of injuries and fatalities caused by the precarious positioning of the truck's fuel tank, including a report from the Center for Auto Safety (CAS), NHTSA refused to take action—which effectively allowed GM to continue producing the vehicle. Additionally, NHTSA misled the public by claiming that the truck met safety standards even though it had not tested the vehicle for side impacts as the standard required. NHTSA claimed to have received "no complaints regarding the subject fuel tank in any collisions as late as 1991, other than the report from CAS."[94] Yet an NHTSA internal newsletter reported a $1.5 million court verdict against GM in 1980. NHTSA's own files contained reports of many other cases.

The Center for Auto Safety exposed the cover-up and formally petitioned NHTSA to take action in August 1992. Four months later NHTSA announced that it would begin a full-scale investigation. At that time, at least three court cases involving the GM truck were in progress, including one class-action case. During the course of the investigation, which continued over the next two years, NHTSA uncovered more than 100,000 pages of documents showing that GM pickup trucks had resulted in more than 650 fire deaths and more than 200 lawsuits and that GM had known about the defect since at least 1973. NHTSA settled the case with GM after the agency made an initial determination of defect in December 1994. Although the settlement required GM to pay $51 million into funding safety programs, it did not require a recall of the trucks. Petitioners settled a national class-action suit against GM with the corporation agreeing to provide a $1,000 coupon toward the purchase of a new truck. Pressure from safety groups arguing that the redemption of coupons for a new truck did precious little to alleviate the safety concerns about the truck, and that the vast majority of truck owners would never use the coupons, caused the settlement to be overturned. A court of appeals remanded the case to the district court for trial in 1996.[95]

Large, and sometimes illegal, campaign contributions given by numerous companies and corporate lobbyists to national and state politicians frequently bring the donors access to and favors from the recipient. In most cases both parties deny any connection between money given and favors received. Indeed, such a connection is generally almost impossible to prove, yet the frequency with which such "coincidences" occur generates considerable suspicion. Members of former President George H. W. Bush's Team 100 (donors who personally or through their corporations each contributed $100,000 or more to his 1988 election campaign and/or the Republican National Committee), for example, received substantial benefits. In one case, a criminal tax evasion investigation of a major utility company was ordered stopped by a DOJ political appointee, even though IRS agents had reportedly collected compelling evidence that company officials had "schemed and conspired to evade federal income taxes" and knowingly filed false tax returns.[96] Agents estimated that the company owed as much as $200 million in back taxes, interest, and penalties. Investigators for Common Cause concluded that "in the absence of any other explanation, one lingering theory is that Southern Co. President Edward Addison's Team 100 membership played some role in the case being killed."[97]

ORGANIZED CRIME, BUSINESS, AND GOVERNMENT

In recent decades much organized crime has changed from a predominantly gangster, back alley operation to a large-scale, illegal business enterprise. Organized crime refers to enterprises set up primarily and intentionally to profit from violating criminal laws. Organized networks control many of the illegal gambling, loan sharking, and narcotics importing and distribution operations and a large portion of the prostitution business in the United States. Virtually every municipality and state has laws prohibiting prostitution and drug abuse, but these activities are still widespread. Organized crime has infiltrated some labor unions and extended operations by "laundering dirty money" into legitimate corporate and other business enterprises such as vending companies, restaurants and bars, hotels, trucking companies, and manufacturing firms.

Organized crime differs from most ordinary street crime in that organized crime involves large-scale organization and is often associated with legitimate politics and businesses. Organized crime operations provide incomes not only for well-heeled racketeers but also for many poverty-area residents.[98] Major drug networks distribute on a national and international scale drugs available from pharmaceutical houses (such as amphetamines) and drugs from South America, Central America, Mexico, and the Far East (such as heroin). These now global crime networks feed the insatiable U.S. demand for these drugs (see Chapter 9).

Over the last decade, federal investigators have linked business officials and politicians to organized crime in cities from Denver to Miami to New York. While the media often limit discussions of organized crime to leading criminal figures, organized crime involves the cooperation and participation of police officers, business officials, city administrators, and other public officials. Large-scale political corruption and organized criminal syndicates are often rolled into one bureaucratic operation. This category of criminality involves not only the activities of the criminal "underworld" but also the day-to-day activities of business officials and politicians and the middle-income and upper-income male clients who often make use of these services. One case, for example, involved the alleged "Hollywood Madam" Heidi Fleiss, the daughter of a prominent pediatrician. Charged with trafficking in prostitution, Fleiss stated in a television interview that some Hollywood figures should be worried about revelations about her clients.[99]

Historically, the federal government has put considerable effort into reducing organized crime in the United States. and, more recently, in Latin America. At times, however, these efforts have culminated in new government crime. After a 2-year investigation into the 40-year history of the FBI's ultrasecret organized-crime informant program in New England, the U.S. House Committee on Government Reform recently reported that the FBI had made scapegoats of innocent people to shield known organized-crime killers. Courts sentenced two men to death for murder convictions obtained through false testimony and the FBI's efforts to protect informants. Two other falsely accused defendants, Joseph Salvati and Peter Limone, languished in prison for more than 30 years. The U.S. Justice Department and the White House directly impeded the congressional probe by refusing to cooperate. One investigator noted that it is interesting that in 2003 President George W. Bush is determined to have the United States root out terror in every corner of Iraq but has refused to let the public see how the FBI waged its own campaign of terror. The Justice Department is also using dubious means to fight the $2 billion worth of civil lawsuits filed by the families victimized by the FBI. The aforementioned congressional report concluded that the FBI's efforts in the investigation of organized crime in the Northeast "must be considered one of the greatest failures in the history of federal law enforcement."[100]

PROSECUTING CRIMINALS

The U.S. criminal justice system includes the police, district attorneys, courts, correctional facilities, and the enforcement arms of regulatory agencies. To some extent, the legal system reflects a consensus of law on the part of most of the population—male and female, capitalist, manager, or worker. Virtually all Americans agree, for example, that laws against murder should exist and that courts should impose stiff penalties for murder.

Administration of the law historically has reflected a strong class and racial bias. Enforcement of the law varies greatly. Higher-income groups tend to receive favored treatment, in part because they can afford to hire talented lawyers. We have seen the lenient treatment that many corporations and other powerful criminals have received for violating a range of laws. Courts usually punish with modest sanctions corporate acts of fraud, price-fixing, massive pollution, and false advertising. On the other hand, the criminal justice system is far more responsive to drug-related crimes (such as theft to support small-scale crack use) and property crimes (for instance, robbery) by poor criminals, typically with prosecutions that are more vigorous and with the imposition of severe punishments. Because the criminal justice system and law enforcement aim much of their activity at conventional street crime, our discussion here focuses primarily on this aspect of law enforcement. However, some power–conflict analysts suggest that the criminal justice system is "primarily designed to guarantee the private property of the capitalists."[101] There is truth to this view, but it overstates the case. While those with the most private property have the most to lose, and usually get the most police protection, an asserted purpose of the justice system is to protect all citizens' property. Nevertheless, police agencies, courts, and such federal law enforcement agencies as the FBI act to protect and reinforce the system of class, racial, and gender inequality in the United States.

The Police

An emphasis on creating more professional police forces and on prevention of street crime accompanied the increasing dominance of U.S. society by large industrial corporations in the late 1800s. As previously stated, this emphasis on street crime continues today. The annual cost of the U.S. criminal justice system is about $150 billion. Nearly 2.3 million people work in the system, including 1 million police officers, 747,000 prison and jail guards, and 488,000 court personnel.[102] The United States has thousands of local police departments as well as such federal police agencies as the FBI, Secret Service, Border Patrol, and Drug Enforcement Administration (DEA).

Recent attempts to improve the quality of police forces have emphasized education, technique, and technology and have relied on experts to create better police forces and crime-control strategies.[103] Federal and state governments have appointed commissions to study law enforcement, and legislatures have passed crime-control laws. Government funding of police agencies has sharply increased. Many have called for large increases in police patrolling to improve law enforcement, yet increasing the number of police or the efficiency of police practices will not necessarily reduce conventional crime rates. Criminologist James Fyfe has noted, "Where crime and violence are the lowest there are no cops. The absence of crime is not because of a heavy police presence but because people there have a sense of community, a sense of ownership. They have things to lose. You see heavy street crime in places where people have nothing to lose."[104]

In recent years, the racist views and actions of white officers have been documented in numerous cities.

Police have great discretion in enforcing laws, and police actions in fighting crime depend partly on political and administrative pressures.[105] To improve their crime solution rate, for example, burglary detectives often permit informants to violate narcotics laws, and other police officers often use liquor laws to control homosexual bars. The behavior of suspects often influences their chances of arrest. Police officers are less likely to arrest youthful offenders that are properly deferential; those too deferential or too hostile fare less well. Police officers often use their discretion in dealing with crime to come down harder on the poor than on the affluent and the rich (especially those who are white).[106]

Differential treatment by police is a major issue in many communities of color. Many residents in these communities cite racial discrimination in quality and character of police services and emphasize the need for more patrolling, better police response times, and greater police civility toward citizens in their communities. Higher rates of crime in many communities of color are compelling reasons for people's concerns about inadequate police protection. The victimization rate for all personal crimes is 40 percent higher for blacks than for whites and 35 percent higher for crimes of violence. Black victims are more likely than white victims to suffer physical injury from criminal victimization.[107] Many black and Latino communities face excesses of policing malpractice, such as the beating of black motorist Rodney King by Los Angeles police officers in 1991, the vicious attack on Abner Louima by New York City police officers in 1997, the punching of 16-year-old Donovan

Jackson by Inglewood police officer Jeremy Morse in 2002, and the police-related fatality involving Nathaniel Jones and the Cincinnati police in 2003. Black and Latino youths have periodically died mysteriously while in police custody.[108] Racist judgments are integral to police brutality because many white officers consider people of color more dangerous and arousing of suspicion than whites.

Pressure from powerful interests to reduce crime and improve the image of a city often compels police officers to look disproportionately for suspects in central city areas and routinely to stop black and Latino men, most of whom have done nothing wrong.[109] Persistent harassment, mistreatment, and brutality contribute to widespread citizen resentment toward police.[110]

In recent years, a number of urban neighborhoods across the country have instituted community-policing programs involving local residents in crime prevention. Recently, in some 100 Houston neighborhoods, more than 4,000 residents carrying citizen band radios volunteered 150,000 hours per year as Citizens on Patrol. The Houston Police Academy provided classes to familiarize community leaders with the justice system and to help them learn to investigate crime, interact with officers, and engage in patrol operations. Community policing focused on getting officers out of the mode of impersonal policing in roving police cars. The goal has been to put officers in direct contact with local residents. In some cases, officers have been encouraged to live in areas they police. In Seattle, where Mothers Against Police Harassment monitors police activities and conducts workshops to educate people in what to do when stopped by the police, officers meet regularly with community groups to develop effective problem-solving strategies. Although some report that community policing can mean neighbors spying on neighbors, police brutality complaints have fallen by almost half, and residents report a decline in problems with drug dealers accosting people in public places. Cities such as Los Angeles, Seattle, Denver, and Houston have experienced dramatic reductions in crime rates over the last few years. While many observers attribute this drop in crime mostly to factors other than community policing, numerous analysts and city residents see community policing as a step in the direction of better police–community relationships.[111]

The Courts

Critics have charged that the U.S. judicial system is too lenient and have called for a tough "law-and-order" solution to crime—more imprisonment and more severe penalties for law violators. This get-tough approach is exactly what has happened over the last several decades. In cities such as Chicago, Kansas City, and St. Louis, more of those arrested for crimes go to jail or prison now than in the 1920s.[112] Mandatory (often draconian) sentencing guidelines in most states, along with harsher drug laws, have dramatically increased the percentage of those arrested and sentenced to prison. Despite a declining crime rate in recent years, the number of prisoners in state and federal prisons and local jails had increased to 2.1 million in 2004.[113] The U.S. rate of incarceration—more than 726 prisoners per 100,000 population in 2004—is the *highest in the world today.*[114] While the prison rate has tripled since over the last few decades, new prison construction has increased 17-fold over this period.[115] Incarceration rates are not equitable, however. In the United States, the black incarceration rate in 2004 was 4,919 black male prison and jail inmates per 100,000 black men, 1,717 Latino male inmates per 100,000 Latino men, and 717 white male inmates per 100,000 white men.[116] These figures mean that the black incarceration rate is nearly *seven times* that of whites, and the Latino incarceration rate is *two and half times* that of whites. Similar racial disparities in the incarceration rates exist for women prisoners. These disparities in incarceration rates among racial groups mean that the law-and-order answer to the country's crime problem is far more burdensome to black and Latino Americans and their communities than for white Americans.

The deterrent effect of punishment rests more on the certainty of its administration than on severity. For example, most students would probably never cheat on exams, regardless of the penalty, if they knew their professors would catch them. Moreover, increases in the severity of punishment gradually lose their ability to add to the deterrent effect. Those not deterred by, say, a $25 fine for illegal parking would not be any more deterred if administrators increased the fine to $30. A report from the Sentencing Project concluded that "incarceration rates set new records each day, while crime rates remain intolerably high. Clearly, large-scale imprisonment provides no panacea for crime."[117]

Harsh approaches to crime affect all citizens. While extreme police repression, such as that in Nazi Germany, reduces conventional crime sharply, such regimes destroy civil liberties of all citizens in the process. Between World War II and the late 1970s, numerous court cases—including many reaching the U.S. Supreme Court—reinforced or expanded the legal rights of criminal defendants and, potentially, all Americans. Many police agencies and prosecutors have resisted and criticized court decisions expanding rights of defendants, yet some of these agencies have a record of civil liberties violations. Increasing their control further could have a negative impact on the rights of citizens, particularly those calling for reform of court and policing systems.

A case in point relates to the security measures stemming from the USA Patriot Act. Six weeks after the murderous events of September 11, 2001, Congress passed the Patriot Act without much debate concerning the effect of the act's provisions on civil liberties. The act enhances federal enforcement agencies' powers in terrorism probes by giving them access to intelligence information previously unavailable to criminal investigators. The act provides for expansive power to government to conduct searches and wiretaps and intercept cell phone calls. Government officials have already used the act's provisions to detain some 1,200 people without identifying them. The act allows government agents to exercise broad authority in holding noncitizens in detention and to deport persons, without proper evidence, thought to be engaged in activities that endanger the national security.[118] Citizens too have reduced legal rights under some provisions of this repressive Patriot Act.

The justice system could address many issues in the courts effectively without such a repressive approach. Noting that fewer than 10 percent of all serious crimes result in arrest, the Sentencing Project report urged authorities to refocus law enforcement policy on community needs and crime prevention. Drug-related penalties are a major cause of the huge increase in incarcerations in recent years, yet researchers have found no evidence that a law enforcement approach to the drug problem has substantially reduced drug abuse or drug-related crime. Indeed, medically oriented researchers recommend that government authorities redefine drug abuse as a public health problem rather than a criminal problem and then redirect funds toward education, prevention, and treatment. (Indeed, one of the most seriously addictive drugs used in the United States is alcohol, and alcoholics usually receive much better societal treatment—usually as persons with a disease—than other drug addicts.) Currently, the waiting period for treatment in a drug-abuse facility is six months or more in many communities.[119]

Plea bargaining, a central part of the overburdened justice system, presents additional difficulties. States such as New York, where prosecutors return tens of thousands of felony indictments each year, have too few courts to try more than a small portion of the cases. Many defendants, especially those who cannot afford an attorney, are urged to plead guilty to a lesser crime—a tactic that cuts court costs and reduces the guilty defendant's sentence, yet does not protect the innocent defendant. The accused pleads guilty to a lesser crime, which often he or she did not commit. The accused also has to say that he or she pled guilty willingly and not because of promises made by state prosecutors, which is usually a lie. Prosecutors will usually promise the defendant that they will not prosecute on a more serious charge if the accused accepts the proposed plea bargain. Prison sentences for the same crime vary widely from one area of the country to another, depending in part on the degree to which prosecutors use the plea-bargaining process. Frequent use of plea bargaining is more likely in areas where prosecutors are very busy. In addition, many poor people, both the guilty and the innocent, plead guilty without adequate legal representation, often after a very brief consultation with a young, inexperienced, or overworked lawyer. Many poor prisoners go to prison believing, justly, that the criminal justice system is unfair, deceptive, or corrupt.[120] In addition, one bar association study concluded that the U.S. legal system is addressing only a small minority of the civil legal problems of poor Americans. Just a few states, such as Ohio, have made some significant efforts to expand legal assistance to the poor.[121] Today, as it is currently structured, the legal system provides justice consistently only to affluent Americans.

Judges tend to come from upper-income families and managerial or professional backgrounds. More than 90 percent are white, and most are male. The election of more conservative national political administrations has brought in ever more archconservative judges who aggressively represent the views of powerful elites. Their decisions tend to reflect a strong and built-in class, racial, and gender bias. Legal representation is seriously class biased. The powerful have greatest access to the best lawyers, and better-paid white-collar employees usually have access to adequate representation. One study finds that the best predictors of contact with lawyers are family income and property ownership—people with higher incomes and with property are more likely than others to have used a private lawyer.[122]

Certain criminals who commit conventional street crimes, such as drug addicts or dealers from high-income, white-collar backgrounds, often receive more lenient treatment from the courts than do those from poorer groups who commit similar crimes. Thus, a Yale Law School research study on white-collar crime found that most judges are reluctant to sentence white-collar criminals to prison.[123] Police will often not even arrest doctors and nurses who are drug addicts, or at least will process them informally. The police or court rationale is often that they are "important, productive members of the community." Many states have lightened punishments for small-scale marijuana possession because of its increased use by well-off Americans, including many white students from affluent families. In 1969, thus, Nebraska became the second state in the nation to reduce possession of marijuana to a misdemeanor, apparently because police arrested a well-known criminal prosecutor's son for possessing marijuana a few months before the state legislators passed the bill.[124]

The Death Penalty Issue

Racial discrimination remains one of the major problems in the use of capital punishment in the United States. Racial disparity in capital sentencing has a long history. Thus, black Americans have made up nearly half of the 4,731 prisoners executed since 1930, the date when the federal government began maintaining information on executions. Death penalty jurisdictions have executed disproportionate numbers of black offenders.[125] Racial disparity in capital sentencing is even more conspicuous when one considers black executions for rape. Although the death penalty is no longer constitutionally permissible for rape convictions where no death results, black perpetrators have made up nearly 90 percent of all persons ever executed for that offense.[126] One of the more troubling historical facts about rape and racial characteristics in the United States is that no court *has ever called for the execution of a white man convicted of raping a black woman.*[127] As Flowers notes, "Black rapists have been far more likely to be put to death when their victims were white females rather than black females, whereas the death penalty has been imposed on white rapists exclusively when their victims were also white."[128] This policing and court bias is especially tragic in light of the long history of white men raping black women, which reached epidemic proportions in many areas of the South under the long eras of slavery and legal segregation (1619–1968).

Not until 1972 did the U.S. Supreme Court finally rule on the obvious racism in capital sentencing. In *Furman v. Georgia,* the court ruled that the arbitrary and capricious nature of the process of imposing capital punishment in the United States amounted to a form

Racist use of peremptory challenges to exclude persons of color from jury participation is another grievous form of prosecutorial misconduct affecting capital cases—particularly in cases involving defendants of color who have victimized whites. One misguided assumption of state prosecutors is that white jurors are more likely than jurors of color to convict defendants of color. One recent case of prosecutorial racism in the use of peremptory challenges involving a black defendant revealed that state prosecutors excluded 91 percent of black persons qualified to serve as jurors. In fact, a training manual used by the prosecutors in the case called for exclusion of "Jews, Negroes, Dagos, Mexicans, or a member of any minority race." Prosecutors in another jurisdiction regularly used video training tapes showing new attorneys how to exclude black jurors, especially "young black women" and "blacks from low-income areas." (State prosecutors also frequently make racist remarks while trying capital cases.) Racist use of the peremptory challenge may explain why death-penalty jurisdictions erroneously convict defendants of color far more frequently than white defendants—nearly 60 percent of exonerated death defendants are persons of color. Wrongfully convicted defendants of color also spend more years in prison between conviction and exoneration than white defendants; innocent defendants of color spend an average of 10.3 years in prison, while innocent white defendants spend an average of 7.4 years in prison.

While state appellate courts appear frustrated with the growing evidence that prosecutors frequently engage in unlawful conduct, they are unwilling to overturn cases on grounds of racial bias. Instead, courts usually assess the relative weight of the racial prejudice to other evidence in the case and explain away racist conduct as having little relevance to the verdict. It is rare for a court to overturn a capital conviction based upon racism in the courtroom. The procedural safeguards established to diminish racism in capital sentencing are relatively ineffectual in practice with the U.S. "justice" system.

Sources: Death Penalty Information Center, *Innocence and the Death Penalty,* available at www.deathpenaltyinfo.org/article.php?did=412&scid=6; The Center for Public Integrity, *Harmful Error: Investigating America's Local Prosecutors,* available at www.publicintegrity.org/pm; Leonard Post, "Open Files Key in Reversals," *National Law Journal,* November 10, 2003, p. 4; Jodi Wilgoren, "Citing Issue of Fairness, Governor Clears Out Death Row in Illinois," *New York Times,* January 12, 2003, p. A1; James S. Liebman, Jeffrey Fagan, Valerie West, and Jonathan Lloyd, "Capital Attrition, Error Rates in Discretionary Powers of 'Public' Prosecutors in Historical Perspective," *American Criminal Law Review* 39, 1309 (2002); Richard Dieter, *Innocence and the Death Penalty: The Increasing Danger of Executing the Innocent,* Death Penalty Information Center (July 1997), available at www.deathpenaltyinfo.org/article.php?scid=45&did=292.

the criminal justice system.[151] The annual cost of corrections is at its highest in the country's history—$2.2 billion.[152]

The majority of those in prisons and jails are poor people and persons of color. Unemployed or low-wage workers disproportionately commit the kinds of crimes for which we most often send people to prison or jail. Inmate populations are disproportionately poor, black, and Latino. While blacks make up about 12 percent of the overall U.S. population, they are slightly more than 28 percent of all persons arrested for crime, 48 percent of prisoners in state and federal institutions, and 40 percent of jail inmates.[153] In fact, the jail incarceration rate for blacks is *five times* that for whites, nearly *three times* that for Latinos, and over *ten times* that for other groups.[154] African Americans constitute just 13 percent of drug users across the country, but they make up nearly 35 percent of those arrested for possession of drugs and three-fourths of those sentenced to prison for drug possession. Indeed, African Americans and Latinos constitute nearly 76 percent of those sent to state prison for drug possession.[155] As one commentator has stated, "Why are there so many minorities in prison when whites make up the overwhelming majority of those in possession of narcotics? The answer is simple: Minorities are the easiest people to catch and convict, according to police, prosecutors, and judges."[156]

Often political authorities describe the purpose of prison as punishing offenders. At other times, they describe prisons as deterring crime. Some mention that the more humane purpose of prisons is rehabilitating prisoners and restoring them as good citizens. Criminologists have returned recently to a debate over whether threat of severe sentences acts as a significant deterrent to crime. Research data from interviews with inmates indicate that many hate prison life, and unpleasantness of prison is for some a deterrent to crime. Criminals say the length of a possible jail term does not deter them from committing crimes but rather certainty of arrest does. Nationally, a substantial percentage of persons released from prison commit new crimes (*recidivism*). Recidivism rates in 15 states have indicated that police rearrest 68 percent of all former prisoners within three years and juries reconvict nearly 47 percent.[157] Recidivism rates, while varying by state, directly challenge the idea that imprisonment deters future criminality.[158]

The criminal justice system relies substantially on maximum-security prisons. Reformers pushing for smaller, nonpunitive treatment and rehabilitation centers have not made much headway. The large, walled maximum-security prisons often have more harmful than beneficial effects on inmates. The National Advisory Commission on Criminal Justice Standards and Goals concluded, "The failure of major institutions to reduce crime is incontestable. Recidivism rates are notoriously high. Institutions do succeed in punishing but do not deter. They protect the community, but that protection is only temporary."[159] Prisons make hardened criminals out of many; many learn how to be better criminals.

Most state prison systems have few rehabilitation programs. Only a small portion of the money for "corrections" goes for rehabilitation, including psychological counseling and work release programs. Most rehabilitation programs are small in scale, and most research on existing rehabilitation programs has showed weak or inconsistent effects on recidivism. One New York study that examined young men found that additional years of education gained while in prison did not significantly reduce the recidivism rate except for the top 7 percent of the prisoners in a special education program. Reviewing data on jobs held by prisoners after release, Martinson notes that job skill programs in prisons fail because they do not provide much help in finding jobs in the outside world. The education and therapy prisons provide are often poor, and poorly funded, and need much improvement before they will have positive effects. Moreover, much crime by the poor is not primarily a "disease" of individuals, but rather something generated by *societal* conditions. Given this reality, rehabilitating offenders during their prison experience should have modest effects at best, particularly for inmates who get a high school diploma or vocational training but cannot translate education into a decent-paying job outside.[160]

Large numbers of criminal offenders have retreated into drugs or alcohol to deal with their poverty-stricken lives. Well-crafted drug treatment programs in prisons can reduce recidivism. A leading Massachusetts judge, Paul J. Liacos, summarized the data: "Criminal justice treatment programs in New York, Oregon and Vancouver report 71 percent to 80 percent success rates. Treatment programs succeed because they cut recidivism, with such programs producing a decrease from the national average of an 80 percent recidivism rate to a recidivism rate of 23 percent to 50 percent."[161] This suggests the need for greater funding of well-crafted drug treatment and other substantial rehabilitation programs in prisons.

Overcrowding: A National Scandal

Severe overcrowding, resulting in large part from the harsh sentencing laws (often for personal crimes like use of small amounts of drugs), has led courts in many states to rule that existing prisons violate human rights or do not provide for minimal needs. Some consequences of prison overcrowding are a lack of privacy for inmates, deleterious physical conditions, inadequate sanitation, inappropriate food and recreation, and a reduction in staff supervision and medical services.[162] Prison overcrowding has forced numerous states to grant early release to their prisoners. Judges have ordered many jurisdictions to reduce their inmate populations, and in one recent case, a judge fined a state department of corrections $2.16 million for not relieving prison overcrowding.[163] Many prisoners have brought lawsuits against state prisons claiming that declining prison conditions violate their Eighth Amendment protection against cruel and unusual punishment.[164] Roughly 21 percent of all state and federal correctional facilities are under a court order or consent decree for the totality of conditions, to limit populations, or for specific conditions of confinement.[165]

Even so, many prisons and jails remain substantially over capacity. In 2000, 110,974 prisoners were in federal prisons, about 134 percent of the capacity of the prisons. Some 1.1 million prisoners reside in state facilities for an occupancy capacity rating of 101 percent, and private facilities housed 93,077 inmates with an occupancy capacity rating of 89 percent.[166] Some state prison systems operate at well above their capacities. In 1995, state prisons in Ohio were reportedly at 176 percent of their capacity, the worst percentage of any state.[167] Many state governments have launched large-scale prison construction programs totaling billions of dollars. In an increasing number of states, however, government fiscal crises fueled by rising prison costs have forced many legislators to rethink commitments to prison building as the main solution to crime.[168]

Prison Riots

Poor prison conditions can generate serious prison riots by human beings pushed to the limits. In terms of lives lost, the most serious riot took place in 1971 at the maximum-security prison in Attica, New York. The riot resulted in the deaths of 43 people, 39 of whom died in the state police gunfire it took to regain control of the prison. According to the New York State Special Commission on Attica, this prison was no worse than most U.S. maximum-security prisons. Overcrowded, Attica had 2,200 inmates at the time of the riot. Inadequately supported, the prison staff had little time for rehabilitation efforts; the central focus was on security and control. "Home" for Attica's male prisoners was a cell six feet wide, nine feet long, and seven feet high, in a nineteenth-century building. The report found personal and institutionalized racism to be a way of life at Attica. White prisoners got better jobs and generally better treatment from the white guards. During the riot, police bullets killed ten of the eleven hostages during the assault on the prison. At first politicians and prison officials refused to believe the autopsy reports. Examinations by additional pathologists, however, confirmed that the stories of "atrocities" committed by the prisoners were official lies and that the police attack on the prison was responsible for all but one of the hostage deaths as well as most inmate deaths.[169]

A federal judge in New York recently determined that 502 former inmates of Attica or their families are to receive from $6,500 to $125,000 each from the settlement of a lawsuit against the state for abuse during the riot. Although the original lawsuit in 1974 sought $100 million in damages, U.S. District Judge Michael Telesca settled the case for $8 million for the inmates and $4 million for their attorneys. In agreeing to the settlement, New York state admitted no wrongdoing.[170] Referring to the atrocities suffered by the inmates at Attica, Judge Telesca wrote in his decision that "the events of the morning of Sept. 13, 1971, left indelible impressions upon each of the plaintiffs after having been subjected to indignities and unwarranted brutal treatment. . . . [a]lthough they have left Attica, Attica has not left them."[171]

Similar violations of human rights like those at the Attica prison prevail in other prisons, and as a result, riots and protests remain pervasive in correctional facilities throughout the United States. In 1993, one guard and nine inmates were killed in an uprising at the Southern Ohio Correctional Facility near Lucasville. A study by state corrections officials reported that the warden's decision to force tuberculosis tests on 159 Muslim inmates who objected to the testing on religious grounds triggered the riot. Ongoing racial tensions and overcrowding at the prison were contributing factors. During the disturbance, some guards displayed white supremacist symbols. This exhibition of symbolic hatred played a role in perpetuating racial tensions since more than half of the inmates were black and fewer than 10 percent of Lucasville's guards were black.[172] Recent reports on the Lucasville prison riot reveal that the Ohio Department of Rehabilitation and Corrections settled a $2.4 million class-action lawsuit brought by the estates of nine inmates killed during the riot and by more than 300 other inmates who suffered mental distress and property damage during the unrest.[173]

In 1995, about 500 prisoners in a jail in Texarkana rioted for several hours. They were Colorado inmates held in Texas because of overcrowding in Colorado. Prisoners complained of poor conditions, of cells that held two dozen people in rows of bunk beds, with lights on all night. When inmates put up blankets to block the light, guards took them down, triggering a riot.[174] Additional riots occurred in other overcrowded prisons. One Memphis prison was 35 percent over capacity; Allenwood, Pennsylvania, and Greenville, Illinois, units were more than 40 percent over capacity; and a Talladega, Alabama, prison was 57 percent over capacity. One Memphis lawyer predicted worse riots in the future because of the "draconian" sentencing laws passed by Congress, and he described the federal system as an "American gulag," the term for the extremely oppressive prisons of the former Soviet Union.[175]

In the past decade, riots have taken place in Connecticut, California, New Mexico, and Texas. An interracial riot erupted at the Eagle Mountain Community Correctional Facility in California, leaving 54 inmates injured and 2 others stabbed and bludgeoned to death. Overcrowding in the state prison system has made inmate violence endemic. In some cases, prison guards deliberately foster violence among prisoners. Prosecutors recently won convictions of two guards at the Pelican Bay State Prison facility for recruiting inmates to attack other inmates. Corcoran State Prison in California was the most deadly prison in the country between 1989 and 1995 when guards wounded 43 inmates and shot to death 7 other inmates. Prosecutors have criminally charged a dozen Corcoran guards but have won no convictions.[176] Roughly 160,000 inmates are held in California prisons, nearly twice as many prisoners as the 33 state facilities are designed to hold—"a level of overcrowding that virtually guarantees violence."[177]

Following the Attica riot, numerous state legislatures passed laws attempting to improve conditions in prisons and to help prisoners realize their rights. But government cost-cutting pressures have fostered a return to a harshness favoring punishment over rehabilitation and creating an atmosphere similar to that preceding the Attica riot. At least 60 percent of state departments of corrections report that they have eliminated some inmate privileges, and correctional facilities in Alabama, Arizona, Florida, Iowa, Massachusetts, and Wisconsin have adopted old forms of the leg-ironed work crews—commonly known as "chain gangs."[178] The Southern Poverty Law Center has challenged such practices as a violation of the Eighth Amendment's protection against cruel and unusual punishment and the Fourteenth Amendment's due process guarantee.[179] The U.S. Supreme Court held in *Hope v. Pelzer* that officials at Limestone Prison in Alabama violate prisoners' rights against cruel and unusual punishment when they handcuff inmates to hitching posts as punishment for disruptive conduct. Officials exposed a shirtless inmate to the summer sun for seven hours while hitched to a post and gave him no bathroom breaks.[180] However, in other rulings supporting a trend to more punitive, "tough and cheap" prisons, a conservative Supreme Court has upheld the view that prison administrators have the right to control local prisons without court interference.[181]

Female Prisoners

The rate of female representation in correctional facilities has increased by over 400 percent since the early 1980s, and the likelihood of women going to prison at some time during their lifetimes is today six times greater than it was in the 1970s.[182] The number of women incarcerated in state and federal prisons rose to 97,491 inmates in 2002, with women now 7 percent of the prison population.[183] As with men, most women inmates are poor, poorly educated, and unskilled. The reason is often the same as for men: U.S. society has forced far too many working-class women to face the societal conditions of unemployment, poverty, and discrimination.[184] State and federal facilities imprison black females at a rate nearly 2.5 times greater than Latinas and at a rate 5.5 times greater than white females. The average female offender is not white, is between the ages of 25 and 29, and has never been married or is a single parent living alone with children.[185]

Gender discrimination and racial discrimination in the justice system account for much of the increase in the female prison population. White law enforcement officials are more likely to arrest and imprison women of color than white women for similar law violations. Stereotyping of women of color among white law enforcement officials increases likelihood of arrest and conviction of these women. On the average, women of color are poorer than white women and cannot easily raise bail. Women released on bail are less likely to suffer incarceration even if convicted, but (mostly white) judges are less likely to release women of color on bail or on their own recognizance. Judges are also more likely to convict women of color than white women for similar offenses and records.[186]

An Alternative Approach

In an article on the federal penitentiary in Lompoc, California, criminal justice expert Mark Fleisher argued that imprisonment under humane conditions can reduce the violent behavior of offenders within prisons, and in the outside world after prisoners are released. One crucial condition is the quality of life provided within the prison. Attica-like conditions breed violence. In the Lompoc penitentiary, inmate industrial work paid at moderate wages was a success. A prison factory employed 60 percent of the prisoners with many earning $300 to $500 monthly. (The rest earned *far less* doing prison chores.) While the manufacturing wages were very low by outside standards, they were far better than what was available in most prisons, and the jobs provided some learning possibilities. The provision of decent working conditions and an opportunity to save money made Lompoc prison a better place for everyone—including the public outside the prison. During the period studied, Lompoc had the lowest rate of serious violence among penitentiaries. As Fleisher notes:

> Staffers and inmates are more-or-less safe and satisfied. Criminals who long have proved themselves to be violent men generally live out their lives in a relatively peaceful environment. As ironic as it might sound, putting criminals in humane, industrial prisons like USP-Lompoc for very long terms gives them a chance to live decent lives and saves others from the pain and anguish of being their prey.[187]

The Federal Bureau of Prisons reports that inmates afforded an opportunity for job training while in prison are far less likely to return to prison after release. One study by the Community Connection Resource Center in San Diego discovered that among ex-prisoners who were able to find a long-term job after prison, not one had engaged in crime again. Sidekick Printers, a company in California, hired a number of ex-offenders as part of its employment policy; one-third of the firm's 40 employees, including some managers, had been convicted of law violations. The company generally found these employees highly motivated and to be good workers.[188] These examples illustrate the link between unemployment and underemployment and street crime, both inside and outside prisons. Effective employment is a way to prevent much crime.[189]

Yet California's general prison policy illustrates the blind-eye approach that some state officials take toward using prison time for the benefit of incarcerated populations. California's recidivism rate is high, with 70 percent of parolees returning to prison within 18 months. The Little Hoover Commission found that "by neglecting to use prison time to educate and train most inmates for jobs on the outside, the Department of Corrections operates a 'revolving door' system that all but assures parolees will resume a life of crime."[190] While 85 percent of the state's 160,000 inmates are incarcerated for crimes related to substance abuse, only 6 percent are in drug treatment programs. In addition, California has all but abandoned literacy and vocational training. Prisons provide only a few thousand inmates with reading and vocational job training, although state law requires that prisons provide literacy programs to all inmates lacking reading skills. Like all other states, California could dramatically reduce its annual $5.2 billion prison and parole costs by providing widespread and meaningful job training. As one commentator points out, though, "California's failure is rooted in its decision decades ago to pour money into bricks and mortar and not into the community- and prison-based educational, job and counseling programs that in other states keep inmates from returning to prison."[191]

SUMMARY

Reports of crime statistics and media discussions often focus excessively on certain violent street crimes, particularly murder, but these crimes are relatively uncommon. The media and politicians focus on street crimes disproportionately committed by working-class Americans, particularly poorer Americans. Crimes "in the suites"—corporate crimes—ordinarily receive less attention, except for a few most sensational cases like that of Enron.

In this chapter, we see that a variety of explanations have been offered to explain "crime in the streets," but the most important explanation from a power–conflict perspective accents the large-scale inequality, unemployment, racism, and poverty of this society. Job discrimination, underemployment, and unemployment, particularly that which confronts groups such as African and Latino Americans over many generations, are major factors in much poverty. The poverty of many working-class Americans links to much of the property and violent personal crime that politicians and the public worry about the most.

Illegal acts by the powerful have received less attention than crimes by the poor. Yet members of the capitalist class and other white-collar groups are also involved in serious crimes. Occupational crime is committed for individual benefit by people acting in their occupational roles. Corporate crime often involves a number of people violating laws in the larger company interest. Such crime is usually organized and typically has a long list of victims, from consumers and employees to competing businesses. One study found that 60 percent of the corporations studied had been charged with violations of federal law, with a significant number being repeatedly charged with violations of financial laws, trade practices laws, and safety laws. All corporate crimes together cost Americans hundreds of billions of dollars annually, far more than conventional street crimes such as robbery and burglary. An unknown but very large number of deaths—in the thousands—results each year from corporate law violations. Illegal corporate actions also affect the general moral climate of the United States.

Crimes by government officials also affect the moral climate. Punishment for felony crimes committed by top officials has tended to be light, as in the case of President Richard Nixon and the assistants to President Ronald Reagan. As serious have been law violations by policing agencies such as the FBI, including their illegal break-ins, wiretapping, and disruption of nonviolent protest organizations.

The operation of the criminal justice system has reflected a class and racial bias. Higher-income earners, especially those committing corporate crimes, tend to receive favored treatment in the system. Punishment for corporate and other crime by well-off Americans is often lenient. Access to legal counsel and to bail is rationed according to income. For the most part, local and federal prisons house the poor, the propertyless, and the powerless—those working people who commit a disproportionate number of the crimes for which we commonly incarcerate people. Most such criminals have suffered lives of poverty, unemployment, or racial discrimination. Many prison facilities are greatly overcrowded, with problems including brutality by guards, inadequate rehabilitation, and inadequate job-training programs. As a result, serious prison riots have erupted in the last few decades, and lawyers for prisoners charging that conditions in prisons are so bad that they constitute "cruel and unusual punishment" have brought dozens of court cases.

Many prison officials agree with calls for expanded educational, vocational, and work programs. If legislators will not provide job training and employment opportunities for unemployed and underemployed people outside prisons, they will not provide such programs inside prisons. Even though jurisdictions spend an estimated $25,000 to $35,000 annually to maintain each prisoner, business and allied political leaders seem to prefer expanded law enforcement expenditures rather than a full-employment economy that guarantees a job at a decent wage to every person who wants to work.

Racial discrimination, both individual and institutionalized, is part of the criminal justice system. Racism pervades the recurring problems of police malpractice in many communities; police brutality precipitated major riots from New York in the 1960s to Miami in the 1980s and Los Angeles in the 1990s. Social scientists and legal scholars find major discrimination in drug laws, in the sentencing practices of some courts, in the treatment of inmates of color in many prisons, and in the disparate application of capital punishment. The racial and class dimensions of the U.S. "injustice system" are now quite conspicuous.

STUDY QUESTIONS

1. As with unemployment, the U.S. government's data collectors routinely overlook several important categories relevant to the measurement of crime. Identify some of the major types of crime that the FBI's *Uniform Crime Reports* do not cover.

2. Explanations of the problem of "conventional" crime take varied forms. Contrast and compare the critical power–conflict position with the conservative views and theories on solutions to the problem of street crime.

3. Despite its relative frequency and its high dollar costs, corporate crime resists sustained public scrutiny. Identify some of the reasons most people usually focus on street crime rather than on corporate crime.

4. U.S. police and security forces have sometimes abridged the civil liberties of citizens, especially of those critical of the government. Cite examples of when this has occurred, including activities reported in the mass media.

5. Describe how the social backgrounds of most judges tend to be different from those of most arrested criminals, and explain the practical implications that such differences have for many defendants in the criminal justice system.

ENDNOTES

1. Quoted in Paul J. Liacos, "Challenges Many, but 'Time Is on Our Side,'" *Massachusetts Lawyers Weekly,* January 22, 1996, p. 11.

2. Cited by Allan Silver, "The Demand for Order in Civil Society," David J. Bordua, ed., *The Police: Six Sociological Essays* (New York: John Wiley, 1967), p. 2.

3. U.S. Department of Justice, *Sourcebook of Criminal Justice Statistics Online,* 2002, Table 2.35, available at www.albany.edu/sourcebook/pdf/t235.pdf.

4. Joseph J. Senna and Larry J. Siegel, *Introduction to Criminal Justice* (Belmont, California: Wadsworth, 1999), p. 424.

5. U.S. Department of Justice, *Sourcebook of Criminal Justice Statistics 2002,* Table 2.41, available at www.albany.edu/sourcebook/pdf/t241.pdf.

6. Philip J. Schwarz, *Twice Condemned: Slaves and the Criminal Laws of Virginia, 1705–1865* (New Jersey: The Lawbook Exchange, Ltd., 1988), p. 119.

7. U.S. Department of Justice, Federal Bureau of Investigation, *Crime in the United States, 2000,* Table 29, p. 216.

8. Michael Tonry, "Rethinking Unthinkable Punishment Policies in America," *University of California Los Angeles Law Review* 46, 1999, pp. 1,751–91; Richard Dvorak, "Cracking the Code: 'De-Coding' Colorblind Slurs During the Congressional Crack Cocaine Debates," *Michigan Journal of Race and Law* 5, 2000, pp. 611–62.

9. Frances A. Allen, "The Borderland of Criminal Law," *Social Service Review* 32 (June 1958): 108–109. In this section we draw on Clayton Hughes, *Crime and Criminalization* (New York: Praeger, 1974), pp. 17–23.

10. Richard Quinney, *Criminology,* 2nd. ed. (Boston: Little, Brown, 1979), pp. 166–67, 221–25, 400–408, and *passim.*

11. U.S. Department of Justice, Federal Bureau of Investigation, *Crime in the United States, 2000,* Table 29, p. 216.

12. Ibid.

13. U.S. Department of Justice, *Criminal Victimization, 2002,* available at www.ojp.usdoj.gov/bjs/pub/pdf/cv02.pdf.

14. U.S. Department of Justice, *Criminal Victimization, 2002,* available at www.ojp.usdoj.gov/bjs/pub/pdf/cv02.pdf.

15. U.S. Department of Justice, *Criminal Victimization 2001: Changes 2000–01 with Trends 1993–2001,* available at www.ojp.usdoj/bjs/pub/pdf/cu01.pdf.

16. For a comparison of the Uniform Crime Reports and the National Crime Victimization Survey, see U.S. Department of Justice, "The Nation's Two Crime Measures," available at www.ojp.usdoj.gov/bjs/pub/html/ntcm.htm.

17. U.S. Department of Justice, *Sourcebook of Criminal Justice Statistics Online,* Table 2.70, available at www.albany.edu/sourcebook/1995/pdf/t270.pdf.

18. U.S. Department of Justice, *Sourcebook of Criminal Justice Statistics 2001,* Table 3.114, p. 228, available at www.albany.edu/sourcebook/1995/pdf/t3114.pdf.

19. U.S. Department of Justice, *Law Enforcement Officers Killed and Assaulted* (LEOKA), 2001, available at www.fbi.gov/ucr/killed/2001leoka.pdf.

20. U.S. Department of Justice, *Sourcebook of Criminal Justice Statistics 2001,* Table 2.79, p. 151, available at www.albany.edu/sourcebook/1995/pdf/t279.pdf; U.S. Department of Justice, *Sourcebook of Criminal Justice Statistics 2001,* Table 2.83, pp. 154, 155, available at www.albany.edu/sourcebook/1995/pdf/t283.pdf.

21. U.S. Department of Justice, *Sourcebook of Criminal Justice Statistics Online,* Table 2.78, available at www.albany.edu/sourcebook/1995/pdf/t278.pdf; U.S. Department of Justice, *Sourcebook of Criminal Justice Statistics 2001,* Table 2.82, p. 153, available at www.albany.edu/sourcebook/1995/pdf/t282.pdf.

22. U.S. Department of Justice, *Sourcebook of Criminal Justice Statistics Online,* Table 3.130, available at www.albany.edu/sourcebook/1995/pdf/t3130.pdf.

23. U.S. Department of Justice, *Sourcebook of Criminal Justice Statistics Online,* Table 3.16, available at www.albany.edu/sourcebook/1995/pdf/t316.pdf.

24. U.S. Department of Justice, *Sourcebook of Criminal Justice Statistics Online,* Table 5.42, available at www.albany.edu/sourcebook/1995/pdf/t542.pdf.

25. U.S. Department of Justice, *Criminal Victimization in the United States, 2001 Statistical Tables,* Table 44, available at www.ojp.usdoj.gov/bjs/pub/pdf/cvus01.pdf.

26. See generally Herbert A. Johnson and Nancy Travis Wolfe, *History of Criminal Justice,* 3rd. ed. (Cincinnati, Oh.: Anderson Publishing Company, 2003).

27. Michael Hakeem, "A Critique of the Psychiatric Approach to Crime and Correction," *Law and Contemporary Problems* 23 (Autumn 1958), pp. 650–82. For a critical discussion of psychological theories, see Quinney, *Criminology,* pp. 8–10.

28. Edwin H. Sutherland, *White Collar Crime* (New York: Holt, Rinehart & Winston, 1949), pp. 243–46.

29. Albert K. Cohen, *Delinquent Boys* (New York: Free Press, 1955), pp. 121–63.

30. Richard A. Cloward and Lloyd E. Ohlin, *Delinquency and Opportunity* (New York: Free Press, 1960), p. 151.

31. Travis Hirschi, *Causes of Delinquency* (Berkeley: University of California Press, 1969); see also George B. Vold and Thomas J. Bernard, *Theoretical Criminology* (New York: Oxford University Press, 1986), pp. 232–46.

32. Judith Blau and Peter Blau, "The Cost of Inequality: Metropolitan Structure and Violent Crime," *American Sociological Review* 47 (1982): 114–29.

33. Richard Morin, "The Surprising Face of Crime in America," *Cleveland Plain Dealer,* October 25, 1994, p. B11.

34. U.S. Department of Justice, *Sourcebook of Criminal Justice Statistics 2001,* Table 6.29, p. 499, available at www.albany.edu/sourcebook/1995/pdf/t629.pdf.

35. Vold and Bernard, *Theoretical Criminology,* pp. 189–200.

36. Mark Warr, "America's Perceptions of Crime and Punishment," in Joseph F. Sheley, ed., *Criminology: A Contemporary Handbook* (Belmont, Calif.: Wadsworth, 1991).

37. Dane Archer and Rosemary Gartner, *Violence and Crime in Cross-National Perspective* (New Haven, Conn.: Yale University Press, 1984), pp. 63–96.

38. Vicki Kemper, "Biting the Bullet," *Common Cause,* Winter 1992, p. 22.

39. Ibid., p. 18.

40. Sutherland, *White Collar Crime,* p. 9.
41. Marshall B. Clinard and Peter C. Yeager, *Corporate Crime* (New York: Free Press, 1980), p. 18; Marshall Clinard, *Corporate Corruption: The Abuse of Power* (New York: Praeger, 1990), pp. 1–20.
42. Charles E. Silberman, *Criminal Violence, Criminal Justice* (New York: Random House, 1980), p. 51.
43. Tom Witom, "Sears Settles Suits Alleging Overcharges on Car Repairs," *Reuter Business Report,* September 2, 1992; "Sears Agrees to Revise Auto-Repair Practices," *New York Times,* October 30, 1992, p. D3.
44. See *Business Week,* January 31, 1977, p. 177; quotation from Carl Madden, "Forces which Influence Ethical Behavior," in *The Ethics of Corporate Conduct* (Englewood Cliffs, N.J.: Prentice Hall, 1977), p. 66.
45. Gilbert Geis, "The Heavy Electrical Equipment Antitrust Cases of 1961," in Gilbert Geis and Robert F. Meier, eds. *White Collar Crime,* rev. ed. (New York: Free Press, 1977), pp. 119–20.
46. Clinard and Yeager, *Corporate Crime,* pp. 112–19.
47. "Trading Places," *Time,* December 28, 1987, p. 63; Jack Egan, Andrea Gabor, and Eva Pomice, "Throwing the Book at Drexel," *U.S. News & World Report,* September 19, 1988, pp. 41–42; "Milken Out of Jail After 22 Months," *New York Times,* January 5, 1993, p. D6.
48. Ronald Sullivan, "Con Ed Admits to Conspiracy to Cover Up Asbestos in Blast," *New York Times,* November 1, 1994, p. A1; James C. McKinley, Jr., "Con Ed Fined and Sentenced to Monitoring for Asbestos Cover-up," *New York Times,* April 22, 1995, p. 25.
49. Alan K. Reichert, M. Lockett, and R. Rao, "The Impact of Illegal Business Activity on Shareholder Returns," *Financial Review* 31(1), February 1, 1996.
50. *United States v. Martha Stewart and Peter Bacanovic,* available at www.corporatecrimereporter. com/steawart_bacano_indictment.pdf.
51. "Corporate Scandals," *Washington Post,* available at www.washingtonpost.com/wp-dyn/business/specials/energy/enron.
52. Elkan Abramowitz, "A Mid-Term Interview with Mary Jo White," *New York Times,* May 2, 1995, p. 3.
53. Carolyn Said, "Boom Trials: The Current High Profile Courtroom Dramas Beg the Question: Will Prosecutions of White-Collar Crimes Change the System," *San Francisco Chronicle,* October 5, 2003.
54. Patsy A. Klaus, "The Costs of Crime to Victims," Bureau of Justice Statistics Crime Data Brief, U.S. Department of Justice, February 1994, available at www.ojp.usdoj.gov/bjs/pub/ascii/coctv.txt.
55. Lee Drutman, "Corporate Crime Acts Like a Thief in the Night," *Los Angeles Times* (November 4, 2003), p. B13.
56. Stephen Pizzo, Mary Fricker, and Paul Muolo, *Inside Job: The Looting of America's Savings and Loans* (New York: McGraw-Hill, 1989), pp. 4, 8; John Miller, "Spring Cleaning at the FDIC: Banking Crisis Redux," *Dollars & Sense,* January–February 1993, p. 7.
57. Lee Drutman, "Corporate Crime Acts Like a Thief in the Night," *Los Angeles Times* (November 4, 2003), p. B13.
58. Russell Mokhiber, *Corporate Crime and Violence* (San Francisco: Sierra Club Books, 1988), pp. 3–6, 16–17.
59. "Testimony of Ann Brown, Chairman, U.S. Consumer Product Safety Commission Submitted Before the VA, HUD, and Independent Agencies Appropriations Subcommittee," Federal News Service, February 27, 1995.
60. Ibid.
61. Robert C. Frederiksen, "AFL-CIO Campaign Aims to Save OSHA," *Providence Journal-Bulletin,* October 18, 1995, p. F1; "Testimony March 22, 1994, John J. Sweeney, International President, Service Employees International Union, Before the Committee on Labor and Human Resources, U.S. Senate," Federal Document Clearing House Congressional Testimony, March 22, 1994.
62. Quoted in Frederiksen, "AFL-CIO Campaign Aims to Save OSHA," p. F1.
63. See Russell Mokhiber, "Don't Buy the Party Line on Corporate Crime," *Legal Times,* November 14, 1994, p. 28.
64. Christopher Stone, *Where the Law Ends* (New York: Harper and Row, 1975), p. xi.
65. *See* Clinard and Yeager, *Corporate Crime,* pp. 11–12.
66. Steven Box, *Power, Crime, and Mystification* (London: Tavistock, 1983), pp. 9–15.
67. Ibid., p. 5.
68. Clinard and Yeager, *Corporate Crime,* pp. 124–25.
69. "Corporate Crime," *U.S. News & World Report,* pp. 25–28.

70. Leonard Buder, "2 Former Executives of Beech-Nut Guilty in Phony Juice Case," *New York Times,* February 18, 1988, p. 1.
71. Mokhiber, "Don't Buy the Party Line on Corporate Crime," p. 28.
72. Robert G. Knowles, "Lawyer Urges Tough Corporate Pollution Governance," *National Underwriter,* February 20, 1995, p. 7.
73. Todd Woody, "Chemical Reaction; Despite Overwhelming Evidence that Unocal Managers Allowed a Harmful Chemical to Contaminate the Town of Crockett, They Have So Far Escaped Prosecution," *The Recorder,* October 4, 1995, p. 1.
74. Donald R. Cressey, *Other People's Money: The Social Psychology of Embezzlement* (New York: Free Press, 1953).
75. William C. Croft, "High Price for White-Collar Crime," *Chicago Tribune,* September 7, 1994, p. 16.
76. Ibid.
77. See Mark Moore, "Notes Toward a National Strategy to Deal with White-Collar Crime," in Herbert Edelhertz and Charles Rogovin, eds., *A National Strategy for Containing White-Collar Crime* (Massachusetts: Lexington Books, 1980), pp. 32–44.
78. National Institute for Occupational Safety and Health, *Occupational Violence,* available at www.cdc.gov/niosh/injury/traumaviolence.html.
79. National Institute for Occupational Safety and Health, *Violence: Occupational Hazards in Hospitals,* available at www.cdc.gov/niosh/2002–101.html#whatare.
80. National Institute for Occupational Safety and Health, *Homicide in the Workplace,* available at www.cdc.gov/niosh/violhomi.html; U.S. Department of Justice, *Sourcebook of Criminal Justice Statistics Online,* Table 3.142, available at www.albany.edu/sourcebook/1995/pdf/t3142.pdf.
81. "Testimony March 22, 1994, John J. Sweeney," Federal Document Clearing House.
82. "Workplace Shooter Described as 'Angry' Man," CNN, available at www.cnn.com/2003/US/South/07/08/plant.shoot/index.html.
83. Workplace Violence Research Institute, "The Cost of Workplace Violence to American Business," available at noworkviolence.com/articles/cost_of_workplace_violence.htm.
84. This and the next paragraph draw on A. James Reichley, "Getting at the Roots at Watergate," in M. David Ermann and Richard J. Lundman, eds., *Corporate and Governmental Deviance* (New York: Oxford University Press, 1978), pp. 186–93; Gilbert Geis and Robert F. Meier, "Political White-Collar Crime," in Geis and Meier, eds., *White Collar Crime,* pp. 209–210.
85. William S. Cohen and George J. Mitchell, *Men of Zeal: A Candid Inside Story of the Iran-Contra Hearings* (New York: Viking Penguin, 1988), p. 311; see also pp. xix–xxxi, 277–310.
86. Quoted in Stephen Pizzo, Mary Fricker, and Kevin Hogan, "Shredded Justice," *Mother Jones,* January–February 1993, p. 19.
87. Kenneth B. Noble, "2 Companies Pay Huge Election Law Fine," *New York Times,* December 24, 1995, p. 12.
88. "Rep. Waldholtz Says She Will not Run for Re-election to House Seat," *Daily Report for Executives,* March 6, 1996, p. F44.
89. Bob Kerrey, "Floundering Campaign," Federal Document Clearing House, Congressional Press Releases, March 5, 1996.
90. "1996 Fund-Raising Scandals Bring Stiff Penalty Politics," *Los Angeles Times* (September 21, 2002), p. A23.
91. "Dirty Money: Corporate Criminal Donations to the Two Major Parties," *Corporate Crime Reporter,* July 3, 2003, available at www.corporatecrimereporter.com/ccrreport.pdf.
92. Nelson Blackstock, *COINTELPRO* (New York: Vintage Books, 1976), pp. 6–23.
93. Tamar Jacoby, "Going After Dissidents," *Newsweek,* February 8, 1988, p. 29; David Corn and Jefferson Morley, "Beltway Bandits," *The Nation,* March 12, 1988, p. 332; "The FBI's Sorry Story," *Time,* September 26, 1988, p. 31.
94. Letter from NHTSA Associate Administrator William Boehly to the Environmental Protection Agency, October 25, 1991.
95. This paragraph is based on information in letters and documents provided to the authors by Clarence M. Ditlow, Executive Director, Center for Auto Safety, Washington, D.C., and a February 1996 interview with Clarence M. Ditlow.
96. "Bush's Ruling Class," *Common Cause,* April–May–June 1992, pp. 11–12; quotation on p. 12.
97. Ibid., p. 11.
98. Donald R. Cressey, *Theft of a Nation* (New York: Harper and Row, 1969), p. xi; Silberman, *Criminal Violence, Criminal Justice,* pp. 134–35.
99. Dan Whitcomb, "Detective Says He Knows Names of Fleiss Customers," Reuters News Service, November 15, 1994.

100. Jonathan Wells and Maggie Mulvihill, "Pack of Lies: House Report—FBI Helped Hub Mobsters 'Destroy' Lives," *The Boston Herald* (November 21, 2003), p. 001; "The FBI's Skeletons, *The Boston Globe* (November 22, 2003); Ralph Ranalli, "FBI Information System Called a Failure, House Report Finds No Proof Against Bulger," *The Boston Globe* (November 21, 2003), p. A18.

101. Albert Szymanski, *The Capitalist State and the Politics of Class* (Cambridge, Ma.: Winthrop, 1978), p. 179.

102. U.S. Department of Justice, *Sourcebook of Criminal Justice Statistics Online,* Table 1.15 available at www.albany.edu/sourcebook/1995/pdf/t115.pdf.

103. See, for example, Larry K. Gaines, Victor E. Kappeler, and Joseph B. Vaughn, *Policing in America* (Cincinnati, Oh.: Anderson Publishing Company, 1999), pp. 517–43.

104. Quoted in Kemper, "Biting the Bullet," p. 22.

105. On discretion, see Frank Schmalleger, *Criminal Justice Today* (Upper Saddle River, N.J.: Prentice Hall, 2003), pp. 224–25.

106. Evelyn L. Parks, "From Constabulary to Police Society: Implications for Social Control," in John F. Galliher and James L. McCartney, eds., *Criminology* (Homewood, Ill.: Dorsey Press, 1977), pp. 216–17; the studies are cited in John F. Galliher and James L. McCartney, "The Administration of Justice: The Police," in Ibid., pp. 180, 185.

107. U.S. Department of Justice, *Criminal Victimization in the United States, 2002,* available at www.ojp.usdoj.gov/bjs/pub/pdf/cv02.pdf.

108. See Joe R. Feagin and Clairece Feagin, *Racial and Ethnic Relations,* 5th ed. (Englewood Cliffs, N.J.: Prentice Hall, 1996), pp. 247–48.

109. See, for example, Kimberly Trone, "Traffic Stops Soar 72 Percent," *Riverside Press-Enterprise,* May 5, 2004, pp. B1, B7.

110. James E. Blackwell, *The Black Community* (New York: HarperCollins, 1991), pp. 456–57.

111. "Crackin' Down on Crack and Crime," *Crisis,* October 1995, pp. 18–20. In contrast to such claims, see David E. Barlow and Melissa Hickman Barlow, "Cultural Diversity Training in Criminal Justice," in *Sources: Notable Selections in Crime, Criminology, and Criminal Justice,* David V. Baker and Richard P. Davin, eds. (Guilford, Conn.: McGraw-Hill/Dushkin, 2001), pp. 203–16.

112. Silberman, *Criminal Violence, Criminal Justice,* pp. 353–54.

113. "More People in Prison Despite Drop in Crime," *Los Angeles Times,* July 28, 2003, p. A9.

114. U.S. Department of Justice, *Prison Statistics—Summary of Findings,* available at www.ojp.usdoj.gov/bjs/prisons.htm#top, U.S. Department of Justice, *Prison and Jail Inmates at Midyear 2004,* available at www.ojp.usdoj.gov/bjs/pub/pdf/pjim04.pdf.

115. Sarah Lawrence and Jeremy Travis, *The New Landscape of Imprisonment: Mapping America's Prison Expansion,* April 2004, The Urban Institute, available at www.urban.org/UploadedPDF/410994_mapping_prisons.pdf.

116. U.S. Department of Justice, *Prison Statistics—Summary of Findings.*

117. Marc Mauer, *Americans Behind Bars: Comparison of International Rates of Incarceration* (Washington, D.C.: The Sentencing Project, 1991), p. 16.

118. Susan Schmidt, "Patriot Act Misunderstood, Senators Say," *Washington Post* (October 22, 2003) p. A04.

119. Ibid., pp. 13–14.

120. See New York State Special Commission on Attica, *Attica* (New York: Bantam Books, 1972), pp. 1–31.

121. James Bradshaw, "Legal Aid Panel Reports Limited Success," *Columbus Dispatch,* August 11, 1994, p. 4C.

122. Leon Mayhew and Albert Reiss, "The Social Organization of Legal Contacts," *American Sociological Review* 34 (June 1969): 309–11.

123. Kenneth Mann, Stanton Wheeler, and Austin Sarat, "Sentencing the White-Collar Offender," *American Criminal Law Review* 17 (Spring 1980): 486.

124. John F. Galliher and James L. McCartney, "The Social Basis of Law," in Galliher and McCartney, eds., *Criminology,* pp. 63–64.

125. U.S. Department of Justice, *Sourcebook of Criminal Justice Statistics 2001,* Table 6.82, p. 536, available at www.albany.edu/sourcebook/1995/pdf/t682.pdf; see also Death Penalty Information Center, *Executions by Year,* available at www.deathpenaltyinfo.org/article.php?scid=8&did=146.

126. *Coker v. Georgia,* 433 U.S. 584 (1977); U.S. Department of Justice, *Sourcebook of Criminal Justice Statistics 2001,* Table 6.82, p. 536, available at www.albany.edu/sourcebook/1995/pdf/t682.pdf.

127. Manning Marable, *How Capitalism Underdeveloped Black America: Problems in Race, Political Economy and Society* (Boston: South End Press, 1983), p. 121.

128. Ronald Barri Flowers, *Minorities and Criminality* (New York: Greenwood Press, 1988), p. 169.

129. *Gregg v. Georgia,* 428 U.S. 153 (1976); *Jurek v. Texas,* 428 U.S. 262 (1976); *Proffit v. Florida,* 428 U.S. 242 (1976); *Woodson v. North Carolina,* 428 U.S. 280 (1976); *Roberts v. Louisiana,* 428 U.S. 325 (1976).

130. *McCleskey v. Kemp,* 481 U.S. 279 (1987).

131. David C. Baldus, Charles Pulaski, and George Woodworth, "Comparative Review of Death Sentences: An Empirical Study of the Georgia Experience," *Journal of Criminal Law and Criminology* 74, 1983, pp. 661, 709–710.

132. *McCleskey v. Kemp.*

133. Deborah Fins, *Death Row U.S.A.: A Quarterly Report by the Criminal Justice Project of the NAACP Legal Defense and Education Fund, Inc.,* available at www.deathpenaltyinfo.org/DEATHROWUSArecent.pdf.

134. David C. Baldus, George G. Woodworth, and Charles A. Pulaski, Jr., *Equal Justice and the Death Penalty: A Legal and Empirical Analysis* (Boston: Northeastern University Press, 1990), p. 316.

135. Death Penalty Information Center, *Persons Executed for Interracial Murders,* available at www.deathpenaltyinfo.org/article.php?scid=5&did=184.

136. Deborah Fins, *Death Row U.S.A.;* see also John H. Blume, Theodore Eisenberg, and Martin T. Wells, "Explaining Death Row's Population and Racial Composition," *Journal of Empirical Legal Studies* 1 (2004): 165.

137. "Carter Symposium on the Death Penalty," *Georgia State University Law Review* 14 (1997): 329.

138. U.S. Department of Justice, *Hispanic Victims of Violent Crime, 1993–2000,* available at www.ojp.usdoj.gov/bjs/pub/pdf/hvvc00.pdf.

139. For a more comprehensive discussion of these legal strategies, see David V. Baker, "Purposeful Discrimination in Capital Sentencing," *Journal of Law and Social Challenges* 5 (2003): 189–223.

140. Death Penalty Information Center, *Number of Executions by State and Region Since 1976,* Washington, D.C., available at www.deathpenaltyinfo.org/article.php?scid=8&did=186; Death Penalty Information Center, *U.S. Military Death Penalty,* Washington, D.C., available at www.deathpenaltyinfo.org/article.php?did=180&scid=32; Death Penalty Information Center, *The Federal Death Penalty,* Washington D.C., available at www.deathpenaltyinfo.org/article.php?scid=29&did=147.

141. Gallup Poll Analysis, May 19, 2003, available at www.deathpenaltyinfo.org/article.php?scid=23&did=592.

142. U.S. Department of Justice, *Sourcebook of Criminal Justice Statistics 2001,* Table 2.66, p. 144, available at www.albany.edu/sourcebook/1995/pdf/t266.pdf.

143. Hugo Adam Bedau, *The Death Penalty in America,* 3rd ed. (New York: Oxford University Press, 1982), pp. 173–80.

144. Lawrence R. Klein, Brian Forst, and Victor Filatov, "The Deterrent Effect of Capital Punishment: An Assessment of the Estimates," in Alfred Blumstein, Jacqueline Cohen, and Daniel Nagin, eds., *Deterrence and Incapacitation: Estimating the Effects of Criminal Sanctions on Crime Rates* (Washington, D.C.: National Academy of Sciences, 1978), pp. 336–60.

145. See Amnesty International, *United States of America: Arbitrary, Discriminatory, and Cruel: An Aide-Memoire to 25-Years of Judicial Killing,* 2002, available at web.amnesty.org/library/print/ENGAMR510032002.

146. National Coalition to Abolish the Death Penalty, *Millions to Kill, Penny to Heal,* available at www.ncadp.org/html/fact3.html.

147. Robert L. Spangenberg and Elizabeth R. Walsh, "Capital Punishment or Life Imprisonment? Some Cost Considerations," *Loyola of Los Angeles Law Review* 23, 1989, pp. 45–58.

148. See Death Penalty Information Center, *Limiting the Death Penalty,* available at deathpenaltyinfo.org/article.php?scid=15&did=411#1996.

149. "Faster Death Penalty Appeals Rejected," *Los Angeles Times,* January 25, 2000.

150. U.S. Department of Justice, Bureau of Justice Statistics, *Prison and Jail Inmates at Midyear 2004,* available at www.ojp.usdoj.gov/bjs/pub/pdf/pjim04.pdf.

151. U.S. Department of Justice, *Sourcebook of Criminal Justice Statistics Online,* Table 6.1, available at www.albany.edu/sourcebook/1995/pdf/t61.pdf.

152. U.S. Department of Justice, *Sourcebook of Criminal Justice Statistics Online,* Table 1.15 available at www.albany.edu/sourcebook/1995/pdf/t115.pdf.

153. U.S. Department of Justice, *Sourcebook of Criminal Justice Statistics Online,* Table 4.10, available at www.albany.edu/sourcebook/1995/pdf/t410.pdf; U.S. Department of Justice, Bureau of Jus-

tice Statistics, *Prison and Jail Inmates at Midyear 2004,* available at www.ojp.usdoj.gov/bjs/pub/pdf/pjim04.pdf.

154. U.S. Department of Justice, Bureau of Justice Statistics, *Prison and Jail Inmates at Midyear 2004,* available at www.ojp.usdoj.gov/bjs/pub/pdf/pjim04.pdf.
155. U.S. Department of Justice, *Prisoners in 2002,* Table 15, available at www.ojp.usdoj.gov/bjs/pub/pdf/p02.pdf.
156. Fredrick McKissack, Jr., "Justice Not Colorblind," *Times Union,* Albany, N.Y., December 10, 1995, p. E1; Gwenn Nettler, *Explaining Crime* (New York: McGraw-Hill, 1984), p. 139.
157. U.S. Department of Justice, *Sourcebook of Criminal Justice Statistics 2001,* p. 506, Table 6.42, available at www.albany.edu/sourcebook/1995/pdf/t642.pdf.
158. Daniel Glaser, *The Effectiveness of a Prison and Parole System* (New York: Bobbs-Merrill, 1964), pp. 481–82; Leon Radzinowicz and Joan King, *The Growth of Crime* (New York: Basic Books, 1977), pp. 126–51.
159. Quoted in Gordon Hawkins, *The Prison* (Chicago: University of Chicago Press, 1976), p. 45.
160. Ibid., p. 50; Robert Martinson, "What Works? Questions and Answers about Prison Reform," *Public Interest* 35 (Spring 1974): 22–50.
161. Liacos, "Challenges Many," p. 11.
162. Susanna Y. Chung, "Prison Overcrowding: Standards in Determining Eighth Amendment Violations," *Fordham Law Review* 68, 2000, pp. 2,351–400.
163. "Alabama Fined for Crowded Prisons," *Corrections Professional* 7(19) July 12, 2002.
164. Susanna Y. Chung, "Prison Overcrowding: Standards in Determining Eighth Amendment Violations," *Fordham Law Review* 68, 2000, pp. 2,351–400.
165. U.S. Department of Justice, *Census of State and Federal Correctional Facilities, 2000,* available at www.ojp.usdoj.gov/bjs/pub/pdf/csfcf00.pdf.
166. U.S. Department of Justice, *Census of State and Federal Correctional Facilities, 2000,* available at www.ojp.usdoj.gov/bjs/pub/pdf/csfcf00.pdf.
167. Kristen Delguzzi, "Plea for New Jail Prompts Study," *Cincinnati Enquirer,* August 31, 1995, p. C2.
168. Charles Sullivan, "Prison Reform Finally Arrives," *Texas Observer,* July 8, 1983, pp. 6–8.
169. New York State Special Commission on Attica, *Attica,* pp. xiv, 4, 33–34, 39–40, 455–64.
170. "Court Decides How to Split $8 Million Awarded Attica Inmates," *Corrections Professional* 6(2), September 22, 2000.
171. Ibid.
172. "The Killing Ground," *Newsweek,* February 18, 1980, pp. 66–75; Kristen Delguzzi, "Ohio Prison Riot," *Gannett News Service,* June 10, 1993.
173. "Ohio DRC Settles Case Related to Lucasville Riot," *Corrections Professional* 2(12), March 7, 1997; "Ohio Inmates Win Settlement Over 1993 Lucasville Riot," *Corrections Professional,* 5(14), April 7, 2000.
174. John Sanko, "Colorado Prisoners Riot for 2 Hours in Texas Jail: No Injuries Reported in Melee," *Rocky Mountain News,* December 12, 1995, p. 6A.
175. Anna Davis, "Crack Sentences: How Long Is Fair?" *Memphis Commercial Appeal,* October 29, 1995, p. 1A.
176. Brian Skoloff, "California Prison Employees Found not Responsible for Inmate's Rape," Associated Press (October 22, 2003).
177. See Vince Beiser, "Sentenced to Death by Doing Time," *Los Angeles Times* (November 4, 2003), p. B13.
178. Peter Morrison, "Punishment on the Cheap: Arizona: A 'Lock 'em Up, Throw Away the Key' State," *National Law Journal,* August 21, 1995, p. A23; Peter Morrison, "The New Chain Gang," *National Law Journal,* August 21, 1995, p. A1.
179. *Austin v. James,* 95-T-637-N.
180. "High Court Strips CO of Qualified Immunity in Cruelty Case," *Corrections Professional* 7(19), July 12, 2002.
181. *Sandin v. Conner,* 63 U.S.L.W. 4601 (1995), and *Farmer v. Brennan,* 114 S. Ct. 1970 (1994).
182. U.S. Department of Justice, Bureau of Justice Statistics, *Prevalence of Imprisonment in the U.S. Population, 1974–2001,* August 2003, available at www.ojp.usdoj.gov/bjs/pub/pdf/piusp01.pdf.
183. U.S. Department of Justice, *Sourcebook of Criminal Justice Statistics Online,* 2002, Table 6.35, available at www.albany.edu/sourcebook/1995/pdf/t635.pdf.
184. D. Stanley Eitzen and Maxine Baca-Zinn, *Social Problems* (Needham Heights, Mass.: Allyn and Bacon, 1992), p. 488.

185. American Correctional Association, *The Female Offender: What Does the Future Hold?* (1990).
186. See generally, Coramae Richey Mann, "Minority and Female: A Criminal Justice Double Bind," *Social Justice* 16, 1989, pp. 95–108.
187. Mark S. Fleisher, "The Costly Business of Warehousing Violent Criminals," *USA Today,* March 18, 1989, pp. 60–62.
188. Elliot King, "San Diego County Firms Give Ex-Convicts 2nd Chance at Life on Outside," *Los Angeles Times,* August 14, 1988, part 4, p. 8.
189. See Thomas Hanlon, David Nurco, Richard Bateman, and Kevin O'Brady, "The Response of Drug Abuser Parolees to a Combination of Treatment and Intensive Supervision," *The Prison Journal* 78, 1998, pp. 31–45.
190. Jenifer Warren, "Panel Calls Prisons a Failure," *Los Angeles Times* (November 14, 2003), pp. B1, B8.
191. Editorial, "State Prisons' Revolving Door: A Siege Against Success," *Los Angeles Times* (November 23, 2003), p. M4; Editorial, "State Prisons Revolving Door: The Guards Own the Gates," *Los Angeles Times* (November 24, 2004), p. B10.

chapter **9**

Problems Labeled "Deviance": Homelessness, Mental Illness, Drug Addiction, and Homosexuality

Many academic departments in colleges and universities have titled social science courses on social problems in U.S. society "deviance" courses, and many other college courses have made substantial use of the concept of deviance in the analysis of societal problems. Four commonly discussed types of "deviant" behavior are *homelessness, mental illness, homosexuality,* and *drug addiction.* Because researchers often consider these types of behavior from the deviance perspective, we specifically focus on them in this chapter and demonstrate how one can view these behaviors from the power–conflict perspective.

GOALS OF THIS CHAPTER

We begin this chapter with a survey of traditional social science perspectives on deviance and deviant individuals. These approaches typically view deviance in terms of maladjusted individuals or families. We emphasize, on the other hand, that behavior identified as deviant often results from such societal conditions as racism and the socioeconomic inequality of capitalism and not necessarily from individual shortcomings. We argue that one should consider homelessness, mental illness, drug addiction, and homosexuality within the larger context of structured social inequality.

PERSPECTIVES ON DEVIANCE

Accenting Maladjusted Individuals

Concern over people who deviate from mainstream norms and values exists in every society. The particular characteristics that define deviance, however, vary according to each society's norms. Traditional social science perspectives on deviance and deviant individuals have viewed social problems primarily in terms of individual and family disorganization, emphasizing individual and family departures from society's established normative rules. Kai Erikson has noted the common practice of picturing "deviant behavior as an alien element in society. Deviance is considered a vagrant form of human activity which has somehow broken away from the more orderly currents of social life and needs to be controlled."[1]

As we noted in Chapter 1, according to Stuart A. Queen and Delbert M. Mann, a sociological interpretation of social problems should accent "maladjustment," "demoralization," and "disorganization." Troubled individuals are considered "pathological," "disorganized," or "maladjusted." Some analysts prefer to interpret cases of deviance such as homelessness and drug use from a psychological or psychoanalytic perspective. We also noted in Chapter 1 that in one of the most influential social problems textbooks of the last few decades, *Contemporary Social Problems,* sociologist Robert Nisbet defined a social problem as behavior patterns regarded by a large part of a society as violating generally accepted or approved norms. He rejects the idea that social problems are deeply rooted in society—that is, that the societal *framework* itself creates major problems. Most social problems textbooks today recognize the role of certain social changes, such as industrialization and geographical mobility, in creating deviant behavior, but many tend to emphasize individual deviations from established norms and roles and neglect oppressive structures and institutions. While industrial and urban changes are usually recognized as forcing individuals to adjust to new situations, most mainstream textbooks give insufficient attention to the problem-generating character of the capitalistic, race-stratified, gender-stratified contexts of the deviant behavior being examined. Moreover, beyond the social science textbooks that consider societal conditions, U.S. politicians and media commentators often view the behavior of certain groups, such as the homeless or gays and lesbians, mostly in pathological or individual maladjustment terms.

Toward a Critical Power–Conflict Approach to "Deviance"

Numerous social scientists reject the tendency toward accenting deviant individuals in traditional analysis of societal problems. Instead, they emphasize how societal conditions, such as racism and the inequality of capitalism, generate behavior stigmatized as deviant. Some analysts, called *labeling theorists,* have underscored the point that deviance is not inherent in behavior but rather a label applied by people to behavior. For example, Howard Becker argues, "Deviance is *not* a quality of the act the person commits, but rather a consequence of the application by others of rules and sanctions to an 'offender.' The deviant is one to whom that label has successfully been applied; deviant behavior is behavior that people so label."[2] One type of stigmatization is labeling certain behavior *criminal*—that is, a violation of formal norms called *law.* Of course, many deviations from established norms are not violations of law. In either case, however, actions are deviant only when they are socially evaluated and stigmatized as such. Thus, defining homeless or mentally ill people as *deviant* and stigmatized targets is a social process.

Edwin Lemert has distinguished between primary and secondary deviance—with the latter taking place when a person reacts to a socially defined status by using his or her "deviance" as a "means of defense, attack, or adjustment to the overt and covert problems created" by the initial societal definition of him or her as deviant. In other words, once defined as deviant, people may behave in the expected deviant role as a defense. Of course, this does *not* mean that certain actions, such as theft and drug use, would not occur if they were not labeled deviant or criminal. Rather, as Edwin Schur underscores, "their nature, distribution, social meaning, and implications and ramifications are significantly influenced by patterns of social reaction. Society, in other words, determines what we make of these acts socially."[3]

Society's definition and stigmatization of deviance are often arbitrary and ambiguous. Behavior regarded in contemporary U.S. society as deviant, such as homosexuality, may not be regarded as deviant in another society or time, such as ancient Greece. In addition, the label of deviance can vary over time within the same society. For instance, the stigma assigned to those who drink alcohol has varied over the course of the last century. During the era of Prohibition in the 1920s, alcohol use became legally defined as deviant. When the law was repealed, the stigma of alcohol consumption declined until the more recent problem of drunk drivers again brought excessive drinking to public attention. The stigma of deviance varies by context. The social context may determine whether people consider certain behavior as deviant. For example, most killing in wartime is not considered deviant, whereas a killing at a bar is considered criminally deviant. In addition, not all deviance is behavior. People with certain characteristics, such as physical handicaps, may be defined as deviant and suffer discriminatory treatment because of that.

How does our society arrive at its definitions of and treatment of deviance? The answer must be sought in our history and in our society's norms and values. Views of who and what are deviant often take time to develop. What is deviant is defined by a majority in society, yet often the deviance is defined, initially or disproportionately, by the powerful members of the dominant class, racial, and gender groups. Not every member of society plays an equal role in defining deviance.

A number of authors, including Edwin Schur and D. Stanley Eitzen, have stressed that the social-labeling process does not exist in isolation from society's powerful interest groups. The deviance-labeling process reflects powerful groups' disproportionate power to define individual or group actions positively or negatively—that is, as socially acceptable or as deviant. From the perspective of a majority of our society's members or from the point of view of powerful groups in our society, some types of deviance are viewed as minor and some as major. A critical question in the defining process is "Whose interest is served by stigmatizing people as deviant?" Many types of harmful behavior are not (yet) considered deviant, or so deviant as to require major societal penalties, including such harmful actions as killing workers by polluting workplaces unnecessarily with toxic chemicals and dust. In this case, the definition of conscious workplace pollution as major deviance has been resisted by powerful groups. The types of deviance that are of greatest concern in the United States are those that challenge deeply held norms and values, especially those of powerful groups. For this reason, even political and ideological diversity is sometimes considered deviant; a person with radical political ideas may be seen as a threat to the status quo and thus defined as deviant. Individuals and groups labeled as deviant are often forced to become outsiders and are stigmatized, feared, shunned, or, on occasion, killed.[4]

A society's norms are part of its basic social system. If the private ownership and control of property are part of society's norms, as they are for the United States, actions that threaten this norm will be considered deviant. This view of private property has developed since the 1600s, at which time there was, among the Puritans, an emphasis on collective ownership and community control of property. Today, the developed concept of private property is held by a majority of Americans, most of whom own only personal goods, the most valuable of which is usually a home. But the inviolability of private property has been extended by the most powerful property holders to cover not only personal private property but also the productive property of the society, such as factories, warehouses, and office buildings. From the perspective of the capitalist, a sit-down strike at a factory by employees protesting unsafe working conditions involves workers' deviance—a trespassing on private property. The workers are not only "deviant" but also "criminal" under present laws. Police and soldiers have been used over the course of U.S. history to evict such strikers. Yet from the workers' perspective the factory is not the same kind of private property as personal property, such as a home or automobile. Indeed, some workers and others have argued that the worth of the productive property of society is created by all the workers building that property and laboring in or on it. Such property, they further argue, should be owned and controlled by the workers, not just by the business elite. From this value position, the sit-down strike is *not* deviant.

The Treatment of Those Labeled Deviant

How are those people labeled deviant actually treated in this society? Deviant groups are often divided into two groups: those viewed as a burden to society but as more or less harmless and those viewed as a burden and a threat to established order.[5] The former group is stigmatized by societal opinion makers as deviant because of its "failure, inability, or refusal . . . to participate in the roles supportive of capitalist society [and] is most likely to come to official attention . . . when the magnitude of the problem becomes significant enough to create a basis for 'public concern.'" Such groups include the mentally retarded. A more threatening group, in contrast, is usually dealt with by "a rapid and focused expenditure of control resources" because of "its potential actively to call into question established relationships, especially relations of production and domination."[6] Societal opinion makers, especially business and political leaders, are often concerned by this latter deviance. Thus, many street criminals are viewed in these terms as very dangerous.

Deviant populations are dealt with in a variety of ways depending upon the degree of threat they are viewed as posing to society. Positive attempts to foster compliance with society's norms are made through the media, educational system, and family and peer groups. During the 1980s, for example, President Ronald Reagan and his wife, Nancy, helped start a mass media campaign proclaiming "Just Say No" to drugs. In addition, social segregation and isolation, such as confinement in prisons or mental hospitals, often separate deviant populations from the rest of society. Punishment of deviant behavior through the prison system is a major method of dealing with deviant individuals and is used for instances of deviance that present the greatest perceived threat. Moreover, some individuals punished as deviant at one point in time become accepted, even heroes, at another. The changes over time in public views of the behavior of women suffragettes seeking the vote for women in the early 1900s, or of civil rights demonstrators in the South in the 1950s and 1960s, are good examples of groups once seen as highly dangerous and deviant but now mostly seen as courageous and heroic.

HOMELESSNESS

Reactions to the Homeless as "Trash"

Today large numbers of Americans are homeless.[7] The Urban Institute estimates that at least 3.5 million people—1.35 million of them children—are homeless each year in the United

States.[8] Some experts distinguish between the "literally" homeless and the "at-risk" homeless. The literally homeless are those who live on the streets or in shelters for the homeless; they do not have a minimally adequate nighttime dwelling.[9] The literally homeless are those who appear in number counts such as those just cited. The at-risk homeless are a broader group, and their number is harder to ascertain than that for the literally homeless. One *Washington Post* reporter framed it this way: "Do the homeless include someone who has lived 'doubled-up' with a relative? A battered wife who spent a week in a shelter last year? A truant teenager running with a gang? Two families 'underhoused' in lodgings designed for one?"[10] It has been estimated that between 5 and 9 million persons have been homeless for some period of time over any specific five-year period in the last decade or two.[11]

Many affluent Americans often view the homeless as highly deviant and as "social refuse" to be discarded, rather than as people suffering because of societal conditions such as unemployment and the lack of affordable housing. In his study of homelessness, researcher Jonathan Kozol reported on negative reactions of people to homeless men, women, and children. For example, one antihomeless activist in Phoenix stated, "We're tired of feeling guilty about these people." In Tucson, voters elected a mayor on a platform that included driving the homeless out of town. Officials in towns such as Laramie, Wyoming, and Lancaster, Ohio, have given homeless people a one-way ticket to another city. Amtrak officials in New York City told the police, "It is the policy of Amtrak to not allow the homeless and undesirables to remain [in the station area]." One Amtrak official wrote in an internal memo, "Can't we get rid of this trash?" Grocers in Santa Barbara, California, have put bleach on discarded food, and a city council member in Fort Lauderdale, Florida, proposed spraying trash with rat poison to discourage homeless families from foraging for food. "The way to get rid of vermin is to cut their food supply," he observed.[12] Such cases are an extreme example of the social labeling process.

Once stigmatized as deviant, individuals can become targets of violence. Homeless individuals are at risk of physical abuse, including muggings, beatings, rape, and murder. One study found that homeless people were 20 times more likely than the general population to be murdered.[13] Still, many Americans seem to be having second thoughts about being hostile to the homeless. In one national survey, 86 percent of respondents said that they had sympathy for homeless people, and just under one-third said that their sympathy had increased in recent years. The majority of the latter group admitted that the reason why they were more sympathetic was their concern that they too might be homeless someday.[14]

Who Are the Homeless?

The aforementioned survey found that the majority of respondents thought of "the average homeless person" as white, male, and single, and in the 18 to 55 age bracket.[15] In addition, many people think of the homeless as lazy derelicts—alcoholics and dropouts from society who do not wish to work. This picture is inaccurate. The homeless include many people of color who face discrimination, many people who have been or are married, and many children. Based on a nationwide survey of homeless people, Martha Burt has concluded that homelessness is "in part rooted in personal vulnerabilities that increase the risk for particular individuals [but is] also a problem of housing availability and affordability. The causes of homelessness include structural factors, personal factors, and public policy."[16] Many of the homeless have lost jobs as plants have closed; and many others are

This photo of homeless Americans was taken by a homeless child. (Shooting Back)

employed at low-wage jobs and cannot afford a place to live because this capitalistic society cannot provide enough adequate housing for all workers. Thus, in one year, two-thirds of the 1,400 residents at a Washington, D.C., shelter were *employed* but could not find an affordable place to live.[17]

The fastest-growing segment of the homeless consists of families with children. A survey of homelessness by the U.S. Conference of Mayors recently found that children make up more than 25 percent of the urban homeless population, and families with children comprise 41 percent of the homeless population. In rural areas these percentages are considerably higher.[18] Often these homeless families are poor women with children escaping abusive domestic relationships. One study found, for example, that one-half of homeless women and children come from abusive domestic situations where they are beaten by husbands or other male relatives.[19] Violent sexism and patriarchalism thus create much homelessness. The International Union of Gospel Missions—which runs 250 missions—has found that children and adolescents make up a growing proportion of the homeless coming to shelters.[20] In addition, millions of poor families are living doubled up with other families in overcrowded conditions. Millions of families spend more than half their income on rent or mortgage payments. All these families are at high risk of eviction and homelessness.

Ironically, in a country that often boasts of caring for its military personnel, about one-third of homeless men are military veterans. One estimate puts the number of homeless veterans at nearly 300,000. Those who served in the late Vietnam and post-Vietnam eras are at the greatest risk of homelessness. Homeless veterans have increased rates of mental health and addiction disorders that may be linked to their military service. Homeless male veterans are more likely to be white, well educated, and married than are nonveteran homeless persons. Homeless female veterans are only about 2 percent of homeless veterans, and they are more often married and more prone to suffer from serious psychiatric disorders than are homeless male veterans. Homeless male veterans, on the other hand, are more often unemployed and suffer from drug addictions.[21]

Causes of Homelessness

Homelessness must be placed in its economic and political contexts. Among the obvious causes of homelessness are unemployment, low family incomes, and the absence of low-cost housing. We saw in Chapter 3 the economic importance of employers and investors who make decisions about where and when to make job-creating investments. By holding back on investments or making investments overseas, top executives eliminate jobs in the United States. During the 1930s Great Depression, capitalists held back on investing, and unemployed homeless people wandered through country and cities, sleeping in parks and subways. This pattern has been repeated in many cities in the last decade. In today's global market, many corporations make capital investments around the world. (In Chapter 10 we examine plant closings and corporate flight from one U.S. community to another and from U.S. cities to locations around the globe.) As a result of this disinvestment activity, large numbers of jobs have been lost, and many unemployed workers have found themselves poor and homeless.

In addition to problems of jobs and income, many Americans face the lack of affordable housing. Because of the rising cost of single-family homes, tens of millions of American households are destined to spend most or all of their lives renting. Renters are now a majority of the households in a number of central cities. Whether in the central cities or in suburbs, apartments are the major alternatives for families unable to afford detached single-family housing. Yet not enough apartments are available at affordable rents. One study found that from 1973 to 1993, some 2.2 million low-rent units disappeared from the U.S. housing market through abandonment, demolition, and conversion to condominiums or expensive apartments, or they became unaffordable because of increases in costs.[22] Yet, during this period the number of low-income renters *increased* by 3.2 million.[23] The disparity between affordable rental units and the number of low-income renter households has now increased to about 4.9 million units available to 7.7 million households.[24] In addition, a federal Housing and Urban Development (HUD) study reported that 5.3 million low-income households that received no governmental assistance had "worst case" housing needs. "Worst case needs" means that renters with incomes below half of an area's median income have been involuntarily displaced, live in substandard housing, or pay more than half their income for rent and utilities. Only one-sixth of very low-income, unassisted households lived in adequate, uncrowded, and affordable housing. Moreover, over the past several years, the households that experienced the sharpest increase in acute housing needs were families with children.[25]

The revitalization of cities and the growth in financial, insurance, and other service industries that began in the 1970s have brought a *gentrification* of many urban neighborhoods as professionals and other white-collar workers are drawn back into central cities. In this gentrification process, many lower-income city residents are displaced by such developments as condo conversions. They often become homeless as the supply of low-cost housing is seriously eroded. Others become homeless when their deteriorating apartment buildings are abandoned by landlords and demolished to make way for office buildings. Still others among the homeless are victims of fires or illness. A large percentage of homeless families have previously lived doubled up with other families. Such precarious living arrangements are also threatened by death or illness in the host family, intolerable overcrowding, or detection by landlords.[26]

Real estate investors, developers, and landlords often blame the shortages of affordable apartment units on high interest rates, high construction costs, rent control laws, or other government interference in the "free market." Conventional housing theorists argue that supply and demand factors determine the cost of housing and that the marketplace will provide enough affordable housing if governments leave it alone. A power–conflict approach, however, suggests that development decisions are governed by our capitalistic system, in which powerful people—such as housing developers, landlords, and bankers—aggressively pursue private profit (and not necessarily societal needs) and thus disproportionately shape the type and pricing of housing available for workers and their families.

As Gilderbloom and Appelbaum have demonstrated, rental housing is *not* a free market; apartment ownership is concentrated in the hands of a modest number of landlords. For example, a study of Cambridge, Massachusetts, found that most of the housing units were owned by just 6 percent of the households. The study found close connections among executives at local banks—which made most of Cambridge's real estate loans—local government officials, and property owners and developers. This powerful network promoted construction of luxury apartments and commercial development by city government; it did not seek to meet the needs of the majority of citizens—the less affluent tenants—such as by implementing effective rent control and enforcing housing codes. The local planning board and zoning board were dominated by real estate interests. In addition, a New York study found that 5 percent of owners held 56 percent of the rent-stabilized units there. Nationwide, rental housing ownership is becoming concentrated. Increasingly, rental housing is controlled by a decreasing number of large owners who cooperate with one another in associations to control rents (that is, to keep them as high as possible) and other aspects of rental housing.[27]

Renters usually find themselves in a very subordinate position. Real estate journals advise apartment managers and developers on how to "deal with delinquent rent payers." One article offers the following tips: "Rent to tenants with a history of paying on time. . . . Assess charges if rent is late. Don't renew leases of tardy tenants. Tie resident manager's bonus to on-time rent collections." The same journal suggests that, if a tenant's rent is ten days late, "the manager should take action to begin court eviction proceedings and follow-up with an attorney to ensure a speedy process."[28] Many landlords have access to computer databases containing the names of people who, for whatever reason, make late rent payments or are conspicuous in ways not related to their rental histories.[29]

Between the 1970s and the 1990s, the average rent more than tripled in the United States, although incomes of renters did not rise as rapidly. Since the 1990s, rents have continued to rise significantly. Many families are unable to find adequate housing without paying exorbitant rents relative to their incomes. Thus, some 4.8 million poor families often spend half or more of their incomes on rent.[30] Younger families and single-parent families are particularly hard hit by housing inflation and other housing problems. Government social-welfare benefits are usually inadequate in meeting the housing needs of low-income families. One survey found that in more than 80 percent of the areas surveyed, total social-welfare benefits for a family of three were less than just the rent for a two-bedroom housing unit in the local area. In half of the areas, total benefits were less than the rent for a one-bedroom unit.[31] In addition, U.S. cities have too few low-rent public housing units to meet the needs of low-income families, and this deficiency has grown worse since 1980. The United States has fewer than 1.5 million public housing units, and only a third of the country's poor renter households live in *any* subsidized housing, either privately owned subsidized units or public housing.[32] A survey of 30 city governments reported that applicants faced an average wait of 21 months for public housing assistance, and 17 of these had stopped taking new applications. In Chicago, applications from nonelderly households have been rejected since 1985.[33] Thus, one of the world's richest countries has no affordable, and adequate, housing units for most of the country's low-income workers and their families. The United States as a nation is thus "deviant" from the world's most respected human rights document, the Universal Declaration of Human Rights. Article 25 of that United Nations document, which was supported by the U.S. government when it was created in 1948, stipulates that governments should live by this human rights code: "Everyone has the right to a standard of living adequate for the health and well-being of himself and his family, including food, clothing, housing."

Deinstitutionalization of Mentally Impaired Persons

About a quarter of homeless adults today suffer from a severe mental impairment.[34] Yet the disproportionality of mentally impaired persons among the homeless has not been the major reason for the enormous growth in homelessness over the last few decades. This is because most patients were discharged from the country's mental hospitals in the 1950s and 1960s, and the enormous growth in homelessness did not take place until the early 1980s. The National Coalition for the Homeless reports that the rise in homelessness resulted more from diminished income and housing opportunities for poor persons than the deinstitutionalization of patients in mental hospitals.[35] Nevertheless, overcrowding of these mental hospitals in the 1980s triggered a shift in national policy for care of the mentally impaired that indeed contributed to homelessness. Accompanying this new wave of deinstitutionalized patients was a rationale that most would be better served, and at a lower cost to the taxpayer, by living in small group homes and receiving outpatient care from small local facilities. By the end of the decade, almost three-fourths of the patients in the country's mental hospitals—some 417,000 persons—were deinstitutionalized. Yet in an increasingly conservative national climate little effort or money has actually been channeled into developing these necessary group homes or clinics for newly released patients. New social welfare programs have been opposed by conservative analysts in government, universities, and the media. The remaining mental institutions continue to receive 70 percent of the still available public mental health funds, and large numbers of the deinstitutionalized mentally impaired, lacking facilities or treatment, do in fact live on the streets of U.S. cities.[36]

Local Responses to Homelessness

Local efforts to deal with homelessness have ranged from policies of deterrence and expulsion to efforts to criminalize the homeless themselves. A recent survey reveals that as homelessness has increased throughout the United States, the number of laws targeting homeless people has also increased. Of the 147 communities surveyed in 42 states, Puerto Rico, and the District of Columbia, well over two-thirds have passed new laws targeting the homeless since

January 2002 while at the same time failing to provide sufficient social services to the homeless. The study documents civil rights violations against people experiencing homelessness taken by local governments that criminalize lifesustaining activities that people are forced to do in public. For example, San Francisco is one of the harshest cities in one of the harshest states for poor and homeless people to live in because of its record of abuse and intolerance of homeless persons. In a one-year period (2000–2001), officials issued over 27,000 citations to homeless people for such public infractions as sleeping or camping in the park, trespassing, or disobeying park signs. During that period, the city spent nearly $31 million incarcerating homeless persons. The study also shows that increases in hate crimes and violent acts against homeless people relate directly to the city's efforts to criminalize homelessness.[37]

Most business and government officials have fostered the idea that the homeless are highly deviant and quite different from the average citizen. These officials seem to believe that if the homeless are made comfortable, they will flock to shelters to live at public expense. Most public and private emergency funds for the homeless are spent to house them in inadequate shelters. Initial placements of homeless individuals and families are usually in barracks-type buildings that provide no privacy and little comfort.[38]

Even placements in these barracks can be painfully slow. Families, including pregnant women and families with infants and young children, have spent weeks sitting in offices day and night before being given a bed. For some years, New York officials offered many homeless families rooms in privately owned hotels; yet these "welfare hotels" were frequently rodent infested, garbage littered, and in desperate need of repair. Police regularly issue citations for disorderly conduct when the homeless complain about living conditions in shelters, however. Homeless families often reside in these shelters for more than two years before finding better housing.[39]

Increases in the homeless are reported periodically by major agencies such as the U.S. Mayors Conference. This recurring demand for housing puts great pressure on public and private agencies to increase available shelters for the homeless. In contrast to public shelters, private shelters in large cities often offer better conditions and more respect for the individual. Yet even in the private shelter industry, far more money goes to the private developers of shelters than to the homeless people. Many of the homeless themselves have noted that for a very small fraction of the cost of group shelters, they could be maintained in regular apartments, avoiding the debilitating and disrupting effects of relocation in shelters. In a few cities some government shelter programs have provided adequate housing and the counseling and employment programs that enable homeless individuals and families to again become self-supporting. However, fully adequate facilities for the homeless still remain uncommon in most U.S. cities.

MENTAL ILLNESS

Labeling the "Mentally Ill"

Mental illness is another label often applied to people whose behavior is considered deviant. While many of those so labeled do have mental impairments, this particular label often is used to suggest a negative stigma of deviance for people with serious personal problems. As with other forms of deviance, mental illness is socially defined. Depression, delusions or hallucinations, defiance of authority, or political dissidence may or may not be labeled as "mental illness," depending on a person's social and economic circumstances and the soci-

etally legitimated diagnostic and labeling procedure. In some politically totalitarian societies, for example, political dissidents have been treated as "mentally ill."

The mass media have played an important role in making the mentally impaired seem
quite different from other people. Ron Schraiber, who describes himself as an "ex–mental
patient," is one patient rights advocate. He has cited the media as a major problem in labeling the impaired: "From the ubiquitous 'psycho' and 'mad bomber' story lines to the sensa-
tionalistic headlines of 'Ex–Mental Patient Kills Two,' violence incarnate goes by the name
of 'psychotic' and its variant terms. Playing into the cultural myth of the 'crazed murderer.'"
He adds, "Such distorted and formulistic images of the 'homicidal maniac' impoverish the
lives of people diagnosed with mental illness, who, research shows, are overwhelmingly not
violent."[40] As Schraiber points out, "normal people" have started world wars and bombed
and killed many civilians in cities such as Hiroshima and Baghdad. The media stereotypes
not only grossly exaggerate the role in social violence of those labeled as mentally ill but
also make life much more difficult for those who must live every day with these stereotypes.

Thomas Szasz has developed the thesis that the creation of the discipline of psychiatry involved redefining as mental illness many human conditions or behaviors that were formerly known as odd behavior, heresy, sin, or even "spirit possession." For example, in the
eighteenth century, Benjamin Rush, an important figure in the American Revolution and the
father of U.S. psychiatry, once defined sanity as *social conformity* and insanity as *social non-
conformity*. Rush classified a "Derangement in the Principle of Faith" as one form of mental
illness and listed as its victims persons who do not believe "in the utility of medicine, as practiced by regular bred physicians, believing implicitly in quacks."[41] Such a definition can lead
to classifying nonconformists in seeking medical treatment as mentally ill. It also awards the
power to define mental illness to (often white) psychiatrists or other psychological therapists.

Many people come to accept social definitions and internalize a negative view of
themselves. People who believe that their actions or feelings are considered inappropriate
by others may believe that "something is wrong with me." Peggy Thoits suggests that this
self-labeling process is particularly likely to occur when individuals experience negative
feelings. It is considered all right to be sad, angry, anxious, or depressed occasionally, but if
such feelings persist, regardless of the material and social circumstances, people may even
come to see themselves as misfits and deviants. In addition, Thoits suggests other ways in
which a person's attempts to conform to society's norms may result in being labeled mentally ill. Sensing society's disapproval, people who experience persistent negative feelings
often make an effort to change or replace these feelings with others that are socially acceptable. However, the very techniques people use to make their emotional reactions socially acceptable may produce thoughts or actions that will be labeled as symptoms of mental illness.
For example, a person whose grief reactions continue for longer than is considered "normal"
may try to justify these reactions by inventing an explanation. However, the explanation
may also seem as inappropriate to some people, just as prolonged grief did to others, resulting in a conclusion that the person is indeed mentally ill.[42]

The social label of mental illness is often reserved for individuals who are hospitalized or institutionalized because of a psychiatric evaluation. However, the same behaviors
that lead to institutionalization can be observed in many other individuals who are *not* institutionalized. As Elaine and John Cumming have pointed out, "Mental illness, it seems,
is a condition which afflicts people who must go to a mental institution, but until they go
almost anything they do is normal."[43] What, then, accounts for the institutionalization of

Criminalizing the Mentally Ill

The release of mentally ill patients from state mental hospitals to community-based facilities—a process called "deinstitutionalization"—began in the early 1960s. A Joint Commission on Mental Illness had condemned the "warehousing of mental patients in huge, dehumanizing, impersonal, and ineffective publicly funded asylums." The commission called for the development of more humane community-based facilities to care for mentally ill persons. In response to the commission's report, President John F. Kennedy signed a federal law mandating local facilities to care for the mentally ill. Policymakers reasoned that deinstitutionalized mentally ill patients, treated with psychotropic drugs, would have better lives if residents in their local communities. Consequently, only the severely ill remained in public mental health hospitals by the mid-1970s.

One major problem arose from this so-called reform. Conservative presidents Richard Nixon, Ronald Reagan, and George H. W. Bush failed to provide the federal funding required for these local treatment centers to operate. The number of public hospital beds available to the mentally ill has decreased by nearly 70 percent since 1982, yet most former patients from the hospitals have not received adequate mental health care at the local level. The mentally ill now constitute a substantial segment of the homeless population. As one scholar notes, the mentally ill are "a silent witness to the heartlessness and befuddlement that has created no better alternative for them than the streets."

Many among the mentally ill have also ended up in prisons and jails, one of the new dumping grounds. While the political establishment has invested billions in prison construction and enacted draconian sentencing laws, it has done little to alleviate the warehousing of 300,000 mentally ill persons in prisons and jails, a number three times that of mentally ill patients in public mental health facilities. About 70,000 of these people suffer from severe illnesses such as schizophrenia, bipolar disorder, and manic depression. While the U.S.Department of Justice claims that most public and private correctional facilities provide mental health services to inmates,

class action lawsuits have swamped federal courts with evidence of the failure of prison officials to provide people with adequate mental health care. The American Civil Liberties Union recently won a case in which a federal judge ruled that the state of Arkansas had violated the rights of the mentally ill by leaving them in jail and denying them court-ordered treatment. Some lawsuits are seeking injunctive relief for prisoner mistreatment; the MacArthur Justice Center recently sued Illinois prison officials for subjecting mentally ill prisoners to the harsh conditions of high security prisons where guards often put prisoners in solitary confinement.

Besides facing homelessness, prior to their imprisonment mentally ill prisoners face high rates of unemployment, alcohol and drug abuse, and physical or sexual abuse. Mentally ill prisoners often serve longer terms than other inmates, with many spending long years in jail for minor offenses. Most prisons and jails are ill equipped to deal with mentally ill inmates because of shortages of personnel trained to handle mental illness. Human Rights Watch found that prison staff frequently punish mentally ill inmates for manifestations of their illnesses, such as noisiness, disobeying orders, and self-mutilation. Because of their illnesses, these prisoners often rant and rave, huddle silently in cells, talk to invisible companions, suffer from hallucinations, and beat their heads against cell walls. Often prison staff use excessive force against mentally ill inmates and, sometimes, have killed them with improper control methods.

Juvenile detention centers are also becoming dumping grounds for mentally ill children. In California, many of the wards in the youth prison system suffer from serious psychiatric conditions. A national survey of children held in juvenile detention centers found that during six months in 2003, nearly 15,000 youths were unnecessarily detained in detention centers while awaiting mental health services. Many of these children have no criminal charges. Authorities are holding many other juveniles for minor offenses such as truancy that result from their mental health problems. According to one report, "the misuse of detention centers as holding areas for mental health treatment is unfair to youths, undermines their health, disrupts the function of detention centers and is costly to society."

Death penalty jurisdictions have executed persons with mental illness and mental retardation. While the Supreme Court has ruled that executing *mentally retarded* prisoners is unconstitutional, the court has only addressed whether death penalty jurisdictions can forcibly medicate *mentally ill* inmates before their execution. The court has qualified the constitutionality of executing mentally ill prisoners to the extent that it prohibits states from executing anyone who does not understand why officials are putting them to death. Yet, in Virginia's execution of Morris Odell Mason, the mentally ill Mason had no idea of his impending execution; he told fellow inmates on his way to the death chamber, "When I get back, I'm gonna show him how I can play basketball as good as he can." Since 1973, death penalty juris-

dictions have executed 34 prisoners despite solid evidence of mental retardation. Significantly, some 10 percent of those on death row today suffer from mental retardation.

Recently, Alabama executed a mentally ill prisoner. In this case, a jury convicted 33-year-old mentally ill prisoner David Hocker for a 1998 stabbing. Hocker killed his employer and splurged on cocaine before turning himself in. He had a long history of mental illness and was the victim of severe abuse as a child, a childhood his lawyer described as a "thoroughgoing regime of terror." Hocker's mental illness was so severe that while on death row he mutilated himself by cutting off his testicles. The director of Equal Justice Initiative, Bryan Stevenson, commented on the execution: "Alabama can take no pride in executing someone who is too unstable or too poor to protect themselves." Indeed, the execution raises serious questions about the civilized values of the criminal justice system.

Sources: Erich Goode, *Deviant Behavior* (Upper Saddle River, N.J.: Prentice Hall, 2001), p. 397; Allen J. Beck and Laura M. Maruschak, *Mental Health Treatment in State Prisons, 2000,* U.S. Department of Justice (July 2001); "300,000 Mentally Ill in U.S. Prisons," *Guardian Newspapers* (March 2, 2003), available at www.buzzle.com/editorials/text3-2-2003-36550.asp; Jamie Fellner and Sasha Abramsky, "Prisons No Place for the Mentally Ill," *San Diego Union* (February 13, 2004); available at www.geocities.com/1union1/mental_health.htm; Kate Randall, "More than a Quarter Million Mentally Ill in America's Jails and Prisons," *World Socialist Web Site* (July 15, 1999), available at www.wsws.org/articles/1999/jul1999/pris-j15_prn.shtml; Human Rights Watch, "United States: Mentally Ill Mistreated in Prison" (October 22, 2003), available at www.hrw.org/press/2003/10/us102203.htm; Human Rights Watch, "Ill-Equipped: U.S. Prisons and Offenders with Mental Illness" (October 22, 2003); Charles J. Kehoe and Robert Bernstein, "Warehousing Youths With Mental Illness," *The Baltimore Sun* (July 21, 2004), p. A15; "Unwell and Untreated," *The Houston Chronicle,* July 23, 2004, p. B10; Karen de Sa, "Harsh Treatment in CYA Perpetuates Violence," *San Jose Mercury News* (February 10, 2004); Death Penalty Information Center, "Mental Illness and the Death Penalty," available at www.deathpenaltyinfo.org/article.php?did=782&scid=66; Death Penalty Information Center, "Mental Retardation and the Death Penalty" available at www.deathpenaltyinfo.org/article.php?scid=28&did=176; National Coalition to Abolish the Death Penalty, "Offending Justice," available at www.ncadp.org/fact_sheet6.html.

some and not others? The existence and proximity of treatment facilities are undoubtedly important factors. So is the orientation of the family to the ideology of mental illness.

Erving Goffman has noted that the degree of irritation an individual's behavior causes family members can be a major factor: "A psychotic man is tolerated by his wife until she finds herself a boyfriend, or by his adult children until they move from a house to an apartment; . . . a rebellious adolescent daughter can no longer be managed at home because she now threatens to have an open affair with an unsuitable companion."[44] In an attempt to observe the social world of patients in mental institutions, Goffman took a job as a minor staff member in a mental hospital. He observed that the hospital's patients included both those who appeared to have mental problems and those who appeared normal by outside norms. He also found that the experience of institutionalization itself had a marked effect on the patients, an effect relatively uniform regardless of the patient's condition at time of entry into the hospital. Goffman found that to preserve some sense of self-respect and self-control, patients often invented "acceptable" biographical sketches for themselves that differed from their actual biographies. They also learned to control and subvert the system within the institution by the use of such techniques as developing underground systems of communication, obtaining and concealing forbidden possessions, and ridiculing therapy sessions among themselves. Goffman concluded that the people in mental hospitals have been *defined* by families and psychologists or psychiatrists as mentally ill. Their actual condition may or may not have coincided with their social definition.

Psychiatrists and psychologists have conducted substantial research on the diagnosis or misdiagnosis of patients as mentally ill. Ronald Laing and Aaron Esterson found that people diagnosed as "schizophrenic" or "psychotic" because of certain symptoms are often showing reactions against extremely tyrannical or bizarre parents. These patients in fact are often reacting normally to "crazy" families. Class, racial, and gender stereotyping and discrimination have also influenced the mental illness definition process. Thomas Scheff suggests from his research that the process of psychiatric screening and diagnosis is "more sensitive to economic, political, and social-psychological pressures on the screening agents than to most aspects of the patient's behavior." Inaccurate diagnoses seem most common in situations where the psychological evaluator is superior in social, racial, or gender status to the client. One psychologist has pointed out, for example, how often black patients have been diagnosed as paranoid schizophrenic on certain standard screening measures (including the Minnesota Multiphasic Personality Inventory) when it was later found that they were normal. Psychologist Melvin Sikes argues that in fact a certain amount of "paranoia" about white people is normal for African Americans in a racist society, for many whites really are "out to get" them. Another basic problem in much diagnostic testing is that many tests have been "normed" on predominantly white populations. As a result, misdiagnosis of black Americans has been more common than it would have been if tests were "normed" on black populations.[45]

Researching the history of the treatment of mental illness in Western societies, Elaine Showalter has demonstrated the gender bias in much psychiatric theory, diagnosis, and treatment. In the nineteenth-century asylum, doing the laundry was standard therapy for female patients. In the 1890s a feminist was committed to an asylum for her opposition to marriage on the grounds that she was unfit to take care of herself. During the 1940s the surgical technique called *lobotomy,* which involves the removal of part of the brain, was prescribed for women more often than men—because housewives, it was said, had less need for their brains. Even today, women are more likely to be diagnosed as mentally ill than are men, and depression is often called the "female malady."[46]

Research on sexist stereotypes of mental health professionals is revealing. In one study researchers asked mental health clinicians to describe the characteristics of a normal healthy man, a normal healthy woman, and a normal healthy adult (sex unspecified). The characteristics considered positive in our culture, such as independence, rationality, and aggressiveness, were associated by the professionals with the healthy masculine personality; and, interestingly, the same characteristics were emphasized for the healthy adult. For the normal woman, though, these clinicians emphasized characteristics that U.S. society generally evaluates as negative: submissiveness, dependence, feelings easily hurt, excitable, and subjective. In the views of these mental health clinicians a mature and "healthy" woman should behave in ways considered as socially undesirable and immature for a healthy male. The sex-role stereotypes held by these highly educated professionals undoubtedly influenced the way they treated patients.[47] In addition, M. Kaplan argues that some categories used in the *Diagnostic and Statistical Manual of Mental Disorder* (DSM), a standard therapist's guide to diagnosis, reflect a masculine bias that defines behaviors considered abnormal for women (such as putting work above family) as normal for men.[48] In addition, Paula Caplan, who has served on DSM committees, has argued that this widely used manual "mislabels as 'mental disorders' the effects of poverty, racism, sexism and ageism, making it seem as though these arise from individuals' psyches rather than from social ills."[49] In the field of mental health diagnosis and treatment, sexism, racism, and other conventional biases and discriminatory practices still intrude in a regular way.

DRUG AND OTHER SUBSTANCE ADDICTION

Junior Rios, the subject of a film documentary titled *Junkie Junior,* started using heroin when he was 15. Later he used cocaine and Valium. At age 29, Junior's face is hollowed and scarred; he looks 60. He has lost his job, his wife, and his family. A few years ago, when caught stealing and thrown in jail, Junior convinced the judge to let him enroll in a rehabilitation program, but he ran away after two weeks. Junior feels disgusted as he stares at the bloody syringe stuck in his arm. He keeps his needles in a filthy bowl under his bed and lives with other junkies in a dark, garbage-littered apartment in a burnt-out building in the South Bronx (New York), an area where it is frequently easier to buy heroin than food. His diet consists of bread soaked in coffee. His drug habit costs $200 a day; for that reason he must steal something every few hours just to get enough drugs to keep him from getting sick. The documentary concludes as Junior stares into the camera and slowly says, "If anyone ever offers you drugs, please remember what happened to me." Junior Rios is the type of person who most readily comes to mind when media commentators, or average Americans, think of drug and substance abuse.[50]

What Substance Use Is Illegal?

Substance abuse is the subject of much political and social concern today. Among the substances that are addictive, physically harmful, and socially disruptive, the most widely used are tobacco, alcohol, and a variety of legal and illegal drugs. The use of some of these substances has been defined as legal; the use of others has been defined as illegal. Users of some of these substances, such as cocaine and heroin, are labeled deviant; users of other substances, such as tobacco, have not been so labeled. On what basis is this seemingly arbitrary determination made? We examine both types of substances in an attempt to answer this question.

Tobacco Use: An Ancient Addiction

Interestingly, in the United States today the most widely used addictive substance is *not* an illegal drug but rather is tobacco, with nicotine its addictive ingredient. Tobacco is the only legal product in the United States today that is addictive for a large percentage of its users and is very dangerous, even in moderation, to both users and those exposed to secondhand smoke. Tar and carbon monoxide gas, by-products of burning tobacco in cigarettes, are major causes of lung cancer and heart disease. Tobacco use is the country's leading yet preventable cause of death—responsible for more than 442,000 deaths annually. Some 38,000 nonsmokers die each year from lung cancer or suffer from serious respiratory illnesses because of exposure to secondhand tobacco smoke.[51] The Environmental Protection Agency has classified environmental tobacco smoke as a Group A carcinogen, putting it in the same category as extremely dangerous carcinogens such as benzene and asbestos. Growing public awareness of tobacco's hazards has reduced the number of smokers in recent years, at least in some segments of the population. Still, the use of this extremely harmful substance has not yet been defined by the majority of Americans as deviance of a major sort.

As early as 1859, published scientific reports documented the connection between tobacco and lung cancer. By the 1930s a substantial body of medical research in Europe and the United States had linked tobacco use with several deadly diseases. In the United States the increased use of tobacco during and following the two world wars was matched by an alarming increase in lung cancer, coronary artery disease, bronchitis, and emphysema. In 1954 the American Cancer Society reported that smokers' death rate from all diseases was 75 percent higher than the death rate for nonsmokers, and smokers' death rate from lung cancer was 16 times that of nonsmokers.[52] Ten years later the U.S. Surgeon General finally and belatedly issued a report certifying that smoking causes disease. The Center for Disease Control reports that since that time, more than 12 million Americans have died from tobacco smoking-related diseases, including 4.1 million deaths from cancer, 5.5 million deaths from cardiovascular diseases, 2.1 million deaths from respiratory diseases, and 94,000 infant deaths related to their mother's smoking. In addition, tobacco use costs the country an estimated $75 billion annually in medical care expenses and another $80 billion resulting from lost productivity.[53] Still, an estimated 66.5 million, or 29.5 percent of the U.S. population, continue to use often addictive tobacco.[54]

The Role of Large Corporations in Tobacco Use

Beginning in 1966, federal legislation required cigarette packages to carry health hazard warnings, and in 1971 cigarette advertising was banned on television. Yet a decade later one-third of the U.S. public was still unaware of the relationship between smoking and heart disease, and some still do not know today about this relationship or about how addictive smoking is. This lack of public knowledge of the dangers of tobacco use is in part the result of effective advertising and heavy pressure on government officials by the tobacco industry, which includes some of the world's most powerful corporations. Through mergers and acquisitions, a few large firms, such as Philip Morris USA, R. J. Reynolds, and Brown and Williamson, have come to dominate the tobacco industry. The huge advertising expenditures of large tobacco corporations give them considerable control over the media that their advertising funds support. For many years, most of the print media, such as magazines and newspapers, refused to publish significant articles on the health hazards of tobacco use. Those that did carry articles often suffered economic reprisals such as cancellation of ads by tobacco firms. Following an article on the health hazards of tobacco use, *Reader's Digest* was dumped by the advertising agency to whom it had paid $1.3 million a year for 28 years. The American Tobacco Company, a client of the same ad agency, had pressured the agency to choose between it and the magazine.[55]

Long years of attempts to suppress medical evidence about the dangers of tobacco use by tobacco firms illustrate the power of top executives to control public health information and to define the use of tobacco as harmless. The power to define what is, or is not, deviant lies disproportionately in the hands of the powerful. The labeling of practices as deviant is a social process. In this case, powerful corporate executives shaped the social definition of a harmful substance used for decades.

During the 1990s hundreds of secret industry documents were uncovered. These papers suggested that cigarette manufacturers had been aware of the addictive nature of tobacco, had conducted years of research on the effects of nicotine on smokers' bodies and behavior, had discussed development of new brands to market to teenagers, and had concealed information on dangers of smoking. As a result, several different criminal investigations into the tobacco industry were conducted.[56]

The efforts of organized citizens' groups challenging the tobacco industry over the public's right to information about the dangers of smoking have increased public awareness of the health hazards of tobacco. This, along with the U.S. Surgeon General's official confirmation of the health hazards to nonsmokers of secondhand smoke, has resulted in laws banning smoking in public places in most states as well as restrictions on where smoking is permitted in private companies. Smoking is now restricted in many public places in cities, towns, and counties across the United States, and cigarette vending machines are banned in most localities.[57] Evidence that smoking is a major cause of heart and lung diseases has prompted a growing number of government agencies to seek financial protection from the high cost of employees' disability pensions by instituting restrictions on smoking. Massachusetts was the first state to prohibit new police officers and firefighters from smoking both on and off the job. Such laws suggest that smoking now has begun to be labeled by some as seriously deviant, a major shift from previous decades.[58]

Over the last decade or two numerous lawsuits against cigarette companies have been filed, including a class action suit seeking damages for illnesses of flight attendants forced to inhale tobacco smoke in airplane cabins. Several states have settled multibillion-dollar civil lawsuits against major cigarette makers to recover public funds spent on treating smoking-related illnesses.[59] One verdict held an employer responsible for an employee's death from lung cancer that was caused by inhaling secondhand smoke in the workplace.[60] Still, the American Lung Association State of Tobacco Control 2003 report card shows that most states are still not taking the necessary measures to protect people from the deadly effects of tobacco smoke.[61]

Though highly addictive, and indeed *more addictive than cocaine,* tobacco is still not a controlled substance in the United States, and most of the general public and most political and business leaders do not label tobacco use as deviant drug use. The multibillion-dollar-a-year tobacco industry remains an important sector of the economy and exerts major influence over lawmakers. Many observers see a connection between the tobacco industry's huge political contributions and the ways in which the lawmakers who receive contributions put tobacco industry interests ahead of both public health issues and the general public's strong support for tobacco regulation. In recent years, legislators receiving industry support have blocked federal legislation to control tobacco as an addictive substance, restrict smoking in public, or tax tobacco to help pay health care costs of smoking-related illnesses. Congress has exempted tobacco from consumer product safety regulations that apply to other toxic products. The tobacco industry contributes millions of dollars to federal candidates and political action committees.[62]

With a shrinking clientele, as millions of cigarette customers quit or die each year, the tobacco industry has increased its advertising expenditures and shifted the focus of its vast advertising campaigns to people in poor countries overseas and to African American, Latino, and Native American communities in the United States. Tobacco companies contribute large sums to African American educational institutions and political organizations; sponsor major musical, social, sporting, and cultural events; advertise heavily in Latino and African American media; and even furnish free feature articles, op-ed pieces, and editorial cartoons to African American newspapers. The Reverend Jesse Brown, founder and president of the National Black Leadership Initiative on Cancer, has stated that "The impact on our communities is devastating and raises the specter of chemical warfare. Tobacco and alcohol are the two most abused, addictive, and lethal drugs in our community. Each of these legal drugs, standing alone, causes more deaths than all of the illegal drugs combined."[63] Tobacco companies have also targeted their advertising at young people in the United States, and as a result the proportion of U.S. youth who are habitual smokers has climbed now to nearly 30 percent.[64]

Alcohol: Another Major Addiction

Alcohol is a widely used addictive substance that, like tobacco, is legally available, though it is a potent drug. However, attempts at government controls, such as Prohibition in the United States during the 1920s, generally have not been successful in preventing alcohol abuse. Although alcoholic beverage use dates back to the dawn of history, the widespread use of manufactured, cheap, high-alcohol-content beverages began after the invention of gin around 1600 and increased in British cities during the Industrial Revolution. Merchant capitalists aggressively sold the new products in the early industrial period, and the deplorable conditions of the working class encouraged the use of alcohol as a means of escape from the oppressive reality of long hours in early capitalist factories.[65]

Almost half of all Americans use alcohol, and an estimated 10 percent are problem drinkers; that is, alcohol is an addictive substance for them.[66] The social and economic costs of heavy drinking include tens of billions of dollars in lost productivity in workplaces and medical treatment each year. Divorce rates are higher for alcoholics and their spouses, and heavy drinking is frequently the cause of child abuse, spouse abuse, and other violence. More than 25 million persons have reported driving under the influence of alcohol at least once in a given year. In 2002 police officers made more than 2.4 million alcohol-related arrests, including 1 million arrests for driving under the influence of alcohol.[67] In that year drunken driving accounted for *41 percent* (more than 17,400) of all highway fatalities.[68] Because of citizen organization and protests in the last two decades, pressure has grown to limit where and when alcohol can be consumed. Legislators have finally strengthened state and local laws increasing punishment for drunken driving, yet enforcement of drunken driving laws is sometimes lenient, especially for affluent offenders. In many states drunken drivers who kill other motorists or pedestrians still pay only a modest penalty. The stigma of drunken driving is increasing, but alcohol abuse has not yet been labeled a serious enough deviance, especially by influential political leaders, for the development of major criminal penalties.[69]

The majority of fire deaths, drownings, and fatal falls are related to alcohol use. In the workplace, alcoholism is responsible for absenteeism, excessive medical bills, and poor job performance, making it perhaps the most costly type of substance addiction for business and industry. A substantial proportion of industrial accidents are alcohol related. Especially stressful working conditions and repetitive jobs frequently result in high levels of alcohol and illegal drug use. One director of an employee assistance program estimates that almost half of all employees in heavy industrial plants are major drug and alcohol users. As for tobacco, production, distribution, and advertising of alcohol are largely controlled by large corporations. In recent years citizen organizations, particularly those involved in fighting drunken driving, have pressured legislators to make citizens more aware of the dangers of alcohol use. However, not until 1989 did a law go into effect requiring warning labels, similar to those for tobacco, to be put on alcoholic beverages. The oligopolistic corporations that dominate the alcoholic beverage industry have fought against government regulation of their products. They spend billions of dollars on advertising to convince the public that alcohol consumption is respectable and desirable. Much marketing of beer and wine is directed at young people to secure a new generation of users. As for tobacco, these corporations are oriented to profits and have played a major role in getting many people addicted to these dangerous substances.[70]

The problem of alcohol abuse can begin at an early age. One national survey found that 19.6 percent of eighth-graders, 35.4 percent of tenth-graders, and 48.6 percent of twelfth-graders reported having used alcohol in the month just preceding the survey; smaller proportions of each age group (6.7 percent, 18.3 percent, and 30.3 percent, respectively) reported having actually been *drunk* in that period. The survey found that 69 percent of college students reported having used alcohol in the month preceding the survey and that 7 percent used alcohol daily. Some 44 percent of college students engage in binge drinking—that is, drinking just to get drunk. Research also shows that alcohol use among adolescents is related to other behaviors, including tobacco use, early sexual activity, violence, drinking and driving, and suicide.[71]

Because alcohol is legal, its use in moderation is not considered deviant behavior by most Americans. The criminal behavior associated with alcohol use results mainly from the effects of significant amounts of alcohol consumption on the individual consumer. The excessive use of alcohol—alcoholism—is primarily labeled and viewed as an illness, not as criminal behavior, except in the case of drunken driving. Significantly, in the United States alcoholics are generally viewed more sympathetically than most other drug addicts. Perhaps because so many influential Americans drink to excess (including President George W. Bush when he was young), the major thrust is to give alcoholics therapeutic treatment rather than to punish them as criminals as we do in the case of illegal drug use (even for less addictive illegal drugs).

Illegal Drug Use

Unlike nicotine or alcohol, many drugs, such as cocaine and heroin, are not legally sold or used in the United States. Treatment of drug addicts as deviant or criminal, and suppression of the illegal drug trade, began in earnest in the early 1900s. Prior to that time, drug addicts were generally tolerated and were scattered throughout society much the same as persons addicted to nicotine or alcohol. Today, varying, but usually severe, penalties for possession and sale of illegal drugs exist in all states. The illegal drug trade is one of the world's largest businesses. Tens of millions of users worldwide support the drug trade upon which millions of people—growers, refiners, financiers, hired killers, wholesale exporters, and retail distributors—depend for their livelihoods.[72] A recent national household survey on drug abuse estimates that in the year preceding the survey, some 25.7 million Americans used marijuana illegally, 5.9 million used cocaine (1.5 million used crack cocaine), and 404,000 used heroin. Other studies have estimated that one-fifth to one-third of cocaine users, and two-thirds of heroin users, are hardcore users.[73]

Another recent survey shows continuing illegal drug use among high school students. About one-quarter of all students used illicit drugs in the preceding year—15.8 percent of

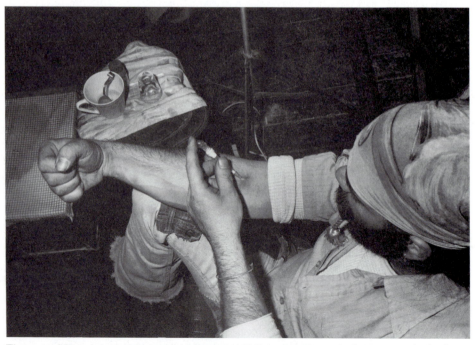

The use of illegal drugs has increased among U.S. teenagers and other groups in the last few years. (Charles Gatewood/Simon & Schuster/PH College)

junior high school students, 32.7 percent of senior high school students, and 37.8 of twelfth-graders. Marijuana is the most frequently used drug, although the use of cocaine, uppers, downers, hallucinogens, inhalants, heroin, and steroids is also reported.[74]

Americans spend an estimated $64 billion annually on illegal drugs. Cocaine accounts for $35.3 billion; marijuana, $10.5 billion; and heroin, $10 billion. Unlike the use of the addictive and harmful substances of tobacco and alcohol, the use of these substances is defined as highly deviant and is usually a criminal offense in the United States. Thus, many millions of Americans frequently violate U.S. drug laws. Law enforcement agents make an estimated 1.6 million arrests annually for drug law violations. Eighty-one percent of these are for possession, not for sale or manufacturing of drugs. Moreover, more than half of the inmates in federal prisons are there on drug charges, which places a huge financial burden on various levels of government.[75]

Drug use crimes are often handled in a racially discriminatory manner. David Lewis, a prominent lawyer, has explained:

> Powder cocaine is a drug of the affluent suburbs, while crack is used and sold in the inner cities. Since 1986, people convicted in federal court of possessing just five grams of crack cocaine . . . face a mandatory sentence of at least five years in prison—and when you get five years of federal time, you do almost all of it. But those caught with powder cocaine must be in possession of 500 grams to get the same five-year sentence. . . . As it stands now, there is one rule of law for crack (a cheap and highly addictive form of cocaine) and another for powder cocaine.[76]

Both types of cocaine are equally potent, and in spite of calls for change, neither recent presidents nor most members of Congress have moved to change these discriminatory drug laws.

People use illegal drugs for many of the same reasons that they use legal drugs: curiosity and boredom; unintentional addiction (for example, children of drug users); a means of escape from unemployment, depression, and helplessness. Most drug users are *not* poor, although police officers are more likely to arrest the poor for drug use. A large proportion of users are young; significant numbers come from affluent families.[77] Take the example of Eric, a young man brought up in a wealthy section of Los Angeles. By age 18, Eric had gone from being an accomplished cellist, varsity baseball player, and honor student to a crack addict who forged checks and stole money from his parents' wallets. In two years he spent $40,000 on crack. Asked to identify those among their 2,000-member student body who were doing drugs, students at Eric's high school replied that it would be easier to identify those who *were not.*[78]

Who Controls the Illegal Drug Trade?

The trade in the legal addictive substances of tobacco and alcohol is controlled by the executives of powerful multinational corporations. The illegal drug trade is also controlled by powerful, wealthy people, but because this trade is illegal, those controlling it operate for the most part in illicit businesses and trade networks. This trade is now very much global and international. The U.S. Foreign Assistance Act stipulates that the president annually make a list of leading drug-producing countries. In the late 1990s then President Bill Clinton sent a list of 31 such countries to the U.S. Congress.

Drug kingpins reside in a number of countries, including Cambodia, Belize, Colombia, Bolivia, Malaysia, and the United States. Some fit the stereotypes of illegal traffickers:

Politics and Organizing in Gay and Lesbian Communities

The first openly gay or lesbian American elected to state political office in the United States was Elaine Noble, elected in Massachusetts in 1975. Over the past three decades, gay and lesbian Americans have developed a number of advocacy organizations and have gained some political power, especially in large metropolitan areas. Now more than 2,000 gay and lesbian political, social, activist, and student organizations can be found nationwide. The gay and lesbian liberation movement has succeeded in weakening some social taboos, eliminating sodomy laws, and lessening repression. For example, in June 2003 the U.S. Supreme Court struck down antisodomy laws nationwide in the pivotal case *Lawrence v. Texas.*[121] In another case, the American Civil Liberties Union urged the U.S. military's highest court to strike down a similar law from its code of conduct.[122] One setback for the gay rights movement was in the case *Boy Scouts of America v. Dale,* when the Supreme Court held that the Boy Scouts of America could terminate an avowed gay rights activist who was an assistant scoutmaster because homosexuality, the court reasoned, is inconsistent with the *private* organization's values.[123] In this case, a conservative high court voted in line with the heterosexist views of many nongay Americans.

One of the major goals of the gay and lesbian liberation movement has been to broaden U.S. civil rights laws to prohibit discrimination against gays and lesbians in the same way that discrimination is legally prohibited against women and people of color in such areas as use of college facilities, employment, and housing. These broader goals have encountered stiff resistance from the U.S. Congress and local legislatures, many of whose members still harbor much homophobia. Nonetheless, in many cities homosexuality is beginning to be recognized by non-homosexuals as a valid lifestyle. For example, some 600,000 same-sex partner households are now reported in the United States, and nationwide some 300 local, state, and federal elected officials are openly gay or lesbian.[124] Moreover, comprehensive state laws or executive orders *prohibiting discrimination* based on sexual orientation are in effect in 38 federal agencies and departments, in 25 states, and in 258 local governments.[125] Only Utah, Florida, and Mississippi prohibit same-sex couples from adopting children, but numerous state governments (including Wyoming, Arkansas, Indiana, and South Carolina) have passed *no* hate crime legislation.[126]

A majority of Americans have gradually adopted a more tolerant attitude toward homosexuality. Most respondents to nationwide opinion polls agree that gays and lesbians should be allowed to live wherever they can afford to live and to stay in public accommodations. Most Americans believe that there should not be laws against homosexuality, and an overwhelming majority believe that same-sex relationships are the participants' business and that discrimination against them is wrong. Even among people who believe that homosexuality is "against God's law," most find that such relationships are a private matter and many express support for gay and lesbian rights. Although a minority of opinion poll respondents favor granting gays and lesbians marriage licenses, a majority support the rights of gays and lesbians to inherit the estates of their partners.[127] For this reason, there is much public support for some sort of legalized relationship for gay and lesbian partners, such as "civil unions," which have a modest number of the benefits of marriage but not the name.

In spite of this general tolerance, opposition to gay rights is still organized, particularly on the religious right, which has pushed a number of antigay legislative measures. For example, two amendments to the Elementary and Secondary Education Act, introduced by antigay members of Congress, sought to bar funding to public schools that include homosexual issues in their curricula, although both were eventually defeated in a House–Senate committee.[128] Numerous attempts have been made in some conservative political areas to legislate discrimination against gays and lesbians at the state level. For example, a majority of Colorado voters approved a state constitutional amendment that bars local governments from prohibiting discrimination in jobs and housing on the basis of sexual orientation, thereby automatically repealing the gay-rights ordinances of Aspen, Boulder, and Denver. Antigay government action can trigger more violent attacks on gay people. Soon after the Colorado election, 23 hate crimes against gay and lesbian individuals and groups were reported in Denver alone.[129] Supporters of gay and lesbian rights organized a boycott of Colorado's tourist industry and filed a lawsuit challenging the federal constitutionality of the anti-gay amendment. The Colorado Supreme Court later ruled that this amendment violated the equal protection guaranteed by the U.S. Constitution, and in 1996 the U.S. Supreme Court upheld the Colorado court's decision. Efforts to pass similar measures in other states have been unsuccessful, although numerous anti-gay measures have been passed at the local level.[130]

Interestingly, efforts to repress gays and lesbians or information about homosexuality have in some areas led to more organizing and openness among gays and lesbians and also to coalition building with nonhomophobic heterosexual groups to fight bigotry and intolerance. Such was the case in Oregon's gay and lesbian business community following the Oregon Citizens Alliance's unsuccessful campaign for an ordinance that would have forced cities to "discourage" homosexuality. Although Oregon's gays and lesbians continue to face significant discrimination and other difficulties in most areas of life, especially in less urbanized areas, their greater openness has brought a new feeling of strength in numbers. They have demonstrated their presence in a variety of area businesses. Individuals have reported personal benefits. The president of a gay and lesbian business association has explained, "As you accept yourself it releases energy. Accepting one's sexual orientation is very freeing. If someone is not out they spend a lot of energy maintaining a fiction."[131] Some have been surprised by the support they have received from the heterosexual community. One building contractor reported that although he had feared his business might go under once he came out, "Nothing happened. In fact I did more business in the next 12 months than I ever had." Numerous local people told him they respected his decision; some even said, "Wow, finally an honest contractor."[132]

AIDS and the Gay and Lesbian Community

Gay and lesbian Americans suffered a significant setback with the arrival of the disease called the acquired immune deficiency syndrome (AIDS), first diagnosed in the United States in 1981. Because AIDS is assumed to have been introduced into the United States by homosexual men, it has become known, erroneously, as a uniquely gay disease and has led to heightened homophobia among heterosexuals. Two years after AIDS was first diagnosed, the ultraconservative columnist Patrick Buchanan, who would later run for president, wrote, "Homosexuals . . . have declared war on nature, and now nature is exacting an awful retribution."[133]

As of 2003, the cumulative estimated number of diagnosed adult and adolescent AIDS cases reported in the United States was 929,985. About 9,419 children under the age of 13 had contracted AIDS; most acquired the disease from their mothers. Roughly 47 percent of AIDS cases involve contracting the disease through male homosexual contact. Significantly, lesbians have the lowest risk for AIDS, although many heterosexuals generalize data regarding gay men to lesbians. Heterosexual contact accounts for about 15 percent of AIDS cases, with women having a much higher rate of contracting AIDS through heterosexual contact than men.[134]

There are many public misconceptions about the human immunodeficiency virus (HIV). Some Americans believe it can be passed by such actions as touching or hugging. However, HIV is only transmitted by the direct exchange of bodily fluids, most commonly semen or blood. Nearly 143,000 Americans whose blood tests indicate that they are infected with HIV, which is believed to cause AIDS, show no symptoms and have not developed AIDS as yet, although the virus can change from a dormant to an active state at any time. Drug use is also linked to the migration of HIV in the U.S. population. Thus, intravenous drug users who share needles with an infected person and individuals receiving a transfusion of infected blood are major at-risk groups for getting the virus. Almost one-third of AIDS cases are intravenous drug users. Although the number of deaths from AIDS has declined by 14 percent since 1998, AIDS has claimed over 501,000 lives.[135] It is still one of the country's, and the world's, most serious public health issues, and many activists have called for much more research on and action toward reducing the impact of AIDS in both homosexual and heterosexual communities.

SUMMARY

In this chapter we have examined major examples of human behavior often labeled as "deviant" in this society: homelessness, mental illness, illegal drug abuse, and homosexuality. In some cases this behavior is regarded as so deviant that it is classified as criminal, as in the case of illegal drug use. Some social science perspectives on deviance have focused heavily on individual deviations; that is, these social problems are viewed mainly in individual and family disorganization terms. Critical power–conflict analysts have rejected this tendency and have instead underscored how societal conditions (such as the unjust inequalities inherent in capitalism, sexism, and racism) generate behavior (such as the street living of the unemployed homeless) that is regarded as socially deviant. Labeling theorists have underscored the point that deviance is *not* inherent in behavior, but rather is an ever-changing label applied to that behavior by other people in society.

Who and *what* are deviant are sometimes defined by a majority of our society, but often the *who* and *what* are defined, initially or principally, by the most powerful members of the dominant class, racial, and gender groups. Not every member of society plays an equal role in defining who is so deviant as to be stigmatized. The deviance labeling process reflects the disproportionate power of the most powerful groups—particularly top corporate executives and other affluent white men—within political, economic, and media organizations to define individual or group actions as socially acceptable or unacceptable.

Today, millions of Americans face the trials of homelessness. These homeless people are often viewed by more affluent Americans not as people suffering because of societal conditions, such as unemployment and the lack of affordable housing, but rather as deviants and as social refuse to be discarded. Many business and political leaders have labeled the homeless in negative terms, yet some obvious causes of homelessness are structural and societal—unemployment, low family incomes, the absence of low-cost housing, and the gentrification of central city neighborhoods. The needs of Americans who can only afford moderate rents are for the most part not being met by our system of private housing investment and development.

We have also seen that *mental illness* is another label often applied to people whose behavior is considered socially deviant. While many of those so labeled do have problems of mental impairment, the labeling of them as *mentally ill*—or, worse, as "crazy"—is often negative and detrimental to the solution of their personal and family problems. It may bring rigid institutionalization when that action is very inappropriate. Moreover, some sexism is apparent in this definition system. Women are more likely to be diagnosed as mentally ill than men, and women are sometimes considered ill simply when they take on stereotypically "masculine" characteristics.

Substance abuse is the subject of much political and social concern today. A number of substances are addictive and physically harmful. Interestingly, the most widely used harmful substances are tobacco and alcohol. The use of some addictive substances has been defined by powerful decision makers as legal; the use of others has been defined as illegal. Users of some of these substances, such as crack cocaine and heroin, are labeled highly deviant and deserving of harsh punishment; users of other substances, such as tobacco and alcohol, are not labeled or punished in a harsh way. People use illegal drugs for the same reasons that people use legal substances—ranging from curiosity and boredom to escape from the pain of serious unemployment and economic recessions.

The illegal drug trade involves many people engaged in otherwise legitimate activities. Money-laundering operations involve college-educated lawyers and business investors whom the general public might never associate with illegal drug trafficking. Moreover, the serious drug-dealing activities of overseas government officials friendly to the United States are sometimes ignored (as during the 1980s in the Reagan–Bush Contras war against the Nicaraguan government or during the early 2005 invasion of Afghanistan), when it is to the benefit of U.S. government officials. Such actions have the side effect of protecting and expanding the power of the major drug operations in Latin America or the Middle East. We have noted the debate over the legalization and decriminalization of illegal drug use, a solution advocated by some Americans, but others oppose such a plan. Many opposed to legalization would prefer that all drugs, legal and illegal, be deglamorized by educational and advertising campaigns. Here again we see the importance of the social definition of harmful behavior as criminal or not criminal.

Finally, gay and lesbian Americans are often considered "deviant" by many heterosexual Americans, not primarily because they present any danger to society but because they do not conform to dominant heterosexist norms. Homosexuality has been variously viewed as a physical or mental disorder, a hereditary defect, and a "sin." Gay and lesbian Americans are often seen as dramatically deviant, yet these men and women are as diverse in their personality characteristics and behavior as heterosexual men and women. Most look and behave outwardly as their neighbors do, and research studies on human sexuality have found that there is a significant group of people naturally inclined toward homosexual relationships. It may be, too, that the hostility that many heterosexuals direct at gays and lesbians signals the strong, sexist gender-role definitions in this society.

STUDY QUESTIONS

1. Explain the social labeling approach to the problems traditionally termed "deviance."
2. What is the stereotypical perception of the homeless and homelessness? Can it be substantiated? What are the primary reasons for homelessness in this country?

3. Perspectives on the homeless vary dramatically. Explain how someone adopting a conservative order–market perspective on the homeless would differ from someone with a power–conflict perspective.

4. What are the major causes and consequences of the affordable housing crisis in the United States? Whom do urban displacement and gentrification affect most? How?

5. Why in this society are tobacco and alcohol users generally treated differently from illegal drug users?

6. Are laws regarding homosexuality changing? How, and why?

7. What is the relationship of sexism in gender roles to public attitudes toward homosexuality? Explain the commonplace male hostility toward gay and lesbian Americans.

8. How does a person come to be defined as "mentally ill"? What is the significance of sexism and racism in the definition and treatment of mental illness?

ENDNOTES

1. Kai T. Erikson, "The Sociology of Deviance," in E. C. McDonagh and J. E. Simpson, eds., *Social Problems* (New York: Holt, Rinehart, & Winston, 1965), p. 457.
2. Howard S. Becker, *Outsiders: Studies in the Sociology of Deviance* (New York: Free Press, 1963), p. 9.
3. Edwin M. Lemert, *Social Pathology* (New York: McGraw-Hill, 1951), p. 75; Edwin M. Schur, *Our Criminal Society* (Upper Saddle River, N.J.: Prentice Hall, 1969), p. 115.
4. Schur, *Our Criminal Society,* pp. 114–95; D. Stanley Eitzen, *Social Problems* (Boston: Allyn & Bacon, 1980), pp. 381–87.
5. Spitzer prefers the terms *social junk* and *social dynamite.* Steven Spitzer, "Toward a Marxian Theory of Deviance," in Delos H. Kelly, ed., *Criminal Behavior: Readings in Criminology* (New York: St. Martin's Press, 1980), pp. 175–91.
6. Ibid., p. 184.
7. The U.S. Congress has formally defined a *homeless person* as an individual who lacks a fixed, regular, and adequate nighttime residence or as an individual who has a primary nighttime residence that is a supervised publicly or privately operated shelter designed to provide temporary accommodations (including welfare hotels, congregated shelters, and transitional housing for the mentally ill; an institution that provides a temporary residence for individuals to be institutionalized; or a public or private place not designed for, or ordinarily used as, a regular sleeping accommodation for human beings). See U.S. Code Title 42, Chapter 119, Subchapter 1, Section 11302(a), available at www4.law.cornell.edu/uscode/42/11302.html#FN1.
8. The Urban Institute, *A New Look at Homelessness in America* (February 1, 2000), available from the Urban Institute, 2100 M Street, N.W. Washington, D.C. 20037. See also, www.urban.org.
9. Guy Gugliotta, "Institute Finds a Number that Adds Up, Has Meaning on the Streets," *Washington Post,* May 16, 1994, p. A3.
10. Ibid.
11. *Priority: Home!* (Washington, D.C.: Interagency Council on the Homeless, 1995); see also the National Coalition for the Homeless, *How Many People Experience Homelessness* (September 2002), available at www.nationalhomeless.org/numbers.html.
12. Jonathan Kozol, *Rachel and Her Children: Homelessness in America* (New York: Crown, 1988), pp. 177–80.
13. James D. Wright and Eleanor Weber, *Homelessness and Health* (New York: McGraw-Hill, 1987), pp. 127–28.
14. "Gallup Survey Uncovers 1 in 6 Americans Fear Becoming Homeless: Also Reveals Public's Confidence That Homeless People Are Not Hopeless," *PR Newswire,* December 12, 1995.
15. Ibid; see also National Coalition for the Homeless, *Who Is Homeless?* (September 2002), available at www.nationalhomeless.org.
16. Martha R. Burt, *Over the Edge* (New York: Russell Sage, 1992), p. 6.
17. Community for Creative Non-Violence, *Newsletter,* November 10, 1992.
18. National Coalition for the Homeless, *Who Is Homeless?*
19. National Coalition for the Homeless, *Domestic Violence and Homelessness* (April 1999), available at www.nationalhomeless.org/domestic.html.

20. Gary Robertson, "More Children Are Homeless: Number Seeking Shelter Is Soaring in Area, Nation," *Richmond Times Dispatch,* November 27, 1995, p. A1.

21. National Coalition for the Homeless, *Homeless Veterans* (January 2004), available at www.nationalhomeless.org/veterans.html.

22. National Coalition for the Homeless, *People Need Affordable Housing* (ret. March 22, 2004), available at www.nationalhomeless.org/facts/housing.html.

23. Paul Leonard and Edward Lazere, *A Place to Call Home: The Low Income Housing Crisis in 44 Major Metropolitan Cities* (Washington, D.C.: Center on Budget and Policy Priorities, 1992).

24. National Coalition for the Homeless, *People Need Affordable Housing.*

25. U.S. Department of Housing and Urban Development, *Worst Case Needs for Housing Assistance in the U.S. in 1990 and 1991: A Report to Congress* (Washington, D.C.: 1994).

26. Kozol, *Rachel and Her Children,* p. 11.

27. John I. Gilderbloom and Richard Appelbaum, *Rethinking Rental Housing* (Philadelphia: Temple University Press, 1988), pp. 9–12, 57–60.

28. "How to Deal with Delinquent Rent Payers," *Professional Builder* 50 (November 1985): 32.

29. "Landlord Intelligence," *Dollars & Sense,* October 1985, p. 11.

30. National Coalition for the Homeless, *People Need Affordable Housing.*

31. U.S. Bureau of the Census, *Statistical Abstract of the U.S.: 1991* (Washington, D.C.: 1991), p. 476; U.S. Bureau of the Census, *Statistical Abstract of the U.S.: 1995* (Washington, D.C.: 1995), p. 493; Adele Blong and Barbara Leyser, *Living at the Bottom: An Analysis of 1994 AFDC Benefit Levels* (Washington, D.C.: Center on Social Welfare Policy and Law, 1994).

32. National Coalition for the Homeless, *People Need Affordable Housing.*

33. Laura Waxman, *A Status Report on Hunger and Homelessness in America's Cities: 1994* (Washington, D.C.: U.S. Conference of Mayors, 1994).

34. National Coalition for the Homeless, *Mental Illness and Homelessness* (April 1999), available at www.nationalhomeless.org/mental.html; *Priority: Home!* p. 24; Federal Task Force on Homelessness and Severe Mental Illness, "Outcasts on Main Street: A Report of the Federal Task Force on Homelessness and Severe Mental Illness," 1992.

35. National Coalition for the Homeless, *Mental Illness and Homelessness.*

36. Jacob V. Lamar, "The Homeless: Brick by Brick," *Time,* October 24, 1988, pp. 34, 38.

37. National Coalition for the Homeless, *Illegal to Be Homeless: The Criminalization of Homelessness in the United States,* August 2003, available at www.nationalhomeless.org/civilrights/crim2003/report.pdf.

38. Kozol, *Rachel and Her Children,* p. 199.

39. Ibid., pp. 159, 194; see also Robert Fitch, "Put 'Em Where We Ain't," *The Nation,* April 2, 1988, pp. 466–69; National Coalition for the Homeless, *Illegal to Be Homeless.*

40. Ron Schraiber, "Stereotyping Mental Illness," *Los Angeles Times,* April 3, 1995, p. F3.

41. Thomas Szasz, *The Manufacture of Madness* (New York: Harper and Row, 1970), pp. 137–59; Benjamin Rush, "Lecture on the Medical Jurisprudence of the Mind," in *The Autobiography of Benjamin Rush,* p. 350; quoted in ibid., pp. 141, 143.

42. Peggy A. Thoits, "Self-labeling Processes in Mental Illness: The Role of Emotional Deviance," *American Journal of Sociology* 91, no. 2 (September 1985): 221–49.

43. Elaine and John Cumming, *Closed Ranks* (Cambridge, Mass.: Commonwealth Fund, Harvard University Press, 1957), pp. 101–2, quoted in Erving Goffman, *Asylums* (Garden City, N.Y.: Anchor Books, 1961), p. 128, n. 2.

44. Goffman, *Asylums,* p. 135.

45. Ronald D. Laing and Aaron Esterson, *Sanity, Madness, and the Family* (London: Tavistock, 1964); Thomas J. Scheff, *Being Mentally Ill,* 2nd ed. (Chicago: Aldine, 1984), p. 205. Dr. Melvin Sikes, in a personal communication, has presented the argument about black patients.

46. Elaine Showalter, *The Female Malady* (New York: Pantheon Books, 1985).

47. Laurel Richardson, *The Dynamics of Sex and Gender,* 3rd ed. (New York: Harper and Row, 1988), pp. 10–12.

48. M. Kaplan, "The Issue of Sex Bias in DSM–III," *American Psychologist* 38 (1983): 802–7.

49. Paula Caplan, "We're All Mentally Ill," *Montgomery Advertiser,* October 29, 1995, p. F3.

50. Summary based on the 1986 documentary, *Junkie Junior: Life in the South Bronx,* available at www.reelplay.com.

51. Centers for Disease Control and Prevention, *Targeting Tobacco Use: The Nation's Leading Cause of Death 2004,* available at www.cdc.gov/nccdphp/aag/pdf/aag_osh2004.pdf.

52. Ben Bagdoloam, "Tobacco Road," *The Harmonist* 2, no. 2 (1987): 14–17, 54–55.

53. Centers for Disease Control and Prevention, *Targeting Tobacco Use.*

54. Substance Abuse and Mental Health Services Administration, *Results from the 2001 National Household Survey on Drug Abuse: Volume I, Summary of National Findings* (August 2001), available at www.samhsa.gov/oas/nhsda/2k1nhsda/PDF/cover.pdf.

55. Bagdoloam, "Tobacco Road," pp. 14–17, 54–55.

56. "Documents Unmask Tobacco Industry," *ASH Smoking and Health Review* 25 (September–October 1995): 4; "ASH Files Secret Documents with FDA," *ASH Smoking and Health Review* 25 (November–December 1995): 1.

57. Vicki Kemper, "Where the Action Is," *Common Cause Magazine,* Spring 1995, p. 21.

58. "One State Says No Smoking for Police and Fire Depts.," *New York Times* (national edition), October 2, 1988, p. 14.

59. "Industry Faces First Round of Mega Suits," *ASH Smoking and Health Review* 25 (March–April 1995): 4–5.

60. "U.S. Government Worker Killed by Secondhand Smoke," *ASH Smoking and Health Review* 26 (January–February 1996): 6.

61. "Report Card Shows Many States Failing to Protect the Public," *Heart Disease Weekly* (February 1, 2004), p. 72.

62. Charles Babington, "Tobacco Aid," *Common Cause,* March–April 1991, pp. 9–10; Vicki Kemper, "The Inhalers," *Common Cause Magazine,* Spring 1995, pp. 18–23.

63. Quoted in Danny R. Johnson, "Tobacco Stains," *The Progressive,* December 1992, p. 28; see also p. 27.

64. Centers for Disease Control and Prevention, *Targeting Tobacco Use: The Nation's Leading Cause of Death 2004,* available at www.cdc.gov/nccdphp/aag/pdf/aag_osh2004.pdf.

65. Drusilla Campbell and Marilyn Graham, *Drugs and Alcohol in the Workplace* (New York: Facts on File, 1988), p. 27.

66. Substance Abuse and Mental Health Services Administration, *Results from the 2001 National Household Survey on Drug Abuse.*

67. U.S. Bureau of Justice Statistics, *Sourcebook of Criminal Justice Statistics, 2003,* available at www.albany.edu/sourcebook/pdf/t427.pdf. This count of alcohol-related offenses includes driving under the influence, liquor law violations, drunkenness, disorderly conduct, and vagrancy.

68. U.S. Bureau of Justice Statistics, *Sourcebook of Criminal Justice Statistics, 2003,* available at www.albany.edu/sourcebook/pdf/t3100.pdf.

69. Elliott Currie, *Confronting Crime* (New York: Pantheon Books, 1985), p. 68.

70. Campbell and Graham, *Drugs and Alcohol in the Workplace,* pp. 23, 28, 220; "Beverage World Top 50," *Beverage World 1988–1989 Data Bank* (Shephardsville, Ky.: Keller, 1988–89), p. 25.

71. Michael Windle, "Alcohol Use Among Adolescent and Young Adults," National Institute of Alcohol Abuse and Alcoholism (December 2003), available at www.niaaa.nih.gov/publications/arh27-1/79-86.htm.

72. U.S. Congress, Committee on the Judiciary, "Hard-Core Cocaine Addicts: Measuring—and Fighting—the Epidemic" (Washington, D.C.: 1990).

73. Substance Abuse and Mental Health Services Administration, (September 2003), *Results from the 2002 National Household Survey on Drug Abuse: Volume I, Summary of National Findings,* available at www.oas.samhsa.gov/nhsda/2k2nsduh/Results/apph.htm#tabh.1.

74. PRIDE Surveys, *Pride Questionnaire Report for Grades 5 thru 12, 2002–2003, PRIDE Surveys National Summary* (August 2003), available at www.pridesurveys.com/main/supportfiles/ns0203.pdf.

75. Office of National Drug Control Policy, *What America's Users Spend on Illegal Drugs, 1988–2000* (December 2001), available at www.whitehousedrugpolicy.gov/publications/pdf/american_users_spend_2002.pdf; U.S. Department of Justice, *Sourcebook of Criminal Justice Statistics: 2003.*

76. David L. Lewis, "Bias in Drug Sentences," *National Law Journal,* February 5, 1996, p. A19.

77. Tom Morganthau et al., "Should Drugs Be Legal?" *Newsweek,* May 30, 1988, p. 38.

78. Jacob V. Lamar, "Kids Who Sell Crack," *Time,* May 9, 1988, pp. 24, 27.

79. Janice Castro, "The Cash Cleaners," *Time,* October 24, 1988, pp. 65–66.

80. Ibid.

81. Currie, *Confronting Crime,* p. 115.

82. Alfred Lindesmith, Anselm Strauss, and Norman Denzin, *Social Psychology,* 6th ed. (Upper Saddle River, N.J.: Prentice Hall, 1988), p. 323.

83. Ibid., pp. 324–26.

84. U.S. Department of Labor, Bureau of Labor Statistics, *Characteristics of Minimum Wage Workers, 2002,* available at stats.bls.gov/cps/minwage2002.htm.

85. Elijah Anderson, "The Code of the Streets: Sociology of Urban Violence," *Atlantic Monthly,* May 1994, p. 80.

86. A. Robert Kaufman, "Stopping the Drug Wars: Part II," *Baltimore Sun,* December 21, 1994, p. 27A.
87. "Junkie King," *Time,* January 28, 1980, p. 70.
88. Jim Atkinson, "The War Zone," *Texas Monthly,* November 1988, pp. 104–11, 172–81.
89. Lamar, "Kids Who Sell Crack," p. 22; see also Tracy Gordon Fox, "Chipping Away at Drug, Prostitution Problems," *Hartford Courant* (Connecticut), October 19, 2003, p. A1.
90. Lamar, "Kids Who Sell Crack," pp. 20, 22.
91. Samantha Stainburn, "Drug Bust," *National Journal,* November 1995, p. 48.
92. Jake Ginsky, "Drug Mistreatment," *Mother Jones,* February 18, 2000, available at www.motherjones.com/news/feature/2000/02/rehab.html.
93. George Church, "Thinking the Unthinkable," *Time,* May 30, 1988, p. 18.
94. Nick Clark, "The Grand Illusion," *Common Cause* 14, no. 3 (May–June 1988): 12.
95. Viveca Novak, "The War on Drugs Gets Serious," *Common Cause,* July–August 1988, p. 35.
96. General Accounting Office, "Heavy Investment in Military Surveillance Is not Paying Off" (Washington, D.C.: 1993); General Accounting Office, "Interdiction Efforts in Central America Have Had Little Impact on the Flow of Drugs" (Washington, D.C.: 1994).
97. Stainburn, "Drug Bust," p. 48.
98. Office of National Drug Control Policy, *The President's National Drug Control Policy* (2003), (ret. April 17, 2004), available at www.whitehousedrugpolicy.gov/publications/policy/ndcs03/index.html
99. Jacqueline Sharkey, "The Contra–Drug Trade Off," *Common Cause,* September–October 1988, pp. 23–33; J. Martinez Vera, "Supplying the 40 Million Who Won't Say No," *World Press Review,* May 1988, p. 28.
100. See *U.S. v. Noriega,* 117 F.3d 1206 (1997).
101. Quoted in Marc Leepson, "Should Drugs Be Legalized?" *Common Cause,* July–August 1988, pp. 31, 32; see also Ernest van den Haag and John LeMoult, "Legalize Illegal Drugs," in Julie S. Bach, ed., *Drug Abuse: Opposing Views* (St. Paul, Minn.: Greenhaven Press, 1988).
102. Leepson, "Should Drugs Be Legalized?" p. 32.
103. Cited in Joshua Wolf Shenk, "Why You Can Hate Drugs and Still Want to Legalize Them," *Washington Monthly,* October 1995, p. 36.
104. Morganthau, "Should Drugs Be Legal?" p. 38.
105. John Boswell, *Christianity, Social Tolerance, and Homosexuality* (Chicago: University of Chicago Press, 1980), p. 135; see also pp. 7–27.
106. Randy Shilts, "What's Fair in Love and War," *Newsweek,* February 1, 1993, p. 59.
107. *Loving v. Virginia,* 388 U.S. 1 (1967).
108. Angie Cannon, "A Legal Maze—And More To Come," *U.S. News & World Report* (March 8, 2004), p. 30.
109. Federal Bureau of Investigation, *Hate Crime Statistics 2003* (ret. June 21, 2005), available at www.fbi.gov/ucr/03hc.pdf.
110. "Anti-Lesbian/Gay Violence in 1995," New York: National Coalition of Anti-Violence Programs and the New York City Gay and Lesbian Anti-Violence Project, 1996; Stanley Kauffmann, "Ballot Measure 9," *New Republic,* July 10, 1995, p. 24.
111. Federal Bureau of Investigation, *Hate Crime Statistics 2003.*
112. The data are cited in Paul Robinson, "The Way We Do the Things We Do," *New York Times,* October 30, 1994, Section 7, p. 3; see also Edward O. Laumann, John H. Gagnon, Robert T. Michael, and Stuart Michaels, *The Social Organization of Sexuality: Sexual Practices in the U.S.* (Chicago: University of Chicago Press, 1994); Robert T. Michael, John H. Gagnon, Edward O. Laumann, and Gina Kolata, *Sex in America: A Definitive Survey* (Boston: Little, Brown, 1994).
113. The previous section also draws generally on Alan P. Bell and Martin S. Weinberg, *Homosexualities: A Study of Diversity among Men and Women* (New York: Simon & Schuster, 1978), pp. 23, 216, cited in Irving M. Zeitlin, *The Social Condition of Humanity* (New York: Oxford University Press, 1984), pp. 331–32; Lindesmith, Strauss, and Denzin, *Social Psychology,* pp. 333–34; Maurice Leznoff and W. A. Westley, "The Homosexual Community," *Social Problems* 3 (1956): 257–63; Zeitlin, *The Social Condition of Humanity,* p. 329.
114. Lindesmith, Strauss, and Denzin, *Social Psychology,* pp. 333–34.
115. Service Members Legal Defense Network, "Ten Year Time Line of Don't Ask, Don't Tell" (ret. April 19, 2004), available at www.sldn.org/templates/dont/index.html?section=42; interview with representative of Service Members Legal Defense Network, February 1996.
116. Ellen Goodman, "Homophobia in the Ranks," *Boston Globe,* January 28, 1993, p. 15.
117. Shilts, "What's Fair in Love and War," p. 59.
118. "Acceptance of Gays on Rise, Polls Show," *Los Angeles Times* (March 30, 2004), pp. B1, B7.

119. Interview with representative of Service Members Legal Defense Network, February 1996; see also Public Agenda, "Military Discharges" (ret. March 27, 2004), available at www.publicagenda.org/issues/factfiles_detail.cfm?issue_type=gay_rights&list=14.

120. Quoted in Shilts, "What's Fair in Love and War," pp. 58–59.

121. *Lawrence v. Texas,* 537 U.S. 1231 (2003).

122. American Civil Liberties Union, "ACLU, SLDN and Lambda Legal Urge Military's Highest Court to Strike Down Law Banning Consensual Sodomy" (October 2, 2003), available at www.aclu.org/LesbianGayRights/LesbianGayRights.cfm?ID=13899&c=41.

123. *Boy Scouts of America v. Dale,* 530 U.S. 640 (2000).

124. Gay and Lesbian Leadership Institute, "Out and Elected Nationwide" (ret. March 25, 2004), available at www.victoryinstitute.org/outofficials/stateofficials/?cState=All.

125. "Acceptance of Gays on Rise, Polls Show," *Los Angeles Times* (March 30, 2004), pp. B1, B7.

126. See, generally, Public Agenda, "Gay Rights" (ret. March 27, 2004), available at www.publicagenda.org.

127. Albert H. Cantril and Susan Davis Cantril, *Live and Let Live* (New York: American Civil Liberties Union Foundation, 1994), pp. 41–48, 174.

128. "Helms Loses Bid to Ban Talk of Gays in Schools," *San Francisco Chronicle,* September 24, 1994, p. 4.

129. Ned Zeman and Michael Meyer, "No 'Special Rights' for Gays," *Newsweek,* November 23, 1992, p. 32; Bill Turque, "Gays Under Fire," *Newsweek,* September 14, 1992, pp. 35–40.

130. Interview with representative of Equality Colorado, February 1996.

131. Steve Dodge, "Out and in Business: Gay and Lesbian Business People Are Increasingly Open About Who They Are, Whether in Portland or the Rest of the State," *Oregon Business,* November 1995, p. 66.

132. Ibid.

133. Quoted in Nick Clark et al., "AIDS," *Newsweek,* August 12, 1985, p. 20.

134. Center for Disease Control, Divisions of HIV/AIDS Prevention, Basic Statistics (December 2002), available at www.cdc.gov/hiv/stats.htm.

135. Ibid.

chapter 10

Problems of Work and Worker Alienation

We are in the early stages of a shift from "mass labor" to highly skilled "elite labor," accompanied by increasing automation in the production of goods and the delivery of services .... This steady decline of mass labor threatens to undermine the very foundations of the modern American state. For nearly 200 years, the heart of the social contract and the measure of individual human worth have centered on the value of each person's labor. How does society even begin to adjust to a new era in which labor is devalued or even rendered worthless?[1]

Work is a significant activity for the majority of adult Americans during most of their lives. Work outside the home brings not only a life-supporting income; it is also a source of self-identity. Performing well or poorly in work has an effect on our self-esteem, on whether we see ourselves as useful or worthless human beings. Who are you? When asked this question, many people respond in terms of their occupation—"I am a plumber," "I am a teacher," or "I am an unemployed laborer"—or in terms of their industry or employer—"I work for the city" or "I work for IBM." Not surprisingly, then, work-related problems often adversely affect workers' entire lives and those of their families—and thus the larger society.

Employers and their political allies view certain work problems (for example, strikes) as a threat to their control of the workplace and thus to profits. In contrast, workers tend to see strikes and much job turnover as rational responses to workplace problems—to tedious jobs, unsafe chemical exposure, or job-threatening automation. Economic conditions of the early twenty-first century, including the global marketplace, have led many company executives to adopt new strategies to enlarge profits. Many corporate strategies for remaining competitive, such as reducing the number of employees, cutting wages, or outsourcing jobs overseas, create heavy burdens for workers. Job destruction and job creation are now frequently discussed issues in the United States.

GOALS OF THIS CHAPTER

In previous chapters we examined a number of important social problems related to work and the workplace, including corporate crime, unemployment, low wages, income inequality, and racial and gender discrimination. This chapter continues our exploration of the interconnectedness of work-related problems by focusing specifically on workplace issues. Here, we analyze the dangers inherent in the U.S. workplace, the consequences of alienation for workers, worker resistance to oppressive conditions in the workplace, and capitalists' resistance to workers' attempts to share control of the workplace.

DANGERS IN THE WORKPLACE

Serious environmental problems still confront people at work. The United States has the worst worker safety and health record of all major industrialized nations; U.S. workers are two to three times as likely to be killed or injured on the job as are European workers. The AFL-CIO reports that each year more than 6 million workers are injured or become seriously ill from their jobs, that at least 50,000 workers die from occupational illnesses, that 5,500 are killed on the job, and that thousands of others are permanently disabled from work-related injuries.[2] Many industries expose workers to a variety of serious health hazards. While some employees are ignorant of workplace hazards, those who do know are often unaware that employers can remove many hazards if they chose to invest profits for that important purpose.

Accidents and Injuries

Occupation-related injury rates vary by industry. Heavy industrial jobs in construction, mining, transportation, and manufacturing generally have the highest injury and fatality rates and the greatest number of days lost. The U.S. Bureau of Labor Statistics reported 4.1 million nonfatal workplace injuries in 2003 alone—an injury rate of 5.0 per 100 full-time workers.[3] That same year, 1.4 million cases required at least one day away from work, and 1 million other cases of injuries required a job transfer or restricted work activity. Roughly half of work-related injuries are sprains and strains resulting from overexertion and contacts with objects or equipment, and falls.[4] In 2002, the Bureau of Labor Statistics also reported 5,524 fatal occupational injuries.[5]

Occupational Illnesses

Occupational illness rates are high among U.S. workers. Private employers reported more than 269,500 occupational illnesses in just one recent year (2002).[6] An occupational illness is an abnormal condition or disorder caused by exposure to factors associated with employment. Occupational illnesses may be acute or chronic and may be caused by inhalation, absorption, ingestion, or direct contact. An estimated 50,000 workers die each year from workplace-caused illnesses.[7]

Official statistics on workplace-related illnesses reflect only the cases reported each year. These tend to be easily identifiable illnesses that are obviously related to workplace activity, such as skin disorders and respiratory conditions caused by toxic agents. Long-term latent illnesses, such as those caused by exposure to cancer-causing agents, are not so

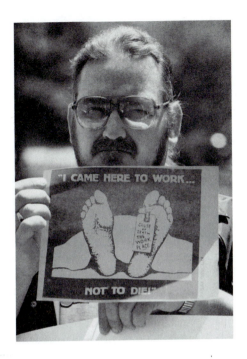

Many U.S. workplaces are dangerous to workers' health and safety. (AFL-CIO News)

easily related to the workplace, and they are seldom included in official statistics. Because they typically take years to develop, these maladies may not become obvious until a worker retires. Yet industries regularly expose millions of workers to toxic substances and high levels of carcinogens; several hundred thousand new cases of long-term, occupation-related illnesses are diagnosed annually. The National Institute for Occupational Safety and Health (NIOSH) warns that long-term exposure to dangerous dust, radiation, and chemicals causes thousands of preventable deaths each year. Black lung, a disease caused by coal dust, has killed or disabled hundreds of thousands of miners. Silicosis (from rock and sand dust), brown lung (from textile dust), white lung (from asbestos fibers), and red lung (from iron dust) kill thousands of other workers each year.[8]

Cancer rates have increased in recent decades. Public health experts believe that workplace and environmental carcinogens are responsible for many cancer deaths. Occupation-related conditions may cause as much as 40 percent of cancers. NIOSH estimates that 20,000 cancer deaths and 40,000 new cases of cancer each year are attributable directly to occupations. This constitutes a major disaster for workers, as well as for the public, many of whom suffer injuries when factories and other workplaces discharge chemicals that pollute air and water. Surprisingly, workplace carcinogens have not received adequate attention from either government or corporate regulators.[9]

Repetitive-motion disorders, such as carpal tunnel syndrome, are the most common workplace illnesses and result in the longest absences from work. These disorders account for one-third of all reported occupational illnesses. Union studies put the annual number of these disorders very high, at 1 million. Repetitive-motion illnesses occur most often in manufacturing jobs but also affect workers using computer keyboards and similar devices in white-collar workplaces, which have traditionally had the lowest injury and illness rates.[10]

Responsibility for Dangers

Who is primarily responsible for the many accidents and injuries in work environments? Business leaders blame most work injuries on worker carelessness and prefer worker education as the solution. The U.S. Chamber of Commerce, the National Association of Manufacturers, and some elected officials have propagated this worker carelessness theory. Even the National Safety Council's exhortation to workers that safety is their responsibility places blame on employees. Little systematic research is available on industrial accidents, but what studies have been done find no evidence that workers are primarily responsible for most job accidents, and they conclude that the worker carelessness theory is often a convenient myth for employers.[11]

Far more evidence exists that the intense drive for profit by employers is to blame for most workplace hazards. Pressure on employees to work faster has frequently led to an increase in the number of accidents and repetitive-motion injuries. In the 1980s, for example, the U.S. Department of Agriculture permitted a speed-up in meat processing plants. Despite efforts by union safety committees and a national safety campaign, the meatpacking industry has generally had one of the highest occupational illness and injury rates of all industries. The average rate of work-related accidents and illnesses in the meatpacking industry rose from 33.4 per 100 full-time workers in 1987 to 44.4 per 100 full-time workers in 1992, but then fell to 24.7 per 100 by 2000. This indicates significant improvement, yet it is still a high rate of casualties. For example, when management at the Morrell meatpacking plant in Sioux Falls, Iowa, accelerated the assembly line speed by as much as 84 percent in some departments, injuries increased 51 percent.[12] One account describes certain work conditions:

> Just after she took the job last summer, Carri Lee Miller knew it was a mistake. Her hands would ache after every day at Morrell's meatpacking house here, where she sometimes had to make 1,900 cuts an hour on the hogs' heads that passed by her station. At night, she would wake up in pain with her fingers clenched in a fist that she could not open alone. The doctors . . . say her fingers may never function the way they did before she went to work at Morrell.[13]

Many of the meatpacking industry's safety problems are attributed to outdated technology and the industry's intense competition. Numerous workers receive cuts, burns, or mutilated hands and arms because of unsafe conditions. Some plants have decreased their workforce but not their expected output, causing worker injuries from a combination of speed and repetitive motion. Some workers' tasks require them to repeat the same motion thousands of times daily. Even with the high rate of repeated-trauma injuries, a meatpacking plant's relatively high wages are attractive for workers, such as undocumented immigrants, who have few work alternatives.

Repeated-trauma disorders reached serious levels in the 1980s when political pressure and funding cutbacks made it difficult for the Occupational Health and Safety Administration (OSHA) to develop needed regulations. Although some employers, including auto manufacturers, have acted to prevent ergonomic (motion-related) injuries, some political conservatives and industry leaders have opposed creation of an ergonomics standard. The trucking and courier industry, which has high rates and numbers of ergonomic injuries, has led the opposition. The American Trucking Association and United Parcel Service of America, Inc. (UPS) led a 300-company business coalition to pressure Congress to stop OSHA from publishing an ergonomics standard and supported a plan to ban OSHA from working on the standard. To keep OSHA from developing ergonomic rules, in the late 1990s UPS spent an estimated $450 per member of the House Appropriations Subcommittee, which came to a UPS "meet and greet" event on the issue. All members of the subcommittee who attended (16 out of 17) voted in favor of UPS.[14]

Through its political action committee, UPS, the world's largest package-delivery service with hundreds of thousands of full- and part-time employees and billions in annual sales, has contributed millions to political campaigns over the last decade. Some UPS employees, former employees, and OSHA officials have charged that UPS endangers its workers by requiring them to lift too much weight or to perform excessive repetitive motions. Ron Carey, president of the Teamsters union and a former UPS driver, has said that "if safety is confronted by production demands, then safety goes out the window."[15] In 2000 the outgoing Bill Clinton administration issued labor regulations designed to protect workers against motion-related injuries, but the 2001 George W. Bush administration quickly called off implementation of the new rules. UPS is one of OSHA's most frequently cited companies, with 1,300 safety violation citations and $4.6 million in fines between 1990 and 1996 alone. UPS continues to have a high rate of injury. UPS has 178 work sites nationwide that appear on OSHA's list of workplaces with high rates of worker injuries. The biggest worker-injury case against UPS thus far involved a $3 million fine for failure to protect workers from hazardous materials spilled from damaged packages.[16]

The previously mentioned business coalition's opposition to worker-protection initiatives, and its preferences for making compliance with job safety laws voluntary and for replacing penalties with warnings, are strongly opposed by unions that represent many transport and delivery workers. The policies favored by this business coalition would keep government regulatory agencies from protecting workers in numerous other industries, from meatcutting to data entry. AFL-CIO job safety director Peg Seminario has commented, "Efforts of Republicans in Congress to stop OSHA's ergonomics standard and to slash OSHA's budget . . . will leave millions of American workers without much-needed protection."[17]

Corporations tend to move slowly on major changes in workplace safety. Executives often wait to make major safety changes until pressured to do so because they fear the costs of changes will lower profit levels. If it costs significantly less to allow deaths and injuries on the job than to prevent them, some employers will delay taking the action necessary to ensure worker safety. However, a representative of the United Food and Commercial Workers (UFCW) union reported that in plants operating under OSHA settlement agreements requiring an ergonomics program, all measures have shown that the programs benefit employers as well as workers: Production goes up while injury incidence rates, surgery rates, insurance rates, compensation claims, and worker turnover decrease, allowing a plant to recoup the cost of implementing the program.[18] Nonetheless, some employers resist even low-cost safety changes if those changes transfer greater workplace control to workers. Much of the human cost of production is today borne by workers themselves.

Robert Reich, secretary of labor during the Clinton administration, told of an experience he had as an official at the Federal Trade Commission:

> We had some obvious problems having to do with consumer protection. We'd put out an initial notice of a proposed rule-making. What happened? Interestingly, the Japanese and many European companies came to my office—not with their lawyers, but with their engineers. And the question was: How can we get on with fixing the problem? The American companies showed up with their lawyers, and their issue was: What evidence do you have?[19]

Workers are directly affected by workplace conditions: noise, heat, dangers of machinery. They often suffer these conditions 40 hours a week, 50 weeks a year, throughout their working lives. In recent decades, corporate management has fought attempts by unions to add health and safety issues in collective bargaining (union negotiation) settings. Employers have frequently been able to avoid bargaining over safety because unions are preoccupied with employers' attempts to force wage concessions. Yet unintentional workplace injuries cost individuals, employers, and the United States nearly $128 billion annually in lost productivity, lost wages, medical expenses, and insurance administration costs.[20] The cost in human suffering is incalculable.

Toxic Exposure

Many chemicals to which industries expose millions in work environments have never been adequately tested for safety. Many of these are toxic; some are known or suspected carcinogens. Chemicals have a negative impact in several ways: the immediate effects on a worker's health, the long-term effects (such as cancers) on a worker, and the effects on family members. Exposure to asbestos, a substance widely used in the manufacture of fire-resistant materials and insulation, is one serious health hazard. The United States is facing an asbestos disease epidemic. Since 1979, an estimated 43,000 people have died from asbestos-related diseases, and experts predict that another 100,000 will die from asbestos exposure in the next decade. A recent insurance industry analysis found that more than $300 billion will be needed to provide for all people injured by asbestos over the next 50 years. Asbestos is a major health concern in states like West Virginia where "thousands of boilermakers, ironworkers and others who toiled in the state's power plants, steel mills and chemical factories are potential victims."[21] Researchers documented asbestos-related diseases as early as the 1930s, and insurance companies had recognized the dangers of asbestos exposure more than a decade earlier. Yet for decades, manufacturers hid this from employees and the public, allowing millions of workers to be exposed unnecessarily to asbestos. Workers also endanger their families with asbestos dust brought home on their clothing. Some compensation has been paid. During the 1980s, for example, thousands of employees and their families sued Johns Manville, a major asbestos producer. In a negotiated settlement, the company set up a $2.5 billion fund to compensate claimants, although even this large fund was inadequate given the damage caused to workers.[22]

The negative impact of indirect asbestos exposure has been high, since unbound asbestos fibers get into food and air from manufactured products, including insulation materials, air ducts, brake linings, and filters for beer and drugs. In some areas, industries have dumped substantial amounts of asbestos waste directly into the air and water. One dumping ground is the Great Lakes, from which numerous cities get drinking water. This type of pollution has obviously affected many people in addition to asbestos workers.[23]

Pesticides and herbicides create serious problems for farm workers who put them on crops or pick the crops after pesticides are used. Of all occupational groups, agricultural workers have one of the highest rates of work-related illnesses, especially skin diseases and poisonings.[24] Frequently, workers are not given adequate information on the dangers of the chemicals they encounter. In a number of documented cases, corporate executives knew about the serious dangers of chemicals but took no action until forced to do so by unions, government officials, or lawsuits brought by workers. Thus, the serious dangers of asbestos dust were hidden by executives from workers and the public for decades, probably out of fear that corporate profits would suffer.

According to Dr. Samuel S. Epstein, most medical researchers and other scientists who work for chemical companies accept their employers' position that the companies' products are safe if used with care. Most industries dealing with toxic materials are reluctant to voluntarily invest a significant amount in protecting workers from hazardous chemicals or testing chemicals for their possible dangers to workers. Older plants have continued to operate without being refitted with safety technologies, and many new plants have not been built safely.[25]

Top industrialists and their managers use various tactics to convince the public there is little risk from exposure to chemicals in the workplace. Some have hired expensive media consultants to prepare campaigns aimed at the public in attempts to get what they view as burdensome government regulations relaxed. Business leaders were successful, for example, in getting the federal government to relax its ban on saccharin, a sweetener whose safety had been challenged. Some chemical companies have spent millions of dollars to market dangerous chemicals claimed to be safe. One corporate tactic is to blame workplace problems on workers or consumers for not handling chemicals properly.[26] Many industry executives contribute substantial sums to congressional candidates and spend huge sums on lobbyists to prevent passage of tougher laws regulating toxic chemicals.

Safety Regulation

The first major occupational safety laws and workers' compensation laws were passed by state legislatures in the early twentieth century, over intense objections from business leaders concerned with profits. Yet most early laws had modest effects on workplace safety because they were weakly enforced by government agencies influenced by industries they were supposed to regulate.

For several reasons, workplace safety has yet to become a central political issue in the United States. One reason is that corporations are allowed to underreport industrial accident and death statistics. Corporate-employed physicians and safety engineers are usually afraid to speak out publicly for fear of losing jobs. State safety regulations are often weakly enforced by often understaffed enforcement agencies. Officials in regulatory agencies are sometimes former participants in the industries they regulate. Federal government officials, with periodic exceptions, have dragged their feet in pressing for worker safety, often because they too are more concerned with business profits than safety.[27]

The 1970 federal Occupational Safety and Health Act (OSHAct) created the Occupational Safety and Health Administration (OSHA). This demonstrated that lobbying by workers and labor unions could produce some measure of federal commitment to workplace safety. Still, OSHA is often seen as a threat to profits by many business leaders, whose pressures have succeeded in obstructing OSHA's worker-oriented goals. OSHA has been inadequately staffed from the beginning. Today, only 2,144 federal and state OSHA inspectors are responsible for *8 million* workplaces; it would take 115 years for them to inspect every U.S. work site. Given the small number of inspectors, in 18 states it would take between 100 and 149 years to visit every workplace once, and in Florida, Georgia, Louisiana, and Mississippi it would take 150 years or more to inspect all workplaces.[28]

The OSHAct requires the agency to set safety standards for toxic materials in workplaces, but OSHA has relied heavily on industry research for much rule making. In its first

Conservative politicians, such as Republican Bob Dole, have helped reduce the number of government health and safety regulations.

nine years, the agency established only five new major permanent standards, including those for asbestos and benzene. By 1990, OSHA had set only 410 advisory standards for the thousands of chemicals used in workplaces. Moreover, even OSHA's official standards for dangerous chemicals do not eliminate serious levels of worker exposure. Corporate pressure has forced standards that are far from "no detectable" exposure, compromises that can mean thousands of unnecessary deaths. Officially, violations carry substantial fines and can result in the closing of a facility, but enforcement is a serious problem. The vast majority of workplaces are unlikely ever to be inspected, and fines have usually been modest.[29] Today, penalties for violations of health and safety laws remain very low—in 2002, the average penalty was only $886![30]

Regulated industries often respond by setting up organizations to fight OSHA, arguing that major restrictions on use of toxic chemicals are costly, cutting profits and jobs. The Center for the Study of Responsive Law has noted numerous examples of OSHA regulations being intentionally ignored. Factories with serious air-pollution and safety violations have been certified as safe or their owners assessed only with token fines. Thus, the workers who died in the Imperial Foods poultry processing plant fire (cited in Chapter 2) would probably have lived had safety codes been enforced at their workplace. This antiregulation policy has especially dominated recent Republican presidential administrations, from that of Ronald Reagan in the 1980s to that of George W. Bush in the early 2000s.[31]

To track workplace safety, OSHA today relies on what is called the OSHA 200 Log, in which employers are supposed to record job-related injuries and illnesses. A report by

Table 10.1 Selected Federal Expenditures for 2005 Fiscal Year

	Federal Expenditure	Funding per Citizen
Savings and loan bailout	$153 billion	$524.00
Environmental Protection Agency	7.8 billion	27.00
Fish and wildlife protection	1.3 billion	4.45
Food safety and inspection service	5.1 billion	17.46
OSHA	737 million	2.52

the Center for the Study of Responsive Law notes that many employers systematically manipulate these OSHA 200 Logs. Doctoring these logs is easy to do since they are maintained by employers, and OSHA has so few inspectors that it is highly unlikely the records will ever be checked by OSHA inspectors. A U.S. Department of Justice investigation found that many companies keep two sets of workplace injury and illness records, "one for the employer's insurer and OSHA, and the other for the companies' health clinics."[32]

The U.S. government has placed a low priority on funding for workplace safety. In Table 10.1 we compare government expenditures on OSHA with other federal expenditures. The government is clearly more concerned with bailing out banks or even with fish and wildlife protection than with the health and safety of workers. Only about two-and-a-half dollars per citizen are spent annually on workplace safety regulation.[33]

Numerous business-oriented conservatives in Congress periodically attack OSHA and seek to placate employers by weakening its regulation further. OSHA is a favorite target of these so-called regulatory reformers. These business interests have affected not only Republican administrations but also Democratic administrations. Thus, the Clinton administration had one of the worst records of protecting workers in the history of OSHA, with the lowest record of annual inspections and the highest percentage of willful violations by employers dismissed or downgraded. The attacks on OSHA continue today. As one informed commentator explains, "Much of what passes for public debate about OSHA today consists of corporate-inspired propaganda, half truths, inventions, and fabrications in the form of anecdotal horror stories about the excesses of the regulatory agency—stories which are frequently exposed as outright lies."[34] Nonetheless, workers continue to speak out strongly on behalf of more OSHA regulations, inspections, and enforcement. In one survey, almost two-thirds of the 800 respondents said that employers would take health and safety issues more seriously if they knew that they could expect OSHA inspections. Altogether, more than eight in ten said that regular OSHA inspections would influence employers' actions.[35]

Indeed, injury rates have decreased in workplaces where OSHA has penalized numerous employers for violations, and the rates of occupational fatalities continue to decline. OSHA has saved thousands of lives in industries where it has focused enforcement activities, but industries that get little attention from OSHA have shown little or no improvement.[36]

The Right-to-Know Movement

Many working people have organized to seek more information about chemicals they handle. The Philadelphia City Council passed the first major right-to-know law. Witnesses for the law included workers in Philadelphia plants who testified that many chemicals had vague labels and cited high cancer rates as a reason for concern. One worker testified that he worked with a chemical, PX-27, which he brought to the hearing in its canister. When he opened the canister to release its contents, the audience heard a loud hiss. One council member asked, "What's that stuff you are releasing?" The worker said, "Oh, it can't be that bad for you. We work with it every day."[37]

Many states do not require employers to label toxic chemicals they use or to disclose the health effects of chemicals. Many chemical containers are marked with brand names, which may not provide detailed information on toxicity. A NIOSH review of 5,000 companies found that most workers do not know the composition of thousands of brand-name substances they use. NIOSH determined that just under half are hazardous. Committees for Occupational Safety and Health—known as COSH groups and composed of union health and safety activists and health and legal professionals—were first organized in the 1970s. They became active in providing information and leadership to workers over subsequent decades and made significant progress in some states. Together with unions, COSH groups continue in getting right-to-know laws passed in many states and cities.[38]

Industry executives have attacked right-to-know legislation, claiming that such will mean unnecessary government interference and that the expense of implementing regulations will lead to plant closings. Supporters of right-to-know reforms believe that industry is actually more concerned about the impact of reforms on labor–management relations. Executives in companies that use toxic chemicals realize that the right-to-know movement will give employees knowledge and may cost profits. They argue that chemical exposure is "just one of the risks" people living in an industrial society must take—just part of industrial progress. But workers and factory-area residents argue that employers have not given them a choice; employees often do not know the long-term consequences of chemicals they are working with until it is too late and they have a terminal illness years later.[39]

In the 1980s, the New Jersey governor signed the Worker and Community Right-to-Know Act, with tough chemical-labeling requirements. Gradually, employers were required to label all chemicals used in the workplace. Regulated industries fought hard against the bill but lost to a coalition including citizens' groups; environmental, community, church, and firefighters' organizations; and unions. After the law passed, the coalition launched "a campaign to insure that workers and the public understand, use, and defend their new rights to information and that the law will be enforced."[40] However, in the 1990s New Jersey's newly elected conservative governor cut more than 2,000 chemicals from the state's right-to-know list. Not surprisingly, a year later three chemicals cut from the list exploded at a New Jersey plant, killing five workers. Dozens of emergency response incidents involving hazardous materials occur in New Jersey every day.[41]

One corporate response to public pressure for health and safety regulations is to move corporate operations from the United States to countries where safety and environmental protection regulations are weak. With expanded federal regulations from agencies such as OSHA, numerous corporations have left the United States. Asbestos, pesticide, textile, and other industries have gone to Mexico, Taiwan, China, Brazil, the Philippines, Malaysia, and South Korea. U.S. workers lose jobs, and overseas workers face a greater chance of contracting diseases from their workplaces. Some worker-oriented analysts see this capital flight as serious corporate "crime" because the injuries, illnesses, and deaths of overseas workers are preventable if workplaces are made safer. Indeed, one of the world's worst industrial accidents occurred in Bhopal, India, in 1984 when a toxic gas used in manufacturing pesticides leaked from a Union Carbide plant, killing nearly 22,000 people and contaminating water and soil near the plant. Union Carbide eventually paid $470 million as part of an out-of-court settlement, yet 20 years after the disaster neither Union Carbide nor the plant's new owner, Dow Chemical International, have yet cleaned up the site. No fewer than *600,000 people* have filed compensation claims against the company complaining of breathlessness, constant fatigue, stomach pain, cardiac problems, and tuberculosis.[42] Recently, survivors and activists from the Bhopal tragedy have called upon Dow Chemical Company and the U.S. government to prevent a similar catastrophe that could be caused by terrorists who might easily turn chemical plants and freight trains into weapons of mass destruction.[43]

ALIENATION AND WORK

The Concept of Alienation

The concept of alienation is useful in understanding work-related problems under capitalism, including problems of unnecessary accidents and diseases. The philosopher G. W. F. Hegel formulated the idea of alienation, and Karl Marx fully developed the idea in his writings on work under capitalism. Much contemporary writing by social scientists emphasizes the subjective side of alienation: personal feelings of loneliness, helplessness, and dissatisfaction. Marx's structural view analyzed alienation in regard to the relations of human beings with each other and with products they create at work. From this viewpoint, alienation under capitalism refers to separation of workers from important productive property (for example, from ownership of machinery), from products and services they create, from one another as competing workers, and from their own deeper selves because of the exploitative work world of capitalism. The ideas of Hegel and Marx remain highly relevant in analyzing the capitalistic economic system today.

In a capitalistic system, most workers have, relative to the power of owners and senior managers, little decision-making power over the structure of the work done in their workplaces. Workers are alienated from—that is, separated from and lacking control over—the major means of production, distribution, and exchange in U.S. society. Capitalist and managerial classes own or control the major productive, distributive, and exchange resources, such as plants, warehouses, stores, and offices. Unlike the U.S. political system, the U.S. economy is intentionally undemocratic. For the most part, owners, managers, and supervisors determine what workers do, what hours they work, and what they earn. Employers choose most of the work that employees do, often with little employee input. Some workers, especially higher-level, white-collar workers, have more control over the workplace than others, and many workers can vary their work and its pace to some degree. In addition, many workers resist the hierarchical character of work and try to change it. In this sense, work under capitalism involves an ongoing dialectical struggle between workers and employers.

Unlike an independent craftsperson such as a potter or sculptor, the nonmanagerial worker in an office, store, or factory sells his or her labor to an employer. Most workers are bought and sold like other goods and services; they labor for wages and salaries determined by others. Workers are generally alienated or separated from the tasks they perform, for once they choose a given workplace, their work's character is largely under the employer's control. Most workers are also separated from the products they produce, in that they have little or no control over what is produced, what happens to the products once they are produced, and what is done with income from sale of the products. The same types of alienation affect workers who provide services and workers who make or distribute manufactured products. Most Americans would not likely tolerate such an undemocratic system if it were in the political sphere.[44]

The capitalistic work structure also tends to alienate workers by separating them in some ways from each other. In large factories, offices, and stores, most workers do not know many of their coworkers. Managers often encourage individualistic competition among workers and may divide work unnecessarily, creating many different positions with differing wage levels. Such job segmentation can isolate workers and set them against one another. Pro-worker organizations, such as unions, are often discouraged.

The ultimate form of alienation is the alienation of a worker from her or his own self. Separated from most productive property, from the product, and from most fellow workers, with little or no control over the work process or product, many workers develop a dulled sense of life and become bored, despairing, or less than fully healthy persons.

This view of alienation applies not only to employees in the private sector but also to many public-sector workers because of government's close links to the needs of private employers. Government bureaucracies have patterns of hierarchical control similar to the hierarchical workplace patterns of capitalistic enterprises. Indeed, many business leaders and some government officials have often spoken of running government "like a business."

Dissatisfaction with Work

Attitudes expressed in surveys illustrate the impact that alienating work has on workers, who often describe their jobs as boring, dull, and repetitive. In one survey an assembly-line worker stated, "God, I hated that assembly line. I hated it. I used to fall asleep on the job standing up and still keep doing my work. There's nothing more boring and repetitive in the world. On top of it, you don't feel human." Similarly, a mail sorter lamented, "When I first started, I kept moving around. I kept looking for a job I'd like. You know, a job where it wouldn't make you tired just to get up in the morning and have to go to work. It took me a number of years to discover that there's not much difference—a job's a job."[45]

Black and Latino workers tend to be more critical of work conditions than are whites. Surveys have found that racial discrimination is a major source of dissatisfaction among black and Latino workers. (See Chapter 4.) Some opinion research suggests that female workers are about as satisfied (or dissatisfied) with their jobs as are men, in spite of lower pay and less control over their work. One possible explanation for these survey results is that most women workers compare themselves with other women, not men. This use of a lower-status reference group may make women feel less exploited.[46]

Decreased job security has accompanied corporate restructuring in recent decades. This is a major source of work dissatisfaction and stress for many workers. Layoffs involving hundreds of thousands of job cuts are commonplace nationwide, and they frequently occur with little notice. Almost half of the American Management Association's 7,000 member firms downsized during just one year, 1993. Large-scale layoffs have continued over the last few years, with employers cutting 3.2 million jobs. The telecommunications industry alone has eliminated a half million jobs.[47] Yet, corporate top executives rarely suffer. In fact, corporations often reward their chief executives after major layoffs. While the pay for CEOs rose by about 6 percent between 2001 and 2002, the median pay for CEOs at the 50 companies with the most layoffs in 2001 rose by 44 percent in 2002.

Hewlett-Packard laid off the most workers in 2001 (25,700) and then increased the CEO's total pay by 231 percent the next year—from \$1.2 million to \$4.1 million. AOL Time Warner's CEO laid off 4,380 workers in 2001, and then increased his total pay by 1,612 percent from \$1.2 million in 2001 to \$21.2 million in 2002.[48]

Downsizing has reduced labor costs per item produced. Yet one American Management Association survey of downsizing firms found that less than half had seen an increase in profits from job cuts. This survey, as well as other studies, discovered that downsizing has a severe effect on the morale of employees who remain. By savaging morale, downsizing frequently reduces productivity and profits, particularly in the long run.[49]

The Health Impact

Job dissatisfaction injures workers as surely, although less visibly, as do physical dangers. Negative job characteristics growing out of lack of control over one's work—such as general job dissatisfaction, tedious work, low self-esteem, fear of job loss because of workforce downsizing, and rapid changes in employment—increase a worker's likelihood of illness, especially heart disease (see Chapter 3). One earlier study of automobile assembly workers found that 40 percent had mental health problems, many of which were related to job dissatisfaction.[50] Other studies have found a causal relationship between serious job stress and depression, alcohol abuse, and suicide.

Desire for More Control

Even though many U.S. workers enjoy material conditions that are better than those found in other countries, many are still unhappy with their work or workplaces. Substantial research indicates that once income needs are satisfied, many workers seek to meet higher-level human needs for self-esteem, more challenging work, and more control over their work lives. Greater control over the workplace would likely lead to substantial improvements in the hazardous working conditions documented earlier. Respondents in one survey ranked "interesting work" as the most important of 25 work characteristics, followed by "enough equipment" and "enough authority" to get the job done.[51] "Good pay" was only fifth on the list. Consistent with the theories of human relations analysts such as Abraham Maslow and Chris Argyris, this finding suggests that after satisfying essential material needs, employees place a higher priority on the actual character of jobs.[52]

Researchers have found that given the availability of genuine alternatives, most blue-collar and white-collar workers would not stay in their same line of work. Desire for self-management in their work can be seen in workers' dreams that they can start their own businesses and become their own bosses. It is widely believed that a person can work hard, put aside some money, start a business, and prosper. Surveys show that a very large proportion of U.S. workers would like to go into business for themselves, but the chances of an employee starting up a successful business are decreasing. As we noted in Chapter 2, the self-employed have declined from a *majority* of the population working outside the home in the mid-1800s to no more than *4.5 percent* of that population today.[53]

The Impact on Dignity and Self-Respect

Employer subordination of workers can destroy workers' dignity in their own eyes as well as in the eyes of other people. Individuals working in lower-status jobs are often encouraged to believe that their positions stem from personal deficiencies in intelligence, weaknesses, and laziness. One effect of the class structure is to pressure people to seek compensation for the damage inflicted by their jobs—to seek more material possessions or higher job status. Richard Sennett and Jonathan Cobb argue that this attempt to compensate comes from trying to restore a psychological balance to lives left empty by alienating work, rather than from an innate materialistic craving.[54]

In this capitalistic society, the heavy emphasis on everything having a market price has led some people to think of themselves, consciously or unconsciously, as commodities. Americans tend to view success in terms of how well a person "sells" herself or himself. Just knowing what one can do is not enough; one has to sell oneself and one's personality. Clothes, cosmetics, and hairstyle become very important. Self-marketing can lead to superficial human relationships and self-destructive attempts to solve the problem of superficiality with drugs or alcohol.[55]

Is White-Collar Work a Way Out?

Many blue-collar workers have worked for decades to give their youngsters more education and the chance to move into clerical, sales, or administrative jobs, which they believe are better paid and not boring. Yet these parents and their children often have been frustrated, since many white-collar jobs actually require little college training. The expansion of white-collar jobs has mostly been at the level of salespersons, typists, bank tellers, file clerks, and other lower-level office workers and not, as widely believed, at the level of prestigious and well-paid professionals such as stockbrokers and computer analysts.

Research has demonstrated the troubled character of most of today's white-collar work. In *White Collar* (1956), sociologist C. Wright Mills documented the factory-like character of much office work.[56] In the late nineteenth century, most white-collar employees were men who were part of a small, privileged fraction of the general class of workers. Then clerical work was relatively prestigious and served as training for promotion to higher-level white-collar positions. Since then the demographic composition of these jobs has been recast, and most clerical workers' prestige and privileges have disappeared. Women now hold most secretarial, typing, bank clerk, and other lower-level white-collar jobs. Most such jobs offer little autonomy and are often routine and mechanized. Work settings are hierarchical, with numerous job titles and pay levels and gradations in rank. A few managers at the top control the work life of most white-collar employees. Today's clerical work, now often feminized, is usually poorly paid in comparison with skilled blue-collar jobs.[57]

Large companies have often used the principles of scientific management in organizing clerical work to be much like factory work. Clerical-management handbooks detail time and other standards for office work. One such manual was developed with the help of companies such as General Electric, Kerr-McGee, and the General Tire and Rubber Company. Table 10.2 lists the standards for certain office activities, in fractions of a minute. And so the standards go, down a long list of office work routines. Other manuals recommend specific time standards for typing operations, computer work, and other clerical tasks. These standards are designed to increase productivity by eliminating as much "brainwork" as possible and making clerical work routine.[58]

Computers and computerized work stations have standardized much office work. Word-processing centers typically break down clerical work into standardized segments. In

Table 10.2   Standards for Selected Office Activities

Activity	Minutes
Opening and closing a file drawer	.040
Opening or closing a folder	.040
Opening a side drawer of a desk	.014

assembly-line style, each employee does a small part of the total work package, and fewer workers are required. Even many college-educated technical and professional workers, including well-paid engineers and scientists, have become wage and salary workers whose jobs are substantially routinized. Some white-collar managers and professionals may supervise a few other workers, but their own professional jobs may also be routine and repetitious.[59]

Bureaucratized work arrangements tend to ritualize the lives of most workers. Even though they sense the alienating character of their work, most adjust to and compensate for the troubling day-to-day labor they find unpleasant. Society's emphasis on the individual and on diligent pursuit of work helps many individuals to justify their own acceptance of alienating work conditions. One study of clerical employees in banks found that the banks' highly organized work arrangements required complete submission to authority, with the usual rewards for conformity. But "in the process, such regularization narrows workers' visions about their lives and about social arrangements, creating a kind of myopia where alternatives do not even occur to them, let alone seem feasible."[60] A recent study of corporate culture and the growing dissatisfaction in the U.S. workplace reveals that millions of white-collar workers are trapped in virtual sweatshops where they contend with excessive workloads; diminishing salaries, pensions, and benefits; the pervasiveness of technology; and persistent job insecurity.[61]

Is High-Tech a Way Out?

Using U.S. Department of Labor projections of future job growth, we have listed in Table 10.3 the top-five categories of job increases expected between 2002 and 2012. Economists predict that total employment over this period will increase by nearly 15 percent—from roughly 144 million jobs in 2002 to about 165 million jobs in 2012. Yet the estimated increase of 21 million jobs will not distribute evenly across industrial and occupational categories. Education and health services are projected to be the fastest-growing areas in number of jobs created. Service-providing industries will account for 96 percent of new jobs created. The newly created jobs will require adequate educational preparation for workers, although several major categories of service jobs will require only a high school degree and/or modest on-the-job training. Among the fastest-growing job categories in numbers of, or percentages of, new jobs, only four require college degrees. An associate's degree is required for registered nurses, a bachelor's degree is required for communications analysts and physician assistants, and a doctorate is often required for college-level teachers.

Potential earnings will also be unevenly distributed among the growing job categories. More low-wage jobs than high-wage jobs will be created in this decade. Although the fastest-growing job categories in terms of percentage increase include low-income and high-income occupations, three of the five job categories expected to grow the fastest *in absolute numbers*

Table 10.3 Occupational Outlook 2002–2012

FIVE FASTEST-GROWING JOBS (IN ABSOLUTE NUMBERS), 2002–2012

Occupation	Existing Number of Jobs	New Jobs Created	Percent Change	Educational Preparation Required
Registered nurses	2.2 million	623,000	27	Associate's degree
Postsecondary teachers	1.6 million	603,000	38	Doctoral degree
Retail salespersons	4.1 million	596,000	15	On-the-job training
Customer service representatives	1.9 million	460,000	24	On-the-job training
Food preparation/service workers	2.0 million	454,000	23	On-the-job training

FIVE FASTEST-GROWING JOBS (IN PERCENT GROWTH), 2002–2012

Occupation	Existing Number of Jobs	New Jobs Created	Percent Change	Educational Preparation Required
Medical assistants	365,000	215,000	59	On-the-job training
Network systems analysts	186,000	106,000	57	Bachelor's degree
Physician assistants	63,000	31,000	49	Bachelor's degree
Social/human service assistants	305,000	149,000	49	On-the-job training
Home health aides	580,000	279,000	48	On-the-job training

are low- or average-wage occupations such as retail sales and food workers. These new jobs require little formal education beyond high school. Most do not offer a way out of the drudgery of traditional blue-collar and clerical work. The "high-tech" character of the new jobs being created in the United States in the late twentieth century and early twenty-first century has been greatly exaggerated.[62]

The Increase in Contingent Work

To cut costs and maximize profits, many corporations are turning to subcontracting, outsourcing, or hiring contingent workers (temporary and part-time workers) rather than full-time, permanent employees. In the early 2000s, the contingent work force accounted for some 5.4 million workers, comprising 4 percent of total employment in the United States.[63] Eileen Appelbaum and Judith Gregory describe this work structure as a "ring and core": Full-time, permanent employees—the core—have job security, predictable incomes, and employee benefits; contingent workers—the ring—have little security, work fewer hours, have fewer chances for promotions, and seldom receive good benefits.[64]

Compared with the noncontingent workforce, contingent workers are more likely to be women and younger. They are more likely to be workers of color. Contingent workers are also less likely to work full-time, more likely to hold more than one job, less likely to be covered by health insurance, and less likely to receive unemployment benefits. One population survey found that fewer than one-third of contingent workers prefer a temporary or part-time work arrangement.[65]

The use of temporaries (temps) in offices and other work sites began after World War II. Since 1980, the number of temporary agencies and the number of temporary workers have increased dramatically. One state saw a 421 percent increase in the number of temporary workers during this period; a large proportion of this increase occurred in manufacturing industries replacing longtime permanent workers with lower-paid temporary workers.[66] Today, temporary workers form the most rapidly growing part of the contingent workforce, accounting for almost 10 percent of the overall gain in employment nationwide. More than 1.2 million workers were employed by temp agencies in the early 2000s.[67]

Temporary help workers include professionals, clerical and other administrative support workers, and blue-collar laborers. Temp agencies typically contract with employers to provide workers, charging employers an hourly rate, and the agency pays workers a portion of the fee. In most jobs, temp workers receive lower hourly wages than traditional employees. Many, especially manual laborers, earn the minimum wage or slightly more, and after the agency's deductions, they take home a low wage. Some work full-time for the same business for years; they are temporary in name only. Although many temp firms offer some benefits, only a small percentage of workers qualify for such major benefits as paid holidays.[68]

Employers see use of temp workers as a good business strategy because they pay such workers less and the latter are ineligible for employer-paid benefits such as holiday or sick pay, worker's compensation, insurance, or pension plans. Temporary labor pools provide a steady supply of workers whom employers see as disposable. Such labor pools offer workers no advantages. Manual temporary jobs are frequently dirty and unsafe. In the words of one activist: "If you work out of a labor pool, you have no say, no control, no nothing. Your humanity is gone. You become a product in the labor pool."[69] This is indeed worker *alienation* under modern capitalism.

Part-time work is another strategy used by employers to cut costs and create a flexible workforce. Only about 60 percent of workers are employed full-time. In some years almost all new jobs are part-time, and some employers intentionally replace full-time employees with part-timers to improve profits. For example, in 1993 BankAmerica, then the nation's second-largest banking corporation (with record profits of $1.5 billion), announced plans to reduce the hours of thousands of employees and eliminate most benefits. Working full-time, BankAmerica tellers averaged $19,000 a year, yet the salary for the chief executive was more than $4 million.[70] Note, too, that hourly wages for part-time workers are usually lower than those for their full-time counterparts. Part-timers usually are denied access to promotion ladders and are seldom eligible for benefits that full-timers receive.

Growing numbers of corporations have also turned to subcontracting and outsourcing, often overseas, for many labor needs. Both practices are a departure from the philosophy of early capitalists such as Henry Ford, who favored vertical integration within one large corporation to control production. Subcontracting and outsourcing reduce the number of full-time permanent personnel the corporation requires and reduce the risk of operating in uncertain, increasingly global, markets.[71] Outsourcing of manufacturing and service jobs has cost millions of U.S. workers their jobs. Estimates are that about 40 percent of *Fortune 1,000* corporations have outsourced 2.8 million manufacturing jobs overseas to India and China since 2002, and that 3 million more jobs will be lost by 2015.[72] One study suggests that as many as 14 million U.S. jobs (11 percent of the total workforce) are now in jeopardy of outsourcing. Corporations are likely to find outsourcing increasingly attractive since savings of up to $300 billion a year are possible if they outsource those jobs.[73]

Many corporations have closed their own plants and rely on a network of lower-cost, often foreign, suppliers. Many U.S. clothing firms outsource clothing production to Central American or Asian manufacturers. One such firm is Mandarin International in El Salvador, which in the mid-1990s paid women workers as little as $43 for an 88-hour week (less than 50 cents an hour). These workers received a mere 16 cents for producing a shirt that sold for $20 or more in U.S. or Canadian stores. The Gap, one of Mandarin's customers, profited some $311 million, and its CEO received millions in compensation. Yet, women workers from Mandarin have described the plant's horrible working conditions: Workers are allowed only two five-minute bathroom breaks a day; drinking water is contaminated; male supervisors sexually abuse female workers; and workers are punished for attempting to join a union. In response to these women's reports, the Gap, which has a code of conduct for its suppliers, said that it had found no violations of its code at Mandarin.[74]

Contract workers predominate in certain job categories, such as building maintenance, that once were composed of full-time, better-paid jobs. Subcontractors are frequently small firms with lower labor costs; their wage and benefit levels are typically low. Small companies in the United States are often willing to accept low profit margins because they are competing with firms in low-wage countries overseas.[75] Some businesses have turned to prison inmates for low-cost labor. Though U.S. law prohibits importation of goods produced by prison labor, more than 80,000 state prisoners and some 21,000 federal prisoners work at low-level jobs for government agencies or private companies.[76] Prison inmates often replace other workers. Lockhart Technologies, for example, fired 150 workers when it moved its Austin, Texas, branch to a privately run prison. Contracting for prisoner labor sharply reduces labor costs—typically minimum wage or less for each worker, paid directly to the prison with no costs for workers' benefits.[77]

Subcontracting and outsourcing, like the use of temporaries and part-timers, are means of union avoidance, cost avoidance, and, many would add, avoidance of public accountability. Organized labor has helped increase public awareness of the job losses to communities when businesses use prison labor. One union boycott forced an Illinois Toys 'R' Us store to stop using inmates to stock shelves. Organized labor convinced Honda Motors to discontinue a parts-assembly subcontracting arrangement that used Ohio prison inmates; the inmates themselves had received only 35 cents from the $2.05 an hour paid to the state for their labor.[78] Unions have engaged in collective bargaining over the issue of subcontracting and offered technical assistance to industries to convince employers of better ways to meet international and domestic competition than using subcontracting at the expense of permanent U.S. workers. Still, many companies spend large amounts of money to defeat union organizing in their facilities.[79]

Workers are not the only ones hurt by the shift from a permanent to a contingent workforce. Jeremy Rifkin has pointed out two dangers for business: declining consumer purchasing power because of reduced earnings and declining capital investment funds because of reduced pension benefits.[80] Pension funds, valued at trillions of dollars, account for the majority of net individual savings and a large percentage of total financial assets in the U.S. economy. Corporations often draw on these funds, directly or indirectly, for investment capital. However, withdrawals of pension funds as millions of baby boomers retire over the next decade or two—combined with declining pension contributions for the new mostly lower-wage, often part-time, workers—will substantially reduce this major source of investment capital, as well as consumer demand for corporate products from many of these new workers.

RESISTANCE AND CHANGE IN THE WORKPLACE

Working life in the United States has alternately taken on the character of workers' acquiescence and of workers' struggle for major improvements. Periodically, U.S. workers react against troubling work situations and try to gain some control over working conditions. Workers' struggles, individual or collective, have improved employment conditions. While it is more overt at some times than others, employers and workers are engaged in an everyday contest for control. This is a dialectical process, with employers struggling to make workers do more work, or more alienating work, and workers resisting in whatever ways they can. (A dialectical process is characterized by recurring opposition between interacting forces, in this case workers on the one hand and owners and managers on the other.)

Sabotage is one major form of worker resistance. The economic analyst Thorstein Veblen once described industrial sabotage as the "conscious withdrawal of efficiency."[81] In some cases, such as the Lordstown, Ohio, autoworkers uprising in the 1970s, industrial sabotage has involved large numbers of workers engaged in widespread disruptive activities. In other situations, single individuals have struck out against an unfavorable work environment. One veteran auto assembly-line worker was quoted about the attitude of workers in his plant before some humanizing reforms: "We'd try to get back. I used a razor to pop vinyl tops like a cantaloupe. Or to cut wiring somewhere hard to get at. It was sabotage, pure and simple."[82]

On a more organized level, during one strike, union leaders angry over antiworker decisions by corporate executives vowed to engage in widespread sabotage against a major airline, including sending baggage to the wrong airports. According to John Jermier, sabotage at work is often a rational act, one "with powerful consequences favoring labor."[83] From this perspective, industrial sabotage is not perpetrated by the stereotypically "mad saboteur" but by ordinary workers expressing deep emotions about alienating work environments. Sabotage has sometimes been an effective tool for workers in struggles against employers they see as highly exploitative.

Some field research provides examples of ingenious methods of workplace resistance. Thus, some construction laborers have worked out ways to reduce their work pace. On a job site, they may work facing their supervisor's office trailer so that they are not surprised when their boss comes out. They may make extra trips to the water jug to vary the pace of work. They may slow their pace to the minimal level supervisors will tolerate. They "play dumb" when a supervisor asks if they know how to run a particular machine, in order to lose work time while being instructed. White-collar workers also fight back against the hierarchical and boring character of their work. One secretary persuaded her boss that she could save him money by making several trips monthly to supply stores to take advantage of sales. At the same time, unknown to her boss, she did her own personal and family shopping. Another secretary started a garden in front of her workplace under the guise of beautifying the area, but she spent as much time as she could caring for the garden, replacing a portion of her less desirable work time with something she enjoyed.[84] Subtle resistance to work can be found even in the most closely supervised settings. High turnover and absenteeism are other indications of worker dissatisfaction and hostility. U.S. workers often resist exploitative and alienating work or try to redesign it to better meet the human needs for diversity and personal autonomy.

The Fight for Better Wages and Conditions

Periodically, workers have made concerted attacks against exploitative or alienating work. The United States has a long history of open, sometimes violent struggle between workers and capitalists. Hundreds of people have been killed in labor struggles since the late nineteenth century. The use of militant tactics such as strikes and picketing by unions and other worker organizations has sometimes resulted in attacks on strikers by the police, the national guard, and private guards under the command of employers. In retaliation, workers and sympathetic community members have sometimes fought back.

Dozens of labor-conflict deaths have occurred since the end of World War II. In most cases, labor disputes have grown out of workers' struggles for greater resources and power against corporate executives seeking to restrict or cut back workers' power. Specific grievances have included the right to unionize, the failure of employers to recognize unions, the use of strikebreakers by employers, the safety of the workplace, subcontracting, employee cutbacks, and cuts in wages and fringe benefits.

Strikes and work stoppages have been numerous since the 1940s. Official statistics show about 4,000 to 5,000 strikes per year in the 1950s and 1960s and 2,300 to 3,800 a year in the 1980s. Major strikes reached a peak in 1974, with 424 involving 1,000 or more workers.[85] Employee fears for jobs in an era of cutbacks, a decline in number of companies employing as many as 1,000 workers, and the nationwide decline in union membership have all contributed to a decline in the number of large-scale strikes over the past decade or so. The number of serious strikes fell to a low of 14 in 2003, the lowest since records have been kept. Still, there were some significant strikes by U.S. workers for better working conditions. Table 10.4 shows work stoppages involving 5,000 or more workers in 2003.[86]

Table 10.4   Work Stoppages Involving 5,000 or More Workers in 2003

Organization and Location	Beginning Date of Work Stoppage	Ending Date of Work Stoppage	Number of Workers Involved
General Electric (Indiana) Communication Workers United Electrical Workers	Jan. 14, 2003	Jan. 15, 2003	17,500
The County of San Joaquin Stockton, CA Service Employees	Aug. 4, 2003	Aug. 8, 2003	5,000
Dierbergs Markets, Schnucks, Shop 'n Save St. Louis, MO United Food & Commercial Workers	Oct. 7, 2003	Oct. 31, 2003	10,200
Albertsons, Ralphs, and Vons Supermarkets Southern CA United Food & Commercial Workers	Oct. 12, 2003	Feb. 26, 2004	67,300
Los Angeles County Metropolitan Transportation Authority Los Angeles, CA United Transportation Union	Oct. 14, 2003	Nov. 17, 2003	6,200

Unions and Worker Protests

The history of strikes and other worker protests has shaped the distinctive character of unions in the United States. Although guild charters existed as early as 1648 in the Massachusetts Bay Colony, the unionization of labor as we know it today dates back to the early 1800s when a variety of workers organized to fight for better wages and working conditions.[87] Labor organizing saw a dramatic increase after the 1860s. The Knights of Labor was organized in 1869 and won a major railroad strike in 1885. The following year the American Federation of Labor (AFL) was created. Early unions were often repressed harshly by capitalists and their political allies, frequently with violence aimed at workers themselves. In contrast, workers' violence was usually aimed at property. Between 1935 and 1938 the Congress of Industrial Organizations (CIO) organized the steel and auto industries and established itself as a militant alternative to the AFL. In 1955 the CIO merged with the AFL, forming the AFL-CIO. Militant action by workers during the 1930s led a number of prominent capitalists and allied politicians to advocate "moderate" unions as a means of creating labor peace and a stable economic system. In return for support of union legalization, employers sought maximum cooperation and union support for the existing capitalistic order. The overwhelming U.S. Senate support for passage of the Wagner Labor Relations Act (1935), which guaranteed the rights of employees to organize and bargain with employers, signaled that powerful business leaders had, however grudgingly, accepted the principle of collective bargaining as a way of reducing workplace strife and preempting more radical worker movements. Of course, many conservatives, then as now, opposed any kind of union, but leading corporate officials saw in moderate unionism a way to save capitalism from revolutionary change.[88]

Leading capitalists did not begin supporting the rights of workers to organize collectively out of a sense of justice for employees. Rather, working people organizing thousands of strikes and demonstrations over poor wages and working conditions forced capitalists to deal more equitably with workers. Early union contracts, such as those growing out of auto industry struggles in the 1930s, brought major concessions by employers—such as better grievance procedures, wage improvements, and recognition of seniority when workers had to be laid off. Gradually, union gains were realized in many industries.

Over the decades, unions have brought many benefits to both workers and employers. Even militant unions such as the CIO helped bring labor peace and industrial order by ending unauthorized strikes. A union that gains the right to exclusive bargaining with employers (a "closed shop") can control dissident members by threatening to throw them out, and thus cause them to lose their jobs. Employers' wage and benefit concessions in union contracts have helped to guarantee a peaceful workforce. In exchange, unions have typically promised labor peace and given up claims to control over the means of production, which have traditionally been the prerogatives of management. Once established, unions also became institutions of socialization to orient inexperienced workers into workplaces, a role that has been useful to the capitalist class.[89]

Historically, union and business leaders have cooperated in efforts to increase worker productivity. Since World War II, AFL-CIO leaders have often cooperated with corporate executives in meeting business objectives. Significantly, many trade union officials have not permitted grass-roots democracy to flourish in their organizations. Regular and close cooperation among these union officials, business leaders, and business-oriented politicians reinforces the commonly held view of many workers that many established union leaders are "sellouts."[90] Not surprisingly, many workers, including union members, have become dissatisfied with mainstream trade unions, seeing them as corrupt or out of touch with the needs and interests of ordinary workers. In the past few decades, hundreds of thousands of employees, from truck drivers to auto workers to postal carriers, have gone out on strike in defiance of union leaders. Unionized workers have also rejected a significant number of collective bargaining agreements negotiated by their leaders. And numerous internal reform movements have occurred within major U.S. unions.

The proportion of U.S. workers in unions dropped from 31 percent in 1970 to 13.3 percent in the 2002. However, this widely cited low percentage of workers in unions is misleading, for almost *38 percent of public-sector workers* are now union members, an increase in recent years. The low national proportion is largely because of the decline of private-sector workers who belong to unions (now just 8.6 percent).[91] The decline in manufacturing jobs in the United States has sharply reduced the number of workers in traditionally unionized industries. Industry's growing use of contingent workers, who are difficult to organize, has further eroded union strength in many sectors.

Nonetheless, many workers in traditionally less-unionized occupations, such as agriculture and textile workers, hospital employees, white-collar workers, and government employees, have come to see unions as an effective way of dealing with exploitation by employers, and unionization in these occupations has increased. Yet some white members in mainstream unions have been reluctant to have their unions organize the low-wage workers. Labor researcher Mary Hollens writes that "Letting low-wage people of color and women in the door through organizing the low-end jobs may mean increased pressure on the union for apprenticeships and training programs that have long been the prerogative of white workers. . . . Union leadership seems more willing to jealously guard its privileges than to actively expand its base into communities of color."[92] Few mainstream unions have focused attention on issues of concern to people of color; within many traditional unions, workers of color are often informally pressured into lower-wage work.[93]

Recognizing the power of worker organizations, some low-wage workers, shunned by the older established unions, have formed independent unions of their own. For example, the Chinese Staff and Workers Association in New York has organized restaurant, construction, and garment workers, and Fuerza Unida in San Antonio, Texas, has organized clothing workers. Other low-wage workers rejected by established unions have formed support organizations, such as the Carolina Alliance for Fair Employment, which keep workers informed of their rights and which have pushed for improved labor laws. In no sense is the U.S. union movement dead. It just seems to shift over time from one group of exploited workers to another.[94]

Progressive labor leaders see workers' desire for a shorter workweek as one of the most relevant issues for organized labor today. They believe that organizing women workers, who now comprise about half of the U.S. workforce, is pivotal to a renewal of union strength. Rifkin reports that "nearly 44 percent of all employed women say they would prefer more time with their family to more money. . . . The call for a 30-hour workweek is a powerful rallying cry that could unite trade unions, women's groups, parenting organizations, churches, and synagogues."[95]

Today, the percentage of the workforce belonging to labor unions in the United States is substantially lower than that in most other industrialized nations. Unionization in European nations ranges from 40 to 90 percent. That is one major reason why wages are lower in the United States than in many European countries.[96] The declining market power of U.S. workers is reflected in the fact that since the early 1970s real wages have declined signifi-

Demonstrations by union members focus public attention on problems of toxic waste as they affect American workers. (AFL-CIO News)

cantly, even though productivity has increased substantially. It is significant that this is the same period during which union membership dropped by almost 50 percent. Still, unionized workers in the United States do have an advantage over their nonunionized counterparts. Research on the effects of unionization show that unions reduce wage inequality by raising wages for low- and middle-wage workers. Compared with the average annual wages of nonunion workers ($30,584), the union worker's advantage averaged about $8,000 ($38,480) a year today.[97] Unionized workers are also more likely to have fringe benefits like paid leave (vacations and holidays), more generous health insurance, and better pension plans.[98]

Ongoing Class Struggle

Employers use numerous antiunion tactics to undermine unions and block unionization efforts. Management-consulting companies specialize in assisting corporations to defeat unionization or decertify existing unions. Employers have benefited from nationwide recessions fostered by top business and government officials who have sought, at least in part, to cut back on workers' wages and benefits. Corporations often threaten to close plants to force unions to accept wage and benefit cuts, thus undermining a union's strength and lowering employee morale. A recent study found that in *fully 62 percent* of the more than 600 union-organizing campaigns across the United States, companies fought the union by threatening to close the plant.[99] A Human Rights Watch investigation of corporate tactics against unionization has found that U.S. companies illegally terminate thousands of workers every year for trying to organize. In one recent year, an estimated 23,580 workers were punished by companies for their union activity. Corporate managers have spied on, harassed, pressured, threatened, suspended, fired, or otherwise victimized many workers who have tried to form unions and to exercise their right of freedom of association. These company tactics have left millions of workers without the protection of organizing and collective bargaining.[100] Some companies even file for bankruptcy to avoid fulfilling union contracts. In addition, some employers who use low-skilled workers recruit recent (and often undocumented) immigrants who are less likely to push for unionization.[101]

Employers' antiunion actions have contributed to the decline in union-organizing activity in the United States over the last several years. For example, the CEO of Whole Food Markets recently refused to recognize company employees' vote to join the United Food and Commercial Workers union in Madison, Wisconsin. The company engaged in a concerted campaign to discredit the union, overturn the election, and decertify the union. When the National Labor Relations Board (NLRB) sided with company employees, management refused to negotiate with the union. The company created a hostile working environment, illegally terminated pro-union workers, and worked diligently to convince new and uniformed workers that a union was unnecessary. The tactics employed by the company were successful in forming an antiunion committee of new employees whom the company rewarded with future management promotions. The union filed several Unfair Labor Practice charges against the company, forcing the NLRB to postpone a decertification election until it can investigate the charges. As one worker who led the fight to unionize puts it, "We knew going into this that it was going to be a tremendous struggle. . . . But seeing the results of the lies and manipulation of a huge corporation is very hard. It is a very sad day for workers."[102]

U.S. workers continue to struggle with employers for better working conditions and wages. Workers at Cook Family Foods, a subsidiary of the huge multinational conglomerate Con Agra, won a four-and-a-half-year struggle for unionization. Frustrated by poverty-level wages, poor safety and health conditions with many unreported injuries, harsh rules, and no bathroom policy, workers voted in favor of the union. The NLRB took almost two years to certify the election. When the company appealed the decision, refused to recognize the union, and continued to engage in unfair labor practices, the workers went on strike. Almost two years later, an appeals court overturned the certification. The striking workers who had not found other jobs returned to work and again started the process of union organizing. Cook began a process of intimidation and hired a union-busting firm that recommended questionable tactics. Some of these tactics were so controversial that Cook's own security guards turned in their boss. He later was arrested for soliciting persons to commit murder, arson, or criminal mischief and to blame that on pro-union workers. An overwhelming majority of the workers voted for the union, and Cook finally agreed not to challenge the election results.[103]

New unions representing service workers have been particularly active, often using the traditional tools of strikes and lawsuits. The mostly female and black workforce at the Delta Pride catfish processing plant in Indianola, Mississippi, went on strike for better wages and for an end to poor working conditions and the discrimination and harassment they faced on the job. Extensive community support of the union's struggle was crucial to victory. Forming coalitions with community and religious organizations to work on environmental, workplace, and racial justice issues is an important strategy of independent unions, such as Black Workers for Justice in North Carolina.[104]

Since the 1980s, the NLRB has been restructured to favor employers even more in its decisions. Today, 70 years after the NLRB law was first passed, this country's basic labor law is still weakly enforced and often ineffective in protecting workers from employers' unfair labor practices.

STRATEGIES FOR CONTROLLING WORKERS

In the ongoing struggle between workers and employers, capitalist employers have powerful resources to resist workers' attempts to gain a share of control of the workplace. Owners have adopted a number of strategies to control workers' behavior, including scientific management, hierarchical control, and technical control.

Scientific Management (Taylorism)

The scientific-management approach uses "efficiency" experts to study the pace of work and structure of the workplace to reduce "soldiering" by workers, that is, employees deliberately restricting their output. Around 1900, time and motion experts such as Frederick Winslow Taylor extended older techniques of closely managing workers. Since then, scientific management has come to mean the timing and pacing of work, its speed-up, the fragmentation of jobs into ever-smaller compartmentalized tasks, and standardization of tools and procedures. Job specialization can increase workers' production, reduce unit labor costs, and increase private profits and management's control over workers. Excessively specialized work, however, is usually repetitive, boring, and, for many, meaningless. Originally designed for blue-collar workers, principles of scientific management have been extended to white-collar work.[105]

The breakup of work into specialized skills and minute operations has shifted much workplace knowledge from workers to management. Workers in offices, factories, and stores now tend to do a limited range of activities repeatedly and with dexterity, but they no longer have the broad skills and knowledge of their more skilled predecessors in early decades of the twentieth century. Capitalistic production of goods and services has separated workers from much knowledge that they once had. For example, traditional cabinetmakers possess much knowledge and broad skills in their craft. They design cabinets, utilize an array of tools, and imagine how custom-designed cabinets will fit into rooms for which they are built. In contrast, an assembly-line worker may only put hinges on cabinet doors all day. A growing number of jobs can be learned in a short period, from just a few minutes to a few months. Yet perfecting the skill of an old-style craftsperson requires years. Modern capitalism's practice of transferring knowledge from workers to management or to machines and computers remains a major source of worker alienation.[106]

The Team Concept: A New Type of Taylorism

The *team concept,* used in industries such as auto manufacturing, emphasizes worker–management cooperation to avoid some plant closings. This system is common in a number of other countries, including Japan. Using a system of standardized work, supervisors specify in great detail every move a worker must make and the order in which the actions are to be performed. Some observers call this system an intensification of Taylorism. Workers sometimes call the system "management by stress."

The team concept is used to push a manufacturing operation to its top capacity by speeding up production lines and cutting the number of workers. It eliminates some job classifications and trains workers to do several operations, ostensibly to add some diversity to their work routines. Such advantages are highlighted in the media. Workers may find more variety in their work, but eventually one assembly-line job becomes as boring as another. Since workers are able to do many jobs, corporate managers can reassign team leaders or other workers to fill in for absentees rather than hiring replacements. The team replaces the union as a decision-making entity. The use of team leaders blurs the line between union and management and, together with the elimination of job classifications and some seniority and work rules, undermines a union's power, thereby decreasing worker protection against employer arbitrariness. Many workers report that they tolerate the stressful "team" conditions because they fear that their plants may otherwise close.[107]

Hierarchical Control

Closely related to scientific management, *hierarchical control* is an older form of worker management. Most U.S. workers are arranged into bureaucratized hierarchies, with the majority toward the bottom, mostly taking orders, and fewer people at middle and upper levels giving orders. Industrial corporations and other business bureaucracies, small and large, use bureaucratic rules—job titles and levels, differing wage scales, and disciplinary rules—to organize and control employees. This bureaucratization of worker control has "institutionalized the exercise of capitalist power, making power appear to emanate from the formal organization itself."[108] Managers and supervisors typically discipline workers by applying company rules. Conventional theories of organization see a work hierarchy as necessary. According to this view, top members in an organization are there because they have the "superior" ability and knowledge and thus the right to see to it that "less able" people toward the bottom contribute the necessary effort. Not surprisingly, research on work organizations reveals that those at higher job levels, particularly managers, not only have higher incomes and material benefits but also are more likely than those at lower ranks to enjoy their jobs, find them satisfying, and feel creative.[109]

A work hierarchy can help to organize the activities of a large number of people, but it creates problems of conflict between people of differing rank. Organizational hierarchies institutionalize inequalities in power and usually create great inequality in the distribution of income. Because hierarchical organizations prevent using people as whole human beings, they help to control employees by developing status gradations (often minute) and refocusing workers' aspirations onto climbing up the organizational ladder. Together with related political, educational, and military hierarchies, work hierarchies play a central role in generating conformity in the general population. In the often-intimidating context of the modern bureaucracy, many people become reluctant to question or talk back to existing institutions and authorities. This lack of citizen questioning makes corporate and government corruption (see Chapter 8) more likely to occur.[110]

Automation and Technical Control

Richard Edwards has suggested the term *technical control* to describe the use of assembly lines, machines, and robots to control the character and pace of work.[111] Technical control by means of computerized automation, such as robots in the automobile industry and computers in business offices, can improve worker efficiency as well as extend employers' surveillance over workers. A central computer can be linked to other computers that control machinery or desktop PCs, providing management with the ability to monitor or time closely workers' activities and to flash back orders for changes in work patterns. Every keystroke can be tallied; time taken for breaks can be registered; and the amount of time consumed loading and unloading products on and off automated equipment can be quantified precisely.[112]

Computers and other automated equipment are part of many plants, warehouses, offices, and stores, often reducing the number of jobs and increasing unemployment. Clerical workers, secretaries, telephone operators, bank tellers, factory workers, librarians, and lower-level managers are particularly vulnerable to technological displacement. Introduction of robots into manufacturing has displaced more jobs than it has created. At least 80,000 robotics jobs have been created over the last decade or so, yet use of robots has permanently eliminated 100,000 to 200,000 jobs in this period. For example, in the auto industry alone, robots are displacing a large number of jobs for welders and production painters.[113] One analyst has noted that as many as 90 million jobs—almost three-fourths of all jobs—are potential casualties of future automation.[114]

Automation, including computerization, often reduces the level of skill required of workers. For example, the automation of bookkeeping replaced many skilled professionals with a hierarchy of numerous less-skilled data entry and clerical workers at the bottom and a few skilled workers such as computer programmers and senior accountants at the top. In Chapter 1 we discussed the argument that ongoing automation has deskilled many U.S. jobs. Several researchers have documented de-skilling as the prevailing pattern following the introduction of automated technology. Abbe Mowshowitz found mainly declining skill requirements for industrial and office workers following the use of automated production methods, and Eileen Appelbaum has identified de-skilling as the predominant pattern following the introduction of new technology in the insurance industry.[115]

Automation illustrates a basic contradiction of modern capitalism. Expanded automation has the potential to liberate many workers from dangerous and boring work and to meet the needs of U.S. workers and their families, such as by shortening workweeks with no reduction in pay. However, top corporate executives introduce machines into their workplaces only when they are profitable to them, not simply because of a technological breakthrough or because machines reduce the dirty work that people do. For example, the hourly cost of operating robots is often lower than workers' hourly wages. Under the direction of corporate executives, automation is a real threat to workers' jobs and generates unemployment, worker anxiety over control, and loss of income.

Job Losses and Capital Flight

The ability of automated machinery, computers, robots, and low-paid workers overseas to do most of the repetitive tasks required of a large majority of U.S. workers is a major contributor to the shrinking number of well-paid jobs in the U.S. economy. Major decisions regarding the number and location of jobs are made by executives who have the power to restructure job markets to meet profit-oriented goals. From senior management's point of view, job layoffs and terminations are "rational" business decisions. From the workers' point of view, however, these decisions are irrational, for they often mean extended periods of unemployment and hardship. Indeed, the commonly used terms "economic restructuring" and "displacement" downplay the often devastating effects of job loss on workers.

A survey by the U.S. Bureau of Labor Statistics reports that plant closings and business failures or declines displaced 9.9 million workers between 1999 and 2001, an increase from the 7.6 million jobs lost over the preceding two-year period. Nearly half of the laid-off workers cited plant or other company closings (or moves) as the reason for their displacement. Another quarter of job losses were because of insufficient work, and another quarter of job losses were because of elimination of positions or shifts abolished. Most job losses were in manufacturing, followed by significant job losses in wholesale and retail trade, transportation and public utilities, and finance, insurance, and real estate.[116]

Many displaced workers found new and decent-paying jobs, but many others could not find jobs or had to take jobs below their previous pay level. Neither the U.S. government nor state governments provide much in the way of dislocated worker services for unemployed workers.[117] Job losses occur during periods of both economic expansion and recession. More than half of those displaced are in manufacturing or construction jobs, although large numbers of white-collar workers also have been laid off.[118] Massive employment reductions have occurred at some of the largest U.S. corporations, including General Motors and IBM.

In recent decades the capitalist market has become global; many corporations now operate around the world. This global market has made low-wage labor and unregulated working situations available to many corporations and encouraged them to shift investments out of moderate-profit industries to higher-profit international ventures, even if that means abandoning basic U.S. industries. From the corporate executives' view, actual or threatened plant closings and capital flight can "discipline" U.S. workers to accept lower wages from employers—and to be docile in the face of corporate decisions. Capital flight is a major reason that displaced manufacturing workers tend to be unemployed for longer periods than displaced service workers, and that only half of displaced manufacturing workers who do find new jobs stay in manufacturing.[119]

The United States has lost millions of manufacturing jobs in recent decades. No public source of information states how many are lost as the result of capital flight. However, considerable evidence suggests that the movement of jobs overseas contributed directly or indirectly to a substantial portion of this job displacement. For example, the National Labor Committee reports that 60 percent of footwear workers in the United States have lost their jobs, while just one large Chinese shoe company employs over 100,000 workers who now assemble Nike, Timberland, Reebok, and New Balance shoes for export to the United States. These Chinese workers earn *only 3 percent* of what U.S. workers earn.[120] Since 1996, some 255 extended mass-layoff events in the United States have resulted from corporate overseas relocations.[121]

Corporate executives have moved investment capital or manufacturing operations overseas for decades. Thus, by the late 1980s capital flight had already brought a 40 percent decline in employment in the U.S. steel industry, a 30 percent decline in primary metals, and a 17 percent decline in the textile industry.[122] A 1990s study of U.S. apparel companies in El Salvador, Guatemala, and Honduras conducted by the National Labor Committee identified "30 U.S. apparel manufacturers with their own plants and another 68 companies with subcontracting relationships in the three countries. Since 1990, these same companies have been involved in at least 58 plant closings and 11 mass layoffs in the U.S., leaving over 12,000 workers jobless."[123]

In spite of claims to the contrary by its business advocates, the North American Free Trade Agreement (NAFTA) has generally hurt U.S. workers. Research shows that as of May 2002, about 403,000 U.S. workers had qualified for special retraining provided for people in the NAFTA agreement who lose jobs because employers have moved production facilities to Mexico or Canada, or who have been hurt by import competition from those countries. Already, thousands of apparel and electronics manufacturing jobs have been lost to Mexico, which particularly hurts white women workers and workers of color who are the primary workers in these U.S. industries.[124]

A variety of U.S. firms are using the relatively low-wage, nonunion labor pools in poorer countries to cut production costs. Computer and electronics industries, which many have counted on to provide jobs to replace the decent-paying ones lost in declining "smokestack" industries, have joined the flight overseas. For example, to help ensure a skilled workforce for plants in Mexico, IBM and Apple have contributed millions of dollars to the Monterrey Technology Institute, a college in Mexico, to train workers who will earn less than one-third as much as their U.S. counterparts.[125] Many white-collar jobs, including insurance claims processing and data entry work, that are being exported overseas are entry-level jobs that are important for new entrants into the U.S. workforce, such as non–college-bound high school graduates. Such a loss has a severely negative effect on the U.S. workforce.[126] Even higher-paying computer programming and engineering jobs are now being exported overseas, to countries such as India.

The governments of newly industrializing countries around the globe compete aggressively for U.S. industry. Governments in prime relocation areas often restrict unionization, provide tax exemptions and liberal foreign exchange rules, and offer a variety of other investment incentives to U.S. multinational corporations. For example, the director of the Dominican Republic's Investment Promotion Council, a private organization funded by the U.S. Agency for International Development (AID), explained that a U.S. apparel plant could save $23,000 in labor costs per worker per year in his country but only $20,000 if it located in Mexico.[127]

U.S. military aid often props up repressive Asian and Central American governments, thereby helping to keep low-wage and less unionized labor there. U.S.-controlled world financial organizations such as the World Bank and the development banks have facilitated corporate flight overseas.[128] In addition, hundreds of millions of dollars of taxpayer money have gone to support corporate flight from the United States. A two-year investigation conducted by the National Labor Committee (NLC) in the 1990s revealed that "the U.S. government had obligated over $1.3 billion to 93 investment and trade promotion projects, at least half of which were directed toward developing Central America and the Caribbean as low-wage assembly production sites for companies fleeing U.S. wages, benefits, unions, and environmental standards."[129]

Most U.S. funds have been provided through AID, which has constructed factory buildings, funded comparative cost analyses for corporations considering moving to Central American and Caribbean locations, paid half the cost of training workers for U.S. firms relocating there, and established a multimillion-dollar credit line to provide loans for these operations. Millions of dollars in Food for Peace aid have also been used to build free-trade-zone factories. AID provided $102 million to the Salvadoran Foundation for Economic and Social Development (FUSADES), a private-sector business that operates three investment promotion offices in the United States.[130] Targeted U.S. industries include apparel, electronic/electrical, and other labor-intensive assembly operations. At least ten other Central American and Caribbean investment and export promotion groups have been funded by the U.S. government. Between 1981 and the present, some U.S. government officials in both political parties have worked to reduce the number of well-paid jobs in the United States and, in effect, to export them to low-wage areas in other countries.[131] (See "The Human Face of CAFTA" on page 400.)

Workers Fighting Back: Plant Closing Laws

The negative impact on workers of plant closings and layoffs is even worse when no advance notice, or inadequate notice, is given. One General Accounting Office survey found that prior to a plant closing or a major layoff, the median notice time given by U.S. plants to their workers was seven days; one-third of the plants that had laid off workers gave no notice.[132] In contrast, laws passed in western European nations, Canada, and Japan require advance warning to workers and government permission to move a plant outside the country.[133] U.S. business interests strongly oppose such requirements, arguing that they restrict the ability of companies to compete internationally. According to market-oriented economists and politicians, unrestrained corporate mobility is necessary for U.S. economic health. The few government interventions that corporate executives approve are tax incentives and other subsidies that actually facilitate capital mobility.

In 1988 Congress passed a modest advance-notice bill requiring larger (with 100 employees or more), stable companies that know beforehand of plans to close plants or lay off large numbers of workers to notify employees 60 days in advance. Known as the Worker Adjustment and Retraining Notification Act (WARN), the law is still the only one in effect nationally. The companies are not required to get approval for plant closings from either government or workers.[134]

The plant closing law gives U.S. workers employed by large organizations a chance to seek new employment prior to being laid off and provides local governments some notice of the major service increases and tax decreases that occur following major plant closings. Labor leaders have called the bill a "very modest step in the direction of fairness."[135] Yet the $500-a-day penalty for noncompliance is seen as a loophole that defeats the law's purpose. Such a small fine does not serve as a deterrent to large employers. In addition, labor advocates note that in nonunionized plants, enforcement is difficult because workers are often afraid to report law violations by employers.[136]

In the 1990s, Ypsilanti, Michigan, won a lawsuit to prevent General Motors (GM) from closing its plant there. The judge stated that GM's acceptance of millions in tax breaks from local government constituted a binding promise to provide long-term employment. Based on a legal doctrine that says that promises must be fulfilled if favors have been accepted on the basis of that promise, the judge ruled that GM could not close the plant. However, GM appealed the court decision and won when a higher court ruled that such a tax abatement does not include a promise of employment over the long term.[137]

The Human Face of CAFTA

In 2004, President George W. Bush asked the U.S. Congress to approve the Central American Free Trade Agreement (CAFTA), creating an international free trade zone between the United States and the Central American countries of Coast Rica, Guatemala, Honduras, Panama, and El Salvador. CAFTA (like the earlier NAFTA agreement) will create new rules for trade in manufactured goods, agricultural products, and services that cross U.S. borders duty-free. Recently, the National Labor Committee investigated the working conditions of laborers working in factories in Central American countries subject to CAFTA and found deplorable conditions. One of these factories is in San Salvador where Marina del Carmen Leiva works.

Marina is a 32-year-old mother of three who earns $152 a month sewing shirts for Copatex, a Korean-owned factory located in the San Marcos Free Trade Zone in El Salvador. Copatex employs 450 mostly young female workers who sew 4,000 shirts per day for the Montreal-based Gildan Activewear label, one of North America's largest shirtmakers. Gildan, a family-owned firm that rivals such major manufacturers as Fruit of the Loom and Hanes, employs about 1,200 workers in Canada and 9,200 workers in factories that it owns or contracts work to in the free trade zone.

Marina and her children live in a cramped bungalow, and each workday she rides an overcrowded bus to the factory. Marina is sure to arrive at the factory on time since her supervisor will dock her one-half hour's wages if she is three to five minutes late. She is also penalized two days' wages if she schedules a medical appointment and misses work without management permission.

Marina is under constant pressure to meet or exceed production quotas. She must sew 154 shirts a day, 17 shirts an hour, or 1 shirt every three-and-one-half minutes. Marina earns less than five cents per shirt she sews, making about three-tenths of 1 percent of the shirt's retail value. Managers at the factory coerce her to produce more by continually reminding Marina that her job depends on achieving high production goals. Marina is re-

quired to work 11- and 12-hour shifts, six days a week. But Copatex pays Marina for only part of those hours; the factory does not pay her for a 20-minute lunch break or one 15-minute break in the morning and one in the afternoon.

Marina labors under extremely oppressive, sweatshop conditions. The physical plant where she works is a large army-type hanger with a rounded sheet-metal roof where the inside temperature can reach more than 90 degrees. Marina is soaked in sweat all day while she works. Marina must ask permission to use the bathroom; Copatex locks worker bathrooms. She can only use the bathroom once during her morning shift and once during her afternoon shift. Even so, the bathroom is always filthy. It usually has no toilet paper, soap, or towels, and at times even no water. The factory does not provide drinking water for workers other than regular tap water. If Marina wants a drink of water during her workday, she risks getting sick since the tap water comes from a cistern and is contaminated with bacterial levels that exceed 225 percent of allowable international standards. The tap water also contains fecal matter.

Marina leaves the factory each night at 6:00 P.M. exhausted with neck pain and arm, wrist, and ankle soreness from performing the same, repetitive motions thousands of times a day. Yet Marina is powerless to improve her working conditions; Copatex prohibits unionization of its workers and fires union activists. Union organizers in the free-trade-zone countries often end up dead or disappear mysteriously. To Marina, her life would be far better if Copatex "would just treat us like human beings."

Marina will have to leave the factory in another three years because Copatex regularly fires or torments women who reach 35 years of age into resigning from their jobs. Copatex replaces its older workers with younger, more energetic teenagers who can work faster. When Marina leaves Copatex, however, the factory will cheat her out of much of her legally entitled severance pay: one month's wages for every year worked.

An independent human rights ombudsman in El Salvador recently reported that the *maquiladora* where Marina works is "a hostile environment for workers, where the business and government sectors see protecting workers' rights as going against the country's economic interests. CAFTA protects the fundamental rights of business, but not the labor rights of the citizens." Human rights organizations have found equally deplorable working conditions in factories throughout the free trade zone where workers manufacture clothing for JCPenney, Kohl's, K-Mart, Wal-Mart, Sears, Nike, Adidas, Hanes, Fruit of the Loom, Gloria Vanderbilt, Bugle Boy, Old Navy/Gap, Tommy Hilfiger, Polo Jeans, and OshKosh. According to a U.S. State Department report, traffickers have forced Central American workers into factories "where they toil under harsh conditions of indentured servitude." Once again, as we have noted throughout this chapter, the goal of corporate capitalists is improving profits and not meeting workers' needs, whether in the United States or overseas.

Sources: National Labor Committee, *Gildan Production in El Salvador*, April 2004, available at www.nlcnet.org/campaigns/copatex/copatex.opt.pdf; Elizabeth Becker, "Central American Deal Ignites a Trade Debate," *New York Times* (April 6, 2004), available at www.nlcnet.org/campaigns/copatex/NYT040604.pdf; National Labor Committee, *AAA Honduras* (ret. May 19, 2004), available at www.nlcnet.org/campaigns/ca03/AAA/aaa.pdf; National Labor Committee, *Sweating for Kohl's* (ret. May 19, 2004), available at www.nlcnet.org/campaigns/archive/sweatingforkohls/thefacts.shtml; National Labor Committee, *KB Manufacturing*, October 2003, available at www.nlcnet.org/campaigns/ca03/kb/kb.report.pdf; National Labor Committee, *Industrial Embroidery* (ret. May 19, 2004), available at www.nlcnet.org/campaigns/ca03/industrial/industrial.pdf; U.S. Department of State, *Trafficking in Persons Report*, June 11, 2003, available at www.state.gov/g/tip/rls/tiprpt/2003/21262.htm.

SUMMARY

Work outside the home is a major life activity for the majority of Americans. Work not only provides an income but also contributes positively or negatively to self-identity. Reflecting alienation about their dissatisfying work, many workers become discontented with the workplace and react with various kinds of protest to such problems as unemployment, unsafe working conditions, automation, capital flight, plant closings, and the hierarchical character of work.

Serious environmental problems confront people at work. Job injuries from accidents and exposure to dangerous chemicals remain commonplace. A major cause of unsafe work environments is the unrestrained drive for private profit. Corporations and other businesses often move slowly in making major changes in workplace safety because such changes can cut into profits and increase worker control over the workplace. A major social cost of our capitalistic system is the harm done to the health and lives of working people in the name of monetary profit.

Millions of individuals are exposed to a long list of dangerous conditions and chemicals, often routinely, at the workplace. Dangerous substances not only cause immediate or long-term health effects on workers but often affect workers' families. Too often, workers are not given adequate information on dangers of the chemicals with which they come into contact. Owners and managers use a variety of tactics to convince the public there is little risk from exposure to accidents and chemicals in the workplace; they have aggressively stalled or minimized the impact of government regulation of workplace safety.

The concept of alienation is useful in making sense of many work-related problems. In this context, alienation refers to the objective separation of workers from productive property, from the products created, from one another, and from themselves. Relative to capitalists and managers, most workers have little control over most of the character and structure of the work they do. Work tasks are mostly determined and structured with relatively little worker input. Unlike independent craftspersons, workers must sell their labor to employers; workers are usually bought and sold like other commodities.

The lack of any real decision-making control over the structure and process of the workplace tends to degrade workers. In numerous opinion surveys many U.S. workers, both blue-collar and white-collar, openly express the alienated view that their work is authoritarian in structure, dull, repetitive, and meaningless. Subordination of workers in an undemocratic workplace also has a negative impact on physical and psychological health.

Many workers not only express negative attitudes toward work but also take action to resist or to change that work's pace or character. The United States has a lengthy history of workers organizing to resist alienating work conditions. Employees have organized many unions, thousands of strikes, and many other protests in their struggles to win concessions from the capitalist and managerial classes. Relative quiet in one period is often replaced by a resurgence of worker organization later. In all periods, organized workers somewhere are struggling for change and improvement in working conditions.

How much work actually gets done is to a great extent the result of an ongoing struggle between the working class and the capitalist class. Workers resist alienating work and struggle by means of individual and collective protests, strikes, and unionizing to improve working conditions. With greater resources, employers and their political allies fight to control the working class by means of such strategies as scientific management, hierarchical control, and automation. Similar situations often face workers struggling with government employers.

Scientific management means controlling workers by, among other things, breaking up jobs into smaller units and by job standardization. Hierarchical control involves arranging people into hierarchies of order givers and order takers, with the magnitude of rewards and privileges growing as one moves up the hierarchy. Automation involves technical control of the workplace through assembly lines, machines, and computerization. Automation has the potential to expand production and to liberate ordinary working people from dangerous and boring work. In our capitalistic system, workers frequently see automation as a threat because it is often used to destroy jobs, create unemployment, and reduce the income of workers.

Capital flight—the movement of companies to locations with lower labor costs and favorable profit-making conditions—is a threat to many U.S. workers. The U.S. government has facilitated the export of many well-paid jobs to low-wage areas in other countries. This process, which already has cost many workers their jobs, has accelerated since the 1980s. With U.S. multinationals now competing aggressively in a global market, union leaders have suggested the need for global worker organizations to match the worldwide scope and power of the corporations. Without some countervailing power, corporations with accountability to no country will go wherever labor is cheapest and most repressed, a process that has steadily eroded the standard of living for many U.S. workers and their families.

STUDY QUESTIONS

1. Each year thousands of Americans die because of their jobs, and hundreds of thousands more are injured or made ill. What are some of the principal causes of workplace deaths and injuries?
2. Explain how workplace hazards can be environmental hazards that affect not only workers but also communities across the country.

3. Describe how political and economic pressures have affected the regulatory policy of the Occupational Safety and Health Administration.

4. What is the right-to-know movement? If successful, what impact will this movement have on workplace safety?

5. Using data on occupational growth, critically examine the argument that high-tech employment will compensate for the jobs lost in "smokestack" industries.

6. Identify the principal strategies used by management for controlling workers, and trace the historical evolution of these approaches.

7. Discuss the importance of plant closings and capital flight for U.S. workers.

ENDNOTES

1. Jeremy Rifkin, "Vanishing Jobs," *Mother Jones,* September/October 1995, p. 60.
2. AFL-CIO, "Safety and Health at Work" (ret. March 29, 2004), available at www.aflcio.org/yourjobeconomy/safety; see also, Linda Chavez-Thompson, testimony before the U.S. Senate Committee on Labor and Human Resources, November 29, 1995, p. 2.
3. U.S. Bureau of Labor Statistics, "Workplace Injuries and Illnesses in 2003," December 2004, available at www.bls.gov/news.release/pdf/osh.pdf.
4. U.S. Bureau of Labor Statistics, "Lost Worktime Injuries and Illnesses: Characteristics and Resulting Days Away from Work, 2002," March 2004, available at www.bls.gov/news.release/pdf/osh2.pdf.
5. U.S. Department of Labor, "National Census of Fatal Occupational Injuries in 2002," September 2003, available at www.bls.gov/news.release/pdf/cfoi.pdf.
6. U.S. Bureau of Labor Statistics, "Workplace Injuries and Illnesses in 2003."
7. AFL-CIO, *Death on the Job: The Toll of Neglect: A National and State-by-State Profile of Worker Safety and Health in the United States,* 12th ed., April 2003, available at www.aflcio.org/yourjobeconomy/safety/memorial/upload/death_2003_intro.pdf.
8. Russell Mokhiber, *Corporate Crime and Violence* (San Francisco: Sierra Club Books, 1988), p. 98.
9. National Institute for Occupational Safety and Health, "Occupation Cancer" (ret. April 14, 2004), available at www.cdc.gov/niosh/topics/cancer; see also, Bill Thomson, "Surviving Cancer," *Natural Health* 23, no. 2 (March–April, 1993): 76; see also Samuel S. Epstein, *The Politics of Cancer* (San Francisco: Sierra Club Books, 1978), pp. 24, 34, 322–24, 327–29.
10. AFL-CIO, "Workers Need Protection from Ergonomic Hazards" (ret. March 31, 2004), available at www.aflcio.org/yourjobeconomy/safety/ergo/ergo_why.cfm.
11. Joseph A. Page and Mary-Win O'Brien, *Bitter Wages* (New York: Grossman, 1973), pp. 145–46.
12. William Glaberson, "Safety Remains Elusive at Morrell," *New York Times,* August 21, 1988, sec. 3, p. 1; U.S. Bureau of Labor Statistics, *Occupational Injuries and Illnesses: Counts, Rates, and Characteristics, 1992,* (Washington, D.C.: 1995), p. 5; U.S. Bureau of Labor Statistics, *Survey of Occupational Injuries and Illnesses, 1993* (Washington, D.C.: 1995), p. 9.
13. Quoted in Glaberson, "Safety Remains Elusive at Morrell," sec. 3, p. 1.
14. Kevin Silverstein, "The 1995 Lobbying Hall of Shame," *Multinational Monitor* (January/February 1996), available at multinationalmonitor.org/hyper/mm0196.12.html.
15. Christopher Drew, "In the Productivity Push, How Much Is Too Much?" *New York Times,* December 17, 1995, sec. 3, p. 1.
16. Polaris Institute, "Corporate Profiles, United Parcel Service (UPS)" (May 2003), available at www.polarisinstitute.org; Colleen M. O'Neill, "Labor Defends Rule to Protect Worker Safety," *AFL-CIO News,* January 22, 1996, p. 3.
17. Colleen M. O'Neill, "Ergonomics Cases Climb Ever Higher," *AFL-CIO News,* January 8, 1996, p. 3.
18. Interview with representative of UFCW, February 1996.
19. Testimony of Robert Reich, U.S. Secretary of Labor, Hearing of the House Education and Labor Committee: Subject: HR 1280, Federal News Service, April 28, 1993.
20. National Safety Council, "Workplace Injuries Cost Americans $127.7 Billion in 1999," (May 2000), available at www.nsc.org/news/nr0522wk.htm.
21. Ken Ward, Jr., "Report Cites U.S. Asbestos Disease 'Epidemic,'" *The Charleston Gazette* (March 8, 2004).

22. "The Asbestos Miracle," *Dollars & Sense,* April 1983, p. 18; Jennifer Stoffel and Stephen Phillips, "Double Jeopardy: Asbestos Is a Hazard That Won't Go Away," *Progressive,* April 1986, pp. 28–31; Randy Hodson and Teresa A. Sullivan, *The Social Organization of Work* (Belmont, Calif.: Wadsworth, 1990), pp. 122–24.

23. Epstein, *The Politics of Cancer,* pp. 85, 94–98.

24. U.S. Bureau of Labor Statistics, "Occupational Injuries and Illnesses in the U.S. by Industry, 1992" (Washington, D.C.: 1995), p. 143.

25. Epstein, *Politics of Cancer,* p. 391; see also pp. 81–83.

26. Ibid., pp. 397–99.

27. Page and O'Brien, *Bitter Wages,* pp. xi–xii.

28. AFL-CIO, *Death on the Job.*

29. Page and O'Brien, *Bitter Wages,* pp. 182–200; Charles Piller, "Toxic Time Bombs in the Factory," *The Nation,* April 4, 1981, pp. 395–98.

30. AFL-CIO, *Death on the Job.*

31. Joel Schufro, "Reforming Reagan's OSHA," *Economic Notes* 56 (November–December 1988): 11–13; "Bush's Ruling Class," *Common Cause,* April/May/June 1992, p. 21.

32. Khalid Elhassan, *The OSHA Mission—Found and Lost, A Public Reminder,* Center for the Study of Responsive Law, February 2000, available at www.csrl.org/reports/OSHA.html#N_49_.

33. This table is constructed from an earlier table produced by the AFL-CIO; see AFL-CIO, *Information and Action Guide* (Washington, D.C.: AFL-CIO, 1995), p. 14; see also Timothy Curry and Lynn Shibut, "The Cost of the Savings and Loan Crisis: Truth and Consequences," *FDIC Banking Review* (December 2000), available at www.fdic.gov/bank/analytical/banking/2000dec/brv13n2_2.pdf; and Office of Management and Budget, Executive Office of the President, Table of Contents (ret. March 31, 2004), available at www.whitehouse.gov/omb/budget/fy2005/budget.html.

34. Khalid Elhassan, *The OSHA Mission.*

35. "OSHA Cuts Unpopular," *AFL-CIO News,* September 25, 1995, p. 4.

36. AFL-CIO, *Death on the Job.*

37. "What's in a Name?" *Dollars & Sense,* April 1983, p. 6.

38. Andrea Hall, ed., *Community Right-to-Know Manual* (Washington, D.C.: Thompson Publishing Group, 1995); see also National COSH Network, available at www.coshnetwork.org/index.htm.

39. "What's in a Name?" p. 18.

40. Rick Engler, "How We Won the 'Right-to-Know' in New Jersey," *Labor Notes,* September 27, 1983, p. 16.

41. "In N.J., Rollbacks Prove Shortsighted," *Working Notes,* May–June 1995, p. 2.

42. Mazhar Ullah, "Thousands Protest on Anniversary of India's Bhopal Industrial Disaster," *Environment News Network,* December 4, 2002, available at www.enn.com/news/wire-stories/2002/12/12042002/ap_49103.asp.

43. Greenpeace, "Bhopal Victims Warn U.S. Government and Dow Chemical of Impending Catastrophe" (ret. April 28, 2004), available at www.greenpeaceusa.org/index.fpl/10386/article/1097.html; see also, Comment, "Bhopal's Legacy," *The Nation,* May 24, 2004, pp. 6–7.

44. This section draws on Karl Marx, *Economic and Philosophic Manuscripts* (Moscow: Progress Publishers, 1959), and Bertell Ollman, *Alienation,* 2nd ed. (London: Cambridge University Press, 1976), pp. 130–34.

45. Lillian Breslow Rubin, *Worlds of Pain* (New York: Basic Books, 1976), pp. 155–56.

46. Faye J. Crosby, *Relative Deprivation and Working Women* (New York: Oxford University Press, 1982); Randy Hodson, "Gender Differences in Job Satisfaction: Why Aren't Women More Dissatisfied?" *Sociological Quarterly* 30 (September 1989): 385–99.

47. Samuel Davidson, "U.S.: 21,000 Verizon Workers Accept Buyout," *World Socialist Web Site,* November 2003, available at www.wsws.org/articles/2003/nov2003/veri/n19.shtml; for weekly updates of the number of U.S. layoffs, see Forbes.com, *The Layoff Tracker,* available at www.forbes.com/2001/01/30/layoffs.html.

48. Sarah Anderson and John Cavanagh, *Executive Excess 2003: CEO's Win, Workers and Taxpayers Lose,* Tenth Annual CEO Compensation Survey, 2003, Institute for Policy Studies and United for a Fair Economy, available at www.stw.org/press/2003/EE2003.pdf.

49. "Upsizing," *The Economist,* February 10, 1996, p. 61.

50. Arthur Kornhauser, *Mental Health of the Industrial Worker* (New York: John Wiley, 1965); National Safety Council, *Accident Facts: 1987,* p. 44.

51. Cited in Special Task Force Report to the Secretary of Health, Education and Welfare, *Work in America* (Washington, D.C.: 1973), pp. 12–13.

52. Abraham H. Maslow, *Motivation and Personality* (New York: Harper and Brothers, 1954); Chris Argyris, "Personality and Organization Theory Revisited," *Administrative Science Quarterly* 18 (1973): 141–67.

53. U.S. Bureau of the Census, *Statistical Abstract of the U.S., 2003,* available at www.census. gov/prod/www/statistical-abstract-03.html; Richard F. Hamilton and James D. Wright, *The State of the Masses* (Chicago: Aldine, 1986); Graham L. Staines and Robert P. Quinn, "American Workers Evaluate the Quality of Their Jobs," *Monthly Labor Review,* January 1979, pp. 3–12; "Current Labor Statistics," *Monthly Labor Review,* November 1995, p. 105.

54. Richard Sennett and Jonathan Cobb, *The Hidden Injuries of Class* (New York: Vintage Books, 1972), pp. 178–86.

55. Erich Fromm, *Man for Himself* (New York: Holt, Rinehart & Winston, 1947), pp. 69–76.

56. C. Wright Mills, *White Collar* (New York: Oxford University Press, 1956).

57. Barbara Garson, *The Electronic Sweatshop* (New York: Penguin Books, 1988).

58. Harry Braverman, *Labor and Monopoly Capital* (New York: Monthly Review Press, 1974), pp. 316–25.

59. Ibid., pp. 336–50.

60. Robert Jackall, *Workers in a Labyrinth* (New York: Allenheld, Osmun, 1978), p. 171.

61. Jill Andresky Fraser, *White-Collar Sweatshops: The Deterioration of Work and Its Rewards in Corporate America* (New York: W.W. Norton, 2002); see also David Ignatius, "Adding Jobs and Anxiety," *The Washington Post,* March 30, 2004, p. A19.

62. U.S. Department of Labor, Bureau of Labor Statistics, *Occupational Outlook Handbook, 2004–05 Edition,* February 2004, available at stats.bls.gov/oco/print/oco2003.htm; Daniel Hecker, "Occupational Employment Projections to 2012," *Monthly Labor Review,* February 2004, available at stats.bls.gov/opub/mlr/2004/02/art5abs.htm.

63. Bureau of Labor Statistics, *Contingent and Alternative Employment Arrangements, February 2001,* available at www.bls.gov/news.release/conemp.nr0.htm.

64. Eileen Appelbaum and Judith Gregory, "Union Responses to Contingent Work: Are Win–Win Outcomes Possible?" in *Flexible Workstyles: A Look at Contingent Labor,* Conference Summary, U.S. Department of Labor, 1988; cited in Camille Colatosi, "A Job without a Future," *Dollars & Sense,* May 1992, p. 9.

65. U.S. Department of Labor, *Report on the American Workforce* (Washington, D.C.: 1995), pp. 26–31.

66. "Disposable Communities," *Dollars & Sense,* March 1992, p. 13.

67. Bureau of Labor Statistics, *Contingent and Alternative Employment Arrangements, February 2001,* available at www.bls.gov/news.release/conemp.nr0.htm; *Report on the American Workforce,* p. 34; "Caught in the Temp Trap," *Economic Notes* 63 (September 1995): 7.

68. *Report on the American Workforce,* pp. 36–37; "Caught in the Temp Trap," p. 7.

69. Randall Williams, "All in a Day's Work," *Dollars & Sense,* December 1988, pp. 12–15.

70. "The Jobless Recovery," *Economic Notes* 61 (April 1993): 1; Sascha Eisner, "Bank of America Makes Most California Employees Part-Timers with No Benefits," *Labor Notes,* May 1993, p. 5.

71. "The Rise of the 'Modular Corporation,'" *Economic Notes* 61 (April 1993): 2.

72. *Lou Dobbs Tonight* (February 10, 2004), Cable News Network, Transcript #021001cb.l10; interview with U.S. Chamber of Commerce CEO Tom Donohue on outsourcing of jobs by U.S. corporations.

73. Sarah Anderson and John Cavanagh, *Outsourcing: A Policy Agenda,* Foreign Policy in Focus, April 2004, available at www.fpif.org/briefs/vol9/v9n02outsource.html.

74. "Crimes of Fashion: Those Who Suffer to Bring You Gap T-Shirts," *Dollars & Sense,* November/ December 1995, pp. 30–31.

75. Colatosti, "A Job without a Future," p. 9.

76. David Leonhardt, "As Prison Labor Grows, So Does the Debate," *New York Times,* March 19, 2000, A1.

77. "Forced Workforce," *Dollars & Sense,* July/August 1995, p. 4; "Captive Labor," *AFL-CIO News,* September 25, 1995, p. 7.

78. "Captive Labor," p. 7.

79. "The Rise of the 'Modular Corporation,'" p. 2.

80. Rifkin, "Vanishing Jobs," pp. 58–64; see also Jeremy Rifkin, *The End of Work: The Decline of the Global Labor Force and the Dawn of the Post-Market Era* (New York: Tarcher/Putnam, 1995).

81. Thorstein Veblen, *The Engineers and the Price System* (New York: Viking, 1921).

82. William L. Chaze, "Who Says the Assembly Line Is History?" *U.S. News & World Report,* July 16, 1984, p. 48.

83. John M. Jermier, "Sabotage at Work: The Rational View," *Research in the Sociology of Organizations* 6 (1988): 101–34.

84. We are indebted to Rogelio Nuñez and Penelope McCalla for these examples of worker resistance.

85. Since the Bureau of Labor Statistics now only reports stoppages involving 1,000 or more workers, current data provide an incomplete picture of strike activity and are not comparable with earlier strike data; see U.S. Bureau of the Census, *Statistical Abstract of the U.S.: 1978* (Washington, D.C.: 1978), pp. 432–33; U.S. Bureau of the Census, *Statistical Abstract of the U.S.: 1992* (Washington, D.C.: 1992), p. 420.

86. Bureau of Labor Statistics, *Major Work Stoppages in 2003,* March 19, 2004, available at www.bls.gov/news.release/pdf/wkstp.pdf.

87. George Gorham Gorat, *An Introduction to the Study of Organized Labor in America* (New York: Macmillan, 1916; BoondocksNet Edition, 2002), available at www.boondocksnet.com/labor/history/ola.

88. John Zerzan, *Creation and Its Enemies: The Revolt against Work* (Rochester, N.Y.: Mutualist Books, 1977), pp. 19–20; Robert J. Goldstein, *Political Repression in Modern America* (Cambridge, Mass.: Schenkman, 1978), p. 3; Wyndham Mortimer, *Organize* (Boston: Beacon Press, 1971), pp. 142–60.

89. Stanley Aronowitz, *False Promises* (New York: McGraw-Hill, 1973), pp. 226–27.

90. Zerzan, *Creation and Its Enemies,* pp. 44–45.

91. U.S. Bureau of the Census, *Statistical Abstracts of the U.S., Labor Union Membership by Sectors: 1983 to 2002* (ret. April 2, 2004), available at www.census.gov/prod/2004pubs/03statab/labor.pdf; "Wages/Unions," *Economic Notes* 64 (January 1996): 4.

92. Mary Hollens, "Catfish and Community," *Third Force,* May–June 1993, pp. 19, 21.

93. Ibid., p. 22.

94. Ibid., pp. 13–14, 19–21.

95. Rifkin, "Vanishing Jobs," p. 64.

96. James B. Parks, "NLRA at 60: Weakened Law Facing New Attacks," *AFL-CIO News,* October 23, 1995, p. 2; U.S. Bureau of the Census, *Statistical Abstract of the U.S.: 1995* (Washington, D.C.: 1995), p. 865.

97. U.S. Bureau of the Census, *Statistical Abstracts of the U.S., Union Members by Selected Characteristics: 2002* (ret. April 2, 2004), available at www.census.gov/prod/2004pubs/03statab/labor.pdf.

98. Moshe Adler, "Unionization and Poverty: The Case of New York City Retail Workers," *Public Interest Economics,* December 2003, available at www.epinet.org/workingpapers/wp127.pdf.

99. Sarah Anderson and John Cavanagh, *Rethinking the NAFTA Record,* Institute for Policy Studies (August 8, 2002), available at www.ips-dc.org.

100. Human Rights Watch, *Unfair Advantage: Workers Freedom of Association in the United States,* August 2000, available at www.hrw.org/reports/2000/uslabor.

101. Alexander Rhoads, "Grinding Workers Down," *Dollars & Sense,* March 1992, p. 19.

102. Whole Workers Unite. "Background on Madison Campaign" (ret. April 22, 2004), available at www.wholeworkersunite.org/ContentExpress-display-ceid-33.html.

103. Parks, "NLRA at 60," p. 2.

104. Hollens, "Catfish and Community," pp. 14, 21.

105. Richard Edwards, *Contested Terrain* (New York: Basic Books, 1979), pp. 104, 130–31; Braverman, *Labor and Monopoly Capital,* pp. 85–21.

106. Braverman, *Labor and Monopoly Capital,* pp. 445–56; M. C. Kennedy, "The Division of Labor and the Culture of Capitalism: A Critique" (Ph.D. dissertation, University of Michigan, 1968), p. 172.

107. Mike Parker and Jane Slaughter, "Running on Yellow," *Dollars & Sense,* September 1988, pp. 10–11, 21.

108. Edwards, *Contested Terrain,* p. 145.

109. Arnold S. Tannenbaum et al., *Hierarchy in Organizations* (San Francisco: Jossey-Bass, 1977), pp. 2–4.

110. Ibid., p. 10; C. George Benello, "Organization, Conflict, and Free Association," in C. George Benello and Dimitrios Roussopoulos, eds., *The Case for Participatory Democracy* (New York: Viking, 1971), pp. 200–201.

111. Edwards, *Contested Terrain,* p. 130.

112. H. Allen Hunt and Timothy L. Hunt, *Human Resource Implications of Robotics* (Kalamazoo, Mich.: W. E. Upjohn Institute for Employment Research, 1983), pp. x–xi.

113. Hodson and Sullivan, *The Social Organization of Work,* p. 182.

114. Rifkin, "Vanishing Jobs," p. 60.
115. Abbe Mowshowitz, *The Conquest of Will: Information Processing in Human Affairs* (Reading, Mass.: Addison-Wesley, 1976); Eileen R. Appelbaum, "The Impact of Technology on Skill Requirements and Occupational Structure in the Insurance Industry, 1960–90," cited in Philip Kraft, ed., *A Review of Empirical Studies of the Consequences of Technological Change on Work and Workers in the U.S.* (Washington, D.C.: National Research Council, 1984).
116. U.S. Department of Labor, Bureau of Labor Statistics, *Displaced Workers Summary, August 2002,* available at www.bls.gov/news.release/disp.no0.htm; see also U.S. Department of Labor, Bureau of Labor Statistics, *Archived Extended Mass Layoffs,* available at www.bls.gov/mls/ #overview.
117. Testimony of Richard McHugh, Associate General Counsel International Union, UAW, before the House Education Committee, June 8, 1994.
118. Michael Podgursky, "The Industrial Structure of Job Displacement, 1979–89," *Monthly Labor Review,* September 1992, p. 19; Diane E. Herz, "Worker Displacement Still Common in the Late 1980s," *Monthly Labor Review,* May 1991, p. 4; Barry Bearak, "Lost in America: Jobs, Trust," *Los Angeles Times,* November 26, 1995, p. A1.
119. Herz, "Worker Displacement Still Common in the Late 1980s," p. 7.
120. National Labor Committee, *Race to the Bottom* (ret. April 3, 2004), available at www.nlcnet.org/campaigns/archive/chinareport/huffybikesdoc.shtml.
121. U.S. Department of Labor, Bureau of Labor Statistics, *Mass Layoff Statistics* (ret. April 3, 2004), available at data.bls.gov/cgi-bin/surveymost?ml.
122. Bennett Harrison and Barry Bluestone, *The Great U-Turn* (New York: Basic Books, 1988), p. 37.
123. Barbara Briggs, "Aiding and Abetting Corporate Flight," *Multinational Monitor,* January–February 1993, p. 41, available at www.ratical.com/corporations/mmCorpFli.html.
124. Sarah Anderson and John Cavanagh, *Rethinking the NAFTA Record,* Institute for Policy Studies (August 8, 2002), available at www.ips-dc.org.
125. Louis Uchitelle, "Mexico's Hope for Industrial Might," *New York Times,* September 25, 1990, p. D1.
126. Robert O. Metzger, "The Ominous Exporting of U.S. Clerical Jobs," *USA Today,* March 1, 1989, p. 30.
127. Briggs, "Aiding and Abetting Corporate Flight," p. 41.
128. Metzger, "The Ominous Exporting of U.S. Clerical Jobs," p. 30.
129. Briggs, "Aiding and Abetting Corporate Flight," pp. 40–41.
130. Quoted in ibid., p. 37.
131. Ibid., pp. 38–39; quotation on p. 38.
132. Frank Swoboda, "Easing Plant-Closing Pain: AT&T, Union Join to Aid the Displaced," *Washington Post,* July 5, 1989, p. A3.
133. Walter S. Mossberg, "Plant-Closings Quarrel Distorts a Modest Idea," *Wall Street Journal,* April 25, 1988, p.1.
134. Ibid.; Clyde H. Farnsworth, "House Passes Bill on Plant Closings by Vote of 286–136," *New York Times,* July 14, 1988, p. A1; Ramona Patterson, "Plants Fear Impact of 60-Day Closing Bill on Workers," *The Business Journal–Charlotte,* February 6, 1989, p. 1; see also U.S. Department of Labor, Plant Closings and Mass Layoffs (ret. April 23, 2004), available at www.dol.gov/asp/programs/guide/layoffs.htm.
135. "Bieber Hails Conclusion of Plant-Closing Notification Fight," *PR Newswire,* August 2, 1988.
136. Patterson, "Plants Fear Impact of 60-Day Closing Bill on Workers," p. 1.
137. "Ypsilanti Says No," *Multinational Monitor,* March 1993, p. 5; Janice Shields, "Getting Corporations Off the Public Dole," *Business and Society Review,* June 22, 1995, p. 4.

chapter 11

Environmental, Energy, and Military-Industrial Problems

Earth's life zone is a fragile belt a few miles deep encircling the globe, a belt that has survived millions of years. This life zone is being threatened by problems so fundamental that the failure to solve them may solve other social problems—by exterminating the human race. Pollution of air, water, and soil has in many areas of the United States and across the rest of the world reached very serious proportions, and despite some gains because of pollution controls, environmental degradation remains a critical issue in the twenty-first century. In addition, major sources of energy, particularly oil, are being rapidly depleted, together with other major mineral resources.

Optimists argue that major strides are being made to deal with pollution and energy problems. Federal laws aimed at control of air and water pollution in the United States have been enacted. A few years back, one research report optimistically stated, "The national commitment now authorizes control over most forms of pollution caused by technological processes, ensuring more rigorous analysis, regulation, enforcement and citizen participation."[1] However, this optimism generally has not been justified. Underfunded government agencies often lack the means to monitor pollution or enforce pollution-control measures effectively. After substantial progress in reducing some pollutants during the 1970s, pressure from many industry leaders and business-oriented politicians for cutbacks in antipollution regulations, especially in the Ronald Reagan 1980s and the George W. Bush (early) 2000s, slowed, and in many cases reversed, this progress against environmental degradation.

GOALS OF THIS CHAPTER

In this chapter, we investigate the effects of *environmental pollution, energy,* and the *military-industrial complex* on U.S. society. We begin with a societal snapshot on how industrial pollution, poor waste management, and the interests of politicians have destroyed the majesty of one of our country's beloved waterways, the Mississippi River. Our discussion on environmental pollution and degradation focuses not only on the extent of pollution in our environment but also on its relationship to health problems. Moreover, we show that corporate profit concerns and the lack of responsible government intervention to protect the environment from corporate greed are major causes of increased pollution. Our discussion of the military-industrial complex furthers the idea that the U.S. military's thousands of toxic waste sites and installations contribute substantially to our pollution problems. The broad societal problem of sufficient energy for commercial and residential use includes the dilemmas of wastefulness in energy consumption, the lack of research into and development of alternative energy technologies, our continued too-heavy dependence on oil, the decline of mass transit, and the resource depletion and pollution generated by millions of autos, trucks, and buses. Nuclear power and related pollution create some of our most serious environmental problems. Here, we also investigate the military-industrial complex and the development of nuclear weapons, its relation to a historical perspective on war, contemporary war in the nuclear age, and "weapons welfarism." We close the chapter by contrasting and comparing two broad perspectives on the environmental and energy crisis confronting the United States: the *individualistic perspective* and the *power–conflict perspective.*

AN ENVIRONMENTAL SNAPSHOT

The Mississippi River is ill and dying, having fallen victim to the profit orientation of hundreds of industrial corporations, the shortsightedness of operators of municipal waste facilities, and the self-interest of politicians directly related to polluting industries. From Minnesota to the Gulf of Mexico, the toxic waste of industries, cities, and agricultural lands along its banks, as well as pollutants carried by its tributaries, have assaulted the Mississippi River. Thousands of toxic waste dump sites are found in the river's basin; hidden dump sites are discovered every year. The Mississippi is considered one of the most polluted rivers in the United States.[2]

The Mississippi River basin, once called the "Body of the Nation," is called today by nearby residents the "Cancer Corridor" or "Chemical Alley." The basin's fertile soil and fresh water once made it one of the world's ideal habitats. Today, it is one of the most dangerous. Chemical manufacturers, power plants, paper mills, and waste incinerators release industrial toxins into the air. Toxic wastes, dumped into the river daily, have poisoned groundwater as well as river water.[3] Wastewater, industrial discharges, and fertilizer runoff from the eastern two-thirds of the United States that drain into the Mississippi River and on into the Gulf of Mexico have turned the river and gulf waters into cocktails of highly toxic substances. Pollution has created a lifeless, oxygen-depleted "dead zone" covering about 3,000 square miles of prime fishing ground from Louisiana to the Texas border.[4]

Areas that rely on the river for drinking water have some of the country's highest disease rates for certain cancers. In Natchez, Mississippi, for example, high rates of cancers and other illnesses among adults, children, and animals prompted investigations that found that private wells have been poisoned by carcinogenic toxic wastes oozing from barrels in abandoned dump sites.[5] In 1993 a 12-year-old Louisiana boy attracted media attention when he told incoming president Bill Clinton that his brother's fatal cancer was caused by pollution from Cancer Alley.[6] In addition, Tennessee officials have prohibited catching fish in the river near Memphis because of high levels of dangerous pesticides.[7]

ENVIRONMENTAL POLLUTION AND DEGRADATION

We Americans have long taken our air, water, forests, and land for granted. For centuries, we have assumed that these natural resources are relatively unlimited, that we could live forever without giving much thought to their pollution, depletion, and degradation. We have come face to face with the hard realities of environmental deterioration over the last few decades. Numerous research studies suggest links between a variety of health problems—including low birth weight, childhood asthma, and the neurodegenerative diseases of aging—and exposure to environmental toxins. Growing numbers of Americans are demanding a more protected environment.

Toxic Chemicals

Toxic chemicals are a major source of environmental pollution. More than 58.1 billion pounds of toxic chemicals entered the environment between 1988 and 2001.[8] Chemicals from metal mining made up about 47 percent of the total; manufacturing facilities accounted for 32 percent; and electric utilities were responsible for 16 percent.[9] Some toxic chemicals also enter the environment accidentally. The National Emergency Response Notification System recorded more than 34,500 spills, explosions, and other accidents that released more than 680 million pounds of toxic chemicals into the environment in just one brief period (1988 to 1992).[10] Toxic chemicals are responsible for many illnesses, including cancers, birth defects, and neurological disorders, as well as ecological damage. Worldwide DDT pollution illustrates the seriousness of using chemicals that have not undergone long-term testing to determine possible dangerous effects. Introduced in the United States in 1942, DDT was widely and effectively used to control disease-carrying insects. Within a few years, DDT's potentially lethal side effects became clear: It and other poisonous chemicals accumulate and become concentrated in the food chain and produce disastrous effects on living tissue. Public outrage led to a ban on its use in 1969. Yet DDT is an extremely stable compound and thus has become part of plankton, fish, and then human beings globally. It remains a permanent part of the world's water and atmospheric systems.[11]

Today, many living creatures have high concentrations of DDT in their bodies. An eagle on Santa Catalina Island off the California coast recently died of DDT poisoning, even though U.S. industries no longer use DDT. One investigative reporter explained: The "food chain around Catalina and the other Channel Islands—from benthic worms and kelp bass to gulls, falcons and eagles—remains contaminated by high DDT concentrations. . . . Although the last drop of DDT in the U.S. was sprayed 23 years ago, the world's largest deposit—100 tons of tainted sediments—remains sprawled across the ocean floor."[12] The sediment was the result of extensive dumping by a Los Angeles area chemical firm many years earlier.

Although DDT has received publicity, other pesticides, some far more toxic than DDT, have continued to be manufactured and widely used in the United States and exported abroad, producing hazards—birth defects, cancers, neurological disorders, and other illnesses—and sometimes death for consumers but large profits for industry. In 1993, Florida growers claimed more than $1 billion in plant damage and serious adverse effects on the health of thousands of farm workers from use of a fungicide (Benlate) manufactured by DuPont. Calling DuPont the country's number-one polluter, Benlate Victims Against

DuPont charged the company with marketing a product that had been insufficiently tested to determine its effects on plants and people and called for a nationwide boycott of DuPont products. The parents of a child born without eyes won a $4 million jury verdict against DuPont after the mother was sprayed with Benlate while pregnant. In 2000, DuPont paid $100 million to two Texas fruit companies for damages to orchards from Benlate. Later that year, Ecuadorian shrimp farmers won lawsuits totaling $22.5 million against DuPont for poisoned shrimp farms from Benlate runoff from banana fields. Litigation for Benlate use has cost DuPont an estimated $1.3 billion. In 2001 DuPont announced it would stop selling Benlate after 33 years of sales. Worldwide sales had earned DuPont roughly $100 million in 2000.[13]

Today, more than 20,000 pesticide products are registered in the United States. Only 32 such products were registered in 1939. Agricultural workers use an estimated 1.2 billion pounds of pesticides each year. Pesticide use has a particularly adverse effect upon farmworkers and their family members, who often suffer elevated levels of leukemia and stomach, uterine, and brain cancer. Each year some 1,000 farmworkers die from exposure to pesticides and another 300,000 are injured.[14] Not surprisingly, agricultural workers had the third-highest fatality rate (per 100,000 workers) from workplace illnesses of any industry in 2003.[15] Government officials have placed restrictions on the use of some highly toxic pesticides, but they have banned very few pesticides. The chemical industry has spent millions to convince people that toxic chemicals are indispensable to agriculture. Interestingly, prior to World War II, U.S. farmers produced huge harvests without pesticides, and recent studies have shown that crop rotation and other organic agricultural methods are still capable of producing bountiful harvests.[16]

Ozone Depletion

Beginning in the 1970s scientists announced concern about continued production and use of nitrogen oxide and chlorofluorocarbon (CFC) gases because of their harmful effects on Earth's ozone layer—the protective shield that filters out harmful radiation. CFC gases, including Freon, have been widely used in air conditioners, refrigerators, and aerosol sprays. Supersonic plane exhausts are a major source of nitrogen oxide. Since that time, atmospheric scientists have produced overwhelming evidence of ozone depletion. By 1977, an area of depleted ozone the size of the United States had formed over Antarctica. In 1986, when the Nimbus satellite detected depletion of the ozone barrier over the North Pole, scientists calculated that Earth had lost 3 percent of its ozone shield since 1920, most since the 1970s.[17] Scientists have found areas over Antarctica *completely without* the protective ozone layer. In just a few years, the area of ozone depletion has periodically increased to an area three times that of the 48 contiguous states of the United States. The ozone in this depleted area is much thinner than normal and scientists predict continued effects on Antarctica. While scientists do not predict similar ozone depletion in the Arctic region, they warn that the region remains vulnerable.[18] This rapid decline in the ozone layer coincided with a dramatic increase in the rate of skin cancers—both the more common basal and squamous cell cancers and the deadly melanoma. Scientists have predicted that severe ozone depletion is likely to occur over North America in the near future.[19] Most life on Earth cannot endure the sun's ultraviolet rays for very long without the protection of an ozone layer.

Since 1981, the conservative politicians' policy of "getting government off the back of industry" has seriously crippled government oversight of the use and disposal of dangerous chemicals in the United States. For example, in 1992 a confidential Environmental Protection Agency (EPA) report revealed that President George H. W. Bush had illegally stalled implementation of many EPA regulations that he considered harmful to business, including provisions to control smog, reduce acid rain, protect the ozone layer, and reduce toxic pollutants.[20]

Methyl bromide, a deadly nerve gas and widely used insecticide, is a powerful ozone destroyer. The United States uses about 60 millions pounds of methyl bromide each year—about 40 percent of the world's use. Farmers use most of it to fumigate soil before planting crops.[21] Methyl bromide kills pests in soil and on harvested crops and is used to fumigate buildings. This chemical is deadly to all forms of life. A few parts per billion in the air can cause headaches and nausea; a few hundred parts per billion can cause death; and exposure of pregnant laboratory animals to it has caused birth defects in offspring. In one eight-year period, 15 deaths and 216 injuries and illnesses from contact with the poison were reported in California alone.[22] About 500 workers at the Diamond Walnut plant in Stockton, California, went on strike in the 1990s to protest workers' exposure to methyl bromide used to fumigate walnuts.[23]

Recently, scientists have estimated that methyl bromide emissions are responsible for a significant part of global ozone loss. Because of the chemical's short atmospheric lifetime, immediate action to cut its use would bring rapid benefits. The EPA has classified methyl bromide as a Class I (most potent) ozone-depleting substance and has ordered a reduction in production and importation of the chemical. In 2001, production and import were reduced to 50 percent of 1991 baseline figures, and in 2003 allowable production and import were reduced to 30 percent of the baseline. As of 2005, production and import of methyl bromide is supposed to be nil, except for critical, emergency, and quarantine uses. Such sharply decreased production and importation of the chemical are unlikely, however, since pressure from the chemical industry has blocked aggressive government action to thus limit its use.[24] Indeed, in 2003 the EPA asked the United Nations to allow U.S. farmers and grain mills to continue using methyl bromide.[25] The chemical is exempt from tax and labeling regulations that apply to all other Class I ozone-depleting chemicals, and the phase-out rule does not cover stockpiles that exist. In the 1990s, an international coalition of users and producers of methyl bromide, including two U.S. producers, became involved in a multibillion-dollar lobbying campaign to keep the chemical on the market. Legislation introduced in the U.S. House of Representatives sought to stop the EPA's announced phaseout.[26] It is this indifference of industrial and agricultural capitalists to hazards of methyl bromide that keeps the emissions of this toxic chemical unchanged as a major contributor to ozone depletion.[27]

Waste Disposal

Waste disposal has become a national crisis. In the early 2000s, U.S. residents, businesses, and institutions produced nearly 230 million tons of municipal solid waste. An average of 4.4 pounds of this waste is created by each person every day. About 30 percent of waste disposal is recovered and recycled or composted, 15 percent is burned at combustion facilities, and the remaining 56 percent is put in landfills. Over the last decade, recycling has doubled the amount of waste (68 million tons) diverted from landfills and incinerators—with 94 percent of batteries, 45 percent of paper and paperboard, and 57 percent of yard trimmings recycled through curbside programs, drop-off centers, buy-back programs, and deposit systems.[28] One result of recycling is that many landfill sites have closed, decreasing from 8,000 in 1988 to 1,858 in the early 2000s.[29] Despite recycling, much solid waste disposal is still deposited in landfills and much of it is extremely dangerous. Toxins from household chemicals and pesticides, mercury in some paints, lead in batteries and newsprint, and cadmium in plastics leach into soil. Hundreds of landfill sites leaking toxins have contaminated groundwater. Although the EPA has issued regulations for garbage dumps calling for liners to prevent seepage and for devices to monitor underground contaminants, formerly unregulated landfills comprise almost one-fourth of the country's worst toxic waste sites.[30]

A portion of U.S. waste is incinerated because burning reduces its volume by 90 percent and its weight by 75 percent. More than 97 combustors with energy recovery systems burn up to 95,000 tons of waste per day.[31] Incineration produces large amounts of ash that must be disposed somewhere. Incineration also produces highly toxic chemicals like dioxin. Even when dioxin and other toxic substances are filtered out of the smoke released from incinerators, they are present in a concentrated form in ashes, making ash disposal problematic. Some cities have installed high-temperature incinerators that limit the production of poisonous pollutants and filter toxic gases. Grassroots pressure and the high costs of upgrades to meet new dioxin emission standards forced the country's most notorious trash-to-energy burner in Columbus, Ohio, to close down. During its many years of operation, that plant spewed huge quantities of dioxin into the environment, contributing to an epidemic of cancer and heart disease among area residents. With assistance from Greenpeace and local activists, the city developed a recycling program and planned ways to reduce waste.[32]

The United States produces many thousands of tons of hazardous waste each day; most is disposed of improperly or unsafely. Unsafe disposal of toxic waste contributes to water, air, and land pollution and the environmental emergencies faced by many U.S. communities. Hazardous waste is sometimes illegally dumped at sea or transported from industrialized countries to impoverished countries desperate for hard currency. In recent years, such "trash imperialism," whereby richer countries can push off their problems onto poorer countries, has been banned by most Pacific island and African countries and some Central American countries. However, these laws can be circumvented by mislabeling waste or exporting it for "recycling," which is often not accomplished. Poorer countries often lack the technical ability to deal safely with toxic waste. U.S. law requires that companies shipping toxic materials abroad notify government officials responsible for ensuring that the receiving countries dispose of waste properly, although shippers frequently ignore this requirement. Some have even tried to *sell* toxic ash to poor countries as landfill, claiming the ash was nonhazardous.[33] Within the United States, dump sites are often located in low-income communities that do not have the power to reject the dumps. Since the 1940s, some local governments have intentionally located hazardous waste disposal sites in numerous African American and Native American communities.[34] This type of action is termed *environmental racism*. Environmental discrimination affects more than Americans of color. Some such discrimination is class-based. Thus, there is environmental inequity in Appalachian mountain areas where poorer whites "are basically dumped on because of lack of economic and political clout."[35]

Toxic wastes are often stored in aboveground or underground containers on back lots or farmland. Other waste is dumped in streams, lakes, or rivers. Some has been disposed of

Incinerators such as this one in East Liverpool, Ohio, emit dioxin and other toxic substances and contribute to air pollution. (Robert Visser/Greenpeace)

openly; in other cases, companies have paid truckers to dump toxic wastes at night in rivers or ditches in rural areas. No one knows for sure how many toxic waste dumps exist. A report by the Insurance Information Institute noted: "Since the original Superfund bill was enacted in 1980, a much larger number of hazardous waste sites has been discovered than had been expected. The EPA has identified about 35,000 inactive or abandoned hazardous waste dumps. Many states have their own hazardous waste clean-up and control programs, some of which are more stringent than the federal Superfund program."[36] Many of these dumps are ticking "time bombs" and pose serious threats to public health. Some of these time bombs have gone off, resulting in major explosions and fires.

In the early 2000s, nearly 18,000 facilities reported releasing 1.4 billion tons of toxic chemicals into the environment.[37] Many of these releases have involved transportation accidents where hazardous materials are being carried across the United States on trains or in trucks. Toxic fumes from chemical explosions following such accidents or from fires at waste dumps have forced mass evacuations in numerous communities. In the 1980s, residents near Eastman Kodak's aging plant in Rochester, New York, learned that highly toxic chemicals from the plant had been seeping into groundwater for years. Although many chemical spills had occurred over time, Kodak had only recently noticed the problem. By the time residents were notified, strong chemical odors were present, and chemicals had leached into adjacent yards and eaten through basement carpets. Many residents and environmentalists suggested that Kodak was negligent in monitoring chemical spills. Exposure to chemicals can cause liver and central nervous system damage. Kodak denied that the chemicals caused any health hazard but promised to upgrade its storage facilities, guarantee the value of houses affected, and clean up the area, treating contaminated soil as well as groundwater.[38] A report in the 1990s found that Rochester's Kodak Park was still the major New York State polluter in terms of discharges of toxic chemicals: "Kodak discharged 12.5 million pounds of toxic chemicals last year, a major component of the 57.2 million pounds discharged throughout New York State."[39] A problematical situation has persisted despite some improvement in chemical discharges at Kodak Park. Today, Kodak reportedly remains a major polluter in New York.[40]

No one knows just how severe the eventual impact on human beings and other living organisms will be from the many billions of pounds of toxic wastes in the environment. The sharp increase in chemical contamination over the last few decades is unprecedented. Human beings and their genetic systems have never had to adapt so quickly to so much chemical bombardment. Today's health problem of many cancers is probably one consequence of this growing chemical contamination of air, water, land, and food.

Frustrated and confused, some people will say to the information presented above, "Everything causes cancer, so why worry?" That is not the case, however. Most physical and chemical elements in our environments do not or cannot cause the cell changes of cancer. One expert has estimated that it is likely that only 700 of the thousands of chemicals in daily use are carcinogens, although many may be toxic in other ways. Experts suggest that the critical task is to get those dangerous chemicals out of our environment and to restrict use. Some companies have begun to respond to public pressures for a cleaner work and living environment. One of the first large corporations to report making significant strides in reducing toxic waste was the Minneapolis-based Minnesota Mining and Manufacturing Company (3M). Using fewer toxic chemicals, substituting nonhazardous raw materials for hazardous ones, and recycling wastes when possible reportedly saved the company $420 million in just one year.[41]

Water Pollution

Today, Florida Bay, an important commercial fishing and sportfishing site between the Everglades and the Florida Keys, is dying from pollution. The once crystal-clear shrimp and lobster breeding ground is stagnant, covered with dead sea grass and surrounded by lifeless banks of mangroves. Over the last few decades, real estate developers have diverted much of the bay's freshwater supply to convert swampland into prime real estate. The bay has heavy concentrations of nitrogen and phosphorus entering the estuary from rainwater runoff that carries agricultural fertilizers to the area. As a result, algae grow rapidly in the water. The algae blooms in turn block sunlight and reduce oxygen levels for other aquatic life.[42] Damage from this real estate activity plus fertilizer runoff and rising water temperatures will cost more than $1 billion to correct. Left uncorrected, the bay's dead water spillover threatens the delicate coral reefs of the Florida Keys, an attraction in a state that relies heavily on tourism.[43]

Widespread pollution of surface water, such as rivers, oceans, and lakes, and underground water systems is a major cost of private enterprise and the private profit orientation. Government assessments of the health of water in the United States reveal that pollution has impaired 39 percent of the country's rivers and streams; 45 percent of lakes, reservoirs, and ponds; 51 percent of estuaries; 78 percent of the Great Lakes shoreline; and 14 percent of ocean shorelines.[44] Pollution's cost is paid for primarily by the public. Water pollution can affect a large number of people who do not know one another and thus have difficulty organizing to prevent it. Its social costs include lost recreational areas, contaminated seafood, lost jobs in the fishing industry, and contamination of drinking water.

Industrial technologies are responsible for much water pollution. The primary goal of most capitalists, who make decisions regarding new technologies, is expanding profits, not protecting the environment. Consider the synthetic detergent story. Following World War II old-fashioned soap was largely replaced by detergents, which brought a sharp increase in profits for capitalists. Soap decays and causes relatively little environmental pollution. Detergents, which biodegrade (break down) very slowly, are often retained in sewage plants and in surface water areas, destroying oxygen needed by fish. The production of detergents requires considerably more energy and contributes three times as much air pollution, compared with the manufacture of soap. No public debate took place on the shift from soaps to detergents, nor were consumers informed about the long-term dangers of the latter.[45] Synthetic detergents are now dominant cleaning products, yet were initially created not to meet consumer demand but to satisfy the desire for profit.

Only 1 percent of Earth's water is drinkable, the rest being salty ocean water (97 percent) or glacial ice (2 percent). Surface waters—streams, rivers, and lakes—supply half of the country's drinking water; the other half is supplied by wells. In 2000, the Environmental Protection Agency (EPA) reported a significant proportion of the 97,321 violations of the Safe Drinking Water Act were health-based violations.[46] Each year nearly one million Americans get sick, thousands get cancer, and hundreds die because of contaminated tap water. In opinion polls, most Americans say that governmental regulations governing drinking water should be strengthened or maintained. At least three-fourths express concern about the

quality of their household water. Yet industries that produce and use toxic chemicals have worked periodically to *weaken* the Safe Drinking Water Act and the Clean Water Act.[47]

Water pollution began to increase sharply in the 1940s, largely because of the introduction of detergents and inorganic fertilizers. Over the next few decades phosphate pollution (from detergents and fertilizers) in surface waters increased 700 percent, and nitrate pollution (from fertilizers) of surface waters increased nearly 800 percent.[48] Beginning with the state of New York in the 1970s, several states have passed laws banning phosphates in detergents. Many European countries have also moved to restrict or ban use of phosphates in detergents. These actions have led most manufacturers to remove phosphates from detergents. While most detergents no longer contain phosphates, phosphates and nitrates still contaminate rivers, lakes, and estuaries. In addition, untreated sewage in many cities pours into streams and rivers from sewage systems that overflow during rainstorms, and much industrial waste is discharged directly into waterways. One EPA survey of U.S. surface water found widespread pollution. Water quality was impaired in more than one-third of the rivers, streams, lakes, reservoirs, and estuaries surveyed. Almost all of the near-shore waters of the Great Lakes were impaired.[49]

Leakage from underground storage tanks, abandoned waste sites, and municipal landfills is polluting a growing number of underground wells. A significant proportion of the 10 million gasoline, heating oil, and chemical storage tanks buried in the United States are leaking at any given time. The EPA has reported that studies of abandoned and uncontrolled hazardous waste sites have found groundwater contamination at 4,000 locations. Many contaminants found in drinking water—pesticides, gasoline additives, cleaning solvents, and heavy metals—are linked to birth defects and cancer. In recent decades many communities have reported outbreaks of various waterborne diseases.[50]

Each year sewage contamination, industrial waste, and polluted water runoff from agricultural and urban areas force the closing of numerous beaches and fishing areas. During one recent year, Florida's beaches were closed more than 200 times because of water contamination.[51] People fishing in the Atlantic, the Pacific, and the Gulf of Mexico have reported fish with blisters, ulcerous lesions, and rotted fins. In some areas, fish have disappeared, unable to survive toxic and oxygen-depleted waters. On Puget Sound in the state of Washington, a sign printed in seven languages warns that bottom fish, crabs, and shellfish may be contaminated. The last commercial fishing boat owner in the Florida Panhandle's onetime fishing village of Destin has reflected, "When you stop to think that we've only really been majorly polluting the Gulf for, what, 40 years, it's really scary that 40 years from now we may have choked it completely to death."[52]

In addition to pollutants that get to the oceans by way of contaminated rivers, oil spills from tankers and offshore oil wells pollute oceans and shorelines, upsetting the balance of the ecosystem for years to come. During one recent year thousands of oil-polluting incidents dumped more than 1.4 million gallons of oil in and around U.S. waters.[53] Incineration ash, sewage sludge, and other hazardous wastes are dumped into oceans despite national and international laws against such practices. Nonbiodegradable plastic trash dumped into oceans is responsible for the death annually of millions of seabirds and tens of thousands of marine mammals. Commercial fishing fleets annually dump tens of millions of pounds of plastic material into the oceans plus hundreds of millions of pounds of plastic fishing nets and lines. Moreover, one report has suggested that each day seagoing vessels dump nearly 5 million metal containers and 750,000 plastic and glass containers into the oceans. Most of the billions of pounds of plastic, glass, and metal dumped over the last decade are still there.[54]

Cruise ships are notorious for dumping waste. These ships carry thousands of passengers and generate daily as much as 30,000 gallons of sewage and 255,000 gallons of gray water from showers, laundries, and kitchens. They also produce 37,000 gallons of oily bilge water, 265,000 gallons of ballast water, and 7 tons of garbage and solid waste.[55] Since 1993, Royal Caribbean Cruise Ships and Celebrity Cruises have incurred millions of dollars in environmental fines for discharging oil and hazardous waste and for falsifying records. Industry analysts expect the number of cruise ship passengers to double by 2010 to nearly 22 million.[56] Recently, two Congressional representatives have introduced a bill to regulate the cruise ship industry. The Clean Cruise Ship Act would make illegal any discharges of untreated sewage, gray water, and bilge water within coastal waters.[57]

Huge quantities of nonbiodegradable plastic debris litter U.S. coastlines. On just one day, volunteers collected 307 tons of litter along the Gulf Coast, two-thirds of it plastic. Sailing vessels have found large quantities of plastic debris floating more than a hundred miles from shore.[58] The oceans provide one-fourth of the animal protein consumed by human beings. Not surprisingly, the incidence of illness from eating contaminated fish is increasing in the United States. Moreover, beaches and seacoasts are favorite vacation spots. The costs to fishing and resort industries of polluted oceans and coastlines run into billions of dollars. Cleanup of ocean pollution is a major task facing U.S. citizens, yet responsibility for water quality and pollution control is shared by a variety of state and federal agencies that often lack coordination and are sometimes in conflict. Existing laws and regulations are often weak or poorly enforced.[59]

In 2004, the U.S. Commission on Ocean Policy released a preliminary report on the condition of the country's surrounding oceans. It revealed that pollution, overfishing, increased coastal development, altered sediment flow, and declines in water quality have had a negative impact on coastal waters. Among the troubling findings in the report are that wetlands are disappearing at a rate of 20,000 acres a year and that 16.3 million gallons of oil (1.5 times the amount of oil spilled from the Exxon *Valdez*) are dumped into the oceans every year as runoff from streets and roadways. The commission urged the federal government to adopt a new ocean policy that is ecosystem-based and balances ocean use with sound science and education.[60]

Air Pollution

Air pollution has a variety of sources, including emissions from gasoline-powered vehicles, waste incineration, electric power generation, and industrial plants. In just one recent year (2001), U.S. industries emitted nearly *1.7 billion tons* of toxic chemicals into the air.[61] The quantities of airborne toxins produced by industry are staggering. A single General Motors plant pumps more than 1,000 pounds of toxic material into the environment every hour.[62] Electric-power generating plants release huge quantities of nitrogen oxide, a major component of smog. Concentrations of ozone, a gas toxic to plant and animal life, often exceed federal standards in metropolitan areas nationwide; emissions of carbon monoxide, a poisonous gas that interferes with people's ability to absorb oxygen, exceed federal safety standards in many areas. In addition, emissions of sulfur dioxide and volatile organic compounds remain high, and emissions of nitrogen dioxide have climbed 13 percent above their 1970 level. A recent study shows that each year the country's eight largest electric utility companies' disposal of sulfur and nitrogen dioxide into the atmosphere at current emission levels is responsible for 6,000 premature annual deaths, 140,000 asthma attacks, and 14,000 cases of acute bronchitis. (The companies are American Electric Power, Cinergy, Duke, Dynegy, FirstEnergy, SIGECO, Southern Company, and the Tennessee Valley Authority.)[63] Millions of Americans live in areas with air quality below EPA air standards; millions of others live in areas in which air quality fails to meet the American Lung Association's stricter standard. Another study has found that mercury levels are so high in about 8 percent of women of childbearing age that both mothers and children are at risk of suffering mental disability.[64]

Industrial air pollution is an environmental cost inflicted on nearby residents, often by aggressively profit-oriented enterprises. This cost is paid by many people who are affected by smog and radioactive discharges from nuclear power plants. Air pollution causes losses to property—such as deterioration of paint on houses and cars—and to human health. Polluted urban air has been linked to cancers, respiratory diseases, eye irritation, and asthma. Those who are already ill, children, the aged, and the poor, who tend to live nearest major pollution sources, are the most likely to be the immediate sufferers from air pollution.

Air pollution has contributed to destruction of trees and crops in all parts of the United States. Decades of air pollution—in particular, ozone and acid rain created by auto exhaust and industrial pollutants—have caused the collapse of the ecological system in North Carolina at the summit of Mount Mitchell, the highest mountain east of the Mississippi. From Maine to Georgia, massive numbers of trees at high altitudes, weakened to the point that they could not withstand natural stresses of temperature extremes, insects, and disease, have died; trees at lower altitudes are deteriorating. Pollution from sulfur dioxide and nitrogen dioxide emissions from burning fossil fuels in power plants, industries, and homes has produced significant damage to agricultural crops in the Midwest. In various states, smog threatens the long-term viability of national parks; it has already hidden from view some of the spectacular scenery in Yosemite, the Grand Canyon, and the Great Smoky Mountains.[65]

The health and safety threats of air pollution have remained very serious under recent presidential administrations. In 2003, for example, the George W. Bush administration announced that it was closing pending Justice Department investigations of 70 power plants for violating the Clean Air Act. That politically conservative administration also reconsidered 13 other cases involving utility companies. Environmentalists asserted that the decision to close the investigations and enforce environmental protection laws was indicative of the Bush administration's efforts to repay the heavy election-year contributions made by utilities and refineries to Republican political candidates and to the Republican party. In addition, policing environmental regulations by the EPA was diminished substantially as the Bush administration cut EPA's enforcement division to the *lowest level* since the EPA was created.[66]

Private Profits and the Costs of Pollution

A major reason for the enormous pollution problems created by modern production technology is that the marketplace has mostly not allowed major environmental costs to be paid for out of private corporate funds. The individualistic values of capitalism place great emphasis on short-term profit making. Corporations hire and promote executives for increasing output and profits. Eliminating production-caused pollution usually involves substantial costs that corporations generally are unwilling to bear. The pressure for pollution controls, for the most part, has come from elsewhere. Most private corporations have resisted pollution controls, which they label *government interference,* because money spent for major pollution-control equipment will usually reduce profits, at least in the short run.[67]

New synthetic products often generate above-average profits for companies, at least until their competition catches up, spurring a continuous drive to create new synthetic products. Water-polluting detergents are an example. This is also the trend for many other synthetic substances that do serious environmental damage. Synthetic fibers usually require more energy to produce and create far more pollution than do natural fibers. Chemical fertilizers and pesticides use more energy and create far more pollution than do natural fertilizers, natural pesticides, and soil conservation programs. Plastics use far more energy and create more pollution than do natural materials such as wood and leather. Environmental regulations have reduced slightly the profits of pesticide, fertilizer, and other chemical companies since the late 1960s, but the profit advantage of innovation keeps these companies creating thousands of new products. The U.S. automotive industry is another example of putting profits over ecological needs. Smaller cars with smaller engines create less pollution; they also mean lower prices and, therefore, lower profits. Reportedly, Henry Ford II once said, "Minicars make miniprofits."[68]

Faced with much citizen and some government pressure to reduce pollution, many companies have moved plants, factories, and refineries to pollution havens overseas in less-developed countries. In 1965, thus, U.S. firms began building factories, called *maquiladoras,* in the northern border region of Mexico to take advantage of low-wage labor and weak environmental and worker-safety standards. Since that time massive amounts of industrial toxins have been discharged from the thousands of maquiladoras in that region, the vast majority of which have not registered their waste discharges with government authorities or treated the waste before illegally dumping or burying it or releasing it into local sewers and canals that flow into the Rio Grande and the Gulf of Mexico. People living near contaminated waterways suffer numerous ailments that doctors attribute to industrial toxins. In 1995, some 40 maquiladora manufacturers reached a $17 million out-of-court settlement in a lawsuit that linked infant deaths and birth defects to toxic factory emissions and toxic fumes from the burning of factory waste. Some of the polluted waterways run through agricultural lands and eventually empty into Pacific coastal wetlands, allowing these industrial toxins the opportunity of working their way up the food chain. While the volume of toxic wastes improperly discarded has declined, partly because of the environmental requirements of the 1990s NAFTA agreement and partly because of the lawsuit, illegal dumping continues. Indeed, one recent study found air pollution from Mexican manufacturing nearly doubling since NAFTA went into effect. Environmental inspections also decreased dramatically after NAFTA was approved.[69] Indeed, industries have done little to clean up the decades of accumulated waste.[70]

Because of this pollution flight overseas, some U.S. communities have faced the dilemma of accepting a polluting plant or losing local jobs. As the U.S. economy cannot now provide enough jobs for everyone willing to work, it is difficult for a community to force a polluting plant to clean itself up. This dilemma is forced on communities because ordinary working people have little say about job creation or export in U.S. society.

Pollution Prevention Measures

Various approaches have been proposed to prevent or at least slow down pollution, including environmental taxes on certain products, such as ozone-depleting chemicals, and deposits paid at the time of purchase, such as on glass bottles or aluminum cans, to encourage recycling. Corporate support for recycling has often been weak, and in some instances recycling has been vigorously opposed by industries that fear it would lower their profit potential. For example, in one case heavy advertising by the producers of paper and plastic packaging materials was largely responsible for failure of a Massachusetts recycling initiative that would have required a certain percentage of recycled materials in packaging.[71] Many critics of industry have called for an end to government subsidies that encourage wasteful and environmentally damaging use of natural resources. Other proposals, supported by some economists and corporate leaders, are "full-cost pricing"—adding a product's environmental costs to its price—and "green taxes"—user fees on polluting products and activities that penalize polluters and energy wasters. Supporters say that such proposals would encourage pollution prevention and provide a fair and economically efficient means to pay the high social costs of cleaning up privately generated pollution, although the full cost of a product's lifetime environmental impact is often difficult to assess at time of purchase.[72]

Those analysts who believe that standards should be set according to what is truly safe for human beings object to allowing industries to pollute as long as they are willing to pay. Some industries are beginning to realize the shortsightedness of polluting technologies because of the huge cleanup costs they face, such as payments to the government-run Superfund. One industry executive has noted: "If we hadn't polluted in the first place, we could cut 80 to 90 percent of the cost of Superfund out."[73]

Still, some private companies and local governments are taking action to remedy pollution problems. San Diego's County Board of Supervisors recognized a company named Cloud 9 Shuttle, the San Diego Gas & Electric Company, and the city of Chula Vista for taking action to prevent pollution. Cloud 9 Shuttle has bought vehicles that run on clean natural gas instead of polluting gasoline. San Diego Gas has offered rebates for energy efficiency to customers and has used natural gas in its vehicles. The city of Chula Vista has set up rebates for businesses purchasing electric vehicles and has made use of "environment-friendly materials" in its operations.[74]

The Military-Industrial Establishment as Polluter

> Imagine, for a moment, that a foreign nation has dispatched a band of terrorists to the U.S. The intruders silently move across the landscape depositing toxic chemicals at a thousand sites around the country. Some of the toxic compounds quickly enter the rivers and underground reservoirs that supply America with drinking water. Other chemicals contaminate our neighborhoods and backyards where our children play. Still others sit like time bombs, destined to contaminate our water supplies after months, years, or even decades. The toxic chemicals carried by these enemies are the products of the most sophisticated laboratories on Earth. They cause birth defects, liver disease, and cancer. Their effects may be felt for generations.[75]

Unfortunately, the terrorist-like pollution described is not imaginary; it has happened. The only imaginary aspect of the account cited is the polluter. It was not a foreign nation. It was the U.S. military-industrial establishment. Today, the military is the largest polluter in the United States—producing more hazardous waste per year than the five largest U.S. chemical companies combined. Over a period of more than four decades, the military has created more than 27,000 known toxic waste sites at more than 18,000 installations. Almost a hundred of these are on the list of the *most* hazardous places in the United States. The largest producer of hazardous waste among domestic military bases is Washington's Fairchild Air Force Base, which generated more than 13 million pounds of waste in just one year (1997).[76] The military's enormous quantities of deadly, environmentally destructive waste products pose long-term threats to the country's overall health; they have contaminated soil and water supplies, in some instances causing irreversible damage. For example, toxic releases from an Air Force plant near Tucson, Arizona, where Hughes Aircraft produced tactical missiles for years, contaminated the drinking water supply. As a result, nearby residents have suffered a high incidence of brain tumors, cancers, and birth defects.[77]

Estimates of cleanup costs for military-industrial pollution run into many billions of dollars. The National Toxic Campaign Fund called for a commitment of $100 billion over a period of ten years, although the Pentagon claims cleanup could run as high as $250 billion.[78] In addition, until cleanup is accomplished much valuable land will remain useless for more productive purposes. Undoubtedly, the multiple toxic pollution sites located on closed military bases will cause major delays in their conversion to civilian use.[79]

Most recently, the U.S. government completed its $460 million, 15-year-long environmental cleanup effort of Kahoolawe Island in Hawaii after decades of military bombing practices. Environmentalists claim, however, that the U.S. military only cleaned the surface of about three-quarters of the island, and it only removed military ordnance and toxins to a depth of four feet below the surface and on only 10 percent of the island. The government now plans a similarly haphazard cleanup of Vieques Island in Puerto Rico.[80]

Consistent with President George W. Bush's policy of systematically dismantling many of the country's environmental standards, during the early 2000s the Department of Defense (DOD) sought exemption from some of the important public health laws concerning hazardous waste. According to the Natural Resources Defense Council (NRDC), DOD officials claimed that environmental laws on hazardous waste, toxic cleanup, and air quality were hindering troop training and military readiness, although the DOD failed to outline how enforcing public health laws affected the military. The DOD's request directly contradicted provisions of the Federal Facilities Compliance Act that the military cannot usurp federal laws safeguarding public health. Specifically, the Pentagon solicited Congress for exemptions from the Resource Conservation and Recovery Act, the Superfund Law, and the Clean Air Act. Heather Taylor, NRDC's deputy legislative director, asked the probing question "Whose interest is the Pentagon really serving by trying to get Congress to relieve the military of its duty to comply with federal health standards? Certainly not our troops, their families and the millions of other Americans who would be left living in contaminated communities."[81]

Citizens Fighting Pollution

Citizen activity directed at improving air and water pollution standards has increased in recent decades. Some groups target government bodies and agencies. For example, one group of more than 300 activists spent several days at the Texas capitol in a "Stand Up for Texas" lobbying effort. They attempted to cajole legislators into voting down legislation damaging to the environment and conducted a daylong training conference to help citizens develop environmental lobbying skills.[82] Similarly, residents of a village in New York learned that the state's powerful Thruway Authority was planning to build a large plaza in their area. Fearing air and water pollution from the project, a citizens' group, the Concerned Citizens of North Chatham, worked hard to fight the new development. They held public meetings, circulated petitions, and displayed bumper stickers. As a writer for an MIT periodical stated, "The Thruway fracas belongs to a vigorous, rapidly growing tradition of American politics. In hundreds of communities across the land, citizens have risen up to protest in-cinerators, landfills, and shopping malls."[83]

In numerous areas, citizens' groups have hit corporations with lawsuits seeking re-straining orders or compensatory damages. Local citizens have held demonstrations to pressure companies to reduce pollution. Angry citizens' groups have formed in places like New York's Love Canal area, near Niagara Falls, where an underground chemical storage area contaminated land and water in a housing subdivision. Residents there had a high in-cidence of cancer. There and elsewhere, citizens' groups, using court action and lobbying government, have forced government authorities to take action to reduce pollution. Citizen demonstrators have gone to jail for their efforts to protect their environment. Today, virtu-ally no community will allow a major toxic waste dump to be opened. Many citizens' groups, such as the Sierra Club, Zero Population Growth, Friends of the Earth, and the Cen-ter for Study of Responsive Law, have helped to keep ecological issues before the public with lawsuits against polluters. Some groups have emerged from local efforts—such as the Citizen's Clearing House for Hazardous Waste, which started in the battle over waste at Love Canal—to become national organizations working against toxic waste dumping.[84]

In a report for Friends of the Earth, Julie Tippett reviewed the actions of local citizens' groups that have protested hazardous waste disposal in landfills in numerous communities. Successful citizen action strategies have involved starting early in the process, maximizing participation with door-to-door recruitment, attending all local government meetings, re-searching the geology of the area and government applications, and distributing fact sheets.[85]

Experience has shown that actions of one or two individuals can make a difference. The efforts of two Oregon citizens, Carol Van Strum and Paul Merrell, brought to public at-tention the growing dioxin contamination of the environment and the collaboration of the paper pulp industry and EPA officials to suppress information regarding the hazards of dioxin and other dangerous chemicals used in paper manufacturing. (Dioxin refers to a fam-ily of compounds that share the same basic chemical structure, and all are toxic. Dioxin is also the deadly ingredient in Agent Orange, widely used during the Vietnam War. Many American military personnel who were exposed to Agent Orange in Vietnam now suffer se-rious illnesses.) Since the 1970s, serious health problems have been common among peo-ple living near forests sprayed with dioxin-laden herbicides. For more than a decade, West Coast forests were sprayed with dioxin-containing herbicides, and dioxin is a by-product of the chlorine bleaching process used in pulp mills. When produced by chemical indus-tries, these carcinogenic compounds are regulated by the EPA, yet they are unregulated when they enter the environment as a waste product of the paper industry.[86]

In May 2004, Chittenden County residents and the Conservative Law Foundation, Friends of the Earth, Sierra Club, and the Vermont Public Interest Research Group won a ma-jor victory when Federal District Court Judge William Sessions ordered work stopped on the $223 million Circumferential Highway in Burlington, Vermont, because the government vi-olated the National Environmental Policy Act and other laws when it approved and funded the construction project. Construction of the highway would have extended the highway another 16.7 miles, would have had no overall effect of alleviating traffic congestion, and would have had a significant environmental impact in the region. The court ruled that the government failed to review adequately the impact of the highway's construction or to consider serious al-ternatives. With the help of nationally recognized environmental protection groups, a local cit-izen group effectively stopped needless environmental damage by government agencies.[87]

Successful actions have been taken against particular polluters. After documenting 40,000 violations of the Clean Water Act by West Coast pulp mills, the Surfrider Foundation, a 15,000-member organization that monitors ocean contamination along the Pacific Coast, brought a lawsuit against the companies. Louisiana-Pacific Corporation and Simpson Paper Company, called by some California's worst industrial polluters, allegedly dumped millions of gallons of untreated waste containing hundreds of chemicals including dioxin into the Pacific daily. The contaminants turned the waves black and caused "a variety of ailments for surfers, including nausea, sinus infections, headaches, sore throats, and skin rashes," according to a Surfrider attorney.[88] Choosing to avoid a long court battle, the two companies agreed to stop polluting the ocean; make an estimated $50 million in improvements in their waste discharge systems; and pay $2.9 million each in federal fines, Surfrider Foundation's legal costs, and money to build a campground and environmental center.[89]

Much of the country's worst pollution disproportionately affects Americans of color. Environmental Defense Fund attorney Karen Florimi told a congressional committee, "Despite the fact that people of color are heavily overrepresented in metropolitan areas with the largest number of uncontrolled hazardous waste sites, some studies have found that the majority of sites which have been scored and slated for cleanup on the [EPA's] NPL [National Priorities List] are in white communities."[90] Moreover, according to the New York Commission of Racial Justice, more than half of the petrochemical and hazardous waste companies in the South are located in predominantly black or Latino areas.[91] Low income, not racism, is often said to be the reason for this pattern. However, some Florida research suggests that discrimination is more than a matter of income. One investigator summarized Florida findings: "Low-income blacks are nearly twice as likely as low-income whites to live within 1.5 miles of an incinerator, landfill or smokestack industry."[92] In Houston, Texas, half the 25 incinerators and landfills were originally located in predominantly black neighborhoods.[93]

Unwilling to accept continued poisoning of communities, black activists in Baton Rouge, Louisiana, organized the North Baton Rouge Environmental Association and "started the fight to make things clean around here again."[94] In Wallace, Louisiana, a coalition of environmentalists and residents of this mostly black village on the Mississippi River helped block plans to build a large pulp and rayon plant that would have worsened their already serious pollution problems, even though the plant would have brought much-needed jobs.[95] In the northwestern United States several environmental organizations, including Heart of America Northwest, Legal Advocates for Washington, Washington Toxics Coalition, People for Puget Sound, and the Sierra Club, have worked aggressively to oppose changes in regulations on the importation of radioactive wastes, to pressure government agencies to conduct appropriate impact studies, and to pressure federal and state agencies to reduce hazardous waste contamination of land areas in the Northwest.[96]

In many instances, corporate leaders have even been slow to recognize the business value of strong environmental standards. Yet, as one *Harvard Business Review* article points out, "Properly designed environmental standards can trigger innovations that lower the total cost of a product or improve its value. Such innovations allow companies to use a range of inputs more productively—from raw materials to energy to labor—thus offsetting the costs of improving environmental impact and ending the stalemate. Ultimately, this enhanced resource productivity makes companies more competitive, not less."[97]

Modest Government Action on Pollution

Periodically, citizens' pressures have led to passage of important environmental pollution legislation, including the Clean Air Act, the Clean Water Act, and the National Environment Policy Act. Largely because of political pressure from industrial corporations, the EPA has been slow to implement and enforce congressionally required regulations, allowing massive pollution to continue. Polluting industries have poured millions into congressional campaigns and lobbying efforts to ensure that congressional action to halt pollution is minimal. In addition, numerous industry associations have been set up to keep government action on pollution and other environmental controls at levels acceptable to corporate interests. For example, chemical companies have lobbied government officials to keep regulations on toxic waste weak enough to guarantee enough disposal sites for the billions of pounds of chemical waste generated each year. Moreover, corporate interests are often better represented than those of the public on distinguished national "citizens" review commissions.

Many government officials are allied with corporate interests they are supposed to regulate. Business-oriented legislators and officials have targeted hundreds of federal regulations for a premature death. This has been particularly true of many top officials in recent Republican presidential administrations and for conservative members of the U.S. Congress. As one commentator has put it, "More than any president in recent history, [George W. Bush] has filled key behind-the-scenes jobs with lawyers and lobbyists plucked from the industries they now regulate—people who have spent their careers seeking to dismantle or circumvent environmental rules and who, in their new jobs, are continuing to do just that."[98] Often defended in terms of the need for "less government bureaucracy," attacks on environmental regulations have signaled a resurgence of corporate power aimed at reducing existing, but for the most part modest, regulations and at preventing the addition of new regulations supported by worker and consumer groups. Many of the largest corporations repeatedly violate pollution-control standards; only occasionally have federal agencies fined these corporations or forced plants to close.[99] As in the case of work safety (see Chapter 10), the federal government has periodically been a battleground for struggles between workers and consumers, on the one hand, and corporate capitalists and managers, on the other.

Congress created its most ambitious toxic waste cleanup plan, known as the Superfund, in 1979. President Jimmy Carter signed the legislation. Initial funding over five years was to be used for cleaning up abandoned toxic waste sites. Under the conservative Ronald Reagan administration's policy of making the EPA more responsive to the needs of industry, however, little cleanup was taken. During the Superfund's first five years, only five toxic waste sites were cleaned up. In 1986, however, Congress passed the Superfund Amendments and Reauthorization Act (SARA), increased the program's funding to $9 billion over the next five years, and imposed several regulations to help ensure that the program would meet its objectives. One important requirement was that the EPA use technologies guaranteed to reduce permanently the amount, toxicity, and mobility of hazardous wastes "to the maximum extent possible."[100]

Still, even after the expenditure of tens of billions of dollars to clean up the toxic waste generated by private enterprise and government agencies, the process has barely begun. In the Superfund cleanup program's first 16 years, more than $60 billion in public and private funds were spent, yet fewer than 100 of 1,300-targeted sites had been cleaned up, and approximately 11,000 additional potential Superfund sites had been identified. One study estimates that from 23 to 49 cleanup sites will be added to the national priority list each year between 2000 and 2009, and that the total estimated yearly cost of implementing the Superfund program over this period will approach $20 billion.[101] The Superfund program, however, may have future financial difficulties since appropriations for the program decreased by 34.5 percent during the 1990s, and the George W. Bush administration decreased funding by another 5.9 percent in the early 2000s.

Those companies that caused the pollution are legally responsible for paying for its cleanup. But in many cases, tracing responsibility for pollution is difficult, and many companies' records are illegible or no longer available. The alternative is for taxpayers to pay for the cleanup. A Congressional Office of Technology Assessment (OTA) report noted that EPA has often selected lower-cost, less-effective cleanup technologies preferred by the polluting industries in order to obtain voluntary or negotiated out-of-court settlements with the polluters. The OTA found that more than half of all Superfund expenditures were going for management, long-range studies, and questionable technology; it also cited fraud by cleanup contractors and laboratories.[102] Various analysts estimate the cost of cleaning up existing toxic waste at $500 billion to $1 trillion over the next half-century.

The U.S. government sometimes acts to cover up ecological catastrophes. For example, a major environmental disaster, *27 times* the size of the famous Exxon *Valdez* oil spill in Alaska, occurred in fall 2000 when 300 million gallons of coal slurry (thick puddinglike waste from mining operations containing such hazardous chemicals as arsenic and mercury) broke through a storage reservoir flooding land, polluting a hundred miles of creeks and rivers, fouling drinking water, and destroying property in Kentucky. Experts warned that the reservoir, owned by Martin County Coal Corporation, a subsidiary of Massey Energy Company (the country's fifth-largest corporation and a major contributor to the Republican party), would inevitably rupture. Company officials claimed that it had taken measures to ensure the integrity of the reservoir after a spill in 1994. But company engineers disputed that the mining company had made the required repairs and indicated that the company knew the reservoir would eventually break, causing a major disaster. What is more, Jack Spadaro, the former superintendent of the federal Mine Health and Safety Academy (MHSA)—a branch of the Department of Labor that trains mining inspectors—alleged in a 2004 CBS *60 Minutes* interview that the George W. Bush administration sabotaged the government's investigation of the spill by severely limiting the MHSA's inquiry and covering up much about the mining company's responsibility by falsifying an official report on the incident. In referring to the Bush administration's whitewash of the investigation, Spadaro claimed that he "had never seen anything so corrupt and lawless . . . as what [he] saw regarding interference with a federal investigation of the most serious environmental disaster in the history of the eastern United States."[103] Industry often depends on politically supported friends in government to protect it from significant environment regulation.

A Global Perspective

Speaking at a conference on business and the environment in Asia and the Pacific, Shridath Ramphal, president of the World Conservation Union, has noted that developed and developing countries perceive Earth's environmental crisis differently. Poorer countries, whose poverty generally increased during the industrialized nations' recent period of prosperity, have far fewer resources with which to tackle serious environmental problems. "Some of the demands being made by affluent states—the preservation of tropical forests, for example, or the linking of aid and trade to environmental standards—provoke genuine fear in developing countries. The idea that poor nations should forsake opportunities for growth in order to attack problems caused largely by the imprudence and profligacy of the rich is often seen as an attempt to preserve the global distribution of wealth and power."[104] The sharp contrast in the position of developed and developing countries has potentially serious consequences for international relations and for the world's environmental health over the long term.

ENERGY PROBLEMS

Energy Consumption and Waste

The United States, with less than 5 percent of the world's population, uses one-fourth of the world's energy. U.S. *per capita* primary energy consumption is more than *twice* that of Great Britain or Japan, more than *12 times* that of China, and more than *85 times* that of Bangladesh.[105] Thus, much of the world views U.S. energy guzzling as irresponsible. Cheap energy over the last several decades has been costly to the U.S. society and economy in the short and long run, since cheap energy makes possible such pollution-producing enterprises as the large-vehicle manufacturing industry, the synthetic packaging industry, and the aluminum industry. If cheap energy had not been available over the last few decades, those industries might well have never developed as they did. Today, these industries use very large quantities of increasingly expensive energy.

Cheap fuels for generating electricity, together with a strong desire for high profits for investors, led many utility companies to encourage wasteful use of electricity. Although they are publicly regulated, privately owned utilities show a very strong profit drive, which has pushed them to increase consumer demand. This increased demand is used to justify requests for rate increases. Many electric utility firms have spent several times as much on advertising to generate consumer demand as they do on research and development (R&D). Even the structure of electricity-generating systems, which are increasingly under the control of large bureaucratized utility companies with centralized operations, has contributed to waste of energy. Although large-scale complexes are justified in terms of efficiency, their very size has resulted in major "diseconomies of scale."[106] As much as two-thirds of every dollar customers pay to large electric utilities goes to maintain utility distribution systems. With increased size, vulnerability increases and reliability often decreases; failures in large operations have created disasters for vast numbers of customers. Also, decisions about utility development are not democratic. Smaller-scale, locally generated energy could be more conducive to local community control.

The price that consumers pay for energy does not include many costs of cleaning up environmental damage created by producing that energy. Marc Breslow has calculated that adding in environmental costs would *double* the price of electricity produced by existing coal-fired plants and add between 30 percent and 80 percent to the cost of electricity produced by other means. He concludes, "If these price increases were instituted, consumers would substantially reduce their consumption of energy. It's no surprise, then, that . . . utilities have vehemently opposed considering such costs."[107]

Alternative Energy Technologies

Over the last few decades, with several Middle East oil-shortage crises, major U.S. energy corporations and government policymakers have focused mostly on developing highly capital-intensive and profit-producing alternative energy sources. Little has been done to develop renewable energy sources or promote serious energy conservation. Since 1948, for example, the majority of federal research and development funds for energy have gone for nuclear power. In recent years, less than 20 percent of federal research and development funds have gone for renewable energy and for increasing energy efficiency.[108] It is thus not surprising that only a tiny portion of energy production is from renewable resources: solar, wind, and geothermal.

In a famous article, "Energy Strategy: The Road Not Taken," published in *Foreign Affairs,* one of the influential policy journals in the United States, Amory B. Lovins argued that with a continuing "hard" technology approach, energy problems would soon be economically impossible to solve and would eventually lead to disaster.[109] Lovins proposed a gradual phasing out of fossil fuels and a massive commitment to "soft" technologies: efficiency and conservation in energy use and the development of solar, wind, and waste-product technologies.[110] The failure of industry and government to heed this advice has contributed to the economic, ecological, and foreign policy dilemmas facing the United States and the world at the beginning of the twenty-first century.

Conservation is the cheapest way to create greater energy independence. High gas and oil prices increase class inequality in U.S. society, while massive conservation could solve energy problems without aggravating that inequality. Renewable technologies of solar, wind, and waste recycling are less expensive than fossil fuel and nuclear technologies. They can redirect control of U.S. energy away from multinational corporations to smaller, localized energy-producing facilities and to homeowners. The public appears to be on the side of renewable energy sources, energy efficiency, and conservation. Most respondents to one nationwide poll favored a national policy ensuring that renewable energy would be responsible for one-quarter of new fuel sources through the year 2005. Large majorities favored tougher government policies to increase the energy efficiency of autos and home appliances.[111] In this sense, the citizenry seems to be ahead of most senior corporate and political leaders.

The international organization Greenpeace has demonstrated that renewable energy is able to replace fossil fuels. Mounted on a tractor-trailer, the group's solar-powered electric generator, which uses 40 solar panels and a 4.5-ton bank of batteries, traveled more than 25,000 miles in the United States and Canada, powering more than 80 events including rock concerts, rallies, radio stations, and the Woodstock "Eco-Village."[112]

Energy, Class, and Race

Rich families consume much more energy (for household needs as well as transportation) than do either poor or middle-income families. Poor and middle-income households spend a much larger proportion of their income on energy than do the well-off.[113] Even racial discrimination has energy costs, since housing discrimination requires many African Americans and other Americans of color to live farther from work than a free choice of housing might allow. People of color are also more heavily concentrated in inner cities and thus are far more likely to endure serious air pollution. One study reveals that 57 percent of whites, 65 percent of African Americans, and 80 percent of Latinos live in counties with substandard air quality. Indeed, inner-city children have the highest rates for asthma, hospitaliza-

tion, and mortality. Asthma—and not gunshot wounds—accounts for most childhood emergency room visits in major central cities.[114]

Oil and Energy Problems

The oil, gas, and auto industries heavily influence U.S. energy policy. Oil will account for almost 45 percent of energy consumption by 2010.[115] Half of oil consumption is for motor vehicle fuel. Because of the increase in cars and limited progress in fuel efficiency, oil use for transportation has increased significantly in recent decades. A large proportion of the oil consumed is imported, making the United States more dependent on imported oil now than during the major oil crises of the 1970s. Yet in recent years, U.S. automakers have spent millions of dollars to block legislation that would require an increase in auto fuel efficiency.[116] By reducing gasoline consumption, fuel-efficient cars reduce toxic emissions that contribute to air pollution, but they also reduce manufacturers' profits—by as much as ten times—compared with large, more powerful luxury cars, trucks, and SUVs.

Burning oil and other fossil fuels creates much pollution of Earth's atmosphere, including chemical compounds that destroy the ozone layer that protects life on Earth from the sun's ultraviolet rays. As with the price of electricity, the price of petroleum products does not include most societal costs of pollution. One analyst calculates that adding the environmental costs to the price of gasoline would increase that price by 40 percent.[120]

The cost of petroleum imports in any given year is a large part of the U.S. trade deficit. The price of a barrel of oil since the early 1980s—escalating from $13 to $60—has been far higher than the $3 a barrel in 1970.[121] The 1970s energy crises, which forced motorists to wait in long gasoline lines, brought the United States to the point of barely veiled threats by government and business leaders about taking over oil-supplying countries *by force* if U.S. economic health was seriously threatened. Indeed, the U.S.–Iraq struggle over control of oil-rich Kuwait in the 1991 Gulf War is one example of this inclination. The U.S. invasion and occupation of Iraq beginning in 2003 also had links to U.S. government and industry concern over oil supplies for the United States.

Even though U.S. energy crises stem from dependence on foreign oil supplies, most media and scholarly discussions about energy and foreign policy do not seriously discuss why and how the United States became so dependent on foreign—particularly Middle Eastern—oil. During World War II, oil-company lobbying and government concern about petroleum reserves for military use led the federal government to intervene in Saudi Arabia on behalf of U.S. oil companies. According to Michael Harrington, Texaco and Standard Oil of California wanted the government to help them fight British dominance in Saudi Arabia. Successfully opposing a government proposal to set up a publicly owned Petroleum Reserves Corporation to acquire reserves outside the United States, U.S. companies persuaded the government that they could supply U.S. petroleum needs forever, mostly from U.S. sources. (The energy crises of the 1970s proved them wrong.) In 1943, President Franklin D. Roosevelt committed the government to spending more money than the British in defending Saudi Arabia, providing military protection to guarantee an environment in which U.S. oil interests could produce profit in the "better business climate" overseas. Oil pumped in the Middle East has traditionally been taxed much less than oil pumped in the United States. These tax breaks constitute a major subsidy that has further encouraged oil companies to make U.S. consumers dependent on Middle Eastern oil. U.S. military involvement in Middle Eastern countries like Saudi Arabia and Iraq, which has involved many thousands of U.S. personnel into the early 2000s, is closely related to protection of U.S. oil interests in the Middle East.[122]

For most of the last century, petroleum and petroleum-based companies have been at the heart of the U.S. economy. Although experts have determined that billions of barrels of recoverable oil remain in the ground in the United States—enough to supply the country for decades—the U.S. oil industry now invests more for exploration and production overseas than at home. Since the early 1980s, the number of jobs in U.S. petroleum exploration, production, and refining has been cut sharply. The aging U.S. oil industry infrastructure suffers from neglect, representing dangers to workers and the environment. An estimated 280 million barrels or more of petroleum products are leaked, spilled, evaporated, or otherwise wasted each year, killing wildlife, contaminating groundwater, and threatening public health. Oil pipelines leak an estimated 20 to 30 million gallons each year and average one water-polluting spill every day. An estimated 175,000 aboveground and 200,000 underground storage tanks are leaking. These leaks create underground oil spills. Hundreds of thousands of pits and tanks filled with oily wastes have been abandoned in U.S. oil fields. Many abandoned oil wells pollute drinking water aquifers. Moreover, almost one-third of the 1.4 billion gallons of used oil generated in the United States each year is discarded into the environment. The economic, environmental, and social costs of these remnants of the oil industry's "culture of waste" are incalculable. Yet, as Jack Doyle explains, "The major oil corporations—with some success—have maneuvered to shift financial responsibility from themselves to the people of the U.S. After years of near-royal treatment and exemption upon exemption from the strictures of law—all for the purported purpose of building a strong national economy—the oil giants, having made substantial profits, are now abandoning America. But left behind are the mounting costs of oilfield pollution, property damage, and economically distressed communities."[123]

The oil industry's political influence—political contributions total millions of dollars each election year—has helped secure numerous exemptions, special provisions, and delayed implementation of regulatory laws and has often blocked proposed regulations. Heavy lobbying succeeded in having all forms of petroleum production waste legally defined as "nonhazardous" and exempt from federal hazardous substance cleanup and federal recovery of cleanup costs. Yet, about 98 percent of petroleum production waste is a highly toxic liquid called *produced water,* which is pumped out of the ground in the drilling process. It can pose a serious threat to public health.[124]

Two gasoline additives have been proposed to meet the auto emissions standards of the 1990 Clean Air Act—ethanol, a corn-distilled product, and methanol, a natural gas derivative. EPA scientists, environmentalists, and refiners have favored methanol because it is less polluting, cheaper, and easier to get to market. The production of ethanol consumes as much energy as the finished product will provide, and its ability to reduce air pollution is questionable. However, the giant agricultural conglomerate Archer Daniels Midland (ADM), the major U.S. manufacturer of ethanol, has lobbied hard for laws favoring its use. ADM has contributed much money to Republican party campaigns and officeholders, which is one likely reason that Republican presidents have favored greater use of ethanol. Yet this ethanol development, and the federal tax subsidies for ethanol, will likely cost taxpayers an estimated $15 billion in 2004–2009.[125]

Resource Depletion and Pollution: Automobiles, Trucks, and Buses

The motor vehicle is a symbol of contemporary life in the United States. Automobiles and trucks have been at the heart of industrial development over the last century. In addition to their role in shaping the gridiron pattern of cities, motor vehicles are major contributors to ecological problems: traffic congestion, air and water pollution, and high gasoline consumption. Henry Ford pioneered in mass-producing cars, including the assembly line, but the conglomerate General Motors developed the marketing, credit, and advertising organization to sell cars throughout the world. Automobiles account for more than 80 percent of passenger traffic in the United States. In 2001, thus, more than 230.4 million autos were registered in the United States, and Americans traveled some 2,782 billion passenger miles by automobile.[126]

The auto industry has long been one of the most concentrated industries. Three automakers—Ford, General Motors, and Chrysler (now owned by Daimler, a German company)—historically dominated the production of cars and trucks designed and built by U.S. companies. Thousands of smaller companies have been heavily dependent on the Big Three, who have considerable power to manipulate prices. Large-scale auto and truck development is mostly driven by corporate profit considerations. Profit-oriented business decisions initially set the automobile at the heart of the U.S. transportation system, with little collective input from rank-and-file Americans. As Larry Sawers has pointed out, "Automobiles . . . were built, not because society in some fashion sat down and figured out that an auto-based urban transportation system was the best, but because it was profitable to build automobiles to sell to a decentralized market."[127] The first automobiles were toys for the wealthy; a significant mass market did not develop until the 1920s. Since then, automobile companies have used aggressive advertising to convince consumers to buy a new car with the newest styling and gadgets every few years, whether they need a new car or not.

For decades auto manufacturers have fought to keep consumers dependent on large automobiles rather than on small ones and on public mass transit. Severe oil shortages in the 1970s forced auto executives to shift their priorities for a time, but when the oil prices declined in the 1980s, auto executives again emphasized larger vehicles. In addition, the auto industry, *not* consumers, has fought government regulation of auto-exhaust pollution. In 1970, three major U.S. auto firms even admitted before the Supreme Court that they had collaborated for decades to prevent antipollution devices from being put on vehicles.[128]

The Decline of Mass Transit

It is rational for consumers to use cheap gas and travel on government-financed highways, especially where mass transit has decayed or disappeared or was never built. Powerful auto industry executives, and allied government elites, engineered this dependence on cars over several decades. Government highway subsidies have favored cars and trucks over more efficient railroads. Over the past several decades, governments have spent far more money on roadway projects than public transit systems.[129] Government subsidies for road systems snowballed under effective lobbying pressure from auto and truck corporations. Not surprisingly, thus, a 1978 President's National Urban Policy Report concluded that building nearly 40,000 miles of interstate highways was the "most powerful direct federal action that has contributed to metropolitan decentralization and central city decline."[130] Today, however, many billions of tax dollars are needed to maintain this superhighway system, which is in substantial disrepair.

Significantly, consumers have demanded longer-lasting cars and more mass transit, but private industry has shown little interest in providing such needs. Indeed, this U.S. corporate attitude led to the huge success of Japanese automakers in the United States. U.S. consumers have increasingly chosen the often more reliable, fuel-efficient Japanese cars over those produced by U.S. companies. In addition, the U.S. industry has historically fought government mass-transit programs. The growth of the automobile industry was accompanied, in fact, by systematic corporate action to *destroy* alternative means of transportation. According to Bradford Snell's research, in the 1930s General Motors (GM) created a holding company through which it and other auto-related companies channeled money to buy electric mass-transit systems and convert them to diesel buses. Through various business arrangements, GM was involved in the conversion of about a hundred transit systems in 45 cities from New York to Los Angeles. In 1949 GM was convicted in federal court of having *conspired* to destroy electric transit and convert electric trolley systems to diesel buses, whose production GM monopolized. The fine, however, was only a modest $5,000. In spite of this conviction, GM continued to play a role, into the 1950s, in converting electric transit systems to diesel buses. Between 1936 and 1955, the number of operating trolley cars in the United States dropped from about 40,000 to 5,000.[131]

Replying to Bradford Snell in a report of its own, General Motors argued that the electric transit systems were already in trouble and that some systems had begun partial conversion to buses before GM began its massive intervention.[132] From GM's viewpoint,

Certain corporate interests and their political allies often oppose the development of mass transit systems

the company's actions only accelerated the destructive process. Perhaps more important in destroying mass transit was GM's aggressive marketing of automobiles and trucks. As autos and trucks flooded the streets, congestion slowed the pace of trolley cars; this decline in efficiency turned some riders away and hastened the decline of mass transit.

The suburbanization of many industries—resulting in part from their quest for cheaper land and lower taxes—accelerated workers' purchase of automobiles. Capitalism's internal logic of market control, private profit, and private consumption fosters a serious neglect of collective consumption, such as public transit, because there is usually less profit to be made from it. In most areas, the consumer has been encouraged since the 1930s to think in terms of high-energy-consumption private transportation rather than public mass transit.

NUCLEAR POWER AND NUCLEAR POLLUTION

Some of the most serious environmental problems of the United States and the world are linked to nuclear energy. Since the mid-1970s, the nuclear power industry in the United States has been on the decline. Reactors have not lived up to the image of "safe," "efficient," and "cheap" sources of power their manufacturers originally portrayed; some have closed because of low performance capacity. Despite public opposition and skepticism among investors because of the high costs of construction, operation, maintenance, and eventual dismantling, in the 1980s the industry launched a multimillion-dollar media campaign to convince the populace that nuclear energy was desirable and necessary. Basing its appeal on growing concern over global warming, which is caused in part by burning of oil and coal to generate electricity, the nuclear power industry sought to ease regulations and to eliminate public participation in the licensing process, particularly involvement of state and local governments; to remove emergency evacuation planning as an issue in reactor siting; to reduce the cost of radioactive waste disposal by deregulating some nuclear waste; and to force taxpayers to pay for development of new "advanced, inherently safe" reactors.[133]

Defenders of nuclear power in the United States see it as a major source of energy for generating electricity. One of the most popular arguments is that nuclear power plants provide thousands of jobs, directly in the plants and indirectly in the businesses that thrive on the electricity they produce. Another defense is to tell consumers that without nuclear-powered plants they will face interruptions in electric power and a lowered standard of living. Today 104, nuclear reactors are operational in the United States, up from just 15 in 1970.[134] A decade earlier the industry had hoped to have 1,000 reactors operating by 2000. Although earlier industry projections forecast that 40 percent of the country's electricity would be generated by nuclear energy in the 1990s, the actual figure was only 20 percent.[135]

Major Problems

Nuclear power plants are extremely expensive to build. Early estimates of $200 million to $800 million in construction costs per plant were soon revised to $2 billion to $7 billion. Construction costs for most plants far exceeded original estimates, some by as much as 7,000 percent. Some have never achieved their projected operating capacity because of safety problems, and all have limited lifetimes. Some utility companies with nuclear power plants have lost hundreds of millions of dollars. In 1994, the Tennessee Valley Authority (TVA) ended construction on three plants after spending $6 billion. TVA estimated that completion of these plants would require an additional $8 billion. In the same year, dismantling was completed at the $5.5 billion Shoreham Nuclear Power Plant on Long Island, New York, because of the impossibility of devising a safe evacuation plan for area residents in the event of an accident. The plant never went into commercial operation, although during testing it generated huge quantities of radioactive waste. Dismantling cost approximately $180 million.[136]

Although nuclear power has been a private industry since 1954, it has been heavily subsidized by taxpayer dollars. At the time of its creation, the private nuclear power industry benefited from billions of dollars in government-funded research and development, and for 20 years government investment in nuclear power research and development exceeded that of private industry. Federal law saves the industry billions of dollars annually in liability insurance (assuming insurers can be found) by limiting private industry's liability for accidents to $200 million per utility and less than $7 billion for the entire industry—an almost insignificant fraction of the hundreds of billions that a major accident might cost. Indeed, because of nuclear power's extremely high risk, without this liability cap it is unlikely that the private nuclear power industry would even have developed.[137]

One Greenpeace study estimated that between 1950 and 1990 the federal government spent $97 billion (calculated in 1990 dollars) for nuclear power research and development, regulation, construction, reactor fuel, and waste handling. This figure does not include expenditures of state and local governments, costs relating to accidents or environmental damage, or costs of closing down and cleaning up nuclear plants and fuel production sites.[138] As aging nuclear reactors are shut down, they need to be dismantled.[139] More than a dozen commercial reactors have been shut down permanently, and more shutdowns have been announced.[140] The U.S. General Accounting Office estimates that the cost of decommissioning reactors to U.S. taxpayers and energy ratepayers will range from $133 to $303 million per plant.[141] Although utilities are required to allocate funds for dismantling reactors, one Public Citizen report revealed that the average utility has put aside only 14 percent of estimated dismantling costs.[142]

Safety problems are an issue with nuclear plants. David E. Lilienthal, the first head of the Atomic Energy Commission (AEC), sharply criticized decisions of private industry and the AEC to use "light water" nuclear reactors to generate electricity. He criticized this technology as "immature" and "too complex" and as having too many places "at which something can go wrong." Lilienthal charged that this technology was "chosen too hastily, largely for short-run commercial reasons."[143] In his view, other types of nuclear reactors should have been carefully considered.

Nuclear reactors contain a core of radioactive material capable of causing massive damage and death if even a small fraction escapes. The reactor's containment system is intended to prevent escape of radioactive material in case of accident. However, containment systems are only required to withstand a certain level of pressure. A study of U.S. nuclear power plants determined that none had a containment system designed to withstand a severe accident that involved a core meltdown. A number of accident situations could trigger a core meltdown, including complete loss of electric power, steam explosions, or the failure of piping systems.[144] In 2000, the Union of Concerned Scientists warned that the Nuclear Regulatory Commission (NRC), the federal agency that has the responsibility to oversee the nuclear power industry, is allowing nuclear plant owners to cut back on tests and inspections of safety equipment, thereby increasing the risk of a national disaster.[145]

The NRC has reported serious shortcomings and possible wrongdoing in the way reactors have been operated.[146] As early as the 1970s newspapers were running headlines about major plant accidents. Many of the accidents, toxic waste problems, and safety and evacuation problems have been covered up or ignored by the industry and brought to public attention only by community and environmental groups. Numerous plants have been plagued by poor management and major construction errors. For example, late in the construction process of California's Diablo Canyon plant it was discovered that the plant's antiearthquake structures were built backward. One investigation found that at least two-thirds of U.S. nuclear power plants were built with some substandard parts.[147] The domination of the nuclear equipment industry by a few corporations limits competition and the quality controls on what they produce.[148]

Age creates additional safety problems for nuclear reactors as parts corrode, degrade, and crack. Aging reactors are subject to multiple problems; repair, when possible,

A local citizens' group calls on the New York governor to close down the Indian Point nuclear power plant. (AP Wide World Photos)

is technically complex and costly, and poses safety risks.[149] The possibility that its brittle steel containment vessel might rupture, thereby releasing massive amounts of radiation, forced the Yankee Rowe nuclear power plant to halt operations in 1991, nine years before its operating license was to expire. Because of the prohibitive cost of analyzing and correcting this problem, Yankee Rowe's owners chose to shut down the reactor permanently. Local citizens blame the reactor for causing environmental damage and "an incredible incidence of birth defects and cancers." By 1995, the plant was largely dismantled. Still, the cost of maintaining the large amount of deadly radioactive material remaining at the site is about $4 million a year.[150]

Pollution from Nuclear Wastes

The nuclear industry generates serious environmental pollution. For example, the three huge coal-burning plants that are required to provide electricity to produce nuclear reactor fuel release into the air each year 661,000 tons of sulfur dioxide, 195,000 tons of nitric oxides, and millions of tons of carbon dioxide. Radioactive waste is dangerous. On a routine basis, even without accidents, nuclear power plants release low-level radioactive pollutants into air and water that over a long period will probably result in an increased number of deaths from cancer in communities near plants. One report found a higher breast cancer death rate for women who live within 100 miles of nuclear reactors than for women who live farther from them.[151] High-level radioactive waste from nuclear power stations also pollutes adjacent air and underground water systems. By 2015, over 75,000 metric tons of highly radioactive waste will have been produced by nuclear reactors. Plutonium, which is lethal in amounts too small to see and which has a half-life of 240,000 years, makes up a large part of this waste. Some of the waste will remain extremely hazardous for an estimated 3 million years.[152]

As yet, the United States has no permanent disposal facility. Radioactive waste is currently maintained at temporary sites at a cost of billions of dollars per year. Most waste is stored in pools of water at each reactor site, but because cracks in cement pools caused by earthquakes or plant accidents could cause leakage of this highly dangerous material, alternative methods of storage have been explored. The U.S. Department of Energy (DOE) has established a permanent waste storage site in Yucca Mountain, Nevada, but it has met with fierce opposition from environmental groups and scientists. Over recent decades, the DOE has conducted environmental impact studies on health and safety issues regarding the proposed storage facility at a taxpayer cost of some $7 billion.[153] Geologist Conrad Krauskoph has expressed the fears of many: "No scientist or engineer can give an absolute guarantee that radioactive waste will not some day leak in dangerous quantities from even the best of repositories."[154] Other scientists believe that many technical issues about the storage facility remain unresolved.[155] Fearing that the EPA might block the DOE's Yucca Mountain plans by ruling the risk of contamination too high, Congress included a provision in a 1992 energy bill transferring the power to establish health standards for long-term nuclear waste storage from the EPA to the National Academy of Sciences, a private group beyond the jurisdiction of the EPA.[156]

Congress and the George W. Bush administration endorsed the Yucca Mountain site in 2002.[157] However, the Nuclear Regulatory Commission has recently discovered a series of private emails from government scientists confirming environmentalists' concerns about the infiltration of nuclear waste into underground water sources at the Yucca Mountain site. The emails involve probably false data supporting computer models showing how slowly rainwater could seep into the mountain and contaminate underground reserves. Recent reports show that the scientists have been under extreme pressure from "higher-ups to reach illegitimate conclusions." A congressional committee, the FBI, and the inspectors general at the Interior and Energy departments have proceeded with criminal probes into the possibility of falsified work by the government scientists. Ironically, the construction of more nuclear power plants has been at the heart of the government's energy plan.[158]

Nuclear Technology: The Military Connection

There has long been a connection between private nuclear power plants and those dedicated to weapons production. Both were designed by the same private sector and government officials and scientists. Indeed, the private nuclear power industry grew out of weapons development and was seen by David Lilienthal and other industry leaders as a way to legitimate in the public mind the high level of expenditures for nuclear weapons. For decades, the government assured the public that residents living near nuclear weapons plants were in no danger of radioactive contamination. However, the immense dangers of nuclear weapons plants became known during the 1980s. Since then a number of officials in weapons production have been charged with complacency, recklessness, or concealing from the public dangers at nuclear weapons plants. It appears that far more problems have occurred than have yet been made public.[159]

Nuclear weapons plant problems include aging and unsafe equipment, poorly trained workers, unsafe operating procedures, and management's disregard of advice from engineers and safety monitors, as well as safety lapses. Accountability is a major problem in the nuclear weapons industry. The DOE, which operates nuclear weapons plants, is answerable only to itself, with no oversight from outside. Another problem stems from the weapons program's goal of maximum security, which has isolated the nuclear weapons industry from the commercial nuclear power industry's technical and safety improvements. Safety protections required on commercial electric-power nuclear reactors do not exist for weapons reactors. The goal of maximum production, intensified during the 1980s, created the additional problem of pushing aging reactors far beyond the limits of safety.[160]

In some cases, workers have been put at risk. In one instance, 19 carpenters in a 28-worker crew employed by a subcontractor at the Department of Energy laboratory in Oak Ridge, Tennessee, were contaminated with radioactive waste leaking from a cut pipe. By the time the problem was discovered, workers had been exposed for six days; some workers' cars and homes had become contaminated. A spokesperson for the workers explained that a health physicist would have detected the presence of radioactive material when the leak first began, but subcontractors are not required to provide such personnel.[161]

Military-industrial firms and defense production facilities have generated millions of tons of highly dangerous waste, and an immense amount of toxic and radioactive material has polluted the environment and caused health problems to people living near nuclear weapons plants. The federal government defense program is the country's most serious nuclear polluter. In its first decade of operation the Hanford (Washington) plant released a large quantity of radioactive iodine into the air without notifying local communities.[162] In the *Bulletin of the Atomic Scientists,* Danielle Gordon writes, "Government contractors released radiation into the environment on hundreds of occasions between 1944 and 1968, mostly around the nuclear weapons complexes where residents already were subject to numerous unintentional releases."[163]

Later, the Hanford plant was responsible for spilling or deliberately dumping 444 billion gallons of radioactive water and liquid waste into the soil and for large deposits of radioactive particles miles from the plant's boundaries. Its radioactive waste has been detected at the mouth of the Columbia River, more than 300 miles away.[164] Thousands of tons of radioactive uranium waste have been released into the atmosphere and water supply by the weapons-related plant at Fernald, Ohio, and thousands of the more than 34 million gallons of radioactive materials stored in underground tanks at the Savannah River Plant (SRP) in South Carolina have leaked into groundwater. The 153 dumps for toxic waste and radioactive debris at the SRP have left South Carolina with the greatest amount of high-level radioactive waste of any place on Earth. Together, Hanford and SRP have produced nearly 100 million gallons of highly radioactive waste, and there is little prospect that such waste can be disposed of permanently.[165]

Liquid wastes are stored at Hanford and the SRP in 220 giant carbon steel tanks holding between 750,000 and 1.3 million gallons each. More than one-third of the Hanford tanks have leaked hundreds of thousands of gallons of nuclear waste.[166] Many of SRP's original tanks have cracked, and the wastes have been transferred to replacement tanks. The Environmental Policy Institute has warned of the danger of a nonnuclear explosion in these tanks that would release huge amounts of radioactivity into the environment. Heavily influenced by the nuclear and utility industries, the DOE favors an underground site for permanent storage of these nuclear wastes. The suitability of using salt caverns was abandoned in the 1960s as unsafe, yet in the 1980s, the DOE returned to this solution and began construction of a $700 million storage site in a New Mexico salt deposit 2,000 feet beneath the desert. Not long after construction began, water, which will quickly corrode the steel storage drums, was discovered leaking into this storage area.[167] The plan is to bury hundreds of thousands of barrels of plutonium-contaminated waste at this site.

The full extent of health problems caused by by-products of nuclear weapons plants will not be known for some time. However, workers at these installations, as well as residents living near them, have experienced much higher-than-average rates of cancers, birth defects, and other health disorders.

U.S. production of plutonium and tritium, elements required for nuclear weapons, came to a halt in 1988 when the SRP was closed. Numerous serious accidents that occurred at the SRP during the 1960s and 1970s were not made public until 1983, when a former waste manager revealed that toxic and radioactive waste—disposed of in pits or buried— was slowly leaking into groundwater. He revealed that the DOE and DuPont, which managed the plant, kept two sets of information about how fast toxic waste seeps into the groundwater—one set based on manipulated data from wells that were flushed before test samples were drawn and another set of accurate information that was restricted to use by DuPont and the DOE. While public records showed tritium levels in groundwater to be two to three times the standard for drinking water, company records showed tritium levels of *1,000 times* the standard. Analysis of SRP data secured by investigators under the Freedom of Information Act showed additional discrepancies between reality and the public statements made by DuPont and the DOE.[168]

Since 1989 the DOE and Westinghouse, the plant's new operator, have been involved in an effort to revive one of the SRP's five reactors—a process replete with problems. Workers have reported numerous safety violations, including unprotected exposure to contaminated areas. Each year hundreds of equipment malfunctions, accidents, procedural violations, and other operating problems have occurred. A failed attempt to restart the reactor in 1991 resulted in radioactive contamination of the Savannah River and a shutdown of public water systems. Radioactive materials from 49 aging storage tanks continue to leak into groundwater. Rust Federal Services signed a five-year contract in 1995 to clean up radioactive waste contamination at the Savannah plant.[169] The most current estimate is that cleaning up the radioactive waste eventually will exceed $40 billion. A National Research Council report claims that the site probably will never be completely clean because the waste is far too entrenched at the site. Yet the federal government plans to build a new $400 million facility at the Savannah plant to extract recycled tritium from decommissioned warheads.[170]

Is a Major Disaster Possible?

As little as one-millionth of a gram of radioactive plutonium can cause cancer. Already a number of studies show high cancer death rates for workers who mine radioactive materials or work in plants with radioactive materials such as uranium. The possibility of a major disaster is even more serious. Serious accidents and near disasters have already occurred. A 1979 accident at Three Mile Island in Pennsylvania, which released significant radioactivity into the environment, came close to being a major disaster. Cleanup costs there have exceeded $1 billion.[171] Columbia University researchers have linked radiation releases from the Three Mile Island disaster to higher cancer rates in nearby communities.[172]

A 1965 Brookhaven National Laboratory report that estimated the casualties from a large nuclear reactor disaster a few miles from a major city—45,000 people killed and 100,000 injured, and an area the size of the state of Pennsylvania unusable for a long time— was not released by the government until 1973, out of fear that the public response might have stopped nuclear reactor construction. A major nuclear reactor accident in 1986 at the Chernobyl nuclear plant in the Ukraine demonstrated the seriousness of a more modest ac- cident than the one projected by Brookhaven. Radiation released by the meltdown of the Chernobyl reactor core contaminated the immediate area and spread through the atmos- phere to much of the world. Thirty people were killed immediately, and almost 100,000 had to be relocated to hastily constructed new towns. Food crops and dairy grazing lands were contaminated in the former Soviet Union and in surrounding European countries. By the 1990s, hundreds of local residents had become ill or were dying because of the disaster. The long-term health effects of this disaster have not yet been fully assessed, but already many thousands of people have been affected. The Nuclear Regulatory Commission has esti- mated that there is still a significant chance of a *major* nuclear power plant accident in the United States in the next few decades.[173]

Can People Bring Change?

Citizen protest movements have played a major role in the cancellation of defective nuclear reactors and safety changes in other nuclear plants. For example, evidence introduced into the licensing process for the Comanche Peak nuclear power plant by the Citizens' Associ- ation for Sound Energy, a group organized by a private citizen, helped convince the Nuclear Regulatory Commission to require Texas Utilities to overhaul its quality assurance pro- gram. Pressure from members of the Citizens Awareness Network contributed to the deci- sion to close the troubled Yankee Rowe plant in Massachusetts. A lawsuit was brought by the 16,000 members of Heart of America Northwest against Westinghouse and the DOE for violating the antipollution standards and failing to report contamination caused by the Han- ford facility, but the court ruled for Westinghouse.[174] In many other instances across the United States, ordinary people working together have made their voices heard and have sometimes achieved success in creating a safer environment.

THE MILITARY-INDUSTRIAL COMPLEX: A SOCIAL PROBLEM?

Nuclear Weaponry

The nuclear power industry developed out of government research designed primarily to create nuclear weapons. U.S. researchers developed the first atomic bomb, and the United States is the only country to drop a nuclear bomb on another country (Japan). For many years the United States has had several times the number of nuclear weapons most experts consider adequate for defense—more than enough to annihilate all life on Earth. But this overkill capability has not reduced government expenditures for nuclear-related technolo- gies. For example, by 1996 the U.S. government had spent 13 years and $30 billion on the

Strategic Defense Initiative (SDI), often called "Star Wars," but had little to show for that huge expenditure. Critics have noted that antimissile programs are escalatory and destabilizing to world disarmament efforts.[175] With the end of the Cold War between the United States and the former Soviet Union, many analysts have argued that there is no longer a need for massive military projects such as "Star Wars."[176] Nonetheless, periodically conservative lawmakers have resurrected the discredited "Star Wars" idea.

At the heart of the weapons production system is the U.S. military-industrial complex, which includes thousands of firms that draw on government funds to make billions of dollars worth of weapons. Nothing reveals more clearly the contradictions of the existing stratification system in U.S. society than the dominance of its military-industrial complex, which outclasses consumer-oriented industries and has made very handsome profits from producing the means of potential destruction of all life on Earth. Military-industrial corporate lobbying to continue the arms race—with its threat of a nuclear holocaust—during the Cold War period, and to continue arms manufacturing after the Cold War was over, indicates the extent to which the military-industrial corporate elite is willing to go to maintain status, profits, and influence. For example, the U.S. Congress voted for more funding for a private military contractor to make more B-2 bombers, even though the program was *opposed* by the U.S. Department of Defense. The company organized a massive national effort, including large-scale advertising and contributions to congressional campaigns. One newspaper editorial noted, "Congressional authorization of continued funding is a testimonial to the power of lobbyists, and the ability of the defense industry to manipulate lawmakers."[177]

Viewed from a power–conflict perspective, a major cause of war is the effort by the dominant business class and its government allies to maintain their power in opposition both to the dominant classes in other countries and to threats to imperialistic U.S. adventures overseas. The costs of preparations for, and the waging of, war are heavily borne by rank-and-file citizens, who are usually the first to die and the first to pay for war by means of heavy taxation, as well as the last to benefit from it. We have seen clear evidence of this in the Vietnam War, with its nearly 60,000 U.S. military deaths (and millions of Vietnamese casualties) and in the thousands of U.S. military dead and wounded (and many thousands of civilian casualties) in the two U.S. invasions of Iraq. Yet during these wars military-industrial companies made very handsome profits. The spoils of "cold" and "hot" wars have gone disproportionately to those capitalists who make and sell expensive weapons of destruction.

War in Historical Perspective

Max Weber, a prominent European social scientist, once defined the *state* (government) as that social institution with a monopoly on the legitimate use of force. The state has the last word on the use of government force; and often the U.S. state acts in the interests of the corporate capitalist elite. A continued U.S. military presence in the Middle East during recent decades, for example, has been designed in part to ensure the flow of oil to fuel U.S. industry and transport, even at the risk of major conflicts with other countries. Moreover, the psychology of war enables the dominant class to solidify its hold over the population by periodically drumming up a patriotic "war fever" and persuading a majority of citizens that they must sacrifice greatly for the adventurous military actions of their country's corporate elite and allied political leaders.[178]

One point of agreement among such different social theorists as Adam Smith and Karl Marx was that the importance of warfare would diminish in the modern era as the orientation of industrial capitalism became international. Their predictions have not come true, however. Approximately 80 million people have been killed in more than 200 wars in the last hundred years. Approximately 36 million died in World War II alone, 60 percent of them civilians. In addition to its tremendous capabilities for destruction, the greatest significance of modern warfare is its expansion to the civilian population and its bureaucratization in military-industrial complexes. Prior to World War I, soldiers generally fought soldiers, with civilians rarely the intentional targets. Beginning with the bombings of civilians in World War I, however, civilians have become principal targets. The bombing of civilians, in fact, accounted substantially for the large number of civilian casualties in World War II, Vietnam, and Iraq. Moreover, as was seen in the Nazi extermination camps in World War II and in the high-altitude bombing of large cities by the United States during World War II, Vietnam, and Iraq, bureaucratic efficiency maximizes violence and distances it from personal contact. The subjects of violence are not spoken of as human beings but rather as impersonal "targets" or "collateral damage"; and the perpetrators are individuals following "orders" given from above in a hierarchical organization.[179]

War in the Nuclear Age

Nuclear weapons were first developed during World War II in a program called the "Manhattan Project." In that program, U.S. scientists tested the first atomic bomb at Alamogordo, New Mexico, on July 16, 1945. A petition signed by many scientists who developed the bomb urged that it be used in a demonstration explosion rather than to destroy a civilian population center. Their efforts were unsuccessful, and U.S. personnel dropped the only atomic bombs ever used in war over the Japanese cities of Hiroshima and Nagasaki in August 1945.

In minutes, tens of thousands of people were killed—and tens of thousands more were injured, some of whom are still suffering today from radiation effects of the bombs. At ground zero, the point of detonation, a fireball was created similar in intensity to the heat of the sun; everything it touched evaporated—steel, concrete, and people. A blast wave moved out from ground zero in all directions, crushing everything in its path. Then the new feature of atomic weapons—radiation—began to take its toll. Weeks and years after the explosion, people became mysteriously ill, began to vomit and have diarrhea, and often died a slow, painful death. The bombs dropped on Hiroshima and Nagasaki in 1945 have long since been dwarfed by vastly more powerful thermonuclear weapons.

Since 1978 numerous U.S. policymakers, most members of or tied to corporate elites, have talked about the possibility of fighting and "winning" a nuclear war. However, studies of the likely effects of nuclear war conclude that this is not the case. The explosion of only 100 megatons of nuclear weapons (a tiny percentage of the U.S. and Russian arsenals) would produce a major firestorm and create a thick cloud of highly radioactive dust and soot that would likely prevent normal levels of sunlight from reaching the planet's surface as the cloud moved over the globe, plunging temperatures to well below freezing and creating a "long nuclear winter." With the death of most plant and animal life on Earth, any human survivors of even a "limited" nuclear war would face a slow death from starvation and radiation sickness, wherever they lived on the globe.[180]

U.S. military adventures abroad have led to the creation of overseas military bases and prisons where foreign nationals have been abused and tortured, contrary to U.S. laws.

The Military-Industrial Complex: Keeping War Alive

President Dwight Eisenhower warned the world in the late 1950s about the vast interlocking system of institutions that profit from military expenditures, the military-industrial complex. It has since grown rapidly, creating what C. Wright Mills called a "permanent war economy."[181]

In 1995, a presidential Advisory Committee on Human Radiation Experiments issued a report with findings indicating that between the end of World War II and the mid-1970s, the U.S. government had funded contractors to do research on radiation's impact on human bodies. The report suggested that this was "one of those times in history in which wrongs were committed by very decent people who were in a position to know that a specific aspect of their interaction with others should be improved. . . . The seeming likelihood that atomic bombs would be used again in war. . . . meant the country had to know as much as it could, as quickly as it could."[182] Much of the military-oriented research used radioactive materials *without* the informed consent of the human guinea pigs. Both children and prisoners were used in the research. In addition, several hundred uranium miners died from lung cancer caused by inhaling radioactive gas; this too was preventable.[183] National security was used as the reason for not informing the victims or the public about what was going on.

Over the last decade, military spending has exceeded that of the previous century. During this period the federal government awarded more than $1.3 trillion in prime military contracts to U.S. corporations.[184] Nuclear weapons, along with nuclear research, personnel, and the ships and planes that carry nuclear weapons, have accounted for half of the U.S. war econ-

The Military-Industrial Complex and Halliburton's War Profiteering

In this chapter, we have defined the *military-industrial complex* as the vast interlocking system of institutions that profit from military expenditures—most notably, the war profits of defense industries from their relationships with the U.S. Congress and the Pentagon. The Halliburton Corporation and its recent multibillion-dollar financial windfall from federal reconstruction contracts in Iraq epitomize concerns about the military-industrial complex.

Halliburton is the world's largest oil and gas services company. Since its founding in 1919, the company has been involved in what critics call "war profiteering" and a series of political scandals. In direct violation of federal law prohibiting U.S. corporations from business dealings with countries that support terrorism, Halliburton has done business with some of the most brutal and corrupt governments, including those in Burma, Iran, Kazakhstan, Libya, and Nigeria, as well as with that of Iraq's former dictator Saddam Hussein.

Despite paying out hundreds of millions of dollars in claims and fines over the years, Halliburton continues to reap enormous profits from its contracts with the federal government. Between the beginning of the Iraqi conflict in 2003 and late 2004, the U.S. government improperly awarded Halliburton $3.9 billion in no-bid contracts for reconstruction projects in war-torn Iraq, thereby increasing the company's earnings many times over its year 2002 earnings. Halliburton re-

ceived these lucrative government contracts despite a history of corruption. In meeting the contracts, Halliburton reportedly overcharged the federal government $61 million for fuel and $24.7 million for meals. Pentagon officials complained that the food Halliburton served to U.S. troops in Iraq fell far below government standards—"the Pentagon found blood all over the floor of kitchens, dirty pans, dirty grills, dirty salad bars and rotting meats and vegetables in four of the military messes the company operates in Iraq." Recently, the Securities and Exchange Commission began an investigation into Halliburton's accounting practices, and the country of Kuwait's parliament announced an investigation into allegations that Halliburton asked for kickbacks from selected contractors.

Because of Halliburton's relationship with Vice President Richard Cheney, the company was able to secure these contracts easily and to make big profits off the Iraq war. Cheney served as Halliburton's chief executive officer from 1995 until his vice presidential candidacy in 2000. During his tenure, Cheney greatly increased Halliburton's federal contracts, and the company compensated Cheney well—in May 2000 Cheney sold stock holdings in the company worth $5 million and the company awarded him a retirement package valued at $20 million. In direct violation of federal ethics standards, moreover, Cheney continued to receive deferred stock salaries as vice president.

Sources: Corpwatch, "Houston, We Have a Problem: An Alternative Annual Report on Halliburton" (April 2004), available at www.corpwatch.org/downloads/houston.pdf; David Phinney, "Kuwait Documents Allege Halliburton Bribe Scandal" (November 11, 2004), available at www.corpwatch.org/article.php?id=11664; Molly Ivins, "Cheney's Mess Worth a Close Look," *Baltimore Sun* (June 10, 2002); On Politics, "A Halliburton Primer" (July 11, 2002), available at www.washingtonpost.com/wp-srv/onpolitics/articles/halliburtonprimer.html; CNN Money, "Cheney May Still Have Halliburton Ties" (September 25, 2003), available at money.cnn.com/2003/09/25/news/companies/cheney/; CNN.com, "Kuwait MPs Start Halliburton Probe" (February 11, 2004), available at www.cnn.com/2004/BUSINESS/02/11/kuwait.halliburton.

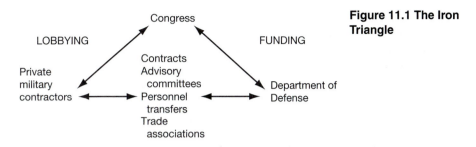

Figure 11.1 The Iron Triangle

omy. Defense spending is an extremely attractive prospect for military-industrial capitalists because of guaranteed profits. The relatively small group of corporations in the military-industrial complex are distinguished from other industries by their position in what is often called the *Iron Triangle*—the Defense Department, military contractors, and members of Congress (Figure 11.1)—which allows them to profit from huge public military expenditures.

The Iron Triangle has a revolving door of money, influence, and jobs among these three sets of actors, involving trillions of dollars. Military contractors who receive contracts from the Defense Department serve on the advisory committees that recommend what weapons they believe are needed. Many people move around the triangle from job to job, serving in the military, then in the Defense Department, then in military industries. As former Assistant Secretary of Defense J. Ronald Fox put it, "Positions are offered to [military] officers who have demonstrated their appreciation for industry's particular problems and commitments."[185] A study of eight major weapons makers found that in one ten-year period about 2,000 individuals moved among the Department of Defense, the National Aeronautics and Space Administration, and eight private military-industrial companies. In some cases, individuals made key decisions about contracts for the Defense Department and then were hired by a contractor to work on the weapons system they had approved.[186]

Military contractors spend millions of dollars annually in congressional campaign contributions and in maintaining lobbyists to influence Congress. The country's largest aerospace and defense contractors spent $8.7 million lobbying Congress just in the 2001–2002 election year.[187]

Large military budgets have a major impact on the U.S. economy since they control the largest single block of capital resources and yet produce neither civilian consumer goods nor much useful material for further production. Whereas most goods that are produced in the United States can lead to direct benefits or further production, military expenditures usually serve no further economic function. A car, for example, can be used to get back and forth to work or to go buy groceries, but a missile just sits in its silo.

Arms Sales Abroad

The breakup of the Soviet Union and the end of the Cold War in the late 1980s destroyed some of the rationale for a continued U.S. arms buildup and caused arms manufacturers to shift their focus to other markets. One Department of Defense report noted that even if the global sale of weapons declines, the sale of weapons by U.S. companies is expected to remain at the high level of $10 to $15 billion annually—roughly half the international weapons business.[188] During the Ronald Reagan and George H. W. Bush administrations, it was actually the United States that sold Iraq the poisonous chemicals and deadly biological viruses (anthrax and bubonic plague) that Saddam Hussein used during the Iran–Iraq war (1980–1988), and U.S. weapons were also used for Iraq's invasion of Kuwait in 1990.[189] Indeed, the U.S. government had helped to put Saddam Hussein in power and assisted him in his military expansion, until the U.S. government decided to fight his regime in the early 1990s. A spokesperson for the Federation of American Scientists has noted that "As old ideological motivations and strong U.S.–Soviet competition for geostrategic influence around the world wane, you find more and more that economics is providing the motivation and determining factor in arms sales."[190]

A number of government actions and policies have increased the potential for worldwide weapons proliferation. Since the 1980s, the U.S. government has provided billions of dollars a year in grants to foreign governments to buy U.S.-made weapons. Several peace groups have protested the actions of the Aerospace Industries Association, a group of major U.S. defense contractors. This organization has aggressively lobbied Congress and made campaign contributions to ensure that members of Congress would allow arms sales overseas, including advanced military aircraft to Middle Eastern countries.[191]

Many observers have pointed out that increased military strength often impedes the democratization of a society. George Lopez wrote in the *Bulletin of the Atomic Scientists* that "One of the clearest correlations in the politics of Third World nations is the relationship between militarization and repression." According to Amnesty International, the use of torture against their own citizens has been commonplace for some government recipients of U.S. military assistance (including Saddam Hussein).[192]

"Weapons Welfarism"

Military industries are organized without many of the checks that make other businesses run efficiently. Because the Department of Defense is not greatly concerned with profits and losses and has had practically unlimited resources, the costs of military equipment have constantly increased. The capital and guaranteed income provided by the Pentagon cannot be matched in the civilian marketplace. The cozy relationship among various parts of the Iron Triangle and the lack of controls affect the number of jobs available, the products made, and the efficiency of production. "Weapons welfarism" spending creates fewer jobs than does comparable federal spending in the private sector. Military spending siphons resources, reducing the ability of the economy to produce goods for civilians, and it makes the United States less competitive in the world market. Defenders of huge military budgets often cite the civilian spin-off from military research and production as justification for a militarized economy. In reality, however, the cost-plus basis on which the military-industrial complex operates offers little incentive for efficient production. Under cost-plus contracts, the federal government pays private corporate contractors whatever cost the contractor claims. Japanese and European companies can often produce better-quality, lower-cost goods than those produced by U.S. corporations that are tied to the military-industrial complex. A good example is the random access memory (RAM) chip, which was pioneered by U.S. electronics companies and which is the heart of many computer systems. U.S. companies once dominated the world market in RAM chips, but by the early 1980s, Japan's cheaper and frequently better-quality chips had won a majority of the world market.[193]

ECOLOGICAL CRISES, CONSUMERISM, AND CAPITALISM

Let us now turn to some broader sociological issues. U.S. analysts offer two broad perspectives on the environmental and energy crises that we have discussed in this chapter. The *individualistic perspective* generally blames problems on personal attitudes and lifestyles—the wastefulness, carelessness, and certain other actions of individuals—without accenting critical societal and stratification contexts. The *power–conflict perspective,* on the other hand, locates the source of most ecological crises in our political–economic institutions that have fostered, if not generated, individual self-centeredness, individual and group wastefulness, and obsessive consumerism. According to this view, the short-run, private-profit drive of the powerful leaders at the top of capitalistic enterprises sets the moral tone for U.S. society; the needs and operation of modern capitalism demand growing consumption no matter what the cost.

While consumers' individual values are important in regard to environmental and energy crises, consumers are not independent. The small number of huge corporations that control this society's major industrial and manufacturing sectors have the power to dictate or shape consumer values and tastes—and what is produced—by means of both market control ("You buy a car like this one or have no transportation") and heavy advertising ("People will like you if you drive a nice car"). The shift to nonreturnable containers, which began in the 1940s, was fostered less by consumer demand than by steel, aluminum, and consumer product companies' quest for higher profits. Competition in many industries is minimal. Large oligopolistic corporations often compete with one another through advertising (the costs of which are passed on to consumers) and product superficialities and, all too often, not in terms of product quality or significant differences in price.

Advertising aimed at convincing consumers to buy products they do not need or products that are of ecologically questionable design is a critical component of environmental and energy problems. Industrial design—which often means developing appealing gadgets and packaging, then devising ways to sell them to consumers—is another contributor to environmental and energy problems. Corporate officials commonly argue that the consumer is "king" or "queen" in the market, that consumers demand the products companies make. But do consumers demand 20 kinds of toothpaste and automobiles that break down too soon? Proponents of a "consumer-driven market" ignore the fact that consumers "demand" many products that corporate executives typically do *not* want to supply, such as affordable rental housing, high-speed mass transit, and long-lasting, high-quality autos that don't pollute.[194]

Much waste is created by business's commitment to *product differentiation*—making small changes in a product so that it can be advertised as something different. Changes in the exterior design of automobiles allow them to be presented as something "new" that consumers cannot do without. Many of the thousands of "new" products introduced by U.S. companies each year are basically the same as existing products. Businesses rely on clever marketing and advertising to turn a constant stream of questionable or useless product changes into profit.

Since the 1970s, consumption of food additives—coloring, artificial flavors, texturizers, preservatives—in the United States has more than doubled. The food technology industry has worked vigorously to design new additives that will imitate natural flavors and colors. Each new chemical additive can potentially bring great new profits to the company developing it. Additives such as texturizers that make food look better to consumers are popular. Food-taste enhancers are created by the hundreds. Ripening of vegetables is speeded up with ethylene gas, and potato sprouting is controlled by a suspected toxic chemical. Coloring is added to orange juice, egg yolks, and butter to make them look "real." Today food technology has become a massive operation attempting to make vegetables, fruits, meats, milk products, and processed foods look better than they are in reality, often helping food corporations disguise lesser-quality products from consumers. However, consumers are becoming more aware of the widespread use of potential poisons in their food. In 1989, when the Natural Resources Defense Council reported that consumers were ingesting dangerous amounts of daminozide, a possible carcinogen, as a result of eating apples sprayed with a product named Alar (used to enhance the appearance of red apples), people across the country reacted with anger.[195] Similar calls for regulation and reform have come from recent episodes of "mad-cow" disease in Great Britain and the United States. Increasing numbers of citizens are now calling for more government action to safeguard food, and demands for poison-free, organically grown foods have increased dramatically.

Critics of modern capitalism argue that many large stores have aisle after aisle of manufactured products no one really needs. This fact illustrates the dilemmas of a capitalistic society substantially oriented toward production for middle- to upper-income consumers. Industry's commitment to hyperconsumerism, driven by its desire for private profit, consumes enormous quantities of U.S. and world resources.

Typically, private-enterprise advocates and their neoclassical economic analyses neglect the unpaid social costs of private enterprise. In many cases, new technologies generate profits only because their total social costs are not factored into a cost–benefit analysis. Many business analysts today, as in the past, regard social costs such as air pollution and waste disposal accidents as minor disturbances, as "externalities," not as the central costs of private enterprise. Big capitalists, because of their power, are able to shift some costs of doing business onto individuals, smaller businesses, and the larger community. This cost shifting is a routine feature of our capitalistic system, not an accidental or occasional phenomenon. Indeed, much mass political protest over the last 150 years has been directed *against* capitalists' shifting of privately generated costs to the general public.[196] Government regulation has periodically attempted to reduce some social costs, to force businesses to pay for some of their air pollution, water pollution, injuries to workers, and so on. Much of this, usually limited, regulation has emerged because of public outcry against the social costs of private enterprise, yet today most social costs of production are still passed along because the regulations tend to be weakly written or enforced.

SUMMARY

Environmental issues have become central concerns for a growing number of the citizens of the United States and many other countries. Earth's fragile life zone is increasingly threatened by pollution of air, water, and soil and by the depletion of basic resources, including energy sources. Widespread pollution of surface and underground water is one major social cost of the U.S. private enterprise system. Worldwide pollution and contamination of drinking water in many areas illustrate the seriousness of introducing toxic chemicals into the natural environment without care. Much water, air, and land pollution is directly linked to the unsafe disposal of toxic wastes. Tens of thousands of potentially toxic chemicals and thousands of disposal sites have the potential of creating serious health hazards. Modern capitalistic production and its expanding technology have fostered, aggravated, or created enormous pollution problems whose costs are heavily borne by the outside community. Top executives in major U.S. firms fear that environmental regulations will make companies uncompetitive and unprofitable.

Rapid depletion of energy and other mineral resources is another environmental problem facing the United States, a country that uses a huge and disproportionate share of the world's resources. The energy crises in recent decades make it clear that energy is no longer a cheap resource, and global oil shortages are predicted for the next several decades. Much blame is placed on consumers and environmentalists for the oil crisis, but the unrestrained profit-seeking actions of major oil companies are substantially responsible for energy problems in the United States and other industrial countries. Similarly, the dominance of auto, bus, and truck transportation over railroads and mass transit has resulted in part from the aggressive profit-seeking behavior of corporate leaders who often ignore the major social costs of their products.

Nuclear power and weaponry both grew out of U.S. efforts to develop nuclear technology before the German Nazis did, yet in one of the great ironies of history, this technological advancement—once seen as the salvation of the human race, with its promise of cheap energy—has come to be a haunting specter threatening annihilation of Earth.

Nuclear power has lost its attractiveness to most of the U.S. citizenry, and even to most investors, because of its tremendous cost, highly toxic wastes, and potential for a major disaster. For these reasons, construction and operation of many nuclear power plants have been canceled. Existing nuclear power plants are not likely to be joined by hundreds more, as industry leaders once forecast. As a result, U.S. multinational corporations engaged in manufacturing reactors and building power plants are moving overseas, selling this dangerous technology to other nations. In addition to the problems mentioned previously, this overseas sales strategy involves yet another problem—nuclear weapons proliferation—since power plants generate materials that can be used for nuclear weapons.

The United States is the only country to have used nuclear weapons against civilians in a war, and this country has led all others in the number of weapons tests and weapons currently in its arsenal. Stronger militarily than the former Soviet Union and China, the United States and its NATO allies provide much of the world's weapon sales and dominate militarily and politically much of the world scene, with hundreds of U.S. and NATO military bases around the globe.

Within the United States, the military-industrial complex is a set of private corporations closely linked to Congress and the Department of Defense by huge, often wasteful, military contracts, exchanges of personnel, advisory committees, and well-paid lobbyists. The Department of Defense and this military-industrial complex have consumed trillions of dollars of the public's tax money in recent decades. Many Americans are increasingly critical of the waste and tragedy of such a raid on the public purse. Such government expenditures, or even a significant portion of them, spent in the civilian sector could, among other things, create jobs for the unemployed, housing for the poor and the homeless, food for hungry children, better health care systems, and improved schools and transportation systems for cities.

Defenders of the established ways of doing things argue that those who raise the issues of the social costs of energy, economic, or military-industrial growth are opposed to all growth and progress. Yet the real issue is not growth or no growth but the *character* and *quality* of that growth and *who* determines its direction. In traditional growth patterns in this society, many new technologies and their products have developed only because their social costs are not brought into a human cost–benefit analysis. This shifting of environmental costs to the general public is a routine feature of capitalistic growth. Narrowly conceived corporate and business investing and profit seeking have had devastating environmental effects. Such activity may seem rational for specific corporations in the short run, but it is irrational at the societal level because it destroys the water, air, and land in the ecosphere for all human beings. Much mass protest by ordinary worker-consumers has been, and likely will continue to be, directed at the shifting of privately generated costs by businesses to the general public.

STUDY QUESTIONS

1. In the United States, profits are privatized while social costs are socialized. Using water and air pollution as reference points, explain how U.S. businesses spread the burden of social costs to workers, consumers, and citizens.

2. How have U.S. businesses reacted to citizen and government pressures to clean up their industries?

3. Explain why alternative forms of energy, such as renewable (e.g., solar) resources, have not been fully developed in the United States.

4. Compare and contrast *soft* (e.g., solar) technologies with *hard* (e.g., nuclear) technologies. Discuss some of the implications for business of a concerted move from the use of hard to soft technologies.

5. Identify several of the most serious problems involved in developing nuclear energy.

6. What is the U.S. military-industrial complex? What role does it play in the perpetuation of the worldwide arms race?

ENDNOTES

1. Michael S. Baram, "Technology Assessment and Social Control," in Albert H. Teich, ed., *Technology and Man's Future,* 2nd ed. (New York: St. Martin's Press, 1977), p. 314.
2. Dick Russell, "You Are My River: The Small-Town Fight to Save the Great Mississippi," *Greenpeace* 13 (September–October 1988): 14–18.
3. Gary Boulard, "Combating Environmental Racism," *The Christian Science Monitor,* March 17, 1993, p. 8.
4. Bill Kaczor, "White Sands and Shiny Sea Belie Gulf of Mexico's Troubled Waters," *Los Angeles Times,* June 28, 1992, p. A8.
5. Russell, "You Are My River," pp. 14–18.
6. Mike Smith, "Region in Brief," *Atlanta Journal and Constitution,* March 7, 1993, p. A3.
7. Larry Ault, "Are the Fish Fit to Eat? Sides Differ," *Arkansas Democrat-Gazette,* April 21, 1995, p. A1; Berry Bass, "TDEC News," *Tennessee Environmental Law Letter,* January 1996, n.p.
8. Scorecard, "Environmental Releases for the Entire U.S." (ret. April 5, 2004), available at www.scorecard.org/env-releases/us.tcl.7.
9. Brad Knickerbocker, "Fewer Toxic Chemicals Sully the Environment," *The Christian Science Monitor,* May, 29, 2002, available at www.csmonitor.com/2002/0529/p02s02-uspo.htm.
10. "Environmentalists Concerned by Rise in Toxic Accidents," *Atlanta Journal and Constitution,* August 18, 1994, p. A8.

11. Dennis C. Pirages and Paul H. Ehrlich, *Ark II* (New York: Viking, 1974), pp. 9–10; John Robbins, *Diet for a New America* (Walpole, N.H.: Stillpoint Publishing, 1987), pp. 313–34.

12. Marla Cone, "DDT Ills Still Haunt the Coast: Years after Scientist Thought Threat from Pesticide Had Ended, a Dispute Rages over Whether a Vast Deposit off Palos Verdes Is Hurting Wildlife," *Los Angeles Times,* August 9, 1995, p. A1.

13. PANUPS (Pesticide Action Network Updates Service), "DuPont Withdraws Benlate from Market," May 7, 2001, available at www.panna.org/resources/panups/panup_20010507.dv.html.

14. Rebecca Clarren, "Fields of Poison," *The Nation,* December 29, 2003, available at www.thenation.com/docprint.mhtml?i=20031229&s=clarren.

15. U.S. Department of Labor, Bureau of Labor Statistics, *National Census of Fatal Occupational Injuries in 2002,* September 2003, available at www.bls.gov/news.release/pdf/cfoi.pdf.

16. Bill Edwards, "DuPont and Benlate: Is There a Coverup?" *FACT,* January 1993, p. 13; Robbins, *Diet for a New America,* pp. 308–49; "Non-chemical Alternatives Promote Sustainable Agriculture," Methyl Bromide Alternatives Network, 1996.

17. "Environmental Timeline," *Washington Times,* April 20, 1990, p. H3.

18. Scientific Assessment Panel of the Montreal Protocol on Substances that Deplete the Ozone Layer, Executive Summary, *Scientific Assessment of Ozone Depletion, 2002,* July 2002, available at www.epa.gov/docs/ozone/science/execsumm-saod2002.pdf.

19. "Ozone," *Greenpeace,* January–February–March 1993, p. 1; Corinna Gilfillan and Brett Hondorp, *Ozone Reality Check: Dispelling the Myths about Ozone Depletion* (Washington, D.C.: Friends of the Earth, 1995), pp. 1–10.

20. "White House Is Holding Up EPA Regulations," *Gainesville* (Fla.) *Sun,* October 1, 1992, p. 2.

21. Agricultural Research Service, *Methyl Bromide Research,* available at www.ars.usda.gov/is/mb/mebrweb.htm.

22. "Methyl Bromide Under Fire," *Environmental Health Perspectives,* 102(9), September 1994, available at ehis.niehs.nih.gov/docs/1994/102–9/forum.html.

23. Dan Strub, "Methyl Bromide: The Pesticide That Kills the Ozone Layer," *Friends of the Earth,* January 1993, pp. 8–10; Methyl Bromide Alternatives Network, "Methyl Bromide and Human Health," 1996.

24. Environmental Protection Agency, *The Accelerated Phaseout of Class 1 Ozone-Depleting Substances,* (ret. April 7, 2004), available at www.epa.gov/docs/ozone/title6/phaseout/accfact.html.

25. World Environmental News, "U.S. Seeks Delay in 2005 UN Methyl Bromide Ban," *Reuters News Service,* October 2, 2003, available at www.planetark.com/avantgo/dailynewsstory.cfm?newsid=19753.

26. "The Politics of Eliminating Methyl Bromide," Methyl Bromide Alternatives Network, 1996.

27. Scientific Assessment Panel of the Montreal Protocol on Substances That Deplete the Ozone Layer, Executive Summary, *Scientific Assessment of Ozone Depletion, 2002.*

28. Environmental Protection Agency, *Municipal Solid Waste* (ret. April 7, 2004), available at www.epa.gov/epaoswer/non-hw/muncpl/facts.htm; see also U.S. Bureau of the Census, *Statistical Abstract of the U.S., 2003,* available at www.census.gov/prod/2004pubs/03statab/geo.pdf.

29. Environmental Protection Agency, *Municipal Solid Waste.*

30. Michael Weisskopf, "EPA Issues First Rules for Landfills," *Washington Post,* September 12, 1991, p. A16.

31. Environmental Protection Agency, *Municipal Solid Waste.*

32. "Trash-to-Energy Goes Up in Smoke," *Greenpeace* 4 (January–February–March 1995): 2.

33. Diane K. Bartz, "America's Garbage," *Multinational Monitor,* November 1988, pp. 7–8; David Clark Scott, "Central American Presidents Seek a Regional Solution to Toxic Waste Imports," *Christian Science Monitor,* March 10, 1992, p. 5.

34. Alva Morrison, "The Nuclear Triangle: Has the Southwest Been Selected as America's Nuclear Waste Dump?" *E* 7 (January 1996): 24.

35. Errol Schweizer, "Environmental Justice: An Interview with Robert Bullard," *Earth First: A Radical Environmental Journal,* July 1999, available at www.ejnet.org/ej/bullard.html.

36. "Environmental Pollution: Insurance Issues," Insurance Information Institute Reports, February 1996.

37. U.S. Bureau of the Census, *Statistical Abstract of the U.S., 2003.*

38. Corie Brown and Vicky Cahan, "Not a Pretty Picture: The Toxic Spills at Kodak Park," *Business Week,* September 12, 1988, p. 39.

39. Mike Vogel, "County 3rd in Toxic Discharges: Three Local Firms among State's Top 10 Emitters," *Buffalo News,* November 23, 1994, p. 6.

40. Barbara O'Brien, "WNY Among 'Dirty Dozen' Polluters," *Buffalo News,* April 3, 2003, p. B3.

41. John Langone, "A Stinking Mess," *Time,* January 2, 1989, p. 45; see also Brian Meyer, "O-Cel-O to Install New Systems to Reduce Emissions," *Buffalo News,* April 21, 1999, p. 7D.

42. Florida Museum of Natural History, "Threats to Florida Bay" (ret. April 27, 2004), available at www.flmnh.ufl.edu/fish/southflorida/threats.html.

43. Spencer Reiss, "What's a Bay without Water?" *Newsweek,* November 2, 1992, p. 83.

44. U.S. Bureau of the Census, *Statistical Abstract of the U.S., 2003.*

45. Barry Commoner, *The Closing Circle* (New York: Alfred A. Knopf, 1971), pp. 155–58.

46. Environmental Protection Agency, "Providing Safe Drinking Water in America," *2000 National Public Water Systems Compliance Report,* July 2002, available at www.epa.gov/ogwdw/annual/sdwcom2002.pdf.

47. U.S. Public Interest Research Groups, March 1996; Gregory Wetstone, legislative director for the National Resources Defense Council, Testimony before the Committee on Commerce, U.S. House of Representatives, January 31, 1996, pp. 1–5.

48. K. William Kapp, *The Social Costs of Private Enterprise* (Cambridge, Mass.: Harvard University Press, 1950), pp. 86–92; Commoner, *Closing Circle,* pp. 140–77.

49. U.S. Environmental Protection Agency, *National Water Quality Inventory: 1994 Report to Congress, Executive Summary* (Washington, D.C.: 1994), pp. 12–25; Jenny Luesby, "Business and the Environment," *Financial Times,* June 7, 1995, p. 13.

50. U.S. Environmental Protection Agency, *Protecting Our Ground Water,* May 1995, pp. 2–3; U.S. Environmental Protection Agency, *National Water Quality Inventory: 1990 Report to Congress* (Washington, D.C.: 1992), pp. xviii, 113–16.

51. "Florida Beaches Closed 215 Times Due to Pollution," *Florida PIRG,* Fall 1995, p. 1; "Our Filthy Seas," *Time,* August 1, 1988, pp. 44–47.

52. Quoted in Kaczor, "White Sands and Shiny Sea Belie Gulf of Mexico's Troubled Waters," p. A8.

53. U.S. Bureau of the Census, *Statistical Abstract of the U.S., 2003.*

54. Friends of the Earth, *Fact Sheet,* November 1991, p. 2; Environmental Defense Fund, *Newsletter,* January 1993, pp. 2–3; "Life's a Beach," *Scotsman,* January 8, 1996, p. 10.

55. Bernard Mallee, "Durbin Wants to Curb Waste-Dumping by Cruise Ships," *St. Louis Post-Dispatch,* April 4, 2004, p. A9.

56. Stop Cruise Pollution, "Royal Carribbean's Environmental Record," (ret. April 7, 2004), available at www.stopcruisepollution.com/index.cfm?fuseaction=page&pageID=976.

57. Gregg Schmidt, "Legislators Promote Better Ocean Stewardship with Introduction of Clean Cruise Ship Act of 2004," The Ocean Conservancy, April 1, 2004, available at www.oceanconservancy.org/dynamic/press/releases/archive.htm?id=040401.

58. "Our Filthy Seas," pp. 47, 50.

59. Ibid., p. 49; see also PEW Oceans Commission, *America's Living Oceans: Charting a Course for Sea Change, A Report to the Nation,* May 2003, available at www.pewoceans.org/oceans/downloads/oceans_report.pdf.

60. U.S. Commission on Ocean Policy, *Preliminary Report of the U.S. Commission on Ocean Policy—Governors' Draft,* April 20, 2004, available at www.oceancommission.gov/documents/prelimreport/welcome.html#quick; see also Pew Oceans Commission, *America's Living Oceans.*

61. U.S. Bureau of the Census, *Statistical Abstracts of the U.S., 2003.*

62. Council on Economic Priorities, "Campaign for Cleaner Corporations," Research Report, December 1992, pp. 2–5; "Toxic Ten," *Mother Jones,* January–February 1993, pp. 40–41.

63. Michael Scherer, "Smoke Screen," *Mother Jones,* February 24, 2003, available at www.motherjones.com/news/update/2003/02/we_304_01.html.

64. "Urban Air Quality Shows Improvement, but," Clean Air Network Online Today, November 9, 1995; Elizabeth B. Thompson and Jayne E. Mardock, *Clean Air at the Crossroads* (Washington, D.C.: Clean Air Network, 1995), p. 1.

65. "Argonne National Lab Study," *Science News,* September 9, 1983, p. 206; "Air Pollution Study Issued," *American City and County* 104 (February 1989): 24; Sue Kirchhoff, "Study Says National Parks Overcrowded, Polluted," *The Reuter Business Report,* August 19, 1992.

66. Eric Pianin, "White House to End Power Plant Probes," *Washington Post,* November 6, 2003, p. A31, available at www.washingtonpost.com/ac2/wp-dyn/A6028–2003Nov5?language=printer.

67. Richard J. Barnet and Ronald E. Muller, *Global Reach* (New York: Simon & Schuster, 1974), pp. 343–44.

68. Commoner, *The Closing Circle,* pp. 262–63.

69. Kevin Gallagher, "Trade Liberalization and Industrial Pollution in Mexico: Lessons for the FTAA," Tufts University, Global Development and Environment Institute, October 2000; noted in Sarah Anderson and John Cavanagh, *Rethinking the NAFTA Record,* Institute for Policy Studies, August 8, 2002, available at www.ips-dc.org.

70. Patrick J. McDonnell, "Foreign-Owned Companies Add to Mexico's Pollution," *Los Angeles Times,* November 18, 1991, p. A1; Judy Pasternak, "Firms Find a Haven from U.S. Environmental Rules," *Los Angeles Times,* November 19, 1991, p. A1; Mark Fineman, "Environmental Nightmare on U.S.-Mexican Border Abates," *Los Angeles Times,* March 12, 1996, p. A8.
71. John Holusha, "Cleanup Industry Expects Growth," *New York Times,* December 1, 1992, p. D8.
72. Martha M. Hamilton, "Making a Product's Cost Reflect Pollution's Costs," *Washington Post,* November 29, 1992, p. H1.
73. Ibid.
74. Billie Sutherland, "Three Leaders in Prevention of Pollution Will Be Honored," *San Diego Business Journal,* September 18, 1995, p. 6.
75. Lenny Seigel, Gary Cohen, and Ben Goldman, *The U.S. Military's Toxic Legacy* (Boston: National Toxic Campaign Fund, 1991), p. 1.
76. Bob Feldman, "War on the Earth," *Dollars and Sense,* March/April 2003, pp. 24–27, available at www.dollarsandsense.org/archives/2003/0303maps.pdf; see also Project Censored, "U.S. Military's War on the Earth" (ret. April 23, 2004), available at www.projectcensored.org/publications/2004/15.html.
77. Ibid., pp. 2–3; Paul Hoversten, "Some Military Bases Will Never Be Cleaned Up," *USA Today,* July 5, 1991, p. 7A; "Crime & Safety Report," *Dayton Daily News,* January 3, 1996, p. 3B.
78. Seigel, Cohen, and Goldman, *The U.S. Military's Toxic Legacy,* pp. 4–5; Helaine Olen, "Huge Military Toxic Cleanup Fund Urged," *Los Angeles Times,* March 14, 1991, p. A34; see also Paul Hoversten, "Base Closings Won't End Problems with Toxic-Waste Sites," *USA Today,* March 22, 1993, p. 3A.
79. Seigel, Cohen, and Goldman, *The U.S. Military's Toxic Legacy,* p. 4.
80. Matt Sedensky, "After Decades of Bombing, Hawaiian Island Begins to Heal," *Environmental News Network,* April 13, 2004, available at www.enn.com/news/2004–04–13/s_22729.asp.
81. Natural Resources Defense Council, "In Harm's Way: The Pentagon's Push to Protect Polluters at the Expense of Public Health," April 21, 2004, available at www.nrdc.org/media/pressreleases/040421.asp.
82. Chuck Lindell, "Environmentalists Aim at Property Measures, Lobbies," *Austin American-Statesman,* April 9, 1995, p. B1.
83. Langdon Winner, "The Mice that Roared: Protest against Commercial Complex Development," *Massachusetts Institute of Technology Alumni Association Technology Review 97* (August 1994): 72.
84. Ibid.
85. Julie Tippett, draft chapter for "The Citizens Guide to Municipal Landfills" (Washington, D.C.: Friends of the Earth, unpublished report, 1994).
86. Peter Von Stackelberg, "White Wash: The Dioxin Coverup," *Greenpeace* 14 (March–April 1989): 7–11.
87. Friends of the Earth, "Cir Construction Stopped," May 7, 2004, available at www.foe.org/new/releases/504circ.html.
88. Richard C. Paddock, "Surfers Force Pulp Mills to Halt Ocean Pollution," *Los Angeles Times,* September 10, 1991, p. A1.
89. Ibid.
90. "Testimony, June 21, 1995, Karen Florimi, Senior Attorney, Environmental Defense Fund, House Transportation Water Resources and Environmental Committee," Federal Document Clearing House Congressional Testimony.
91. Boulard, "Combating Environmental Racism," p. 8.
92. Craig Quintana, "Why Are Poor, Black Neighborhoods a Dumping Ground for Pollution?" *Orlando Sentinel,* March 12, 1995, p. G1.
93. "Environmental Racism," *Race Relations Reporter,* August 15, 1994, p. 1.
94. Boulard, "Combating Environmental Racism," p. 8.
95. "No Plant, No Jobs, but a Louisiana Victory," *Atlanta Journal and Constitution,* November 1, 1992, p. M6.
96. Perkins Coie, "Environmental Groups Challenge New Dangerous Waste Rules," *Washington Environmental Compliance Update,* November 1995, n.p.; Heart of America Northwest is available at www.heartofamericanorthwest.org; Washington Toxics Coalition is available at www.watoxics.org/pages/root.aspx; People for Puget Sound is available at www.pugetsound.org; Sierra Club is available at www.sierraclub.org.
97. Michael E. Porter and Claas van der Linde, "Green and Competitive: Ending the Stalemate," *Harvard Business Review,* September–October 1995, p. 120.
98. "Behind the Curtain," *Mother Jones,* September/October 2003, available at www.motherjones.com/news/feature/2003/09/ma_534_01.html.

99. Council on Economic Priorities, "Campaign for Cleaner Corporations," Research Report, December 1992, pp. 2–5; "Toxic Ten," pp. 40–41.
100. Susan Q. Stranahan, "Broken Promises," *Sierra* (May–June 1988): 52–56.
101. Katherin N. Probst and David M. Konisky, *Superfund's Future: What Will It Cost?: A Report to Congress City & State?* (Washington, D.C.: Resources for the Future, 2001).
102. "Reilly Reiterates Superfund Successes," *Daily Report for Executives,* April 9, 1992, p. A33; John Nielsen, "The Failure of the Superfund Law: Part 5," *Morning Edition,* National Public Radio, September 16, 1994; Phillip Davis, "Superfund Law about to Run Out of Time and Money," Morning Edition, National Public Radio, February 7, 1995; Phillip Davis, "Republicans Want to Revamp Superfund Program," *Morning Edition,* National Public Radio, September 29, 1995.
103. Associated Press, "Ex-Official: Agency Covered up Ky. Spill," April 3, 2004; "Ex-Mine Official Alleges Spill Coverup," *Riverside Press-Enterprise,* April 3, 2004, p. A5; Bob Simon, "Who Is Jack Spadaro? "Mining Safety Advocate Blows the Whistle on Investigation Cut Short by Federal Government," *CBS News Transcript, 60 Minutes,* April 4, 2004, available at www.lexisnexis.com.
104. Shridath Ramphal, "In a North–South Gap, Seeds of Environmental Discord," *International Herald Tribune,* January 24, 1992.
105. U.S. Bureau of the Census, *Statistical Abstract of the U.S., 2003.*
106. Amory B. Lovins, "Prepared Testimony," in Hugh Nash, ed., *The Energy Controversy* (San Francisco: Friends of the Earth, 1979), pp. 23–24.
107. Marc Breslow, "Gluttons for Energy," *Dollars & Sense,* March 1993, pp. 7–9; quotation on pp. 7–8.
108. Breslow, "Gluttons for Energy," pp. 6–8; U.S. Bureau of the Census, *Statistical Abstract of the U.S., 1995,* pp. 601, 607.
109. Amory B. Lovins, "Energy Strategy: The Road Not Taken?" *Foreign Affairs* 55 (October 1976): 65–83.
110. Lovins, "Prepared Testimony," pp. 21–24.
111. "Toward Energy Efficiency," *The Polling Report,* March 22, 1993, p. 8.
112. "Cyrus Generates Interest in Solar Power," *Greenpeace* (January–February–March 1995): 2.
113. U.S. Bureau of the Census, *Statistical Abstract of the U.S., 2003.*
114. Robert D. Bullard, Glenn S. Johnson, and Angel O. Torres, "Race, Equity, and Smart Growth: Why People of Color Must Speak for Themselves," The Center for Environmental Justice (ret. April 29, 2004), available at www.ejrc.cau.edu/raceequitysmartgrowth.htm#nrg%20consump.
115. U.S. Bureau of the Census, *Statistical Abstract of the U.S., 2003.*
116. Ibid.; Jack Doyle, *Crude Awakening: The Oil Mess in America* (Washington, D.C.: Friends of the Earth, 1994), p. 5; Breslow, "Gluttons for Energy," p. 6; Jeffrey Denny, "King of the Road," *Common Cause,* May–June 1991, pp. 19–20.
117. U.S. Bureau of the Census, *Statistical Abstract of the U.S., 2003.*
118. "Scientific Symposium Examines Exxon *Valdez* Aftermath," *All Things Considered,* National Public Radio, February 5, 1993; "Damages of $5 Billion Awarded for '89 Exxon Oil Spill," *Weekend Edition,* National Public Radio, September 17, 1994.
119. Lieff, Cabraser, Heinman & Bernstein, LLP (plaintiff's attorney), "Exxon *Valdez* Oil Disaster" (ret. April 27, 2004), available at www.lieffcabraser.com/wbh_exxart.htm.
120. Breslow, "Gluttons for Energy," p. 9.
121. U.S. Bureau of the Census, *Statistical Abstract of the U.S., 1995,* pp. 711, 814.
122. Michael Harrington, *The Twilight of Capitalism* (New York: Simon & Schuster, 1976), pp. 239–50.
123. Doyle, *Crude Awakening,* pp. 3–7, 14–56, 85–144; quotation on p. 7.
124. Ibid., pp. 145–71; see also Harrington, *The Twilight of Capitalism,* pp. 239–50.
125. "Common Cause Urges Senate to Act to End Corporate Welfare Programs," *Common Cause* (ret. April 27, 2004), available at www.ccsi.com/~comcause/news/corwel.html; "Energy Bill Agains Sinks on Ethanol Tax Fight," *World Environmental News* (ret. April 27, 2004), available at www.planetark.com; "Bush's Ruling Class," *Common Cause,* April–May–June 1992, pp. 16–17, 22–23; "The Real Cost of Ethanol," *Mother Jones,* July–August 1995, p. 47.
126. See U.S. Bureau of the Census, *Statistical Abstract of the U.S., 2003;* Barry Weisberg, *Beyond Repair* (Boston: Beacon Press, 1971), p. 105.
127. Larry Sawers, "Urban Form and the Mode of Production," *Review of Radical Political Economics* 7 (Spring 1975): 54.
128. Victor Papanek, *Design for the Real World* (New York: Random House, 1971), pp. 300–301.
129. Robert D. Bullard, Glenn S. Johnson, and Angel O. Torres, "Race, Equity, and Smart Growth: Why People of Color Must Speak for Themselves," The Center for Environmental Justice (ret. April 29, 2004), available at www.ejrc.cau.edu/raceequitysmartgrowth.htm#nrg%20consump.

130. President's National Urban Policy Report, quoted in Eric Goldstein and Steven Jurow, "Community Conservation Guidance," *Amicus Journal* 2 (Summer 1980): 8; see also Emma Rothschild, *Paradise Lost* (New York: Random House, 1973), pp. 246–47.

131. Bradford C. Snell, "American Ground Transport," in Joe R. Feagin, ed., *The Urban Scene* (New York: Random House, 1979), pp. 239–66.

132. See General Motors' reply to U.S. Senate Subcommittee on Antitrust and Monopoly in Larry Sawers, "American Ground Transportation Reconsidered," *Review of Radical Political Economics* 11 (Fall 1979): 66–69; see also Stuart Ewen, *Captains of Consciousness* (New York: McGraw-Hill, 1976), pp. 23–24, 31–32, 45.

133. Michael Mariotte, "The Resurgence of Nuclear Power in America," *Multinational Monitor,* January–February 1989, pp. 9–11.

134. U.S. Bureau of the Census, *Statistical Abstracts of the U.S., 2003;* see also Energy Information Administration, U.S. Department of Energy, "U.S. Nuclear Reactors" (ret. April 28, 2004), available at www.eia.doe.gov.

135. David Lapp, "The Price of Power: Atomic Energy's Free Ride," *Multinational Monitor,* January–February 1993, p. 23; "Is There a Future for Nuclear Power?" *Nucleus* 3 (Fall–Winter 1980): 5–6; Robert Weissman, "A Nuclear Tombstone," *Multinational Monitor,* April 1992, p. 7; Dan Charles, "No More Nuclear Power Plants Being Built in the U.S.," *Morning Edition,* National Public Radio, December 13, 1994.

136. "As Shoreham Goes," *The Nation,* June 11, 1988, p. 811; Gary Lee, "NRC Expands Investigation at Connecticut Nuclear Plant," *Washington Post,* March 9, 1996, p. A2; Charles, "No More Nuclear Power Plants Being Built in the U.S."; "Dismantling of the Shoreham Nuclear Plant Is Completed," *New York Times,* October 13, 1994, p. B6.

137. Lapp, "The Price of Power," p. 22.

138. Ibid., p. 21.

139. Matthew L. Wald, "Dismantling Nuclear Reactors," *Scientific American,* March 3, 2003.

140. "How Nuclear Power Works," The Union of Concerned Scientists (ret. April 28, 2004), available at www.ucsusa.org/clean_energy/renewable_energy/page.cfm?pageID=85.

141. Charlie Higley, Public Citizen's Critical Mass Energy Project, "The Future of Nuclear Energy," December 2, 1999, available at www.citizen.org/cmep/energy_enviro_nuclear/nuclear_power_plants/nuclear_revival/articles.cfm?ID=4167; "How Nuclear Power Works," The Union of Concerned Scientists.

142. Lapp, "The Price of Power," p. 9–10.

143. David E. Lilienthal, *Atomic Energy: A New Start* (New York: Harper and Row, 1980), pp. 12–16; quotation on p. 16.

144. "Nuclear Reactor Containments: Sieve or Shield?" Briefing Paper, Union of Concerned Scientists, January 1993.

145. David Lochbaum, *Nuclear Plant Risk Studies: Failing the Grade,* Union of Concerned Scientists, August 2000, available at www.ucsusa.org/clean_energy/nuclear_safety/page.cfm?pageID=181.

146. Gary Lee, "NRC Expands Investigation at Connecticut Nuclear Plant," *Washington Post,* March 9, 1996, p. A2.

147. Julie Gozan, "Nuke Leaks," *Multinational Monitor,* September 1992, p. 4.

148. Jim Donahue, "The Westinghouse Web," *Multinational Monitor,* March 1992, p. 28.

149. Robert Pollard, *U.S. Nuclear Power Plants—Showing Their Age: Case Study: Core Shroud Cracking* (Washington, D.C.: Union of Concerned Scientists, 1995), pp. 1–10; Robert Pollard, *U.S. Nuclear Power Plants—Showing Their Age: Case Study: Steam Generator Corrosion* (Washington, D.C.: Union of Concerned Scientists, 1995), pp. 1–14; Robert Pollard, *U.S. Nuclear Power Plants—Showing Their Age: Case Study: Reactor Pressure Vessel Embrittlement* (Washington, D.C.: Union of Concerned Scientists, 1995), pp. 1–11.

150. David L. Chandler, "Dismantling Yankee Rowe," *Boston Globe,* June 5, 1995, p. 25.

151. "Occupying Reactor Cooling Tower to End Nuclear Nightmare," *Greenpeace* 4 (October–November–December 1995): 3.

152. "Yucca Mountain, Nevada," *Scientific American,* June 1988, p. 18; Lapp, "The Price of Power," p. 23.

153. Editorial, "Is Nuclear Power Ready," *Scientific American,* January 13, 2002; John Nielsen, "Nuclear Waste Disposal Bill Draws Controversy," *Weekend Edition,* National Public Radio, December 24, 1995.

154. Quoted in Lapp, "The Price of Power," p. 23.

155. Steve Nadis, "Man against a Mountain," *Scientific American,* February 10, 2003, available at www.sciam.com/article.cfm?articleID=0004CF54–4981–1E40-89E0809EC588EEDF&sc=I100322; see also Greg Mone, "Scientists Voice Concerns About Yucca Mountain Repository,"

Scientific American, April 26, 2002, available at www.sciam.com/article.cfm?articleID= 000C21B5–1263–1CD0-B4A8809EC588EEDF&sc=I100322.

156. Lapp, "The Price of Power."
157. Nadis, "Man against a Mountain."
158. Jeff Nesmith, "E-mails Could Foil Nuclear Disposal Plan," *The Atlanta Journal-Constitution* (April 5, 2005), p. 13A; "Toxic E-Mails," *The Washington Post* (April 10, 2005), p. B06; "Falsified Data Alleged in Nuke Waste Project," *The Times-Picayune* (April 17, 2005), p. 5.
159. Donahue, "The Westinghouse Web," p. 31.
160. Tom Morganthau, "Nuclear Danger and Deceit," *Newsweek,* October 31, 1988, p. 29.
161. "Outrage at Oak Ridge," *Multinational Monitor,* March 1993, p. 33.
162. Ed Magnuson, "They Lied to Us," *Time,* October 31, 1988, p. 63; Morganthau, "Nuclear Danger and Deceit," p. 29.
163. Danielle Gordon, "The Verdict: No Harm, No Foul; Report of the Advisory Committee on Human Radiation Experiments," *Bulletin of the Atomic Scientists* 52 (January 1996): 32.
164. Magnuson, "They Lied to Us" Morganthau, "Nuclear Danger and Deceit" Donahue, "The Westinghouse Web." p. 30.
165. Dick Thompson, "Bad Scene at Rocky Flats," *Time,* October 24, 1988, p. 77; Dick Thompson, "Big Trouble at Savannah River," *Time,* October 17, 1988, p. 55; Andre Carothers, "The Death of Ellenton," *Greenpeace,* June 1988, p. 14.
166. "National News Briefing," *Rocky Mountain News,* February 21, 1996, p. 41A.
167. Minard Hamilton, "Nuclear Waste Dilemma," *USA Today,* March 1989, pp. 45–46.
168. Carothers, "The Death of Ellenton," p. 15; Donahue, "The Westinghouse Web," p. 31; George Lobsenz, "Environmentalists Contest Savannah River Restart Plan," *The Energy Daily,* May 24, 1994, n.p.
169. Donahue, "The Westinghouse Web," p. 31; "Consortium to Study Chernobyl," *Nuclear News,* April 1995, p. 51.
170. Charles Seabrook, "The Bomb's Legacy," *The Atlanta Journal and Constitution,* November 26, 2000, p. 1C.
171. "Three Mile Island: The Lesson Avoided," *Nucleus* 3 (Fall–Winter 1980): 9; see also McKinley C. Olson, *Unacceptable Risk* (New York: Bantam Books, 1976), pp. 21–33; "The Browns Ferry Scram Failure," *Nucleus* 3 (Fall–Winter 1980): 4.
172. Joby Warrick, "Study Links Three Mile Island Radiation Releases to Higher Cancer Rates," *Washington Post,* February 24, 1997, p. A06, available at www.washingtonpost.com/wp-srv/national/longterm/tmi/stories/study022497.htm.
173. Lapp, "The Price of Power," p. 22.
174. Todd Mason and Corie Brown, "Juanita Ellis: Antinuke Saint or Sellout?" *Business Week,* October 24, 1988, pp. 84, 86; Weissman, "A Nuclear Tombstone," p. 7; Donahue, "The Westinghouse Web," p. 31.
175. Jeffrey Denny, "Star Struck," *Common Cause,* March–April 1991, pp. 25–29.
176. Quoted in Lee Siegel, "USU Infrared Telescope Has Role in Controversial Missile-Defense System *Spirit III,*" *Salt Lake Tribune,* April 4, 1996, p. C1.
177. "B-2 Funding a Tribute to Lobbyists," *Sun-Sentinel* (Fort Lauderdale), December 30, 1995, p. 14A.
178. This section and the following two sections were written with the help of Lester Kurtz; Max Weber, *The Religion of China* (New York: Free Press, 1951); Roland Bainton, *Christian Attitudes toward War and Peace* (New York: Abingdon Press, 1960).
179. Michael Mann, "Capitalism and Militarism," in Martin Shaw, ed., *War, State and Society* (New York: St. Martin's Press, 1984), p. 27; Andrew Wilson, *The Disarmer's Handbook* (Harmondsworth: Penguin Books, 1983); Ruth Leger Sivard, *World Military and Social Expenditures: 1985* (Washington, D.C.: World Priorities, 1985); Randall Collins, "Three Faces of Cruelty: Towards a Comparative Sociology of Violence," *Theory and Society* 1 (1974): 415–40.
180. Paul R. Ehrlich, Carl Sagan, Donald Kennedy, and Walter Orr Roberts, *The Cold and the Dark: The World after Nuclear War* (New York: W. W. Norton & Co., Inc., 1984).
181. C. Wright Mills, *The Causes of World War Three* (Westport, Conn.: Greenwood Press, 1976).
182. The report is quoted in Gordon, "The Verdict: No Harm, No Foul," p. 32.
183. Ibid.
184. U.S. Bureau of the Census, *Statistical Abstract of the U.S., 2003.*
185. Quoted in Helen Caldicott, *Missile Envy* (New York: William Morrow, 1984), p. 82.
186. Gordon Adams, *The Politics of Defense Contractors: The Iron Triangle* (New Brunswick, N.J.: Transaction Books, 1982).
187. See "Just the Facts," *Common Cause,* January–February–March 1992, p. 4.

188. Jeff Erlich, "Loan Support Will Not Boost U.S. Arms Sales," *Defense News,* February 27, 1995/March 5, 1995, p. 26.

189. Michael Dobbs, "U.S. Had Key Role in Iraq Buildup: Trade in Chemical Arms Allowed Despite Their Use on Iranians, Kurds," *Washington Post,* December 20, 2002, p. A01, available at www.washingtonpost.com/ac2/wp-dyn/A52241-2002Dec29?language=printer.

190. Peter Montgomery, "Re-Arm the World," *Common Cause,* May–June 1991, pp. 25–29, 36; quotation on p. 27.

191. Michael Remez, "Disarmament Groups Go on Attack Against Defense Industry Lobbying," *Hartford Courant,* November 14, 1995, p. A5.

192. Montgomery, "Re-Arm the World"; quotation on p. 29.

193. Seymour Melman, *Profits without Production* (New York: Alfred A. Knopf, 1983), pp. 43, 262.

194. Papanek, *Design for the Real World,* p. xxi.

195. Orville Schell, "What This Country Needs Is a Stronger White Rat," *Mother Jones* 4 (February–March 1979): 37–38; Margaret Carlson, "Do You Dare to Eat a Peach?" *Time,* March 27, 1989, pp. 24–27.

196. Kapp, *The Social Costs of Private Enterprise,* pp. 9–16.

chapter 12

Remedying Social Problems

When Joe Gunton left the Army, he'd seen the sights of Vietnam, South Korea, and Germany. After 21 years in uniform, he looked forward to coming home to America. He settled into the pastel suburb of Coral Springs, outside Fort Lauderdale.

And then he fled the country in dismay. "The first time I saw a guy standing by a freeway ramp holding a sign saying, 'Will Work for Food,' I thought, 'What the hell is going on?' Law and order was not present. The crime rate was more than I wanted to tolerate."

Today, Gunton and his family live outside Heidelberg, Germany, a 1,000-year-old university town set among castles and vineyards. Life is pleasant.[1]

Joe Gunton is one of many former U.S. military personnel who have decided to stay abroad. As one young lieutenant explained, "A lot of soldiers get out and stay here [Germany]. There's very little crime. . . . You don't see people in the street hungry. . . . You don't see trash and garbage and ghettos."[2]

In the United States, we often celebrate the "free market" as a solution for social and economic problems here and overseas, even though that capitalistic market has created serious problems and crises everywhere. Some analysts of the U.S. domestic economy predict its significant decline in coming decades. U.S. firms are now part of a global system and are competing with firms in Europe and Japan. Moreover, large U.S. multinationals are directing more and more of their profit-making and investment activities overseas—to low-wage areas such as Brazil, Mexico, Malaysia, Sri Lanka, India, and China—even as they close U.S. plants and cut the number of decent-paying jobs in the United States.

The real wages of U.S. workers, as well as the income and standard of living of many families, have declined in recent decades. While many large corporations have made huge profits during this period, these economic "advances" have come at great cost to workers and have been accompanied by increasing signs of trouble within the business sector itself. As Berch Berberoglu has pointed out, the "decline in capacity utilization in the manufacturing industry, record trade deficits, growing unemployment, decline in real wages and purchasing power, small-business bankruptcies and farm foreclosures, bank failures, a shaky international financial system, record government deficits, and a highly speculative stock market" are all grave symptoms of a seriously troubled U.S. economy, albeit one often ignored or rationalized by politicians and the media.[3]

This sorry state of affairs need not be a cause for great pessimism. Progressive change is possible and, more importantly, quite necessary. The United States can become a better place, socially and economically, for all. Citizen action has brought progressive change in the past, and it can bring similar change in the future.

GOALS OF THIS CHAPTER

This concluding chapter explores views on how the American people could replace or rebuild the existing social system. We examine people's movements and the problems they target. This chapter reviews alternative political–economic systems and examines the ways we could restructure U.S. society to better meet all its citizens' needs. We begin the chapter with a critical analysis of the role of the mass media and its control over the information that Americans receive.

THE MASS MEDIA AND INFORMATION CONTROL

The Mass Media

Some readers may wonder why they have heard or seen little power–conflict analysis of the problems discussed in this book. A major reason is that the mass media, their assertions to the contrary notwithstanding, are in fact *controlled* media. A small handful of corporations own most of the mass media. Both the concentration and centralization of control of the media—including the news services that provide most news carried by local TV, radio, and newspapers—have increased steadily in recent decades. In 1983, 50 corporations owned and controlled most U.S. news media, but this number has shrunk to *six* huge conglomerates (Time Warner, Disney, Bertelsmann, Viacom, New Corporation, and Vivendi Universal) dominating the media of the entire Western world in the early 2000s.[4] The profit orientation of large corporations often conflicts with the news media's objective of bringing accurate information to the public. Advertisements almost totally support television; magazines and newspapers depend on advertising revenue for much of their income. Fairness and Accuracy in Reporting (FAIR), a media watch group, has shown that corporate ownership and sponsorship of the media often inhibit the point of view from which journalists present information, which information they include, and which sources they consult.[5] In the vast majority of cases, FAIR studies have found, journalists rely heavily on "official government sources" or corporate experts to the exclusion of truly independent analysts and critics. Rather than serving the function of keeping watch over the three official branches of the U.S. government, FAIR spokesperson Martin Lee says, "the media seem to function as a fourth branch of government."[6] Media analyst Edward Herman has noted the relationship between network TV's increased competition from cable news channels and the increased control over programming that networks have given to corporate advertisers.[7]

A high degree of homogeneity characterizes the U.S. news media; most news sources present similar coverage from roughly the same politically moderate-to-conservative point of view. Most of the news media are *not* liberal in their dominant point of view. A broad diversity of political and economic perspectives is *not* part of regular news programming in the United States, and a consumer's "free choice" of information is limited. Systematic power–conflict perspectives exploring class, racial, and gender issues *in depth* are indeed quite *rare* in the mainstream TV, radio, and print media. A poll that included questions about both domestic issues and foreign policy, commissioned by FAIR found that "the *more* television news people watched, the less they knew about the issues being raised in the campaign. . . . People were more familiar with trivia and less important matters than with . . . more important issues. . . . Something was wrong in terms of where they were getting their information."[8] Almost two-thirds of the members of the nonpartisan consumer group Common Cause who responded to a similar poll agreed, "The role played by television in American politics has been a major factor in the breakdown of our political system."[9]

Frequent or in-depth explorations of the fundamental role of class, racial, and gender stratification in social problems are not in the self-interest of the media's conservative owners. While the journalists' code of ethics pressures them to sever ties with organizations on which they are reporting to avoid conflicts of interest, media owners routinely violate this ethical standard. Media companies are generally part of large diversified conglomerates. Media people interviewed by FAIR noted that "when the same corporations that own and sponsor the media are the ones to be investigated," the whole notion of freedom of the press in the United States is problematic. For example, in the mid 2000s General Electric (GE) owns the large media network NBC. GE is a builder of nuclear plants and weapons and one of the country's biggest polluters. Yet GE's polluting activities receive little coverage in the mainstream media. When asked in a televised debate why NBC had not covered the pollution of the Hudson River, into which GE dumped more than 4,000 pounds of toxic PCBs a few years ago, the executive producer of the *NBC Nightly News* stated that he did not have enough money to

cover every story. Yet as Martin Lee of FAIR has pointed out, NBC found money for a documentary, "Nuclear Power: In France It Works," promoting nuclear power.[10]

The media's self-censorship process limits coverage of controversial issues. Many news reports are brief or superficial rather than comprehensive, and they generally omit the names of corporations responsible for problems under discussion. Commercial media analysts seldom criticize the capitalistic system in any systematic way. Edward Herman has pointed out that GE is one of several corporations funding a variety of "allegedly 'non-partisan' but ideologically directed research institutes, who finance and publicize the work of approved 'experts'"[11]

Even though the U.S. Constitution protects freedom of expression (freedom of the press) under the First Amendment, a fundamental dilemma with the media is that it lacks sustained, regular, and in-depth coverage of many societal problems detailed in previous chapters of this book. Rarely do journalists produce *in-depth* and *critical* stories on these major social problems.

PREPOLITICAL THOUGHT?

As a result of home, school, church, and media socialization and training, many Americans often sound conservative in their views on personal and societal problems. Many people are harshly critical of the poor, welfare recipients, feminists, and gays and lesbians. They also can be supportive of free markets, corporate profits, traditional gender roles, and the right of business to dispose of property as it sees fit. Many say they fear a "welfare state" and "socialism." Some people are consistently conservative on major social issues, while a small minority holds a consistently radical perspective on the same issues. Yet many people who are conservative on the aforementioned issues hold liberal or radical beliefs on other issues. They can be very critical of big oil companies for overpricing and oil spills, of political corruption, and of pollution-producing corporations. They can be very critical of the corporate corruption and multinationals moving jobs overseas. They can be very critical of governmental adventures overseas, such as recent invasions of Iraq. Eric Hobsbawm calls this inconsistency in ordinary people's views *prepolitical thought* or consciousness. Prepolitical thought has not yet reached the level of full political or class-consciousness. The U.S. majority's perspective on personal and social problems is not yet consistent enough to enable them to see the *deep* roots of societal problems and to organize to work for large-scale social and political change.[12]

Most rank-and-file Americans continue to tell pollsters that they want a healthier environment and a better health care system. Large majorities express strong criticisms of business and industry. For example, more than two-thirds of Americans agree with the statement "The way most companies work, the only thing management cares about is profits, regardless of what workers want or need," and three-quarters agree that corporations should pay more of their profits to workers and less to shareholders.[13]

Most people are critical of big government as well, although many are inconsistent. They see the size of the federal government and its high level of spending as contributing to inflation and other economic problems. Two-thirds of respondents favor smaller government with fewer services.[14] At the same time, most of these same people believe strongly in existing government programs that benefit them, such as Social Security, Medicare, and unemployment insurance, as well as in the expansion of government programs in such areas as health care and safety. More than three-quarters of respondents believe that the government should *guarantee* medical care for all who do not have health insurance, and more than half believe that the government should see to it that everyone who wants a job has a job.[15]

In addition, relatively *small* percentages of Americans have "a great deal of confidence" in people running Congress, the executive branch of the federal government, and the White House.[16] Respondents believe that the federal government wastes more than one-third of the money it collects.[17] This widespread distrust of government may reflect why relatively low numbers of citizens (as compared to citizens of European countries) participate in most local, state, and federal elections.

Over the last few decades, there has been a dramatic rise in the "religious right" in the United States, including groups such as the Christian Coalition. These archconservative groups draw on the discontent of people with their government. Ralph Reed resigned from the leadership of the Christian Coalition in 1997, but before his departure he argued that U.S. voters overwhelmingly support the coalition's archconservative positions. Yet a national survey found that a majority of voters reject nearly every position in the coalition's "Contract with the American Family." A majority of voters believe, for example, that they are more likely to support a political candidate who holds to the position that the "choice on abortion should generally be left up to the woman and her doctor, with few legal restrictions." Even born-again Christian voters *support* pro-choice candidates. Majorities of these same voters reject vouchers for private and religious schools, replacing public welfare programs with private charity, abolishing the U.S. Department of Education, and abolishing federal aid for the arts and public broadcasting. In spite of their concerns about "big government" in the abstract, a majority of U.S. voters are relatively liberal on most of these major issues and reject much of a right-wing political agenda.[18]

PEOPLE PROTESTING AND ORGANIZING FOR CHANGE

From the founding of the United States, Americans have regularly organized themselves to try to solve some of the problems created by a capitalist, racist, and sexist system. A strong strain of democratic reform has supported a democratizing of the economy and a greater democratization of politics. People's movements and organizations vary in the extent of societal reform that they seek. Some seek limited reforms only in one area; others seek massive reforms in one area; and yet others seek major society-wide reforms, which, if implemented, would transform U.S. capitalism into a quite different sociopolitical system.

In the late nineteenth century, for example, organizations such as the Farmers Alliance spread throughout the South and the Midwest. Hundreds of thousands of poor farmers joined in organizations whose goals included greater regulation of railroads, banks, and grain combines, which were routinely exploiting the country's poorer farmers. The key state of Texas had 2,000 units of the Farmers Alliance, with 100,000 members. These people's organizations drew up lists of demands protesting abuse of farmers and urban workers by powerful employers. Specific demands included legal recognition of unions and farmer organizations, stiff regulation of railroads, corporate taxes, a federally administered banking system, a flexible currency system, high taxes on speculative land deals, and an end to speculation in farm commodities. Numerous U.S. socialist movements developed in the early part of the twentieth century. In 1912, a thousand members of the Socialist Party of America held elected office as mayors and state legislators in the United States. In that same year, the eloquent Eugene V. Debs received almost a million votes as a Socialist candidate for president. Government repression and internal organizational factors brought a sharp decline in that political party's regular members by the 1920s, but social legislation eventually implemented many of its reform proposals. Most public discussions today have forgotten these large-scale progressive movements.[19]

Movements for state Communism, such as existed in Eastern Europe and the former Soviet Union from the 1920s through the 1980s, have never taken root in U.S. soil. Imitators of foreign radicalism have been unimportant. Rather, homegrown radicalism has been far more important—the populist, union, democratic socialist, and civil rights movements that have demonstrated large-scale, working-class resistance to repressive political and economic authorities. According to David De Leon, we find "the spirit of our radicalism not in Lenin but in Debs, not in the USSR, but in the IWW, not in the Chinese peasants, but in the Populists. . . . Our radicals have concentrated on emancipation, on breaking the prisons of authority, rather than on planning any reconstruction."[20] In other words, organized Americans working for progressive change have usually been clearer about what oppression they are against than about the political–economic system they would prefer to see replace advanced monopoly capitalism.

Our troubled society has provided fertile soil for the emergence of people's groups of many kinds. Grassroots movements, such as women's organizations, black and Latino civil rights groups, gay rights organizations, and unions of many kinds, have used a variety of strategies to bring progressive changes. Civil disobedience and class-action lawsuits have expanded the rights and opportunities of subordinated Americans. For example, some of the modest civil rights and equal opportunity legislation of the 1960s and 1970s, often activated by court cases, has led to improvements in the conditions of women and people of color. Today, grassroots pressure for progressive reform continues to manifest itself—sometimes at the ballot box and sometimes with civil disobedience or rioting. People are still fighting back against the dominant class, racial, and gender groups that are burdening and exploiting them. Many working-class Americans continue to fight the established authorities by joining unions. People of color join civil rights organizations and struggle for equal rights and equal opportunities. Progressive movements are often small groups, but they can have an impact far greater than their numbers. Gay and lesbian groups have pressed for expanded civil rights, including the right to legally recognized marriages (as was recently achieved in the state of Massachusetts). Workers' unions have forced positive wage and benefit changes affecting large numbers of workers and have tried to force reconsideration of corporate commitments to overseas investments that cost U.S. jobs. Since 1900, unions have frequently forced business leaders and their government allies to implement a variety of important social programs, ranging from unemployment compensation to environmental and workplace protection laws.

Numerous progressive movements have changed the face of government at local and national levels. Demands from ordinary Americans have been critical to the growth of government social programs. Sometimes dominant groups' concessions to progressive reform efforts have allowed limited reforms, with the goal of further perpetuating or legitimizing the capitalistic system. The compromises that reform-oriented groups have had to make with business interests indicate the limitations of progressive reform movements in the United States. We can only wait and see whether a larger-scale progressive movement that can restructure society in more massive and progressive ways will yet arise in the United States.[21]

In recent years, millions of activists have taken part in citizens' groups across the country. In his book *The Great Divide,* Studs Terkel writes:

> A bantam housewife in Chicago leads her blue-collar neighbors in a challenge to the Waste Management Corporation, a powerful multinational. She beats the outfit: there will be no toxic-waste dump in the neighborhood. A local, Bob Bagley, let Congress know about

Thousands of pro-choice women demonstrate on the Washington, D.C. mall in opposition to conservative Republican policies on abortion and family planning. (Rick Steele/UPI/ Landov LLC)

somebody's spray trucks hauling dioxin through his forgotten town in the Ozark foothills. He won the battle. Name a place, a big-city block or a village square, and you'll find corporate dumpers with tigers by the tails.[22]

Many organizations have been relatively successful in dealing with local social problems, although they have had fewer successes uniting with one another to deal with national problems. Still, nationwide organizing for progressive issues does take place from time to time. In 1989, 1992, and again in 2004, abortion-rights supporters demonstrated in Washington, D.C., to protest the threatened movement of the Supreme Court away from the right of women to have legal abortions and to oppose the erosion of reproductive freedoms under recent conservative presidential administrations.[23] Thousands of Americans—men and women; young and old; black, Latino, Indian, Asian, and white; low-income and middle-income; gay and heterosexual—have learned the problems of organizing and the successes that come from organizing and have the strong feeling that they *can* fight back successfully against powerful establishments that often oppress them.

Women's Groups

The contemporary women's movement for greater equality came dramatically onto the national stage in the 1960s. More women were working outside the home, but wages and working conditions often remained poor, and male domination in the economy and government remained entrenched. Women have long joined in movements for progressive reform, such as those for black civil rights. In recent decades, women have pressed for their own women's causes. Protesting women became the target of rage for many in the dominant male group, who often stereotyped them as "bra burners," but the counterattacks did not stop the movement. New progressive organizations sprang up, such as the National Organization for Women.[24]

Women have organized many feminist groups in all types of communities; these groups discuss and implement feminist ideas in many areas, often without specific reference to the term *feminism.* One major example was the organization of women flight attendants to fight sexist working conditions, discriminatory management practices, and sexist advertising by airlines, such as, "Hi, I'm Cheryl. Fly Me!"[25] Various groups of working women have organized to cope with discrimination in jobs and careers. These women have worked together on problems with male superiors and coworkers, with bureaucratic red tape, and with institutionalized sexist practices. One organization, Women Employed, formed in 1973, combats discrimination in pay and working conditions.[26] Women Employed provides career counseling, networking information, and professional development seminars, as well as advice and counseling services on job problems and workplace discrimination, to its 1,800 members in the Chicago area. It is a national leader in research and advocacy to advance women's rights and opportunities in the workplace. Through its lobbying activities, Women Employed brings to national policymakers a grassroots perspective on issues affecting women.

Another national women's organization, 9 to 5: National Association of Working Women, whose membership has grown dramatically since its founding in 1973 by a group of office workers in Boston, has representatives in 250 U.S. cities and operates a toll-free job problem hotline to help women in white-collar jobs with problems of discrimination. This organization's lobbying efforts helped ensure that the 1991 Civil Rights Act covered the victims of sexual harassment and contributed to the passage of the 1993 federal Family Leave Act.[27] More recently, the organization was involved in speaking out against President George W. Bush's proposed cuts to the Equal Employment Opportunity Commission created under Title VII of the 1964 Civil Rights Acts to eliminate illegal discrimination in the workplace.[28]

Other grassroots organizations have sprung up to address particular problems. For example, following the 1992 Los Angeles riot, women from that city's ravaged area formed a coalition to pressure the leaders of the organization Rebuild L.A. to include women's concerns for housing, child care, and transit in its renewal plans.[29] Similarly, the Asian Immigrant Women Advocates organization, founded in 1983 in Oakland, California, addresses labor and other economic concerns and works to empower its members.[30]

La Mujer Obrera, founded in El Paso, is a community-based workers' organization of low-wage, mostly Latina garment workers.[31] The group includes domestic workers and restaurant workers. Workplace issues are a focus of La Mujer Obrera. As Carmen Dominguez has explained, "High production quotas and long work days provoke exhaustion, and accidents are common. There is no unemployment or disability insurance, and women frequently suffer racial and sexual harassment. These women workers are the least organized, least empowered, and most exploited people in the country. Many of the women working in the factories don't realize that they have a right to struggle for better conditions. Part of our work is to make people realize they have rights."[32] La Mujer Obrera members have joined union strikes against small garment sewing shops, pressing for paid overtime and sick leave, adequate ventilation, fire protection, and safe machinery. To meet members' needs, La Mujer Obrera launched the El Puente Community Development Corporation in 1998 to provide social, educational, and economic opportunities for Latinas.[33] It has operated a food cooperative, a clinic, and a credit bank for members. La Mujer Obrera is among many groups concerned about the U.S.–Mexico Free Trade Agreement, which will make it more profitable for U.S. corporations to take manufacturing, and jobs, out of the United States. The situation of garment workers is similar to that of auto, electronics, and other manufacturing workers who are under increasing pressure to accept whatever conditions corporate management offers for fear their companies will abandon U.S. communities.[34]

Sometimes one woman can make a difference. Consider Geraldine Jensen, the mother of two children who received child support for only six months after her divorce. When local child support officials could not help her collect child support, she put an ad in a paper that brought a dozen mothers together to create an organization that became the Association for Children for the Enforcement of Support (ACES).[35] With help from the Center for Community Change, the group has grown to 300 chapters across the United States. Local chapters have worked effectively to collect millions in child support for thousands of mothers and children. ACES has used a variety of strategies. When one judge was uncooperative in hearing support cases, ACES successfully picketed the judge. ACES has attracted media attention, and the ABC network broadcast a movie about Jensen's efforts.[36] ACES has been instrumental in getting congressional mandates involving the welfare of children from divorced families, including making federal employees provide health insurance for their children when support orders grant coverage and enacting the Deadbeat Parents Punishment Act making nonsupport a federal offense. ACES has won several lawsuits against states for illegally withholding families' support payments and has successfully advocated for employer income-withholding compliance laws. Recently, ACES investigators have found that state government child support agencies are holding $738 million in child support payments in violation of federal law.[37]

Union Movements

For more than a century, unions have improved U.S. workers' wages, benefits, and working conditions. However, some established leaders of large national unions have sold out workers by working in collusion with the management of their industry's firms. As one observer noted, "Procapitalist, anticommunist, corrupt union 'leaders' such as Gus Tyler of the International Ladies' Garment Workers Union (ILGWU), Walter Reuther of the UAW, George Meany of the AFL-CIO, Tony Boyle of the United Mineworkers of America (UMWA), Joe Curran of the National Maritime Union (NMU), and Jimmy Hoffa and Frank Fitzsimmons of the Teamsters Union, to name only a few, were in the forefront of the reactionary, collaborationist process that led to the crisis of organized labor."[38] Although union reformers have challenged the authoritarian, probusiness leadership of unions in recent decades, collusion and corruption, along with aggressive antiunion policies of many large firms, increasing automation, the movement of jobs overseas, and the shift from manufacturing to service jobs, have led to the decline in union membership. Among the major industrialized countries, the United States is the least unionized, with only 13 percent of its workers in unions. This compares with about 95 percent of workers in Denmark and Sweden, 50 percent in the United Kingdom, 43 percent in Germany, 28 percent in Japan and France, and 36 percent in Canada.[39] Those democratic countries with *higher* levels of unionization generally have a *better* standard of living for their workers, often provided by means of a government "welfare state."[40]

Over the last few decades union reformers have sought to reform their unions or to create new ones. Reform movements have included Steelworkers Fight Back, which fought for a democratic United Steelworkers union, better grievance procedures, and safer work-places, and Teamsters for a Democratic Union, which fought to rid the Teamsters union of corrupt leaders.[41]

Gaining community support and building coalitions with local political leaders have helped union activists win more rights for workers. Negotiating with building owners, many of whom care about their public image, the nationwide Justice for Janitors campaign of the Service Employees International Union (SEIU) has won better wages and benefits for janitors in major cities.[42] The campaign has aroused public awareness of the exploitation of low-wage workers by calling attention to the fact that full-time janitorial employees earning a minimum wage could not afford to pay for a place to live anywhere near where they worked. Justice for Janitors workers have found direct action, such as invading the bars and restaurants patronized by owners or managers of buildings they clean, to be effective. A Justice for Janitors' worldwide boycott persuaded Apple computers to hire a contractor that would provide janitors with decent wages and benefits. Justice for Janitors' efforts to organize contract workers in the building maintenance industry target the contract firms that formally hire workers and the employers where workers actually work. Unionization of a contract firm or a temporary agency may be of little value, since the larger corporation may switch to a nonunion temporary agency or contractor. The nonunionized firm may hire workers formerly employed by the unionized firm.[43] In recent years, Justice for Janitors has continued to win major wage and health care benefits for janitors in several states.[44]

Jobs with Justice, a nationwide campaign involving communications and transportation workers, as well as people in other occupations, owes its success to its network of unions and organizations representing a diversity of racial and gender groups, such as the National Organization for Women (NOW), the National Association for the Advancement of Colored People (NAACP), and the Southern Christian Leadership Conference (SCLC).[45] Jobs with Justice has operated from Miami to Oregon and has sought to secure for workers enforced rights to bargain collectively, to a decent standard of living, and to a secure job. Thousands have demonstrated in support of Jobs with Justice in cities across the country. The campaign has supported prolabor political candidates, new contracts for workers, and labor law reforms that stop union busting by employers and make stronger the National Labor Relations Board, which has been weakened by recent conservative presidential administrations.[46]

Following the relocation of a Levi Strauss plant from San Antonio, Texas, to Costa Rica, displaced garment workers formed Fuerza Unida (United Force).[47] Fuerza staged public demonstrations and held a four-city hunger strike to protest company actions. Fuerza also filed a class-action lawsuit alleging that Levi Strauss violated workers' compensation laws and another charging the company with discriminatory policies in laying off women of color. Fuerza has worked to protect employees at the company's other plants by making them aware of "symptoms of plant closings."[48]

Persistence and civil disobedience paid off for maintenance workers who sought permanent employee status in the Dallas, Texas, Independent School District. For several years they had been classified as temporary workers (they were hired for one semester, then laid off and rehired) and denied job security and other benefits received by permanent employees. The school board at first denied formal grievances filed by their local union. The workers won permanent status only by visiting the offices of school administrators in person and refusing to leave until the school board took action.[49]

Overall, unions have improved the lot of U.S. workers. The media and conservative commentators have attacked unions as having a negative effect on U.S. society. However, an analysis by Richard Freeman and James Medoff shows that unions significantly reduce economic inequality and that the presence of unions reduces wage inequality. Freeman and Medoff found that the internal affairs of most unions are now much more democratic and much less corrupt than the media and public images of unions suggest. In addition, the outside political activity of unions has benefited workers generally, as well as union members. Union lobbying tends to be more effective in bringing social legislation for the public than in bringing favors for unions. In regard to efficiency and productivity, the Freeman and Medoff analysis suggests that having a workplace union improves working conditions and practices at no extra cost to management and in most settings increases or has no significant effect on worker productivity.[50]

Older Americans

Older Americans have created a number of effective reform groups. Before the burst of civil rights activity in the 1960s, the most successful people's organizations were among the needy aged. Beginning in the 1930s, movements such as that led by Francis Townsend proposed to end poverty by giving regular payments to the needy aged. The Townsend movement was still active into the 1950s. It and other organizations in the 1940s and 1950s, which were oriented toward improving old-age assistance, had some effect on the improvement of benefits in such programs as Social Security.

Today, groups such as the American Association of Retired Persons (AARP), with 35 million members, and the National Council of Senior Citizens, with still more millions of members, have fought successfully for programs such as Medicare and for increases in Social Security payments and benefits.[51] These groups will likely gain even greater importance in realizing the social, political, and economic interests of older Americans in coming decades, since one-third of the population will likely be 55 years or older by 2050.[52] AARP provides drugs to its members at discounts, and it has provided tax assistance to members and sued in court on behalf of the aged. Despite these efforts, however, some analysts have called into question AARP's position in regard to recent Medicare debates and laws, such as the new Medicare prescription-drug bill passed by Congress in 2004. In that process AARP officials, some suggest, compromised longstanding AARP goals by working closely with a conservative (George W. Bush) presidential administration to begin the restriction or privatization of Medicare and related programs.[53]

Groups that are more militant include the Gray Panthers, an intergenerational assemblage of people.[54] The Gray Panthers have worked aggressively against what they term the "fuddy-duddy" image of the aged. They are much more willing to lead demonstrations to secure fair play and support progressive legislation than are groups like AARP. Members and supporters of this group now total tens of thousands of people of all ages. Under the motto "Age and youth in action," the Gray Panthers have developed task forces to address vital national issues: economic and tax justice, including a real jobs policy; defense reductions and other budgetary issues; preservation of the environment; national health care reform; affordable housing for all; and an end to discrimination, including ageism, sexism, and racism. The group has created the Panther Media Watch to pressure the media to present better images of older citizens. At the local level, its members have worked successfully for such community needs as better transportation services for the poor.[55]

Americans of Color

Among the oldest people's organizations still in existence are civil rights organizations of African Americans and other Americans of color, which have played an important role in breaking down racial discrimination barriers in the United States. Nonviolent civil disobedience increased in the 1950s and 1960s in boycotts such as that of segregated buses in Montgomery, Alabama (a successful movement that brought the Reverend Martin Luther King, Jr., into prominence), and the later sit-in movement and freedom rides. The 1960 Greensboro, North Carolina, sit-in by black students at a whites-only lunch counter touched off a series of similar actions by thousands of black southerners and their white allies throughout the South. The freedom rides of the 1960s—designed to test court orders desegregating public transportation and to demonstrate the lack of compliance throughout the South—began a long series of demonstrations and marches that expanded liberty and freedom in the United States.

Direct action against racial segregation in the North began in earnest in the 1960s with boycotts in Harlem, sit-ins in Chicago, school sit-ins in Englewood, New Jersey, and demonstrations in Cairo, Illinois. The Nation of Islam aggressively pressed for black pride and black-controlled businesses.[56] The Congress of Racial Equality (CORE) accelerated protest campaigns against housing and employment discrimination. School boycotts, picketing at construction sites, and rent strikes became commonplace.[57] The growing group of organizations oriented toward greater black political and economic power included the Student Nonviolent Coordinating Committee (SNCC) and the Black Panthers.[58]

Since the 1960s, the civil rights movement has periodically expanded and contracted. Pressure from civil rights groups has secured the passage of legislation prohibiting

The black civil rights leader Dr. Martin Luther King, Jr., here leads the 1963 "March on Washington for Jobs and Freedom." (UPI/Corbis-Bettmann)

responsible for the National Highway Traffic Safety Administration's decision to ask General Motors to recall millions of hazardous pickup trucks.[76] Similar public research groups have examined monopoly control of industries and political corruption in the U.S. Congress.

Public Citizen led a large coalition of consumer, labor, and environmental organizations in opposing the North American Free Trade Agreement (NAFTA) and proposed revisions to the General Agreement on Tariffs and Trade (GATT), agreements which were mostly designed to benefit multinational corporations and which remain a threat to U.S. jobs. NAFTA has led to the exploitation of workers and to the weakening of pollution control and safety standards in numerous countries. The Economic Policy Institute estimates that NAFTA has cost the United States nearly 1 million jobs and contributes "to rising income inequality, suppressed real wages for production workers, weakened workers' collective bargaining powers and ability to organize unions, and reduced fringe benefits."[77]

Young people have organized many groups seeking to create a better society. Thousands of high school and college graduates have signed a Graduation Pledge of Environmental and Social Responsibility that states, "I pledge to explore and take into account the social and environmental consequences of any job opportunity I consider and will try to improve these aspects of any organization for which I work."[78] The Graduation Pledge Alliance (GPA) began at Humboldt State University in California, and the program has spread to roughly 150 college campuses across the United States, Canada, and Western Europe. Student GPA leaders have organized public discussions, workshops, and art shows relating to social and environmental implications of various employment opportunities. Although some have criticized the pledge as vague and ineffectual, the statements and actions of numerous former college students indicate otherwise. Some students have turned down jobs after considering the employment position's social and environmental aspects. In some cases, pledged students have made changes in their workplaces. One recent graduate of Manchester College stated, "I told my boss of the pledge and my concerns. He understood and agreed . . . and the company did not pursue the (chemical weapons related) project." Other pledged students have established recycling programs at their jobs, called for greater involvement of women in high school athletic programs, and edited workplace training manuals for biased language; and still others have made conflict resolution services more available to underserved populations.[79]

Antinuclear and Antiwar Protest

In recent decades, concerned Americans have organized numerous antinuclear and antiwar groups. The antinuclear movement has periodically received attention from the media because its civil disobedience provides dramatic fare. For example, in 1978 the Clamshell Alliance brought together more than 20,000 people, including students, college-educated workers, blue-collar workers, farmers, and fishing interests to demonstrate against the building of a nuclear plant in Seabrook, New Hampshire, and they succeeded in slowing the project.[80] At the other end of the continent, 300 people protesting nuclear pollution participated in a nonviolent occupation of a nuclear submarine base near Seattle, Washington.[81] Since that time hundreds of thousands of Americans have participated in legal demonstrations and nonviolent disobedience directed at nuclear power facilities across the country. Citizen protest has been a major factor in decisions to shut down permanently a number of nuclear power plants.[82]

INFACT, a Boston-based grassroots organization whose position is that among the various life-threatening corporate practices, the production of nuclear weapons poses the greatest threat to human survival, is a national leader in the antinuclear movement. In 1985, INFACT launched a public education campaign to reveal corporate influence in the U.S. government's nuclear weapons decisions and issued a public challenge to General Electric (GE), the nation's largest nuclear weapons producer, to stop its promotion and production of nuclear weapons. GE's failure to respond to this challenge led INFACT to call for a nationwide boycott of GE products the following year.[83] In 1992 INFACT's film *Deadly Deception: General Electric, Nuclear Weapons, and Our Environment,* which focuses on the health risks and management oversights at two nuclear facilities managed by GE, won an Oscar for best short documentary.[84] INFACT continues as an important citizens' organization that monitors the questionable and dangerous activities of large corporations, most notably the tobacco industry.[85]

Wars still spark citizen protests. During the 1991 Gulf War, although the majority of citizens supported the war, tens of thousands of antiwar protestors demonstrated in cities and towns across the United States. Many people who felt obliged to support U.S. troops expressed opposition to war as a means of protecting U.S. access to Middle East oil.[86] Massive protests against the 2003 invasion and postwar occupation of Iraq occurred in March 2004. Demonstrations took place in more than 250 U.S. cities and towns, including those by 50,000 people in San Francisco, 20,000 in Los Angeles, 10,000 in Chicago, and 100,000 in New York City.[87] Since then, organized protests have continued against U.S. military intervention in the Middle East.

Information revealed after the first Iraq invasion—much of which citizens' groups have made public—illustrates the incomplete and even distorted media coverage that reached the U.S. population while the war was in progress. For example, 70 percent of the 88,500 tons of bombs dropped on Iraq during the 1991 Gulf War missed their targets, although the Pentagon did not release any of these misses shown on the gun-camera videos.[88] Peace activist Kathy Kelly, who spent months in Iraq and Jordan with the 73-member international Gulf Peace Team during the war, tells of receiving replies of "We didn't know. We didn't realize" from people in the United States when she described the Gulf War's devastation upon the many thousands of Iraqi civilians she observed.[89] Similar ignorance on the part of the general public was also demonstrated during the 2003–2004 invasion of Iraq. The U.S. government refused to report on the number of civilian casualties, apparently out of fear of public reaction, and also refused to let the media photograph the coffins of U.S. soldiers killed in the invasion and during the subsequent occupation. The U.S. government also engaged in a cover-up of the scale of damage done to many thousands of civilians, including those held in Iraqi prisons by the U.S. military. Indeed, it was CBS *(60 Minutes II)* that first released photographs of the abuse and torture of Iraqi civilians by U.S. soldiers in Iraqi prisons. Large numbers of those killed, imprisoned, and tortured by U.S. forces during the Iraqi war were innocent civilians. One veteran U.S. sergeant, who has now left the Marines because of what he saw and had to do in Iraq, has reported these painful words: "I killed innocent people for our government. For what? What did I do? Where is the good coming out of it? I feel like I've had a hand in some sort of evil lie at the hands of our government. I just feel embarrassed, ashamed about it."[90]

Environmental Action Groups

Numerous citizens' groups, sometimes called the *Greens,* have organized around environmental protection issues and brought pressure for change. Some groups, such as the Green

Greenpeace activists demonstrate for more medical aid for survivors of DOW Chemical Company's poison gas release in Bhopal, India, which killed 20,000 people. (Ronald Wittek/dpa/Landov LLC)

Party of California, have become political parties. Many such groups have engaged in successful demonstrations. For example, citizens concerned about the Alaska Railroad Corporation's use of chemical herbicides to clear tracks ended the practice after a protest campaign that had lasted more than two decades.[91] Environmental groups have also called for a rethinking of the corporate definitions of concepts such as *profit* and *efficiency*.

With some 250,000 members in the United States and 2.5 million members worldwide, Greenpeace is one of the best-known environmental protection groups. For several decades Greepeace has brought major environmental problems to public attention across the globe.[92] Following the success of its campaign to persuade the U.S. government to end nuclear testing on an earthquake-prone Alaskan island, the organization has worked to end numerous environmental abuses worldwide through aggressive but nonviolent resistance, education, and lobbying. Among the environmental abuses that Greenpeace has targeted are industrial chemical emissions that produce acid rain; nuclear and other toxic waste dumping in oceans and in less industrialized nations; ozone layer depletion; and toxic waste incineration.[93] Opposition mobilized by Greenpeace against Atlanta's Blue Circle Cement's attempts to secure a permit to burn toxic waste led the plant to abandon this plan. Greenpeace also participated with local groups in barring construction of the world's largest chlorine-bleaching rayon pulp mill in Wallace, Louisiana, a plant that would have dumped chemical poisons into the already-polluted Mississippi River.[94] In 2003 Attorney General John Ashcroft moved to indict the entire organization for its protest activities in Florida. His Justice Department charged Greenpeace under an old 1872 "sailormongering" law, after a few Greenpeace activists climbed aboard a commercial ship well off the coast of Florida and posted a banner that read, "President Bush, Stop Illegal Logging." The ship was carrying mahogany wood illegally exported from Brazil's Amazon rainforest.[95] In May 2004, however, the federal judge granted Greenpeace's motion to dismiss the case for lack of evidence after the Justice Department rested its case.[96]

Other Community Action Groups

The thousands of community organizations that have sprung up in recent decades reflect dissatisfaction with existing political and economic leadership and show a resurgence of grassroots democracy. Neighborhood groups often use three strategies: (1) They pressure business and political officials; (2) they work to replace political officials in elections; and (3) they develop their cooperative, self-help organizations.[97] Groups that have the most success are those with a full-time staff, good fund-raising, sophisticated organizing and lobbying techniques, and the ability to build coalitions with other groups.

Neighborhood movements are often effective in forcing local officials to take action benefiting low- and moderate-income families. Several national support networks, such as the Center for Community Change in Washington, D.C., have emerged, as have numerous centers for training community organizers, such as the Industrial Areas Foundation (IAF) founded by Saul Alinsky in Chicago in 1940.[98] The major goal of IAF organizers is to build confidence and hope in poor and oppressed people, empowering them to address their communities' problems. In the late 1990s, the IAF had 55 affiliated community organizations active in 21 states and the District of Columbia, as well as groups in Canada, England, and Germany. IAF represents several million families.[99] One of these organizations, South Bronx Churches (SBC), built a coalition of 46 churches and politicized substantial numbers of local citizens to challenge the local political leadership. The group collected 100,000 signatures on petitions demanding better schools, affordable housing, and other civic reforms; won improvements in a local hospital's emergency room services; and organized a housing rally that involved 8,000 residents.[100]

The Philadelphia Unemployment Project (PUP) is another example of effective grassroots organizing. Its members have staged demonstrations to prevent evictions and to pressure mortgage companies to stop home mortgage foreclosure procedures against unemployed people.[101] PUP helped influence Philadelphia's city council to pass a plant-closing ordinance and the state legislature to pass the Emergency Mortgage Assistance Act, which established a loan fund for unemployed workers who fall behind on house payments. In the 1990s, PUP members traveled to Washington, D.C., to participate in demonstrations to support extending unemployment benefits to the long-term unemployed and sponsored a conference for unemployed workers to discuss strategies for obtaining extended unemployment benefits, tax relief for unemployment compensation, and job placement programs. PUP has organized protests against cuts in health care programs for the working poor and has helped unemployed people in other states to form grassroots organizations.[102]

In cities as diverse as Little Rock, Arkansas, and Spartanburg, South Carolina, public housing residents have organized to bring change to their communities. For example, in the 1990s, 25 low-income residents from nine Little Rock housing projects went on a retreat with housing staff members to discuss project problems. This retreat was facilitated by an organizer from the Center for Community Change in Washington, D.C., which helps low-income Americans to organize. Working in partnership with local housing managers, the residents have helped improve conditions and move the housing authority off the government's troubled authorities list. By coming together and organizing, these public housing residents were able to bring change.[103]

The Association of Community Organizations for Reform Now (ACORN) has become the umbrella organization for hundreds of community groups fighting for solutions to local and national problems.[104] ACORN has more than 150,000 member families organized into 750 neighborhood chapters in more than 60 cities across the country; most member families are poor, low-middle-income, or elderly. The thousand delegates at ACORN's first national convention (1978) in Memphis, Tennessee, passed a strong platform with planks calling for guaranteed jobs for all, fair taxes, an end to redlining by banks, national health insurance, and greater people's representation in major societal institutions. Attended by a variety of people—including truck drivers, the unemployed, retirees, and farmers—the next convention passed an even stronger People's Program, including not only antiredlining planks* but also strong demands for public ownership of banks. Since that time, local ACORN groups have worked through the electoral system to get some members elected to local government. ACORN delegates regularly attend national political conventions and have pressed their progressive "People's Platform"—with its theme "Our freedom shall be based on the equality of the many, not the income of the few"—on both Democrats and Republicans. Among its many successes, ACORN has done the following:

1. Established or improved homesteading programs that turn over vacant houses to low-income residents in Philadelphia, Bridgeport, Phoenix, Chicago, Detroit, and Brooklyn.
2. Won a national homesteading bill.
3. Forced the federal Housing and Urban Development (HUD) agency to make it easier for low- and moderate-income people to purchase HUD-owned properties.
4. Negotiated agreements with banks in numerous cities, making much money available for loans in low-income neighborhoods.
5. Improved school facilities and governance in Chicago, New York, and Bridgeport and stopped school closings in Des Moines.
6. Registered more than a half million new voters since 1980 and struck down barriers to voter registration in a number of cities.
7. Forced companies to clean up, move, or cancel plans for toxic chemical plants, dumps, or discharges in at least ten cities.
8. Secured ordinances or agreements requiring developers to hire low-income unemployed residents in at least eight cities.
9. Improved hospital care in Little Rock, Dallas, and New York and expanded childhood immunization in New Orleans.
10. Won drug-abuse-prevention and rape-prevention programs and forced police and city officials to respond more effectively to rapes in low-income neighborhoods in several cities.[105]

Prospects for Expanded Progressive Grassroots Action

Many community and neighborhood groups that focus on local concerns have difficulty organizing national reform campaigns. Some critical observers note that local groups' victories are too scattered and thus doubt that such groups can become part of a national movement for large-scale social justice reform. However, local victories can, with great ef-

---

Redlining is the practice of some banks and insurance companies of designating areas (often low- and moderate-income areas) in cities in which mortgage or business loans or insurance policies will not be approved. Such denial of financial support usually hastens the decay of the inner city.

fort, accumulate to the level of significant redistributions of goods and services to workers and consumers. In addition, when people learn how to pressure established centers of power, they are learning how the U.S. economic structure and politics really operate. They are learning that people, when well organized, can bring important changes.

Progressive movements, composed of less than a majority of the population, vary considerably in the degree of reform in society they seek. Some desire moderate reforms. Others, such as ACORN, aim for extensive reforms in society's structure. Some reform-oriented community groups accept the capitalistic system and focus on one area of interest. Others are groping toward full "political consciousness," in Eric Hobsbawm's sense of that phrase. Some are beginning to develop a consistent language in which to express their vision of an alternative political–economic system for the United States and to assert their view of practical strategies to reach that larger goal.

In 1992, for example, a diverse group of several hundred citizens founded a new political party, simply called the "New Party," with the goal of establishing a significant progressive presence in U.S. politics and building a genuine working democracy.[106] This political party is committed to racial and gender justice. Because it is difficult for third-party candidates to win elections in the United States, most third parties have been short-lived. Many voters feel that a vote for a third-party candidate is wasted, yet large numbers of voters are dissatisfied with both major political parties. A spokesperson for the New Party summed up this view: "This country is not doing well as a democracy, and the natural default of American politics in the future is 'more of the same, only worse.' We honestly don't think we can afford that. We know we don't want it."[107]

The 1993 election of two of the three New Party candidates in the city council election in Jennings, Missouri, near St. Louis, illustrates this new political vehicle's success in mobilizing a multiracial grassroots effort to attack old-style political problems. The entrenched all-white city council in Jennings was notorious for abuse of public power. New Party candidates campaigned for a full audit of city finances, improvements in the public schools, and an end to redlining. One newly elected official was the first African American ever to serve on that city council, even though half of the city's population is African American. Today, the New Party has several thousand members, dozens of national organizers, chapters in seven states, and active organizing in several other states. Since its founding, the New Party has lent its support to candidates in hundreds of local elections, such as school board and state legislative races, and numerous candidates have won. The party has succeeded in electing state legislators in Missouri and Wisconsin and has built successful political coalitions with union and civil rights groups. The New Party has pressed for the ability of a small party to cross-endorse a good candidate of another political party.[108]

In addition to the New Party, other reform-oriented political groups have been created in recent years. These vary considerably in the degree of social and political change they envision. One such group was United We Stand, formed by supporters of Ross Perot, an independent presidential candidate who polled nearly a fifth of the vote in the 1992 presidential election. The party resurfaced in 1996, renamed the Reform Party, with Perot again as its presidential candidate. In 2000, the Reform Party nominated the conservative Patrick Buchanan for president, and in 2004 it endorsed the more liberal Ralph Nader for president. The Reform Party has advocated a mixture of social and political reforms, including restrictions on lobbyists, reduction of the federal budget deficit, a plan to increase jobs across the country, elimination of political action committees (PACs), and major reform of public schools. The Reform Party has consistently supported increasing citizen participation in local and federal governments.[109]

Recently, a number of Internet-based political organizations have been developed to press hard for expanding democracy in the United States. One of these is MoveOn, which was started by Joan Blades and Wes Boyd, two businesspeople in California. Joined by Eli Pariser, who had organized an online petition campaign called MoveOn Peace, they have developed a major Web site and organizational efforts designed to bring millions of Americans back into the democratic political process. According to the MoveOn Web site, the grassroots organization is "a catalyst for a new kind of grassroots involvement, supporting busy but concerned citizens in finding their political voice. Our nationwide network of more than 2,000,000 online activists is one of the most effective and responsive outlets for democratic participation available today."[110] Its major political tactic is to build online advocacy groups working progressively on such issues as "campaign finance, environmental and energy issues, media consolidation, or the Iraq war." So far, its efforts have gotten millions of people involved in political action efforts and have helped raise millions of dollars in contributions for progressive political candidates.

Conservative and Reactionary Groups

Not all citizens' groups, local or national, are progressive. Some are very conservative; others are reactionary. Leaders in these organized groups tend to be consistently conservative, although many of the followers may, inconsistently, hold conservative and liberal views.

Some Americans have sought to solve the serious social and economic problems they face through conservative and even extreme right-wing movements committed to reinforcing the structures of classism, racism, sexism, and authoritarianism. For example, white supremacy organizations such as the Ku Klux Klan have frequently blamed black, Jewish, and immigrant Americans for various social and economic ills and have periodically threatened members of these groups with violence. White supremacy organizations, which were strong politically in the 1920s, began gaining strength again in the 1970s. Today, these groups are still numerous. For example, the number of racist Skinhead groups doubled in 2003, and the neo-Nazi Aryan Nations created 11 new chapters in that one year. Antigovernment "patriot" groups, such as private militias, also increased their numbers by 20 percent in 2003. Nearly 500 hate Web sites are now on the Internet. Overall, one count estimates 751 hate groups active in the United States, with combined membership in the tens of thousands.[111] Some groups regularly hold rallies and put out literature attacking non-European groups as a threat to "American jobs" and the Anglo-Saxon core culture. Members of white supremacist groups have been involved in the burning of numerous black churches since 1995. Although no white supremacist has as of summer 2005 been convicted for the majority of these crimes, a South Carolina jury awarded the Macedonia Baptist Church $37.8 million from the Christian Knights of the Ku Klux Klan for its role in a conspiracy to burn the church in 1995.[112]

The resurgence of racist, reactionary, and extreme right-wing groups signals that their members, mostly ordinary (white) working-class Americans, are very unhappy with conditions in the United States, yet they have not found an adequate explanation for the problems in the mass media or from politicians. The media do not provide a systematic progressive, critical explanation of U.S. problems, nor can one find such explanations in most public schools. For that reason, many people fall back on the extremist right-wing perspective of blaming the

In recent years the U.S. government has sometimes engaged in actions threatening the liberties and freedoms of Americans.

victims—especially politically weak groups—for U.S. economic and political troubles, even though it can be demonstrated that these targeted groups have nothing to do with these societal problems. Indeed, we have provided much countering data throughout this book.

ALTERNATIVE SOCIAL SYSTEMS

Varieties of Socialism

Historically, a major alternative social system to capitalism has taken the form of some type of socialism. Dictionaries define *socialism* as a political–economic system with extensive public or government ownership and control of the major means of production and distribution of goods and services. For most Americans, however, *socialism* is a fuzzy word associated somehow with everything from government health insurance to totalitarian Communist countries such as the former Soviet Union and contemporary China. Most Americans have been taught by politicians, the mass media, and schoolteachers to consider a capitalistic market economy as the best political–economic system available and to view any type of socialism as repressive in the style of the old Soviet Communism. In fact, different types of socialist systems range from the totalitarian to the genuinely democratic.

The American people perceive realistically that the type of socialism long practiced in the former Soviet Union and in contemporary China is indeed totalitarian, antidemocratic, and undesirable. They understand that totalitarian countries repress their citizens. The centralized bureaucratic control characteristic of totalitarian countries, socialist and otherwise, has given workers little input into the decision-making process; arbitrary and impersonal decisions by distant bureaucrats have shaped their lives. In fact, the discontent of workers over the lack of democracy in the former Soviet Union helped bring an end to Communism there in the early 1990s.

A Social Welfare State

Since 1900 virtually all capitalistic societies, including the United States, have seen considerable government intervention on behalf of the needs of ordinary working people. Some capitalistic societies have seen considerably more government intervention than others. Indeed, countries such as Germany and Sweden are often, mistakenly, seen by many Americans as "socialist" because of the extent of social intervention by their governments. These are *not* socialist countries, however; they are countries, with capitalistic economies and developed social-welfare states.

For example, in the 1930s Sweden began moving in the direction of large-scale social service reforms, including modest nationalization of industry, public ownership of some major enterprises, and expanded educational and other social services that greatly benefited rank-and-file citizens. Yet most production of goods and services in the Swedish economy has remained in the hands of capitalist-controlled private enterprises, with government ownership confined primarily to railroads, mineral resources, a public bank, and liquor and tobacco operations. Historically, Sweden's blue-collar and white-collar workers have organized strong unions and been able to force considerable concessions from the Swedish capitalist class. The social democratic government, in power for most of the time since the 1930s, has developed one of the world's most successful social welfare systems. It implemented a broad range of people-oriented social service programs, supported by taxes on larger incomes and the profits of corporations, to protect all citizens from poor housing, poor health care, poverty incomes, and lack of jobs.[113]

In Sweden a laid-off worker has access to a state-run employment agency with which employers must list job openings. Once a job is found, the worker receives government assistance for relocation. If no job is available, job-retraining programs and unemployment insurance benefits are provided. Swedish law requires substantial advance notification of layoffs to give workers time to find new jobs. When necessary, the government has expanded public employment programs to reduce unemployment levels. As a result, unemployment rates since World War II have been relatively low. Sweden's well-developed welfare state has resulted in a wealthy and productive country; its per capita gross national product has been among the highest in the world.[114]

In the 1950s Sweden became one of the first countries to implement a national health insurance program. Patients choose their physicians. Prenatal care, delivery, and postnatal care are free, and new mothers receive paid leave from work. Schoolchildren receive free medical and dental care. A special program provides most of a worker's income for time lost because of sickness. Sweden's excellent health statistics include infant and maternal mortality rates that are among the lowest in the world. In the 1950s a government-supported pension plan was initiated, and since then numerous other social programs have been implemented. Working fathers, as well as working mothers, may take leave from work to help care for an infant, and if they are insured they receive an income supplement for time missed from work. A large proportion of Swedish children of working parents are provided with safe government child care facilities.[115]

One early 2000s analysis of the Swedish social welfare state concluded that it is still strong and effective in providing a relatively egalitarian society: "Sweden has achieved remarkable economic success *and* egalitarian outcomes in recent years. It is clear to virtually all analysts that the key to these redistributive outcomes has been the universalistic social programs which provide benefits to all citizens regardless of wealth and income. Because they are universalistic, however, they are very expensive. At the same time, because they are universalistic they generate enormous popular support."[116]

Conservative criticism of the Swedish welfare state claims that taxes are twice as high in Sweden as in the United States. It has been estimated that all direct and indirect taxes on individuals and corporations amounted to about 30 to 35 percent of the gross national product in the United States and 50 to 60 percent in Sweden. The Swedes, particularly those who are better off, do pay more taxes, but not as much more as many critics claim. In opinion surveys, the majority of Swedes have said that they are willing to pay higher taxes in order not to have such problems as chronic unemployment, homelessness, and health care rationed by income. For their taxes, all Swedes receive an array of benefits and services that help to prevent major social problems such as the inadequate health care received by many moderate-income Americans, homelessness, and widespread unemployment with no hope of employment. In addition, if we were to add to the taxes Americans pay, the cost of the private medical insurance carried by many Americans (estimated at 10 to 30 percent of a typical household's income), as well as the cost of medical care *not* covered by insurance and the cost of private social services such as day care centers, the total Swedish and U.S. "taxes" are more nearly equal. Much of what the Swedes pay for through the tax system, Americans buy, if they can get it at all, from private enterprise—and they often get less adequate health care, child care, and other services as a result. Indeed, Americans probably pay more per capita for all such support services than do the Swedes—and Americans receive less.

Conservative criticism of Sweden's welfare state also targets its alleged lack of personal freedom; the laziness it creates; and the problems of suicide, alcoholism, and inefficiency. Yet, Sweden has *greater* political and press freedoms than the United States. The Swedish national media present a wider array of political and economic opinions on a regular basis than do the U.S. media. By providing working-class and lower-income Swedes with the means to think beyond struggling for food and shelter to higher needs such as active political participation, Sweden's welfare state has *expanded* political freedom. Moreover, the welfare state has not made Swedes lazy; Sweden has had one of the world's highest postwar growth rates, high earned per capita incomes, and advanced educational programs. Accusations that suicide and alcoholism are correlated with the growth of the Swedish welfare state are not supported. Suicide and alcoholism are problems, but they have been problems since *before* the welfare state developed, and Sweden's national health care system has provided major remedial responses to both problems, unlike the U.S. situation where much less support is provided for people with these problems.[117]

The only criticism that seems to have some truth in it is inefficiency. Hospital beds are adequate in number, but sometimes not enough doctors are available. Health services are specialized and heavily used, and waits for *elective* health care are sometimes long. This problem exists because *all* Swedes, not just the affluent, avail themselves of medical facilities. Indeed, some argue that the U.S. system is much more inefficient: It probably costs hundreds if not thousands of lives yearly, such as those of poor mothers and infants who could be saved if a Swedish-type infant and maternal care system were widely available.[118]

The progressive critique of the Swedish welfare state seems more serious. This critique points out that for all its advances in human services, Sweden still has a sharply unequal income distribution, a small capitalist class that owns and controls most of the production facilities, and a large group of modest-wage workers. Organizations of capitalists still have a greatly disproportionate influence on day-to-day societal and government operations. Labor unions are much more influential in Sweden than in the United States because a very large proportion of workers belong to them, but capitalists are yet more powerful than labor.[119]

Since 1989 Sweden has experienced economic problems, caused to a substantial degree by some powerful multinational corporations taking capital out of the country. In 1991 the Swedish Social Democratic Party was replaced by a coalition of conservative parties. Responding to the needs of large corporations for higher profits, the new government dealt with the economic crisis by cutting some government social programs and humanitarian aid and by supporting policies that led to the transfer of income from working people to corporations.[120] Not surprisingly, however, in 1994 the Social Democratic Party was voted back into power because rank-and-file Swedes like the benefits of a social welfare state.[121] In Sweden, just as in the United States, the class struggle between workers and employers can be seen regularly in the struggle over state-provided social services for ordinary citizens. Despite business pressures, and facing calls for cutbacks in social services, the majority of Swedes still strongly support the movement of their country in the direction of democratic socialism.

A Note on Government Intervention in the United States

A few enterprises in the United States, such as public utilities, are government controlled. The Tennessee Valley Authority (TVA) is a major example of a successful government enterprise.[122] Created in the 1930s, the TVA has built dams and power plants that provide electricity, flood control, and recreation to millions. The TVA has thousands of employees and millions of customers. Although the TVA has long been regarded as an efficient publicly owned enterprise, in recent years its nuclear power plants have endangered its economic health and efficiency.[123]

The extent to which government should intervene in the private economy in the United States has been the subject of much debate. Many Americans who think of themselves as conservatives argue that federal programs should be cut back severely. Yet even they do *not* really support "small government" in practice, for they too look to federal intervention to pay for highway systems, airport complexes, river levees, and military weapons, even if these mean huge federal deficits. Moreover, the U.S. government has been substantially involved in supporting private enterprise, small and large, since at least the early 1900s. It has granted taxpayer dollars for many infrastructure projects such as new highways, dams, levees, and port development projects proposed by private entrepreneurs. Government has also provided much research and development money for private industry over many decades.

In addition, even during conservative Republican administrations, such as the Ronald Reagan and George Bush administrations, the federal government has bailed out numerous private corporations in financial trouble. In the mid-1980s, for example, the Reagan administration used federal funds for the multibillion-dollar bailout of Continental Illinois, the country's eighth-largest bank. Hundreds of billions of taxpayer dollars have been used to bail out poorly managed savings and loan associations. These bailouts demonstrate that many conservatives who oppose government intervention in public statements favor such intervention when it supports particular business interests. Yet over the last two decades, many thousands of small businesses have been allowed to fail by "conservative" legislators, and benefits for unemployed workers and the poor have been cut in the name of getting government out of the U.S. economy.

Democratic Socialism in the Kibbutz

As yet there is no fully democratic socialist country on the globe, but there are examples of democratic socialism within some countries. Israel's 268 predominantly rural kibbutz communities, which range in size from 34 to more than a thousand persons and involve about 3 percent of Israel's population, are a major example. Going back several decades, these kibbutzim have a strong democratic socialist philosophy and explicitly reject the more autocratic, hierarchical organization of both capitalistic and totalitarian Communist societies. A typical kibbutz is an independent economic community with separate agricultural and industrial divisions. Until recently, the traditional pattern has been this: Residents generally do not earn wages; income goes into a common treasury, out of which are paid annual personal expense allowances and the costs of a large number of communal services; and food, housing, child care, and health services are typically provided on a communal basis and are distributed according to need.[124]

Agricultural operations and industrial plants are worker controlled. Supervisors are democratically elected and are replaced every few years, giving a large proportion of kibbutz workers a chance to be managers. A workers' assembly controls the production plan, decides on investment and development, lays out the organization of work, and decides on training programs. Workers' committees take responsibility for technical problems and marketing arrangements. The general assembly for the kibbutz usually elects the managers, who have the authority to solve technical and professional problems. This assembly also provides a democratic government for the kibbutz in dealing with a broad range of noneconomic issues, including social services. Because the industrial plants and agricultural cooperatives are not hierarchical, managers and other supervisors cannot use coercion; they must use persuasion.

In recent years many kibbutzim have experienced changes in these traditional arrangements, and some have experienced financial problems. Beginning in the 1980s a number of kibbutzim began borrowing heavily to expand rapidly and were later caught in the sharp interest rate increases and other problems of the troubled capitalistic Israeli economy surrounding them. In the 1990s many kibbutzim had to restructure their debts and receive subsidies from the Israeli government. Moreover, to some extent, the kibbutzim's material success and prosperity have endangered the kibbutz philosophy. For example, because many families now own their own television sets, watching television in groups, a traditional communal activity on kibbutzim, is declining. Kibbutzim have also had problems persuading their youth to stay. National television has brought individualism, hyperconsumerism, and greater materialism to children and adults even in strong socialist homes. Once they have completed their military service, many youth leave what they regard as boring rural areas for

Israel's urban centers, which they see as more exciting. However, kibbutzim leaders have not capitulated in the face of these changes. They have started colleges and other incentive programs to encourage their own youth to stay and to recruit other youth from the cities. The impersonality of city life has caused a number of young people in the cities to consider life on a kibbutz. As one woman returning to a kibbutz put it, "On kibbutz, you're somebody. In the city, you're nobody. In the city I was always working to create money; here, I am free to change and influence other matters of my life, work with the elderly, and give of myself."[125]

Despite their periodic problems, kibbutzim generally have had a high standard of living and a higher level of economic democracy than one finds in Israeli society generally. Many business and political leaders in capitalistic countries have argued that hierarchy is necessary for organizations to perform efficiently in industrial societies, yet Israeli kibbutzim, as well as the worker-control arrangements in some U.S. plants, demonstrate that there is no universal requirement for complex hierarchies and supervisory authoritarianism. The kibbutzim demonstrate that democratic socialism can be made to work. Ordinary people, particularly if they are well educated, certainly can run their own economies and communities without capitalists.

THE POSSIBILITY OF ECONOMIC DEMOCRACY

Democratic socialism is one possible alternative to the trouble-filled late-capitalist system we have in the United States. The socialist tradition is a complicated one, with many different kinds of socialism being proposed and tried in its long history. Some forms of socialism have been autocratic, while others have been very democratic. Although the idea that existing capitalistic institutions maim the bodies and souls of working people has been at the heart of all democratic socialist thinking and experimentation, most of the implemented examples of socialism, such as those in the former Soviet Union and contemporary China, have moved so far away from these humanistic ideals that they provide no models for better social, political, and economic systems.

What would be a better political–economic system for the United States? What system might reduce or eliminate the many problems discussed in this book? These are questions that some Americans have been asking for many decades. The answers may lie, many progressives argue, in a new U.S. system that has not been seen as yet. We should remember that in the late eighteenth century many residents of the North American colonies thought that the ideas of political rights and democracy expressed by revolutionaries such as Thomas Jefferson (in, for example, the Declaration of Independence) were foolish, impossible, and utopian. Expanded rights and democracy were seen as too radical and as too experimental. King George and the British government were too powerful. Yet the idea of expanded democracy was made to work, even if it had not been tried before. The challenge today is to think futuristically about how to expand political, economic, and social democracy in the United States beyond that which is now in place.

Advocates of major progressive reforms suggest that the implementation of greatly expanded worker control in workplaces and in corporate boardrooms, of thoroughgoing political democracy where money does not buy influence and elections, and of expanded social service programs to provide safety nets for working people in need could be accomplished while strengthening the existing democratic tradition. Civil liberties and democratic politics in the United States are essential to a democratic socialism or democratic populism that seeks to meet a broader range of human needs. The cry of the French Revolution was "Liberty,

Equality, Fraternity." The cries of the American Revolution were "All men are created equal" and the "Unalienable rights of life, liberty, and the pursuit of happiness." The U.S. republican political system promises and provides a substantial degree of political liberty, albeit a system compromised and corrupted by the great influence of money. Moreover, as we saw in Chapters 2 and 3, the capitalistic United States economic system has neither promised nor achieved economic equality or even equality of economic opportunity. While some totalitarian Communist countries have provided greater economic equality, neither capitalist nor totalitarian socialist countries have adequately met the full range of basic human needs, including materialistic needs and the needs for substantial work control, self-mastery, and human creativity.[126]

Many observers have emphasized the oppressiveness of state Communism and have also argued for limits to government's power in any society. Numerous conservative analysts have argued forcefully that government should be limited and that voluntary associations of individual citizens should be encouraged to play a critical role in protecting individuals from too much government control of their lives.[127] There is much truth to this view; all governments should be controlled by the governed. Yet these same analysts generally have *not* been willing to recognize and examine the severely negative impact of the capital investments of privately controlled corporations headed by *unelected* and very powerful business elites, and they have not been willing to examine closely and to alter other negative features of late capitalism such as economic inequality, racial and gender discrimination, environmental pollution, corporate crime, and low-wage exploitation of workers in the United States or overseas.

The present U.S. political–economic system is part capitalism and part social welfare state. Many defenders of modern capitalism believe that the solution to today's social problems is to roll back social-welfare and government regulative programs and return to the days when capitalism was supposedly unfettered by "big government." What was life like for most Americans in the period from 1850 to 1930, when capitalism was relatively unfettered and no big government was heavily shaping the U.S. economy and society? Life included extensive child labor, extremely unsafe working conditions, wages of $1 to $2 per day for many, poor or no health care, no Social Security, and regular economic depressions with very severe levels of unemployment. Life was shorter and more painful for most Americans.

Democratic Socialism in the United States

The *democratic* socialist tradition in the United States is important and indigenous. Its most vigorous period was the last decade of the nineteenth century and the first two decades of the twentieth century. More than a thousand Socialist party members served as local and state government officials in the key year of 1912, the same year that Eugene V. Debs received nearly 1 million votes as a presidential candidate. Three hundred socialist newspapers and other periodicals were being published. Socialist party members were influential in U.S. labor unions. This socialism was very much a homegrown class-oriented radicalism, colored by events and issues in the United States and only distantly related to European socialism. U.S. socialists pressed vigorously for the right of workers to organize. Some were early supporters of civil rights and women's rights efforts. Most pressed for the collective ownership of the means of production and distribution. The movement declined after 1917, for a number of reasons. One major factor was government repression. Leaders were jailed for making antiwar speeches. Considered subversive, progressive periodicals were banned from the mails by the postal service. The movement splintered into factions favoring different political strategies. Still another reason for the decline in these democratic socialistic movements was the rise of corporate liberalism, whose moderate government reforms, which often copied socialist ideas, satisfied many people, at least for a time.[128]

In recent decades a number of progressive groups in the United States have suggested that democratic socialism is a far better system than modern capitalism. Indeed, many citizen groups have pressed for expanded economic democracy. One of these is the Democratic Socialists of America (DSA), which was led until 1989 by Michael Harrington, a major democratic socialist thinker.[129] Today the DSA has several thousand members. The DSA has aggressively pressed for better health care, better working conditions, and better wages for U.S. workers. It has pressed for economic democracy. Such economic democracy could provide some solutions for certain societal problems discussed in this book. The present political–economic system is fundamentally shaped by the decisions of business owners and executives, particularly those who head large corporations. Replacing these executives and owners with worker-controlled organizations is one goal of those advocating greater economic democracy in the United States.

Workplace Democracy

Workers in the United States are raised on a political diet of democracy, equality, and representation, but most spend their lives working in *inegalitarian hierarchies* where they must submit routinely to the orders of higher-ups. Still, workplace democracy is not a foreign idea. In some places, especially where corporations are planning to close subsidiary companies because of low profits, workers have taken over U.S. enterprises. For example, in the 1970s more than 300 employees, including secretaries, file clerks, and mail room clerks, at the Consumers United Group, Inc., a large insurance company, took over the company and governed themselves with a worker congress and a worker-elected board of directors. The workers voted to give each employee the same productivity bonus as the president and to set a high minimum salary for lower-level workers; and they voted for an excellent health plan for all workers. Since the 1970s this worker-owned firm has sought to invest money in the poverty-stricken inner-city areas of major cities.[130] In another example, when the GAF Corporation decided to liquidate an asbestos operation in a high-unemployment area of Vermont, the workers and other community residents gained control of the facility by buying shares of stock and then elected their own board of directors.[131]

Many employee buyouts are not wholly successful, in part because employees get the chance to own facilities only when they are neglected or considered unprofitable by corporate executives. Yet employee efforts can be made to work. In McCaysville, Georgia, in the late 1960s, some 60 women garment makers who lost a strike for decent working conditions at a Levi Strauss factory formed a cooperative. The women rotated membership on their board of directors and made decisions by democratic vote. Their small factory survived for some time in spite of problems obtaining good contracts and fair financing and the loss of some employees because the company could afford to pay only meager wages.[132]

Today, an estimated 200 U.S. companies are owned entirely by their employees. For several decades, some of the largest worker-owned and worker-managed corporations were the numerous plywood cooperatives in the Pacific Northwest. Begun in 1921, these cooperatives were for some decades substantially controlled by their employees, who owned shares in the factories and voted in key elections. The boards of directors were composed of elected workers who made decisions about basic issues including sick leave, wages, and investments. Workers owned shares in the company. Some were democratically managed; others hired managers who operated more in the fashion common to capitalist-controlled industry. In hard times, such as recessions, workers were usually not laid off. Instead, all workers took a cut in pay. And owner-workers received equal shares of the income from sales. These cooperatives became multimillion-dollar operations producing for a time a significant proportion of all the plywood in the United States. The cooperatives legally established the right of worker control and roughly equalized the income distribution of most workers in the plants. While the cooperatives were hit hard by recent economic troubles in the plywood and timber industry (which affected non–co-ops as well), and eventually all but a few were closed, they nonetheless showed how workplace democracy can be made to work in the U.S. economy.[133]

In discussions of worker control of business enterprises, this question sometimes arises: Don't owners have the right to run their businesses and invest their hard-earned money without worker input? Steve Babson and Nancy Brigham have suggested that those who ask this question have not dug deeply into the ownership and financing of most corporate enterprises.[134] For some companies, ownership and control are inherited. Many owners did not work hard to build billion-dollar businesses from the bottom up. Many other capitalist owners, large and small, have borrowed the money to start their enterprises, with much of this money coming from the savings ordinary workers have put into banking institutions. Capitalists play a role in the work process by financing and directing operations, but because of the power they have, they can generally take a disproportionately large share of the profits from their businesses, profits mostly generated by the work of their blue-collar and white-collar workers.

Views of Democratic Socialism and Economic Democracy: The Future?

Advocates of progressive reform have written about what a thoroughgoing democratic socialism might look like in the United States, as well as about the transitional period during which people might work to bring about a more democratic economy and politics. For example, Michael Albert and Robin Hahnel have discussed economic democracy in detail. They suggest that economic democrats want all people to have what is necessary for their physical and emotional security, for material survival, and for growth and development. People need adequate food, housing, and shelter, but they also need the freedom to control their lives and to develop their own lifestyles, as long as their activities do not hurt other people. To meet these needs for *all* Americans, capitalistic, racist, sexist, ageist, homophobic, and bureaucratic–authoritarian social structures must be dismantled so that personal, family, and community life can continue without the restrictions of discrimination or exploitation.[135]

The current U.S. political system is *in principle* a democracy, but *in reality* it is actually shaped by the capitalistic economic system, which is not even democratic in principle. Most workplaces are hierarchies in which the "boss" is usually "right." For the most part, blue-collar and white-collar workers must do what they are told. Outside the workplace, employees generally have freedom of speech and freedom to question publicly the actions of their political leaders. The U.S. political system provides certain basic rights: freedom of speech, freedom of organization, freedom of the press, and so on, yet within small businesses, corporations, and government agencies, these rights are generally restricted, if they exist at all. Employees may be fired for speaking critically of their bosses and for participating in grassroots protest organizations on their own time.[136]

Decision making in workplaces would still be necessary under a system of democratic socialism in the United States, but according to Albert and Hahnel, it would be thoroughly democratic and much less centralized than it is today. A more democratic U.S. political–economic system would be composed of thousands of groups, workplaces, and communities, some small and some as large as a few thousand persons. The existing hierarchical decision-making structures in most U.S. factories, offices, and communities would be replaced by a popularly elected council of workers to make the key daily decisions about economic, production, political, and other matters. Power and production would be greatly decentralized. Small groups would govern themselves as democracies of the whole; larger groups would elect representatives to governing councils. To protect against the constant threat of oligarchies (rule by a few) emerging, membership on the governing councils would rotate, with no representative being able to serve several terms in a row. A bill of rights guaranteeing such rights as freedom of speech and of assembly in *all* sectors of society, political and economic, would be required to protect dissenters.[137]

In this vision of U.S. society, productive and distributive facilities would be owned and controlled by working people as a whole, not by a small capitalist class with little or no concern for the collective good. Decisions, economic and political, would thus be made democratically. The civil liberties of all could be protected by law, including those who dissent from decisions of the majority. In the workplace, decision-making units that allow significant face-to-face relations would have the powers that come with decentralized ownership and control. In face-to-face relations, people can learn how to do democratic decision making. Currently, large organizations usually centralize power in the hands of a few and seem to have more hierarchy than smaller organizations. Large industrial organizations, with their hierarchies and decision-making authoritarianism, were first created in capitalist countries and reflect primarily the need to make private profit. Significantly, Communist leaders such as Vladimir Lenin and Joseph Stalin introduced such large-scale economic organizations in the former Soviet Union and *intentionally imitated* this capitalistic hierarchy in an attempt to catch up with the industrialization of capitalist countries. In the United States, real economic democracy would require a substantial decentralization of economic power and much development of smaller-scale organizations in both the political and economic spheres.[138]

In their idealistic model, Albert and Hahnel note that democratic councils at workplaces might decide to emphasize the well-being of all workers. Both unpleasant and pleasant and rewarding jobs might be rotated. In other jobs, spreading knowledge could improve personal relations. For example, in hospitals, doctors might be strongly encouraged to teach many more medical skills to nurses and aides, so that knowledge could be spread to all willing and able to learn and so that the hierarchical structure of many health care organizations could be sharply revised and reduced. Spreading knowledge and rotating less desirable jobs are likely to (1) increase the commitment of all workers to improve the workplace so that fewer jobs are unpleasant and unrewarding and (2) reduce antidemocratic authoritarianism and increase solidarity among workers now placed on different hierarchical rungs in organizations.[139]

Direct democracy seems to work best in relatively small settings of just a few thousand people. One can see this type of direct democracy in New England town meetings. Representative democracy, as exemplified in the U.S. House of Representatives, works well only if representatives are actually a cross-section of all Americans and can be in close contact with most of their constituents. (The U.S. House and Senate are currently very unrepresentative of the American people, socially and demographically.) That contact is generally impossible, however, if each elected official must represent several hundred thousand citizens. Studies of political participation in the United States confirm that citizens are more politically active and feel more influential in *smaller* cities than in larger ones. Real democracy seems to be possible only in relatively small-scale settings. Kirkpatrick Sale has suggested that to maximize democracy and citizen participation, our cities need to be divided into self-governing neighborhoods of perhaps just 5,000 to 10,000 residents, with 10 to 12 neighborhoods in a city of 50,000 to 100,000 people. Perhaps 100,000 residents is the maximum city size for a city to be able to have truly democratic local government. Sale notes that "small cities can be more efficient and responsive than large cities. There is likely to be more two-way communication, more and better message sending from people to the government and back again, and easier access to the offices that get things done."[140] Those who are elected in such cities are more likely to be known to and to have contact with those they serve.

A decentralized society could democratically control certain problematical technologies that are implemented in society. A new technology that reduced the need for workers could be used to decrease the total number of working hours without cutting back on the number of workers. No worker would need to fear being thrown out of work by new technologies. This would work only if workers, not just a few capitalists, have democratic control of their workplaces. Moreover, a reasonably decentralized society could make better use of such alternative energy technologies as solar energy. U.S. society, with its huge centralized organizations, such as multinational corporations and the Pentagon, has a huge appetite for the world's energy and mineral resources. Earth cannot easily continue to provide the resources and waste disposal required. Jeremy Rifkin has argued that a basic law of nature, the Second Law of Thermodynamics, destroys the notion that ever more sophisticated and complex technologies can bring progress and prosperity to Earth. Complex technologies—and the bureaucratic organizations they require—tend to create ever more waste, pollution, and centralized authoritarianism. Complexity usually breeds new and serious problems for humanity. In Rifkin's view, a smaller-scale, decentralized, and democratic organization of human beings is necessary for our planet's ultimate physical survival. A decentralized U.S. society can make better use of ecologically sound, community-controlled technologies.[141]

From this perspective, all rural and urban neighborhoods should have democratically elected councils—with rotating memberships representing *all* residents—that are empowered to make significant decisions about collective consumption issues such as the building of new mass transit, roads, and parks. These local councils would decide how much of taxpayer funds would be spent on collective needs and how much would be spent to facilitate individual materialistic needs. Resources would be allocated as the democratic council decides. Thus, it might well choose more public transportation over an increase in roads for private cars.

The more numerous and newly empowered neighborhood and workplace councils would need to be integrated with one another through the means of new regional and national confederations. In a country with nearly 300 million people, it would be necessary to coordinate the decisions of local groups by means of a national democratic assembly. One community's decision to build a paper mill, for example, might have a negative effect on another community's water quality. Not all important decisions could be made at the local level. Higher-level democratic assemblies—not unrepresentative bodies of mostly elite politicians like the U.S. Congress—would be necessary to resolve intercommunity conflicts and other problems.[142]

Democratic planning is better than undemocratic central planning, since all local units would have representation and power at regional and national levels. Federations of democratic

more income and wealth would be available to low- and middle-income Americans. Most poverty could be eliminated. More important than wealth is the power over society that ownership and control of wealth-creating facilities confer. If plants, offices, stores, natural resources (like oil and minerals), and such were owned publicly and controlled democratically, the people of the United States would no longer be heavily controlled by decisions made by an elite capitalist class, usually with their own business interests in mind. People themselves could decide much more democratically how their workplaces and other major organizations would be run, how their natural resources would be developed and used, and how national economic surpluses would be used.

As previously noted, the goal of greater control over powerful institutions has periodically appeared in U.S. history, from the Farmers Alliance in the late 1800s to the ACORN and union movements more recently. Greater worker and community control, by definition, reduces some of the powerlessness and alienation problems discussed in previous chapters. Those pressing for economic democracy would carry the idea of control by the people to the point of full workplace and community democracy.

While any society is going to have planning and distribution problems, progressive analysts suggest that a more democratic economy would not have severe recessions or depressions in which the bottom two-thirds of the society would suffer while capitalists and managers continue to live in luxury as they work out their investment and private profit difficulties. No capitalist class would delay investment in jobs now in order to realize larger profits later. In hard times, all citizens would broadly share the suffering. Jobs would be more or less guaranteed. The goal of full employment at decent wages has been well articulated by some progressive members of Congress in recent years, but only a handful have recognized that full employment is not possible without major structural changes in the existing economy. If full employment were to be implemented, it would do away with some major problems associated with chronic unemployment and underemployment.

As we noted in Chapter 6, progressives have often analyzed the problems of class-structured schools. From a democratic socialist point of view, major reforms in schooling are necessary. An alienated society is one with troubled and inegalitarian schools. A democratic socialist society would have decentralized community schools oriented toward a cooperative rather than an individualistic ethic. Children would learn in a cooperative environment, where class, racial, and gender stratification would no longer track students into segregated educational environments and job channels. Education would be more of an omnipresent, lifelong process. Critical thinking and exploration would be encouraged. There would be no complex educational or workplace hierarchies to break down communication among individuals and groups.

In an economic democracy, a reasonably equal distribution of wealth and income, and thus of dignity, would likely reduce sharply most crime rates by removing the causes of much property and personal crime. There would be much less economic need for people to steal, and the economic pressures underlying many crimes of assault and murder would be reduced substantially. In addition, much of the economic and political pressure for the poor to riot or revolt would be removed from the society. Corporate crime would also be eliminated from the society, since no secretive corporate class could, for example, embezzle from their corporations, charge artificially high prices, or export needed jobs overseas for corporate profit.

Today, unnecessary defense expenditures waste huge sums of tax dollars. In recent decades, about one-third of the country's newly available capital has been used for military purposes. According to Seymour Melman, who once headed the National Commission for Economic Conversion and Disarmament, some 32,000 prime-contractor industrial facilities and 100,000 additional subordinate factories are more or less controlled by the Pentagon, whose annual budget was greater than the total net profits of all U.S. corporations in the mid-1990s.[149] Melman has recommended that economic conversion of the massive U.S. defense industry be directed toward the production of the goods needed to rebuild and modernize the decaying infrastructure—such as roads, bridges, schools, waterworks, and sewers. Huge defense expenditures are a source of public investment capital that could help solve the problem of toxic and nuclear waste cleanup and could modernize and electrify our railroad system. Melman argues that "Building and operating these industries gives new value to peoples' lives and will counter the human decay that now devalues whole communities and feeds rightist extremism and racism."[150] In his view, this process of channeling extraordinarily wasteful defense expenditures to much more critical societal needs would create millions of new jobs, thereby helping to revitalize many of the country's economically troubled rural and urban communities.

THE FUTURE OF DEMOCRACY

Greater economic and political democracy will not come easily—this is a point recognized by many progressive Americans. Established economic and political power is a major barrier to greater democracy. Indeed, powerful business and political leaders today seem to fear an expansion of democracy, particularly a sharp increase in ordinary Americans' control over large political and economic institutions. The expansion of democracy has been strongly criticized by powerful leaders in numerous capitalist countries, including the United States.

For example, a major report of the high-level Trilateral Commission, an international organization composed primarily of top capitalists, managers, and allied political leaders from Japan, Europe, and the United States and founded by Rockefeller interests, has argued that the Western capitalist nations are becoming more and more ungovernable.[151] The report argued that the "democratic surge" since World War II has significantly challenged powerful elites at the top in the United States. Fear of expanding democracy is at the heart of the argument made in the report by the U.S. social scientist Samuel P. Huntington, writing on behalf of the Trilateral Commission. Huntington complained that existing hierarchies of power and established authorities have been weakened by the attacks by various citizens' groups seeking expanded rights and greater equality. Even the "authority of wealth was challenged and successful efforts made to introduce reforms to expose and to limit its influence." Huntington has asserted that a major problem in the United States is an "excess of democracy," that government and other established institutions have been challenged so much by people's movements that they no longer have the necessary authority. He has called for moderation in democratic action and a submission of the people to the authority of established leaders and their experts. From this conservative viewpoint, which prominent analysts like Huntington continue to vigorously articulate today, those Americans with grievances against the existing political–economic system must quit making heavy demands on it. It is significant that Jimmy Carter, George H. W. Bush, Bill Clinton, and Dick Cheney were all members of the Trilateral Commission before they became president or vice-president of the United States.[152]

Such antidemocratic views as these are seldom discussed publicly by business and political leaders. The public statements and positions of business-oriented leaders have preferred to emphasize people-oriented issues that are more appealing to the general public. Indeed, U.S. progressives have allowed conservative groups to seize and use many issues that seem much closer to the ideals of progressives than to business-oriented conservatives. Today, many Americans feel betrayed by their institutions. As Harry C. Boyte has expressed it, they have a deep sense of grievance, a "skepticism about all large institutions coupled with the feeling that an unresponsive and arrogant elite has dishonored and exploited the American people and their traditions and values."[153] This sense of grievance is often radical in its tone, since many people feel that they have been hurt by their political institutions and that they must somehow take the institutions back, yet they do not know how.

Since the late 1970s, conservatives have manipulated this sense of grievance in the general population and focused it heavily on one large bureaucratic institution—the big federal government. Since the late 1960s, conservative politicians—such as presidents Richard Nixon, Gerald Ford, Ronald Reagan, and George H. W. Bush, as well as House Speaker Newt Gingrich and, most recently, President George W. Bush—have seized on this popular distrust and have channeled it for the political purposes of business elites. Yet from the nineteenth century to the 1960s, many progressive groups have also articulated the people's distrust of large government, corporate, and other bureaucratic institutions. As Robert Zevin has pointed out, unrepresentative big government was *originally* a progressive issue, and

Zevin has suggested that to win back the people, as well as to win elections, progressives should strongly support decentralized, smaller-scale governments, reduced property taxes, improved government services without waste and red tape, and improved public schools.[154]

Today, most of those in top business and government positions are committed to the needs and profit goals of modern capitalism much more so than to the needs of the general population. As we have seen in earlier chapters, corporate capitalists seek the lowest production costs across the globe. This tendency has led to first blue-collar and now clerical as well as higher-level professional jobs being exported offshore to countries with lower labor costs, along with weaker regulation of businesses and pollution. The fact that this system does not benefit most workers everywhere does not seem to be of much concern to most capitalists. One business analyst wrote about this changing job situation:

> Today's youth in America must reject previous years' beliefs in some form of entitlement to the good life and return to a values-driven ethic which states that you only obtain what you work hard for. Nothing is guaranteed without continuous, career-long efforts. Young people [must] recognize that the only thing they can be promised is commensurate with the quality of their work.[155]

Only a member of the elite could come to such a notion that most Americans, young or old, are unwilling to work. Ironically, U.S. sweatshop workers earning well below federal and state minimum wage requirements are some of this country's hardest-toiling, most work-ethic–driven workers. Yet their compensation—and that of growing numbers of better-paid workers—is not commensurate with the quality of their work effort (often 60 to 80 hours per week).[156]

The profit-centered view of capitalism sees U.S. workers mostly as commodities serving the business economy rather than as people whose interests should be served by that economy. From this common business perspective, U.S. workers should be thankful for what they get from a system controlled by a small capitalist elite. Conservative order–market view analysts cannot hide the fact that most influential political leaders in the United States are tied closely to corporate and smaller-scale capitalism and will work hard to meet the needs of businesses for such things as capital flight, automation, reindustrialization, lower business taxes, expanded profits, control of organized workers, and world markets safe from unions. Where big government is helpful to capitalist leaders, it will usually be expanded. There are, for example, numerous federal subsidies for corporations (at least $100 billion today), including those for airlines, defense contractors, and agribusinesses, as well as federal bailouts of major corporations in economic difficulties, such as Lockheed, Continental Illinois, Penn Central, Chrysler, and savings and loan institutions.[157] The antigovernment rhetoric of many business-oriented leaders is for the most part insincere, a smoke screen covering up an underlying commitment to continuing and heavy local, state, and federal government support of privilege, wealth, and corporate power.[158]

Nonetheless, as we have seen in previous sections of this chapter, people's groups and movements periodically challenge the business philosophy of profits before people, and they have periodically succeeded, often with great effort, in moving this society in the direction of expanded social, economic, and political democracy. As we move well into the twenty-first century, class, racial, and gender struggles for yet more democracy and justice show no sign of lessening in the United States.

SUMMARY

We Americans face serious societal problems. In previous chapters of this book we have raised critical questions about our capitalistic system, because that system generates and aggravates many major societal problems. The average American encounters little sustained, in-depth attention to the character and real causes of these social problems in the media. Deep structural analyses of the societal roots of such collective troubles as racial, gender, and antigay discrimination, urban decline, corporate and street crime, and environmental pollution are infrequently presented in the commercial print media or on commercial television and radio networks.

Nonetheless, in opinion polls many Americans say that they want a better environment, a better health care system, a more democratic workplace, and a more responsible business community, yet these criticisms have not been focused into an integrated, generalized power–conflict perspective on social problems. Periodically, substantial groups of Americans have protested problematical conditions and have pressed for major societal changes. From the Farmers Alliance in the nineteenth century to more recent union reform movements, civil rights movements, women's liberation movements, tenants' groups, and community action groups, organized groups of rank-and-file Americans have pressed for, and sometimes won, significant reforms in the structure and operation of the U.S. economy and polity. Today many progressive organizations operate at the grassroots level, and a major concern is how to move from the local concerns of many of these successful organizations to a larger-scale, national people's movement that brings real democracy to major U.S. institutions.

Historically, a major alternative to a capitalist system has been some type of socialism. Totalitarian Communism has been described by some as a type of "state capitalism" with repressive political institutions in which rank-and-file citizens have little voice. Neither capitalistic nor totalitarian socialist systems have adequately met the full range of human needs, including materialistic needs, needs for self-mastery, and needs for democratic control over the political and market institutions in which people live their lives. In recent years the people of Communist countries, such as the former Soviet Union and contemporary China, have pressed for greatly expanded political and economic democracy.

As envisioned by millions of progressive Americans, a democratic socialist United States would have a political–economic system with much greater democracy in the workplace, much more worker control over major institutions, a thoroughgoing political democracy, much expanded social service and health programs, and truly protected civil liberties. Democratic forms of socialism have often been proposed in the United States, and some capitalistic countries in western Europe have developed in that direction, but as yet no full-fledged democratic socialist country can be found on the face of the globe. Economic democracy is suggested by many progressive Americans in all regions as a better system than present-day capitalism, and such a real democracy could resolve, wholly or in part, most serious societal problems discussed in this book.

People must have their own and their families' material needs met, but they also need the power to control their major economic and political institutions. To meet these needs for real freedom and power, many progressives argue that it will be necessary to dismantle capitalistic, racist, sexist, and heterosexist structures and replace them with a more egalitarian, democratic system. In principle the U.S. political system is a democracy, but in reality it is greatly shaped by class inequality in the economic system, which is not democratic even in principle. Progressives argue that economic democracy is a significant step toward solving such problems as class exploitation in the economic system, including serious income inequality and chronic unemployment, as well as such related problems as street crime and corporate crime, environmental degradation, and health care rationed by income.

Finally, greater economic and political democracy in the United States, most progressives realize, will not come easily. Established political and economic power is a major barrier. Most capitalist leaders and their political allies fear what they call an "excess of democracy" and prefer to reshape the U.S. system so that it better meets their needs. Insofar as big government is helpful to capitalist leaders, it will likely be expanded or maintained, not reduced. Thus, Americans themselves, organized in progressive movements from 1776 to the present, remain the main hope for putting the old American ideal of democracy into much fuller economic and political reality.

STUDY QUESTIONS

1. Despite our constitutional guarantees of a free press, the mass media are not fully open. In what sense are the mainstream mass media "controlled"?

2. Why do many Americans not draw a connection between their personal problems and society-wide problems? What kinds of mechanisms have created the conservative order–market view?

3. Identify three examples of change-oriented, grassroots social movements in the United States. What kinds of victories have these progressive movements achieved?

4. How does the form of totalitarian socialism as practiced in the former Soviet Union differ from the democratic socialism found in kibbutz communities in Israel?

5. In what sense is *democratic socialism* partially practiced in the United States? Define it. Identify possible examples.

6. How would decentralization enhance the practice of democracy in the United States? How would a decentralized city work? What is the relationship between city size and democratic practice?

7. Characterize the benefits and drawbacks of a modern social welfare state, such as that exemplified by Sweden.

ENDNOTES

1. Tim Weiner, "For Some, Leaving Service Doesn't Mean Going Home," *Gainesville* (Fla.) *Sun,* April 25, 1993, p. G6.
2. Ibid.
3. Berch Berberoglu, *The Legacy of Empire* (New York: Praeger, 1992), p. 50.
4. Columbia Journal Review, *Who Owns What* (ret. April 6, 2004), available at www.cjr.org/tools/owners/index.asp.
5. Fairness and Accuracy in Reporting is available at www.fair.org.
6. Martin Lee, "Media: Too Close to Power," lecture presented at Chapel Hill, North Carolina, November 11, 1992.
7. Edward S. Herman, *Beyond Hypocrisy* (Boston: South End Press, 1992), p. 192, note 20; Joanne Lipman, "Brand-Name Products Are Popping Up in TV Shows," *Wall Street Journal,* May 15, 1991.
8. Lee, "Media: Too Close to Power."
9. "Common Cause Issues Poll," *Common Cause,* Fall 1992, p. 36.
10. Lee, "Media: Too Close to Power."
11. Herman, *Beyond Hypocrisy,* p. 12.

12. E. J. Hobsbawm, *Primitive Rebels* (New York: W. W. Norton & Co., Inc., 1959), p. 2; this point was suggested to the senior author in a draft paper by Janice E. Perlman.
13. Roper Center for Public Opinion Research, General Social Survey, 1991; see also "Meeting Health Care Needs," *The Polling Report,* March 22, 1993, p. 1; "Toward Energy Efficiency," *The Polling Report,* March 22, 1993, p. 8.
14. The Pew Research Center, "How Americans View Government," March 10, 1998, available at people-press.org/reports/display.php3?ReportID=95; "The Way Washington Works," *The Polling Report,* March 22, 1993, p. 8.
15. The Pew Research Center, "How Americans View Government"; "The Government's Role," *The Polling Report,* July 27, 1992, p. 8.
16. The Pew Research Center, "How Americans View Government"; "Confidence in Institutions," *The Polling Report,* March 8, 1993, p. 4.
17. The Pew Research Center, "How Americans View Government"; "The Way Washington Works," *The Polling Report.*
18. Peter Montgomery, "On Our Side: Americans Reject Right-Wing Agenda," *People for the American Way News,* Fall 1995, p. 1.
19. Lawrence Goodwyn, *Democratic Promise* (New York: Oxford University Press, 1976), pp. 60–64, 593–99; John M. Laslett and S. M. Lipset, eds., *Failure of a Dream?* (New York: Anchor Books, 1974).
20. Quoted in C. Vann Woodward, "Home-Grown Radicals," review of David De Leon, *The American as Anarchist: Reflections on Indigenous Radicalism* (Baltimore: Johns Hopkins University Press, 1979), *New York Review of Books,* April 5, 1979, p. 5.
21. David Hapgood, *The Average Man Fights Back* (New York: Doubleday, 1977), pp. 1–2.
22. Studs Terkel, *The Great Divide* (New York: Pantheon Books, 1988), p. 16.
23. Associated Press, "Abortion Rights Protest Packs National Mall," April 25, 2004, available at www.cnn.com/2004/US/04/25/abortion.protest.ap/index.html.
24. National Organization for Women is available at www.now.org.
25. Alexsandra Sett and Harold Silverman, "Coffee, Tea and Dignity," *Perspectives: The Civil Rights Quarterly* 12 (Spring 1980): 4–11.
26. Women Employed Online is available at www.womenemployed.org.
27. Interview with Barbara Otto, Program Director for 9 to 5: National Association of Working Women, April 12, 1993.
28. "Campaign Updates," 9 to 5: National Association of Working Women (ret. May 1, 2004), available at www.9to5.org/updates.
29. Loyola Marymount University, The Center for the Study of Los Angeles, "Rebuild L.A. Collection, 1992–1997" (ret. May 1, 2004), available at www.lmu.edu/csla/index.html.
30. Asian Immigrant Women Advocates is available at www.aiwa.org; see also, Mary Hollens, "Catfish and Community," *Third Force,* May–June 1993, p. 21.
31. Mujer Obrera is available at www.mujerobrera.org.
32. Micah Fink, "Weaving Workers Together," *Multinational Monitor,* January–February 1992, p. 8.
33. See "Building the Bridges Mexican Immigrant Women Workers" (ret. April 30, 2004), available at www.mujerobrera.org/about.
34. Ibid.
35. The Association for Children for the Enforcement of Support is available at www.childsupport-aces.org.
36. Center for Community Change, Annual Report—1994, Washington, D. C., 1994, pp. 10–11.
37. The Association for Children for the Enforcement of Support, "Accomplishments of ACES" (ret. April 30, 2004), available at www.childsupport-aces.org.
38. Berberoglu, *The Legacy of Empire,* p. 96.
39. Steve Brouwer, *Sharing the Pie* (New York: Henry Holt and Company, 1998); See also www.thirdworldtraveler.com/Economics/SocialDemocracy.html.
40. Berberoglu, *The Legacy of Empire,* pp. 100–101.
41. James Green, *The World of the Worker* (New York: Hill and Wang, 1980), pp. 241–48; Laura McClure, "The New Teamsters," *Dollars & Sense,* April 1993, pp. 10–11, 21–22; United Steelworkers of America is available at www.uswa.org/uswa/program/content/index.php.
42. Service Employees International Union is available at www.seiu.org.
43. "The Justice for Janitors Campaign: Organizing against the Odds," *Economic Notes* 56 (September–October 1988): 3–8; Mary Hollens, "Catfish and Community," p. 22; Camille Colatosi, "A Job without a Future," *Dollars & Sense,* May 1992, pp. 11, 21.
44. Justice for Janitors, "Health Care Victories" (ret. May 1, 2004), available at www.seiu.org/building/janitors/campaign_central/health_care_/victories.cfm.

45. Jobs with Justice is available at www.jwj.org/AboutJWJ/AboutJWJ.htm; National Organization for Women is available at www.now.org; National Association for the Advancement of Colored People is available at www.naacp.org; Southern Christian Leadership Conference is available at sclcnational.org/home.asp?siteid=2607.

46. "Jobs with Justice: Rebuilding Solidarity," *Economic Notes* 56 (September–October 1988): 9–11.

47. Fuerza Unida is available at fuerzaunida.freeservers.com.

48. "Blue Jeans Boycott," *Multinational Monitor,* November 1991, p. 4.

49. "Huge Win in Dallas!" Local 100, *Service Employees International Union News,* January 1993, p. 1.

50. Richard B. Freeman and James L. Medoff, *What Do Unions Do?* (New York: Basic Books, 1984), pp. 4–5, 246–50.

51. The American Association of Retired Persons is available at www.aarp.org.

52. U.S. Bureau of the Census, *Statistical Abstracts of the U.S., 2003* (ret. May 1, 2004), available at www.census.gov/prod/2004pubs/03statab/pop.pdf.

53. Barbara T. Dreyfuss, "The Seduction: The Shocking Story of How AARP Backed the Medicare Bill," The American Prospect—Online Edition (July 7, 2004), available at www.prospect.org/web/page.ww?section=root&name=ViewPrint&articleId=7702.

54. The Grey Panthers Web site is available at www.graypanthers.org.

55. Activity information and membership statistics were secured from the national offices of each organization.

56. The Nation of Islam is available at www.noi.org.

57. The Congress for Racial Equality is available at www.core-online.org.

58. Joe R. Feagin and Harlan Hahn, *Ghetto Revolts* (New York: Macmillan, 1973), pp. 92–94; Lerone Bennett, Jr., *Confrontation: Black and White* (Baltimore: Penguin Books, 1966), pp. 164–69; Inge P. Bell, *CORE and the Strategy of Nonviolence* (New York: Random House, 1968), pp. 13ff. The Student Nonviolent Coordinating Committee is available at www.ibiblio.org/sncc/index.html. For further information on the Black Panthers see www.hartford-hwp.com/archives/45a/index-be.html.

59. Frances Piven and Richard Cloward, *Poor People's Movements* (New York: Pantheon Books, 1977).

60. The NAACP Legal Defense and Educational Fund is available at www.naacpldf.org/welcome/index.html; the National Leadership Conference on Civil Rights is available at www.civilrights.org/about/lccr; and the Leadership Conference on Civil Rights Education Fund is available at www.civilrights.org/about/lccref.

61. The various civil rights campaigns involving these groups are available at www.civilrights.org/index.html.

62. Quoted in Don Aucoin, "Black Leaders Agree It's Time to Fertilize the Grass Roots," *Boston Globe,* January 22, 1992, p. 19.

63. Ibid.

64. Sheila D. Collins, *The Rainbow Challenge* (New York: Monthly Review Press, 1986), pp. 128–43; Michael Oreskes, "Voters and Jackson," *New York Times,* August 13, 1988, p. 1.

65. The Rainbow/PUSH Coalition is available at www.rainbowpush.org.

66. "AJ Congress, National Rainbow Coalition Launches 'New Mobilization' on Common Legislative Agenda," PR Newswire, December 14, 1992.

67. The Southern Poverty Law Center is available at www.splcenter.org.

68. Terry Lefton, "Building Bridges in the Big Apple," *Teaching Tolerance,* vol. 1, no. 1 (Spring 1992): 8–13; quotation on p. 13.

69. "Soft Replies Have Strong Impact on Racist Remarks," *Detroit News,* December 22, 1992, pp. 1A, 6A.

70. Woodrick Institute for the Study of Racism and Diversity, "Institutes for Healing Racism" (visited on May 14, 2004), available at woodrick.aquinas.edu/about.html; Nathan Rutstein, *Healing in America* (Springfield, Mass.: Whitcomb Publishing, 1993), pp. 163–71.

71. I draw here on Joe R. Feagin, *Racist America* (New York: Routledge, 2000), pp. 256–257, and on Eileen O'Brien, *Whites Confront Racism: Antiracists and Their Paths to Action* (Lanham, Maryland: Rowman & Littlefield, 2001).

72. Katherine Isaac, "LA Tax Dodgers," *Multinational Monitor,* March 1993, pp. 7–8. Citizens for Tax Justice is available at www.ctj.org.

73. Public Citizen is available at citizen.org.

74. Quoted in Joanne Ball Artis, "Clinton Expected to Pay Heed to Concerns of Consumers," *Boston Globe,* November 22, 1992, p. 19.

75. The Center for Auto Safety is available at www.autosafety.org.

76. National Highway Traffic Safety Administration is available at www.nhtsa.dot.gov.
77. Robert E. Scott, "The High Price of 'Free' Trade: NAFTA's Failure Has Cost the United States Jobs Across the Nation," Economic Policy Institute, Briefing Paper, November 17, 2003, available at www.epinet.org/content.cfm/briefingpapers_bp147.
78. Graduation Pledge Alliance is available at www.graduationpledge.org.
79. See Graduation Pledge at www.graduationpledge.org/pldgback.html.
80. E. M. Cohen, *Ideology, Interest-Group Formation, and Protest: The Case of the Anti-nuclear Power Movement, the Clamshell Alliance, and the New Left,* January 1981, available at www.osti.gov/energycitations/product.biblio.jsp?osti_id=6774861.
81. Stephen Zunes, "Seabrook: A Turning Point," *Progressive* 42 (September 1978): 28–31.
82. "Green Victories," *Greenpeace,* April–May–June 1993, p. 8.
83. "Building a Winning Campaign," *INFACT: Nuclear Weaponmakers Campaign Update,* Winter–Spring 1992, p. 1.
84. Debbie Dover, "Bringing Bad Things to Light," *Dollars & Sense,* June 1992, pp. 9–11.
85. INFACT is available at www.infact.org.
86. Jill Walker, "San Francisco March Draws About 35,000," *Washington Post,* January 20, 1991, p. A32.
87. International A.N.S.W.E.R., press release from the organizers of the March 20 antiwar protest (ret. May 14, 2004), available at www.internationalanswer.org/news/update/032004m20report2.html#pr.
88. "Just the Facts," *Common Cause,* May–June 1991, p. 10.
89. Kathy Kelly, "When the Hysteria Subsides," *Progressive,* May 1993, p. 39.
90. Paul Rockwell, "A Soldier of Conscience," *Sacramento Bee,* May 18, 2004, at www.alternet.org/waroniraq/2004/05/001956.html.
91. Judy Price, "Pushing Pesticides," *Multinational Monitor,* March 1993, p. 13.
92. Greenpeace USA is available at www.greenpeaceusa.org.
93. "A Brief History of Greenpeace," *Greenpeace,* Fall 1992, pp. 1–6.
94. "Green Victories," *Greenpeace,* p. 8.
95. Greenpeace, "Unprecedented Federal Prosecution of Greepeace to Proceed with Jury Trial," April 15, 2004, available at www.greenpeace.org/usa/press/releases/unprecedented-federal-prosecut.
96. Greenpeace, "Greenpeace Acquitted: Judge Finds Greenpeace Not Guilty in Landmark Free Speech Case," May 19, 2004, available at www.greenpeace.org/usa/press/releases/greenpeace-acquitted-judge-fi.
97. Janice Perlman, "Grassroots Empowerment and Government Response," *Social Policy* 10 (September–October 1979): 16–19.
98. Industrial Areas Foundation is available at www.industrialareasfoundation.org.
99. *IAF: 50 Years of Organizing for Change* (New York: Industrial Areas Foundation, 1990); Bill Broadway, "A Promising Moment to Make a Difference," *Washington Post,* June 1, 1996, p. B7.
100. Jim R. Rooney, *Organizing the South Bronx,* unpublished Ed.D. dissertation, Harvard University, 1991; Jeff Simmons, "Beep Pushes School Vote," *Daily News* (New York), March 29, 1996, p. 2.
101. Philadelphia Unemployment Project is available at www.philaup.org.
102. Allen Hornblum, "Fighting Foreclosures in Philly," *Dollars & Sense,* May–June 1984, pp. 15–17; "Unemployed Seek Solutions," United Press International, January 17, 1992; Michael Remez, "State Residents Push for Action to Help Unemployed," *Hartford* (Conn.) *Courant,* January 18, 1992, p. D1.
103. Center for Community Change, Annual Report—1994, p. 2.
104. ACORN is available at www.acorn.org.
105. Information about ACORN in this section is based on pamphlets and newsletters published by ACORN.
106. For a comprehensive list of Internet links to other other progressive organizations and resources, see the New Party's homepage at www.newparty.org.
107. "Questions and Answers about the New Party," Pamphlet, April 1992, pp. 1–2; see also *New Party: Building the New Majority* (New York: New Party, 1992).
108. "A Race in Missouri," *New Party News,* Spring 1993, p. 3; conversation with Daniel Cantor, national organizer, May 11, 1993; Linda Puner, "New Party Offers Hope for Those Dissatisfied with Political Process," *New York Times,* December 3, 1995, sec. 13WC, p. 7; Todd Gitlin, "There Is an Alternative: The New Party," *Los Angeles Times,* July 4, 1996, p. B9.
109. The Reform Party is available at www.reformparty.org; David Jackson, "Perot Organizing United We Stand," *Dallas Morning News,* January 12, 1993, p. 1A; Jack W. Germond, "His Party Looks for Ways to Supplement Perot's Wallet," *Baltimore Sun,* May 13, 1996, p. 9A.

110. The MoveOn organization is available at www.moveon.org.
111. Mark Potok, "The Year in Hate," Southern Poverty Law Center (ret. May 14, 2004), available at www.splcenter.org/intel/intelreport/article.jsp?aid=374.
112. Southern Poverty Law Center, "Day of Reckoning" (ret. May 14, 2004), available at www.splcenter.org/intel/intelreport/article.jsp?aid=413.
113. The Swedish Institute's "Fact Sheets on Sweden" series, 1979–1990; see also Norman Furniss and Timothy Tilton, *The Case for the Welfare State* (Bloomington: Indiana University Press, 1977), pp. 134–36.
114. "Plant Closings in Sweden," *Dollars & Sense,* December 1983, pp. 9–12.
115. "Fact Sheets on Sweden"; Furniss and Tilton, *Case for the Welfare State,* pp. 131–43.
116. Sven Steinmo, "Bucking the Trend? The Welfare State and the Global Economy: The Swedish Case Up Close," (December 18, 2001), p. 22 available at stripe.colorado.edu/907/Esteinmo/bucking.pdf.
117. Furniss and Tilton, *Case for the Welfare State,* pp. 144–47.
118. Ibid., pp. 144–45.
119. Ibid., pp. 147–49.
120. Eero Carroll, "Swedish Austerity: Benefits at Risk," *Multinational Monitor,* January–February 1993, p. 35.
121. Michael Binyon, "New Leader Sees Years of Austerity for Sweden," *The Times,* March 19, 1996, n.p.
122. The Tennessee Valley Authority is available at www.tva.gov.
123. John N. Howley, "Public Ownership in the U.S.," *Economic Notes* 51 (June 1982): 4.
124. Arnold S. Tannenbaum et al., *Hierarchy in Organizations* (San Francisco: Jossey-Bass, 1977), pp. 32–36, 208–9.
125. Stephanie Fried, "All for One," *Jerusalem Post,* April 30, 1993, n.p.; Leora Frankel-Sholsberg, "Kibbutzim Struggle Amid Economic Changes," *Dallas Morning News,* March 8, 1996, p. 43A.
126. David Mermelstein, "Austerity, Planning, and the Socialist Alternative," in *Urban Scene,* Joe Feagin, ed. (New York: Random House, 1979), pp. 300–304.
127. Robert A. Nisbet, *Community and Power* (New York: Oxford University Press, 1962); see also Gar Alperovitz, "Socialism as a Pluralist Commonwealth," in R. C. Edwards, M. Reich, and T. E. Weisskopf, eds., *The Capitalist System* (Englewood Cliffs, N.J.: Prentice Hall, 1972), pp. 524–26.
128. James Weinstein, "The Problems of the Socialist Party," in Laslett and Lipset, eds., *Failure of a Dream?* pp. 300–40.
129. Democratic Socialists of America is available at www.dsausa.org/dsa.html.
130. Daniel Zwerdling, "Workplace Democracy," *Progressive* 42 (August 1978): 16.
131. Daniel Zwerdling, *Democracy at Work* (Washington, D.C.: Association for Self-Management, 1978), pp. 53–55.
132. Zwerdling, "Workplace Democracy," pp. 9–13.
133. Ibid., pp. 91–99; William Foote Whyte and Joseph Raphael Blasi, "Quality of Work Life in the 1980s," United Press International, November 22, 1981; "Worker Cooperatives Survive in Northwest Plywood Industry," *Bureau of National Affairs Daily Labor Report,* March 14, 1990, p. C1.
134. Steve Babson and Nancy Brigham, *What's Happening to Our Jobs?* (Somerville, Mass.: Popular Economics Press, 1978), pp. 54–55.
135. Michael Albert and Robin Hahnel, *Unorthodox Marxism* (Boston: South End Press, 1978), pp. 254–55.
136. David Ewing, *Freedom Inside the Organization* (New York: McGraw-Hill, 1977), pp. 219–39.
137. Ibid., pp. 257–58.
138. Mermelstein, "Austerity, Planning, and the Socialist Alternative," pp. 300–4; Tannenbaum et al., *Hierarchy in Organizations,* pp. 224–25.
139. Albert and Hahnel, *Unorthodox Marxism,* pp. 258–59.
140. Kirkpatrick Sale, "The Polis Perplexity: An Inquiry into the Size of Cities," *Working Papers for a New Society* 5 (January–February 1978): 71–72.
141. Jeremy Rifkin, *Entropy: A World View* (New York: Viking, 1980); Albert and Hahnel, *Unorthodox Marxism,* pp. 261–62.
142. Mermelstein, "Austerity, Planning, and the Socialist Alternative," pp. 302–3.
143. Alperovitz, "Socialism as a Pluralist Commonwealth," in *Capitalist System,* pp. 527–28; Albert and Hahnel, *Unorthodox Marxism,* pp. 270–73.
144. Alperovitz, "Socialism as a Pluralist Commonwealth," in *Capitalist System,* p. 528.

145. See, for example, Michael Albert et al., *Liberating Theory* (Boston: South End Press, 1986).

146. Martin Luther King, Jr., "I Have a Dream," in A. Meier, E. Rudwick, and F. L. Broderick, eds., *Black Protest Thought in the Twentieth Century,* 2nd ed. (New York: Bobbs-Merrill, 1971), pp. 349–50.

147. Michael Harrington, "Full Employment and Social Investment," *Dissent* 25 (Winter 1978): 125–36.

148. Tannenbaum et al., *Hierarchy in Organizations,* pp. 214–15.

149. National Commission for Economic Conversion and Disarmament is available at www.webcom.com/ncecd/index.htm.

150. Seymour Melman, "America Can Turn Civilian, Successfully," *Los Angeles Times,* December 29, 1992, p. B7.

151. The Trilateral Commission is available at www.trilateral.org.

152. Michael J. Crozier, Samuel P. Huntington, and Joji Watanuki, *The Crisis of Democracy: Report on the Governability of Democracies to the Trilateral Commission* (New York: New York University Press, 1975), pp. 75–114.

153. Harry C. Boyte, "Building a Populist Politics," *Social Policy* 11 (November–December 1980): 38.

154. Robert Zevin is interviewed in Alexander Cockburn and James Ridgeway, "Reagonomics: Facts, Follies and Faults," *Mother Jones* 6 (February–March 1981): 53–54.

155. Robert O. Metzger, "The Ominous Exporting of U.S. Clerical Jobs," *USA Today,* March 1989, p. 31.

156. See "The Garment Industry," *Sweatshop Watch* (ret. May 7, 2004), available at www.sweatshopwatch.org/swatch/industry.

157. See the Congressional testimony of Stephen Moore, Director of Fiscal Policy Studies, Cato Institute, "Corporate Subsidies in the Federal Budget," June 30, 1999, available at www.cato.org/testimony/ct-sm063099.html.

158. See the speech by Steve Max, a veteran community organizer, to the Conference on Alternative State and Local Policies, Pittsburgh, July 18, 1980, reprinted in *Social Policy* 11 (November–December 1980): 34–35.

Index